CLOSE RELATIONSHIPS

Key Readings in Social Psychology

General Editor: ARIE W. KRUGLANSKI, University of Maryland at College Park

The aim of this series is to make available to senior undergraduate and graduate students key articles in each area of social psychology in an attractive, user-friendly format. Many professors want to encourage their students to engage directly with research in their fields, yet this can often be daunting for students coming to detailed study of a topic for the first time. Moreover, declining library budgets mean that articles are not always readily available, and course packs can be expensive and time-consuming to produce. *Key Readings in Social Psychology* aims to address this need by providing comprehensive volumes, each one of which will be edited by a senior and active researcher in the field. Articles will be carefully chosen to illustrate the way the field has developed historically as well as current issues and research directions. Each volume will have a similar structure to include:

- an overview chapter, as well as introduction to sections and articles
- questions for class discussion
- annotated bibliographies
- full author and subject indexes

Published Titles

The Self in Social Psychology	Roy F. Baumeister
Stereotypes and Prejudice	Charles Stangor
Motivational Science	E. Tory Higgins and Arie W. Kruglanski
Social Psychology and Human Sexuality	Roy F. Baumeister
Emotions in Social Psychology	W. Gerrod Parrott
Intergroup Relations	Michael A. Hogg and Dominic Abrams
The Social Psychology of Organizational Behavior	Leigh L. Thompson
Social Psychology: A General Reader	Arie W. Kruglanski and E. Tory Higgins
Social Psychology of Health	Peter Salovey and Alexander J. Rothman
The Interface of Social and Clinical Psychology	Robin M. Kowalski and Mark R. Leary
Political Psychology	John T. Jost and James Sidanius
Close Relationships	Harry T. Reis and Caryl E. Rusbult

Titles in Preparation

Attitudes	Richard E. Petty and Russell Fazio
Group Processes	John Levine and Richard Moreland
Language and Communication	Gün R. Semin
Persuasion	Richard E. Petty and Russell Fazio
Social Cognition	David L. Hamilton
Social Comparison	Diederik Stapel and Hart Blanton
Social Neuroscience	John T. Cacioppo and Gary Berntson

For continually updated information about published and forthcoming titles in the Key Readings in Social Psychology series, please visit: **www.keyreadings.com**

CLOSE RELATIONSHIPS
Key Readings

Edited by

Harry T. Reis
University of Rochester

Caryl E. Rusbult
University of North Carolina

Psychology Press
New York and Hove

Cover illustration: "The Park" by Lynne Feldman (www.lynnefeldman.com). Details from the painting are in the Community Room of the Anthony Square Affordable Housing Development, Rochester, NY.

Published in 2004 by
Psychology Press
270 Madison Avenue
New York, NY 10016
www.psypress.com

Published in Great Britain by
Psychology Press
27 Church Road
Hove, East Sussex
BN3 2FA
www.psypress.co.uk

Copyright © 2004 by Taylor & Francis Books, Inc.

Psychology Press is an imprint of the Taylor & Francis Group.
Printed in the United States of America on acid-free paper.

10 9 8 7 6 5 4 3 2 1

Library of Congress Cataloging-in-Publication Data

Close relationships: key readings/edited by Harry T. Reis, Caryl Rusbult.
    p. cm. – (Key readings in social psychology)
Includes bibliographical references and index.
    ISBN 0-86377-595-0 (hardback: alk. paper)—ISBN 0-86377-596-9 (pbk.: alk. paper)
1. Interpersonal relations. 1. Reis, Harry T. II. Rusbult, Caryl E. III. Series.

HM1106.C552 2004
302—dc22

2004011225

Contents

Relationship Science: A Casual and
Somewhat Selective Review   1

About the Editors

Harry T. Reis is a professor of psychology at the University of Rochester. His research interests include influences on social interaction, patterns of socializing for health and psychological well-being, and psychological processes that affect the course and conduct of close relationships, including intimacy, attachment, and emotion regulation. He is the past President of the International Society for the Study of Personal Relationships and the Executive Officer of the Society for Personality and Social Psychology.

Caryl E. Rusbult is the William Friday Professor of Psychology at University of North Carolina-Chapel Hill, where she is also the director of the Social Psychology Program. Her research interests include motivation and behavior in close relationships and commitment processes. Her awards include the New Contribution Award from ISSPR and the Reuben Hill Award from the National Council on Family Relations.

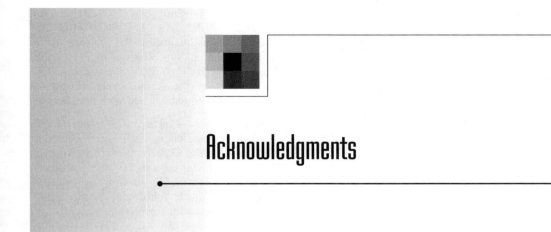

Acknowledgments

The Editors and Publishers are grateful to the following for permission to reproduce the articles in this book:

Reading 1: E. Berscheid, The Greening of Relationship Science. American Psychologist, 54, 260–266. Copyright © 1999 by the American Psychological Association. Reprinted with permission.

Reading 2: N.L. Collins, C. Dunkel-Schetter, M. Lobel and S.C.M. Scrimshaw, Social Support in Pregnancy: Psychosocial Correlates of Birth Outcomes and Postpartum Depression. Journal of Personality and Social Psychology, 65, 1243–1258. Copyright © 1993 by the American Psychological Association. Reprinted/adapted with permission.

Reading 3: H.T. Reis, Y. Lin, M.E. Bennett and J.B. Nezlek, Change and Consistency in Social Participation During Early Adulthood. Developmental Psychology, 29, 633–645. Copyright © 1993 by the American Psychological Association. Reprinted/adapted with permission.

Reading 4: D. Byrne, C.R. Ervin and J. Lamberth, Continuity Between the Experimental Study of Attraction and Real-Life Computer Dating. Journal of Personality and Social Psychology, 16, 157–165. Copyright © 1970 by the American Psychological Association. Reprinted/adapted with permission.

Reading 5: R.L. Moreland and S.R. Beach, Exposure Effects in the Classroom: The Development of Affinity among Students. Journal of Experimental Social Psychology, 28, 255–276. Copyright © 1992, Elsevier Science (USA). Reprinted/adapted with permission from the publisher.

Reading 6: M. Snyder, E. Berscheid and E. Decker Tanke, Social Perception and Interpersonal Behavior: On the Self-Fulfilling Nature of Social Stereotypes. Journal of Personality and Social Psychology, 35, 656–666. Copyright © 1977 by the American Psychological Association. Reprinted/adapted with permission.

Reading 7: D.T. Kenrick and M.R. Trost, Evolutionary Approaches to Relationships. From Handbook of Personal Relationships, 2nd Edition, 151–177. Copyright © 1997. Reprinted/adapted by permission of John Wiley & Sons Limited.

Reading 8: D.M. Buss, Sex Differences in Human Mate Preferences: Evolutionary Hypotheses Tested in 37 Cultures. Behavioral and Brain Sciences, 12, 1–49. Copyright © 1989 by Cambridge University Press. Reprinted/adapted with permission.

Reading 9: C. Hazan and P.R. Shaver, Attachment as an Organizational Framework for Research on Close Relationships. Psychological Inquiry, 5, 1–22. Copyright © 1994 by Lawrence Erlbaum Associates, Inc. Reprinted/adapted with permission.

Reading 10: M. Mikulincer, Attachment Working Models and the Sense of Trust: An Exploration of Interaction Goals and Affect Regulation. Journal of Personality and Social Psychology, 74, 1209–1224. Copyright © 1998 by the American Psychological Association. Reprinted/adapted with permission.

Reading 11: J.P. Laurenceau, P.R. Pietromonaco and L. Feldman Barrett, Intimacy as an Interpersonal Process: The Importance of Self-Disclosure, Partner Disclosure, and Perceived Partner Responsiveness in Interpersonal Exchanges. Journal of Personality and Social Psychology, 74, 1238–1251. Copyright © 1998 by the American Psychological Association. Reprinted/adapted with permission.

Reading 12: R.J. Sternberg, A Triangular Theory of Love. Psychological Review, 93, 119–135. Copyright © 1986 by the American Psychological Association. Reprinted/adapted with permission.

Reading 13: R. Levine, S. Sato, T. Hashimoto and J. Verma, Love and Marriage in Eleven Cultures. Journal of Cross-Cultural Psychology, 26, 554–571. Copyright © 1995 by Sage Publications, Inc. Reprinted/adapted with permission.

Reading 14: M.S. Clark and J. Mills, Interpersonal Attraction in Exchange and Communal Relationships. Journal of Personality and Social Psychology, 37, 12–24. Copyright © 1979 by the American Psychological Association. Reprinted/adapted with permission.

Reading 15: B.R. Schlenker and T.W. Britt, Beneficial Impression Management: Strategically Controlling Information to Help Friends. Journal of Personality and Social Psychology, 76, 559–573. Copyright © 1999 by the American Psychological Association. Reprinted/adapted with permission.

Reading 16: D.M. Wegner, P. Raymond and R. Erber, Transactive Memory in Close Relationships. Journal of Personality and Social Psychology, 61, 923–929. Copyright © 1991 by the American Psychological Association. Reprinted/adapted with permission.

Reading 17: C.E. Rusbult, N. Olsen, J.L. Davis and P.A. Hannon, Commitment and Relationship Maintenance Mechanisms. Close Romantic Relationships: Maintenance and Enhancement, 87–113. Copyright © 2001 by Lawrence Erlbaum Associates, Inc. Reprinted/adapted with permission.

Reading 18: J. Simpson, M. Lerma and S.W. Gangestad, Perception of Physical Attractiveness: Mechanisms Involved in the Maintenance of Romantic Relationships. Journal of Personality and Social Psychology, 59, 1192–1201. Copyright © 1990 by the American Psychological Association. Reprinted/adapted with permission.

Reading 19: S.L. Murray, J.G. Holmes and D.W. Griffin, The Benefits of Positive Illusions: Idealization and the Construction of Satisfaction in Close Relationships. Journal of Personality and Social Psychology, 70, 79–98. Copyright © 1996 by the American Psychological Association. Reprinted/adapted with permission.

Reading 20: W. Ickes and J.A. Simpson, Managing Empathic Accuracy in Close Relationships. From W. Ickes (Ed), Empathic Accuracy, 218–250. Copyright © 1997 by Guilford Publications, Inc. Reprinted/adapted with permission.

Reading 21: A. Aron, E.N. Aron, M. Tudor and G. Nelson, Close Relationships as Including Other in the Self. Journal of Personality and Social Psychology, 60, 241–253. Copyright © 1991 by the American Psychological Association. Reprinted/adapted with permission.

Reading 22: S.M. Andersen, I. Reznik and L.M. Manzella, Eliciting Facial Affect, Motivation, and Expectancies in Transference: Significant-Other Representations in Social Relations. Journal of Personality and Social Psychology, 71, 1108–1129. Copyright © 1996 by the American Psychological Association. Reprinted/adapted with permission.

Reading 23: S. Gabriel and W.L. Gardner, Are There "His" and "Hers" Types of Interdependence? The Implications of Gender Differences in Collective Versus Relational Interdependence for Affect, Behavior and Cognition. Journal of Personality and Social Psychology, 77, 642–655. Copyright © 1999 by the American Psychological Association. Reprinted/adapted with permission.

Reading 24: F.D. Fincham, Attribution Processes in Distressed and Nondistressed Couples: 2. Responsibility for Marital Problems. Journal of Abnormal Psychology, 94, 183–190. Copyright © 1985 by the American Psychological Association. Reprinted/adapted with permission.

Reading 25: G. Downey, A.L. Freitas, B. Michaelis and H. Khouri, The Self-Fulfilling Prophecy in Close Relationships: Rejection Sensitivity and Rejection by Romantic Partners. Journal of Personality and Social Psychology, 75, 545–560. Copyright © 1998 by the American Psychological Association. Reprinted/adapted with permission.

Reading 26: L. Carstensen, R.W. Levenson and J.M. Gottman, Emotional Behavior in Long-Term Marriage. Psychology and Aging, 10, 140–149. Copyright © 1995 by the American Psychological Association. Reprinted/adapted with permission.

Reading 27: M.P. Johnson, Patriarchal Terrorism and Common Couple Violence: Two Forms of Violence Against Women. Journal of Marriage and the Family, 57, 283–294. Copyright © 1995 by the National Council on Family Relations. Reprinted/adapted with permission.

Relationship Science: A Casual and Somewhat Selective Review

> No attempt to understand behavior, in the individual case or in the collective, will be wholly successful until we understand the close relationships that form the foundation and theme of the human condition.
>
> —Ellen Berscheid and Anne Peplau (1983, p. 19)

We spend about two-thirds of our waking hours in the presence of other humans. The lion's share of that time is spent in the company of "close others," including family, friends, and co-workers. Indeed, since the time that our ancestors climbed out of the trees and began walking upright on the plains of Africa, we've lived our lives with other humans, hunting in groups, cooking and eating together, and raising our children in concert with other families. Not surprisingly, the exceptional sociability of human life colors nearly every phenomenon studied in the social and behavioral sciences: Close others exert a powerful impact on our psychological and physical health. Our cognitive and affective experiences are fundamentally interpersonal. Our "selves"— including our values, dispositions, and behavioral tendencies—are shaped by our relations with close partners. Indeed, virtually all societal structures and processes—formal and informal, economic, legal, and political—are colored by our relations with others. As such, it's not hyperbole to assert that "no attempt to understand behavior . . . will be wholly successful until we understand the close relationships that form the foundation and theme of the human condition" (Berscheid & Peplau, 1983, p. 19).

The Scientific Study of Attraction and Relationships

Lay Knowledge versus Scientific Knowledge

In light of the exceptional sociability of human life, it comes as no surprise that even before reading the articles collected in this volume, you already know a good deal about interaction and relationships. After all, you have almost two decades (or more) of experience with interpersonal relations. Over the course of these decades, you've developed relationships with family, friends, neighbors, and classmates; you've experienced conflict and learned various methods (some better, some worse) for resolving conflict and reconciling with others; you've learned when and how to reciprocate, as well as when and how to compromise; you've learned how to (and how not to) initiate interactions and become closer to the people to whom you're attracted; you've learned about opening up to confidantes and trying to just "be there" for a friend in need; you may have fallen in love once or twice; and you may have developed one or two enemies. You've also learned a good deal about interaction and relationships from fiction, poetry, religion, philosophy . . . and from "Friends," the Indigo Girls, and Bill and Hillary Clinton.

However, there's an important difference between lay knowledge and scientific knowledge: The things we "know" based on our experiences in everyday life are not particularly well articulated or reliable. Many of our beliefs about interactions and relationships are ambiguous, inconsistent, or contradictory. Indeed, much of what we "know" is misleading or even incorrect. Why so? One important reason is that our lay understanding is based on unsystematic observation, and frequently is distorted by the fact that (a) we typically have a rather restricted set of experiences with a given sort of phenomenon, and (b) those experiences are limited by the relatively small number of partners with whom we've interacted. Our lay understanding of relationships is also colored by what we "want to believe" or "need to believe," as well as by various other biases in information processing and memory. And importantly, although we learn a

good deal from observing our own interactions and relationships, personal experience provides a biased sample of information, in that it is based on observations including a common denominator . . . ourselves: You've never had a conversation in which you weren't there, you've never kissed a person when you weren't there, and you've never had an argument in which you weren't there. For these reasons, if we're to fully and accurately "understand the close relationships that form the foundation and theme of the human condition," we must turn to the scientific study of interaction and relationships.

When we speak of "relationship science," we refer to *scientific knowledge*—to knowledge based on findings from empirical research, to the regularities identified via systematic observation, to that which has been established using methods that provide a reasonable degree of objectivity, reliability, and validity, to the results of work that adheres to the process of scientific inquiry that you've learned in your courses in the social and natural sciences. These rules maximize the probability that our findings are interpretable, reliable, and valid. For example, we can replicate studies to demonstrate that the obtained findings are dependable, we can employ alternative procedures to demonstrate that findings don't rest on peculiar manipulations or measurement techniques, and we can determine if a set of results is limited to one age group or culture or historic period. In short, these rules help assure that over the long run, the claims of science are valid, and that our understanding of the world—the understanding embodied in our libraries and lectures and journals—constitutes "knowledge."[1]

A Brief History of Relationship Science

We (this time we literally mean "we," Harry and Caryl, the editors of this volume) were

---

[1]Of course, this is not to suggest that there are no other valid "ways of knowing." You may know many things on the basis of logical reasoning (e.g., Plato's Republic) or religious faith (e.g., the Bible or Koran) or received wisdom (e.g., the Bill of Rights). Such ways of knowing are not necessarily wrong. These alternative ways of knowing simply lack the objectivity of the scientific method—the method on which this volume is based.

undergraduates during what has come to be called "the 60s"—the late 1960s and early 1970s. Although we matriculated on opposite sides of the country—one of us at CCNY, the other at UCLA—many of our experiences were similar. Over the course of our education we learned a bit about interaction and relationships from our classes in psychology and sociology, we read a few journal articles concerning marital relations, and we encountered some theories and empirical work regarding parent–child interactions and encounter groups (a then-innovative method for creating a microcosm of personal relationships in a laboratory setting). In our undergraduate social psychology courses, we read one slim textbook chapter and enjoyed one or two lectures on interpersonal attraction.[2] In terms of accumulated knowledge regarding relationship science, there was not much to write home about.

Granted, many early theories of personality emphasized the importance of interpersonal relations, including the theories of Sigmund Freud, Erik Erikson, and Harry Stack Sullivan (Freud, 1917; Erikson, 1950; Sullivan, 1953). And during the 60s, humanistic psychologists began to argue for the importance of "rapport": Erich Fromm described the "art of loving," Sidney Jourard emphasized the importance of "self-disclosure," and Abraham Maslow argued for the centrality of "being love" (Fromm, 1962; Jourard, 1964; Maslow, 1968). Unfortunately, these authors' claims were based largely on casual observation or case study, not on empirical evidence garnered from scientific research (although we hasten to add that over the intervening decades, many of their claims have been confirmed by scientific evidence). But despite the dearth of data, even then we greatly appreciated being exposed to these theories—they were an interesting and thought-provoking departure from the prevailing behaviorist orientation.

And importantly, things were beginning to change. A few pioneers had begun to gather solid

scientific evidence about interpersonal relations: Theodore Newcomb had studied the acquaintance process among undergraduates at Bennington College, Leon Festinger and his colleagues had examined friendship formation in a married student housing complex at MIT, Donn Byrne had initiated a program of experimental research regarding the impact of attitudinal similarity on attraction, Ellen Berscheid and Elaine Walster had commenced their studies of physical attractiveness and the character of passionate love, and Zick Rubin had conducted his landmark research contrasting the experiences of liking and loving. Also, George Levinger had developed a compelling theory of persistence versus breakup in a review of the sociological literature regarding divorce, and Irwin Altman and Dalmas Taylor had begun their seminal studies of the role of self-disclosure in the acquaintance process. Nevertheless—and as noted earlier—at that time, relationship science was a very small empirical literature.

Despite its youth, the budding relationship science was really very exciting: It was sufficiently promising to pique our interest, sufficiently exciting to entice us—and many others in our generation—to pursue graduate education in the social sciences, particularly in social psychology, clinical psychology, developmental psychology, communications, and sociology. Most of us began our studies in alternative subfields prior to becoming relationship scientists (e.g., prejudice and discrimination, fairness and justice, the environment). By the early 1980s, we were surprised to find that the interests of many of us were converging on something that has come to be called "relationship science." We began to meet one another at conferences, convene formal meetings at which we discussed our work, develop specialized journals and organizations, produce edited volumes summarizing emerging findings and theories, and move to positions of prominence and esteem in our respective fields.[3] More and more young scientists were attracted to the field;

---

[2]And of course, both of us were model students—we worked hard, earned good grades, ignored distractions such as the civil rights movement and anti-war protests, and shunned the culture of sex, drugs, and rock 'n roll.

[3]One watershed event was the first International Conference on Personal Relationships, held in Madison, Wisconsin in the summer of 1982.

more and more established scientists joined what they regarded as a promising new enterprise. The following decades were a tremendously energetic, vital period in the field—a time filled with a lot of hard work, along with great insights, innovation, and discovery. Relationship science took its place as a large and valued presence in the social sciences.

Although there are many good reasons to be interested in relationship science, in the final analysis—at "rock bottom"—some of the best reasons concern the link between relationships and health. Countless studies have been conducted on this topic—and scores of reviews have summarized this literature—all of which reach the same general conclusion: As Michael Argyle noted in his 1987 book, *The Psychology of Happiness*, "social relationships are a major source of happiness, relief from distress, and health" (p. 31). It's remarkable to note the number and variety of health and well-being indices that have been linked to relationship circumstances. Just consider a few: The development and treatment of depression, social anxiety, and most varieties of mental illness; survival longevity among patients with congestive heart failure; retrospective reports of life satisfaction among the elderly; the strength of the immune system in preventing colds and in facilitating wound healing; children's adaptation following parental divorce; school and work effectiveness; cardiovascular reactivity to stress; smoking, and drug and alcohol abuse; and adherence to treatment regimes for a broad array of illnesses and conditions. In other words, it's no exaggeration to conclude that any comprehensive intervention involving mental or physical health must take account of people's relationships. Healthy relationships are good for the body, mind, and soul.

What is a Relationship?

When people learn that we are relationship scientists, their most common question is: "What is a relationship?"[4] The question is humbling, in that the field has no clear and consistent answer. Often, it seems that laypeople (and even some scholars) adopt a stance like Supreme Court Justice Potter

Stewart adopted in a 1964 decision when trying to define pornography: They don't know how to define it [pornography, or in our case, a relationship], but they know it when they see it. Of course, good science requires a clear definition of the phenomenon under scrutiny. The most widely accepted definition is that a *relationship* exists to the extent that two people exert strong, frequent, and diverse effects on one another over an extended period of time (Kelley et al., 1983). That is, when people are in a relationship, each affects the other's behavior and well-being—each person's actions have some bearing on what the other does, as well as on whether the other enjoys good or poor outcomes, feels happy or unhappy, experiences pleasure or pain. This is what we mean when we speak of *interdependence*—interdependence describes the ways in which and the degree to which people depend on one another, exert power over one another, and encounter congenial versus not-so-congenial interactions. A close relationship, then, is simply a relationship with relatively strong interdependence.

Sometimes people also inquire about the range of relationships to which relationship science applies. Many empirical studies (including those collected in this volume) examine special types of relationship. Empirical studies of dating and marital relationships are common; studies of same-sex friendships are somewhat less common. Relationship scientists generally *intend* that their theories and empirical findings apply across the board, describing important processes in any and all of the interpersonal relations that fit the definition proffered above—to friendships and romantic relationships of varying degrees of closeness, to relationships involving teammates and neighbors and co-workers, to student–teacher, physician–patient and supervisor–subordinate dyads, and to familial relations involving cousins and siblings and children. Whenever an ongoing association involves strong, frequent, and diverse influence over an extended period of time, the processes and findings of relationship science are pertinent.

Prominent Theoretical Orientations

Relationship science is wonderfully diverse, in that different scientists approach the study of

---

[4]Their second question is usually something like, "How come most relationships are so screwed up?"

relationships from different—sometimes dramatically different—theoretical orientations. This means that when they study a given phenomenon, they're likely to emphasize different sorts of processes, identify different sorts of causal factors, and study different sorts of effects. The fact that relationship scientists have differing "takes" on interaction and relationships is one of the great strengths of our field. Over time, such diversity tends to produce a rich and multifaceted understanding of human behavior. Three theoretical orientations have proven to be particularly popular in the social psychological literature. In the following paragraphs we briefly describe each orientation in turn.

Evolutionary orientation. Some relationship scientists adopt an *evolutionary orientation*, emphasizing the role of inherited biological make-up in shaping contemporary behavior (for an excellent review, see Buss & Kenrick, 1998). From this point of view, if a specific human tendency—an impulse to think, feel, or behave in a particular manner—has a genetic basis, to the degree that the tendency enhances one's "fitness" (i.e., probability of successful reproduction), the tendency will become more prominent over the course of generations. For example, back in the Pleistocene Era, if some but not all men inherited a genetically based tendency to enjoy mating with women in their 20s (at which age women are maximally fertile), those men who possessed this tendency would have been more likely to produce offspring; in turn, those offspring themselves would be more likely to exhibit this tendency, and would be more likely to successfully pass the tendency on to their offspring. Men who inherited a genetically based tendency to enjoy mating with women in their 50s would have been less likely to produce offspring, and therefore would have become no one's ancestors—their genetically based tendency would become less prominent in the next generation, and would eventually disappear from the gene pool. The evolutionary orientation has been particularly successful at explaining what might be construed as "primitive" components of behavior in relationships—mate selection, sexual exclusivity, jealousy, patterns of childrearing, and the like. However, this orientation is increasingly

being applied to more complex forms of relationship-relevant behavior. Indeed, Darwin's (1859) earliest analyses of evolutionary processes recognized that many important tasks of human survival—establishing shelter from the elements, raising offspring to maturity, food gathering, and defense against predators and competitors—rested on the ability to live and work in relationships and groups.

Attachment orientation. Some relationship scientists adopt an *attachment orientation*, emphasizing not only our genetic inheritance, but also our childhood experiences (see Cassidy & Shaver, 1999, for a collection of essays reviewing both classic and contemporary theory and research). Attachment theory was first proposed by John Bowlby, a British psychiatrist whose observations—described in a three-volume masterwork—spawned the explosion of research that followed (Bowlby, 1969, 1973, 1980). Attachment theorists propose that humans are born with genetically based tendencies that regulate attachment and caregiving. For example, infants are biologically prepared to bond with adult caregivers (e.g., to smile at adult faces and to seek proximity with caregivers when distressed), and adults are biologically prepared to respond to and bond with infants (e.g., to comfort and soothe distressed infants). The manner in which infant–caregiver interactions unfold during infancy and early childhood are thought to exert profound effects on the developing child's "mental models" of relationships—that is, what the child comes to expect from significant others in terms of support, empathy, and trustworthiness. Some children have adult caregivers who are appropriately responsive to their needs—their caregivers readily perceive the child's needs, and gratify them in ways that help the child feel safe and secure. Other children have adult caregivers who are less responsive (or even unresponsive) to their needs—their caregivers misunderstand or ignore their needs, and are essentially inattentive or inappropriately responsive (e.g., indifferent, neglectful, intrusive, abusive). As a consequence of such interactions, children develop expectations about how others will respond to them; later in life, these expectations color a wide range of important behaviors. Thus, the attachment orientation has been used to explain why some people are secure and trusting in close relationships, whereas others tend to be worried and unsure about their partners, and still others have learned that relationships are so fraught with danger and unpleasantness that it's best to keep others at a distance or avoid relationships altogether. These general principles help to explain a surprisingly diverse array of behaviors, including love, sexuality, self-confidence, empathy, grief, mental health, and exploratory behavior.

Interdependence orientation. Some relationship scientists adopt an *interdependence orientation*, emphasizing the nature of the relationships *between* people (rather than focusing on the people themselves, as is characteristic of many theories; Kelley, 1979; Kelley & Thibaut, 1978; Rusbult & Van Lange, 2003). From this point of view, if we're to understand interactions and relationships, we must first understand the nature of the interdependence between people: Does each person affect the other's well-being, how much power does each have over the other, are the two equally dependent on one another, are the things that they seek from their interaction in harmony or in conflict? These properties have enormous relevance for the pair: They define what the two are likely to experience in interaction; they specify the sorts of traits and norms that will guide their interactions; they limit what the two can learn about one another and reveal to one another; and they shape the character of their cognitive, affective, and motivational experiences. The interactions two people experience—and the nature of their overall relationship—are a product of (a) the properties of their interdependence with one another, along with (b) the unique characteristics of each person and (c) the distinctive ways in which their characteristics interact in the context of their interdependence with one another. A metaphor conveys the gist of this orientation: In modern physics, the relations *between* particles are as real and influential as the particles themselves; in interdependence theory, the relations *between* people are as real and influential as the people themselves. This orientation has been particularly successful at explaining why people become committed to their relationships, how they come to trust (or mistrust) one another, why they experience conflict and how they resolve it, how they coordinate their behavior to achieve shared goals, and what makes them willing to sacrifice for one another.

Other orientations. At present, evolutionary theory, attachment theory, and interdependence theory are the most prominent "grand theories" in relationship science. You'll see these perspectives reflected in the articles included in this reader, along with a number of prominent "mid-level theories" (e.g., intimacy theory, self-expansion theory, theory of exchange versus communal relationships). But of course, other orientations are also popular, and you'll see them represented in this reader as well. For example, many researchers adopt theories and perspectives from cognitive psychology to investigate the mental events and processes that accompany and drive interaction. Emotion theories occupy a similarly prominent position in the literature. In addition, a number of relationship scientists seek to identify individual differences that will help explain key aspects of interaction and relationships, exploring personal traits such as empathy, self-esteem, narcissism, or depression. As noted earlier, the fact that relationship scientists have differing "takes" on interaction and relationships is one of the great strengths of our field. (We really like this aspect of the field, and hope you do as well!)

Research Methods

Relationship science is wonderfully diverse not only in its theoretical orientations, but also in its methods of research. This means that when different scientists study similar processes and phenomena, they're likely to employ different sorts of research designs and tools. Some relationship scientists conduct experiments, wherein key variables are actively manipulated, extraneous variables are controlled, and participants are randomly assigned to experimental conditions. Experiments sometimes are carried out in artificial environments (laboratory experiments), and sometimes are carried out in the relatively more natural environments in which the phenomenon of interest normally takes place (field experiments). Other relationship scientists conduct nonexperimental research, studying the naturally occurring associations among independent variables and dependent variables. For example, existing friendships, families, or romantic relationships are often investigated in cross-sectional survey studies or in extended longitudinal studies. In addition, over the past few decades many scientists have become committed to examining interactions and relationships in such a manner as to capture the natural, "everyday character" of these phenomena. For example, to study daily interactions, scientists may ask participants to carry interaction records with them over a 10-day period, instructing participants to report on specified events immediately following each such event (e.g., following each interaction involving disagreement or conflict).

Relationship scientists also employ diverse measurement techniques. Some scientists rely on *self-report techniques*, whereby participants describe themselves and their relationships by recording answers to questionnaire items with fixed-response formats (e.g., "I can rely on my partner to keep the promises he/she makes to me"; respond to this item using a 9-point scale ranging from $0 =$ do not agree at all, to $8 =$ agree completely). Sometimes scientists obtain both self-report measures *and* "other-report" measures. For example, each participant may report on both his or her own commitment level *and* the partner's commitment level, or both participants *and* outside observers (e.g., parents, teachers, peers) may provide reports of a child's bullying behavior. Comparing two or more sources of data does more than simply verify self-reports; it also informs researchers about the influence of perspective on the interpretation of interpersonal behavior.

Other scientists employ *observational techniques*. For example, they may videotape couples' conversations about an area of disagreement in their relationship, develop a coding scheme to characterize partners' interactions, and ask trained coders to rate each partner's behavior during each segment of the conversation (e.g., during each two-minute segment, counts of the number of critical comments or of positive nonverbal gestures).

Relationship scientists generally embrace the concept of *converging operations*, testing a given hypothesis using two (or more) methods, using two (or more) measurement techniques, and using two (or more) participant populations (e.g., both gay/lesbian and straight relationships, both North American and Asian samples). Via converging operations, the possible limitations of one method (or measurement technique, or participant population) can be compensated for by another, such that collectively, the multiple studies that address a given phenomenon provide comprehensive and convincing evidence regarding that phenomenon. Also, via the use of multiple methods, measures, and participant populations, we can learn a good deal about the external validity of our findings, or the extent to which our findings are generalizable beyond the specifics of the study in which a finding was obtained. Not all fields are as dedicated to methodological diversity as relationship science is. The fact that relationship scientists have different "takes" on methodology is a second strength of our field, in that over time, this diversity tends to produce a rich and multifaceted understanding of relationships. (This is another aspect of the field that we really like. Again, we hope that you like it, too!)

In the sections that follow, we provide a brief review of some of the topics and phenomena that have occupied relationship scientists over the years. (Actually, we might more accurately describe this enterprise in terms of topics that have "consumed" relationship scientists, in light of the passion and enthusiasm that our colleagues bring to their work.) Naturally, a presentation this brief can only hope to point out the most general, widely examined themes, phenomena, and tendencies. Readers will find more in-depth analysis in the articles included in this volume, as well as in textbooks and scholarly reviews. (And importantly, we hope that as a result of reading these articles and thinking through the broad themes that comprise relationship science, you'll identify other issues that you'll want to examine in research of your own!)

Attraction and Initiating Relationships

During the early years of relationship science, much of what we knew about interactions and relationships concerned the initial encounters between people—the first impressions they form about one another, whether they're inclined to affiliate further, and whether they feel attracted to each other. In part, this emphasis made good sense: If we want to understand relationships, we should begin with the initial encounters from which they emerge. In addition, this emphasis to some extent reflected the field's early commitment to experimentation, which dictated the study of initial encounters between strangers—a situation in which the specific properties of encounters could be carefully manipulated and controlled. For example, we can manipulate whether the person to whom a participant is introduced is very physically attractive versus not so physically attractive, controlling all other components of the interaction. Or, for example, we can present participants with "potential dates" in the context of an Internet dating study, controlling the information we provide about the date's personal characteristics and manipulating whether the person is described as having a good or bad sense of humor.[5]

First Impressions

Early research regarding first impressions examined how the initial information we receive about another person can shape our impressions of that person. For instance, Kelley (1950) examined whether learning that someone is cold (rather than warm) can color our interpretations of other traits that

person might possess. In comparison to people who are described as cold, those described as warm are also perceived more positively on many other dimensions—they're better liked, are perceived as more capable, and are thought to possess other desirable attributes. The phrase halo effect was coined to describe the impact of so-called central traits—including not only warmth, but also physical attractiveness—on judgments regarding another's sociability, competence, and integrity (Asch, 1946). As you might imagine, relationship scientists have examined the impact of scores of factors on first impressions—for example, attractiveness, height, ethnicity, age, and information about a person's attitudes, values, and personality.

Other work has revealed that the way in which information is presented, sought, or received can influence the impressions we form. For example, researchers have studied: (a) *primacy effects*, examining when and why early information about another tends to carry greater weight in shaping people's impressions than does later information (e.g., Jones et al., 1968); (b) *confirmation bias*, or how perceivers may unconsciously seek out information that confirms rather than disconfirms their initial impressions of people (e.g., Darley & Gross, 1983); (c) *overconfidence effects*, or when and why perceivers tend to overestimate the accuracy of their judgments about others (e.g., Swann & Gill, 1997); and (d) *self-presentation*, or the manner in which people attempt to influence the impressions that others form of them (e.g., Leary, 2001).

Affiliation

Some of the earliest work that is relevant to understanding interaction and relationships examined affiliation, or the simple inclination to seek the company of others. For example, Stanley Schachter and his colleagues studied the association between emotions and affiliation, demonstrating that humans are particularly inclined to seek the company of others when they're fearful (i.e., when they anticipate physical or psychological pain; Schachter, 1959). This work has served as a basis for later studies of phenomena such as seeking social support from others. Later studies

[5]For both practical and ethical reasons, people in longstanding relationships typically cannot be randomly assigned to experimental conditions. For example, it's difficult to randomly assign couples to low versus high commitment conditions, "forcing" half to feel low commitment and the other half to feel high commitment. This is why experimental methods tend to be employed more frequently in studies of initial impressions than in studies of ongoing relationships.

demonstrated that some but not all strong emotions promote affiliation. For example, when people feel anxious or concerned about possible embarrassment, they tend to avoid contact with others (Sarnoff & Zimbardo, 1961).

People also seek the company of others in order to better understand themselves. Research regarding *social comparison* demonstrates that, in part, we figure out whether our opinions are acceptable by comparing our beliefs to other people's beliefs (e.g., "are my religious beliefs viable—do other people think as I do?"), and we figure out if our abilities are adequate by comparing our abilities to other people's abilities (e.g., "is my sexual behavior 'normal'—do others enjoy the same things with the same frequency as I do?"; Festinger, 1954). Indeed, it appears that humans affiliate with others for a variety of reasons—because the presence of others is comforting, because others can help us gain a more accurate understanding of ourselves, because others can help us feel better about ourselves, or because others can help us develop strategies for improving ourselves (Sedikides & Strube, 1997).

Attraction

One of the most enduring topics of interest among relationship scientists concerns initial attraction—who is attracted to whom, and why. Some of the most influential early work examined proximity. For example, Leon Festinger and his colleagues studied students' natural patterns of friendship formation in a married-student housing complex at MIT. Their work demonstrated that the probability of forming a friendship is governed in part simply by the immediacy and availability of others in our everyday lives (Festinger et al., 1950). Over the years, other scientists have extended these early findings by identifying some of the mechanisms underlying the impact of proximity. For example, simple repeated exposure to another person tends to enhance our attraction to that person (e.g., Zajonc, 1968). In fact, all other things being equal, the simple act of interacting with another person—for example, talking to each other, asking questions—causes us to become more strongly attracted to that person (e.g., Insko & Wilson, 1977).

Affect also contributes to attraction. For example, work on the *person positivity effect* reveals that people are generally inclined to regard others favorably—humans are evaluated more favorably than are non-human objects, and specific individuals are evaluated more favorably than are the groups to which those individuals belong (e.g., Americans tend to like their own senators more than they like the U.S. Senate as a whole; Sears, 1983). Also, work regarding the *target positivity effect* reveals that people tend to feel more attracted to others who say and do positive things (e.g., evaluating films favorably, making positive comments about politicians) than to others who say and do negative things (Folkes & Sears, 1977). (At the same time, negative targets are regarded as more intelligent [Amabile, 1983].) In addition, researchers have identified what may be one of the most fundamental and reliable effects in all of social psychology, the *reciprocity of affect effect*: People tend to like others who like them, and tend to dislike others who dislike them (Backman & Secord, 1959).

Some of the field's most concerted attention has addressed the *similarity versus complementarity* question: Are we more attracted to people who are similar to ourselves or to people who are different from ourselves? Theodore Newcomb's early work regarding friendship formation in university dormitories demonstrated that roommate relationships tend to flourish to the extent that roommates hold common preexisting attitudes and values (Newcomb, 1961). Extending this literature, Donn Byrne and his colleagues used laboratory experimentation to study *attitudinal similarity and attraction*. They identified the so-called *law of attraction*—the fact that on average, a given increase in the proportion of similar attitudes yields a comparable percentage increase in attraction to another (Byrne, 1971).

It's interesting that work regarding attitudinal similarity has revealed stronger and more clear-cut support for the impact of similarity than has work examining personality similarity. Some research suggests that we like others whose personalities are similar to our own, whereas other research has revealed weak or inconsistent findings, or—mainly in the case of dominance and submissiveness—has revealed support for complementarity. Some researchers attempt to explain such inconsistencies by proposing *filter theories* of developing relationships. Filter theories suggest that (a) some variables influence attraction early in a relationship (but not during later stages), serving to filter out unsuitable partners (e.g., those with dissimilar backgrounds or values), whereas (b) other variables influence attraction later in a relationship (but not during early stages), promoting movement toward deeper involvement (e.g., complementary needs, role compatibility; e.g., Murstein, 1976). Other scientists attempt to explain such inconsistencies by examining possible confounds with key variables. For example, Insko and his colleagues suggest that the real issue in understanding the impact of similarity is *similarity to the ideal self*—that is, we're attracted to people who are similar to our ideal selves, not necessarily to people who are similar to what we think we're actually like (e.g., Wetzel & Insko, 1982).

Before moving on, it is important to mention a final class of attraction phenomenon. During the late 1960s and early 1970s, Ellen Berscheid, Elaine Walster, and their colleagues carried out seminal work regarding the impact of *physical attractiveness*, demonstrating that—far more than we might imagine or want to admit—we're attracted to others who are pleasing to the eye (many of their early studies are reviewed in Berscheid & Walster, 1974b). Later research demonstrated that in addition to being strongly attracted to those who are physically beautiful, we're also inclined to perceive others through the halo (or horns) of their physical appearance: Attractive people (both women and men) are perceived to possess superior skills and capacities on almost every dimension and outcome that has been studied; for example, social skill, leadership, performance (i.e., the quality of their work), and even virtue. This research has led scientists to examine such issues as: (a) the *kernel of truth question*, or whether there is any validity to the

so-called "what is beautiful is good" stereotype (answer: yes, mainly for social skill; Reis et al., 1982); (b) the *universal standards question*, or whether the standards used to judge beauty transcend time and culture (answer: yes, to a startling degree; Langlois & Roggman, 1990); and (c) the *assimilation versus contrast question*, or whether affiliating with physically attractive people makes us look better versus worse in the eyes of others (answer: it depends, although we generally seem to benefit from affiliating with attractive opposite-sex partners, and suffer from comparison to attractive same-sex friends; Kenrick & Gutierres, 1980). Attractiveness is a richer and much more complex phenomenon than it might initially seem, however—it's not simply a case of rampant unfairness. In this regard, we invite you to consider findings obtained by Snyder, Tanke, and Berscheid (1977), reprinted in this volume.

Developing Relationships

Of course, relationships involve more (much more!) than initial interactions and first impressions. Whereas all relationships begin with an initial encounter, we live our lives in a network of relatively more extended involvements. Although some initial encounters evolve into lasting relationships, many more do not. Just think of the many people with whom you've come into contact during the past month, most of whom never made it past square one. Researchers have therefore become quite interested in understanding how relationships develop from their earliest stages to increasing levels of involvement. The processes that have received the most attention are communication, intimacy, and (in the case of romantic relationships) love.

Communication

Communication is enormously important in developing relationships. At the same time, effective communication is difficult. In order for a "sender" to convey his or her intentions to a "target," the sender must effectively translate his or her private thoughts and feelings into verbal and nonverbal actions. If the sender has poor social skills or there are noisy distractions in the environment, the target may find it difficult to receive the sender's message. Moreover, once a message is received by the target, it must be correctly decoded. Far more frequently than one might imagine, interacting individuals face an interpersonal gap, or a disparity between what the sender intended to communicate and what the target actually received. This gap can be a source of misunderstanding and conflict in developing relationships. Indeed, it's not so much the intent of communication (what a sender intended to convey) as it is the impact of communication (what the target actually received) that differentiates between satisfactory and unsatisfactory interactions: In unsatisfying interactions, targets interpret messages as substantially less positive and more negative than senders intended their messages to be (Gottman, 1979).

Nonverbal communication refers to all of the things that people do during interaction except for their spoken words, including eye contact, facial expressions, gestures, touch, voice pitch, rate of speech, and the like. Nonverbal communication serves several functions—it can provide information about the sender's mood and inner state, it can regulate interaction by conveying interest or by instigating turn-taking, and it can define the character of a relationship (e.g., expressing intimacy, displaying power or status; e.g., Patterson, 1988). It's been argued that when there is a discrepancy between what's communicated verbally and nonverbally (e.g., when people are lying or being sarcastic), the true intent of communication is better conveyed through the nonverbal channel (e.g., Burgoon, 1994). In general, researchers have found that women's skills at both encoding and decoding are somewhat greater than those of men (e.g., Noller, 1980).

Relationship scientists have also dedicated a good deal of effort to the study of *verbal communication*. Much of this work has been carried out by marital researchers, and is oriented toward identifying differences between the communication styles of well-functioning and poorly functioning couples. Given that the ultimate goal of

this work is to teach poorly functioning couples to interact as well-functioning couples do, research in this tradition tells us a good deal about "what works," or about effective verbal communication. For example, researchers have discovered that in comparison to well-functioning relationships, partners in poorly functioning relationships spend a lot of time *cross-complaining*, without ever responding in a meaningful way to what the other is saying or feeling; partners in well-functioning relationships are better at establishing an *agenda of issues* to discuss, listening to the other's concerns, and proceeding to discuss them. Partners in poorly functioning relationships also are more likely to engage in mindreading, especially *negative mindreading*—rather than asking why the other behaved as he or she did, each person simply assumes that he or she understands the reasons for the other's behavior (and the "reasons" tend to be negative or blameful). These are only a few of the many documented differences that distinguish communication patterns in well-functioning and poorly functioning marriages (a more detailed list may be found in Gottman, 1998). Relationship scientists believe that the consequences (good or bad) of these communication patterns are similar across most types of close relationships, although empirical studies of such generalizability are relatively rare.

Intimacy

One of the most important functions of communication is to regulate intimacy, either increasing closeness between two people or widening the gap that separates them. In lay language, the term "intimacy" is often used as a synonym for closeness, sexuality, or privacy. However, most relationship scientists prefer a more sharply defined usage—namely, to refer to the process of becoming more deeply knowledgeable about, and connected to, another person. Thus, a major focus of intimacy research concerns *self-disclosure*, or the ways in which we reveal private information about ourselves to others. Existing research supports three broad conclusions: (a) self-disclosure proceeds from superficial to intimate topics as partners become acquainted (e.g., Altman &

Taylor, 1973); (b) partners tend to reciprocate each other's level of self-disclosure (in other words, relationship development is impeded by too little or too much disclosure, in comparison to personal standards, situational norms, or the present closeness of a relationship; e.g., Derlega et al., 1993); and (c) we tend to like those who self-disclose to us, and tend to disclose to those whom we like (e.g., Collins & Miller, 1994). Importantly, intimacy is established not only through spoken messages but also through nonverbal communications, especially those that signal the communicator's affective state.

More sophisticated models have broadened the definition of intimacy, in recognition of the fact that self-disclosure is only part of what creates intimacy in a relationship. For example, the *interpersonal model of intimacy* stresses the role of perceived partner responsiveness, suggesting that intimacy is enhanced when another's response to one's self-disclosure communicates understanding, validation, and caring (Reis & Shaver, 1988). This and similar models are helpful in focusing attention on the fundamentally interactive nature of intimacy: That is, it's not just whether the sender discloses, but *also* whether the receiver is responsive. In fact, many relationship theorists share this perspective, conceptualizing intimacy as a complex process that cuts across two levels of analysis: (a) the psychology of the individual self; and (b) the psychology of interaction and relationships. In this sense, intimacy parallels other important interactive processes in relationships, including trust, conflict resolution, and cooperation.

Love

Few topics in relationship science tend to capture readers' attention to the extent that love does. (In fact, perhaps you've skipped ahead to this section!) Substantial energy has gone into simply defining and classifying the many types of love that people experience. Rubin (1970) was one of the first researchers to do this, establishing distinctions between *liking* versus *loving*. More recently, the field has adopted Berscheid and Walster's (1974a) distinction between *passionate* versus *companionate love*. The former refers to "a state of intense longing for union with another person," whereas the latter characterizes "the affection we feel for those with whom our lives are deeply entwined." Other schemes have been offered, too, such as the *colours of love* model, which differentiates styles of love such as passionate, friendship, possessive, and game-playing (e.g., Lee, 1977).

To a greater or lesser extent, all of these models posit that the dynamics of love—that is, its causal and motivational antecedents, its behavioral, biological, and cognitive manifestations—depend on the specific variety under consideration. Models of love that emphasize changes in the self suggest that passionate love arises when a relationship—whether imagined, embryonic, or longstanding—provides novel opportunities for *self-expansion*, including such experiences as personal growth, acquiring new resources, or developing new social identities (Aron & Aron, 1997). In contrast, evolutionary theorists suggest that passionate love exists because it redirects one's attention away from routine activities and instead toward the existence of a potential mating partner, thereby facilitating the initiation and development of mating relationships (e.g., Diamond, 2003). This orientation may help explain one of the better-supported findings in the literature—that level of passionate love tends to be a poor predictor of long-term marital satisfaction and longevity. (Some scientists suggest that this is because passionate love tends to diminish over the early years of marriage, once the function of attracting reproductive partners to each other has been fulfilled.) In contrast, companionate love fares better as a predictor of relationship success, in all likelihood because of the importance of intimacy in maintaining relationships (we say more about this in a later section).

In recent years, spurred by the seminal theorizing of Hazan and Shaver, some relationship scientists have conceptualized romantic love as an attachment process (Hazan & Shaver, 1987). In part, this is because romantic relationships serve many of the same functions in adulthood that infant–caregiver relationships serve earlier in life. Irrespective of whether one agrees with this theorized connection between love and attachment (and to be sure, there are important differences), it is readily apparent that across all stages of the life cycle, some of the closest relationships we develop are attachment relationships, or relationships in which the partner: (a) serves as a secure base for exploration and a safe haven during times of distress; (b) is a person to whom we feel very attached, and for whom we long when his or her absence is prolonged; (c) is someone we trust to be sensitive to our most important needs, and whose lack of support causes us to feel upset; and (d) upon whose availability and responsiveness our emotional well-being rests. Some of the most influential work in the attachment tradition has shown just how pervasively *internal working models of attachment*—that is, beliefs about our own worthiness and expectations about the trustworthiness of others—formed during early childhood influence a variety of relationships and relationship-related behaviors "from the cradle to the grave" (as Bowlby himself expressed it).

Maintaining Relationships

In the early years of relationship science, researchers paid little heed to relationship maintenance processes. Initiating relationships, developing relationships, and even deteriorating relationships came under scrutiny, but the question of how people maintain ongoing relationships did not. It was almost as though the field assumed that nothing interesting happens after a relationship is established, until it begins to fall apart. We scarcely need to say that this isn't so. Maintaining a close relationship involves its own set of processes and considerations, which differ in meaningful ways from the processes that are involved in beginning or ending a relationship. The care and feeding of ongoing relationships require something different from merely continuing to do whatever attracted you and your partner to each other in the first place. Similarly, maintaining a satisfying relationship entails more than simply *not* doing the things that cause a relationship to deteriorate.

Fortunately, in recent years relationship scientists have recognized the importance of investigating maintenance processes. We suspect that part of the field's reluctance to instigate such work was methodological: The study of maintenance processes typically requires a pool of research participants who are engaged in reasonably long-standing, committed relationships, which adds to the complexity of carrying out research on a college campus. Moreover, relationship maintenance research often tends to rest on nonexperimental designs, inasmuch as many of the relevant variables are difficult—if not impossible or unethical—to manipulate experimentally. (Try randomly assigning participants to low versus high trust conditions!) Finally, relationship maintenance research sometimes involves comparing two partners' differing perspectives, a fascinating but complex addendum to research design. Although all of this may sound daunting, to us it's clear that the extra effort is worth it—relationship maintenance research includes some of the most interesting and important topics in the field.

Interdependence

Relationships are prime examples of *interdependence*. Building on the definition advanced earlier, relationship partners exert causal effects on each other with regard to both important and trivial matters, and depend on each other for significant outcomes. Most work in this tradition builds on *interdependence theory*, first proposed by Thibaut and Kelley (1959) and later extended by Kelley and Thibaut (1978). Their theory provides a systematic account of the interpersonal properties that shape social interaction. These properties include (a) *degree of dependence* (the extent to which each partner's outcomes depend on, or are influenced by, the other's behavior), (b) *mutuality of dependence* (the extent to which two people depend on a relationship to the same degree), (c) *basis of dependence* (whether the partners' dependence on one another is absolute or contingent), and (d) *correspondence of outcomes* (whether the partners' outcomes correspond or conflict). One of the most important contributions of interdependence theory is the simple proposition that living life in ongoing relationships—as most people do, whether at home, at work, or even in recreation—typically requires that partners coordinate their actions and, consequently, that people often act in ways that go against their immediate self-interest in order to benefit the partner (e.g., choosing to vacation where a partner prefers to go). This sort of analysis provides a critical "relationship-based" perspective that nicely complements more "individualistic" theories of motivation.

Interdependence theory defines *norms* as a broad set of rules for solving specific problems of interdependence that commonly arise. For example, nearly all societies have norms about acceptable versus unacceptable sexual behavior; such rules help to prevent conflict about sexual partners and activities. Many norms regarding prosocial actions—behavior enacted for the primary purpose of helping another person—apply most strongly to close relationships. For example, we expect our close friends and family to be helpful to us, especially when our need is great; in turn, we expect to help them when they're in need. Clark and Mills (1979) propose an important distinction between relationships governed by two distinct types of norm. They suggest that *communal relationships* are those in which needs take precedence: We respond to our partners' needs, and expect them to respond to our needs; both partners tend to behave in such a manner without much attention to who has given how much to whom. In contrast, in *exchange relationships* we're more concerned with principles of *equity*—preserving a fair balance of what each person puts into the relationship and what each gets out of it. Both types of relationship can be "close." For relationship scientists, the important difference is in the rules that regulate the giving and receiving of benefits.

Commitment and Trust

Some of the more influential aspects of maintaining relationships involve commitment and trust. Although these terms describe different processes, they share a common functional role: When commitment and trust exist, it's easier to engage in

behaviors that tend to bolster relationships over the long haul (e.g., sacrificing for the other's welfare, revealing an important personal secret). Also, both constructs involve willingness to become dependent on another. *Commitment* describes an individual's intention to persist in a relationship. This definition emphasizes behavioral intent, distinguishing intent from affective state, which may or may not be positive. (After all, people sometimes feel strongly committed to relationships that aren't very satisfying.) According to the *investment model*, three factors contribute to the emergence of commitment— increases in satisfaction, declines in the desirability of available alternatives (i.e., other relationships, being alone), and increases in the investment of resources in a relationship (e.g., time, effort; Rusbult, 1983). This model has led to many useful insights about why people persist in relationships, for good or ill (e.g., even in abusive relationships, jobs they dislike). At the same time, commitment often brings with it a sense of emotional linkage to a partner and a tendency to think about long-term circumstances in a relationship, both of which increase people's willingness to engage in costly or effortful behaviors for the good of the relationship—for example, to sometimes sacrifice their immediate interests in order to sustain the relationship.

In complementary manner, trust involves willingness to place oneself in a position of vulnerability relative to another person. *Trust* describes the strength of one's conviction that a partner consistently will be responsive to one's needs. According to existing theories, trust begins to develop when we observe our partners place our needs and interests above their own—for example, when we take a risk and make ourselves vulnerable, and the partner responds with behavior that provides evidence of his or her trustworthiness (Holmes & Rempel, 1989). In some sense, then, commitment and trust are reciprocal processes: When we're committed to our partners, we often place their needs above our own, and we come to trust our partners when we observe them place our needs above their own. As such, one might think of trust as an "implicit gauge" of the strength of a partner's commitment (Wieselquist et al., 1999). The emerging sense of trust—"I know you would never do anything to hurt me"—is a crucial element in coping with the uncertainty and vulnerability that are inherent in needing others and depending on them.

Sustaining Ongoing Relationships

As you might imagine, people engage in a variety of behaviors that help sustain their ongoing relationships. That is, they enact strategically motivated behaviors that (at some level) are intended to foster the well-being of the partner or relationship. There are many different ways to think about these behaviors. For example, some researchers have attempted to list the diverse ways in which partners strive to be kind and thoughtful to each other—avoiding sensitive topics, using affectionate nicknames, running errands for a partner, and so on. Other researchers have focused on strategies that are aimed at defusing negativity. The latter focus arises out of the rather extensive empirical evidence demonstrating that negative interactions erode even the most rewarding relationships. Thus, this class of strategy may be important in preventing erosion from beginning in the first place. Some of these strategies involve overt actions, whereas others are somewhat more psychological. We list just a few such mechanisms, to give you a feel for the kinds of (very cool) things that partners do—either consciously or unconsciously—to sustain their relationships:

Behavioral maintenance mechanisms: (a) *sacrifice*—foregoing one's personal desires and needs, engaging instead in behaviors that are valued by the partner (e.g., Van Lange et al., 1997); (b) *accommodation*—controlling the impulse to retaliate in response to a partner's destructive act (e.g., lack of consideration, rudeness), "biting one's tongue" and reacting constructively (e.g., Rusbult et al., 1991); and (c) *forgiveness*—finding one's way to forgiving a partner's act of betrayal (e.g., McCullough et al., 1998).

Cognitive maintenance mechanisms: (a) *derogation of alternatives*—dealing with tempting alternative partners by exhibiting cognitive distor-

tions, such as perceiving the alternative as less desirable (e.g., "he probably has an awful sense of humor"; e.g., Simpson et al., 1990); (b) *positive illusion*—thinking about a partner's faults in such a manner as to minimize them or transform them into virtues, as well as idealizing a partner's strengths by perceiving them in a very positive light (Murray & Holmes, 1993); and (c) *cognitive interdependence*—exhibiting perceptual and cognitive tendencies that rest on "relational" thought rather than "self-based" thought (e.g., "we, us, our," rather than "I, me, mine"; e.g., Agnew et al., 1998).

Deteriorating Relationships

It's a sad fact that many relationships deteriorate over time; many relationships end. No matter how close two people are, the interactions that once made friendships, romances, and relations between relatives, co-workers, teammates, classmates, and neighbors gratifying may at some point become less frequent or less enjoyable. As you've probably discovered on your own, sometimes these interactions actually become distasteful, perhaps even nasty. Why have relationship scientists had such a longstanding interest in the antecedents, processes, and consequences of deteriorating relationships? As Kenny (1995) noted, "society has an interest in preventing destructive relationships, and we are the people who are best equipped to assist society in this endeavor" (p. 598). It's well documented that "toxic" relationships—relationships characterized by destructive interactions—may have devastating consequences not only for the partners themselves, but also for others in their social network, including children, family, friends, or co-workers. Few factors exert a stronger causal role in the problems that confront people in the modern world—drug and alcohol abuse, loneliness, sexually transmitted diseases, violence, depression, the destruction of families, and the like. However one construes the costs and societal effects of relationship toxicity, it's clear that the effects of deteriorating relationships are profound and widespread. Perhaps this is why—likely more than at any other time in human history—relationships have entered the arena of public policy.

It seems unlikely that these problems will simply go away on their own. Moreover, relationship scientists tend to believe that the solutions are unlikely to be found in the "fixes" championed by pop self-help gurus, political commentators, bible-thumping preachers, or media celebrities. Instead, what's called for is rigorous, thoughtful research into the factors that cause relationships to deteriorate, as well as the interventions that are likely to prevent or reverse such deterioration. In fact, many scientists became relationship researchers in the first place because of a deeply felt desire to contribute to improving relationship life. As Bradbury (2002) expressed this social concern ("life goal" might be more apt, given the dedication that many relationship scientists bring to their work), "the key feature of applied relationships research is that it is designed with the eventual goal of bringing about better relationships." (p. 572).

Given the importance of marriage, it should come as no surprise that a great many studies have focused on marital dissatisfaction and instability (separation, divorce). Existing research tends to fall into one of three general traditions (Berscheid & Reis, 1998). The *sociological tradition* asks whether various demographic and descriptive variables predict dissatisfaction and divorce. The list of potentially relevant variables is seemingly infinite, including religion, age, prior divorce, cohabitation, length of courtship, socioeconomic status, fertility, illness, and so on. (Any good relationships textbook will review these findings.) The *clinical tradition* tends to focus its attention on discovering how the behavior of distressed couples differs from that of nondistressed couples. Couples are classified as distressed versus nondistressed using some valid criterion (e.g., whether they seek counseling, scores on a marital adjustment inventory); then their behavior on putatively relevant variables is compared. This approach led to the growth of *behavioral observation methods*, whereby couples are observed while they attempt to resolve an important conflict. The pioneers of this approach were Robert Weiss at the University of Oregon and John Gottman, first at Indiana

University and later at the University of Illinois and the University of Washington. These scientists believe that direct observation is the best way to determine objectively what really transpires during couple interaction (rather than relying on self-report, which may be colored by numerous biases). A third approach, the *social psychological tradition*, is most concerned with identifying the underlying causes of the processes that regulate interaction between partners (e.g., commitment, working models of attachment). Although each of these approaches has emphasized somewhat different issues, there is remarkable consistency among them in the causes of relationship deterioration that have been found to be most central.

Communication

One thing that clearly differentiates between functional and dysfunctional couples is the manner in which they communicate about conflictual issues. Of course, all relationships involve disagreements and competing interests. Relationship science has determined that it is not the frequency or character or even intensity of conflict that matters; rather, the key issue is how couples go about resolving conflict. *Negative affect reciprocity*—a pattern of increasing negativity that escalates as the conversation shifts from one partner to the other—is the hallmark of interaction in distressed couples, whereas nondistressed couples tend to exhibit behaviors that are likely to deescalate conflict and facilitate constructive solutions, such as accommodation (defined earlier; Margolin & Wampold, 1981), responsive listening, and soothing (Gottman et al., 1998). John Gottman— whose extensive observational analyses of marital problem-solving conversations represent some of the most comprehensive analyses in the field— characterizes distressed couples' destructive patterns of communication in terms of the so-called "four horsemen of marital apocalypse": *criticism*, *contempt* (focusing on the partner's moral or dispositional shortcomings as opposed to concrete behaviors), *defensiveness* (unwillingness to engage the partner's requests or complaints openly and honestly), and *withdrawal* (Gottman, 1994). Other researchers have identified related tendencies. For example, Christensen and Heavey (1993) examine the *demand–withdraw pattern*, which is characterized by one partner's tendency to withdraw in response to the other's request for a change in behavior. Relationship scientists continue to explore the details that differentiate between distressed and nondistressed communication. But very generally speaking, the fundamental difference is clear: Distressed couples communicate in ways that yield escalating negativity, foster withdrawal from the relationship, and preclude constructive problem-solving, whereas successful couples deal with problems by deescalating negativity and engaging one another in constructive and mutually respectful ways.

Conflict

Because conflict has many causes, scientists have sought to understand the many ways in which it can arise. One of the more common types of disagreement involves incompatibility. Because close partners' outcomes are interdependent, achieving important personal goals necessarily involves coordination of activity. Applying the principles of interdependence described earlier, partners can experience incompatibility because their outcomes do not mesh or because they cannot find ways of coordinating their actions so that both persons' desires may be satisfied. Sometimes incompatibility results from personality traits or dispositions that don't fit together or complement one another—for example, when both partners insist on being the dominant decision-maker. But although the effects of personality factors are noteworthy, this sort of variable typically accounts for only a small portion of couple conflict. Partners' values and predispositions toward each other tend to be more influential factors (Rusbult & Van Lange, 2003). For example, among romantic couples in North America, the division of labor is a common source of conflict.

Relationship scientists have also found that attributions about conflict—that is, the factors that each person judges to be the cause of each person's behavior—play a central role in couple functioning. Several systematic attributional tendencies have been identified. For example, there's

the so-called *actor–observer bias*: All other things being equal, people tend to perceive that they, themselves, make a larger contribution to the day-to-day functioning of the relationship than their partners do (e.g., when both partners estimate their personal contributions, their estimates typically sum to more than 100%; e.g., Orvis et al., 1976). For another example, there's the *self-serving bias*: When disagreements occur, we tend to think that our own perspectives are more justified than our partners' perspectives (e.g., Bradbury & Fincham, 1990). The most important reason for studying attributional tendencies is that they contribute importantly to couple functioning. For example, in unhappy couples, partners tend to blame each other for negative events while not giving each other credit for positive events. In happy couples the opposite pattern is evident; partners give each other credit for positive events but tend not to blame each other for negative events (e.g., Fincham et al., 2000). It's easy to see why the former pattern of attribution is termed *distress–maintaining*, whereas the latter pattern is *relationship–enhancing*.

Deception, Jealousy, and Betrayal

When a relationship is going well, it can be a source of great satisfaction and joy; when a relationship is going badly, it can cause distress and woe. To better understand distress and woe, many researchers study the "dark side" of relationships. For example, topics such as violence, betrayal, jealousy, bereavement, unrequited love, loneliness, and deception have received significant attention in recent years. This research is important not only in increasing basic scientific knowledge, but it also has enormous practical value: The better we understand the causes and consequences of relationship dysfunction, the better we become at developing effective interventions to address social problems. One important consideration in such research is that although relationship problems are distressing, they may also provide opportunities for growth and renewal. For example, although betrayal is surely corrosive to relationships and painful for all parties, it may provide an opportunity for forgiveness to occur (Fincham &

Beach, 2002). Similarly, jealousy has roots in the importance of the relationship to both parties; as such, the occurrence of jealousy offers relationship partners an opportunity to think through and discuss the ways in which each person's behavior affects the other's feelings (Buunk, 1991). As noted earlier for the phenomenon of conflict, it's not so much the problem itself as the manner in which partners go about trying to solve their problems that ultimately shapes couple functioning.

Conclusion

Before closing we want to note that in many ways, we feel blessed (and once again we literally mean "we," Caryl and Harry). We've managed to spend the better parts of our lives conducting scientific research regarding phenomena that many people find to be the most important and fascinating aspects of human existence—the interpersonal relationships in which our lives are deeply embedded. The ability to blend our personal curiosity about relationships with the urgent need for fuller, more accurate knowledge about how relationships operate and how they affect human welfare has made our professional lives both challenging and satisfying.[6] Our students sometimes wonder why we occasionally send them e-mail messages at 3:00 AM. The answer is simple: For both of us, when the itch to know more about relationships is awakened, we cannot help but scratch it.

There's no question that relationships are important, using nearly any definition of "important" that one might adopt. This central truth is acknowledged in diverse theories of human behavior, from the biological to the philosophical to the historical to the psychological. (In fact, this claim is so obvious that it's typically neither elaborated nor defended.) Empirical evidence regarding the impact of social relations is conclusive—indeed, it's no overstatement to describe it as overwhelming—in studies of both mental and physical health, across all parameters of human development, in virtually all domains of human activity, including productivity and creativity at

work, in school, or in recreation. It's not surprising that scholars in the natural and social sciences—from economics and political science to cognitive and affective science to genetics and medicine—increasingly incorporate principles of relationship science into their theories and research (although in many cases, these efforts are still in their infancy). As the quotation at the beginning of this essay asserts, it's simply impossible to understand the human condition without understanding the relationship context in which most human behavior takes place.

Although relationship science may no longer be in its infancy, it's at best in its early adolescence. Like all adolescents, the field is active, vibrant, and full of possibilities; perhaps more than some might like, it can also be sprawling, unruly, and difficult to fathom. Although much has been learned, those of us who work in this field appreciate how much more remains to be understood. To us, this is a cause for optimism: Interest in relationship science is burgeoning, and recent advances in the field's theoretical concepts and methodological tools offer unprecedented opportunities for deeper, more accurate understanding. We hope that the articles selected for inclusion in this reader convey to you the potential and excitement of relationship science. We invite you to join us in this endeavor.

REFERENCES

Agnew, C. R., Van Lange, P. A. M., Rusbult, C. E., & Langston, C. A. (1998). Cognitive interdependence: Commitment and the mental representation of close relationships. *Journal of Personality and Social Psychology, 74,* 939–954.

Altman, I., & Taylor, D. A. (1973). *Social penetration: The development of interpersonal relationships.* New York: Holt, Rinehart, & Winston.

Amabile, T. M. (1983). Brilliant but cruel: Perceptions of negative evaluators. *Journal of Experimental Social Psychology, 19,* 146–156.

Argyle, M. (1987). *The psychology of happiness.* London: Methuen.

Aron, A., & Aron, E. N. (1997). Self-expansion motivation and including other in the self. In S. Duck (Ed.), *Handbook of personal relationships: Theory, research, and interventions* (2nd Ed., pp. 251–270). Chichester: Wiley.

Asch, S. E. (1946). Forming impressions of personality. *Journal of Abnormal and Social Psychology, 41,* 258–290.

Backman, C. W., & Secord, P. F. (1959). The effect of perceived liking on interpersonal attraction. *Human Relations, 12,* 379–384.

---

[6]Besides which, this stuff makes for excellent dinner party conversation!

Berscheid, E., & Peplau, L. A. (1983). The emerging science of relationships. In H. H. Kelley, E. Berscheid, A. Christensen, J. H. Harvey, T. L. Huston, G. Levinger, E. McClintock, L. A. Peplau, & D. R. Peterson (Eds.), *Close relationships* (pp. 1–19). New York: W. H. Freeman.

Berscheid, E., & Reis, H. T. (1998). Attraction and close relationships. In D. T. Gilbert, S. T. Fiske, & G. Lindzey (Eds.), *Handbook of social psychology* (4th Ed.; Vol. 2, pp. 193–281). New York: McGraw-Hill.

Berscheid, E., & Walster, E. (1974a). A little bit about love. In T. L. Huston (Ed.), *Foundations of interpersonal attraction* (pp. 355–381). New York: Academic Press.

Berscheid, E., & Walster, E. (1974b). Physical attractiveness. In L. Berkowitz (Ed.), *Advances in experimental social psychology* (Vol. 7, pp. 157–215). New York: Academic Press.

Bowlby, J. (1969). *Attachment and loss: Vol. 1. Attachment.* New York: Basic Books.

Bowlby, J. (1973). *Attachment and loss: Vol. 2. Separation.* New York: Basic Books.

Bowlby, J. (1980). *Attachment and loss: Vol. 3. Sadness and depression.* New York: Basic Books.

Bradbury, T. N. (2002). Research on relationships as a prelude to action. *Journal of Social and Personal Relationships, 19,* 571–599.

Bradbury, T. N., & Fincham, F. D. (1990). Attributions in marriage: Review and critique. *Psychological Bulletin, 107,* 3–33.

Burgoon, J. K. (1994). Nonverbal signals. In M. L. Knapp & G. R. Miller (Eds.), *Handbook of interpersonal communication* (2nd Ed., pp. 229–285). Thousand Oaks, CA: Sage.

Buss, D. M., & Kenrick, D. T. (1998). Evolutionary social psychology. In D. T. Gilbert, S. T. Fiske, & G. Lindzey (Eds.), *Handbook of social psychology* (4th Ed.; Vol. 2, pp. 982–1026). Boston: McGraw Hill.

Buunk, B. P. (1991). Jealousy in close relationships: An exchange-theoretical perspective. In P. Salovey (Ed.), *The psychology of jealousy and envy* (pp. 148–177). New York: Guilford.

Byrne, D. (1971). *The attraction paradigm.* New York: Academic Press.

Cassidy, J., & Shaver, P. R. (Eds.) (1999). *Handbook of attachment: Theory, research, and clinical applications.* New York: Guilford.

Christensen, A., & Heavey, C. L. (1993). Gender differences in marital conflict: The demand/withdraw interaction pattern. In S. Oskamp & M. Costanzo (Eds.), *Gender issues in contemporary society* (pp. 113–141). Newbury Park, CA: Sage.

Clark, M. S., & Mills, J. (1979). Interpersonal attraction in exchange and communal relationships. *Journal of Personality and Social Psychology, 37,* 12–24.

Collins, N. L., & Miller, L. C. (1994). Self-disclosure and liking: A meta-analytic review. *Psychological Bulletin, 116,* 457–475.

Darley, J. M., & Gross, P. H. (1983). A hypothesis-confirming bias in labeling effects. *Journal of Personality and Social Psychology, 44,* 20–33.

Darwin, C. (1859). *On the origin of species by means of natural selection.* London: Murray.

Derlega, V. J., Metts, S., Petronio, S., & Margulis, S. T. (1993). *Self-disclosure.* Newbury Park, CA: Sage.

Diamond, J. (1998). *Why is sex fun? The evolution of human sexuality.* New York: Basic Books.

Erikson, E. (1950). *Childhood and society* (2nd Ed.; pp. 247–269). New York: W. W. Norton.

Festinger, L. (1954). A theory of social comparison processes. *Human Relations, 7,* 117–140.

Festinger, L., Schachter, S., & Back, K. W. (1950). *Social pressures in informal groups: A study of human factors in housing.* New York: Harper & Brothers.

Fincham, F. D., & Beach, S. R. (2002). Forgiveness in marriage: Implications for psychological aggression and constructive communication. *Personal Relationships, 9,* 239–251.

Fincham, F. D., Harold, G. T., & Gano-Phillips, S. (2000). The longitudinal association between attributions and marital satisfaction: Directions of effects and role of efficacy expectations. *Journal of Family Psychology, 14,* 26–285.

Folkes, V. S., & Sears, D. O. (1977). Does everybody like a liker? *Journal of Experimental Social Psychology, 13,* 505–519.

Freud, S. (1917). *Introductory lectures on psycho-analysis.* London: Hogart.

Fromm, E. (1962). *The art of loving.* New York: Harper.

Gottman, J. M. (1979). *Marital interaction: Experimental investigations.* New York: Academic Press.

Gottman, J. M. (1994). *What predicts divorce?: The relationship between marital processes and marital outcomes.* Hillsdale, NJ: Erlbaum.

Gottman, J. M. (1998). Psychology and the study of marital processes, *Annual Review of Psychology, 49,* 169–197.

Gottman, J. M., Coan, J., Carrere, S., & Swanson, C. (1998). Predicting marital happiness and stability from newlywed interactions. *Journal of Marriage and the Family, 60,* 5–22.

Hazan, C., & Shaver, P. (1987). Romantic love conceptualized as an attachment process. *Journal of Personality and Social Psychology, 52,* 511–524.

Holmes, J. G., & Rempel, J. K. (1989). Trust in close relationships. In C. Hendrick (Ed.), *Review of personality and social psychology* (Vol. 10, pp. 187–220). London: Sage.

Insko, C. A., & Wilson, M. (1977). Interpersonal attraction as a function of social interaction. *Journal of Personality and Social Psychology, 35,* 903–911.

Jones, E. E., Rock, L., Shaver, K. G., Goethals, G. R., & Ward, L. M. (1968). Pattern of performance and ability attribution: An unexpected primacy effect. *Journal of Personality and social Psychology, 10,* 317–340.

Jourard, S. M. (1964). *The transparent self.* New York: Van Nostrand.

Kelley, H. H. (1950). The warm-cold variable in first impressions of persons. *Journal of Personality, 18,* 431–439.

Kelley, H. H. (1979). *Personal relationships: Their structures and processes.* Hillsdale, NJ: Erlbaum.

Kelley, H. H., Berscheid, E., Christensen, A., Harvey, J. H., Huston, T. L., Levinger, G., McClintock., E., Peplau, L. A., & Peterson, D. R. (Eds.) (1983). *Close relationships.* New York: W. H. Freeman.

Kelley, H. H., & Thibaut, J. W. (1978). *Interpersonal relations: A theory of interdependence.* New York: Wiley.

Kenny, D. A. (1995). Relationship science in the 21st century. *Journal of Social and Personal Relationships, 12*, 597–600.

Kenrick, D. T., & Gutierres, S. E. (1980). Contrast effects and judgments of physical attractiveness: When beauty becomes a social problem. *Journal of Personality and Social Psychology, 38*, 131–140.

Langlois, J. H., & Roggman, L. A. (1990). Attractive faces are only average. *Psychological Science, 1*, 115–121.

Leary, M. R. (2001). The self we know and the self we show: Self-esteem, self-presentation, and the maintenance of interpersonal relationships. In G. J. O Fletcher & M. S. Clark (Eds.), *Blackwell handbook of social psychology: Interpersonal processes* (pp. 457–477). Oxford: Blackwell.

Lee, J. A. (1977). A typology of styles of loving. *Personality and Social Psychology Bulletin, 3*, 173–182.

Margolin, G., & Wampold, B. E. (1981). Sequential analysis of conflict and accord in distressed and nondistressed marital partners. *Journal of Counseling and Clinical Psychology, 49*, 554–567.

Maslow, A. (1968). *Toward a psychology of being* (2nd Ed.). New York: Van Nostrand.

McCullough, M. E., Rachal, K. C., Sandage, S. J., Worthington, E. L., Jr., Brown, S. W., & Hight, T. L. (1998). Interpersonal forgiving in close relationships II: Theoretical elaboration and measurement. *Journal of Personality and Social Psychology, 75*, 1586–1603.

Murray, S. L., & Holmes, J. G. (1993). Seeing virtues in faults: Negativity and the transformation of interpersonal narratives in close relationships. *Journal of Personality and Social Psychology, 65*, 707–722.

Murstein, B. I. (1976). The stimulus-value-role theory of marital choice. In H. Grunebaum & J. Christ (Eds.), *Contemporary marriage: Structures, dynamics, and therapy* (pp. 165–168). Boston: Little, Brown.

Newcomb, T. M. (1961). *The acquaintance process.* New York: Holt, Rinehart & Winston.

Noller, P. (1980). Misunderstandings in marital communication: A study of couples' nonverbal communications. *Journal of Personality and Social Psychology, 39*, 1135–1148.

Orvis, B. R., Kelley, H. H., & Butler, D. (1976). Attributional conflict in young couples. In J. H. Harvey, W. J. Ickes, & R. E. Kidd (Eds.), *New directions in attribution research* (Vol. 1, pp. 353–386). Hillsdale, NJ: Erlbaum.

Patterson, M. L. (1988). Functions of nonverbal behavior in close relationships. In S. Duck (Ed.), *Handbook of personal relationships: Theory, research, and interventions* (pp. 41–56). New York: Wiley.

Reis, H. T., Wheeler, L., Spiegel, N., Kernis, M. H., Nezlek, J., & Perri, M. (1982). Physical attractiveness in social interactions: II. Why does appearance affect social experience. *Journal of Personality and Social Psychology, 43*, 979–996.

Reis, H. T., & Shaver, P. (1988). Intimacy as an interpersonal process. In S. Duck (Ed.), *Handbook of personal relationships: Theory, relationships, and interventions* (pp. 367–389). Chichester: Wiley.

Rubin, Z. (1970). Measurement of romantic love. *Journal of Personality and Social Psychology, 16*, 265–273.

Rusbult, C. E. (1983). A longitudinal test of the investment model: The development (and deterioration) of satisfaction and commitment in heterosexual involvements. *Journal of Personality and Social Psychology, 45*, 101–117.

Rusbult, C. E., & Van Lange, P. A. M. (2003). Interdependence, interaction, and relationships. *Annual Review of Psychology, 54*, 351–375.

Rusbult, C. E., Verette, J., Whitney, G. A., Slovik, L. F., & Lipkus, I. (1991). Accommodation processes in close relationships: Theory and preliminary empirical evidence. *Journal of Personality and Social Psychology, 60*, 53–78.

Sarnoff, I., & Zimbardo, P. (1961). Anxiety, fear, and social affiliation. *Journal of Abnormal and Social Psychology, 62*, 356–363.

Schachter, S. (1959). *The psychology of affiliation.* Stanford, CA: Stanford University Press.

Sears, D. O. (1983). The person-positivity bias. *Journal of Personality and Social Psychology, 44*, 233–250.

Sedikides, C., & Strube, M. J. (1997). Self-evaluation: To thine own self be good, to thine own self be sure, to thine own self be true, and to thine own self be better. In M. P. Zanna (Ed.), *Advances in experimental social psychology* (Vol. 29, pp. 209–269). New York: Academic Press.

Simpson, J. A., Gangestad, S. W., & Lerma, M. (1990). Perception of physical attractiveness: Mechanisms involved in the maintenance of romantic relationships. *Journal of Personality and Social Psychology, 59*, 1192–1201.

Snyder, M., Tanke, E., & Berscheid, E. (1977). Social perception and interpersonal behavior: On the self-fulfilling nature of social stereotypes. *Journal of Personality and Social Psychology, 35*, 656–666.

Sullivan, H. S. (1953). *The interpersonal theory of psychiatry.* New York: W. W. Norton.

Swann, W. B., Jr., & Gill, M. J. (1997). Confidence and accuracy in person perception: Do we know what we think we know about our relationship partners? *Journal of Personality and Social Psychology, 73*, 747–757.

Thibaut, J. W., & Kelley, H. H. (1959). *The social psychology of groups.* New York: Wiley.

Van Lange, P. A. M., Rusbult, C. E., Drigotas, S. M., Arriaga, X. B., Witcher, B. S., & Cox, C. L. (1997). Willingness to sacrifice in close relationships. *Journal of Personality and Social Psychology, 72*, 1373–1395.

Wetzel, C. G., & Insko, C. A. (1982). The similarity-attraction relationship: Is there an ideal one? *Journal of Experimental Social Psychology, 18*, 253–276.

Wieselquist, J., Rusbult, C. E., Foster, C. A., Agnew, C. R. (1999). Commitment, pro-relationship behavior, and trust in close relationships. *Journal of Personality and Social Psychology, 77*, 942–966.

Zajonc, R. B. (1968). Attitudinal effects of mere exposure. *Journal of Personality and Social Psychology Monograph Supplement, 9*, Part 2, 1–27.

SECTION 1

Relationships in Our Lives

Never believe that you know the last word about any human heart.

— Henry James

The bird a nest, the spider a web, man friendship.

— William Blake

What role do relationships play in our lives? Although few would deny
that people care deeply about their ongoing connections with others, a full
appreciation of the impact of relationships involves more than simply
declaring that "humans are social animals." Relationships have been
an ever-present theme throughout human history, as evidenced in literature,
music, Biblical tales and precepts, anthropological studies of any and all
human societies, and the chronicles of kings, queens, emirs, emperors,
chiefs, and their nation-states and alliances. As discussed in the
introduction to this volume, the social psychological perspective to
understanding relationships differs from these and other approaches by its
focus on underlying processes, broad theoretical analysis, and rigorous
empirical scrutiny.

The articles in this section address several of the many ways in which
relationships affect our lives and everyday activities. Berscheid's article
provides a fitting introduction to this volume. In sounding a clarion call for
relationship science, Berscheid refers to the empirical study of relationships
as an "essential science." By this she means that relationships—not only
between two individuals but also the larger social networks in which dyadic
relationships reside—inherently and importantly influence many or most
phenomena in the social, behavioral, and biological sciences (Reis, Collins, &

21

Berscheid, 2000). Berscheid further notes that because relationships have profound implications for human health and welfare, researchers in this field have an obligation to contribute to public policy debates and to the design of treatments and interventions. Berscheid's paper stirringly articulates a fundamental rationale for the field to which many researchers resonate.

Research regarding physical and psychological health powerfully demonstrates the importance of relationships for human welfare—a fact that may account for the ever-growing popularity of this research topic. That these effects can be substantial is evident in House, Landis, and Umberson's (1988) analysis of five ambitious, long-term prospective epidemiological studies, which concluded that the risk for premature death associated with poor social integration exceeds the risk associated with such well-known health hazards as tobacco use. Similarly, relational circumstances are among the most potent factors affecting mental health, as demonstrated in numerous studies of depression, loneliness, life satisfaction, emotional distress, and happiness (Myers, 1992; Ryff, 1995). Conducting this sort of research—research that spans the social, physical, and medical sciences—often requires collaboration among scientists with diverse specializations. The social psychologist's contribution is to identify and document the interpersonal mechanisms involved in these dramatic effects on personal well-being.

Collins and her colleagues provide a compelling example of the health effects of relationships in their study of social support among pregnant, low-income women. Their research shows that social support predicts not only lesser postpartum depression among these women, but also the well-being of their babies: Women with more support had healthier babies with higher birth weight. To the medical community, studies such as this highlight the need to consider relationship circumstances when providing health care. To researchers, studies such as this stimulate our desire to more fully understand the mechanisms by which these and many other similar effects come about.

In the final article in this section, Reis and his colleagues explore the role of relationships in our lives by examining how social participation changes during early adulthood. Lifespan developmental theorists—such as Erikson (1950) and Hartup and Stevens (1997)—have a longstanding interest in describing and understanding developmental changes in the form and function of social interaction from infancy to old age. Reis et al.'s research relies on a diary method. Using participants' brief, structured descriptions of all of their social interactions lasting 10 minutes or longer, these researchers provide a detailed social ecology of the college years and later (around age 30). Their study reveals, for example, that as Dave and Anna move from their college years into adulthood, they come to spend somewhat less time with same-sex friends, spending more time with opposite-sex partners. Moreover, as they proceed into adulthood, Dave's and Anna's relationships become increasingly intimate, or personally meaningful to them; this increase in intimacy is evident not only in opposite-sex interactions, but also in same-sex interactions. Importantly, this study reminds us that although social relations matter greatly throughout life, the particular manner in which social needs are manifested and satisfied is likely to change as we mature and age (Hartup & Stevens, 1997).

REFERENCES

Erikson, E. (1950). *Childhood and society*. New York: Norton.

Hartup, W. W., & Stevens, N. (1997). Friendships and adaptation in the life course. *Psychological Bulletin, 121*, 355–370.

House, J. S., Landis, K. R., & Umberson, D. (1988). Social relationships and health. *Science, 241*, 540–545.

Myers, D. G. (1992). *The pursuit of happiness: Who is happy—and why*. New York: William Morrow & Co.

Reis, H. T., Collins, W. A., & Berscheid, E. (2000). The relationship context of human behavior and development. *Psychological Bulletin, 126*, 844–872.

Ryff, C. D. (1995). Psychological well-being in adult life. *Current Directions in Psychological Science, 4*, 99–103.

Suggestions for Further Reading

Baumeister, R. F., & Leary, M. R. (1995). The need to belong: Desire for interpersonal attachments as a fundamental human motivation. *Psychological Bulletin, 117*, 497–529. This paper reviews evidence from diverse sources in support of the claim that the "need to belong" is an abiding force in shaping human behavior and everyday experience.

Berkman, L. F. (1995). The role of social relations in health promotion. *Psychosomatic Medicine, 57*, 245–254. A useful overview of research illustrating how relationship factors influence health in diverse ways.

Brown, G. W., & Harris, T. (1978). *Social origins of depression: A study of psychiatric disorder in women*. London: Tavistock. A classic study in the area, this research was one of the first to link intimate relationships to depression.

Cohen, S., Underwood, L. G., & Gottlieb, B. H. (Eds.). (2000). *Social support measurement and intervention*. New York: Oxford University Press. How to measure social support and how to design interventions that improve social support.

Collins, W. A., & Laursen, B. (Eds.). (1999). *Relationships as developmental contexts: Minnesota Symposia on Child Psychology* (Vol. 30). Mahwah, NJ: Erlbaum. A collection of essays by some of the leading scholars who have studied the impact of relationships on development.

Diener, E., Suh, E. M., Lucas, R. E., & Smith, H. L. (1999). Subjective well-being: Three decades of progress. *Psychological Bulletin, 125*, 276–302. Many studies have examined the correlates of subjective well-being; this comprehensive review summarizes that research, including sections on relationships and social involvement.

Hartup, W. W. (1989). Social relationships and their developmental significance. *American Psychologist, 44*, 120–126. An insightful review of both changes and continuities in the impact of relationships across the human lifespan from infancy to old age.

Kiecolt-Glaser, J. K., & Newton, T. (2001). Marriage and health: His and hers. *Psychological Bulletin, 127*, 472–503. A comprehensive review of evidence regarding the impact of marriage on physical health, with an emphasis on behavioral and physiological mechanisms.

Leary, M. R., & Baumeister, R. F. (2000). The nature and function of self-esteem: Sociometer theory. In M. P. Zanna (Ed.), *Advances in experimental social psychology* (Vol. 32, pp. 1–32). San Diego: Academic Press. Sociometer theory argues that self-esteem is an internal, psychological monitor of social belongingness. This article describes the theory and presents supporting studies.

Stroebe, M. S., & Stroebe, W. (1983). Who suffers more? Sex differences in the health risks of the widowed. *Psychological Bulletin, 93*, 279–301. This article reviews empirical evidence regarding the consequences of bereavement and discusses why men frequently suffer even more devastating effects than women.

Uchino, B. N., Cacioppo, J. T., & Kiecolt-Glaser, J. K. (1996). The relationship between social support and physiological processes: A review with emphasis on underlying mechanisms and implications for health. *Psychological Bulletin, 119*, 488–531. This paper discusses three specific physiological processes that appear to underlie social support effects on health and well-being.

Discussion Questions

1. When Berscheid says that relationships are "the foundation and the theme of the human condition," what does she mean? Give an example of an important human behavior that is influenced by people's relationships with others.

2. What public programs and policies might our legislatures enact if they took relationship science research to heart? What sort of research should relationship scientists conduct in order to generate a knowledge base tailored to the needs of policymakers?

3. Discuss at least one specific mechanism by which the social support a pregnant woman receives might influence the health of her baby.

4. Discuss the qualities that, in your experience, make a relationship supportive. How might these qualities contribute to your health?

5. What are the advantages and disadvantages of the diary method that Reis and his colleagues used? For what sorts of scientific phenomena is this method best suited?

6. Using concepts and variables discussed by Reis et al., describe ways in which your patterns of social participation have changed over the past few years. What principles might you use to explain these changes?

The Greening of Relationship Science

Ellen Berscheid • University of Minnesota, Twin Cities Campus

This article briefly outlines the salutary implications for psychology of the development of a science of interpersonal relationships, which has emerged as multidisciplinary in nature and international in scope. Discussed are the potentials of relationship science: to unite psychological scholars with other social, behavioral, and biological scientists; to help integrate many subdisciplines within psychology; to bridge the chasm between researcher and practitioner; to extend knowledge of human behavior to people's daily lives and natural surroundings; and to inform issues of national concern. The realization of these potentials, however, requires transcendence of psychologists' traditional individualistic orientation, as well as more research on the impact of affect on cognition and research on the impact of relationships' exterior environments on their interior dynamics.

Garrison Keillor has observed that those of us who live in Lake Wobegon country were assigned three seasons rather than the customary four—we're either getting over winter, or we're getting ready for winter, or it *is* winter. But he forgot to mention that we were gifted with a very special day that separates our winter season from our getting-over-winter season: We awaken one morning and discover that if we squint our eyes and cock our heads just so, we can see that overnight Mother Nature has cloaked our trees in a diaphanous haze of green. It is then that we know winter is over and that our bleak landscape has begun its magical metamorphosis.

Today, if you squint your eyes and cock your heads just so, you can see the greening of a new science of interpersonal relationships. In this article, I discuss its potential to transform the landscape of psychology and, in accordance with the 1998 American Psychological Association Convention theme of "Prevention: Building Strength, Resilience, and Health in Young People," its potential to inform issues of national concern. If APA President Martin Seligman is correct that we psychologists, in trying "to undo the worst things in life . . . , forgot the mission of building the best things in life" (Seligman, 1998, p. 2), then psychology's contributions to the development of relationship science will go a long way to redressing that imbalance, for virtually every study of human happiness reveals that satisfying close relationships constitute the very best thing in life; there is nothing people consider more meaningful and essential to their mental and physical well-being than their close relationships with other people (see Berscheid & Reis, 1998). In outlining the potential of relationship science to change our disciplinary landscape, two nascent research areas will be highlighted—the impact of affect on cognition and the impact of relationships' exterior environments on their interior dynamics—for both are vital to realizing the promise of what many believe is not only the newest frontier of the social and behavioral sciences, but perhaps their last and greatest challenge.

In his classic work, *The Psychology of Affiliation: Experimental Studies of the Sources of Gregariousness*, Stanley Schachter observed that all of the social and behavioral sciences are "in good part devoted to the study of the process and products of human association" (Schachter, 1959, p. 1). Thus, it perhaps was inevitable that the evolution of these sciences would lead to a collaborative and direct confrontation of the core mysteries of human relationship. As this suggests, relationship science is not the exclusive province of psychology, or even of American social and behavioral sciences. The field has emerged as both international in scope and multidisciplinary in nature. In addition to psychology, it encompasses, for example, sociology, anthropology, communication studies, marital and family therapy, and even economics (e.g., University of Chicago economist Gary Becker recently received the Nobel Prize for his extension of microeconomic analysis to a wide range of personal relationship behavior, including marriage and divorce; Royal Swedish Academy of Sciences, 1992). Relationship science encompasses, as well, many of the health sciences, including epidemiology, traditional and alternative medicine, nursing, pharmacology, and veterinary science with its interest in human–companion-animal relationships.

Within psychology, the principal contributors to the development of relationship science have been clinical, counseling, developmental, and social psychology, with other subfields, such as cognitive psychology, playing strong supporting roles and with several others now appearing in the wings. Thus, as well as acting as an integrating force for scientific disciplines outside psychology, relationship science is proving to be an integrating force within psychology—one that has the potential to stem the much-lamented balkanization of our discipline.

Relationship science also has the potential to build a sorely needed bridge between psychological scholars and practitioners. Many studies have documented that a troubled relationship, especially a distressed marital or family relationship, is the most common presenting problem of those seeking psychotherapy (see Berscheid & Reis, 1998), as is reflected in the phenomenal and still-rising number of licensed marital and family therapists (e.g., Schrof, 1998). Many practitioners are actively supporting the development of a body of relationship knowledge to inform their therapeutic activities, while relationship scholars, in turn, are becoming more aware that they need the clinical wisdom of those serving on psychology's frontlines. To facilitate a continuing dialogue, the Minnesota Psychological Association, composed largely of practitioners, has begun to sponsor Bridging the Gap conferences that bring together scholars and practitioners on the common ground of their interest in understanding relationship dynamics, and such conferences to facilitate dialogue between relationship researchers and practitioners are now appearing nationally as well (e.g., the March 1998 Successful Relating in Couples, in Families, Between Friends, and at Work conference sponsored by the University of Arizona).

Although relationship science promises to be a cohesive force for many subdisciplines of psychology and to bridge the present chasm between researcher and practitioner, relationship science requires a departure from business as usual for psychological researchers. It especially requires surmounting the *individualistic* orientation to human behavior that historically has pervaded the field (see Sears, 1951). Psychology traditionally has been individualistic in at least two ways: First, psychologists usually search for laws that govern the behavior of a single individual, and second, in searching for the causes of an individual's behavior, psychologists typically look inside the individual. Attitudes, personality traits, skills, aptitudes, genes, and most other causes investigated by psychologists are located in the individual. Moreover, these causes are often assumed to have a physical, often neurophysiological, representation of some kind, whether or not that material representation explicitly figures into our theories, which it often does not.

In contrast, relationship scholars seek laws governing individuals' *interactions* with each other—or the influence each person's behavior exerts on his or her partner's behavior. Thus, the tissue of a relationship, and the object of study, is the oscillating rhythm of influence observed in the interactions of two people. This rhythm is displayed in regularities in their interaction pattern, and the goal of relationship science is to identify the causal conditions responsible for that rhythm. A relationship thus does not reside in the individual. Moreover, the rhythm of a relationship is revealed only over time; relationships are inherently temporal rather than static. Further, a relationship's rhythm is not presumed to have a direct material representation. Finally, like the other great forces of nature—such as gravity, electricity, and the four winds—a relationship itself is invisible; its existence can be discerned only by observing its effects.

Thinking dyadically, about recurring interconnections between individuals rather than properties within individuals, is foreign to some psychologists. It may seem especially foreign to our brethren in the psychobiological wings of our field who are currently pressing their claims in psychology and who sometimes seem to identify more with the hard, material sciences than with the so-called softer areas of their own discipline. But it shouldn't. Just one example of why it shouldn't is provided by subatomic physics, the exemplar of the study of matter, or of material "things." Physicists long ago were forced to recognize that the properties of isolated material particles are, as Niels Bohr observed, "definable and observable only through their interaction with other systems" (Bohr, 1934, p. 37). As one contemporary physicist elaborated, "Subatomic particles . . . are not 'things' but are interconnections between 'things,' and these 'things' in turn,

are interconnections between other 'things,' and so on. In quantum theory you never end up with 'things'; you always deal with interconnections" (Capra, 1982, p. 80). Thus, the growing attempt by the social and behavioral sciences to transcend the study of individuals—our material "things"—to the study of interconnections between individuals, as exemplified by relationship science, is neither without precedent nor revolutionary.

That the study of interconnections is not a new endeavor in the history of science needs to be underscored for a number of reasons, including the apparent belief of some of our colleagues, and many laypersons, that such subareas of psychology as neuropsychology or psychophysiology, where the focus of study engages matter, are more susceptible to scientific analysis than a field of study that focuses on interconnections that have no material substance. Another reason is that just as the shift from the study of things to the study of interconnections in subatomic physics required a shift in methodological and analytical technique—most notably in the use of probability theory—so too does relationship science require a shift away from our own traditional methodological and analytical techniques. Reflecting psychology's individualistic orientation, virtually all of our methodologies and statistics are predicated on the individual as the unit of analysis. As a consequence, relationship scholars often find themselves jerry-rigging old methodologies and statistics to accommodate the dyadic unit of analysis, but some, such as David Kenny and his associates (e.g., Kenny & La Voie, 1984), are creatively constructing new ones.

The most important potential of relationship science, of course, is to improve our understanding of human behavior. It cannot fail to do so because relationships with other humans are both the foundation and the theme of the human condition: We are born into relationships, we live our lives in relationships with others, and when we die, the effects of our relationships survive in the lives of the living, reverberating throughout the tissue of their relationships. Relationships thus are the context in which most human behavior occurs, and so understanding and predicting that behavior is difficult, if not impossible, if that context is ignored. It is for this reason that in *Close Relationships* (Kelley et al., 1983), my coauthors and I characterized relationship science as an essential science—essential in the sense of being necessary to the further development of the social, behavioral, and biological sciences.

Relationship science clearly is essential to the further development of social psychology. The ultimate intended destination of social psychological insights has always been the understanding of people behaving in their natural habitat—which is to say, then, of people behaving in the context of their ongoing relationships with others. But despite our Lewinian origins, social psychology in recent years has become almost as individualistic as other areas of psychology. Social psychology's shift from a focus on people's behavior in relationships, at least in small groups, to a focus on the individual, has been traced by Steiner (1974) to the publication of cognitive dissonance theory (Festinger, 1957). Subsequently fueled by the cognitive revolution in psychology, it was then that social psychologists began to tunnel into the minds of individuals—albeit, of course, with the worthy purpose of learning more about how people perceive and think about other people. Experimentally, however, the other people usually were strangers to the individuals, or even hypothetical constructions of people; that is, they were people with whom the individuals had never interacted in the past, were not interacting with in the present, and did not expect to interact with in the future. In short, the other people were persons with whom the individuals had no relationship—in the past, present, or future.

Despite the remarkable achievements of cognitive social psychology, the suspicion is growing that our understanding of many social phenomena not only is incomplete, but actually may be misleading in terms of its generalizability to behavior in the very situations to which we wish to predict: to naturalistic situations where people are almost always enmeshed in a web of ongoing relationships with others. The suspicion, in other words, is that the omnipresent relationship context of

human behavior makes a difference—that the properties of individuals do not exert simple and sovereign effects independent of context and that, in fact, the influence of the relationship context on behavior is often so powerful that it overturns what we think we know about behavior.

The disturbing corollary to this suspicion is that principles derived from studies of human behavior conducted in a relationless context cannot be expected to transfer in whole to behavior in the relationship context typical of naturalistic settings. Although there are many reasons for this, only two are mentioned here. First, encounters with others in our laboratory settings, even where actual interaction is permitted, usually are viewed by individuals as unlikely to be repeated in the future, whereas in ongoing relationships, there is almost always the prospect of future interaction. The prospect of future interaction, all by itself, makes a difference along many dimensions, as three decades of research have shown (e.g., Darley & Berscheid, 1967). The second reason, not unrelated to the first, is that passive and noninteractive encounters with others, typical of our laboratory settings, are usually devoid of motivational and affective import to individuals, whereas interactions with others in ongoing relationships almost never lack this import, as reflected in the fact that people experience emotion most frequently and most intensely in the context of their close relationships (see Kelley et al., 1983). The absence in so many of our studies of just these two features of relationships can be expected to produce surprises when we attempt to transfer our findings from relationless settings to even minimal relationship contexts (see Berscheid, 1994; Reis & Downey, in press).

An illustrative case in point is a study conducted over two decades ago by Miller and Norman (1975), who examined what we now call the "fundamental attribution error," or the tendency of people to underestimate the situational causes of another's behavior and overestimate the extent to which it reflects the other's dispositions, and the "actor–observer effect," where actors are more likely to attribute their own behavior to situational causes than observers are. What made

Miller and Norman's study different from most others before or since is that some participants actively interacted with each other in a prisoner's dilemma game, whereas other participants were simply passive observers of the others' interaction, as is typical of attribution studies. Following the interaction, the interactants and the passive observers were asked what caused the interactants' behavior.

Because the actor–observer effect already had been well-established, Miller and Norman (1975) predicted that in contrast to passive observers, active interactants would be more likely to attribute their own behavior to their situation—namely, the constraints of the prisoner's dilemma game—than to their dispositions, but that is not what they found. Contrary to prediction, the interactants "attributed more behavioral responsibility to themselves and perceived more disposition in their [own] behavior than did observers" (Miller & Norman, 1975, p. 507), who saw the situational constraints of the game as more responsible for the interactants' behavior. Moreover, the interactants saw themselves as more responsible for their partners' behavior than passive observers did, and not unexpectedly, the interactants' affective responses to their partners' behavior were much stronger than those of observers. In summary, the fact of relationship—even the minimal relationship of a brief laboratory interaction—made a difference. Miller and Norman gave a motivational explanation of their findings. They speculated, for example, that people need to feel in control of their interactions with others; the interactants' tendency, relative to passive observers, to see themselves as the cause of their own and their partners' interaction behavior may have served such a need.

Although more social psychologists are beginning to infuse motivational import into the settings in which they study social cognition, with the work of Forgas (e.g., 1994) and Clark (e.g., 1998) being prominent examples, there is a pressing need for more studies of cognition under conditions where motivational and emotional systems are activated, as they typically are in relationship contexts. That need has been underscored by recent neuroscience findings. Arnsten (1998), for example, has reviewed neurobiological evidence suggesting that during stressful experiences often associated with emotion, catecholamine neuromodulators released in the peripheral and central nervous systems appear to activate opposing actions in the brain—actions that turn on the amygdala (long associated with the expression of emotion) and turn off the prefrontal cortex (associated with working memory and also with the inhibition of inappropriate responses and distractions, both contributors to effective problem solving). In addition, at least one possible mediator of improved memory for emotional events has been identified by Gold (e.g., 1992), who has found that the arousal accompanying emotional states may affect neuroendocrine processes regulating memory storage; specifically, he has demonstrated that epinephrine release appears to modify brain function and enhance memory storage through an increase in blood glucose level.

Such neuropsychological findings are not only consistent with clinical observations by therapists that quarreling couples sometimes seem to be behaving without the full benefit of their prefrontal cortex, but they are consistent with many previous findings by relationship researchers as well. For example, relationship-interaction events tend to be better remembered than other kinds of events (e.g., see Berscheid, 1994), and Knapp and Clark (1991) have shown that people interacting in bad moods make poor problem solvers, whereas good moods do not have a commensurate beneficial effect.

It seems likely, then, that cognitive processing in active relationship-interaction situations is different from that observed in our typical research paradigms and that some, but probably not all, of the difference is due to the fact that when people are up close and personal, as they usually are in relationships, they constitute highly "emotogenic stimuli," as Albert Ellis (e.g., 1962) so aptly put it. If only for this reason, relationship scholars cannot automatically export findings obtained from passive, interactionless settings to relationship settings without knowing much more than we curently do about the association between affect and cognition.

A better understanding of behavior in relationship contexts will help us realize another potential of relationship science, and that is to inform public policy. Many issues of concern to state and federal policy makers engage close relationships, with the high rate of dissolution of marital and parental relationships in this country perhaps the most central. But legislative remedies depend on the identification of causes, and these, at least with respect to marital instability, still remain the subject of speculation and contentious debate, as was illustrated by a recent *Meet the Press* (Dukert, 1997) panel discussion.

The panel included Laura Schlessinger, a radio talk show host and columnist, also known as Dr. Laura; Reverend Jerry Falwell; Representative Jesse Jackson, Jr., congressman from Illinois; and Mario Cuomo, former governor of New York. After initial discussion, all agreed that the source of many of this country's troubles is, as one panel member put it, "the virtual extinction of the family as we know it." The threatened extinction of the family was the last thing they agreed on, however, for they then proceeded to expound their personal views of the causes of the problem and likely remedies. According to Schlessinger and Falwell, the cause is a deterioration of strong personal moral values, especially a sense of personal responsibility. Jackson and Cuomo, on the other hand, put the cause in widespread environmental changes that have weakened family relationships.

As for remedies, Schlessinger and Falwell, in line with their individualistic causal attributions, argued vigorously for actions that would change individuals' dispositions (e.g., Schlessinger emphasized educating people on the need to "honor covenantal vows"). In contrast, Jackson and Cuomo argued that the debilitating environment in which many marital and parental relationships are currently embedded needs to be changed. As Jackson put it, "The United States government can provide an environment for families to survive," a view subsequently elaborated by Cuomo, but loudly protested by Schlessinger and Falwell, who argued that governmental actions to improve stability would be ineffectual and therefore a waste of time and money.

It is not only the promise but the obligation of relationship science to inform such debates. And, as a matter of fact, the question of relationship stability in general, and marital stability in particular, has been the single most frequently addressed question by relationship scholars. However, this massive body of research isn't contributing much to public debate. It isn't—and it can't—because the lion's share of our stability research looks as though it was personally designed by Schlessinger and Falwell; that is, it overwhelmingly reflects an individualistic orientation to the question, and unfortunately, our myriad attempts to find an association between stability and properties of the individual haven't been very successful (see Glenn, 1990). As Karney and Bradbury (1995) detailed in their review of the stability literature, even the association between an individual's satisfaction with a marriage and its stability is not large; these authors concluded that "although there can be little doubt that an unstable marriage is marked by dissatisfaction, the experience of dissatisfaction does not strongly predict instability" (p. 20).

Political psychologists would not be surprised that the causes and remedies endorsed by the *Meet the Press* panel members broke along political lines. They have found that with respect to causal attributions for social problems, conservatives take an individualistic view and see the individual as responsible, whereas liberals are more likely to causally implicate the environment (e.g., Sitka & Tetlock, 1993). What is surprising, however, is that the stability literature suggests that relationship scholars are dyed-in-the-wool conservatives. More likely, we have been prey to the fundamental attribution error in our overemphasis on the causal role of individual dispositions and our neglect of relationships' environments—a neglect fostered by our individualistic perspective.

Still, it is disconcerting that social psychologists have neglected the impact of relationships' environments, because most of us are Lewinians and subscribe to his thesis that behavior is a function of the interaction between the properties of people and the properties of their environments (e.g., Lewin, 1951). Lewin (1951), it will be recalled, was inspired by the revolutionary experiments of Faraday and Maxwell, who banished the concept of ether from physics by demonstrating that knowing the properties of an individual particle (e.g., its mass and velocity) was not sufficient to predict its behavior; one also needed to know the properties of the electromagnetic field in which it was embedded because the particle's behavior was a function of the interaction between its properties and the field's properties. Given the present individualistic orientation of stability research, as well as most other relationship research, relationship science thus currently resembles pre-field theory in physics; that is, a relationship's environment currently tends to be viewed just as ether was—as a nebulous, undifferentiated, and causally innocuous surround.

Our treatment of relationships' environments as ether is both reflected in, and reinforced by, laypersons' beliefs that close, committed, and loving relationships are impermeable and unsinkable vessels that can sail through any environmental storm with impunity. The adages that "love conquers all" or "no third party can break up a happy relationship" reflect this popular belief, as do the results of studies my students and I have been conducting on the causal attributions people make for the quality of their relationships, including their ongoing romantic relationships (Berscheid, Ammazzalorso, Langenfeld, & Lopes, 1998). Few spontaneously mention their relationships' physical and social environments as having any impact whatsoever on the quality of their relationships. Their attributions focus not on their relationships' environments, or even on their own dispositions or on their partners' dispositions. Rather, they make Person × Partner causal attributions; that is, they almost invariably refer to the felicitous (or sometimes disastrous) fit between their own properties and their partners' properties to account for relationship quality.

When our respondents looked in the rearview mirror at one of their past (and now defunct) romantic relationships, however, we found, just as Heider (1958) would predict, that the role their relationship's environment played in producing its quality was then significantly more apparent to

them. Consistent with the thesis that psychological distance allows the influence of the surround to be better appreciated, they also were significantly more aware of the impact of the environment on a friend's romantic relationship than on their own relationship. When people are deep in the woods of an ongoing relationship, apparently they can't see the contextual forest for the tree of the relationship.

The problem this presents, of course, is that to the extent that people believe their relationships are unsinkable Titanics invulnerable to environmental assault, the probability that the partners will be vigilant for icebergs decreases and the chance that the relationship will drift into dangerous waters increases. Kelley (1992) has observed that the commonsense psychology people use to guide their behavior typically resides at the mesolevel of analysis; causal events occurring at the microlevel (i.e., rapidly occurring events invisible to the eye) and causal events at the macrolevel (i.e., events occurring slowly and at a distance) are much harder for people to detect and incorporate into their personal causal theories. Perhaps even relationships' immediate physical and social environments are too macro—too diffuse and slowly changing—for people to be aware of their effects on their relationships. If so, relationship scholars have the important job of mapping out the locations of environmental icebergs that will cripple if not sink relationships—environmental features that people need to avoid or change if they can and that legislators, who are in the business of changing environments, might try to modify to increase the stability of societally valued relationships.

Unfortunately, and congruent with our treatment of relationships' exteriors as ether, information about the effects of the physical and social environments in which relationships are embedded is sparse, as Levinger (1994) has eloquently detailed. But at least with respect to the stability question, some scholars are now turning their attention to the environments of relationships. For example, one iceberg deservedly receiving more attention is the extent to which the social environment contains attractive alternative partners to a present partner. The importance of this factor to stability was first empirically reported by Udry (1981), who found that spouses' perceptions of their marital alternatives not only predicted disruption longitudinally, but it independently was a better predictor of stability than was satisfaction with the relationship. More recent testimony to the potency of alternatives in the environment was reported by South and Lloyd (1995), who found that the risk of marital dissolution in this country is highest in geographical areas where there is an abundance of potential alternatives to a present spouse.

Other evidence of the influence of environmental conditions on relationships is slowly accumulating. For example, several recent studies have shown that the degree to which people in the partners' social environment approve of the relationship is a significant factor in premarital romantic relationship dissolution (e.g., Sprecher & Felmlee, 1992), and other studies, some recently conducted by Conger and his associates (e.g., Conger et al., 1990), have shown that economic strain not only promotes hostility in marital interaction, but reduces the frequency of supportive behaviors. Not surprisingly, job stress also influences couple interaction; for example, Repetti (1989) found a significant association between air traffic controllers' exposure to job stressors and anger and aggression in their family interactions.

However, much more research on the effects of environment on relationships is needed. Happily, the prospect for obtaining such research has been enhanced by Karney and Bradbury's (1995) stability model. Their vulnerability–stress model assumes that different couples inhabit different environments, different environments present different stressors, and different couples possess different vulnerabilities to those stressors. The fate of a relationship is theorized to hinge on the interaction between a couple's vulnerabilities and the nature of the stressors present in their relationship's environment. Another recent environmental stability model assumes that a single relationship is likely to inhabit several different environments as it moves through time, and it attempts to predict the temporal interplay between such changes in a relationship's environment and changes in the nature and quality of its interior dynamics (Berscheid & Lopes, 1997).

Although the predictive usefulness of these environmental models remains to be seen, at the least they may broaden our view of constructs traditionally associated with stability. "Commitment" and "closeness" are examples, with the current assumption being that the more committed the partners are to the relationship and the closer it is, the stronger and thus the more enduring the relationship will be. But both commitment and closeness tend to be measured as properties of individuals; that is, we measure individuals' intent to maintain the relationship or individuals' subjective feelings of closeness. But environmental models of stability suggest that our predictions might be enhanced if we adopted the perspective of civil engineers who typically calculate a structure's durability relative to the environmental forces it can withstand without disintegrating; that is, the strength of a bridge is calculated relative to the force of wind and water to which it will be exposed, a car relative to the speed with which it can hit a brick wall without crumpling, and as memorably demonstrated by John Cameron Swayze, a Timex watch by its plunge into a washing machine where it "took a licking but kept on ticking."

In short, it is not enough to know partners' vulnerabilities, or strengths, in a vacuum—or in ether, as it were. To predict a relationship's future, we also have to predict the nature of the environments the relationship will inhabit as it moves through time. About this we currently know little, but for certain types of relationships, especially romantic relationships, there may be relatively common environmental progressions over a relationship's life span (see Berscheid & Lopes, 1997). In addition to our need to learn more about the impact of relationships' exteriors, environmental models also suggest that our discourse, both among ourselves and with the public, should acknowledge more than it has that some fragile relationships survive forever because they never encounter a relationship-toxic environment, but some very strong relationships dissolve—not because they weren't close, or committed, or loving—but because fate, or the partners' ignorance of the vulnerability of their relationships to external forces, or perhaps even uninformed governmental policy decisions put their relationships in harm's way.

As new environmental models of stability suggest, there is reason to believe that one fine day, relationship scholars will have identified the environmental conditions that are healthy and those that are especially toxic to marital and parental relationships, and that not only will therapists be able to provide relationship risk probabilities to couples considering actions whose secondary result will be a change in their relationships' environments, but "environmental therapy" will be added to therapists' treatment arsenal for troubled relationships. Perhaps, then, we also can look forward to the day when legislators, before taking actions that change the environments of important relationships, routinely obtain environmental impact statements similar to those they now mandate for the Spotted Owl and the Mississippi Darter Fish.

If public opinion leaders and policy makers really believe that the family as we know it is threatened with extinction, and if they view this constellation of close relationships to be as precious and vital to human welfare and to the future of our culture as they obviously believe endangered species of wildlife are, then they will put their money and their influence alongside their beliefs and support the further development of relationship science. For example, they might well consider investing in a far-ranging big science initiative for the social, behavioral, and biological sciences focused on close relationships, especially marital and parent–child relationships.

In summary, the emergence of relationship science is a salutary event for psychology. In addition to its potential to unite psychological scholars with other social, behavioral, and biological scientists, to help integrate many subdisciplines within psychology, to narrow the gap between psychological researchers and practitioners, and to extend our knowledge of human behavior to people's daily lives and natural surroundings, it also has the potential to inform many issues of national concern. The emergence of relationship science represents the flag of a higher truth that

has now been planted in the individualistic soul of our discipline. Whether that flag will continue to stand or even someday wave over a new synthesis in psychology depends on whether future generations of scholars can conquer the daunting problems relationship science presents. About these problems, I have said little because—for those of us who personally are concerned about the future of valued human relationships, as well as those of us who professionally believe that our discipline needs to better address the fact that most human behavior occurs in the causally potent context of relationships—it is that very special morning when, at long last, we truly can see the green of a science of relationships.

NOTES

A version of this article was originally presented as part of an Award for Distinguished Scientific Contribution address at the 106th Annual Convention of the American Psychological Association, San Francisco, CA, August 1998.

Author's note. The comments of Gene Borgida and Mark Snyder, University of Minnesota, are gratefully acknowledged.

Correspondence concerning this article should be addressed to Ellen Berscheid, Department of Psychology, University of Minnesota, Twin Cities Campus, N309 Elliott Hall. Minneapolis, MN 55455. Electronic mail may be sent to bersc001@maroon.tc.umn.edu.

REFERENCES

Arnsten, A. F. T. (1988, June 12). The biology of being frazzled. *Science, 280*, 1711–1712.

Berscheid, E. (1994). Interpersonal relationships. *Annual Review of Psychology, 45*, 79–129.

Berscheid, E., Ammazzalorso, H. L., Langenfeld, N. W., & Lopes, J. (1998). *Studies in the attribution of cause of relationship quality.* Manuscript in preparation, University of Minnesota.

Berscheid, E., & Lopes, J. (1997). A temporal model of relationship satisfaction and stability. In R. J. Sternberg & M. Hojjat (Eds.), *Satisfaction in close relationships* (pp. 129–159). New York: Guilford Press.

Berscheid, E., & Reis, H. T. (1998). Attraction and close relationships. In D. T. Gilbert, S. T. Fiske, & G. Lindzey (Eds.), *The handbook of social psychology* (Vol. 2, 4th ed., pp. 193–281). New York: McGraw-Hill.

Bohr, N. (1934). *Atomic physics and the description of nature.* Cambridge, England: Cambridge University Press.

Capra, F. (1982). *The turning point: Science, society, and the rising culture.* New York: Simon & Schuster.

Clark, M. S. (1998, June). *Emotional states and the adoption of distributive justice norms*. Paper presented at the Ninth Biennial Conference of the International Society for the Study of Personal Relationships, Skidmore College, Saratoga Springs, New York.

Conger, R. D., Elder, G. H., Jr., Lorenz, F. O., Conger, K. J., Simons, R. L., Whitbeck, L. B., Huck, S., & Melby, J. N. (1990). Linking economic hardship to marital quality and instability. *Journal of Marriage and the Family, 52*, 643–656.

Darley, J. M., & Berscheid, E. (1967). Increased liking as a result of the anticipation of personal contact. *Human Relations, 20*, 29–40.

Dukert, B. C. (Executive Producer). (1997, December 21). *NBC News' Meet the Press*. New York and Washington, DC: National Broadcasting Corporation.

Ellis, A. (1962). *Reason and emotion in psychotherapy*. New York: Lyle Stuart.

Festinger, L. (1957). *A theory of cognitive dissonance*. Evanston, IL: Row, Peterson.

Forgas, J. P. (1994). The role of emotion in social judgments: An introductory review and an affect infusion model (AIM). *European Journal of Social Psychology, 24*, 1–24.

Glenn, N. D. (1990). Quantitative research on marital quality in the 1980s: A critical review. *Journal of Marriage and the Family, 52*, 818–831.

Gold, P. E. (1992). A proposed neurobiological basis for regulating memory storage for significant events. In E. Winograd & U. Neisser (Eds.), *Affect and accuracy in recall: Studies of "flashbulb" memories* (pp. 141–161). New York: Cambridge University Press.

Heider, F. (1958). *The psychology of interpersonal relations*. New York: Wiley.

Karney, B. R., & Bradbury, T. N. (1995). The longitudinal course of marital quality and stability: A review of theory, method, and research. *Psychological Bulletin, 118*, 3–34.

Kelley, H. H. (1992). Common-sense psychology and scientific psychology. *Annual Review of Psychology, 43*, 1–23.

Kelley, H. H., Berscheid, E., Christensen, A., Harvey, J. H., Huston, T. L., Levinger, G., McClintock, E., Peplau, L. A., & Peterson, D. R. (1983). *Close relationships*. New York: Freeman.

Kenny, D. A., & La Voie, L. (1984). The social relations model. *Advances in Experimental Social Psychology, 18*, 142–182.

Knapp, A., & Clark, M. S. (1991). Some detrimental effects of negative mood on individuals' ability to solve resource dilemmas. *Personality and Social Psychology Bulletin, 17*, 678–688.

Levinger, G. (1994). Figure versus ground: Micro- and macroperspectives on the social psychology of personal relationships. In R. Erber & R. Gilmour (Eds.), *Theoretical frameworks for personal relationships* (pp. 1–28). Hillsdale, NJ: Erlbaum.

Lewin, K. (1951). *Field theory in social science*. New York: Harper.

Miller, D. T., & Norman, S. A. (1975). Actor–observer differences in perceptions of effective control. *Journal of Personality and Social Psychology, 31*, 503–515.

Reis, H. T., & Downey, G. (in press). Introduction to special issue on cognition and relationships. *Social Cognition*.

Repetti, R. L. (1989). Effects of daily workload on subsequent behavior during marital interaction: The roles of social withdrawal and spouse support. *Journal of Personality and Social Psychology, 57*, 651–659.

Royal Swedish Academy of Sciences. (1992, October 13). *This year's laureate has extended the sphere of economic analysis to new areas of human behavior and relations*. Stockholm, Sweden: Author.

Schachter, S. (1959). *The psychology of affiliation: Experimental studies of the sources of gregariousness*. Stanford, CA: Stanford University Press.

Schrof, J. M. (1998, January 19). Married . . . with problems. *U.S. News & World Report*, pp. 56–57.

Sears, R. R. (1951). A theoretical framework for personality and social behavior. *American Psychologist, 6*, 476–482.

Seligman, M. E. P. (1998, June). Striking a healthy balance in ethics. *APA Monitor*, p. 2.

Sitka, L. J., & Tetlock, P. E. (1993). Providing public assistance: Cognitive and motivational processes underlying liberal and conservative policy preferences. *Journal of Personality and Social Psychology, 65*, 1205–1223.

South, S. J., & Lloyd, K. M. (1995). Spousal alternatives and martial dissolution. *American Sociological Review, 60*, 21–35.

Sprecher, S., & Felmlee, D. (1992). The influence of parents and friends on the quality and stability of romantic relationships: A three wave longitudinal investigation. *Journal of Marriage and the Family, 54*, 888–900.

Steiner, I. D. (1974). Whatever happened to the group in social psychology? *Journal of Experimental Social Psychology, 10*, 93–108.

Udry, J. R. (1981). Marital alternatives and marital disruption. *Journal of Marriage and the Family, 43*, 889–897.

Social Support in Pregnancy: Psychosocial Correlates of Birth Outcomes and Postpartum Depression

Nancy L. Collins, Christine Dunkel-Schetter, Marci Lobel, and Susan C. M. Scrimshaw

This prospective study examined the effects of prenatal social support on maternal and infant health and well-being in a sample of low-income pregnant women ($N = 129$). Three aspects of support (amount received, quality of support received, and network resources) and four outcomes (birth weight, Apgar scores, labor progress, and postpartum depression) were studied. Results indicated that women who received more support had better labor progress and babies with higher Apgar scores. Women with higher quality support had babies with higher Apgar scores and experienced less postpartum depression. Also, women with larger networks had babies of higher birth weight. Further analyses indicated that the outcomes as a whole were more consistently predicted by instrumental rather than emotional forms of support. Finally, although there was some evidence for stress-buffering effects of support, the overall findings were more consistent with a main effect model.

Social relationships play a central role in shaping the quality of people's lives. Yet surprisingly little is known about the specific social resources that influence health and well-being. This may be due, in part, to inconsistencies between the way that social support is defined and the way it is operationalized (Coyne & Bolger, 1990; Coyne & DeLongis, 1986; Lakey & Cassady, 1990). Empirical research on support and health has been largely intrapersonal despite the interpersonal emphasis of social support theory. As noted by Gottlieb (1985), "investigators have settled into a way of measuring social support that makes it a property of the person rather than an environmental resource or at least an interpersonal exchange that has some basis in actual experience" (p. 357).

In seeking to understand the role of supportive relationships in well-being, it is important to distinguish between the effects of social support on psychological versus physical health. Although there is fairly strong evidence that social support is beneficial to psychological well-being (see Kessler & McLeod, 1985, for a review), research on physical health outcomes has been less conclusive (for reviews, see Berkman, 1985; Schwarzer & Leppin, 1991; Wallston, Alagna, DeVellis, & DeVellis, 1983). Here, shortcomings in the measurement of social support, coupled with methodological weaknesses, have made it difficult to draw definitive conclusions (Cohen & Syme, 1985). For example, the dependent measure of health used in most studies is self-reported symptomatology, a highly subjective index that is influenced by a variety of personality, mood, and cultural factors (Pennebaker, 1982). Unfortunately, the few studies that have included more objective outcomes such as mortality and morbidity (e.g., Berkman & Syme, 1979; House, Robbins, & Metzner, 1982; Schoenbach, Kaplan, Fredman, & Kleinbach, 1986) have used structural measures of support that provide little information about the functional aspects of relationships that may contribute to people's health (Berkman, 1985; Cohen & Syme, 1985). Thus, after years of research, many questions about the health benefits of social support remain.

The present article addresses some of these questions by examining the effects of enacted support in a prospective study of women during pregnancy. Our primary focus was on objective indicators of maternal and infant health, although significant psychological outcomes were studied as well. Examining social support in the context of pregnancy is valuable for a number of reasons. First, unlike illnesses such as coronary heart disease or cancer, pregnancy is relatively short in duration and has specific endpoints. Second, pregnancy is a health event for which there is a defined set of physical and mental health outcomes. Measures such as infant birth weight provide reliable and objective indicators of infant health, and maternal postpartum depression is a well-researched mental health outcome. Finally, there is a pressing need for further research on the psychosocial variables that contribute to birth outcome. The United

States has an alarmingly high infant mortality rate, and biomedical risk factors alone are poor predictors of adverse birth outcomes (Institute of Medicine, 1985). As a result, researchers have become increasingly interested in the psychosocial factors that may contribute to maternal and infant health (e.g., Bragonier, Cushner, & Hobel, 1984; Istvan, 1986; Lobel, in press). Indeed, in his classic review, Sidney Cobb (1976) highlighted the importance of social support in pregnancy.

Conceptualizing Social Support

There is some agreement that support involves the exchange of social resources between individuals (Cohen & Syme, 1985; Kahn & Antonucci, 1980; Shumaker & Brownell, 1984; Thoits, 1985). A number of taxonomies have been developed to identify these resources (e.g., House, 1981; Weiss, 1974; Wills, 1985), and there is consensus on at least three broad categories of provisions: (a) emotional support (expressions of caring and esteem), (b) informational support (advice or guidance), and (c) instrumental support (tangible goods or assistance with tasks).

Although theoretical definitions of social support emphasize the interpersonal exchange of resources, the vast majority of studies operationalize support by asking people to report on whether support is available to them rather than whether they have actually received support from others. Measures of *available support* concern a person's general perception or belief that people in their social network would provide assistance in times of need. In contrast, *received* or *enacted* support refers to supportive exchanges that have actually occurred within a specific context. These exchanges may be directly observed, but they are most often measured by asking people to report on support that they have received in some recent time period (e.g., Barrera, Sandler, & Ramsey, 1981).

As noted by Schwarzer and Leppin (1991), perceived available support is anticipatory, whereas received support involves behaviors that are perceived to have actually occurred. And, whereas we might expect the two forms of support to be closely associated, they appear, instead, to be largely independent constructs. For example, in a review on this topic, Dunkel-Schetter and Bennett (1990) found that in studies that measured both constructs, expectations of available support were associated only modestly or not at all with actual support received in specific situations (also see Barrera, 1986). In addition, researchers are beginning to conclude that perceptions of available support are more closely tied to stable individual differences than to environmental provisions that exist outside the individual (Bolger & Eckenrode, 1991; Lakey & Cassady, 1990; Sarason, Sarason, & Shearin, 1986).

Both aspects of social support—its availability and its receipt—are likely to be important in understanding the various ways in which social relationships may influence health and well-being. Nevertheless, when ongoing events require the continued regulation of emotional and environmental demands and it becomes necessary to seek the help of others, a person's well-being should depend largely on the amount and quality of supportive provisions received from his or her network (Gottlieb, 1985). As Gore (1985) stated, "the question of a stress-buffering effect of social support, strictly speaking, is contingent upon evidence that support is mobilized, not that it exists as a potential" (p. 269). Understanding these processes calls for increased attention to environmental and behavioral perspectives of social support, which have been underemphasized in the research literature.

A shift from studying available support to studying aspects of received support requires that a number of important conceptual issues be considered. First, received support is complex and multidimensional (Dunkel-Schetter & Bennett, 1990; Shinn, Lehmann, & Wong, 1984; Tardy, 1985). Past research has often simply measured the frequency of supportive acts or the number of network members who provided types of support. Yet, whether support is given in a considerate manner and whether the recipient is satisfied with it are likely to be crucial in determining whether such provisions are beneficial (Barrera, 1981; Dunkel-Schetter, Blasband, Feinstein, & Herbert, 1992). Thus, quality of support received may need to be distinguished

from the amount or quantity of support given. Other important distinctions can be made between different types of support received (i.e, instrumental vs. emotional) and between different providers of support (e.g., friends vs. family). Support researchers and theorists have tended to emphasize the value of emotional support, but several studies suggest that the provision of instrumental support may be a critical resource for successfully managing many life challenges (Kaniasty & Norris, 1992; Schaefer, Coyne, & Lazarus, 1981).

A second concern in assessing received support is that the demands of a particular stressor and the ecological context must be considered (Cohen & Wills, 1985; Dunkel-Schetter & Bennett, 1990; Vaux, 1988). Different recipients of social support and different stressors may vary in the extent to which they benefit from specific types of social support (Cutrona & Russell, 1987; Hobfoll, 1989).

Finally, an important issue to consider is the timing of the support measures with respect to the developmental time course of a health outcome. As noted by Cohen (1988), short-term changes in a person's behavior or in one's environment are unlikely to have an impact on outcomes that have a long developmental sequence. Hence, repeated measures of social support would provide a more valid assessment of the social provisions received over the course of a stressor as well as a more reliable and powerful basis for detecting their effects. Many past studies have been cross-sectional, and longitudinal studies have failed to measure support on more than one occasion.

In sum, strong tests of the effects of received support in correlational studies will require that researchers be responsive to a number of important conceptual issues not addressed in past work. In the present study, we responded to these issues in several ways. First, we studied social support in a group of individuals experiencing a common life challenge—pregnancy—increasing the likelihood that support effects could be detected. Second, our support measures were specifically designed with consideration of the support needs and experiences of this population, and our instruments were tailored to our particular sample, which was composed of women of diverse ethnic backgrounds, low levels of education, and low income. Third, we assessed several types of support and measured the amount of support received, as well as satisfaction with that support. Finally, we measured support on multiple occasions throughout pregnancy.

Role of Social Support in Pregnancy

How might social support promote maternal and infant health? Although pregnancy and the birth of a child are often joyful, they are also typically stressful experiences characterized by substantial psychological and physical change (Lederman, 1984; Reading, 1983). Supportive relationships may enhance feelings of well-being, personal control, and positive affect, thereby helping women to perceive pregnancy-related changes as less stressful (Norbeck & Anderson, 1989; Tietjen & Bradley, 1985). This may result in lowered rates of stress-induced biochemical responses and fewer stress-related health behaviors such as smoking and alcohol use (Pagel, Smilkstein, Regen, & Montano, 1990). Pregnancy is also a health challenge that requires specific health-care regimens. Informational support may provide guidance with respect to adequate prenatal care, proper nutritional and health-care practices, and preparation for labor and delivery (Aaronson, 1989; Burnes-Bolton, 1988; Zweig, LeFevre, & Kruse, 1988). In addition, help with daily tasks such as household chores and child care can provide needed assistance with physically taxing demands that may be harmful to expectant mothers, especially late in pregnancy (Mamelle, Laumon, & Lazar, 1984; McDonald et al., 1988).

Although social support should be valuable to all expectant mothers, life circumstances may place some women in greater need than others. For example, adolescents, unmarried women, and women with few economic resources may be especially likely to benefit from support. Pregnancy is not uniformly stressful for all women, and there is growing evidence that women with especially high prenatal stress are at greater risk for poor outcomes (Lobel, Dunkel-Schetter, & Scrimshaw, 1992;

Turner, Grindstaff, & Phillips, 1990; see Lobel, in press, for a review). Consequently, the effects of social support on maternal and infant health may be more pronounced among women who experience high levels of environmental stress. Interactions between support and stress are generally interpreted as evidence for a stress-buffering effect of social support (Cohen & Wills, 1985).

Present Study

The present study examines the effects of prenatal social support on birth outcomes and maternal depression in a sample of economically disadvantaged women. This research had three primary goals. The first goal was to test the effects of different aspects of enacted support (e.g., quality vs. quantity) on maternal and infant health and well-being. It was predicted that women who received more social support and higher quality support during pregnancy would have healthier babies, better progress in labor, and fewer depressive symptoms after childbirth. A second goal was to determine whether specific types of support (i.e., instrumental vs. emotional) were more strongly associated with particular outcomes (e.g., physical vs. psychological health). Given the needs of the population being studied, we predicted that instrumental support would emerge as especially beneficial. Our final goal was to determine whether social support was more strongly associated with health and well-being in women who experienced the highest levels of stressful life events. Because our sample was composed of low-income women with many sources of stress in their lives, we expected there to be stronger evidence for main effects of support than for stress-buffering effects.

Method

Overview

The current study used a subset of data from a larger investigation of psychosocial factors in pregnancy conducted in the public prenatal clinic of a university-affiliated hospital (also see Dunkel-Schetter, Lobel, Collins, Hobel, & Scrimshaw, 1993; Lobel et al., 1992). The clinic serves women from the local area, most of whom are economically disadvantaged. Information was gathered on a variety of psychological and social variables, but this report is concerned only with findings related to social support. Women were interviewed on multiple occasions throughout pregnancy. Some aspects of social support (amount and quality of received support) were measured repeatedly; other aspects (social network and satisfaction with support from baby's father and from health-care providers) were measured at a single interview only. Birth outcomes were abstracted from medical charts, and maternal postpartum depression was assessed in a single postpartum interview. Multivariate analyses were conducted using structural equation modeling, which allowed us to simultaneously examine the impact of different aspects of support on several correlated birth outcomes while controlling for background factors and medical history.

Subjects

Eligibility and recruitment. To participate in the study, subjects were required to be at least 18 years of age, at 15 weeks or less gestation, and able to speak either English or Spanish.[1] Of all the eligible women approached during a 3-year span, 88% agreed to participate. Reasons for not enrolling included not wanting to discuss personal topics, feeling too tired, and husband's disapproval.

Current sample description. The current sample was composed of 129 women enrolled in the project who delivered a live infant at the study hospital and completed a postpartum interview. On average, subjects were 12.4 (*SD* = 3.2) weeks

pregnant upon entry into the study. Participants ranged in age from 18 to 42 (*M* = 27.7, *SD* = 5.1) years and had an average of 10.8 (*SD* = 3.3) years of education. The sample was primarily Latina (65%), with a small percentage of African-Americans (20%), Anglos (13%), and others (2%). The majority of women (68%) were multiparas (had previously borne children), and more than half chose to be interviewed in Spanish. A total of 58% of the subjects were married, although 78% reported living with the baby's father at the time of entry into the study. Although we did not gather information on income, approximately one in five subjects (21.5%) reported that they received no monetary support from the baby's father. In addition, 70% of the women in the sample reported that they had difficulty paying for medical care and meeting monthly expenses, and over 50% reported difficulty in paying for food. Most subjects paid for prenatal care on a visit-by-visit basis or had public medical assistance.

During the period of data collection, an additional 134 clinic patients enrolled in the project, but did not complete all components of the study and are therefore not included in this report. Known reasons include spontaneous abortions, therapeutic abortions, transfer to private care or to other medical facilities, moving, and no return for postpartum care, with attempts at telephone contact unsuccessful. Analyses of partial questionnaire data showed that these women were not significantly different from the present sample with respect to age, education, parity, or marital status. However, the current sample was significantly more likely to be Latino and living with the baby's father. Additional analyses of 65 women who had medical records data showed that women in the present sample were at lower medical risk and delivered babies that weighed slightly more and had higher Apgar scores than women not in the sample (all *ps* < .05). Although these differences tended to be small, they indicate that the current sample was somewhat better off than those who did not complete all components of the study, as might be expected. These differences, however, suggest that any results obtained with the current sample may underestimate, rather

---

[1] Near the end of data collection, the eligibility requirement based on weeks of gestation was relaxed to allow medically high-risk women who had reached as many as 20 weeks of gestation to participate in the study. This change was initiated to increase the number of high-risk subjects in the study.

than overestimate, the effects of support on birth outcomes.

Measures

The selection of measures was made with particular concern for the sample's cultural and linguistic diversity, low level of education, and the necessity to administer interviews in the clinic quickly and with ease. Standard scales and specially developed sets of structured questions were used to assess the major study variables. All measures required equivalent Spanish and English versions, and the selection, adaptation, and translation of measures took place during 1 year of pretesting in the clinic. Instruments were chosen and developed so that they yielded equivalent meaning in Spanish and English and could be easily understood by women with little formal education. All instruments were translated in a forward and backward fashion by experienced translators. Because there are national and dialect differences in the way that Spanish is spoken, translations were also confirmed by a group of Spanish-speaking research team members with varying national backgrounds.

Received social support. On the basis of the guidelines discussed above, we developed a measure of social support that would be appropriate for low-income pregnant women and would be meaningful to administer repeatedly. Of the forms of support identified in the theoretical and empirical literature, it was expected that four types would be most applicable to this sample: (a) material aid, (b) assistance with tasks, (c) advice or information, and (d) listening while one expresses beliefs or feelings.

The social support instrument had four sections, one corresponding to each type of support. For each section, subjects were first asked whether they had received that type of support in the previous week. For example, to assess task support, women were asked, "In the past seven days, did you get help from anyone with things you had to do such as errands, household tasks, or child care?" Responses were recorded as yes or no. If subjects answered yes, they were asked to

list who provided that type of support and to rate how satisfied they were with the support that person had provided on a scale from 1 (*not at all*) to 4 (*very much*). The current sample was queried about received support an average of four times during pregnancy, with the number of interviews ranging up to nine. The vast majority of women (93%) had at least three prenatal assessments.

Several indexes were computed from this measure. First, to provide an overall summary score of the support each woman received during pregnancy, an index of average amount of received support was computed. For each interview, receipt of the four types of support was counted, with 0 indicating no support received, 1 indicating one type of support, 2 indicating two types, and so on. Thus, for any one interview, subjects reported from 0 to 4 types of support received. Scores across interviews were then averaged so that amount of support was not confounded with the number of interviews completed.[2] On average, women reported receiving 1.7 ($SD = 0.94$) types of support at each interview. Four percent of the sample reported no support at each interview, and only 2% reported receiving all four types of support at each interview. Because we also wanted to explore the relative effects of different types of support, separate indexes were also computed for each of the four types. Thus, women received scores that reflected the average amounts of material, task, informational, and emotional support they received over the course of pregnancy. These scores could range from 0 (for women who never reported receiving that type of support at *any* interview) to 1 (for women who reported receiving that type of support at *every* interview). Thus, higher scores on these indexes indicate that women received that type of support more often over the course of pregnancy.

---

[2] An examination of the consistency in these measures over time indicated moderate stability in the amount of social support a woman reported each week and in her satisfaction with that support. Because there was some fluctuation, averaging over the course of pregnancy provides the best overall summary index of the quantity and quality of support received during that time.

Next, an index of satisfaction with received support was computed. Average satisfaction ratings from each interview were computed, then averaged across interviews. This score ranged from 1 to 4. The mean satisfaction rating was 3.7 ($SD = 0.41$). Separate satisfaction indexes were also computed for each of the four types of support.

Baby's father support. An eight-item scale was developed to assess overall support received during pregnancy from the baby's father. This measure was administered once in the third trimester (at 30 weeks gestation, on average) and women were asked to respond in terms of the father's behavior since they became pregnant. Respondents were asked how much the baby's father had provided money, helped with errands, listened to worries and concerns, helped solve problems, and showed that he cared. Two additional items asked how often the baby's father disappointed them and was critical or short-tempered. These seven items were rated on a scale from 0 (*never*) to 4 (*almost always*). A final item asked subjects how satisfied they were, overall, with the support given by the baby's father since they became pregnant, on a scale from 1 (*not at all*) to 4 (*very much*). When factor analyzed, all eight items loaded highly on one factor and were therefore summed to form a single composite. Scores ranged from 6 to 34, with a mean of 26.9 ($SD = 6.9$). The scale had high internal consistency in both English ($\alpha = .94$) and Spanish ($\alpha = .90$).

Health care provider support. A six-item scale was developed to assess satisfaction with support received from health care providers. This measure was also administered in a single interview during the third trimester. Three items asked how satisfied subjects were with the emotional support, information, and overall care they had received from nurses at the clinic. Three identical items asked about support from their doctors. Responses were made on a scale from 1 (*not at all*) to 4 (*very much*). When factor analyzed, all items loaded highly on a single factor and were therefore summed. Scores ranged from 9 to 24, with a mean of 20.59 ($SD = 3.7$). Cronbach's alpha was .92 for assessments conducted in English and .81 for assessments in Spanish.

Network resources. To assess social network resources, a variable was computed on the basis of number of kin, number of close friends, and whether the subject was living with the baby's father. Subjects were given one point each if they (a) had at least one relative living in the area, (b) had at least one close friend in the area, and (c) were living with the baby's father. The mean network score was 2.7 ($SD = 0.50$). None of the women reported having no network resources, but 25% of the sample were lacking at least one of the three.

Depression. Postpartum depressive symptoms were measured with the Center for Epidemiological Studies Depression scale (CESD; Radloff, 1977). This 20-item scale is a widely used measure of depressive symptomatology and has been shown to be valid and reliable in many samples, including pregnant women (Turner et al., 1990; Zuckerman, Amaro, Bauchner, & Cabral, 1989). Subjects were asked to respond in terms of how they felt during the previous week. Scores ranged from 20 to 63, with a mean of 33.67 ($SD = 10.6$). Cronbach's alpha in this sample was .88 in English and .89 in Spanish.

A brief measure of depressive symptoms was also included in each prenatal interview. Women were asked the extent to which they felt sad, felt hopeless, and had been crying during the previous 7 days. Responses to each of these three items were given on a scale from 1 (*not at all*) to 4 (*very much*). Cronbach's alpha ranged from .59 to .83 within interviews, with a mean reliability of .78 in English and .71 in Spanish. The three items were summed for each interview and then averaged across interviews. The mean prenatal depression score was 1.65 ($SD = 0.56$). When computed across interviews, the reliability was .86 in English and .85 in Spanish, indicating a fair degree of stability in depressive symptoms over the course of pregnancy.

Prenatal life events. A measure of stressful life events was adapted from the Los Angeles Epidemiological Catchment Area study (Golding, 1989) and was administered in the postpartum interview. This measure contained 22 events such as moving, being robbed, having troubles with immigration, and having someone close die. Subjects were asked whether they or a close family member had experienced these events at any time during their pregnancy. Women reported an average of 2.3 life events during pregnancy, with a range from 0 to 10. Twenty-eight subjects (21.5%) experienced no event.

Parity and medical risk. Because women giving birth for the first time have been shown in some studies to experience more adverse outcomes (e.g., Zax, Sameroff, & Farnum, 1975), it was important to control for this variable (parity). Nearly one third (31.5%) of the sample was giving birth for the first time.

Medical risk was scored from information recorded in each woman's medical chart. Although medical risk is often used as a dichotomous variable (i.e., high vs. low risk), a more sensitive continuous measure was developed here that took both prepregnancy and pregnancy conditions into account. A list of 62 criteria considered as contributing to risk was developed after a review of the medical literature and consultation with obstetric experts. Six categories of maternal risk were included on the basis of major medical risk classification instruments (Selwyn, 1982): (a) subject's medical history (e.g., renal disease or epilepsy), (b) family history of diabetes or hypertension, (c) gynecological and obstetric history (e.g., previous stillbirths or second trimester spontaneous abortions), (d) complications of past pregnancies (e.g., preeclampsia or placenta abruptio), (e) unusual features of current pregnancy (e.g., multiple gestation or Rh negative status), and (f) current pregnancy complications (e.g., edema or incompetent cervix). Each item was rated 1 if present and 0 if absent. Medical risk was calculated by summing these ratings. Scores ranged from 0 (6.2% of the sample) to 14 (0.8% of the sample). Average medical risk was 3.5, and the median was 3. Although most subjects experienced at least one risk-contributing condition, risk scores for the majority were at the low end of the scale, as would be expected.

Labor and infant outcomes. Birth outcomes were selected on the basis of several criteria. First,

we chose outcomes that have the greatest clinical significance and have been examined in prior research on psychosocial and medical predictors of pregnancy outcome. In addition, to be used in regression analyses, the outcome had to be measured on either an interval or an ordinal scale. Finally, to reduce redundancy in our dependent measures, we sought outcomes that were expected to be somewhat independent from one another. On the basis of these considerations, two infant outcomes (birth weight and 5-min Apgar score) and one maternal outcome (abnormal labor progress) were selected.

Birth weight is one of the most important objective determinants of newborn health. In this sample, birth weight ranged from 1,000 to 4,470 g, with a mean of 3,370 g ($SD = 636$). Eight percent of the sample delivered babies weighing 2,500 grams or less (approximately 5 1/2 pounds), which is generally defined as low birth weight (Cunningham, MacDonald, & Gant, 1989). No infant in the sample weighed more than 4,500 g, which is considered abnormally high birth weight.

Because birth weight is confounded with gestational age, we wanted a measure of infant birth weight that was independent from variations in weeks of gestation. Following procedures suggested by Turner et al. (1990), we regressed birth weight onto gestational age and then computed residual scores (observed scores minus predicted scores). These residual birth weight scores were then used in all subsequent analyses.[3]

Infant Apgar score is the most widely used measure of newborn status. Infants are rated 1 min and 5 min after delivery on five criteria: heart rate, respiratory effort, muscle tone, reflex irritability, and skin color. Each criterion is rated

---

[3]Two thirds of low birth weight infants are explained by preterm delivery, and the remaining third by growth retardation. As a result, weeks gestation and birth weight are largely redundant and were therefore not included here as separate outcomes. By removing variations in gestational age from birth weight, we are able to disentangle the effects of growth retardation from those of premature delivery.

from 0 (*worst*) to 2 (*best*), and these ratings are summed to form the Apgar score. We used the 5-min Apgar score because it is more clinically significant than the 1-min Apgar score (Cunningham et al., 1989). Apgar scores in this sample ranged from 1 to 10, with a mean of 8.7 (*SD* = 1). Two percent of the sample had a 5-min score below 7, which is considered an adverse outcome.

Maternal labor difficulties were indexed by assessing abnormal labor progress during first-stage labor. Labor progress was coded as 0 if normal, 1 if the mother experienced primary dysfunction, and 2 if she experienced secondary arrest. *Primary dysfunction* refers to a slowdown in the normal progression of first stage labor, and *secondary arrest* refers to the complete arrest of first stage labor for 2 or more hours (Friedman, 1982). Thirty-four percent of the sample experienced some abnormality of labor.

Procedure

Interviewers. Twelve bilingual female interviewers were trained in group sessions and individually on site with the assistance of a survey interviewing consultant, an obstetric nurse, a cultural anthropologist, and clinic staff.

Sequence and timing of interviews. Women were interviewed at each clinic visit throughout pregnancy and once postpartum. Each interview was administered at least 10 days after the preceding one to space interviews for those receiving frequent care. Postpartum interviews were typically scheduled for 4 to 8 weeks after birth. Initially, these interviews were conducted in the clinic when subjects returned for their first visit after birth. However, the number of missed appointments turned out to be extremely high, so telephone interviewing was initiated. The mean number of interviews completed was 7, with a range from 2 to 11.

Medical charts. Medical risk factors, prenatal care variables, and labor and delivery outcome variables were abstracted from subjects' medical charts by obstetric nurses. To calculate interrater reliability, an independent coder, also an obstetric nurse, coded the medical charts of 45 randomly

selected subjects a second time. Agreement averaged 92% and ranged from 86% to 100% across five variables appearing in different sections of the medical chart.

Results

Overview

We began with structural equation modeling (SEM) to test the main effects of social support on pregnancy outcomes while controlling for relevant background variables. Next, we examined these effects more closely in correlational analyses to determine whether particular types of support were contributing more strongly to these relationships. Finally, stress-buffering effects were tested by examining the interaction of social support and stressful life events in hierarchical regression models.

Multivariate Analyses of Social Support and Birth Outcomes

We conducted SEM to examine the main effects of social support on birth outcomes while controlling for biomedical risk factors and prenatal depression. This is analogous to fitting several multiple regression equations simultaneously. SEM has many advantages over traditional multiple regression. Among them is the ability to incorporate latent factors, which are composed of several correlated predictors and which enable one to separate error variance from the more meaningful common variance among the measures (Newcomb, 1990). These techniques also allow one to model relationships among the independent and dependent variables, which is especially useful here because the predictors and outcomes were expected to covary.

Specifying the model. An exploratory factor analysis was conducted first to determine whether the five support indexes, or some subset of them, should form a latent variable in the model. A principal-components analysis with orthogonal (and oblique) rotation resulted in a three-factor solution. Three of the support measures (satisfaction with received support, baby's father support, and satisfaction with health-care provider support) loaded on a single factor, whereas the amount of support index and the network index each formed a separate factor. Social network and amount of support may be viewed as reflecting two different conceptualizations of quantity of support. In contrast, the remaining measures appeared to reflect the quality of support received and shared enough variance to be modeled as a single latent variable.

The hypothesized model included six independent variables: (a) a latent construct, labeled *support quality*, composed of baby's father support, health-care provider support, and satisfaction with received support, (b) amount of received support, (c) social network resources, (d) maternal medical risk, (e) parity, and (f) prenatal depression.[4] Several relationships among the predictors were specified in the model. First, it was predicted that more and better support would be associated with less prenatal depressed mood. Thus, our initial model specified correlations between the three support variables and prenatal depression. Second, the three support indexes were allowed to freely correlate with each other. No other relationships were expected among the predictors.

The dependent variables in the model were the four pregnancy outcomes (birth weight, Apgar score, labor progress, and postpartum depression). Two relationships among these variables were predicted. First, because bigger babies are more difficult to deliver, a directional path was included from birth weight to abnormal labor progress. Second, because bigger babies are likely to be healthier, a correlation between birth weight and Apgar score was also predicted.

Finally, the existing research literature was used as a guide for specifying directional paths from the independent to the dependent variables.

First, regression paths from all three support indexes to all four outcomes were included in the initial model. In addition, higher medical risk was expected to predict lower birth weight, and medical risk and primiparity were expected to predict more difficulties in labor. Finally, prenatal depression was expected to predict postpartum depression.

Testing the model. Model testing was conducted using EQS software (Bentler, 1989). Two indexes were used to assess model fit, the chi-square statistic and the Comparative Fit Index (CFI; Bentler, 1990). A nonsignificant chi-square and a CFI (which can range from 0 to 1.0) greater than .95 indicated a good-fitting model.

The test of our initial model resulted in a chi-square of 48.24 ($df = 39$, $N = 129$, $p = .15$) and a CFI of .92. Although these statistics indicated an acceptable model fit, the CFI suggested that the model could be improved. Several adjustments were made following procedures suggested by Bentler (1989).

The chi-square statistic for the final model was 41.40 ($df = 49$, $N = 129$, $p = .77$) and the CFI was 1.0, indicating that this model was a very good representation of the data. The final model is presented in Figure 2.1. All paths are significant at $p < .05$ or greater. Paths with double-headed arrows are interpreted as correlations, and those with single-headed arrows are standardized regression paths.

Relationships among predictors. As shown on the left side of Figure 2.1, the social support variables were unrelated to each other, with the exception of one significant correlation between the amount of support received and the residual of a single component of the latent construct, satisfaction with support received ($r = .31$). This indicates that women who reported receiving more support during pregnancy tended to be more satisfied with that support. However, this association is unique to this one support quality indicator and is not shared with the other components of the latent factor (satisfaction with baby's father support and with health-care provider support). This may be partly due to shared method variance because, unlike the other support variables, these two were

---

[4]Two additional control variables, age and education, were excluded because they were uncorrelated with all predictor and outcome variables. Although there were some ethnic differences in social support, this variable was also excluded from the model because it was uncorrelated with the birth outcomes and, when partialed out, did not alter relationships between social support and these outcomes.

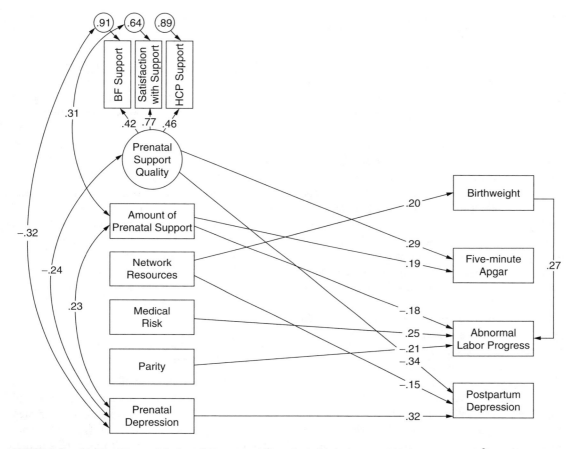

FIGURE 2.1 ■ Multivariate model of social support, biomedical risk factors, and birth outcomes. (χ^2[49, N = 129] = 41.40, p = .77; Comparative Fit Index = 1.0; all paths significant at $p < .05$ or less. BF = baby's father; HCP = health care provider.)

measured on multiple occasions and were always assessed together within each interview. As expected, there were no significant correlations between prenatal social support and medical risk or parity.

As predicted, there were several significant relationships between prenatal support and depressed mood during pregnancy. First, women who reported higher quality support (as indicated by the latent construct) reported less depression during pregnancy ($r = -.24$). In addition to this overall relationship, there was also a unique relationship between prenatal depression and the residual of one component of the latent factor, satisfaction with support from the baby's father

($r = -.32$). This indicates that baby's father support was associated with less prenatal depression in ways not already shared by the other two support quality indicators. Finally, women who received greater amounts of support were more likely to feel depressed ($r = .23$).

Relationships between predictors and outcomes. First, with regard to infant and maternal health outcomes, women with more network resources delivered babies of higher birth weight ($\beta = .20$). Next, women who were more satisfied with their support and who received more support had babies with higher Apgar scores ($\beta = .29$ and $\beta = .19$, respectively). Finally, women who received more support had fewer difficulties in labor ($\beta = -.18$), after controlling for medical risk, parity, and birth weight.

With regard to maternal mental health, women who reported lower quality support and who had fewer network resources were significantly more depressed after childbirth (βs $= -.34$ and $-.15$, respectively, after controlling for prenatal depression). Postpartum depression was unrelated to the amount of prenatal support received.

In sum, this model provides considerable evidence for main effects of prenatal social support on infant and maternal health and well-being. The three components of support studied (amount, quality, and network resources) are largely independent from each other and are differentially related to the various birth outcomes. Moreover, relationships between social support and outcomes remained significant after considering the contributions of relevant biomedical factors. The total variance accounted for in each outcome by all predictors in the model was 4% for birth weight, 12% for Apgar scores, 23% for abnormal labor progress, and 30% for postpartum depression.

Testing an alternative model. Because many models may fit a data set equally well, increased confidence in an obtained model can be gained by demonstrating that it fits better than a reasonable alternative model. This is especially important if the sample size is somewhat small, as in the present case, because reduced power may lead one to accept even a poorly fitting model (because a nonsignificant chi-square indicates a good fit). In the current instance, the most reasonable alternative is to assume that birth outcomes are predicted only by biomedical factors, and that postpartum depression is predicted only by prenatal depression. Thus, a second model was tested in which the three birth outcomes were predicted by medical risk alone, except for labor progress, which was also predicted by parity. Postpartum depression was predicted only by prenatal depression. Correlations among the social support variables were allowed to remain the same, as were correlations between social support and prenatal depression. Relationships among the outcomes also remained the same. In sum, this model was identical to the obtained model except that all regression paths from the social support variables to the outcome variables were removed and thus assumed to be zero.

This alternative model resulted in a chi-square of 77.42 ($df = 53, N = 129, p = .01$) and a CFI of .81, both of which indicated that the model could be clearly rejected as a good representation of these data. In addition, chi-square difference tests were computed to compare the fit of this alternative model with the fit of the final modified model (shown in Figure 2.1) as well as with the fit of the original hypothesized model. Results indicated that both the final model, $\chi^2_{\text{difference}} (16, N = 129) = 29.18, p < .01$, and the original hypothesized model, $\chi^2_{\text{difference}} (4, N = 129) = 36.02, p < .01$, fit the data significantly better than the alternative model. In sum, a model that assumes no effects of social support on birth outcomes and postpartum depression is not supported by these data.

Relationships Broken Down by Type of Support

Because the two repeated measures of received support (average amount of support received and satisfaction with support received) were created by summing across four different types of prenatal support, it was important to explore whether any one type was contributing more strongly to relationships involving these indexes. (Recall that separate receipt and satisfaction indexes were computed for each type of support.) To accomplish this, partial correlations were computed between the support subscales and the four outcomes. For each outcome, the effects of relevant control variables were partialed out, as indicated by the previous multivariate model.

As shown in the upper panel of Table 2.1, the relationship between amount of support and Apgar score appears to be primarily due to receipt of task and information support, and the association with labor progress is primarily a function of task and material support. In addition, it is interesting to note that although the overall index of support received had not been significantly related to postpartum depression in the structural model, these results indicate that women who received more

TABLE 2.1. Correlations Between Birth Outcomes and Social Support Received, Broken Down by Type of Support

Support measure	Birthweight	5-min Apgar	Abnormal labor[a]	Postpartum depression[b]
Amount received				
Task	−.058	.157*	−.220***	.008
Material	.071	.044	−.157*	−.197**
Confiding	−.078	.111	−.070	−.031
Information	−.041	.179**	−.102	−.116
Satisfaction with support				
Task (n = 94)	−.003	.296**	−.136	−.145
Material (n = 71)	−.071	.393***	−.057	−.252**
Confiding (n = 113)	−.002	−.060	.196**	−.179*
Information (n = 81)	.149	.168*	.020	−.043

Note. n = 129, unless otherwise noted.
[a]Medical risk, parity, and birth weight partialed out. [b]Prenatal depression partialed out.
*p < .10 **p < .05. ***p < .01

material support tended to be less depressed after childbirth.

As shown in the lower panel of Table 2.1, the relationship between satisfaction with received support and Apgar score was primarily due to the quality of task and material support, whereas postpartum depressive symptoms were significantly predicted by satisfaction with material and confiding support. In summary, some types of support were more strongly related to various birth outcomes. Although no one type is clearly superior, task and material support appear to be more consistently related to the various outcomes.

Stress-Buffering Analyses

Although we were interested primarily in the main effects of support on birth outcomes, we wanted to explore the possibility that support effects would be more pronounced among women experiencing high levels of life stress, as indicated by the number of prenatal life events. To accomplish this, a series of hierarchical regression analyses was conducted to examine the interactions of social support and life events, which is the conventional method of testing stress-buffering effects (Cohen & Wills, 1985). For each support index, the main effects of social support and life events were entered first, followed by the interaction term. In addition, for each birth outcome, we included the social support variable after controlling for other relevant factors,

as indicated by the structural model. For these analyses, we computed a single index of support quality by standardizing and averaging the three components of the latent construct.

First, analyses for the three health outcomes yielded a single significant interaction, which was between life events and support quality for the prediction of birth weight. To illustrate this interaction, the regression of birth weight on support quality was plotted at one standard deviation above and below the mean on life events (Cohen & Cohen, 1983). As shown in Figure 2.2, support quality was unrelated to birth weight when life events were low ($\beta = -.06$), but when life events were high, better support quality predicted higher birth weight ($\beta = .26$).

Next, the analyses for postpartum depressive symptoms revealed a single interaction, which was between life events and amount of prenatal support received. To illustrate this interaction, the regression of CESD scores on support received was plotted at one standard deviation above and below the mean on life events. As shown in Figure 2.3, the amount of support received was unrelated to depression when life events were low ($\beta = .08$), but when life events were high, women who received more support were significantly less depressed ($\beta = -.41$). Viewed another way, life events was unrelated to depression for women with high support ($r = .16$, *ns*), but was associated with increased depression for women with low

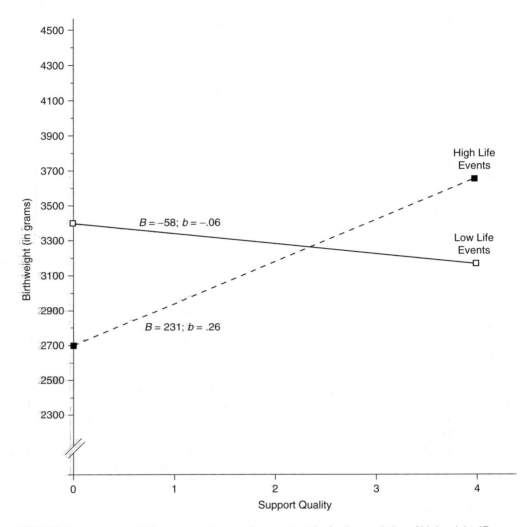

FIGURE 2.2 ■ Interaction of life events and prenatal support quality for the prediction of birthweight. (B = unstandardized regression coefficient; b = standardized regression coefficient.)

support ($r = .33$, $p < .01$). In sum, receiving social support appears to have buffered women against the increased risk of depression associated with stressful life events.

Discussion

Behavioral and social scientists have long been interested in the effects of interpersonal relationships on health. This topic is clearly social psychological in nature and calls for increased atten-

tion to environmental and behavioral perspectives of social support, which have been underemphasized in the existing research literature. This investigation addressed this gap in a prospective study of ethnically diverse and economically disadvantaged pregnant women. The findings presented here provide some of the strongest evidence to date linking social support to physical and mental health in pregnancy.

Our primary goal was to test the prediction that women who received more prenatal social

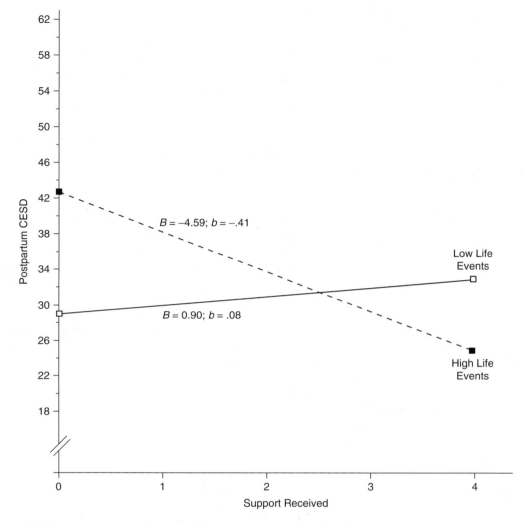

FIGURE 2.3 ■ Interaction of life events and prenatal support received for the prediction of postpartum depression (B = unstandardized regression coefficient; b = standardized regression coefficient; CESD = Center for Epidemiological Studies Depression Scale.)

support and who were more satisfied with that support would experience fewer difficulties in labor and would give birth to healthier babies. Results provided considerable evidence for the main effects of prenatal support on these objective indicators of maternal and infant health. Women who received more prenatal support experienced better progress in labor and delivered babies who appeared healthier 5 min after birth, as indicated by their Apgar rating. Independent from the amount of support a woman received, those who were more satisfied with that support delivered babies with higher Apgar scores. When broken down by the type of support received, prenatal task, material, and informational support appeared most important for infant Apgar score, whereas prenatal task, material, and confiding support contributed disproportionately to labor progress. Finally, women with more social network resources delivered babies of higher birth weight.

A second focus of this research was to examine psychological well-being during pregnancy and after childbirth. Results provided clear evidence that women who were dissatisfied with the prenatal support they received (especially from the baby's father) were at greater risk for depressed mood during pregnancy and depressive symptomatology 6–8 weeks postpartum. Having fewer prenatal network resources was also associated with depression after childbirth.

Although other studies have demonstrated positive links between social support and mental health, these findings are some of the first to show clear benefits of enacted support. Past work has tended to find either no effects or negative relationships between received support and well-being. One reason for this may be that researchers have focused almost exclusively on the amount of support received and have failed to measure the quality of that support. In addition, most studies have been cross-sectional. Like a number of these researchers (e.g., Cutrona, 1986; Dunkel-Schetter, Folkman, & Lazarus, 1987; Revenson & Majerovitz, 1990), we found a positive association between distress and the amount of support received when assessed concurrently. This has sometimes been interpreted as a negative effect of support on well-being. To be sure, support transactions may often involve costs to the recipient (such as decreased self-efficacy or increased feelings of indebtedness), which can have adverse effects on adaptation (Antonucci & Jackson, 1990; Rook, 1984). Nevertheless, this probably reflects a mobilization process whereby women who are distressed seek or elicit more support from their network (Barrera, 1986; Dunkel-Schetter, 1984; Schwarzer & Leppin, 1990; Wethington & Kessler, 1986). Consistent with this, the positive relationship between depression and support in this sample did not remain when tested prospectively. Moreover, among women with high prenatal life events, those who received more social support during pregnancy reported less depression after childbirth.

Although we were primarily interested in the main effects of social support, results provided some evidence for stress-buffering effects. It is interesting to note, however, that none of the main effects resulting from the structural model were qualified by an interaction. Instead, two new effects emerged. Among women with high prenatal life events, those with better support delivered babies of higher birth weight, and those who received more support experienced less postpartum depression. Although our sample size was somewhat small for detecting reliable interactions between social support and life events, that the evidence for stress-buffering was weak is consistent with our belief that behavioral provisions of support should be beneficial to all expectant mothers, especially if, as in the current sample, they face environmental or social-structural stresses that place them at risk. Interactions of social support and life events may be more likely to emerge within samples that are less homogeneous with respect to these variables. Consistent with this, stress-buffering effects in pregnancy have been reported most often with samples of middle-class women (Norbeck & Tilden, 1983; Nuckolls et al., 1972), whereas main effects have occurred more often with adolescents, for whom pregnancy and motherhood are likely to carry additional physical and psychological burdens (Boyce et al., 1985; Cutrona, 1984; Turner et al., 1990).

What are some of the mechanisms that may explain links between social support and health and well-being? A number of specific mechanisms were mentioned earlier, and these can be viewed as mapping onto two general pathways suggested by Cohen (1988): (a) emotion- or stress-induced physiological and biochemical processes, and (b) health-related behavioral patterns. For instance, social support may reduce the extent to which circumstances are appraised as stressful, or might promote positive affect by enhancing self-esteem or feelings of self-efficacy. These may in turn influence susceptibility to illness through effects on neuroendocrine or immune system function or through changes in health-care behaviors such as decreased substance use and improved diet or exercise patterns (Cohen, 1988; Cohen & Williamson, 1991; Cohen & Wills, 1985; Jemmott & Locke, 1984). In the present sample, information abstracted from medical charts and patient interviews provided some preliminary evidence for some of these pathways. For example, women who were satisfied with the support they received experienced le*ss stress during pregnancy (r =* $-.34$, $p < .001$), reported less prenatal substance use ($r = -.19, p < .05$), and tended to initiate prenatal care earlier ($r = -.16, p < .10$). In addition, women with more network resources reported feeling less prenatal stress ($r = -.24, p < .01$) and made more visits to the clinic for prenatal care ($r = .20, p < .05$). These findings, while very preliminary, suggest important avenues for future research. Additional mediators, such as physical strain or fatigue, may also be useful to examine. For example, providing women with child care or household assistance might reduce heavy lifting or prolonged standing, which have been linked to poor birth outcomes (Mamelle et al., 1984; McDonald et al., 1988).

Considered together, the findings presented here have a number of general implications for research on interpersonal relations and health. First, the dimensions of social support that were examined in this study—amount of support received, quality of support received, and social network resources—were largely independent from each other and had distinct relationships with measures of health and well-being. Thus, as suggested by Vaux (1988), it seems useful to conceptualize social support as a metaconstruct comprised of a number of theoretically and empirically distinct components. Distinctions between types of supportive provisions were also apparent in this study. For instance, task and material support predicted physical health outcomes more consistently than did emotional support. A similar pattern has occurred in other studies using different populations (Schaefer, Coyne, & Lazarus, 1981; Seeman, 1984). It is likely that various types of support operate through somewhat different processes (Dunkel-Schetter et al., 1987; House, Umberson, & Landis, 1988), and future research might benefit from giving greater attention to instrumental aid, which has been underemphasized in the support literature.

Whatever factors contribute to support satisfaction, the current findings suggest that a recipient's subjective interpretations of his or her interactions are likely to play a role in determining whether they are beneficial. We speculate that support quality will be especially critical for physical and psychological health outcomes that are mediated by cognitive processes (such as stress perceptions), whereas the amount of support may have more direct links to other outcomes. For example, if emotional support protects against depression by enhancing self-esteem, then the subjective appraisal of that support should be critical. On the other hand, if assistance with household chores affects a health outcome by reducing a woman's strenuous activity, we need not assume that she subjectively evaluate this support as helpful (or even that she is aware of it). In this way, the amount of support may be directly associated with positive health outcomes regardless of support quality.

Although structural aspects of support were not the main focus of this study, it is noteworthy that women with more network resources did not report greater amounts of support, as might be expected. This may be due to limitations in our index of network resources, but our finding that women with larger networks delivered higher birth weight infants suggests that social ties influence well-being through processes other than, or in addition to, enacted support. For example, network researchers have argued that social and community ties promote feelings of belonging and attachment, provide positive models and reference groups, and exert pressures to conform to normative standards and to social roles (Fischer et al., 1977; Mitchell & Tricket, 1980; Moos & Mitchell, 1982). Larger networks may also be associated with greater perceptions of available support or with increased opportunities for shared activities and companionship (Rook, 1987).

Before concluding, a few additional limitations of this work should be noted. First, although the prospective design and rigorous methodology increase our confidence that prenatal support contributed to outcomes of pregnancy in this sample, causal inferences are still not permitted. Controlled intervention studies are needed to draw definitive conclusions (Elbourne & Oakley, 1990). Another issue not addressed in this study is whether personality or contextual variables affect one's ability to develop supportive networks or one's appraisal of support transactions (Gottlieb, 1985). Past research indicates that help-seeking beliefs (Eckenrode, 1983; Hobfoll & Lerman, 1988), social anxiety and social competence (Cohen, Sherrod, & Clark, 1986), self-esteem (Hobfoll & Lerman, 1989), attachment style (Collins & Read, 1990; Simpson, Rholes, & Nelligan, 1992), and family and cultural norms (Vaux, 1988) are among the many factors that affect one's ability or willingness to make use of social resources. Our finding that different aspects of support were differentially related to various outcomes makes it unlikely that any one personality trait (such as neuroticism) is responsible for our study results. Nevertheless, personality factors are likely to contribute in complex ways to the nature and quality of one's relationships, and research is needed to clarify these links. Finally, our sample was composed of lower income, primarily Latino women, and it is unclear whether these findings would generalize to other populations. We might expect that different types of support, for example, would be more or less beneficial to populations of women who share different life circumstances or cultural histories. Nevertheless, there are strong theoretical reasons, and some empirical evidence using different samples, that suggest that the provision of social support in pregnancy will be beneficial to most, if not all, women.

In conclusion, these findings provide evidence that in the context of a life transition that is stressful for many women, especially those who are economically and socially disadvantaged, the assistance and support provided by others may indeed be consequential to physical and psychological health. This research is an early step toward what we hope will be an increasing empirical focus on the interpersonal and relational aspects of social support. One continuing challenge is to identify the mechanisms through which supportive interactions affect health and the complex ways in which social and personality factors interact. These issues are central to the development of more comprehensive theoretical models of social support, and they are likely to be critical to the design of interventions aimed at promoting the health and well-being of mothers and their infants.

NOTES

Nancy L. Collins and Christine Dunkel-Schetter, Department of Psychology, University of California, Los Angeles (UCLA); Marci Lobel, Department of Psychology, State University of New York at Stony Brook; Susan C. M. Scrimshaw, School of Public Health, University of California, Los Angeles.

Funding for the UCLA Psychosocial Factors in Pregnancy Project was provided by Grant 12–130 from the March of Dimes Foundation and National Institute of Health Biomedical Research Support Grant funds (RR07009–19). Nancy L. Collins and Marci Lobel received support during work on this project from National Institute of Mental Health Training Grant MH 15750.

We thank Charles Brinkman, Linda Burnes-Bolton, Rose Garcia, Calvin Hobel, Cheryl Killion, Betsey Patterson, Andrea Rapkin, our interviewers, many undergraduate research assistants, and the staff of the UCLA Prenatal and Family Planning Clinics for their assistance or encouragement in the conduct of this research. We would also like to express our gratitude to the women who participated in this project.

Correspondence concerning this article should be addressed to Nancy L. Collins, who is now at the Department of Psychology, University of California, Santa Barbara, California, 93106 or Christine Dunkel-Schetter, Department of Psychology, University of California, 405 Hilgard Avenue, Los Angeles, California 90024–1563. Electronic mail may be addressed to ncollins@psych.ucsb.edu.

REFERENCES

Aaronson, L. S. (1989). Perceived and received support: Effects on health behavior during pregnancy. *Nursing Research, 38,* 4–9.

Antonucci, T. C., & Jackson, J. S. (1990). The role of reciprocity in social support. In I. G. Sarason, B. R. Sarason, & G. R. Pierce (Eds.), *Social support: An interactional view* (pp. 111–128). New York: Wiley.

Barrera, M., Jr. (1981). Social support in the adjustment of pregnant adolescents: Assessment issues. In B. H. Gottlieb (Ed.), *Social networks and social support* (pp. 69–96). Beverly Hills, CA: Sage.

Barrera, M., Jr. (1986). Distinctions between social support concepts, measures, and models. *American Journal of Community Psychology, 14,* 413–445.

Barrera, M., Jr., Sandler, I. N., & Ramsey, T. B. (1981). Preliminary development of a scale of social support: Studies on college students. *American Journal of Community Psychology, 9,* 435–447.

Bentler, P. M. (1989). *Theory and implementation of EQS: A structural equations program.* Los Angeles, CA: BMDP Statistical Software.

Bentler, P. M. (1990). Comparative fit indexes in structural models. *Psychological Bulletin, 107*, 238–246.

Berkman, L. F. (1985). The relationship of social networks and social support to morbidity and mortality. In S. Cohen & S. L. Syme (Eds.), *Social support and health* (pp. 241–262). San Diego, CA: Academic Press.

Berkman, L. F., & Syme, S. L. (1979). Social networks, host resistance, and mortality: A nine-year follow-up study of Alameda County residents. *American Journal of Epidemiology, 109*, 186–204.

Bolger, N., & Eckenrode, J. (1991). Social relationships, personality, and anxiety during a major stressful event. *Journal of Personality and Social Psychology, 61*, 440–449.

Boyce, W. T., Schaeffer, C., & Uitti, C. (1985). Permanence and change: Psychosocial factors in the outcome of adolescent pregnancies. *Social Science and Medicine, 11*, 1279–1287.

Bragonier, J. K., Cushner, I. M., & Hobel, C. J. (1984). Social and personal factors in the etiology of preterm birth. In F. Fuchs & D. G. Stubblefield (Eds.), *Preterm birth: Causes, prevention, and management* (pp. 64–85). New York: Macmillan.

Burnes-Bolton, L. (1988). *Analysis of social support and stress factors within a preterm and fullterm birth outcome.* Unpublished doctoral dissertation, University of California, Los Angeles.

Cobb, S. (1976). Social support as a moderator of life stress. *Psychosomatic Medicine, 38*, 300–314.

Cohen, S. (1988). Psychosocial models of the role of social support in the etiology of physical disease. *Health Psychology, 7*, 269–297.

Cohen, J., & Cohen, P. (1983). *Applied multiple regression/correlation analysis for the behavioral sciences.* Hillsdale, NJ: Erlbaum.

Cohen, S., Sherrod, D. R., & Clark, M. S. (1986). Social skills and the stress-protective role of social support. *Journal of Personality and Social Psychology, 50*, 963–973.

Cohen, S., & Syme, S. L. (1985). Issues in the study and application of social support. In S. Cohen & S. L. Syme (Eds.), *Social support and health* (pp. 3–22). San Diego, CA: Academic Press.

Cohen, S., & Wills, T. A. (1985). Stress, social support, and the buffering hypothesis. *Psychological Bulletin, 98*, 310–357.

Cohen, S., & Williamson, G. S. (1991). Stress and infectious disease in humans. *Psychological Bulletin, 109*, 5–24.

Collins, N. L., & Read, S. J. (1990). Adult attachment, mental models, and relationship quality in dating couples. *Journal of Personality and Social Psychology, 58*, 644–663.

Coyne, J. C., & Bolger, N. (1990). Doing without social support as an explanatory concept. *Journal of Social and Clinical Psychology, 9*, 148–158.

Coyne, J. C., & DeLongis, A. (1986). Going beyond social support: The role of social relationships in adaptation. *Journal of Consulting and Clinical Psychology, 54*, 454–460.

Cunningham, F. G., MacDonald, P. C., & Gant, N. F. (1989). *Williams obstetrics* (18th ed.). Norwalk, CT: Appleton & Lange.

Cutrona, C. E. (1983). Causal attributions and perinatal depression. *Journal of Abnormal Psychology, 92*, 161–172.

Cutrona, C. E. (1984). Social support and stress in the transition to parenthood. *Journal of Abnormal Psychology, 98*, 378–390.

Cutrona, C. E. (1986). Behavioral manifestations of social support: A microanalytic investigation. *Journal of Personality and Social Psychology, 51*, 201–208.

Cutrona, C. E., & Russell, D. W. (1987). The provisions of social relationships and adaptation to stress. In W. H. Jones & D. Perlman (Eds.), *Advances in personal relationships* (Vol. 1, pp. 37–67). Greenwich, CT: JAI Press.

Cutrona, C. E., & Troutman, B. R. (1986). Social support, infant temperament, and parenting self-efficacy: A mediation model of postpartum depression. *Child Development, 57*, 1507–1518.

Dunkel-Schetter, C. (1984). Social support and cancer: Findings based on patient interviews and their implications. *Journal of Social Issues, 40*, 77–98.

Dunkel-Schetter, C., & Bennett, T. L. (1990). Differentiating the cognitive and behavioral aspects of social support. In B. R. Sarason, I. G. Sarason, & G. R. Pierce (Eds.), *Social support: An interactional view* (pp. 267–296). New York: Wiley.

Dunkel-Schetter, C., Blasband, D. E., Feinstein, L. F., & Herbert, T. B. (1992). Elements of supportive interactions: When are attempts to help effective? In S. Spacapan & S. Oskamp (Eds.), *Helping and being helped in the real world*. Newbury Park, CA: Sage.

Dunkel-Schetter, C., Folkman, S., & Lazarus, R. (1987). Correlates of social support receipt. *Journal of Personality and Social Psychology, 53*, 71–80.

Dunkel-Schetter, C., Lobel, M., Collins, N., Hobel, C., & Scrimshaw, S. M. (1993). *Psychosocial risks in adverse birth outcomes: Effects of prenatal stress and social support in low income women.* Manuscript submitted for publication.

Eckenrode, J. (1983). The mobilization of social support: Some individual constraints. *American Journal of Community Psychology, 11*, 509–528.

Elbourne, D., & Oakley, A. (1990). An overview of trials of social support in pregnancy: effects on gestational age at delivery and birthweight. In H. W. Berendes, W. Kessel, & S. Yaffe (Eds.), *Advances in the prevention of low birthweight*. New York: Perinatology Press.

Fischer, C., Jackson, R., Stueve, C., Gerson, K., Jones, L., & Baldassare, M. (1977). *Networks and places: Social relations in urban settings*. New York: Free Press.

Friedman, E. A. (1982). Assessment of progress in labor. In J. R. Bolognese, R. H. Schwarz, & J. Schneider (Eds.), *Perinatal medicine: Management of the high risk fetus and neonate* (pp. 215–222). Baltimore, MD: Williams & Wilkins.

Golding, J. M. (1989). Role occupancy and role-specific stress and social support as predictors of depression. *Basic and Applied Social Psychology, 10*, 173–195.

Gore, S. (1985). Social support and styles of coping. In S. Cohen & L. Syme (Eds.), *Social support and health* (pp. 263–278). San Diego, CA: Academic Press.

Gottlieb, B. H. (1985). Social support and the study of personal relationships. *Journal of Social and Personal Relationships, 2*, 351–375.

Henderson, S., Byrne, D. G., & Duncan-Jones, P. (1981). *Neurosis and the social environment.* San Diego, CA: Academic Press.

Hobfoll, S. E. (1989). Conservation of resources: A new attempt at conceptualizing stress. *American Psychologist, 44*, 513–524.

Hobfoll, S. E., & Lerman, M. (1988). Personal relationships, personal attitudes, and stress resistance: Mothers' reactions to their child's illness. *American Journal of Community Psychology, 16*, 565–589.

Hobfoll, S. E., & Lerman, M. (1989). Predicting receipt of social support: A longitudinal study of parents' reactions to their child's illness. *Health Psychology, 8*, 61–77.

House, J. W. (1981). *Work stress and social support.* Reading, MA: Addison-Wesley.

House, J. S. Robbins, C., & Metzner, H. L. (1982). The association of social relationships and activities with mortality. *American Journal of Epidemiology, 116*, 123–140.

House, J. S., Umberson, D., & Landis, K. R. (1988). Structures and processes of social support. In W. R. Scott & J. Blake (Eds.), *Annual review of sociology* (Vol. 14, pp. 293–318). Palo Alto, CA: Annual Reviews.

Institute of Medicine. (1985). *Preventing low birthweight.* Washington, DC: National Academy Press.

Istvan, J. (1986). Stress, anxiety, and birth outcomes: A critical review of the evidence. *Psychological Bulletin, 100*, 331–348.

Jemmott, J. B., & Locke, S. E. (1984). Psychosocial factors, immunologic mediation, and human susceptibility to infectious diseases: How much do we know? *Psychological Bulletin, 95*, 78–108.

Kahn, R. L., & Antonucci, T. (1980). Convoys over the life course: Attachment, roles, and social support. *Lifespan Development and Behavior, 3*, 254–286.

Kaniasty, K., & Norris, F. H. (1992). Social support and victims of crime: Matching event, support, and outcome. *American Journal of Community Psychology, 20*, 211–241.

Kessler, R. C., & McLeod, J. D. (1985). Social support and mental health in community samples. In S. Cohen & S. L. Syme (Eds.), *Social support and health* (pp. 219–240). San Diego, CA: Academic Press.

Lakey, B., & Cassady, P. B. (1990). Cognitive processes in perceived social support. *Journal of Personality and Social Psychology, 59*, 337–343.

Lederman, R. P. (1984). *Psychosocial adaptation in pregnancy.* Englewood Cliffs, NJ: Prentice-Hall.

Lobel, M. (in press). Conceptualizations, measurement, and effects of prenatal maternal stress on birth outcomes. *Journal of Behavioral Medicine.*

Lobel, M., Dunkel-Schetter, C., & Scrimshaw, S. C. M. (1992). Prenatal maternal stress and prematurity: A prospective

study of socioeconomically disadvantaged women. *Health Psychology, 11*, 32–40.

Mamelle, N., Laumon, B., & Lazar, P. (1984). Prematurity and occupational activity during pregnancy. *American Journal of Epidemiology, 199*, 309–322.

McDonald, A. D., McDonald, J. C., Armstrong, B., Cherry, N. M., Nolin, A. D., & Robert, D. (1988). Prematurity and work in pregnancy. *British Journal of Industrial Medicine, 45*, 56–62.

Mitchell, K. E., & Tricket, E. J. (1980). Task force report: Social networks as mediators of social support: An analysis of the effects and determinants of social networks. *Community Mental Health Journal, 16*, 27–44.

Moos, R. H., & Mitchell, R. E. (1982). Social network resources and adaptation: A conceptual framework. In T. A. Wills (Ed.), *Basic processes in helping relationships* (pp. 213–232). San Diego, CA: Academic Press.

Newcomb, M. D. (1990). What structural equation modeling can tell us about social support. In I. G. Sarason, B. R. Sarason, & G. R. Pierce (Eds.), *Social support: An interactional view* (pp. 26–63). New York: Wiley.

Norbeck, J. S., & Anderson, N. J. (1989). Psychosocial predictors of pregnancy outcomes in low-income Black, Hispanic, and White women. *Nursing Research, 38*, 204–209.

Norbeck, J., & Tilden, V. (1983). Life stress, social support and emotional disequilibrium in complications of pregnancy: A prospective multivariate study. *Journal of Health and Social Behavior, 24*, 30–46.

Nuckolls, K. B., Cassel, J. C., & Kaplan, B. H. (1972). Psychosocial assets, life crisis, and prognosis of pregnancy. *American Journal of Epidemiology, 95*, 431–441.

Pagel, M. D., Smilkstein, G., Regen, H., & Montano, D. (1990). Psychosocial influences on newborn outcomes: A controlled prospective study. *Social Science and Medicine, 30*, 597–604.

Pennebaker, J. W. (1982). *The psychology of physical symptoms.* New York: Springer-Verlag.

Radloff, L. (1977). The CESD scale: A self-report depression scale for research in the general population. *Applied Psychological Measurement, 1*, 385–401.

Reading, A. (1983). *Psychosocial aspects of pregnancy.* New York: Longman.

Revenson, T. A., & Majerovitz, D. (1990). Spouses' support provision to chronically ill patients. *Journal of Social and Personal Relationships, 7*, 575–586.

Rook, K. (1984). The negative side of social interaction: Impact on psychological well-being. *Journal of Personality and Social Psychology, 45*, 1097–1108.

Rook, K. (1987). Social support versus companionship: Effect on life stress, loneliness, and evaluations by others. *Journal of Personality and Social Psychology, 52*, 1132–1147.

Sarason, I. G., Sarason, B. R., & Shearin, E. N. (1986). Social support as an individual difference variable: Its stability, origins, and relational aspects. *Journal of Personality and Social Psychology, 50*, 845–855.

Schaefer, C., Coyne, J., & Lazarus, R. S. (1981). The health related functions of social support. *Journal of Behavioral Medicine, 4*, 381–406.

Schoenbach, V. J., Kaplan, B. H., Fredman, L., & Kleinbach, D. G. (1986). Social ties and mortality in Evans County Georgia. *American Journal of Epidemiology, 123*, 577–591.

Schwarzer, R., & Leppin, A. (1990). Social support, health, and health behavior. In K. Hurrelmann & F. Losel (Eds.), *Health hazards in adolescence* (pp. 363–384). Berlin: de Gruyter.

Schwarzer, R., & Leppin, A. (1991). The possible impact of social ties and social support on morbidity and mortality. In U. Baumann & H. Yeiel (Eds.), *The meaning and measurement of social support* (pp. 65–83). Washington, DC: Hemisphere.

Seeman, T. (1984). *Social networks and coronary artery disease.* Unpublished doctoral dissertation, University of California, Berkeley.

Selwyn, B. J. (1982). Review of obstetrical risk assessment methods. In *Institute of Medicine and National Research Council, Research issues in the assessment of birth settings* (pp. 149–170). Washington, DC: National Academy Press.

Shinn, M., Lehmann, D., & Wong, N. W. (1984). Social interaction and social support. *Journal of Social Issues, 40*, 55–76.

Shumaker, S. A., & Brownell, A. (1984). Toward a theory of social support: Closing conceptual gaps. *Journal of Social Issues, 40*, 11–36.

Simpson, J. A., Rholes, W. S., & Nelligan, J. S. (1992). Support-seeking and support-giving within couple members in an anxiety-provoking situation: The role of attachment styles. *Journal of Personality and Social Psychology, 62*, 434–446.

Tardy, C. H. (1985). Social support measurement. *American Journal of Community Psychology, 13*, 187–202.

Tietjen, A. M., & Bradley, C. F. (1985). Social support and maternal psychosocial adjustment during the transition to parenthood. *Canadian Journal of Behavioural Science, 17*, 109–121.

Thoits, P. A. (1985). Social support processes and psychological well-being: Theoretical possibilities. In I. G. Sarason & B. R. Sarason (Eds.), *Social support: Theory, research, and applications* (pp. 51–72). Dordrecht, The Netherlands: Martinus Nijhoff.

Turner, R. J., Grindstaff, C. F., & Phillips, N. (1990). Social support and outcome in teenage pregnancy. *Journal of Health and Social Behavior, 31*, 43–57.

Vaux, A. (1988). *Social support.* New York: Praeger.

Wallston, B. S., Alagna, S. W., DeVellis, B. M., & DeVellis, R. F. (1983). Social support and physical health. *Health Psychology, 2*, 367–391.

Watson, J. P., Elliot, S. A., Rugg, A. J., & Brough, D. I. (1984). Psychiatric disorder in pregnancy and the first postnatal year. *British Journal of Psychiatry, 144*, 453–462.

Weiss, R. (1974). The provisions of social relationships. In Z. Rubin (Ed.), *Doing unto others* (pp. 17–26). Englewood Cliffs, NJ: Prentice-Hall.

Wethington, E., & Kessler, R. C. (1986). Perceived social support, received support and adjustment to stressful life events. *Journal of Health and Social Behavior, 27*, 78–89.

Wills, T. A. (1985). Supportive functions of interpersonal relationships. In S. Cohen & S. L. Syme (Eds.), *Social support and health* (pp. 61–82). San Diego, CA: Academic Press.

Zax, M., Sameroff, A. J., & Farnum, J. E. (1975). Childbirth education, maternal attitudes, and delivery. *American Journal of Obstetrics and Gynecology, 123*, 185–190.

Zuckerman, B., Amaro, H., Bauchner, H., & Cabral, H. (1989). Depressive symptoms during pregnancy: Relationship to poor health behaviors. *American Journal of Obstetrics and Gynecology, 160*, 1107–1111.

Zweig, S., LeFevre, M., & Kruse, J. (1988). The health belief model and attendance for prenatal care. *Family Practice Research Journal, 8*, 32–36.

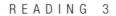

Change and Consistency in Social Participation During Early Adulthood

Harry T. Reis, Yi-Cheng Lin, M. Elizabeth Bennett, and John B. Nezlek

This article reports a longitudinal study of the social interaction patterns of college students and adults. Adults ($N = 113$) from 26 to 31 years old who had participated in similar studies in college kept detailed records of social activity for 2 weeks. Three hypotheses were supported. First, from college to adulthood, opposite-sex socializing grew, whereas same-sex, mixed-sex, and group interactions decreased. Second, intimacy increased in adulthood, whereas satisfaction did not. Contrary to theories that focus on the formation of primary intimate relationships in early adulthood, intimacy increased in all interaction categories. Sex differences in the development of intimacy were also noted. Third, correlations revealed marked consistency over time in several variables. Implications of these findings for social development during early adulthood were examined.

Social interaction occupies a position of considerable importance in the lives of young adults. Much waking time is spent participating in and thinking about social activity with friends, family, and romantic partners (Csikszentmihalyi & Larson, 1984; Robinson, 1977). Satisfying social bonds are a primary source of psychological well-being and happiness (Argyle, 1987), and through the vehicle of social support, have been shown to benefit physical health (Cohen, 1988; Reis, 1984). Moreover, the absence of desired levels of social contact and closeness with friends and relatives typically produces distress, ranging from mild loneliness and dysphoria to extreme depression and suicidal tendencies (Peplau & Goldston, 1984; Reis, 1990; Veroff, Kulka, & Douvan, 1981). Retrospections by older persons about sources of satisfaction during their lifetimes also assign a preeminent role to warm relationships with both family and friends (e.g., Sears, 1977; Vaillant, 1977).

Not surprisingly, therefore, most theories of life span development discuss the nature and development of relationships from infancy to old age. These theories commonly describe young adulthood as a period in which the social patterns of adolescence are replaced by a focus on primary close relationships. We review several models in the following section. The purpose of this research was to provide empirical evidence about changing patterns of social interaction during this period. More specifically, we report the results of a longitudinal study examining continuity and change in social activity from the college years to adulthood.[1]

Models of Relationship Development in Early Adulthood

In a review of gender differences in children's friendships, Maccoby (1990) discussed two widely supported findings. One is gender segregation, or the tendency of children and adolescents to socialize mostly with same-sex others. A second tendency Maccoby noted is for friendships among girls to be more intimate than friendships among boys. This latter difference has been shown in many studies, with subjects ranging from fifth graders (Buhrmester & Furman, 1987) to junior and senior high school students (Blyth & Foster-Clark, 1987; Fischer, 1981) and adults (Dindia & Allen, 1992; Reis, in press). Gender differences (which are discussed later) notwithstanding, both sexes begin to value intimacy as a basis for friendship during early adolescence (Berndt & Perry, 1990; Steinberg, 1989). The centrality of intimacy to close friendship continues to grow through late adolescence (J. L. Fischer, 1981). Moreover, although intimacy first emerges within same-sex friendships, as Sullivan (1953) noted, intimacy also becomes important in cross-sex friendships, as they become more prevalent during adolescence.

Few developmental studies of friendship patterns have been conducted during young adulthood. In a broad review of normal development, Arnstein (1984) described the development of intimacy as one of five major life tasks facing young adults.

This view is consistent with many models of life span development, which assert that the period from roughly 18 to 30 years of age is preoccupied with finding, establishing, and stabilizing adult patterns of social interaction. To Erikson (1950), this age range is critical for resolving the crisis of intimacy versus isolation—whether or not one forms a meaningful, intimate bond with another person. Much research on intimacy status, while not necessarily concurring on the particulars of this process, supports the timeliness of these issues within this period (see Orlofsky, 1988, for a review). Similarly, Levinson (1978) and Neugarten (1969) portray the interval from 22 to 28 years of age as a time for choosing adult peer and love relationships. Even Sullivan's (1953) interpersonal theory, which mostly focuses on childhood and adolescence, asserts that the nature of close relationships, particularly regarding intimacy and companionship, continues to mature into adulthood. That adolescent social behavior evolves into young adulthood may not be surprising, given that, in 1986, the median age of first marriages in the United States was 23.0 years for women and 25.1 years for men (*Statistical Abstract of the United States*, 1990).

These general concepts notwithstanding, little direct evidence exists concerning the manner in which maturation of social goals and personality is reflected in everyday socializing. Particularly in terms of intimacy, for example, most theories concern the desire for a primary (and single) intimate relationship, but it would be important to show how this focus is manifested in ongoing social activity. Existing literature tends to be based on cross-sectional studies, global indicators of social activity (e.g., shyness or marital status), or self-summarized retrospective reports, often spanning lengthy time periods. As Reis and Wheeler (1991) have discussed, retrospective accounts are not reliable indicators of actual social activity, because the cognitive and motivational processes involved in event selection, recall, aggregation, and interpretation frequently alter recollections. The present research was designed to fill this gap with longitudinal comparisons of daily social activity reports collected with the Rochester Interaction Record (RIR), a

---

[1] For convenience, we label the period spanning from college to approximately age 30 as *early* or *young* adulthood. We also refer to the former time as *college* and the latter as *adulthood* for simplicity. Even first-year college students, half of our sample, should be considered adults, but it will be clearest to use this label to describe the data we collected around age 30.

diarylike procedure that provides contemporaneous accounts of social participation. The benefits of the RIR procedure are described later.

Our reasons for studying continuity and change in social activity during early adulthood go beyond the logic of "critical-period" maturation. Having graduated from a residential college, the sample we studied has encountered one of the most abrupt and complete transitions in life: Social networks, work and financial arrangements, and physical settings all change at once, necessitating new adaptations. It remains to be demonstrated whether college students will socialize similarly in the very different environments they face in later life. This point has implications for the various theories cited earlier, which use traitlike constructs in a manner that implies, if not requires, substantial continuities over the life span. Other theories, such as that of Lewis (1982), suggest that the determinants of social activity are to be found in the structure of the individual's social system. And still others, such as Main, Kaplan, and Cassidy (1985), propose that possibilities for changing mental models of relationships (and hence social behavior) are greatest during major life transitions. If so, the many differences between a university dormitory and independent adult life (e.g., privacy, opportunities for spontaneous contact, shared tasks, physical proximity, common eating and bathing facilities, and scheduling constraints) should engender considerable differences in social activity.

Hypotheses

The specific purpose of this research was to determine whether the age-related changes in social relationships posited by many life span theories would be manifested in everyday socializing. A second purpose was to determine whether interaction patterns would show consistency from the college years to adulthood. We conducted this study with a sample of 113 adults between the ages of 26 and 31 who kept the RIR for 2 weeks. All had taken part in prior RIR studies as college students, half during their first year and half as seniors.

The first hypothesis concerned changes in the frequency and distribution of social interaction. The various theories described earlier suggest that adult subjects should have established, or be in the process of establishing, primary intimate heterosexual relationships. Accordingly, we predicted that opposite-sex interactions, notably those involving primary opposite-sex partners, would be more common in adulthood than in college. At the same time, we expected that interaction with same-sex others and in groups would decrease. This derives from Maccoby's (1990) description of the lessened significance of same-sex contact during adolescence, which may continue into adulthood. Also, if social needs are met through increasingly intimate, opposite-sex relationships, reliance on same-sex partners may decrease. We further expected that group interactions would decrease, because it is often speculated that social interaction in late adolescence is group-focused.

Hypothesis 2 dealt with two subjective variables: perceived intimacy and satisfaction. Based on the notion that intimacy is a fundamental concern during early adulthood, we expected that interaction intimacy would increase from college to adulthood. This hypothesis was offered not only for opposite-sex interaction, but also for all other types of interaction. Our earlier research (e.g., Wheeler, Reis, & Nezlek, 1983) suggests that intimacy appears in traitlike fashion; that is, persons who interact intimately in one relationship also tend to interact intimately in other relationships. Also, if the increase in opposite-sex intimacy represents a preference for more meaningful social contacts, it would be reasonable to expect generalization to other relationships. It is not clear whether increases in intimacy ought to be accompanied by increases in satisfaction, and we therefore had no predictions for this variable.

An interesting sidelight of Hypothesis 2 concerns sex differences in the timing of the predicted gains. In a cross-sectional study, J. L. Fischer (1981) found that although college students of both sexes reported more intimate interactions than high school students did, women were more advanced in this characteristic than men were. This trend is consistent with peer friendship results obtained by Buhrmester and Furman (1987) with fifth and eighth graders and by Blyth and Foster-Clark (1987) with high school students. In all of our previous studies, women have been found to interact more intimately than men do, particularly with same-sex others (Reis, in press), a finding consistent with Dindia and Allen's (1992) meta-analysis of 205 self-disclosure studies. It is possible, however, that what appears as a sex difference in college students is actually a developmental difference: Women may attain intimacy sooner than men. Comparisons of first- and senior-year data, as well as comparisons of both years with mid-adulthood data, may shed light on this issue.

Hypothesis 3 concerned stability in interaction patterns from college to adulthood. To the extent that everyday social activity is influenced by environmental factors, relatively little within-individual consistency should be found. On the other hand, if traits and capacities determine social activity, then relative consistency should be evident despite variations in the social environment.[2] Several longitudinal studies have demonstrated stability of interaction style (e.g., Caspi, Bem, & Elder, 1989) and personality traits and values relevant to socializing, such as sociability, need for affiliation, and the value placed on affection (Bakteman & Magnusson, 1981; Block, 1969; Costa, McCrae, & Arenberg, 1980; Haan, 1977; Jessor, 1983). Focusing on actual social activity offers a somewhat more stringent test of developmental consistency, because these data examine behavioral manifestations of social traits rather than the traits themselves. Very few longitudinal studies have done so, however, and these span a period of less than 1 year. Shaver, Furman, and Buhrmester (1985) found evidence of continuity from the summer before college to the end of the first year of college, and two previous RIR studies have demonstrated continuity within a single college year (Nezlek, in press; Wheeler & Nezlek, 1977). Based on these studies, as well as on our belief that interaction patterns derive from relatively stable mental representations of past relational experience (Main et al., 1985), we hypothe-

sized that social participation in adulthood would be correlated with college social participation, over and above general developmental shifts.

Why Focus on Social Activity in Everyday Life?

The RIR is a fixed-format diary procedure that requires subjects to complete a short record after every interaction lasting 10 min or longer. These records include standard descriptors and rating scales, from which summary indexes are computed. This approach offers three advantages over standard questionnaire or interview methods. First, the RIR deals with voluntary social activity in its natural, everyday context. Researchers have recently become interested in the nature of daily experience as a complement to traditional paradigms that focus on major life events or global perceptions of relationships (see DeVries, 1992; Tennen, Suls, & Affleck, 1991, for overviews). Rather than focusing solely on primary relationships or highly salient social behavior, the RIR considers all social activity within a given period.

Second, standard questionnaire and interview methods require that subjects first recollect, then evaluate, and finally summarize many events, often over lengthy periods. Such accounts possess substantial possibilities for error attributable to cognitive and motivational processes (Fiske & Taylor, 1991; Nisbett & Ross, 1981; Schwarz, 1990). Although retrospective self-reports of social activity provide useful data about interpretations of social life, they are not as accurate as contemporaneous accounts are. (In fact, the discrepancy between retrospective summaries and contemporaneous diary accounts has been used to study the biasing impact of personal theories on recollections of past experience; Ross, 1989.) The RIR minimizes these complications by having subjects describe each interaction separately rather than in aggregation and by obtaining reports soon after the interaction has occurred.

Third, perceptions of social experiences are often imprecise and undifferentiated. Retrospective questionnaires typically ask subjects to simultaneously estimate several features of social interac-

---

[2]Of course, this alternative encompasses the notion that traits lead individuals to choose particular social environments.

tion (e.g., frequency or degree of closeness) across many separate events or many different partners. Although lay impressions may be nonspecific, social interaction theories are nevertheless precise about their constituent processes. Consequently, it is important to distinguish the various types and features of social activity from one another.

Method

Subjects

Adults eligible to participate in this research were drawn from three separate studies conducted while they were college students at the University of Rochester. Two of these studies were conducted during their first year of college—academic years 1974–1975 and 1976–1977. (Data from these studies were published in Wheeler and Nezlek, 1977, and Reis, Nezlek, and Wheeler, 1980, respectively.) The third study was conducted during the students' senior year, 1979–1980 (Reis et al., 1982). In all three samples, subjects were recruited through posted flyers or advertisements in campus newspapers. Subjects were paid a small amount for participation. Adult data were collected during 1985–1986, when participants were between the ages of 27 and 31. Consequently, freshman–adult comparisons span 9 to 11 years, whereas senior–adult comparisons span 6 years.

The two freshman-year studies included multiple assessments. Wheeler and Nezlek (1977) collected data twice, during the latter half of the fall and spring semesters. Nezlek (1978) used four assessments, roughly during the 5th and 13th weeks of the fall semester, and the 3rd and next-to-last weeks of the spring semester. These data were averaged across time periods. Assessment intervals varied from 1 week to 2 weeks, depending on the study. All quantitative indexes were adjusted to equate for this variation.

Two hundred and nine individuals had participated in the previous studies. We located 167 (79.9%), of whom 114 (68.3%) agreed to take part in this research. Forty-one percent resided in New York State; the remainder were dispersed widely throughout the United States. Data from

1 subject were discarded because of failure to follow instructions, leaving a sample of 113 individuals (56 women and 57 men). Rates of failure to locate subjects and refusals varied less than 3% between men and women. Given response rates typical in such research, we believe our efforts were very successful.

Sixteen persons (12 women and 4 men) participated in both the second first-year study and the senior study. Including their data in both groups would have confounded the analyses, because unadjusted dependencies can affect between-groups comparisons unpredictably (Kenny & Judd, 1986). Accordingly, this group was split randomly, such that half (6 women and 2 men) was assigned to the first-year group and half to the senior group. There were no significant differences between these two subgroups.

Procedure

A letter describing the study's general purposes and specifying what would be required of participants was sent to all potential subjects. Addresses were obtained from several sources: university records, alumni mailing lists, the New York State Motor Vehicles Bureau, and from other subjects. In addition, a recruitment letter was sent through the Social Security Administration to all individuals not otherwise contacted.

Those individuals expressing interest were contacted by telephone and scheduled for the 2-week RIR period at a point of mutual convenience. Intervals were selected that avoid major holidays, vacations, or prolonged atypical personal circumstances; we wanted a representative 2-week slice of life. Subjects were scheduled in staggered intervals ranging from June 1985 to June 1986, although the majority participated during September–October 1985, January–February 1986, and April 1986.

Shortly before they were to begin the RIR, subjects were mailed a package of forms along with detailed instructions (described later). They were also telephoned by the coordinator, who reinforced the instructions and answered questions. At the end of the 2 weeks, subjects were called again and interviewed, as well as probed for potential problems or inaccuracies. On receipt of completed RIRs, we sent subjects $50, along with a thank-you letter.

Rochester Interaction Record. The record form used for the adult data is shown in the Appendix. One record was completed for every interaction lasting 10 min or longer. *Interactions* were defined as any encounter with another person(s) in which the participants attended to one another and adjusted their behavior in response to one another. For example, sitting next to someone in a lecture was not appropriate, whereas talking during the lecture for 10 min was. A more detailed description of the RIR procedure may be found in Reis and Wheeler (1991). Subjects were instructed to complete the RIR immediately after each interaction or as soon afterward as possible. In all instances, records were to be completed no less than once or twice a day. A scratch sheet was provided to facilitate memory. Throughout the study, a collaborative, nondeceptive atmosphere was maintained, which we believe aided the gathering of valid data. Confidentiality of the records was emphasized and was closely guarded throughout.

The RIR has evolved since the three college-student studies from which our subjects were drawn. The two first-year studies used a similar form, except that there were only two rating scales (intimacy and pleasantness). The senior study used virtually the same record as that shown in the Appendix, except that there was no social integration scale. Because the forms varied, the analyses reported in this article are necessarily limited to variables that were included in all three studies and whose format remained essentially identical. These variables include the following:

1. *Daily interactions*: mean number of interactions per day.
2. *Length*: mean reported length of interactions. To minimize skew, we set the maximum length for any single interaction at 360 min.
3. *Time per day*: mean number of minutes per day spent in social interaction.
4. *Intimacy*: mean level of perceived intimacy across all interactions. Intimacy was defined as "the personal meaningfulness of an interaction. It does not refer to sexual behavior, because

sexual interactions may or may not be meaningful."
5. *Satisfaction/pleasantness*: mean level of perceived pleasantness across all interactions. (The pleasantness scale was titled Satisfaction in the two freshman studies and Quality in the senior and adult studies.)
6. *Number of different others*: number of different interaction partners. These data were adjusted to equate the number of days the RIR was kept.
7. *Nature*: percentage of all interactions falling into each of several descriptive categories. The early RIR had three additional categories: Sharing thoughts and feelings, which was combined with Conversation presently; and Party and Date/Party, which were combined with Date. Pastime was an interaction whose primary aim was to "pass time without any particular goal or focus."

As is standard in RIR studies, each of these variables was computed according to the sex composition of the encounter: *same sex*—interactions including up to three other persons of the same sex; *opposite sex*—interactions including up to three members of the opposite sex; *mixed sex*—interactions including up to three others, at least one of each sex; and *group*—interactions including more than three others. *Total* measures incorporated all interactions.

Each of the RIR indexes was also calculated for interactions involving the subject's same-sex best friend and opposite-sex best friend. Because the original Wheeler and Nezlek (1977) research used a behavioral criterion for defining best-friend status (the subject's most frequent interaction partner), we were constrained to use the same criterion.[3] The appropriateness of frequency to define closeness

---

[3]It would have been better to have subjects identify their best friends and spouses in the adult interaction records. Unfortunately, because such information was not collected in the college data, longitudinal comparisons would not have been possible. In other studies, we have found that married persons' opposite-sex best friends are almost always their spouses. Also, we wanted to maximize confidentiality in the present records.

has been discussed earlier (Wheeler & Nezlek, 1977). In their sample, 93% of respondents named one of the three most frequent interactants as their best friend. Also, in Berscheid, Snyder, and Omoto's (1989) model of closeness, frequency of contact is one of three criteria defining closeness.

Some categories contained no observations for a few subjects. These entries were coded as zero for daily interaction and time per day and as missing data for all other variables.

It should be noted that we excluded interactions classified as work from the RIR data sets. *Work* was defined as any interaction mandated by job requirements: meetings, interviews, appointments with patients and clients, and so on. (Interaction that takes place at work but that is not central to the work itself was coded in one of the other categories and is included in our analyses.) We sought to exclude those interactions that were mandated by work assignments and that did not pertain to voluntary social activity. Also, because the vast majority of subjects did not work as college students, including adult work interactions would have compromised interpretation of longitudinal comparisons.[4]

Reliability. To check on the assumption that 2 weeks would provide stable and generalizable estimates of social activity, we computed split-half intraclass correlations for representative variables. Separate composites were calculated for even and odd days and were then correlated. The following correlations were obtained: daily interactions, .85; mean length, .85; intimacy, .89; and satisfaction, .76. Thus, the internal consistency of the RIR indexes appears high.

Interview

The following questions were designed to probe for difficulties in recording interactions, inaccuracies, or misunderstandings of the instructions. (a) How difficult was the recording process (1 = *not difficult at all*, 7 = *very difficult; M* = 3.41)? (b) Did the recording process become easier as the study progressed (1 = *easier*, 2 = *no change*, 3 = *harder; M* = 1.65)? (c) How accurate does the subject consider her or his records (1 = *very accurate*, 7 = *very inaccurate; M* = 2.46)? (d) What percentage of interactions would the subject guess were not recorded (*M* = 5.94%)? (e) Were there any regular or ritual interactions that were not recorded (0 = *no*, 1 = *yes; M* = 0.02)? (f) How many interactions lasting less than 10 min were recorded (*M* = 1.03)? (g) Did accuracy change over the course of the study (1 = *decreased*, 2 = *no change*, 3 = *increased; M* = 2.11)? (h) Did the record keeping interfere with interactions (1 = *not at all*, 7 = *a great deal; M* = 1.40)? (i) Did such interference change over the course of the study (1 = *decreased*, 2 = *no change*, 3 = *increased; M* = 2.01)? There were no significant sex differences on any questions.

These data indicate that subjects perceived their records to be largely accurate and that they generally followed instructions. They also reported little interference of the record keeping with social activity. The moderate degree of difficulty reported apparently did not compromise the self-perceived accuracy of their reports. We have obtained similar interview means in prior research. Although these self-reports are not objective measures of accuracy, we would expect them to have reflected any substantial problems.

Results

Comparability Analyses

We first sought to ensure that the adult sample was representative of the college samples from which they were drawn. We conducted analyses of variance (ANOVAs) within each of the three samples, comparing college interaction records of subjects who took part in the adult study with

---

[4]The decision to drop work interactions was based on our desire to focus on voluntary social activity. Psychotherapists or receptionists are required by their jobs to interact in very different ways than novelists or computer technicians. Including these data would have distorted the meaning of the obtained indexes. Student jobs were also excluded, but classwork-related interactions were not deleted in either data set. Past research indicates that few in-class interactions achieve the 10-min criterion. We felt that the social nature of course-relevant activity outside of class was indeed discretionary in a way that work is not. Furthermore, such activities were coded as *tasks*, and we could not distinguish coursework tasks from other tasks.

those who did not. These analyses consisted of 2 (followed/not followed) × 2 (sex) ANOVAs on the central RIR variables of this study.

In general, the rate of significant differences (i.e., main effects or interactions with sex) was only slightly greater than chance (7.7%). In no instance did any RIR variable reveal a significant difference between followed and nonfollowed subjects in more than one of the three original samples. These results suggest that the sample studied presently was largely representative of its college cohort.

Longitudinal Analyses

Quantity of interaction. We conducted 2 (college year) × 2 (sex) × 2 (time) ANOVAs, with repeated measures on the last factor. Separate analyses were conducted for each composition category, because our aim was to highlight consistencies and differences. We focus on time main effects and interactions involving time; sex main effects and interactions are noted in the tables. We are particularly interested in College Year × Time interactions, because they indicate differential change over time of the first-year and senior groups and therefore may reflect changes that occurred between the first and senior year of college.

Table 3.1 shows means and F values for the average number of daily interactions. Although there was a highly reliable drop from college to adulthood in the total number of interactions (from 6.93 to 5.08, $p < .001$), as predicted in Hypothesis 1, the composition categories revealed

a more differentiated pattern: Same-sex and group interaction decreased, mixed-sex interaction was unchanged, and opposite-sex interaction increased significantly. Separate analyses of interaction with same-sex and opposite-sex best friends, not shown in Table 3.1, revealed the same general trend, namely, that interaction with same-sex best friends decreased over time (from 1.50 to 1.06), $F(1, 109) = 13.55, p < .001$, whereas interaction with opposite-sex best friends became more common (from 1.16 to 1.91), $F(1, 109) = 23.71$, $p < .001$. In only one instance was the time trend qualified by a significant interaction with sex or college year: The decrease over time in group interactions was greater for first-year students than for seniors, but was significant for both groups.

Analyses of time per day spent socializing, reported in Table 3.2, supported these results. There were highly reliable decreases overall (from 340.6 min to 277.5 min per day) and in same-sex, mixed-sex, and group interactions. In contrast, time per day in opposite-sex interaction increased significantly. Best-friend analyses, not shown in Table 3.2, confirmed the increase in opposite-sex socializing (from 71.9 to 128.0 min per day), $F(1, 108) = 27.51, p < .0001$, but the drop for same-sex best friends was not significant (70.4 to 61.8 min), $F(1, 109) = 1.17, ns$. There were no significant interactions involving time.

We also examined two other measures of interaction quantity. First, the average interaction

TABLE 3.1. Number of Interactions Per Day

Group	All interaction		Same sex		Opposite sex		Mixed sex		Group	
	College	Adult	College	Adult	College	Adult	College	Adult	College	Adult
Men										
1st yr	6.44	4.71	3.26	1.79	1.11	1.79	0.63	0.75	1.45	0.38
Seniors	5.82	4.45	2.63	1.72	1.54	1.68	0.52	0.68	1.13	0.37
Women										
1st yr	8.00	5.81	3.27	2.03	2.36	2.41	0.98	0.92	1.40	0.46
Seniors	7.48	5.37	3.56	1.84	2.08	2.41	0.72	0.64	1.12	0.48
Time F	56.07**		65.22**		3.93*				137.45**	
Sex F	12.68**				19.20**		3.72			
Year F							4.17*			
Sex × Time							2.96			
Year × Time									4.45*	

Note. Degrees of freedom are 1, 109.
*$p < .05$. **$p < .001$.

TABLE 3.2. Time (in Minutes) Per Day Spent Socializing

Group	All interaction		Same sex		Opposite sex		Mixed sex		Group	
	College	Adult	College	Adult	College	Adult	College	Adult	College	Adult
Men										
1st yr	329.0	263.5	143.6	86.2	53.5	89.3	32.2	53.0	100.8	34.8
Seniors	299.5	232.0	109.7	63.0	90.4	94.2	22.3	48.9	79.3	26.7
Women										
1st yr	390.7	332.6	131.2	86.6	118.8	145.4	41.4	58.8	91.7	41.7
Seniors	344.3	283.2	135.7	67.3	104.6	134.9	32.8	39.9	70.2	40.9
Time F	23.57***		42.04***		6.52*		17.16***		87.02***	
Sex F	9.62**				14.02***					
Year F	4.59*		3.92*				3.44		3.90	
Sex × Time									3.44	

Note. Degrees of freedom are 1, 109.
*$p < .05$. **$p < .01$. ***$p < .001$.

increased in length from 51.4 min during college to 56.7 min during adulthood, $F(1, 109) = 5.78$, $p < .02$. This increase was evident in opposite-sex interaction (49.6 min to 54.9 min), $F(1, 109) = 2.95$, $p < .10$; mixed-sex interaction (47.8 min to 69.6 min), $F(1, 103) = 20.93$, $p < .001$; group interaction (71.6 min to 92.3 min), $F(1, 95) = 10.07$, $p < .005$; same-sex best-friend interaction (47.8 min to 58.9 min), $F(1, 109) = 6.80$, $p < .01$; and opposite-sex best-friend interaction (60.8 min vs. 69.3 min), $F(1, 108) = 4.15$, $p < .05$. No other effects were significant in this analysis.

Second, the number of different interaction partners also decreased significantly. Subjects reported more same-sex others (22.7 vs. 14.4), $F(1, 109) = 72.26$, $p < .001$, and opposite-sex others (16.2 vs. 9.8), $F(1, 109) = 66.90$, $p < .001$, as college students than as adults. The latter decrease was moderated by sex, however, $F(1, 109) = 23.09$, $p < .001$. Whereas as college students, women had more opposite-sex interaction partners than men did (19.8 vs. 12.5), as adults, men and women did not differ (both $M = 9.8$).

Let us briefly summarize these findings. When compared with their experiences as college students, adults interacted less frequently for less time with members of the same sex and in groups. Interaction with opposite-sex others, and in particular with their opposite-sex best friend, increased during this interval. The decrease in group interaction was greater for first-year subjects because group interactions had already become less prevalent by their senior year. Adults' interac-

tions lasted longer than college students' did. Finally, the number of different interaction partners decreased from college to adulthood, with women showing a larger drop than men in the number of opposite-sex partners.

Subjective quality of interaction. The two subjective variables, intimacy and satisfaction, were examined in separate 2 (college year) × 2 (sex) × 2 (time) ANOVAs, with repeated measures on the final factor. As documented in Table 3.3, perceived intimacy levels were consistently and significantly higher in adulthood. This was true overall and in three of the four composition categories (in group interaction, the increase was not significant, $p < .14$). There were parallel increases in intimacy with same-sex best friends, $F(1, 109) = 9.30$, $p < .005$, and opposite-sex best friends, $F(1, 108) = 5.23$, $p < .05$. Hypothesis 2 therefore received strong support.

The time effect was qualified by several interactions with college year. College Year × Time interactions were significant ($ps < .01$) in the total and same-sex categories. As shown in Table 3.3 and confirmed by simple effects tests, the rise in intimacy was greater for the first-year group (across all interactions, from 3.44 to 4.10) than for seniors (from 3.91 to 4.09). Inspection of Table 3.3 indicates, however, that this effect stemmed mostly from women. Senior women reported significantly higher intimacy levels in all categories than first-year women did (simple effect $ps .02$); in contrast, senior and first-year men differed significantly only in mixed-sex interaction. Moreover, intimacy levels reported by senior women in no instance increased

TABLE 3.3. Intimacy

Group	All interaction		Same sex		Opposite sex		Mixed sex		Group	
	College	Adult	College	Adult	College	Adult	College	Adult	College	Adult
Men										
1st yr	3.47	4.10	3.36	3.93	4.00	4.31	3.74	4.10	3.27	3.43
Seniors	3.48	3.95	3.41	3.61	4.17	4.41	3.15	3.83	2.74	3.08
Women										
1st yr	3.41	4.11	3.47	4.21	3.73	4.22	3.11	3.99	2.72	3.18
Seniors	4.34	4.22	4.49	4.25	4.48	4.44	3.97	3.85	3.47	3.25
Time F	25.26***		10.48***		6.01*		18.52***			
Sex F	4.48*		13.08***							
Year F	3.09				4.64*					
Sex × Time										
Year × Time	8.68**		12.06***							
Sex × Year × Time	3.81						10.11**		3.11	

Note. Degrees of freedom vary from 1, 96 to 1, 109.
*$p < .05$. **$p < .01$. ***$p < .001$.

from college to adulthood, whereas for senior men, all means rose from college to adulthood (although the rise was significant only in total and mixed-sex interaction). Therefore, it appears that for men, intimacy increases occurred largely after college, whereas for women, they tended to occur between the first and senior years of college.

There was an interesting divergence from this pattern in best-friend interactions. As shown in Table 3.4, for same-sex best friends, the three-way interaction was significant and similar to that described earlier (namely, all groups increased from college to adulthood except senior women). However, with opposite-sex best friends, only the College Year × Time effect approached significance ($p < .07$). Inspection of the relevant means suggests

that this is because senior men's intimacy was somewhat higher than that of first-year men, resembling the pattern shown by women. Our speculation is that age-related intimacy increases for men may reveal themselves earliest in this category of interaction.

Satisfaction revealed only one significant effect involving time: College students found opposite-sex interaction ($M = 5.15$) more pleasant than adults did ($M = 4.99$), $F(1, 108) = 8.54, p < .01$. In all other categories, satisfaction decreased over time, but the drops were small and nonsignificant. The absence of time effects on satisfaction ratings also has useful methodological implications. Because reported satisfaction did not increase over time, the rise in intimacy described earlier should not be attributed to global increases in positive

TABLE 3.4. Intimacy With Best Friends

Group	Same-sex best friend		Opposite-sex best friend	
	College	Adulthood	College	Adulthood
Men				
1st year	3.50	3.81	3.99	4.43
Seniors	3.42	3.94	4.27	4.40
Women				
1st year	3.43	4.12	3.68	4.22
Seniors	4.39	4.30	4.66	4.63
Sex F	6.03*			
Year F	3.40		6.00*	
Time F	9.30**		5.23*	
Year × Time F			3.59	
Year × Sex × Time F	4.56*			

Note. Degrees of freedom vary from 1, 108 to 1, 109.
*$p < .05$. **$p < .01$.

TABLE 3.5. Correlations Between College and Adult Interaction

Type of interaction	No. of interactions	Time per day	M length	M intimacy	M satisfaction
All interactions					
1st yr	.47***	.42***	.28*	.16	.27*
Seniors	.38**	.32*	.31*	.59***	.52***
Difference				< .01	< .12
Same sex					
1st yr	.23	.08	.13	.21	.14
Seniors	.23	.11	.03	.54***	.46***
Difference				< .05	< .07
Opposite sex					
1st yr	.22	.32*	.15	.13	.21
Seniors	.24	.23	.35**	.49***	.58***
Difference				< .05	< .05
Mixed sex					
1st yr	.35**	.35**	.19	.28 *	.17
Seniors	.32**	.22	.33*	.51***	.24
Difference				< .16	
Group					
1st yr	.39**	.36**	.06	.26	.32*
Seniors	.21	.10	.11	.46***	.11
Difference		< .17			
Same-sex best					
1st yr	.03	−.04	.10	.04	.18
Seniors	.30*	.08	.13	.51***	.18
Difference	< .15			< .01	
Opposite-sex best					
1st yr	.22	.34**	.17	.16	.09
Seniors	.24	.12	.05	.49***	.43***
Difference				< .06	< .06

Note. First-year correlation ns vary from 50 to 57; senior ns vary from 49 to 56. All significance tests are two-tailed. If no p value is listed, p was greater than .20.
*$p < .05$.   **$p < .01$.   ***$p < .001$.

feelings about social interaction or to longitudinal changes in socially desirable responding.

Nature of interactions. Overall, the percentage of interactions classified as pastime increased from 16.4% in college to 20.2% in adulthood, $F(1, 109) = 4.35$, $p < .05$, whereas the percentage of conversations decreased from 66.3% to 61.3%, $F(1, 109) = 5.78$, $p < .02$. Simple effects tested revealed that the growth in pastimes at the expense of conversations was consistently stronger among first-year students than seniors, who showed no significant differences between college and adulthood. There were no interactions with sex.

Consistency Across Time

To determine whether relative interaction patterns were consistent from college to adulthood, we computed a series of simple correlation coefficients between the two time periods for the five major variables of this research.[5] These correlations were computed separately for the first-year and senior samples, so that differences, which might give evidence of the establishment of stable interaction patterns during college, could be evaluated. The sample was not large enough to permit further breakdown into female and male subgroups; however, visual inspection showed few consistent sex differences in the pattern of correlations.

Table 3.5 lists these correlations. Looking first at the total number and time of social interaction, significant college-to-adult correlations were found in both groups. Correlations within the separate composition categories were more variable. Among first-year students, significant correlations with adult interaction were obtained for

---

[5]The reader is reminded that first-year to adult correlations span 9 to 11 years, whereas senior to adult correlations span 6 years.

opposite-sex, mixed-sex, group, and opposite-sex best-friend interaction. Among seniors, only time per day in mixed-sex and same-sex best-friend interaction correlated significantly. However, the correlation differences between groups were not significant. For these two measures, then, the most general finding appears to be the significant correlation across time in total interaction.

Perceived intimacy produced striking results. For seniors, correlations between college and adult interaction were uniformly and highly significant. For the first-year group, the comparable correlations were positive, but significant only in mixed-sex interaction. The senior and first-year correlations differed significantly ($ps < .05$) in total interaction and in three of six specific categories. Thus, intimacy levels reported in the senior year of college showed greater long-term stability than intimacy levels reported in the first year of college.

Correlations for reported satisfaction, shown in the final column of Table 3.5, revealed a similar pattern, although less definitively so. Over all interactions and in the same-sex, opposite-sex, and opposite-sex best-friend categories, seniors showed strong and significant correlations over time, whereas first-year students' correlations were significant overall and in group interaction. Once again, seniors' correlations tended to be greater than those of first-year students, although the difference was significant only for opposite-sex interaction.

The mean length of all interactions was significantly correlated in both groups. Finally, for seniors, the number of same-sex, $r(56) = .41, p < .005$, and opposite-sex, $r(56) = .28, p < .05$, partners were significantly correlated over time. For first-year subjects, the comparable correlations, $rs(57) = .22$ and $.17$, were not significant, but did not differ significantly from the seniors.

Do Marriage and Parenthood Qualify These Results?

Two obvious potential qualifications to our results are marital status and parental status, given that these factors might substantially alter a person's social environment. Unfortunately, this information was available for only 96 subjects. Only 5 subjects had children, so this factor was not examined

further. Forty subjects were married (24 women and 16 men), whereas 56 were not (24 women and 32 men). Using marital status as a fourth between-groups factor (cell ns varied from 8 to 16), we repeated the prior analyses for number of interactions, time per day spent socializing, the number of different partners, intimacy, and satisfaction.

For the number of different partners, intimacy, and satisfaction, marital status produced no significant effects. Consequently, for these variables, none of the prior results can be attributed to the special characteristics of marriage. Opposite-sex best-friend intimacy means were nearly identical for married ($M = 4.40$) and unmarried ($M = 4.41$) adults.[6]

An important qualification did emerge for interaction quantity, however. In the opposite-sex and opposite-sex best-friend categories, there were significant Marital Status × Time effects for the number of interactions, $Fs(1, 88) = 15.37$ and 16.48, respectively, both $ps < .001$, and time per day, $Fs(1, 88) = 6.85$ and 7.69, respectively, both $ps < .01$. In all opposite-sex interactions, married subjects showed large increases from college to adulthood, whereas means for unmarried subjects were virtually unchanged. With opposite-sex best friends, both groups increased the number and time of interactions, but the gains by married subjects were significantly greater than those of unmarried subjects. Only one other category produced an effect for marital status: time per day spent socializing with same-sex others. Although both married and unmarried subjects showed significant decreases ($p < .02$), the married subject drop was significantly greater than the unmarried subject drop, Marital Status × Time $F(1, 88) = 5.19, p < .05$.

Thus, with the exception of opposite-sex interaction, the changes in interaction patterns described earlier generally did not depend on marital status. Even among unmarried subjects, however, opposite-sex interaction became proportionally more common in adulthood—whereas all other

---

[6]Because of the procedures used to ensure confidentiality, we do not know the initials of subjects' spouses and therefore cannot identify interactions that occurred between subjects and their spouses. However, we believe it is highly likely that most married subjects' opposite-sex best friends were their spouses.

categories decreased in prevalence, opposite-sex interaction remained steady.

Discussion

We begin by summarizing findings relevant to our three hypotheses. Hypothesis 1 proposed an increase in the frequency of opposite-sex socializing along with a decrease in other categories. This hypothesis received strong and consistent support for both measures of social contact: number of daily interactions and time per day spent socializing. Moreover, these effects were usually not qualified by sex or college year, with one exception: The decrease in group interactions (more than three others present) in adulthood was significantly greater for first-year students than seniors. This may mean that group interactions are most representative of late adolescents' social behavior and begin declining during college. It may also be that students adjust to their new social environment by relying on group interactions.

These results indicate that the ecology of social participation shows a marked shift from college to adulthood. That opposite-sex interactions, including those involving best friends, became more prevalent in adulthood is consistent with trends that begin during adolescence (cf. Maccoby, 1990). Of course, many theorists characterize adult social behavior in terms of its focus on primary heterosexual relationships. It is interesting to note, however, that this increase occurred at the expense of same-sex interaction. Indeed, the decrease in the number of same-sex interactions (1.34 per day) was more than three times greater than the increase in opposite-sex interactions (0.30 per day). There is no particular reason why increases in one category necessitate decreases in another category (aside, perhaps, from time constraints), and the drop in same-sex socializing is therefore psychologically interesting. In Sullivan's (1953) interpersonal theory, same-sex friendships are the foundation of identity and intimacy development during adolescence. This is because the benefits of shared world views are most available with similar, same-sex others. As people mature, and as they become more comfortable with the opposite sex, they may have less need to limit their social contacts in this manner. In fact, adults had roughly equal levels of same-sex and opposite-sex socializing, suggesting that the preference for same-sex partners ends in adulthood.

Two results demonstrated greater reliance on close relationships in adulthood. Adult interactions were significantly longer than college interactions, and adults reported more than one third fewer different partners than college students. Although adults might have fewer partners because of differences in their social environment (i.e., fewer opportunities for spontaneous contact), the drop might also reflect adults' desire to focus their social time on a smaller number of good friends. This is consistent with the greater length of adult interactions.

Hypothesis 2 proposed intimacy increases from college to adulthood across all interaction categories. This hypothesis was supported by a strong main effect in total interaction and by main effects in four of six specific composition categories. Most theories, including Erikson's (1950), speak about early adulthood in terms of the establishment and growth of a primary intimate relationship. Our data suggest that age-related intimacy gains occur in a far less differentiated fashion. Increases in intimacy were not limited to a single heterosexual relationship, but rather were evident in all categories. The increase of intimacy in early adulthood may therefore mark a developmental shift in social preferences, goals, or abilities. In the future, it might be profitable to conceptualize intimacy as a global interaction style variable with traitlike characteristics and not just as a characteristic of single relationships. That is, people who prefer to interact intimately with one partner may prefer to do so with many partners and across varying contexts.

This general trend was qualified by a three-way interaction with college year and sex, significant in two categories and marginally significant in two others. Inspection of the means in Tables 3.3 and 3.4 plainly shows that for senior women, intimacy remained unchanged from college to adulthood. The time effects noted earlier apparently derived from first-year women and all men. By their senior year of college, women seem to have attained adult levels of interaction intimacy, whereas men did not do so until after college. Rather, men's interaction intimacy was essentially stable during college, but increased from senior year to adulthood in all interaction categories except opposite-sex best friend. Thus, the developmental trends discussed earlier may take place somewhat earlier for women (between ages 18 and 22) than for men (between ages 22 and 30). (These trends may relate to the uniqueness of a college environment, which is discussed later.)

Just why intimacy increases during this interval is not indicated by our research. One set of possible reasons relate to maturation. Previous studies examined intimacy gains during adolescence, and ours is the first to show continued advances in early adulthood. Certain forms of cognitive development that occur during early adulthood may be essential for true adult intimacy. K. W. Fischer, Hand, and Russell (1984) proposed that the capacity to relate several aspects of two or more abstractions to one another may not emerge until age 19 or 20 (Level 9) and that people's ability to form general principles by systematically coordinating various aspects of two or more abstractions may not develop until approximately age 25 (Level 10). Personal understandings of relationships between people qualify as abstractions in their model, and it seems likely that intimacy would be facilitated by these cognitive skills (Chelune, Robison, & Kommor, 1984; Reis & Shaver, 1988). It would be interesting to directly verify the role of these cognitive skills in close relationships with subsequent studies.

It is also possible that intimacy changes from the first year of college may be due to the instability of friendships during this transitional period. Although we cannot rule out this explanation, we believe it is unlikely for several reasons. First, for men, intimacy increased from the first to senior year in only one category—opposite-sex best friend—and then not significantly. It would therefore be necessary to posit that instability applies only to first-year women or that men's social networks remain unstable for all 4 years of college. We see no particular reason to support this logic. Second, Shaver et al. (1985) examined various social network variables at four points during the college year. Their data indicate that

network involvement and satisfaction had stabilized by the winter quarter. Our freshman-year data averaged across multiple assessments, at least half of which occurred after the equivalent of winter quarter on a semester system. Moreover, the original analyses of our data sets revealed no significant differences in intimacy as a function of assessment time (Nezlek, 1978; Wheeler & Nezlek, 1977). Third, note that quantitative measures of social participation in college, which should also show first-year instability, correlated equally well with adult data, regardless of college year.

We also found, as J. L. Fischer (1981) did, that regardless of age, men's socializing with other men was less intimate than both their socializing with women and women's socializing with either sex. This pattern has been shown in many prior studies (Dindia & Allen, 1992; Reis, in press). Consequently, the quantitative changes discussed earlier—that adults have more opposite-sex interaction and less same-sex interaction—may hold considerable intimacy benefits for men, but little advantage for women (cf. Reis, 1990).

Hypothesis 3 was concerned with consistency of interaction patterns from college to adulthood. Substantial across-time correlations were found for the amount of socializing and for mean levels of intimacy and satisfaction. Caspi et al. (1989) described two consistency processes that may have contributed to these findings. Interactional consistency occurs when an individual's interaction style repeatedly evokes similar responses from others. Cumulative consistency, in contrast, stems from the individual's choice of similar social environments at various points in the life cycle. In both cases, social behaviors, such as the variables we studied, reflect stable preferences and capabilities for interacting in particular ways. In turn, these interaction styles arise from personality traits, idiosyncratic needs, and cognitive representations (such as schemas and prototypes) relevant to socializing. Evidence for the longitudinal stability of such dispositional variables has been provided elsewhere (e.g., Caspi et al., 1989; Costa et al., 1980; Main et al., 1985), and Nezlek (in press) has shown that interaction patterns tend to be consistent within a single college year. The present research is unique in demonstrating consistency over a considerable time span in one product of these dispositions: everyday social behavior. This consistency was evident despite extensive differences in social environments. Interaction patterns apparently transcend differences in social networks and opportunities (cf. Lewis, 1982), consistent with the notion that people are active producers of their social experience.

For intimacy, correlations between adult and senior-year socializing were significantly greater than between adult and first-year socializing. This difference has important implications for understanding age-related trends in the development of intimacy. One explanation is that, at age 18, the traits and skills necessary for interacting intimately have not yet developed fully. By age 21, in contrast, enduring styles of interaction had apparently emerged, such that notwithstanding the general developmental shift among men noted earlier, those who interacted more or less intimately were likely to continue doing so at age 30. Future research is needed to identify the nature of the traits and skills that become established during this interval and the manner in which they affect daily interaction.

Two alternative explanations for this difference are plausible. One stems from the previously noted instability of first-year students' social networks. Although we cannot discount this possibility, we believe it is unlikely for the reasons discussed earlier. A second alternative concerns a confound in interpreting differences between the first-year and senior samples. As noted earlier, adult data were collected from the first-year group between 9 and 11 years after their college data, whereas the senior group was studied only 6 years later. This discrepancy might account for several of our results, notably the lack of mean intimacy increase among senior women and the higher across-time correlations for intimacy and satisfaction. We think this explanation is unlikely, however, for three reasons. First, if correct, similar results should have appeared for all variables, and they did not. Only intimacy consistently yielded significantly greater correlations for seniors than first-year students. In fact, across-time correlations in the amount and distribution of interaction were actually somewhat larger for first-year students than for seniors.

Second, we believe that 4 years of college are generally a time of significantly more meaningful psychological and personal change than 4 years around age 30. Finally, there were no consistent differences in the college–adult comparisons between the two groups of first-year students for whom the time interval differed by two years (9 vs. 11 years). Thus, had we waited another 4 years to follow the senior group, we think it unlikely that our findings would have been noticeably different.

Conclusion

Additional limitations of this research warrant note. First, the sample was composed of graduates of a single university, who may not be representative of university graduates in general or individuals who do not attend college. It will be particularly important to determine whether noncollege samples show similar developmental trends, because it is possible that the unique characteristics of residential college life were to some extent responsible for our findings. Second, because our study spanned the postgraduation transition, it was not possible to distinguish changes attributable to development and maturation from changes caused by differences in social environment. It would of course be important to separate these influences.

Future studies should examine longitudinal changes later in life, as well as changes brought on by specific life events (e.g., birth of a child, retirement, or relocation). Structured event-recording procedures such as the RIR make it possible for researchers to examine in some detail how changing life circumstances affect everyday activity. This perspective offers a useful complement to paradigms focusing only on the most significant relationships or on global impressions of one's social involvement. After all, it is in everyday social activity that people spend most of their conscious time, energy, and thought. The data reported in this article describe several key differences in the manner that college students and adults socialize. Given the importance of social activity in human functioning and well-being, our findings suggest that early adulthood may be a fruitful period for developmental research.

NOTES

Harry T. Reis and Yi-Cheng Lin, Department of Psychology, University of Rochester; M. Elizabeth Bennett, School of Dental Medicine, University of Pittsburgh; John B. Nezlek, Department of Psychology, College of William and Mary.

This research was supported by National Science Foundation Grant BNS 8416988. We are grateful for the foundation's help, and we are also grateful to the 113 persons who took part in this study. We also wish to thank David Kenny for his statistical advice.

Correspondence concerning this article should be addressed to Harry T. Reis, Department of Psychology, University of Rochester, Meliora Hall, Rochester, New York 14627. E-mail: reis@psych.rochester.edu.

REFERENCES

Argyle, M. (1987). *The psychology of happiness*. London: Methuen.

Arnstein, R. L. (1984). Young adulthood: Stages of maturity. In D. Offer & M. Sabshin (Eds.), *Normality and the life cycle* (pp. 108–144). New York: Basic Books.

Bakteman, G., & Magnusson, D. (1981). Longitudinal stability of personality characteristics. *Journal of Personality, 49*, 148–160.

Berndt, T. J., & Perry, T. B. (1990). Distinctive features and effects of early adolescent friendships. In R. Montemayor, G. R. Adams, & T. P. Gulotta (Eds.), *From childhood to adolescence: A transitional period* (pp. 269–287). Newbury Park, CA: Sage.

Berscheid, E., Snyder, M., & Omoto, A. M. (1989). The Relationship Closeness Inventory: Assessing the closeness of interpersonal relationships. *Journal of Personality and Social Psychology, 57*, 792–807.

Block, J. (1969). *Lives through time*. Berkeley, CA: Bancroft Books.

Blyth, D. A., & Foster-Clark, F. S. (1987). Gender differences in perceived intimacy with different members of adolescents' social networks. *Sex Roles, 17*, 689–718.

Buhrmester, D., & Furman, W. (1987). The development of companionship and intimacy. *Child Development, 58*, 1101–1113.

Caspi, A., Bem, D. J., & Elder, G. H., Jr. (1989). Continuities and consequences of interactional styles across the life span. *Journal of Personality, 57*, 375–406.

Chelune, G. J., Robison, J. T., & Kommor, M. J. (1984). A cognitive interactional model of intimate relationships. In V. J. Derlega (Ed.), *Communication, intimacy and close relationships* (pp. 11–40). San Diego, CA: Academic Press.

Cohen, S. (1988). Psychosocial models of the role of social support in the etiology of physical disease. *Health Psychology, 7*, 269–297.

Costa, P. T., Jr., McCrae, R. R., & Arenberg, D. (1980). Enduring dispositions in adult males. *Journal of Personality and Social Psychology, 38*, 793–800.

Csikszentmihalyi, M., & Larson, R. (1984). *Being adolescent*. New York: Basic Books.

DeVries, M. W. (1992). *The experience of psychopathology*. Cambridge, England: Cambridge University Press.

Dindia, K., & Allen, M. (1992). Sex differences in self-disclosure: A meta-analysis. *Psychological Bulletin, 112*, 106–124.

Erikson, E. (1950). *Childhood and society*. New York: Norton.

Fischer, J. L. (1981). Transitions in relationship style from adolescence to young adulthood. *Journal of Youth and Adolescence, 10*, 11–23.

Fischer, K. W., Hand, H. H., & Russell, S. (1984). The development of abstractions in adolescence and adulthood. In M. Commons, F. A. Richards, & C. Armon (Eds.), *Beyond formal operations* (pp. 43–73). New York: Praeger.

Fiske, S. T., & Taylor, S. E. (1991). *Social cognition* (2nd ed.). New York: McGraw-Hill.

Haan, N. (1977). *Coping and defending: Processes of self-environment organization*. San Diego, CA: Academic Press.

Jessor, R. (1983). The stability of change: Psychosocial development from adolescence to young adulthood. In D. Magnusson & V. L. Allen (Eds.), *Human development: An interactional perspective* (pp. 321–341). San Diego, CA: Academic Press.

Kenny, D. A., & Judd, C. M. (1986). Consequences of violating the independence assumption in analysis of variance. *Psychological Bulletin, 99*, 422–431.

Levinson, D. (1978). *The seasons of a man's life*. New York: Random House.

Lewis, M. (1982). The social network systems model: Toward a theory of social development. In T. M. Field, A. Huston, H. C. Quay, L. Troll, & G. E. Finley (Eds.), *Review of human development* (pp. 189–214). New York: Wiley.

Maccoby, E. E. (1990). Gender and relationships: A developmental account. *American Psychologist, 45*, 513–520.

Main, M., Kaplan, N., & Cassidy, J. (1985). Security in infancy, childhood, and adulthood: A move to the level of representation. In I. Bretherton & E. Waters (Eds.), *Growing points of attachment theory and research* (pp. 66–104). Chicago: Society for Research in Child Development.

Neugarten, B. L. (1969). Continuities and discontinuities of psychological issues in adult life. *Human Development, 12*, 121–130.

Nezlek, J. B. (1978). *The social behavior of first-year college students*. Unpublished doctoral dissertation, University of Rochester.

Nezlek, J. B. (in press). The stability of social interaction. *Journal of Personality and Social Psychology*.

Nisbett, R., & Ross, L. (1981). *Human inference: Strategies and shortcomings of social judgment*. Englewood Cliffs, NJ: Prentice Hall.

Orlofsky, J. (1988). *Intimacy status: Theory and research*. Unpublished manuscript, University of Missouri—St. Louis.

Peplau, L. A., & Goldston, S. E. (1984). *Preventing the harmful consequences of severe and persistent loneliness*. Rockville, MD: National Institute of Mental Health.

Reis, H. T. (1984). Social interaction and well-being. In S. Duck (Ed.), *Personal relationships: V. Repairing personal relationships* (pp. 21–45). San Diego, CA: Academic Press.

Reis, H. T. (1990). The role of intimacy in interpersonal relations. *Journal of Social and Clinical Psychology, 9*, 15–30.

Reis, H. T. (in press). The interpersonal context of emotions: Gender differences in intimacy and emotional support. In V. E. O'Leary & J. Sprock (Eds.), *Gendered emotions*. Newbury Park, CA: Sage.

Reis, H. T., Nezlek, J., & Wheeler, L. (1980). Physical attractiveness in social interaction. *Journal of Personality and Social Psychology, 38*, 604–617.

Reis, H. T., & Shaver, P. (1988). Intimacy as an interpersonal process. In S. Duck (Ed.), *Handbook of personal relationships* (pp. 367–389). New York: Wiley.

Reis, H. T., & Wheeler, L. (1991). Studying social interaction with the Rochester Interaction Record. *Advances in Experimental Social Psychology, 24*, 269–318.

Reis, H. T., Wheeler, L., Spiegel, N., Kernis, M. H., Nezlek, J., & Perri, M. (1982). Physical attractiveness in social interaction: II. Why does appearance affect social experience? *Journal of Personality and Social Psychology, 43*, 979–996.

Robinson, J. (1977). *How Americans use time: A social–psychological analysis of everyday behavior*. New York: Praeger.

Ross, M. (1989). Relation of implicit theories to the construction of personal histories. *Psychological Review, 96*, 341–357.

Schwarz, N. (1990). Assessing frequency reports of mundane behaviors: Contributions of cognitive psychology to questionnaire construction. In C. Hendrick & M. S. Clark (Eds.), *Research methods in personality and social psychology* (pp. 98–119). Newbury Park, CA: Sage.

Sears, R. R. (1977). Sources of life satisfactions of the Terman Gifted Men. *American Psychologist, 32*, 119–128.

Shaver, P., Furman, W., & Buhrmester, B. (1985). Aspects of a life transition: Network changes, social skills, and loneliness. In S. Duck & D. Perlman (Eds.), *Understanding personal relationships* (pp. 193–219). Beverly Hills, CA: Sage.

Statistical Abstract of the United States. (1990). Washington, DC: U. S. Government Printing Office.

Steinberg, L. (1989). *Adolescence*. New York: Knopf.

Sullivan, H. S. (1953). *The interpersonal theory of psychiatry*. New York: Norton.

Tennen, H., Suls, J., & Affleck, G. (1991). Special issue on studying small events. *Journal of Personality, 59*, 313–662.

Vaillant, G. E. (1977). *Adaptation to life*. Boston: Little, Brown.

Veroff, J., Kulka, R. A., & Douvan, E. (1981). *Mental health in America: Patterns of help-seeking from 1957 to 1976*. New York: Basic Books.

Wheeler, L., & Nezlek, J. (1977). Sex differences in social participation. *Journal of Personality and Social Psychology, 35*, 742–754.

Wheeler, L., Reis, H. T., & Nezlek, J. (1983). Loneliness, social interaction, and sex roles. *Journal of Personality and Social Psychology, 45*, 943–953.

Appendix

Rochester Interaction Record (Adult Data)

Date _____   Time _____   a.m. _____   Length: _____ hr _____ min

p.m. _____

Initials: _____ _____ _____   If more than 3 others:

Sex: _____ _____ _____   No. of females _____   No. of males _____

Intimacy:...superficial	1	2	3	4	5	6	7	meaningful
I disclosed:..very little	1	2	3	4	5	6	7	a great deal
Other disclosed:.....................................very little	1	2	3	4	5	6	7	a great deal
Social integration: did not feel like part of a group	1	2	3	4	5	6	7	felt like part of a group
Quality:..unpleasant	1	2	3	4	5	6	7	very pleasant
Satisfaction:.............................less than expected	1	2	3	4	5	6	7	more than expected
Initiation:...I initiated	1	2	3	4	5	6	7	other initiated
Influence:................................I influenced more	1	2	3	4	5	6	7	other influenced more

Nature: Job   Task   Pastime   Conversation   Date

First Impressions and Interpersonal Attraction

They gave each other a smile with a future in it.

— Ring Lardner

Friendship needs a certain parallelism of life, a community of thought, a rivalry of aim.

— Henry Brooks Adams

Only God, my dear,
Could love you for yourself alone
And not your yellow hair.

— William Butler Yeats

It has been said that you don't get a second chance to make a good first impression, underscoring the importance of first impressions in social life. First impressions are influential for several reasons, one of which is that because all relationships begin with an initial meeting between strangers, these encounters serve as "gatekeeper" to the acquaintance process. Throughout our lives, we come into contact with scores of people, only a few of whom receive more than momentary attention. Anna's first impressions of Dave—Is this new guy interesting? Is interaction with him likely to be enjoyable or rewarding?—play a key role in determining whether she will seek to know him better or disregard him. Moreover, because our behavior toward new acquaintances depends on our thoughts and feelings about them, first impressions can affect ensuing interaction. Thus, although Anna's first impressions of Dave may be fleeting, vague, and founded upon minimal, sometimes inaccurate information, they nevertheless are pivotal in shaping her early interactions with him as well as the odds that she will take him seriously as a potential partner. (It bears noting, however, that first impressions tend to be more accurate than we typically give them credit for; Ambady & Rosenthal, 1992.)

Attraction is usually studied in terms of very general positive or negative sentiment about another person, reflecting a fundamental theme of social judgment (Heider, 1958): Does this person seem "good for me or bad for me?" In fact, recent research using sophisticated psychophysiological methods suggests that the evaluation of a novel stimulus as hospitable or hostile is one of the quickest, most automatic judgments in human cognition (Ito & Cacioppo, 2001). Presumably, such judgments conferred an adaptive advantage over the course of evolution: Effective coping with the demands of the environment and survival itself were facilitated by the ability to classify a novel entity as desirable or dangerous, and to do so quickly, easily, and without deliberate intent. As such, it may not be coincidental that in the field of social psychology, nothing about relationships has been studied as extensively as the determinants of initial attraction. Some of the most influential initial studies were conducted by Theodore Newcomb, including a classic longitudinal study of friendship formation among new University of Michigan students who were strangers prior to being assigned to share living quarters (Newcomb, 1961). Together with studies using Byrne's experimental paradigm for manipulating the degree of similarity between research participants and their potential partners (described below), the early flurry of research focused on attitudinal and personality similarity as key determinants of attraction.

Another watershed event in the study of attraction was the publication in 1969 of *Interpersonal Attraction*, by Ellen Berscheid and Elaine Walster. In this slim yet insightful volume, these authors suggested that attraction is based on "rewards others provide," and went on to describe a variety of specific factors and mechanisms that underlie the processes of attraction. It is fair to say that hundreds of studies of initial attraction have built upon this foundation. Many of these studies are laboratory experiments: Participants are randomly assigned to meet and interact with a stranger (who may be real, hypothetical, or a confederate) who possesses or enacts a constellation of personal qualities that are of interest to the researchers. Although other methods have also been popular (e.g., field experiments, surveys), the predominance of laboratory experiments involving strangers with little in common beyond the experimental scenario—and with virtually no chance of future interaction—has been criticized for spawning a knowledge base with little generality to the development of relationships in the real world (except, perhaps, to speed-dating). On the other hand, the well-known benefits of laboratory experimentation have led to an impressively detailed literature, the main principles and established findings of which have endured remarkably well across time, replications, settings, and samples (e.g., ages, cultures). If nothing else, the value of methodological diversity seems clear.

The articles reproduced in this section represent three principles of initial attraction that have received excellent support in the empirical literature. The first article, by Byrne, Ervin, and

Lamberth, demonstrates that following an initial interaction between Dave and Anna, the two are more likely to be attracted to one another to the extent that they possess similar attitudes, and to the extent that each regards the other as physically attractive. Although the study proper did not involve random assignment, an experimental manipulation was included—a "simulated stranger" condition, in which a hypothetical partner is described as being similar to Dave or Anna with regard to either one third (low similarity) or two thirds (high similarity) of the questionnaire items. No interaction took place in the simulated stranger condition, in order to provide a baseline for the dating study—in other words, to establish that Dave will feel more attracted to a partner he perceives as similar to himself, independent of anything that might take place during actual interaction with that person. This manipulation constitutes Byrne's "attraction paradigm"—a paradigm that was very popular in early research (Byrne, 1971).

The second paper, Moreland and Beach's study of "mere exposure" in the classroom, addresses another important principle, that of familiarity. Social psychological research suggests that repeated exposure to a stimulus tends to increase liking for it (Bornstein, 1989). The stimulus category of "other people" is no exception to this rule. Many researchers believe that this principle helps explain the oft-replicated finding that the closer two individuals are in proximity to each other, and hence the more accessible they are to each other for interaction, the more likely they are to become friends. Moreland and Beach demonstrate in their research that the mere exposure effect extends to something as simple as merely seeing another person walk into one's classroom frequently. Although no one would deny that attraction is a complex process, these authors' striking results suggest that interpersonal processes with important outcomes may be triggered when people simply come into contact with each other more frequently, whether at work, at school, or at the neighborhood coffee shop or local health club.

Finally, Snyder, Tanke, and Berscheid's research makes two important points about first impressions. First, their study provides compelling evidence for the positive impact of physical attractiveness, reflecting the "what is beautiful is good" stereotype: Attractive individuals are perceived to possess socially desirable traits. Second, this work illustrates how first impressions can serve as self-fulfilling prophecies, via a process termed "behavioral confirmation": Dave tends to develop expectations about Anna based in part on her outward appearance. He tends to interact with her in a manner that is consistent with those beliefs, thereby eliciting from Anna behaviors that actually confirm his expectations. In short, Dave's expectations—and not Anna's actual qualities—are causally responsible for the nature of their interactions. The behavioral confirmation process represents an important reason why first impressions are so important. (Incidentally, although Snyder et al.'s study was limited to male perceivers, other research has revealed similar effects with female perceivers [Andersen & Bem, 1981]. In general, Anna is just as likely to be prone to this stereotype as is Dave.)

REFERENCES

Ambady, N., & Rosenthal, R. (1992). Thin slices of expressive behavior as predictors of interpersonal consequences: A meta-analysis. *Psychological Bulletin, 111*, 256–274.

Andersen, S. M., & Bem, S. L. (1981). Sex typing and androgyny in dyadic interaction: Individual differences in responsiveness to physical attractiveness. *Journal of Personality and Social Psychology, 41*, 74–86.

Berscheid, E., & Walster, E. H. (1969/1978). *Interpersonal attraction.* Reading, MA: Addison Wesley.

Bornstein, R. F. (1989). Exposure and affect: Overview and meta-analysis of research, 1968–1987. *Psychological Bulletin, 106,* 265–289.

Byrne, D. (1971). *The attraction paradigm.* New York: Academic Press.

Heider, F. (1958). *The psychology of interpersonal relations.* New York: Wiley.

Ito, T. A., & Cacioppo, J. T. (2001). Affect and attitudes: A social neuroscience approach. In J. P. Forgas (Ed.), *Handbook of affect and social cognition* (pp. 50–74). Mahwah, NJ: Erlbaum.

Newcomb, T. M. (1961). *The acquaintance process.* New York: Holt, Rinehart, and Winston.

SUGGESTIONS FOR FURTHER READING

Berscheid, E. (1985). Interpersonal attraction. In G. Lindzey & E. Aronson (Eds.), *Handbook of social psychology* (3rd ed.)(pp. 413–484). New York: Random House. A full discussion of theoretical underpinnings and empirical findings regarding interpersonal attraction. Includes a history of the field.

Byrne, D., Clore, G. L., & Smeaton, G. (1986). The attraction hypothesis: Do similar attitudes affect anything? *Journal of Personality and Social Psychology, 51,* 1167–1170. Provides a reply to Rosenbaum (1986), listed below.

Caspi, A., & Herbener, E. S. (1990). Continuity and change: Assortative marriage and the consistency of personality in adulthood. *Journal of Personality and Social Psychology, 58,* 250–258. An impressive study that shows how similarity influences the choice of marital partners, and how stability in one's personality may be promoted by interaction with partners over the course of a lifetime.

Fehr, B. (1996). *Friendship processes.* Thousand Oaks, CA: Sage. This accessible volume includes a useful update of work regarding similarity effects in friendship formation.

Festinger, L., Schachter, S., & Back, K. (1950). *Social pressures in informal groups: A study of human factors in housing.* Stanford, CA: Stanford University Press. An early and vivid account of the importance of proximity in promoting attraction.

Hatfield, E., & Sprecher, S. (1986). *Mirror, mirror: The importance of looks in everyday life.* Albany, NY: State University of New York Press. A thoughtful and comprehensive review of research concerning physical attractiveness.

Langlois, J. H., Kalakanis, L., Rubenstein, A. J., Larson, A., Hallam, M., & Smoot, M. (2000). Maxims or myths of beauty? A meta-analytic and theoretical review. *Psychological Bulletin, 126*, 390–423. An update on physical attractiveness research, with a focus on the validity of the stereotype.

Rosenbaum, M. L. (1986). The repulsion hypothesis: On the nondevelopment of relationships. *Journal of Personality and Social Psychology, 51,* 1156–1166. This research suggests that the similarity-liking effect may be less important than the dissimilarity-repulsion effect.

Sears, D. O. (1983). The person-positivity bias. *Journal of Personality and Social Psychology, 44*, 233–250. This research suggests that we are prepared to react positively to the extent that a given entity is more "person-like"; for example, students evaluate specific professors more favorably than they evaluate professors in general, and Americans typically like their own senators and representatives yet distrust politicians more generally.

Snyder, M. (1992). Motivational foundations of behavioral confirmation. In M. P. Zanna (Ed.), *Advances in experimental social psychology* (pp. 67–114). San Diego, CA: Academic Press, Inc. A clear and complete theoretical statement regarding the behavioral confirmation process in social interaction.

DISCUSSION QUESTIONS

1. Why does similarity promote attraction? What specific processes might be responsible for this effect?

2. Think about several close friends, and then think about some other people you know but who are not your friends. To what extent do you feel more similar to the former than the latter? With regard to what sorts of qualities? How has similarity played a role in your developing close friendships with the former but not the latter?

3. How has familiarity and "mere exposure" influenced your friendships and romantic relationships?

4. Discuss the "mere exposure" effect. What specific mechanisms might be responsible for it?

5. Describe a situation in which you were on either the perceiving end or the receiving end of the behavioral confirmation process. How might that interaction have proceeded differently had there been a different initial expectation?

6. What is the "what is beautiful is good" stereotype? How might this stereotype influence the course of a job interview or the outcome of a political election?

7. Beyond the principles discussed in these articles, what factors influence your initial impressions of a new acquaintance? Are these factors unique to you, or do you think that they influence others' first impressions as well? If you believe that a factor is generally influential, why do you think that factor has not (yet) been examined by relationships researchers?

8. Do you think that the variables identified as important causes of initial attraction continue to influence our feelings of attraction to a partner beyond the first impression stage? Which ones continue to be important, and which ones fade in importance? Why?

READING 4

Continuity Between the Experimental Study of Attraction and Real-Life Computer Dating[1]

Donn Byrne[2] • SUNY Albany
Charles R. Ervin • University of Texas
John Lamberth • Purdue University

As a test of the nonlaboratory generalizability of attraction research, a computer dating field study was conducted. A 50-item questionnaire of attitudes and personality was administered to a 420-student pool, and 44 male–female pairs were selected on the basis of maximal or minimal similarity of responses. Each couple was introduced, given differential information about the basis for their matching, and asked to spend 30 minutes together at the Student Union on a "coke date." Afterward, they returned to the experimenter and were independently assessed on a series of measures. It was found that attraction was significantly related to similarity and to physical attractiveness. Physical attractiveness was also significantly related to ratings of desirability as a date, as a spouse, and to sexual attractiveness. Both similarity and attractiveness were related to the physical proximity of the two individuals while they were talking to the experimenter after the date. In a follow-up investigation at the end of the semester, similarity and physical attractiveness were found to predict accurate memory of the date's name, incidence of talking to one another in the interim since the coke date, and desire to date the other person in the future.

A familiar but never totally resolved problem with any experimental findings is the extent to which they may be generalized to the nonlabora- tory situation. At least three viewpoints about the problem may be discerned. First, and perhaps most familiar, is instant generalization from the

[1]This research was supported in part by Research Grant MH-11178-04 from the National Institute of Mental Health and in part by Research Grant GS-2752 from the National Science Foundation. The authors wish to thank James Hilgren, Royal Masset, and Herman Mitchell for their help in conducting this experiment.

[2]Requests for reprints should be sent to Donn Byrne, Department of Psychology, SUNY Albany, Albany, New York 12222.

specific and often limited conditions of an experiment to any and all settings that are even remotely related. This tendency is most frequently seen at cocktail parties after the third martini and on television talk shows featuring those who popularize psychology. Second, and almost as familiar, is the notion that the laboratory is a necessary evil. It is seen as an adequate substitute for the real world, only to the extent that it reproduces the world. For example, Aronson and Carlsmith (1968) ask, "Why, then, do we bother with these pallid and contrived imitations of human interaction when there exist rather sophisticated techniques for studying the real thing [p. 4]?" They enumerate the advantages of experiments over field study, but emphasize that good experiments must be realistic in order to involve the subject and have an "impact" on him. Concern with experimental realism often is expressed in the context of positing qualitative differences between the laboratory and the outside world; it is assumed that in moving from simplicity to complexity, new and different principles are emergent. Third, and least familiar in personality and social psychology, is a view that is quite common in other fields. Laboratory research is seen not as a necessary evil, but as an essential procedure that enables us to attain isolation and control of variables and thus makes possible the formulation of basic principles in a setting of reduced complexity. If experiments realistically reproduce the nonlaboratory complexities, they provide little advantage over the field study. Continuity is assumed between the laboratory and the outside world, and complexity is seen as quantitative and not qualitative. To move from a simple situation to a complex one requires detailed knowledge about the relevant variables and their interaction. Application and the attainment of a technology depend upon such an approach.

With respect to a specific psychological phenomenon, the problem of nonlaboratory generalization and application may be examined more concretely. The laboratory investigation of interpersonal attraction within a reinforcement paradigm (Byrne, 1969) has followed a strategy in which the effect of a variety of stimulus variables

on a single response variable was the primary focus of interest. A model has evolved that treats all relevant stimuli as positive or negative reinforcers of differential magnitude. Attraction toward any stimulus object (including another person) is then found to be a positive linear function of the proportion of weighted positive reinforcements associated with that object. Attitude statements have been the most frequently employed reinforcing stimuli, but other stimulus elements have included personality variables (e.g., Griffitt, 1966), physical attractiveness (e.g., Byrne, London, & Reeves, 1968), economic variables (Byrne, Clore, & Worchel, 1966), race (e.g., Byrne & Ervin, 1969), behavioral preferences (Huffman, 1969), personal evaluations (e.g., Byrne & Rhamey, 1965), room temperature (Griffitt, 1970a), and sexual arousal (Picher, 1966).

Considering just one of those variables, attitude similarity–dissimilarity, why is it not reasonable to propose an immediate and direct parallel between laboratory and nonlaboratory responses? One reason is simple and quite obvious, but it seems often to be overlooked. Laboratory research is based on the isolation of variables so that one or a limited number of independent variables may be manipulated, while, if possible, all other stimulus variables are controlled. In the outside world, multiple uncontrolled stimuli are present. Thus, if all an experimental subject knows about a stranger is that he holds opinions similar to his own on six out of six political issues, the stranger will be liked (Byrne, Bond, & Diamond, 1969). We cannot, however, assume that any two interacting individuals who agree on these six issues will become fast friends because (a) they may never get around to discussing those six topics at all, and (b) even if these topics are discussed, six positive reinforcements may simply become an insignificant portion of a host of other positive and negative reinforcing elements in the interaction. A second barrier to immediate applicability of a laboratory finding lies in the nature of the response. It is good research strategy to limit the dependent variable (in this instance, the sum of two 7-point rating scales), but nonlaboratory responses may be as varied and uncontrolled as the stimuli. The relationship between that paper-and-pencil measure of attraction and other interpersonal responses is only beginning to be explored (e.g., Byrne, Baskett, & Hodges, 1969; Efran, 1969). The third barrier lies in the nature of the relationship investigated. For a number of quite practical reasons, the laboratory study of attraction is limited in its time span and hence might legitimately be labeled the study of first impressions. Whether the determinants of first impressions are precisely the same as the determinants of a prolonged friendship, of love, or of marital happiness is an empirical question and one requiring a great deal of research.

In view of these barriers to extralaboratory application of experimental findings, how may one begin the engineering enterprise? The present research suggests one attempt to seek a solution. Specifically, a limited dating situation is created in which the barriers to application are minimized. Independent variables identified in the laboratory (attitude similarity, personality similarity, and physical attractiveness) are varied in a real-life situation, and an attempt is made to make the variables salient and to minimize the occurrence of other stimulus events. Even though similarity has been the focus of much of the experimental work on attraction, the findings with respect to physical attractiveness have consistently demonstrated the powerful influence of appearance on responses to those of the opposite sex and even of the same sex. Both field studies (Megargee, 1956; Perrin, 1921; Taylor, 1956; Walster, Aronson, Abrahams, & Rottmann, 1966) and laboratory investigations (Byrne et al., 1968; McWhirter, 1969; Moss, 1969) have shown that those who are physically attractive elicit more positive responses than do those who are unattractive. The laboratory response measure was retained so that a common reference point was available, but additional response variables were also used in order to extend the generality and meaning of the attraction construct. Finally, in this experiment, the interaction was deliberately limited in time so that it remained close to a first-impression relationship. Given these deliberately limited conditions, it was proposed that the positive relationship between

the proportion of weighted positive reinforcements and attraction is directly applicable to a nonlaboratory interaction. Specifically, it was hypothesized that in a computer dating situation (*a*) attraction is a joint function of similarity and physical attractiveness, and (*b*) the greater the extent to which the specific elements of similarity are made salient, the greater is the relationship between similarity and attraction.

The variety of ways in which similarity and attraction could be investigated in a field situation raises an interesting question of strategy. It should be kept in mind that there is no magic about the similarity effect. Similarity does not exude from the pores; rather, specific attitudes and other characteristics must be expressed overtly. It would be relatively simple to design a computer dating experiment in which no similarity effects would be found. For example, one could lie about the degree of similarity, and in a brief interaction, the subjects would not be likely to discover the deception. Another alternative would be to provide no information about similarity and then to forbid the subjects to talk during their date. Negative results in such studies would be of no importance as a test since they are beyond the boundary conditions of the theory. Another possible study would give no initial similarity information and then require an extended interaction period, but that has already been done. That is, people in the real world do this every day, and numerous correlational studies indicate that under such conditions, similarity is associated with attraction. The strategy of the present research was frankly to maximize the possibility of securing a precise similarity attraction effect in a real-life setting; in subsequent research, the limiting conditions of the effect may be determined.

Method

Attitude-Personality Questionnaire

In order to provide a relatively broad base on which to match couples for the dating process, a 50-item questionnaire was constructed utilizing five variables. In previous research, a significant similarity effect has been found for authoritarianism (Sheffield & Byrne, 1967), repression–sensitization (Byrne & Griffitt, 1969; Byrne, Griffitt, & Stefaniak, 1967), attitudes (Byrne, 1961, 1969), EPPS items and self-concept (Griffitt, 1966, 1970b). Each variable was represented by 10 items, which were chosen to represent the least possible intercorrelations within dimensions; the rationale here was the desire to maximize the number of *independent* scale responses on which matching could be based.

Simulated Stranger Condition

In order to provide a baseline for the similarity effect under controlled conditions, a simulated stranger condition was run in which the other person was represented only by his or her purported responses to the attitude–personality questionnaire. The study was described as an investigation of the effectiveness of the matching procedures of computer dating organizations. Subjects were told, "Instead of arranging an actual date, we are providing couples with information about one another and asking for their reactions." The simulated scales were prepared to provide either a .33 or .67 proportion of similar responses between stranger and subject. The subject was asked to read the responses of an opposite-sex stranger and then to make a series of evaluations on an expanded version of the Interpersonal Judgment Scale. This scale consists of ten 7-point scales. The measure of attraction within this experimental paradigm (Byrne, 1969) consists of the sum of two scales: liking and desirability as a work partner. This attraction index ranges from 2 to 14 and has a split-half reliability of .85. In addition, four buffer scales deal with evaluations of the other person's intelligence, knowledge of current events, morality, and adjustment. These variables are found to correlate positively with attraction, but they have somewhat different antecedents and are included in the analysis simply as supplemental information. Three new scales, added for the present study in order to explore various responses to the opposite sex, asked the subject to react to the other person as a potential date, as a marriage partner, and as to sexual attractiveness.

Finally, a tenth scale was added in order to assess a stimulus variable, the physical attractiveness of the other person. In addition, the physical attractiveness of each subject was rated by the experimenter on the same 7-point scale on which the subjects rated one another.

Computer Dating Condition

Selection of dating couples. The attitude–personality questionnaire was administered to a group of 420 introductory psychology students at the University of Texas, and each item was scored in a binary fashion. By means of a specially prepared program, the responses of each male were compared with those of each female; for any given couple, the number of possible matching responses could theoretically range from 0 to 50. The actual range was from 12 to 37. From these distributions of matches, male–female pairs were selected to represent either the greatest or the least number of matching responses. There was a further restriction that the male be as tall as or taller than the female. Of the resulting pairs, a few were eliminated because (*a*) one of the individuals was married, (*b*) the resulting pair was racially mixed, or (*c*) because of a failure to keep the experimental appointment. The remaining 88 subjects formed 24 high-similar pairs, whose proportion of similar responses ranged from .66 to .74, and 20 low-similar pairs, whose proportion of similar responses ranged from .24 to .40.

Levels of information saliency. The experiment was run with one of the selected couples at a time. In the experimental room, they were introduced to one another and told:

> In recent years, there has been a considerable amount of interest in the phenomenon of computer dating as a means for college students to meet one another. At the present time, we are attempting to learn as much as possible about the variables which influence the reactions of one individual to another.

In order to create differential levels of saliency with respect to the matching elements, subjects in the salient condition were told:

> Earlier this semester, one of the test forms you filled out was very much like those used by some

of the computer dating organizations. In order to refresh your memory about this test and the answers you gave, we are going to ask you to spend a few minutes looking over the questions and your answers to them.

The answers of several hundred students were placed on IBM cards and run through the computer to determine the number of matching answers among the 50 questions for all possible pairs of male and female students. According to the computer, the two of you gave the same answers on approximately 67% (33%) of those questions.

In the nonsalient condition, they were told:

Imagine for the purposes of the experiment that you had applied to one of the computer dating organizations and filled out some of their information forms. Then, imagine that the two of you had been notified that, according to the computer, you match on approximately 67% (33%) of the factors considered important.

All subjects were then told:

For our experiment, we would like to create a situation somewhat like that of a computer date. That is, you answered a series of questions, the computer indicated that you two gave the same responses on some of the questions, and now we would like for you to spend a short time together getting acquainted. Specifically, we are asking you to spend the next 30 minutes together on a "coke date" at the Student Union. Here is 50¢ to spend on whatever you would like. We hope that you will learn as much as possible about each other in the next half hour because we will be asking you a number of questions about one another when you return.

Measures of attraction. When they returned from the date to receive their final instructions, an unobtrusive measure of attraction was obtained: the physical distance between the two subjects while standing together in front of the experimenter's desk. The distance was noted on a simple ordinal scale ranging from 0 (touching one another) to 5 (standing at opposite corners of the desk). The subjects were then separated and asked to evaluate their date on the Interpersonal Judgment Scale.

Follow-up measures. At the end of the semester (2–3 months after the date), it was possible to

locate 74 of the 88 original subjects who were willing to answer five additional questions. Each was asked to write the name of his or her computer date and to indicate whether or not they had talked to one another since the experiment, dated since the experiment, and whether a date was desired or planned in the future. Finally, each was asked whether the evaluation of the date was influenced more by physical attractiveness or by attitudes.

Results

Simulated Stranger Condition

The mean attraction responses of two simulated stranger conditions are shown in Table 4.1. Analysis of variance indicated that the similarity effect was significant ($F = 4.00$, $df = 1/46$, $p < .06$; $Ms = 9.47$ and 10.78 for the low and high similarity conditions).

Predicting Attraction in the Computer Dating Condition

The mean attraction responses for male and female subjects at two levels of information saliency and two levels of response similarity are shown in Table 4.1. Analysis of variance indicated the only significant effect to be that of proportion of similar responses ($F = 13.67$, $df = 1/40$, $p < .001$). The attempt to make the matching stimuli differentially salient did not affect attraction, and there were no sex differences.

TABLE 4.1. Mean Attraction Responses of Males and Females with Similar and Dissimilar Dates at Two Levels of Saliency Concerning Matching Information

| | Proportion of similar responses | |
Level	Low	High
Male *Ss* Information		
Salient	10.00	11.91
Nonsalient	10.56	11.38
Female *Ss* Information		
Salient	10.73	11.82
Nonsalient	10.33	12.15

TABLE 4.2. Correlations Between Ratings of Physical Attractiveness of Date and Evaluations of Date

Variable	Attractiveness of date Rated by Ss		Attractiveness of date Rated by E	
	Male Ss	Female Ss	Male Ss	Female Ss
Attraction	.39**	.60**	.07	.32*
Dating	.66**	.57**	.21	.33*
Marriage	.56**	.55**	.18	.34*
Sex	.77**	.70**	.53**	.44**

Note. *$p < .05$. **$p < .01$.

The other variable that was expected to influence attraction was the physical attractiveness of the date. It is interesting to note in the simulated stranger condition that while the manipulation of similarity influenced attraction, it had no effect on guesses as to the other person's physical attractiveness ($F < 1$). Thus, data in the computer dating condition indicating a relationship between attractiveness and attraction would seem to result from the effect of the former on the latter. Two measures of attractiveness were available: ratings by the experimenter when the subjects first arrived and by each subject of his or her own date following their interaction. The correlation between these two measures was significant; the correlation between the experimenter's ratings of male subjects and the females' ratings of their dates was .59 ($p < .01$) and between the experimenter's ratings of female subjects and the males' ratings of their dates was .39 ($p < .01$). As might be expected, the subject's own ratings proved to

be better predictors than did the experimenter's ratings. In Table 4.2 are shown those correlations between physical attractiveness ratings and Interpersonal Judgment Scale responses, which were consistent across sexes.

Thus, the first hypothesis was clearly confirmed, but there was no support for the second hypothesis.

With respect to the prediction of attraction, it seems likely that a combination of the similarity and attractiveness variables would provide the optimal information. In Table 4.3 are shown the mean attraction responses toward attractive (ratings of 5–7) and unattractive (ratings of 1–4) dates at two levels of response similarity. For both sexes, each of the two independent variables was found to affect attraction. The physical attractiveness variable was significant for both males ($F = 3.85$, $df = 1/39$, $p < .05$) and for females ($F = 10.44$, $df = 1/40$, $p < .01$). The most positive response in each instance was toward similar attractive dates, and the least positive response was toward dissimilar unattractive dates. An additional analysis indicated no relationship between an individual's own physical attractiveness (as rated by the date) and response to the other person's physical attractiveness.

Other Effects of Similarity and Attractiveness

On the additional items of the Interpersonal Judgment Scale, similarity was found to have a significant positive effect on ratings of the date's intelligence ($F = 4.37$, $df = 1/40$, $p < .05$), desirability as a date ($F = 8.92$, $df = 1/40$, $p < .01$),

TABLE 4.3. Mean Attraction Responses of Males and Females with Similar and Dissimilar Dates Who Are Relatively Attractive and Unattractive

Physical attractiveness of date	Proportion of similar responses	
	Low	High
Male Ss		
Attractive	10.55	12.00
Unattractive	9.89	10.43
Female Ss		
Attractive	11.25	12.71
Unattractive	9.50	11.00

and desirability as a marriage partner ($F = 4.76$, $df = 1/40$, $p < .05$).

The simplest and least obtrusive measure of attraction was the proximity of the two individuals after the date, while receiving their final instructions from the experimenter. If physical distance can be considered as an alternative index of attraction, these two dependent variables should be correlated. For females, the correlation was $-.36$ ($p < .01$) and for males, $-.48$ ($p < .01$); in each instance, the greater the liking for the partner, the closer together they stood. Another way of evaluating the proximity variable is to determine whether it is influenced by the same independent variables as is the paper-and-pencil measure. For both sexes, physical separation was found to correlate $-.49$ ($p < .01$) with similarity. Thus, the more similar the couples, the closer they stood. Because similarity and proximity are necessarily identical for each member of a pair, it is not possible to determine whether the males, the females, or both are responsible for the similarity–proximity relationship. When the physical attractiveness measure was examined, however, there was indirect evidence that proximity in this situation was controlled more by the males than by the females. For females, there was no relationship between ratings of the male's appearance and physical separation ($r = -.06$). For males, the correlation was $-.34$ ($p < .05$).

In the follow-up investigation at the end of the semester, 74 of the 88 original subjects were available and willing to participate. For this analysis, each subject was placed in one of three categories with respect to the two stimulus variables of similarity and attractiveness. On the basis of the same divisions as were used in the analysis in Table 4.3, subjects were either in a high-similarity condition with a physically attractive date, a low-similarity condition with a physically unattractive date, or in a mixed condition of high-low or low-high. In response to the question about the date's name, the more positive the stimulus conditions at the time of the date, the more likely was the subject to remember correctly the date's name ($\chi^2 = 8.47$, $df = 1$, $p < .01$). With respect to talking to the other individual during the period since the experiment, the relationship was again significant ($\chi^2 = 4.95$, $df = 1$, $p < .05$). The same effect was found with regard to whether the individual would like or not like to date the other person in the future ($\chi^2 = 5.38$, $df = 1$, $p < .05$). The only follow-up question that failed to show a significant effect for the experimental manipulation was that dealing with actual dating; even here, it might be noted that the only dates reported were by subjects in the high-similarity, high-attractiveness condition.

Conclusions

Perhaps the most important aspect of the present findings is the evidence indicating the continuity between the laboratory study of attraction and its manifestation under field conditions. At least as operationalized in the present investigation, variables such as physical attractiveness and similarity of attitudes and personality characteristics are found to influence attraction in a highly predictable manner.

The findings with respect to the physical distance measure are important in two respects. First, they provide further evidence that voluntary proximity is a useful and unobtrusive measure of interpersonal attraction. Second, the construct validity and generality of the paper-and-pencil measure of attraction provided by the Interpersonal Judgment Scale is greatly enhanced. The significant relationship between two such different response measures is comforting to users of either one. In addition, the follow-up procedure provided evidence of the lasting effect of the experimental manipulations and of the relation of the attraction measures to such diverse responses as remembering the other person's name and engaging in conversation in the weeks after the termination of the experiment.

The failure to confirm the second hypothesis is somewhat puzzling. It is possible that present procedures, designed to vary the saliency of the elements of similarity, were inadequate and ineffective, that the actual behavioral cues to similarity and dissimilarity were sufficiently powerful to negate the effects of the experimental manipulation, or that the hypothesis was simply incorrect. There is no basis within the present experiment on which to decide among these alternatives.

In conclusion, it must be emphasized that striking continuity has been demonstrated across experiments using paper-and-pencil materials to simulate a stranger and to measure attraction (Byrne, 1961), more realistic audio and audiovisual presentations of the stimulus person (Byrne & Clore, 1966), elaborate dramatic confrontations in which a confederate portrays the stimulus person (Byrne & Griffitt, 1966), and a quasi-realistic experiment such as the present one, in which two genuine strangers interact and in which response measures include nonverbal behaviors. Such findings suggest that attempts to move back and forth between the controlled artificiality of the laboratory and the uncontrolled natural setting are both feasible and indicative of the potential applications of basic attraction research to a variety of interpersonal problems.

REFERENCES

Aronson, E., & Carlsmith, J. M. Experimentation in social psychology. In G. Lindzey & E. Aronson (Eds.), *The handbook of social psychology.* Vol. 2 (2nd ed.). Reading, Mass.: Addison-Wesley, 1968.

Byrne, D. Interpersonal attraction and attitude similarity. *Journal of Abnormal and Social Psychology,* 1961, 62, 713–715.

Byrne, D. Attitudes and attraction. In L. Berkowitz (Ed.), *Advances in experimental social psychology.* Vol. 4. New York: Academic Press, 1969.

Byrne, D., Baskett, G. D., & Hodges, L. Behavioral indicators of interpersonal attraction. Paper presented at meeting of the Psychonomic Society, St. Louis, November 1969.

Byrne, D., Bond, M. H., & Diamond, M. J. Response to political candidates as a function of attitude similarity–dissimilarity. *Human Relations,* 1969, 22, 251–262.

Byrne, D., & Clore, G. L., Jr. Predicting interpersonal attraction toward strangers presented in three different stimulus modes. *Psychonomic Science,* 1966, 4, 239–240.

Byrne, D., Clore, G. L., Jr., & Worchel, P. Effect of economic similarity–dissimilarity on interpersonal attraction. *Journal of Personality and Social Psychology,* 1966, 4, 220–224.

Byrne, D., & Ervin, C. R. Attraction toward a Negro stranger as a function of prejudice, attitude similarity, and the stranger's evaluation of the subject. *Human Relations,* 1969, 22, 397–404.

Byrne, D., & Griffitt, W. Similarity versus liking: A clarification. *Psychonomic Science,* 1966, 6, 295–296.

Byrne, D., & Griffitt, W. Similarity and awareness of similarity of personality characteristics as determinants of attraction. *Journal of Experimental Research in Personality,* 1969, 3, 179–186.

Byrne, D., Griffitt, W., & Stefaniak, D. Attraction and similarity of personality characteristics. *Journal of Personality and Social Psychology,* 1967, 5, 82–90.

Byrne, D., London, O., & Reeves, K. The effects of physical attractiveness, sex, and attitude similarity on interpersonal attraction. *Journal of Personality,* 1968, 36, 259–271.

Byrne, D., & Rhamey, R. Magnitude of positive and negative reinforcements as a determinant of attraction. *Journal of Personality and Social Psychology,* 1965, 2, 884–889.

Efran, M. G. Visual interaction and interpersonal attraction. Unpublished doctoral dissertation, University of Texas, 1969.

Griffitt, W. B. Interpersonal attraction as a function of self-concept and personality similarity–dissimilarity. *Journal of Personality and Social Psychology,* 1966, 4, 581–584.

Griffitt, W. B. Environmental effects of interpersonal affective behavior: Ambient effective temperature and attraction. *Journal of Personality and Social Psychology,* 1970, 15, 240–244. (a)

Griffitt, W. B. Personality similarity and self-concept as determinants of interpersonal attraction. *Journal of Social Psychology,* 1970, in press. (b)

Huffman, D. M. Interpersonal attraction as a function of behavioral similarity. Unpublished doctoral dissertation, University of Texas, 1969.

McWhirter, R. M., Jr. Interpersonal attraction in a dyad as a function of the physical attractiveness of its members. Unpublished doctoral dissertation, Texas Tech University, 1969.

Megargee, E. I. A study of the subjective aspects of group membership at Amherst. Unpublished manuscript, Amherst College, 1956.

Moss, M. K. Social desirability, physical attractiveness, and social choice. Unpublished doctoral dissertation, Kansas State University, 1969.

Perrin, F. A. C. Physical attractiveness and repulsiveness. *Journal of Experimental Psychology,* 1921, 4, 203–217.

Picher, O. L. Attraction toward Negroes as a function of prejudice, emotional arousal, and the sex of the Negro. Unpublished doctoral dissertation, University of Texas, 1966.

Sheffield, J., & Byrne, D. Attitude similarity–dissimilarity, authoritarianism, and interpersonal attraction. *Journal of Social Psychology,* 1967, 71, 117–123.

Taylor, M. J. Some objective criteria of social class membership. Unpublished manuscript, Amherst College, 1956.

Walster, E., Aronson, V., Abrahams, D., & Rottmann, L. Importance of physical attractiveness in dating behavior. *Journal of Personality and Social Psychology,* 1966, 4, 508–516.

Exposure Effects in the Classroom: The Development of Affinity Among Students

Richard L. Moreland and Scott R. Beach • University of Pittsburgh

Affinity is a complex blend of familiarity, attraction, and similarity that strengthens social relations by fostering a sense of closeness among people. We studied the development of affinity among students in a large college course. Four women of similar appearance attended class sessions, posing as students in the course. To create conditions of mere exposure, they did not interact with any of the other students. Each woman attended a different number (0, 5, 10, or 15) of class sessions. At the end of the term, students ($N = 130$) were shown slides of the women, and measures of each woman's perceived familiarity, attractiveness, and similarity were obtained. Mere exposure had weak effects on familiarity, but strong effects on attraction and similarity. Causal analyses indicated that the effects of exposure on familiarity and similarity were mediated by its effects on attraction. The potential role of affinity in several kinds of social relations is discussed. © 1992 Academic Press, Inc.

Propinquity often leads to interpersonal attraction (Nahemow & Lawton, 1975; Priest & Sawyer, 1967; Segal, 1974). When people live in the same neighborhood, work in the same office building, or shop in the same stores, they are likely to become friends. There are at least two ways in which such friendships could arise. First, a shared environment provides opportunities for social interaction, and if those interactions are rewarding, then the participants may learn to like one another. But many social encounters seem to involve little or no interaction—the participants exchange (at most) a nod of the head or some brief greeting. Could these "passive contacts" (cf. Festinger, Schachter, & Back, 1950) also lead people to like one another? Research on the mere exposure phenomenon suggests that they could.

Zajonc (1968) claimed that mere exposure to a novel stimulus is a sufficient condition for the enhancement of our attitudes toward it. A great deal of evidence supports his claim (see Bornstein, 1989; Harrison, 1977), and much of that evidence involves the effects of mere exposure on interpersonal attraction. Many researchers have demonstrated these effects using social stimuli, such as names or photographs (e.g., Colman, Hargreaves, & Sluckin, 1981; Grush, McKeough, & Ahlering, 1978; Hamm, Baum, & Nikels, 1975; Mita, Dermer, & Knight, 1977; Zajonc, Markus, & Wilson, 1974). Mita and his colleagues, for example, photographed many subjects to produce a regular-image and reversed-image print for each person. These prints were later shown to the subjects and their friends, all of whom were asked to choose which photograph they preferred. Most of the subjects chose the reversed-image print, which provided a view of themselves that was familiar to them from mirrors. But their friends often chose the regular-image print, which provided a view of the subjects that was familiar to their friends from everyday activities.

A few researchers have actually manipulated how often people encounter one another in a laboratory setting (e.g., Brockner & Swap, 1976; Saegert, Swap, & Zajonc, 1973; Swap, 1977). Saegert and her colleagues, for example, recruited subjects for an experiment on the "psychophysics of taste." During that experiment, the subjects moved from one laboratory cubicle to another, sampling and evaluating various liquids according to a prearranged schedule. Some of these liquids had a pleasant taste, whereas others tasted unpleasant. The schedule was arranged so that the frequency with which subjects encountered one another, as they moved from cubicle to cubicle, was systematically varied. Afterward, the subjects were asked to evaluate many aspects of the experiment, including their fellow participants. Feelings of attraction were stronger among subjects who had encountered one another more often, even if those encounters involved tasting unpleasant liquids.

Clearly, mere exposure to someone can make us feel attracted to him or her. Could it have other effects as well? When we feel attracted to someone, we often believe that he or she is similar to us in important ways (e.g., Gold, Ryckman, & Mosley,

1984; Granberg & King, 1980; Marks, Miller, & Maruyama, 1981; Moss, Byrne, Baskett, & Sachs, 1975). Perhaps, by making someone more attractive, mere exposure could increase his or her perceived similarity as well. This hypothesis was tested by Moreland and Zajonc (1982). Once a week for 4 weeks, their subjects were shown a photograph of someone and asked to evaluate him on a variety of measures. Some of these measures assessed the subjects' feelings of attraction for the person. Other measures assessed how similar the person seemed to the subjects. Half of the subjects saw a photograph of a *different* person each week. Each of those persons was equally familiar to these subjects, who thus evaluated him as equally attractive and similar to themselves. But the remaining subjects saw a photograph of the *same* person each week. As weeks went by, that person became more familiar to these subjects and was thus evaluated as more attractive *and* similar to themselves. There was also some evidence that the effects of familiarity on perceived similarity were mediated by its effects on attraction.

In a second experiment, Moreland and Zajonc (1982) explored the relationships among familiarity, attraction, and similarity from another direction. When someone is similar to us in important ways, we often feel attracted to him or her (e.g., Buss, 1985; Byrne, Gouax, Griffitt, Lamberth, Murakawa, Prasad, Prasad, & Ramirez, 1971; Davis, 1984; Smeaton, Byrne, & Murnen, 1989). And an attractive person can seem very familiar to us (cf. Gerard, Green, Hoyt, & Conolley, 1973; Matlin & Stang, 1978). Perhaps, by making someone more attractive, similarity could increase his or her perceived familiarity as well. To test this hypothesis, subjects were shown a series of slides depicting several different persons. Each slide was shown the same number of times, so that the subjects became equally familiar with each person. Afterward, the subjects were given (false) information indicating that some of the people they had seen were more similar to them than others. They were then asked to evaluate those people on a variety of measures. Some of those measures assessed the subjects' feelings of attraction for each person, whereas other measures assessed how familiar each person seemed to the subjects. People who were more similar to the subjects were evaluated as more attractive *and* as more familiar. And there was some evidence that the effects of similarity on perceived familiarity were mediated by its effects on attraction.

Moreland and Zajonc (1982) argued, on the basis of their results, that familiarity, attraction, and similarity are strongly related to one another, combining to produce a sense of "affinity" that brings people together psychologically. Attraction appears to be a key factor in the development of affinity. As we become familiar with someone, we begin to feel attracted to him or her, and that attraction makes the person seem more similar to ourselves. When we discover that someone is similar to ourselves, we begin to feel attracted to him or her, and that attraction makes the person seem more familiar to us. All of these effects are consistent with Heider's (1958) views on the role of balance in social relations. In Heider's terms, familiarity and similarity are positive unit relations, whereas attraction is a positive sentiment relation. Sentiment and unit relations must be congruent or balanced—otherwise, we feel (and appear) foolish. So when a positive unit relation arises between ourselves and another person, we must develop a positive sentiment relation with that person in order to remain balanced. And once that sentiment relation is established, balance dictates that any other unit relations still unspecified (or capable of distortion) be made positive too.

Although the concept of affinity is intriguing, much research remains to be done. The field experiment we are about to describe was an attempt to explore the development of affinity among people occupying a natural social setting. We arranged for several women to pose as students in a large college course by attending various class sessions. Each woman visited the class a different number of times, under conditions of mere exposure. At the end of the term, students in the course were shown slides of the women and asked to evaluate them on many measures of familiarity, attraction, and similarity. These data were valuable in several ways. First, no one has studied the effects of mere exposure on attraction (or similarity)

under such realistic conditions. Few researchers have tried to manipulate how often people actually encounter one another, and all of their experiments were carried out in simple and highly controlled laboratory settings. In more complex natural settings, exposure effects (of any sort) might be much weaker. Second, only Moreland and Zajonc (1982) have thus far shown that mere exposure can affect similarity as well as attraction. This important finding, which links two large research literatures, deserves to be replicated. Finally, the availability of several measures of familiarity, attraction, and similarity made it possible to perform more sophisticated causal analyses of their relationships with one another. We were especially interested in discovering whether attraction is indeed a key factor in the development of affinity.

Method

Before our field experiment could be performed, some pretesting was needed to assess how the classroom visitors were evaluated by students who had never encountered them before. This pretesting was important, because if those women differed significantly in their initial levels of familiarity, attraction, or similarity, then the results of our field experiment would have been compromised. The methods used in the pretesting will thus be described here, along with those used in the field experiment.

Subjects

The pretesting sample was drawn from an undergraduate course on social psychology. Eighty-two students from that course were invited to earn extra credit by completing a questionnaire at the end of the term. Fifty of them agreed to do so. Six students were later dropped from the sample because they failed to answer all of the questionnaire items. The final sample thus consisted of 44 students, 24 men and 20 women. Sixty-six percent of these students were freshmen or sophomores; the rest were juniors or seniors.

The sample for our field experiment was drawn from an undergraduate course on personality psychology. One hundred and ninety-one students from that course were invited to earn extra credit by completing a questionnaire at the end of the term. One hundred and fifty of them agreed to do so. Fifteen students were later dropped from the sample because they failed to answer all of the questionnaire items. Another five students were dropped because of their unusual ages (greater than 25 years) or poor attendance (fewer than half of the class sessions). The final sample thus consisted of 130 students, 63 men and 67 women. Seventy percent of these students were freshmen or sophomores; the rest were juniors or seniors.

Materials

Four women (A, B, C, and D) were chosen to serve as "stimuli" for our research. These women were all similar in age and appearance and looked to us like typical college students. A color photograph was taken of each woman, dressed in casual clothing and standing in an outdoor setting. These photographs were later converted to slides, which were used for both the pretesting and our field experiment.

Similar questionnaires were used for both the pretesting and our field experiment. These questionnaires, which every student completed anonymously, were divided into five sections. The first four sections of each questionnaire were identical; each section contained measures of familiarity, attraction, and similarity for one of the women. The final section of each questionnaire contained items measuring various characteristics of the students (e.g., age and sex; class and major; guesses about the purpose of the research). There was only one difference between the pretesting questionnaire and the questionnaire used for our field experiment: The final section of the latter questionnaire was a bit more extensive, requesting information about the students' enjoyment of the course and expected grade, attendance record, typical seating position, etc.

Three measures of familiarity were obtained for each woman. First, students were asked whether they actually knew the woman (YES/NO). Those who claimed to know her were asked to provide the woman's name and describe the conditions under which they first met. Second, students were asked whether they had ever seen the woman before (YES/NO). Finally, students were asked to rate (1 to 7) how familiar the woman seemed to them. Higher ratings indicated greater perceived familiarity.

Four measures of attraction were obtained for each woman. First, students were asked to rate (1 to 7) the woman on 10 trait dimensions (INTERESTING/BORING, UNATTRACTIVE/ATTRACTIVE, UNSELFISH/SELFISH, UNPOPULAR/POPULAR, UNCONCEITED/CONCEITED, UNINTELLIGENT/INTELLIGENT, WARM/COLD, UNSUCCESSFUL/SUCCESSFUL, HONEST/DISHONEST, INSINCERE/SINCERE), all chosen for their strong affective connotations. These 10 ratings were later rescored, so that higher ratings always indicated greater attraction, and then averaged across trait dimensions to produce a single index of attraction. Next, students were told to imagine meeting the woman and learning more about her. They were then asked to estimate the probabilities (0 to 100%) that they would (a) like the woman and become friends with her, (b) enjoy spending time with the woman, and (c) work with the woman on some project of mutual interest.

Finally, four measures of similarity were also obtained for each woman. First, students were asked to compare themselves to the woman on the same 10 trait dimensions, by rating (1 to 7) whether each trait was stronger or weaker in their own personalities. Higher ratings indicated that a trait (e.g., selfishness, honesty) was stronger in the woman than it was in the students. These ratings were later rescored by "folding" the measurement scale around its midpoint. This created a new set of ratings that ranged from 0 to 3, with higher ratings indicating more similarity. These new ratings were then averaged across trait dimensions to produce a single index of perceived similarity. Next, the students were told to imagine meeting the woman and learning more about her. They were then asked to estimate the probabilities (0 to 100%) that (a) the woman would turn out to come from the same social background as themselves, (b) they would be able to understand the woman's personality fairly well, and (c) they would discover that the woman's plans for the future were similar to their own.

Procedure

The pretesting procedures were fairly simple. During the last week of classes, students in the social psychology course were invited to participate in a study assessing their "social perception skills." Those who agreed to take part attended a special testing session held several days after the term ended. At this session, students were first given their questionnaires, along with some brief instructions for completing them. The four slides were then shown to everyone in a randomly determined order. Each slide was shown for 10 min, enough time for the students to complete the relevant familiarity, attraction, and similarity measures. After the last slide was shown, students were given another 10 min to complete the final section of the questionnaire. They were then debriefed, allowed to ask any questions about the research, and thanked for participating.

The procedures for our field experiment were somewhat more complex. The personality psychology course was held in a large lecture hall capable of seating 200 students. This hall was fan-shaped, broader at the back, where the doors were located, and narrower at the front, where the lecturer stood. The hall was also elevated, rising from the front to the back. This allowed every student to have a clear view downward to the front of the hall. Forty class sessions were held during the term. Class attendance varied from one session to another, but averaged about 75% of the students.

We arranged for the four women to pose as students in this course. Each woman, dressed in casual clothing like the other students, attended a different number of class sessions. Woman A attended 0 class sessions; Woman B attended 5 class sessions; Woman C attended 10 class sessions; and Woman D attended 15 class sessions. These visits began during the eighth session and continued (except for examinations) for the rest of the term. Only one of the women attended each class session; the order of these visits was randomly determined.

The same "script" was used for every visit. One of the women arrived at the lecture hall a few minutes before class began, walked slowly down toward the front of the hall, and sat where she could be seen by all the other students. During the lecture, she simply listened and took notes. A few minutes after class ended, the woman rose, walked slowly up toward the back of the hall, and left. In order to create conditions of mere exposure, none of the women was allowed to interact (verbally or nonverbally) with the other students. On those rare occasions when one of the women was approached by a student, she simply turned away and ignored that person.

During the last week of classes, students in this course were also invited to participate in a study assessing their "social perception skills." Those who agreed to take part attended a special testing session held in the regular lecture hall several days after the term ended. At this session, we simply repeated the procedures used for the pretesting.

Results

A review of the data from both research projects indicated that male and female students responded to the four women in similar ways. Sex was therefore dropped as a variable in all subsequent data analyses.

A series of single-factor (Woman: A/B/C/D) repeated measures analyses of variance was performed on the various measures of familiarity, attraction, and similarity. None of these analyses was significant (all p's > .30), and the effect sizes were very small, ranging from .001 to .050 (M = .017). Apparently, the students regarded all four women as comparably familiar, attractive, and similar. This finding had important implications for interpreting the results of our field experiment. If, as we expected, the students in that experiment regarded women who attended more class sessions as more familiar, attractive, or similar, then those effects must have been due to mere exposure, rather than to any differences in the appearance or demeanor of the women themselves.

The actual results of our field experiment are summarized in Table 5.1. The effects of mere

TABLE 5.1. Effects of Mere Exposure on Familiarity, Attraction, and Similarity

Dependent measure	Number of visits				F(1, 387)
	0	5	10	15	
Familiarity					
Know her?	0.00	0.00	0.00	0.00	—
Seen her?	0.13	0.08	0.08	0.12	0.09
	(0.34)	(0.27)	(0.28)	(0.33)	
Familiar?	2.87	2.95	3.39	3.15	4.87*
	(1.82)	(1.93)	(1.83)	(1.83)	
Attraction					
Index	3.62	3.88	4.25	4.38	101.44**
	(0.83)	(0.71)	(0.55)	(0.67)	
Become friends?	0.41	0.43	0.57	0.60	72.81**
	(0.27)	(0.26)	(0.24)	(0.25)	
Enjoy time?	0.36	0.37	0.49	0.54	56.63**
	(0.27)	(0.26)	(0.24)	(0.25)	
Work together?	0.32	0.37	0.41	0.44	29.63**
	(0.25)	(0.26)	(0.25)	(0.25)	
Similarity					
Index	1.88	1.93	2.11	2.23	42.76**
	(0.64)	(0.61)	(0.52)	(0.51)	
Same background?	0.34	0.37	0.47	0.45	35.35**
	(0.25)	(0.25)	(0.25)	(0.24)	
Understand her?	0.44	0.44	0.55	0.57	54.90**
	(0.26)	(0.25)	(0.23)	(0.23)	
Similar plans?	0.34	0.35	0.39	0.40	7.75**
	(0.25)	(0.24)	(0.24)	(0.22)	

Note. Table entries include means and standard deviations. The first two measures were coded 0 = No and 1 = Yes. All significance tests are for the linear effects of mere exposure.
$*p < .05.$ $**p < .01.$

exposure on the various measures of familiarity, attraction, and similarity were assessed through another series of single-factor (Number of Visits: 0/5/10/15) repeated-measures analyses of variance. Trend analyses were performed whenever significant ($p < .05$) exposure effects were observed. These analyses always revealed strong linear trends. Few curvilinear trends emerged and they contributed little (10 to 15%) to the observed exposure effects. Thus, only significance tests for the linear effects of mere exposure are reported in the table.

Mere exposure had its weakest effects on familiarity. None of the students knew any of the women. Only a few of the students (8 to 13%) remembered seeing even one of the women, and women who attended more class sessions were not significantly more likely to be remembered. All of the women were rated as unfamiliar ($M < 4.00$) by the students. Women who attended more class sessions were indeed rated as significantly

more familiar, but this effect was very small in size (.012). These results indicated that familiarity was largely unaffected by exposure. Given the conditions under which exposure occurred, this may not seem surprising.

We were surprised, however, by the relatively strong effects of mere exposure on attraction. These effects ranged in size from .056 to .603, with a mean of .273. Women who attended more class sessions earned significantly higher scores on the attraction index, and the students believed that they would be significantly more likely to befriend those women, enjoy spending time with them, and work with them on some project. The fact that students liked these women better, without necessarily regarding them as more familiar, is reminiscent of several laboratory experiments (e.g., Bornstein, Leone, & Galley, 1987; Moreland & Zajonc, 1977; Seamon, Brody, & Kauff, 1983; Wilson, 1979) demonstrating exposure effects in the absence of stimulus recognition.

Finally, mere exposure also affected similarity, although these effects were weaker than those for attraction. The effects of exposure on similarity ranged in size from .023 to .122, with a mean of .077. Women who attended more class sessions earned significantly higher scores on the similarity index, and the students believed that they would be significantly more likely to share the social backgrounds of those women, understand their personalities, and have similar plans for the future. These results replicated the earlier finding (Moreland & Zajonc, 1982) that mere exposure to others can enhance not only their attractiveness, but also their perceived similarity.

Discussion

We are the first researchers to study the effects of mere exposure on interpersonal attraction in a natural social setting. The setting was a large college classroom, in which nearly 200 students spent a semester together studying personality psychology. We arranged for four women to visit that classroom, posing as students in the course. Each woman attended a different number of class sessions. There was no reason for the other students to pay special attention to these women—no one knew that an experiment was in progress, nor was there anything unusual about the appearance or demeanor of the women. And there were certainly many other things going on in the classroom that could (should) have captured the students' attention. Under these conditions, it seems unlikely that mere exposure to the four women could have affected the students' evaluations of them at all. Nevertheless, we found clear evidence of exposure effects.

The strongest effects of mere exposure involved the students' feelings of attraction for the women. Women who attended more class sessions were perceived as significantly more attractive. For example, their personalities were evaluated more positively on a variety of trait dimensions, and the students believed that they would be more likely to befriend these women, enjoy any time spent with them, and work together with them on some project of mutual interest. Mere exposure also af-

fected the perceived similarity of the women, though these effects were weaker than those for attraction. Women who attended more class sessions were perceived as significantly more similar to the students. For example, their personalities were evaluated as more similar on a variety of trait dimensions, and the students believed that they would be more likely to share the social backgrounds of these women, understand their personalities, and have similar plans for the future. These results replicate those of Moreland and Zajonc (1982), who found that mere exposure not only enhances a person's attractiveness, but can increase his or her perceived similarity as well.

Despite its strong effects on the attractiveness and perceived similarity of the women, mere exposure had only weak effects on their perceived familiarity to the students. On the average, only about 10% of the students remembered seeing any of the women before, and this figure did not vary from one woman to another. Women who attended more class sessions were indeed evaluated as significantly more familiar by the students, but all of their evaluations were low. A more accurate interpretation of this finding might be that these women seemed less *unfamiliar* to the students.

The fact that mere exposure made the women seem more attractive and similar to the students, without necessarily increasing their perceived familiarity, reminds us of several laboratory experiments in which exposure effects occurred in the apparent absence of stimulus recognition. In fact, a recent meta-analysis of research on exposure effects (Bornstein, 1989) showed that those effects are often *stronger* when stimuli are presented below the subjects' threshold of awareness. Bornstein has offered an "attributional discounting" explanation for this phenomenon. He argues that most subjects are aware of the positive relationship between familiarity and attraction. When stimuli are presented above their threshold of awareness, subjects are more attracted to stimuli that seem more familiar, but they discount some of that attraction by attributing it to their familiarity. Exposure effects are weakened as a result. But when stimuli are presented below the subjects' threshold of awareness, no attributional discounting takes place, so any exposure effects that occur remain strong. We suspect that few of our students engaged in the attributional discounting described by Bornstein, because most of them seemed unaware that the four women had visited their classroom. This may have strengthened (or left intact) the effects of mere exposure on the attractiveness and perceived similarity of those women.

One purpose of our experiment was to explore the concept of affinity. Moreland and Zajonc (1982) argued that familiarity, attraction, and similarity often blend together to form a sense of affinity among people, and that attraction is the key factor in the development of that affinity. Affinity seems worthy of all this research effort because of the role that it may play in many kinds of social relations. For example, some romantic relationships seem to develop quickly and almost inexplicably—people who are strangers to one another feel a special "chemistry" that encourages them to become intimate. Perhaps these people are not really strangers at all, but have encountered one another many times at restaurants, parties, and so on. If those encounters involved minimal social interaction (mere exposure), then they might not be remembered. But the participants would still feel more attracted to one another, and if an opportunity for more meaningful interaction occurred, then they might also seem surprisingly familiar and similar to one another. Affinity, created through mere exposure, would thus allow their relationship to develop faster than it could have otherwise.

Affinity may also play a role in the relationships among members of small groups. For example, newcomers often find it difficult to gain the acceptance of oldtimers in such groups (Moreland & Levine, 1989). Acceptance may be withheld until newcomers prove their worthiness to oldtimers. One tactic that newcomers might use to win acceptance more quickly is to participate as often as possible in group activities. Simply appearing at those activities (mere exposure) could make newcomers seem more attractive to oldtimers. That attraction could lead oldtimers to perceive newcomers as more familiar and similar than they really are. Newcomers who seem less "new" and "different" to oldtimers are more likely to be accepted as full members of the group.

Finally, the role of affinity in the behavior of crowds might be worth investigating. Crowds often behave in unusual ways, committing acts that observers find inexplicable. When asked to justify their behavior, crowd members describe strong feelings of camaraderie that led them to take collective rather than individual action. There are, of course, many reasons why the members of a crowd might feel such camaraderie (see Milgram & Toch, 1969). But one factor that could be important is affinity. A common feature of many crowds is the constant "milling" of their members. Crowds are nearly always in motion—people circulate rapidly from one place to another, often centering their movements around some object of special interest (e.g., a building or speaker). Milling provides the opportunity for mere exposure to occur. If that exposure leads a crowd's members to view one another as more familiar, attractive, and similar, then feelings of camaraderie may indeed arise, making collective action more likely to occur.

The authors thank Charles Judd and David Kenny for their helpful advice regarding structural equations analyses. Requests for reprints should be sent to Dr. Richard Moreland, 432 Langley Hall, Psychology Department, University of Pittsburgh, Pittsburgh, PA 15260.

REFERENCES

Bornstein, R. F. (1989). Exposure and affect: Overview and meta-analysis of research, 1968–1987. *Psychological Bulletin*, **106**, 265–289.

Bornstein, R. F., Leone, D. R., & Galley, D. J. (1987). The generalizability of subliminal mere exposure effects: Influence of stimuli perceived without awareness on social behavior. *Journal of Personality and Social Psychology*, **53**, 1070–1079.

Brockner, J., & Swap, W. C. (1976). Effects of repeated exposure and attitude similarity on self-disclosure and interpersonal attraction. *Journal of Personality and Social Psychology*, **33**, 531–540.

Buss, D. M. (1985). Human mate selection. *American Scientist*, **73**, 47–51.

Byrne, D., Gouax, C., Griffitt, W., Lamberth, J., Murakawa, N., Prasad, M., Prasad, A., & Ramirez, M. (1971). The ubiquitous relationship: Attitude similarity and attraction. *Human Relations*, **24**, 201–207.

Colman, A. M., Hargreaves, D. J., & Sluckin, W. (1981). Preferences for Christian names as a function of their experienced familiarity. *British Journal of Social Psychology*, **72**, 3–5.

Davis, J. M. (1984). Attraction to a group as a function of attitude similarity and geographic distance. *Social Behavior and Personality*, **12**, 1–5.

Festinger, L., Schachter, S., & Back, K. (1950). *Social pressures in informal groups*. New York: Harper.

Gerard, H. B., Green, D., Hoyt, M., & Conolley, E. S. (1973). Influence of affect on exposure frequency estimates. *Journal of Personality and Social Psychology*, **28**, 151–154.

Gold, J. A., Ryckman, R. M., & Mosley, N. R. (1984). Romantic mood induction and attraction to a dissimilar other: Is love blind? *Personality and Social Psychology Bulletin*, **10**, 358–368.

Granberg, D., & King, M. (1980). Cross-lagged panel analysis of the relation between attraction and perceived similarity. *Journal of Experimental Social Psychology*, **16**, 573–581.

Grush, J. E., McKeough, K. L., & Ahlering, R. F. (1978). Extrapolating laboratory exposure research to actual political elections. *Journal of Personality and Social Psychology*, **36**, 257–270.

Hamm, N. H., Baum, M. R., & Nikels, K. W. (1975). Effects of race and exposure on judgments of interpersonal favorability. *Journal of Experimental Social Psychology*, **11**, 14–24.

Harrison, A. A. (1977). Mere exposure. In L. Berkowitz (Ed.), *Advances in experimental social psychology* (Vol. 10, pp. 39–83). New York: Academic Press.

Heider, F. (1958). *The psychology of interpersonal relations*. New York: Wiley.

Marks, G., Miller, N., & Maruyama, G. (1981). Effect of target's physical attractiveness on assumptions of similarity. *Journal of Personality and Social Psychology*, **41**, 198–206.

Matlin, M. W., & Stang, D. J. (1978). *The Pollyanna principle: Selectivity in language, memory, and thought*. Cambridge, MA: Schenkman.

Milgram, S., & Toch, H. (1969). Collective behavior: Crowds and social movements. In G. Lindzey & E. Aronson (Eds.), *The handbook of social psychology* (2nd ed., Vol. 4, pp. 507–610). Reading, MA: Addison-Wesley.

Mita, T. H., Dermer, M., & Knight, J. (1977). Reversed facial images and the mere exposure hypothesis. *Journal of Personality and Social Psychology*, **35**, 597–601.

Moreland, R. L., & Levine, J. M. (1989). Newcomers and old-timers in small groups. In P. Paulus (Ed.), *Psychology of group influence* (2nd ed., pp. 143–186). Hillsdale, NJ: Erlbaum.

Moreland, R. L., & Zajonc, R. B. (1977). Is stimulus recognition a necessary condition for the occurrence of exposure effects? *Journal of Personality and Social Psychology*, **35**, 191–199.

Moreland, R. L., & Zajonc, R. B. (1979). Exposure effects may not depend on stimulus recognition. *Journal of Personality and Social Psychology*, **37**, 1086–1089.

Moreland, R. L., & Zajonc, R. B. (1982). Exposure effects in person perception. *Journal of Experimental Social Psychology*, **18**, 395–415.

Moss, M. K., Byrne, D., Baskett, G. D., & Sachs, D. H. (1975). Informational versus affective determinants of interpersonal attraction. *Journal of Social Psychology*, **95**, 39–53.

Nahemow, L., & Lawton, M. P. (1975). Similarity and propinquity in friendship formation. *Journal of Personality and Social Psychology*, **32**, 205–213.

Priest, R. F., & Sawyer, J. (1967). Proximity and peership: Bases of balance in interpersonal attraction. *American Journal of Sociology*, **72**, 633–649.

Saegert, S. C., Swap, W. C., & Zajonc, R. B. (1973). Exposure, context, and interpersonal attraction. *Journal of Personality and Social Psychology*, **25**, 234–242.

Seamon, J. G., Brody, N., & Kauff, D. M. (1983). Affective discrimination of stimuli that are not recognized: Effects of shadowing, masking, and cerebral laterality. *Journal of Experimental Psychology: Learning, Memory, and Cognition*, **9**, 544–555.

Segal, M. W. (1974). Alphabet and attraction: An unobtrusive measure of the effect of propinquity in a field setting. *Journal of Personality and Social Psychology*, **30**, 654–657.

Smeaton, G., Byrne, D., & Murnen, S. K. (1989). The repulsion hypothesis revisited: Similarity irrelevance or dissimilarity bias? *Journal of Personality and Social Psychology*, **56**, 54–59.

Swap, W. C. (1977). Interpersonal attraction and repeated exposure to rewarders and punishers. *Personality and Social Psychology Bulletin*, **3**, 248–251.

Wilson, W. R. (1979). Feeling more than we can know: Exposure effects without learning. *Journal of Personality and Social Psychology*, **37**, 811–821.

Zajonc, R. B. (1968). Attitudinal effects of mere exposure. *Journal of Personality and Social Psychology Monographs*, **9**, 1–27.

Zajonc, R. B., Markus, H., & Wilson, W. R. (1974). Exposure effects and associative learning. *Journal of Experimental Social Psychology*, **10**, 248–263.

READING 6

Social Perception and Interpersonal Behavior: On the Self-Fulfilling Nature of Social Stereotypes

Mark Snyder • University of Minnesota
Elizabeth Decker Tanke • University of Santa Clara
Ellen Berscheid • University of Minnesota

Thoughts are but dreams
Till their effects be tried

— William Shakespeare[1]

This research concerns the self-fulfilling influences of social stereotypes on dyadic social interaction. Conceptual analysis of the cognitive and behavioral consequences of stereotyping suggests that a perceiver's actions based upon stereotype-generated attributions about a specific target individual may cause the behavior of that individual to confirm the perceiver's initially erroneous attributions. A paradigmatic investigation of the behavioral confirmation of stereotypes involving physical attractiveness (e.g., "beautiful people are good people") is presented. Male "perceivers" interacted with female "targets" whom they believed (as a result of an experimental manipulation) to be physically attractive or physically unattractive. Tape recordings of each participant's conversational behavior were analyzed by naive observer judges for evidence of behavioral confirmation. These analyses revealed that targets who were perceived (unknown to them) to be physically attractive came to behave in a friendly, likeable, and sociable manner in comparison with targets whose perceivers regarded them as unattractive. It is suggested that theories in cognitive social psychology attend to the ways in which perceivers create the information that they process in addition to the ways that they process that information.

---

[1]From *The Rape of Lucrece*, lines 346–353.

Cognitive social psychology is concerned with the processes by which individuals gain knowledge about behavior and events that they encounter in social interaction, and how they use this knowledge to guide their actions. From this perspective, people are "constructive thinkers" searching for the causes of behavior, drawing inferences about people and their circumstances, and acting upon this knowledge.

Most empirical work in this domain—largely stimulated and guided by the attribution theories (e.g., Heider, 1958; Jones & Davis, 1965; Kelley, 1973)—has focused on the processing of information, the "machinery" of social cognition. Some outcomes of this research have been the specification of how individuals identify the causes of an actor's behavior, how individuals make inferences about the traits and dispositions of the actor, and how individuals make predictions about the actor's future behavior (for reviews, see Harvey, Ickes, & Kidd, 1976; Jones et al., 1972; Ross, 1977).

It is noteworthy that comparatively little theoretical and empirical attention has been directed to the other fundamental question within the cognitive social psychologist's mandate: What are the cognitive and behavioral consequences of our impressions of other people? From our vantage point, current-day attribution theorists leave the individual "lost in thought," with no machinery that links thought to action. It is to this concern that we address ourselves, both theoretically and empirically, in the context of social stereotypes.

Social stereotypes are a special case of interpersonal perception. Stereotypes are usually simple, overgeneralized, and widely accepted (e.g., Karlins, Coffman, & Walters, 1969). But stereotypes are often inaccurate. It is simply not true that all Germans are industrious or that all women are dependent and conforming. Nonetheless, many social stereotypes concern highly visible and distinctive personal characteristics; for example, sex and race. These pieces of information are usually the first to be noticed in social interaction and can gain high priority for channeling subsequent information processing and even social interaction. Social stereotypes are thus an ideal testing ground for considering the cognitive and behavioral consequences of person perception.

Numerous factors may help sustain our stereotypes and prevent disconfirmation of "erroneous" stereotype-based initial impressions of specific others. First, social stereotypes may influence information processing in ways that serve to bolster and strengthen these stereotypes.

Cognitive Bolstering of Social Stereotypes

As information processors, humans readily fall victim to the cognitive process described centuries ago by Francis Bacon (1620/1902):

> The human understanding, when any proposition has been once laid down . . . forces everything else to add fresh support and confirmation . . . it is the peculiar and perpetual error of the human understanding to be more moved and excited by affirmatives than negatives. (pp. 23–24)

Empirical research has demonstrated several such biases in information processing. We may overestimate the frequency of occurrence of confirming or paradigmatic examples of our stereotypes simply because such instances are more easily noticed, more easily brought to mind, and more easily retrieved from memory (cf. Hamilton & Gifford, 1976; Rothbart, Fulero, Jensen, Howard, & Birrell, Note 1). Evidence that confirms our stereotyped intuitions about human nature may be, in a word, more cognitively "available" (Tversky & Kahneman, 1973) than nonconfirming evidence.

Moreover, we may fill in the gaps in our evidence base with information consistent with our preconceived notions of what evidence should support our beliefs. For example, Chapman and Chapman (1967, 1969) have demonstrated that both college students and professional clinicians perceive positive associations between particular Rorschach responses and homosexuality in males, even though these associations are demonstrably absent in real life. These "signs" are simply those that comprise common cultural stereotypes of gay males.

Furthermore, once a stereotype has been adopted, a wide variety of evidence can be interpreted readily as supportive of that stereotype, including events that could support equally well an opposite interpretation. As Merton (1948) has suggested, in-group virtues ("We are thrifty") may become outgroup vices ("They are cheap") in our attempts to maintain negative stereotypes about disliked out groups. (For empirical demonstrations of this bias, see Regan, Straus, & Fazio, 1974; Rosenhan, 1973; Zadny & Gerard, 1974).

Finally, selective recall and reinterpretation of information from an individual's past history may be exploited to support a current stereotype-based inference (cf. Loftus & Palmer, 1974). Thus, having decided that Jim is stingy (as are all members of his group), it may be all too easy to remember a variety of behaviors and incidents that are insufficient one at a time to support an attribution of stinginess, but that taken together do warrant and support such an inference.

Behavioral Confirmation of Social Stereotypes

The cognitive bolstering processes discussed above may provide the perceiver with an "evidence base" that gives compelling cognitive reality to any traits that he or she may have erroneously attributed to a target individual initially. This reality is, of course, entirely cognitive: It is in the eye and mind of the beholder. But stereotype-based attributions may serve as grounds for predictions about the target's future behavior and may guide and influence the perceiver's interactions with the target. This process itself may generate behaviors on the part of the target that erroneously confirm the predictions and validate the attributions of the perceiver. How others treat us is, in large measure, a reflection of our treatment of them (cf. Bandura, 1977; Mischel, 1968; Raush, 1965). Thus, when we use our social perceptions as guides for regulating our interactions with others, we may constrain their behavioral options (cf. Kelley & Stahelski, 1970).

Consider this hypothetical, but illustrative, scenario: Michael tells Jim that Chris is a cool and aloof person. Jim meets Chris and notices expressions of coolness and aloofness. Jim proceeds to overestimate the extent to which Chris' self-presentation reflects a cool and aloof disposition and underestimates the extent to which this posture was engendered by his own cool and aloof behavior toward Chris, which had in turn been generated by his own prior beliefs about Chris. Little does Jim know that Tom, who had heard that Chris was warm and friendly, found that his impressions of Chris were confirmed during their interaction. In each case, the end result of the process of "interaction guided by perceptions" has been the target person's *behavioral confirmation* of the perceiver's initial impressions of him.

This scenario makes salient key aspects of the process of behavioral confirmation in social interaction. The perceiver (either Jim or Tom) is not aware that his original perception of the target individual (Chris) is inaccurate. Nor is the perceiver aware of the causal role that his own behavior (here, the enactment of a cool or warm expressive style) plays in generating the behavioral evidence that erroneously confirms his expectations. Unbeknownst to the perceiver, the reality that he confidently perceives to exist in the social world has, in fact, been actively constructed by his own transactions with and operations upon the social world.

In our empirical research, we proposed to demonstrate that stereotypes may create their own social reality by channeling social interaction in ways that cause the stereotyped individual to behaviorally confirm the perceiver's stereotype. Moreover, we sought to demonstrate behavioral confirmation in a social interaction context designed to mirror as faithfully as possible the spontaneous generation of impressions in everyday social interaction and the subsequent channeling influences of these perceptions on dyadic interaction.

One widely held stereotype in this culture involves physical attractiveness. Considerable evidence suggests that attractive persons are assumed to possess more socially desirable personality traits and are expected to lead better lives than their unattractive counterparts (Berscheid & Walster, 1974). Attractive persons are perceived to have virtually every character trait that is socially desirable to the perceiver: "Physically attractive people, for example, were perceived to be more sexually warm and responsive, sensitive, kind, interesting, strong, poised, modest, sociable, and outgoing than persons of lesser physical attractiveness" (Berscheid & Walster, 1974, p. 169). This powerful stereotype holds for male and female perceivers and for male and female stimulus persons.

What of the validity of the physical attractiveness stereotype? Are the physically attractive actually more likable, friendly, and confident than the unattractive? Physically attractive young adults are more often and more eagerly sought out for social dates (Dermer, 1973; Krebs & Adinolphi, 1975; Walster, Aronson, Abrahams, & Rottman, 1966). Even as early as nursery school age, physical attractiveness appears to channel social interaction: The physically attractive are chosen and the unattractive are rejected in sociometric choices (Dion & Berscheid, 1974; Kleck, Richardson, & Ronald, 1974).

Differential amount of interaction with the attractive and unattractive clearly helps the stereotype persevere, for it limits the chances for learning whether the two types of individuals differ in the traits associated with the stereotype. But the point we wish to focus upon here is that the stereotype may also channel interaction so that it behaviorally confirms itself. Individuals may have different styles of interaction for those whom they perceive to be physically attractive and for those whom they consider unattractive. These differences in interaction style may in turn elicit and nurture behaviors from the target person that are in accord with the stereotype. That is, the physically attractive may actually come to behave in a friendly, likable, sociable manner—not because they necessarily possess these dispositions, but because the behavior of others elicits and maintains behaviors taken to be manifestations of such traits.

Accordingly, we sought to demonstrate the behavioral confirmation of the physical attractiveness stereotype in dyadic social interaction. In order to do so, pairs of previously unacquainted individuals (designated, for our purposes, as a perceiver and a target) interacted in a getting-acquainted situation that had been constructed to allow us to control the information that one member of the dyad (the male perceiver) received about the physical attractiveness of the other individual (the female target). To measure the extent to which the actual behavior of the target matched the perceiver's stereotype, naive observer judges, who were unaware of the actual or perceived physical attractiveness of either participant, listened to and evaluated tape recordings of the interaction.

Method

Participants

Fifty-one male and 51 female undergraduates at the University of Minnesota participated, for extra course credit, in a study of "the processes by which people become acquainted with each other." Participants were scheduled in pairs of previously unacquainted males and females.

The Interaction Between Perceiver and Target

To insure that participants would not see each other before their interactions, they arrived at separate experimental rooms on separate corridors. The experimenter informed each participant that she was studying acquaintance processes in social relationships. Specifically, she was investigating the differences between those initial interactions that involve nonverbal communication and those, such as telephone conversations, that do not. Thus, she explained, the participant would engage in a telephone conversation with another student in introductory psychology.

Before the conversation began, each participant provided written permission for it to be tape recorded. In addition, both dyad members completed brief questionnaires concerning such infor-·mation as academic major in college and high school of graduation. These questionnaires, it was explained, would provide the partners with some information about each other with which to start the conversation.

Activating the perceiver's stereotype. The getting-acquainted interaction permitted control of the information that each male perceiver received about the physical attractiveness of his female target. When male perceivers learned about the biographical information questionnaires, they also learned that each person would receive a snapshot of the other member of the dyad, because "other people in the experiment have told us they feel more comfortable when they have a mental picture of the person they're talking to." The experimenter then used a Polaroid camera to photograph the male. No mention of any snapshots was made to female participants.

When each male perceiver received his partner's biographical information form, it arrived in a folder containing a Polaroid snapshot, ostensibly of his partner. Although the biographical information had indeed been provided by his partner, the photograph was not. It was one of eight photographs that had been prepared in advance.

Twenty female students from several local colleges assisted (in return for $5) in the preparation of stimulus materials by allowing us to take Polaroid snapshots of them. Each photographic subject wore casual dress, each was smiling, and each agreed (in writing) to allow us to use her photograph. Twenty college-age men then rated the attractiveness of each picture on a 10-point scale.[2] We then chose the four pictures that had received the highest attractiveness ratings ($M = 8.10$) and the four photos that had received the lowest ratings ($M = 2.56$). There was virtually no overlap in ratings of the two sets of pictures.

Male perceivers were assigned randomly to one of two conditions of perceived physical attractiveness of their targets. Males in the attractive target condition received folders containing their partners' biographical information form and one of the four attractive photographs. Males in the unattractive target condition received folders containing their partners' biographical

information form and one of the four unattractive photographs. Female targets knew nothing of the photographs possessed by their male interaction partners, nor did they receive snapshots of their partners.

The perceiver's stereotype-based attributions. Before initiating his getting-acquainted conversation, each male perceiver rated his initial impressions of his partner on an Impression Formation Questionnaire. The questionnaire was constructed by supplementing the 27 trait adjectives used by Dion, Berscheid, and Walster (1972) in their original investigation of the physical attractiveness stereotype with the following items: intelligence, physical attractiveness, social adeptness, friendliness, enthusiasm, trustworthiness, and successfulness. We were thus able to assess the extent to which perceivers' initial impressions of their partners reflected general stereotypes linking physical attractiveness and personality characteristics.

The getting-acquainted conversation. Each dyad then engaged in a 10-minute unstructured conversation by means of microphones and headphones connected through a Sony TC-570 stereophonic tape recorder that recorded each participant's voice on a separate channel of the tape.

After the conversation, male perceivers completed the Impression Formation Questionnaires to record final impressions of their partners. Female targets expressed self-perceptions in terms of the items of the Impression Formation Questionnaire. Each female target also indicated, on 10-point scales, how much she had enjoyed the conversation, how comfortable she had felt while talking to her partner, how accurate a picture of herself she felt that her partner had formed as a result of the conversation, how typical her partner's behavior had been of the way she usually was treated by men, her perception of her own physical attractiveness, and her estimate of her partner's perception of her physical attractiveness. All participants were then thoroughly and carefully debriefed and thanked for their contribution to the study.

[2]The interrater correlations of these ratings of attractiveness ranged from .45 to .92, with an average interrater correlation of .74.

Assessing Behavioral Confirmation

To assess the extent to which the actions of the target women provided behavioral confirmation for the stereotypes of the men perceivers, 8 male and 4 female introductory psychology students rated the tape recordings of the getting-acquainted conversations. These observer judges were unaware of the experimental hypotheses and knew nothing of the actual or perceived physical attractiveness of the individuals on the tapes. They listened, in random order, to two 4-minute segments (one each from the beginning and end) of each conversation. They heard *only* the track of the tapes containing the target women's voices and rated each woman on the 34 bipolar scales of the Impression Formation Questionnaire as well as on 14 additional 10-point scales; for example, "How animated and enthusiastic is this person?", "How intimate or personal is this person's conversation?", and "How much is she enjoying herself?". Another group of observer judges (3 males and 6 females) performed a similar assessment of the male perceivers' behavior based upon only the track of the tapes that contained the males' voices.

Results

To chart the process of behavioral confirmation of social stereotypes in dyadic social interaction, we examined the effects of our manipulation of the target women's apparent physical attractiveness on (a) the male perceivers' initial impressions of them and (b) the women's behavioral self-presentation during the interaction, as measured by the observer judges' ratings of the tape recordings.

The Perceivers' Stereotype

Did our male perceivers form initial impressions of their specific target women on the basis of general stereotypes that associate physical attractiveness and desirable personalities? To answer this question, we examined the male perceivers' initial ratings on the Impression Formation Questionnaire. Recall that these impressions were recorded *after* the perceivers had seen their partners' photographs, but *before* the getting-acquainted

conversation.[3] Indeed, it appears that our male perceivers did fashion their initial impressions of their female partners on the basis of stereotyped beliefs about physical attractiveness, multivariate $F(34, 3) = 10.19$, $p < .04$. As dictated by the physical attractiveness stereotype, men who anticipated physically attractive partners expected to interact with comparatively sociable, poised, humorous, and socially adept women; by contrast, men faced with the prospect of getting acquainted with relatively unattractive partners fashioned images of rather unsociable, awkward, serious, and socially inept women, all $Fs(1, 36) > 5.85$, $p < .025$.

Behavioral Confirmation

Not only did our perceivers fashion their images of their discussion partners on the basis of their stereotyped intuitions about beauty and goodness of character, but these impressions initiated a chain of events that resulted in the behavioral confirmation of these initially erroneous inferences. Our analyses of the observer judges' ratings of the women's behavior were guided by our knowledge of the structure of the men's initial impressions of their target women's personality. Specifically, we expected to find evidence of behavioral confirmation only for those traits that had defined the perceivers' stereotypes. For example, male perceivers

[3]These and all subsequent analyses are based upon a total of 38 observations, 19 in each of the attractive target and unattractive target conditions. Of the original 51 dyads, a total of 48 male–female pairs completed the experiment. In each of the remaining three dyads, the male participant had made reference during the conversation to the photograph. When this happened, the experimenter interrupted the conversation and immediately debriefed the participants. Of the remaining 48 dyads who completed the experimental procedures, 10 were eliminated from the analyses for the following reasons: In 4 cases, the male participant expressed strong suspicion about the photograph; in 1 case, the conversation was not tape recorded because of a mechanical problem; and in 5 cases, there was a sufficiently large age difference (ranging from 6 years to 18 years) between the participants that the males in these dyads reported that they had reacted very differently to their partners than they would have reacted to an age peer. This pattern of attrition was independent of assignment to the attractive target and unattractive target experimental conditions ($\chi^2 = 1.27$, *ns*).

did not attribute differential amounts of sensitivity or intelligence to partners of differing apparent physical attractiveness. Accordingly, we would not expect that our observer judges would "hear" different amounts of intelligence or sensitivity in the tapes. By contrast, male perceivers did expect attractive and unattractive targets to differ in sociability. Here we would expect that observer judges would detect differences in sociability between conditions when listening to the women's contributions to the conversations, and thus we would have evidence of behavioral confirmation.

To assess the extent to which the women's behavior, as rated by the observer judges, provided behavioral confirmation for the male perceivers' stereotypes, we identified, by means of a discriminant analysis (Tatsuoka, 1971), those 21 trait items of the Impression Formation Questionnaire for which the mean initial ratings of the men in the attractive target and unattractive target conditions differed by more than 1.4 standard deviations. This set of "stereotype traits" (e.g., sociable, poised, sexually warm, outgoing) defines the differing perceptions of the personality characteristics of target women in the two experimental conditions.

We then entered these 21 stereotype traits and the 14 additional dependent measures into a multivariate analysis of variance. This analysis revealed that our observer judges did indeed view women who had been assigned to the attractive target condition quite differently than women in the unattractive target condition, $Fm(35, 2) = 40.003$, $p < .025$. What had initially been reality in the minds of the men had now become reality in the behavior of the women with whom they had interacted—a behavioral reality discernible even by naive observer judges, who had access *only* to tape recordings of the women's contributions to the conversations.

The differences between the behavior of the women in the attractive target and the unattractive target conditions were in the same direction as the male perceivers' initial stereotyped impressions for fully 17 of the 21 measures of behavioral confirmation. The binomial probability that at least 17 of these adjectives would be in the predicted direction by chance alone is a scant .003.

By contrast, when we examined the 13 trait pairs that our discriminant analysis had indicated did *not* define the male perceivers' stereotype, a sharply different pattern emerged. Here, we would not expect any systematic relationship between the male perceivers' stereotyped initial impressions and the female targets' actual behavior in the getting-acquainted conversations. In fact, for only 8 of these 13 measures is the difference between the behavior of the women in the attractive target condition in the same direction as the men's stereotyped initial impressions. This configuration is, of course, hardly different from the pattern expected by chance alone if there were no differences between the groups (exact binomial $p = .29$). Clearly, then, behavioral confirmation manifested itself only for those attributes that had defined the male perceivers' stereotype; that is, only in those domains where the men believed that there did exist links between physical attractiveness and personal attributes did the women come to behave differently as a consequence of the level of physical attractiveness that we had experimentally assigned to them.

Moreover, our understanding of the nature of the difference between the attractive target and the unattractive target conditions identified by our multivariate analysis of variance and our confidence in this demonstration of behavioral confirmation are bolstered by the consistent pattern of behavioral differences on the 14 additional related dependent measures. Our raters assigned to the female targets in the attractive target condition higher ratings on *every* question related to favorableness of self-presentation. Thus, for example, those who were thought by their perceivers to be physically attractive appeared to the observer judges to manifest greater confidence, greater animation, greater enjoyment of the conversation, and greater liking for their partners than those women who interacted with men who perceived them as physically unattractive.

In Search of Mediators of Behavioral Confirmation

We next attempted to chart the process of behavioral confirmation. Specifically, we searched for evidence of the behavioral implications of the perceivers' stereotypes. Did the male perceivers present themselves differently to target women whom they assumed to be physically attractive or unattractive? Because we had 50 dependent measures of the observer judges' ratings of the males—12 more than the number of observations (male perceivers)—a multivariate analysis of variance is inappropriate. However, in 21 cases, univariate analyses of variance did indicate differences between conditions (all $ps < .05$). Men who interacted with women whom they believed to be physically attractive appeared (to the observer judges) more sociable, sexually warm, interesting, independent, sexually permissive, bold, outgoing, humorous, obvious, and socially adept than their counterparts in the unattractive target condition. Moreover, these men were seen as more attractive, more confident, and more animated in their conversation than their counterparts. Further, they were considered by the observer judges to be more comfortable, to enjoy themselves more, to like their partners more, to take the initiative more often, to use their voices more effectively, to see their women partners as more attractive, and, finally, to be seen as more attractive by their partners than men in the unattractive target condition.

It appears, then, that differences in the level of sociability manifested and expressed by the male perceivers may have been a key factor in bringing out reciprocating patterns of expression in the target women. One reason that target women who had been labeled as attractive may have reciprocated these sociable overtures is that they regarded their partners' images of them as more accurate, $F(1, 28) = 6.75$, $p < .02$, and their interaction style to be more typical of the way men generally treated them, $F(1, 28) = 4.79$, $p < .04$, than did women in the unattractive target condition. These individuals, perhaps, rejected their partners' treatment of them as unrepresentative and defensively adopted more cool and aloof postures to cope with their situations.

Discussion

Of what consequence are our social stereotypes? Our research suggests that stereotypes can and do

channel dyadic interaction so as to create their own social reality. In our demonstration, pairs of individuals got acquainted with each other in a situation that allowed us to control the information that one member of the dyad (the perceiver) received about the physical attractiveness of the other person (the target). Our perceivers, in anticipation of interaction, fashioned erroneous images of their specific partners that reflected their general stereotypes about physical attractiveness. Moreover, our perceivers had very different patterns and styles of interaction for those whom they perceived to be physically attractive and unattractive. These differences in self-presentation and interaction style, in turn, elicited and nurtured behaviors of the target that were consistent with the perceivers' initial stereotypes. Targets who were perceived (unbeknownst to them) to be physically attractive actually came to behave in a friendly, likable, and sociable manner. The perceivers' attributions about their targets based upon their stereotyped intuitions about the world had initiated a process that produced behavioral confirmation of those attributions. The initially erroneous attributions of the perceivers had become real: The stereotype had truly functioned as a self-fulfilling prophecy (Merton, 1948).

We regard our investigation as a particularly compelling demonstration of behavioral confirmation in social interaction. For if there is any social–psychological process that ought to exist in "stronger" form in everyday interaction than in the psychological laboratory, it is behavioral confirmation. In the context of years of social interaction in which perceivers have reacted to their actual physical attractiveness, our 10-minute getting-acquainted conversations over a telephone must seem minimal indeed. Nonetheless, the impact was sufficient to permit outside observers who had access only to one person's side of a conversation to detect manifestations of behavioral confirmation.

Might not other important and widespread social stereotypes—particularly those concerning sex, race, social class, and ethnicity—also channel social interaction so as to create their own social reality? For example, will the common stereotype that women are more conforming and less independent than men (cf. Broverman, Vogel, Broverman, Clarkson, & Rosenkrantz, 1972) influence inter- action so that (within a procedural paradigm similar to ours) targets believed to be female will actually conform more, be more dependent, and be more successfully manipulated than interaction partners believed to be male? At least one empiri- cal investigation has pointed to the possible self- fulfilling nature of apparent sex differences in self-presentation (Zanna & Pack, 1975).

Any self-fulfilling influences of social stereo- types may have compelling and pervasive societal consequences. Social observers have for decades commented on the ways in which stigmatized social groups and outsiders may fall "victim" to self-fulfilling cultural stereotypes (e.g., Becker, 1963; Goffman, 1963; Merton, 1948; Myrdal, 1944; Tannenbaum, 1938). Consider Scott's (1969) observations about the blind:

> When, for example, sighted people continually insist that a blind man is helpless because he is blind, their subsequent treatment of him may preclude his even exercising the kinds of skills that would enable him to be independent. It is in this sense that stereotypic beliefs are self- actualized. (p. 9)

And all too often it is the "victims" who are blamed for their own plight (cf. Ryan, 1971) rather than the social expectations that have constrained their behavioral options.

Of what import is the behavioral confirmation process for our theoretical understanding of the nature of social perception? Although our empiri- cal research has focused on social stereotypes that are widely accepted and broadly generalized, our notions of behavioral confirmation may apply equally well to idiosyncratic social perceptions spontaneously formed about specific individuals in the course of everyday social interaction. In this sense, social psychologists have been wise to devote intense effort to understanding the processes by which impressions of others are formed. Social perceptions are important pre- cisely because of their impact on social interac- tion. Yet, at the same time, research and theory in social perception (mostly displayed under the banner of attribution theory) that have focused on

the manner in which individuals process informa- tion provided them to form impressions of others may underestimate the extent to which information received in actual social interaction is a product of the perceiver's own actions toward the target indi- vidual. More careful attention must clearly be paid to the ways in which perceivers *create* or *construct* the information that they process in addition to the ways in which they *process* that information. Events in the social world may be as much the *effects* of our perceptions of those events as they are the *causes* of those perceptions.

From this perspective, it becomes easier to ap- preciate the perceiver's stubborn tendency to fash- ion images of others largely in trait terms (e.g., Jones & Nisbett, 1972), despite the poverty of evidence for the pervasive cross-situational con- sistencies in social behavior that the existence of "true" traits would demand (e.g., Mischel, 1968). This tendency, dubbed by Ross (1977) as the "fundamental attribution error," may be a self- erasing error. For even though any target individ- ual's behavior may lack, overall, the trait-defining properties of cross-situational consistency, the actions of the perceiver himself may produce consistency in the samples of behavior available to that perceiver. Our impressions of others may cause those others to behave in consistent trait- like fashion for us. In that sense, our trait-based impressions of others are veridical, even though the same individual may behave or be led to behave in a fashion perfectly consistent with opposite attributions by other perceivers with quite differ- ent impressions of that individual. Such may be the power of the behavioral confirmation process.

NOTES

1. Rothbart, M., Fulero, S., Jensen, C., Howard, J., & Birrell, P. *From individual to group impressions: Availability heuris- tics in stereotype formation.* Unpublished manuscript, Univer- sity of Oregon, 1976.

Research and preparation of this manuscript were sup- ported in part by National Science Foundation Grants SOC 75–13872, "Cognition and Behavior: When Belief Creates Reality," to Mark Snyder and GS 35157X, "Dependency and Interpersonal Attraction," to Ellen Berscheid. We thank Marilyn Steere, Craig Daniels, and Dwain Boelter, who assisted in the empirical phases of this investigation; and J. Merrill Carlsmith, Thomas Hummel, E. E. Jones, Mark Lepper, and Walter

Mischel, who provided helpful advice and constructive commentary.

Requests for reprints should be sent to Mark Snyder, Laboratory for Research in Social Relations, Department of Psychology, University of Minnesota, 75 East River Road, Minneapolis, Minnesota 55455.

REFERENCES

Bacon, F. [*Novum organum*] (J. Devey, Ed.). New York: P. F. Collier & Son, 1902. (Originally published, 1620.)

Bandura, A. *Social learning theory.* Englewood Cliffs, N.J.: Prentice Hall, 1977.

Becker, H. W. *Outsiders: Studies in the sociology of deviance.* N.Y.: Free Press, 1963.

Berscheid, E., & Walster, E. Physical attractiveness. In L. Berkowitz (Ed.), *Advances in experimental social psychology* (Vol. 7). New York: Academic Press, 1974.

Broverman, I. K., Vogel, S. R., Broverman, D. M., Clarkson, F. E., & Rosenkrantz, P. S. Sex-role stereotypes: A current appraisal. *Journal of Social Issues*, 1972, *28*, 59–78.

Chapman, L., & Chapman, J. The genesis of popular but erroneous psychodiagnostic observations. *Journal of Abnormal Psychology*, 1967, *72*, 193–204.

Chapman, L., & Chapman, J. Illusory correlations as an obstacle to the use of valid psychodiagnostic signs. *Journal of Abnormal Psychology*, 1969, *74*, 271–280.

Dermer, M. *When beauty fails.* Unpublished doctoral dissertation, University of Minnesota, 1973.

Dion, K. K., & Berscheid, E. Physical attractiveness and peer perception among children. *Sociometry*, 1974, *37*(1), 1–12.

Dion, K. K., Berscheid, E., & Walster, E. What is beautiful is good. *Journal of Personality and Social Psychology*, 1972, *24*, 285–290.

Ebel, R. L. Estimation of the reliability of ratings. *Psychometrika*, 1951, *16*, 407–424.

Goffman, E. *Stigma: Notes on the management of spoiled identity.* Englewood Cliffs, N.J.: Prentice Hall, 1963.

Hamilton, D. L., & Gifford, R. K. Illusory correlation in interpersonal perception: A cognitive basis of stereotypic judgments. *Journal of Experimental Social Psychology*, 1976, *12*, 392–407.

Harvey, J. H., Ickes, W. J., & Kidd, R. F. *New directions in attribution research.* Hillsdale, N.J.: Erlbaum, 1976.

Heider, F. *The psychology of interpersonal relations.* New York: Wiley, 1958.

Jones, E. E., & Davis, K. E. From acts to dispositions: The attribution process in person perception. In L. Berkowitz (Ed.), *Advances in experimental social psychology* (Vol. 2). New York: Academic Press, 1965.

Jones et al. *Attribution: Perceiving the causes of behavior.* Morristown, N.J.: General Learning Press, 1972.

Jones, E. E., & Nisbett, R. E. The actor and the observer: Divergent perceptions of the causes of behavior. In E. Jones,

D. Kanouse, H. Kelley, S. Valins, & B. Weiner (Eds.), *Attribution: Perceiving the causes of behavior.* New York: General Learning Press, 1972.

Karlins, M., Coffman, T. L., & Walters, G. On the fading of social stereotypes: Studies in three generations of college students. *Journal of Personality and Social Psychology*, 1969, *13*, 1–16.

Kelley, H. H. The process of causal attribution. *American Psychologist*, 1973, *28*, 107–128.

Kelley, H. H., & Stahelski, A. J. The social interaction basis of cooperators' and competitors' beliefs about others. *Journal of Personality and Social Psychology*, 1970, *16*, 66–91.

Kleck, R. E., Richardson, S. A., & Ronald, L. Physical appearance cues and interpersonal attraction in children. *Child Development*, 1974, *45*, 305–310.

Krebs, D., & Adinolphi, A. A. Physical attractiveness, social relations, and personality style. *Journal of Personality and Social Psychology*, 1975, *31*, 245–253.

Loftus, E., & Palmer, J. Reconstruction of automobile destruction. *Journal of Verbal Learning and Verbal Behavior*, 1974, *13*, 585–589.

Merton, R. K. The self-fulfilling prophecy. *Antioch Review*, 1948, *8*, 193–210.

Mischel, W. *Personality and assessment.* New York: Wiley, 1968.

Myrdal, G. *An American dilemma.* New York: Harper & Row, 1944.

Raush, H. L. Interaction sequences. *Journal of Personality and Social Psychology*, 1965, *2*, 487–499.

Regan, D. T., Straus, E., & Fazio, R. Liking and the attribution process. *Journal of Experimental Social Psychology*, 1974, *10*, 385–397.

Rosenhan, D. L. On being sane in insane places. *Science*, 1973, *179*, 250–258.

Ross, L. The intuitive psychologist and his shortcomings: Distortions in the attribution process. In L. Berkowitz (Ed.), *Advances in experimental social psychology* (Vol. 10). New York: Academic Press, 1977.

Ryan, W. *Blaming the victim.* New York: Vintage Books, 1971.

Scott, R. A. *The making of blind men.* New York: Russell Sage, 1969.

Tannenbaum, F. *Crime and the community.* Boston: Ginn, 1938.

Tatsuoka, M. M. *Multivariate analysis.* New York: Wiley, 1971.

Tversky, A., & Kahneman, D. Availability: A heuristic for judging frequency and probability. *Cognitive Psychology*, 1973, *5*, 207–232.

Walster, E., Aronson, V., Abrahams, D., & Rottman, L. Importance of physical attractiveness in dating behavior. *Journal of Personality and Social Psychology*, 1966, *4*, 508–516.

Zadny, J., & Gerard, H. B. Attributed intentions and informational selectivity. *Journal of Experimental Social Psychology*, 1974, *10*, 34–52.

Zanna, M. P., & Pack, S. J. On the self-fulfilling nature of apparent sex differences in behavior. *Journal of Experimental Social Psychology*, 1975, *11*, 583–591.

Evolution, Experience, and Later Relationships

I have called this principle, by which each slight variation, if
useful, is preserved, by the term Natural Selection.

— Charles Darwin

Love is the farce invented by nature to ensure that humans
propagate.

— August Strindberg

She: "I do love you. When is one of us going to start feeling tied
up and run for life?"

He: "Never, is my plan. I not, because tied up is exactly what I
want to feel. You not, because I mean to give you so much
space to move about in you'll begin to miss me and seek
me out."

— Amanda Cross

Over the years, the nature–nurture distinction has served as the basis for
some of the most enduring research questions in psychology. This is no
less true in relationship science as in other social sciences. It would be fair,
although overly simplistic, to summarize this body of research with the
conclusion "yes—nature matters, and so does nurture." Decades of studies
support the conclusion that Anna and Dave behave as they do in part
because of their biological makeup, and in part because of what they have
learned through previous experience and observation of others' adaptations.
The problem with this conclusion is that it begs an even more compelling
question: How do these two factors—our human biological makeup and

our unique developmental experiences—interact to create the patterns of interaction and the relationships that constitute our social lives?

The papers reprinted in this section represent both general theories and specific empirical studies that seek to explore this important question. Evolutionary approaches have become increasingly influential during the past two decades, as researchers have begun to articulate specific implications and hypotheses for the broad principles first described by Darwin (who was plainly aware of the importance of social relations in evolution; see Darwin, 1859, 1872). Many scholars believe that evolutionary forces relevant to living in small cooperative groups have shaped human nature. This is because, across human history, living in groups served as our species' primary strategy for contending with such basic survival problems as protection from predators and competitors, reliable access to food and shelter, procreation, and caring for offspring. As a consequence of natural selection, the many and diverse social processes that characterize interactions and relationships in small cooperative groups have come to be fundamental, innate, and universal human capacities (e.g., Bugental, 2000; Buss & Kenrick, 1997; Caporael, 1997).

Kenrick and Trost's article describes many of these fundamental processes, including, for example, mating, parental investment, kinship, alliance formation, and dominance hierarchies. Their review highlights important "adaptive" functions of relationships: In evolutionary terms, precisely how might a particular behavioral tendency have conferred a survival or reproductive advantage? For example, why might female "choosiness" in mate selection have been selected for, and what is the adaptive value of male attentiveness to partners' youth and attractiveness? Another point that Kenrick and Trost highlight concerns the importance of subjecting hypotheses derived from evolutionary theorizing to the rigorous empirical scrutiny to which we subject hypotheses from other theoretical orientations. As they note, evolution-based predictions have not always been tested in such a manner as to rule out plausible alternative explanations.

Buss's study of mate preference criteria in 37 cultures illustrates the sort of rigorous empirical test that even opponents of the evolutionary orientation find convincing. Sex differences in preferred mate characteristics have long been a popular topic among relationship researchers, especially those interested in evolution. In part, this is because of the unambiguous predictions that evolutionary mechanisms suggest. Buss finds that whether raised in a Middle Eastern metropolis or an Eastern European village, women tend to pay relatively greater attention than men do to qualities associated with resource acquisition, whereas men, whether they were born in the South Seas or the southern US, tend to pay relatively greater attention than women do to reproductive potential. Buss's research is impressive because it involved participants from every continent on Earth (except Antarctica), and because participants were from diverse ethnic, religious, educational, and socioeconomic backgrounds. Although some scholars have disagreed with Buss's evolutionary interpretation (for example, see Wood & Eagly,

2002), the near-universality of his findings across diverse cultures is not easily explained through other principles.

Evolutionary mechanisms also figure prominently in attachment theory, one of the most influential theories of social and emotional development. The founder of attachment theory was John Bowlby, a British psychiatrist with extensive psychoanalytic training. Bowlby sought to explain the vitally important relationship between infants and their caregivers by reference to mechanisms that are compatible with evolutionary principles, cognitive psychology, and ethological observations of animal behavior. The resulting theory, which Bowlby detailed in a masterful trilogy (*Attachment: Attachment and loss*, 1969; *Separation: Anger and anxiety*, 1973; *Loss: Sadness and depression*, 1980), has for several decades spurred systematic empirical studies and myriad theoretical elaborations and refinements among developmentally oriented researchers. A particularly appealing feature of attachment theory is its insightful integration of nature—the innate drive for proximity between infants and caregivers that nearly all higher species display—and nurture—the qualities of responsiveness and warmth in the infant–caregiver relationship that shape the child's developing self-concept, emotional makeup, and willingness to depend on others.

Bowlby postulated that attachment processes were significant "from the cradle to the grave," but it was not until 1987—when Cindy Hazan and Phillip Shaver published their initial research examining adult romantic love from the perspective of attachment theory—that this theory became

prominent among researchers studying relationships later in life. Attachment theory has become one of the field's most generative and influential theories—so much so that even an extensive new handbook (Cassidy & Shaver, 1999) barely does justice to the burgeoning literature. Hazan and Shaver's theoretical review, reprinted herein, illustrates how attachment theory can provide a coherent theoretical framework for explaining many important phenomena in adult relationships—for example, how Dave's early experiences shape his confidence that later partners will be responsive to his needs, or why Anna finds it difficult to openly communicate her thoughts and feelings.

The final paper in this section, by Mikulincer, explores several specific mechanisms by which working models of attachment affect adult relationships. A hallmark of these studies is their use of varied and rigorous experimental methods, including both open-ended probes and measures of response latencies. Mikulincer's research shows that systematic differences in trust—as well as in the cognitive accessibility of certain trust-related emotions, memories, and goals—can be explained by attachment theory. Because trust and contending with potential betrayals of trust are consequential in all close relationships, his research illustrates one important set of processes by which early interpersonal experiences can affect relationships much later in life.

REFERENCES

Bugental, D. B. (2000). Acquisition of the algorithms of social life: A domain-based approach. *Psychological Bulletin, 126*, 187–219.

Buss, D. M., & Kenrick, D. T. (1998). Evolutionary social psychology. In D. T. Gilbert, S. T. Fiske, & G. Lindzey (Eds.),

Handbook of social psychology (4th Ed., pp. 982–1026). New York: McGraw Hill.

Caporael, L. R. (1997). The evolution of truly social cognition: The core configurations model. *Personality and Social Psychology Review, 1,* 276–298.

Cassidy, J., & Shaver, P. R. (Eds.). (1999). *Handbook of attachment: Theory, research, and clinical applications.* New York: Guilford.

Darwin, C. (1859). *The origin of species.* London: Murray.

Darwin, C. (1872). *The expression of the emotions in man and animals.* London: Murray.

Hazan, C., & Shaver, P. R. (1987). Romantic love conceptualized as an attachment process. *Journal of Personality and Social Psychology, 52,* 511–524.

Wood, W., & Eagly, A. H. (2002). A cross-cultural analysis of the behavior of women and men: Implications for the origins of sex differences. *Psychological Bulletin, 128,* 699–727.

Suggestions for Further Reading

Barkow, J. H., Cosmides, L., & Tooby, J. (Eds.). (1992). *The adapted mind: Evolutionary psychology and the generation of culture.* New York: Oxford University Press. This collection of essays was and is a "call to arms" for the evolutionary psychology movement. Collectively, these papers touch on many important psychological and cultural processes and phenomena from the evolutionary perspective.

Bowlby, J. (1988). *A secure base.* New York: Basic Books. A very accessible collection of several of John Bowlby's lectures.

Bowlby, J. (1991). *Charles Darwin: A new life.* New York: W. W. Norton. A fascinating, albeit controversial, biography of Charles Darwin, written by the admiring founder of attachment theory.

Buss, D. (1995). *The evolution of desire: Strategies of human mating.* New York: Basic Books. An overview of our understanding of love and sexual desire, written from an evolutionary perspective.

Cassidy, J., & Shaver, P. R. (Eds.). (1999). *Handbook of attachment: Theory, research, and clinical applications.* New York: Guilford. The most comprehensive and scholarly review of attachment theory yet available, this collection includes chapters by many leading researchers in the attachment "camp."

Diamond, J. (1998). *Why is sex fun? The evolution of human sexuality.* New York: Basic Books. An engaging discussion of sex and pair bonding research from the perspective of an evolutionary biologist.

Kenrick, D. T., Keefe, R. C., Bryan, A., Barr, A., & Brown, S. (1995). Age preferences and mate choice among homosexuals and heterosexuals: A case for modular psychological mechanisms. *Journal of Personality and Social Psychology, 69,* 1166–1172. Using an analysis of singles ads, this article demonstrates that as men (both heterosexual and homosexual) age, they develop an increasing preference for partners younger than themselves. In early adulthood, women prefer partners older than themselves; among lesbians, this tendency diminishes with age.

Kurzban, R., & Leary, M. R. (2001). Evolutionary origins of stigmatization: The functions of social exclusion. *Psychological Bulletin, 127,* 187–208. Nearly all mammalian species use social exclusion (rejection) to regulate the behavior of individuals. This paper addresses this process from an evolutionary perspective, with an eye toward understanding human behavior.

Mikulincer, M., & Shaver, P. R. (2003). The attachment behavioral system in adulthood: Activation, psychodynamics, and interpersonal processes. In M. P. Zanna (Ed.), *Advances in experimental social psychology* (Vol. 35, pp. 53–152). San Diego: Academic Press. Two leading researchers review and discuss research investigating social-cognitive processes related to the operation of the attachment system.

Simpson, J. A., Rholes, W. S., & Phillips, D. (1996). Conflict in close relationships: An attachment perspective. *Journal of Personality and Social Psychology, 71,* 899–914. An excellent example of an observational study of the impact of attachment style on behavior during problem-solving interactions.

Sroufe, L. A. (1996). *Emotional development: The organization of emotional life in the early years.* New York: Cambridge University Press. How attachment affects early emotional development.

Tidwell, M. O., Reis, H. T., & Shaver, P. R. (1996). Attachment, attractiveness, and social interaction: A diary study. *Journal of Personality and Social Psychology, 71,* 729–745. This diary study demonstrates the impact of attachment processes on everyday social interaction.

Waters, E., & Cummings, M. (2000). A secure base from which to explore relationships. *Child Development, 71,* 164–172. Attachment research has often emphasized insecurity and individual differences; this important paper reviews the secure base concept as a fundamental characteristic of healthy adult relationships.

Wright, R. (1995). *The moral animal: Evolutionary psychology and everyday life.* New York: Vintage Books. Evolutionary theorizing, it turns out, can help explain many phenomena that at first glance seem to tell a very different story.

Discussion Questions

1. Why is it difficult to test hypotheses derived from evolutionary theory using the usual methods of psychological research?
2. Pick one phenomenon or process that operates in relationships. Discuss how that phenomenon or process might have been adaptive in the evolutionary past.
3. What is the difference between a proximate and an ultimate explanation? Suggest a proximate explanation of why men's and women's mate preferences differ.
4. What criteria contribute to mate preferences besides those Buss discusses? Which are more important, and why?
5. Have any of the evolutionary processes discussed by these authors outlived their usefulness? Which ones?

6. Attachment theory was originally designed to explain the bonds between infants and their caregivers. In what ways are adult romantic relationships also "attachment" relationships? In what ways do adult romantic relationships differ from attachment relationships earlier in life?

7. Select an aspect of adult romantic relationships that you have observed, and explain it in terms of attachment theory principles.

8. Explain the differences in trust that secure, anxious–ambivalent, and avoidant persons might be expected to display. How might these differences influence the manner in which friendships and romantic relationships develop?

9. How do the trust-related goals of secure, anxious–ambivalent, and avoidant persons differ? According to Mikulincer, why do they differ in this way?

Evolutionary Approaches to Relationships

Douglas T. Kenrick and Melanie R. Trost

• Arizona State University

Evolutionary theory is arguably the most powerful set of ideas in the life sciences. No natural scientist studying the wing of a bat or the flipper of a seal or the long neck of a giraffe would ignore Darwin's theory of evolution by natural selection. Likewise for the behaviors of bats or seals or giraffes—obviously the unique bodies of these animals evolved to do something, and evolutionary theory helps to understand the co-evolution of physical morphology and behavior. Neither would many disagree that an evolutionary perspective is essential to understand the human body, with its upright posture, prehensile grasping hands, and large brain capable of producing complex language. Yet many social scientists have not yet realized that an evolutionary perspective is just as essential for a full understanding of human behavior. Just as bats are designed to survive by flying through the night sky, seals by swimming through the ocean depths, and giraffes by walking through the African plains, so human beings are designed to behave in certain ways in certain environments. To a large extent, humans are designed to live in social groups with other humans, and an evolutionary perspective can enhance our understanding of every aspect of personal relationships considered in this volume—including love, interdependence, social support, parent-child relationships, and family conflicts. Indeed, an evolutionary perspective can help us see how all of these different aspects of human relationships are connected with one another and, at the next level, how they are connected with the evolved design of the human body and brain, and ultimately with the fundamental principles that underlie the design of all living creatures.

Basic Assumptions of Evolutionary Psychology

Evolutionary explanations of life begin with Darwin's (1859) set of simple assumptions:

1. Organisms reproduce very rapidly, so by normal processes of geometric multiplication, even slowly reproducing animals such as elephants could cover the globe in a few centuries, if unrestrained. Any given species would therefore rapidly exhaust the limited resources available to it, if not for the fact that other animals are also competing for those same resources.
2. Animals vary in ways that influence their ability to survive in competition with members of their own and other species (some giraffes have longer necks, some have shorter necks).
3. Those organisms whose genetic traits provide an advantage in access to resources will survive longer and be more successful in mating. As a result, their genes will increase in the population relative to less well-adapted competitors.

(Of course, the population growth of even relatively well-adapted animals is still limited by resource availability, competition with members of other species, predators, parasites, and so on.) These processes of random variation and selective retention form the basis of natural selection. Analogous to the artificial selection exercised by animal breeders, as in selecting for short hair or a peaceful disposition in a dog, the forces of nature select certain characteristics over others.

As Darwin (1872) spelled out in his classic work on emotion, the process of natural selection also applies to behavior. Snarling communicates an intention to attack, and animals who recognize the signal and avoid a snarling adversary save themselves costly and bloody encounters. The abilities to both transmit and receive emotional communications are thus selected. Although the pioneering textbooks in social psychology were written from a Darwinian perspective (James, 1890; McDougall, 1908), later behavioral scientists largely ignored the implications of natural selection for humans. During the 1970s, however, stimulated in part by Wilson's *Sociobiology* (1975), social scientists began to incorporate evolutionary theory into their models of human social behavior.

Misunderstandings of the relationship between genetic predispositions and psychological development have led to misguided controversies about the extent to which human behavior is controlled by genes vs. cultural environment, or by genes vs. rational thought. The human capacities to create culture and to engage in complex cognition are themselves made possible by our genetic predispositions. These predispositions influence the choice of certain cultural practices over others and the inclination to attend to, think about, and remember certain features of the environment (Lumsden & Wilson, 1981; Tooby & Cosmides, 1992). Genetic predispositions unfold in interaction with experience, resulting in cognitive and behavioral mechanisms that are themselves triggered by, and attuned to, events in the social and physical environment (Buss, 1995; Crawford & Anderson, 1989). Language provides a clear example. As Pinker (1994) notes, language is undoubtedly a species-specific evolved feature of humans: there are brain mechanisms dedicated to its production and understanding; the level of linguistic complexity is the same in all human groups, children acquire it with little effort, sign language shows some of the same deep structure as spoken language, and so on. However, the specific language that a child learns is determined by environmental inputs. No set of genes determines whether a child will say: "Come vanno le cose, signore?", "Hoe gaat het met je, mijnheer?", or "How's it going, man?"

Depending partly on environmental inputs, genetic predispositions may unfold very differently for different members of a species. Within one fish species, for instance, some males grow into large territorial animals that attract harems, others grow into small animals that look like females and attempt to "sneak-copulate", and still others begin life as females and only turn into males when a large territorial male dies (e.g., Gross, 1984; Warner, 1984). Hence evolutionary theory does not posit static immutable genes working *against* the environment. It proposes a set of general principles that shape the behavioral and cognitive mechanisms underlying human behavior across cultures, some of which may be shared with other species by common ancestry or ecological demands. These general principles may sometimes produce incredibly flexible mechanisms and may sometimes produce more rigid mechanisms. Even so, evolutionary theorists assume that to ignore the general principles underlying the evolutionary design of a behavior is to be blind to the ultimate causal mechanisms underlying that behavior.

Some Important General Principles

In this section, we consider several general principles that have been used to generate evolutionary hypotheses about behavior. Before beginning, it is important to distinguish between ultimate and proximate levels of explanation. A *proximate explanation* considers behavior in terms of immediate determinants, such as the current environment or internal hormonal states. Laboratory experimenters tend to consider proximate causes-events in the immediate environment such as an aggressive prime or a confederate's remark. *Ultimate explanations* consider behavior in terms of more enduring background factors, such as the cultural norms that make a remark an insult, individual differences that make some people more prone to take offense, or an evolutionary past in which males were more concerned than females with challenges to their dominance. Evolutionary theorists are not unconcerned with proximate explanations, they are simply less likely to be satisfied without asking "why" a particular event might or might not elicit a particular response in a particular setting.

Reproduction, Kin Selection, and Inclusive Fitness

The name of the evolutionary game is gene replication. Gene replication is accomplished directly via the production of offspring, hence evolutionary theorists have taken a strong interest in sexuality and heterosexual relationships. However, gene replication can be accomplished indirectly by helping those who share copies of one's genes. Thus, the theory applies not only to sexual behavior, but to mate attraction and selection, mate retention, and kin relationships as well. Even foregoing the opportunity to reproduce directly may increase the "ultimate payoff"—more copies of one's genes. For instance, under conditions of resource scarcity and low survival rates for hatchlings, male birds may fare better by helping their brothers raise a clutch than by mating on their own (Trivers, 1985). Hatchlings receiving the extra resources provided by a helper are more likely to survive than birds raised with only two parents. Because brothers share half of their genes, the net benefit to both is greater if they cooperate than if they go it alone. This is an example of the general process of *kin selection*, which involves sacrificing direct reproductive opportunities to favor the survival and reproduction of relatives. The kin selection model helps explain the widespread occurrence of altruistic and cooperative behavior in animals. It has replaced the "red in tooth and claw" view of evolution as a process that exclusively involves survival by individual competition.

Before notions such as kin selection were developed, evolutionary biologists evaluated an animal's reproductive potential in terms of individual "fitness". This concept was sometimes operationally defined as the number of offspring that were successfully raised to reproductive age. At its base, however, fitness in an evolutionary sense meant not simply to survive, but to successfully reproduce one's genes. *Inclusive fitness* is simply the logical extension of this notion, referring to the net number of one's genes passed on to future generations, a number that includes not only the individuals' direct contribution via personal offspring, but also their indirect contribution to the survival and reproduction of relatives who share copies of their genes (Hamilton, 1964).

Sexual Selection

As we just noted, a characteristic can be naturally selected because it provides a survival advantage to the individual or to kin. Darwin believed, however, that features such as peacocks' feathers or large horns on male mammals were selected through a process of *sexual selection*. Sexual selection occurs when a trait provides an advantage in attracting mates, even though it may hinder individual survival. There are two forms of sexual selection—*intersexual choice*, in which a trait gains an advantage because (like the feathers on a male bird) it is attractive to the opposite sex, and *intrasexual competition*, in which a trait gains an advantage because (like the horns on a male mammal) it helps an individual compete with same-sex rivals. Modern evolutionary theorists believe that sexual selection is just a special case of natural selection, in which the culling force is other members of one's species. The same sex provides obstacles to stop one another from mating; the opposite sex provides tests that must be passed before mating.

Parental Investment

Darwin noted that, when it comes to sexual selection, females are more likely to be the selectors, and males are more likely to be banging their heads against one another to win the females' attention. Trivers (1972) developed Darwin's insight into the theory of *differential parental investment*. According to this theory, the sex with the initially higher investment in the offspring has more to lose from a poor mating choice and will demand more before agreeing to mate. In general, females have a higher initial investment and should be more selective about choosing mates. There are, however, species in which males make the larger investment (e.g., by caring for the eggs and young offspring, as in seahorses), and in those species males tend to be more selective about their mates (Daly & Wilson, 1983; Trivers, 1985). In mammals, however, the normal discrepancy between males and females is especially pronounced, because females carry the young inside their bodies and nurse them after birth. Male mammals can reproduce with little cost, and frequently the male's direct input does not go beyond a single act of copulation. In such species, males tend to be nonselective about their mates, whereas females demand evidence of superior genetic potential before mating and will often mate only with males who

have demonstrated superior capabilities. Humans also sometimes have sexual relations within less committed relationships, in the typical mammalian mode. Under those circumstances, an evolutionary perspective would predict typical mammalian differences—females high and males low in selectivity (Kenrick et al., 1990).

Unlike most mammals, however, humans tend to form long-term pair-bonds. Human males, therefore, often invest resources such as effort, time, money, and emotional support in their offspring. Under those circumstances, men's selectivity is expected to approach that of women. However, to the extent that men and women make different contributions to the offspring, they should select partners along somewhat different dimensions. Women contribute their bodies, through internal gestation and nursing. Men would therefore be expected to value indications of fertility, including a healthy appearance and a waist-hip ratio characteristic of youthful sexual maturity (Singh, 1993). On the other hand, men primarily contribute their genes and indirect resources such as money and shelter. Presumably, women could appraise a man's genetic potential from physical attractiveness and his position in a dominance hierarchy (Thornhill & Gangestad, 1994; Sadalla, Kenrick, & Vershure, 1987). His ability to provide resources could be gauged indirectly by his ambition and directly by his social status and acquired wealth (Buss & Barnes, 1986; Daly & Wilson, 1983; Symons, 1979). Even with these differential tendencies, humans cooperate in raising their offspring. Hence, a number of characteristics should be (and are) desired by both sexes, such as agreeableness, kindness, and faithfulness (Buss, 1989; Kenrick et al., 1993).

Evolutionary Hypotheses Are Subject to the Same Standards of Empirical Evidence as Any Other Hypotheses

The principles described above have been tested in a number of studies of animal behavior, and several of them (such as kin selection and differential parental investment) are very well-established (Alcock, 1993; Daly & Wilson, 1983; Trivers, 1985; Wilson, 1975). Nevertheless, their application to any given instance of human behavior may or may not be appropriate. There is nothing any less refutable about a hypothesis derived from evolutionary principles than there is about a hypothesis derived from principles of information processing or classical conditioning. Some derivations are astute, others are stretched, and others are dead wrong. Consequently, some derivations receive empirical support, and some are refuted (Buss, 1995; Buss & Kenrick, in press; Kenrick, 1994). As we will describe below, evolutionary principles have proven fruitful in explaining gender differences in sexual behavior, mate preferences, and aggressive behavior. In some cases, findings seem to refute alternative explanations from traditional social science models; in other cases, traditional models and evolutionary hypotheses have been used to complement one another. In other areas, such as kinship and friendship, there have been fewer tests of evolutionary hypotheses, and their utility remains to be seen.

The Adaptive Functions of Relationships

From an evolutionary perspective, the primary question about a physical or behavioral characteristic is: "What was it designed to do?" In discussing the functional design of human cognitive and behavioral mechanisms, evolutionary theorists often discuss the environment of evolutionary adaptedness (EEA). Although the distribution of alternative genes can change in a few generations, it is assumed that the redesign of a functional feature (such as the development of a giraffe's neck) will take, at a minimum, thousands of years (Lumsden & Wilson, 1981). There is thus considerable "lag time" in evolution, and any evolved human cognitive mechanisms were designed not for life on the freeways or malls of modern Los Angeles, but for co-existence in small hunter-gatherer groups. The hunting and gathering lifestyle set the stage for human social arrangements for well over a million years, as agriculture was only introduced within the last few thousand years (and then only for a minority of our ancestors), and large urban centers only began to predominate within the past few hundred years. Hence, evolutionary psychologists assume that the human mind was constructed for

life in a small group of closely related individuals, in which there was a well-established dominance hierarchy, division of labor by sex (females devoting more time to parenting and gathering, males more to hunting), marriage to someone from a very similar background (usually a cousin from a neighboring group), and so on (Lumsden & Wilson, 1981; Tooby & Cosmides, 1992). Hunter-gatherers everywhere shared some very similar problems as a function of that lifestyle and, as a consequence, evolutionary theorists expect to find a number of human universals beneath the surface diversity of modern cultures (Brown, 1991). Undoubtedly there are psychologically important differences across cultures, and modern life has introduced many new problems for the human mind. However, there is an assumption that we can better understand how humans respond to contemporary cultural variations if we consider the social arrangements within which our ancestors evolved. Evolutionary theorists also assume that modern cultures are not randomly created, but include many customs and institutions actively constructed by organisms designed for a prehistoric lifestyle (Lumsden & Wilson, 1981; Kenrick, 1987; Tooby & Cosmides, 1992). In the following sections, we consider some of the functions that relationships might have served in the human environment of evolutionary adaptedness.

Romantic Relationships

The primary adaptive functions of romantic relationships are assumed to be sexual reproduction and bonding for the care of offspring (Kenrick & Trost, 1987; Mellen, 1981; Morris, 1972). Romantic relationships also provide secondary adaptive benefits such as mutual sharing, social support, and protection. The joint investment in offspring should facilitate such sharing, moving couples into a strong, communal mode with little accounting of individual contributions or resources. Therefore, men and women should have some shared goals, such as finding a cooperative and compatible partner or ensuring the survival of the offspring.

In line with our earlier discussion, however, men and women are also assumed to have some different goals in romantic relationships (Buss, 1995; Kenrick & Trost, 1987, 1989). For instance, women ought to be concerned that the man contributes his part (i.e., resources) to the child-rearing responsibility. A woman should thus be concerned if her partner is possibly squandering resources on outside mating opportunities. Men should be more concerned with ensuring paternal certainty; that is, that the offspring in whom he is investing are indeed his (obviously, maternal certainty is not an issue for women). In addition, a man is more likely to be concerned with gaining access to additional mates, a goal that is not as beneficial for a woman.

Kin Relationships

Relationships with close relatives primarily serve the ultimate goal of gene replication. By helping one's kin, one helps one's own genes. From an evolutionary perspective, one would expect to find, among close relatives, a higher prevalence of Clark & Mills' (1979) communal relationships than tit-for-tat exchange relationships. In fact, explicit accounting of exchanged rewards should diminish as an inverse function to r (an index of relatedness, which would be 0.5 for a woman and her sister, 0.25 for a woman and her mother's sister, 0.125 for a woman and her first cousin, and so on). It is expected that one's willingness to benefit one's kin is also a function of their future reproductive potential (Burnstein, Crandall, & Kitayama, 1994). So, whereas a 40-year-old woman has the same degree of relatedness to her 17-year-old daughter and her 70-year-old mother, she would be expected to feel more positively about investing resources in her daughter (whose reproductive potential is quite high) than in her 70-year-old mother (who, although she may still be capable of providing the indirect benefits of grandmothering to the kin group, has a relatively low reproductive potential).

Friendships

Evolutionary theorists have devoted some attention to reciprocal alliances between non-relatives. Vampire bats, for instance, will often share their nightly take of blood with others. Research on this sharing indicates that it occurs between relatives, or between individuals who have forged a reciprocal exchange relationship (Wilkinson, 1988, 1990). The same sort of arrangement is found in hunter-gatherer groups (Hill & Hurtado, 1989). In traditional hunter-gatherer societies, the likelihood of capturing game may be quite low on any given occasion for any given individual. If one individual catches a large fish or a deer, however, it is often too much to consume alone, and will rot if not shared. By sharing, the individual helps the other members of the group survive, and accrues credit for the future when his or her own luck may be down.

In most traditional societies even today, one's best friends are usually related in some way (Moghaddam, Taylor, & Wright, 1993). Even in modern urban societies, most women list a close relative when asked to name someone with whom they are intimate. In hunter-gatherer societies like those in which our ancestors evolved, individuals were all closely related. Thus, the immediate selfish obstacles to reciprocal sharing in humans were diminished by potential kin selection. It would be expected, however, that our ancestors would have benefited from sensitivity to differences between close and distant relatives, and that reciprocal alliances with more distant relatives would involve more direct accounting. In addition to the benefits of trading resources, friendships would have served other functions for our ancestors. In chimpanzees, friends protect one another and also form mating alliances (deWaal, 1989). Although the most dominant male in a group can monopolize the mating attention of the females, he can be toppled by an alliance of less dominant males. In humans, of course, one's social position is also often related to "who one knows", and cooperative alliances often involve large groups of individuals.

Dominance Hierarchies

In addition to cooperating to survive, group members also sometimes compete with one another. Dominance hierarchies serve to reduce continual competition in stable groups—once everyone knows who can defeat whom, there is less need to struggle over every new resource. When a new member is introduced into an existing group, there is often a period of conflict until a new hierarchy is established (e.g., deWaal, 1989). In addition to reducing conflict, male dominance hierarchies also define the most desirable mates for females to choose from. Thus, male mammals tend to be more concerned than females with their status within dominance hierarchies. Note that there is no assumption of altruism here; animals do not take their place within a hierarchy to reduce conflict or to help the other sex make mating decisions. They jockey for the best available position, and will occasionally re-challenge those just above them in line. However, it is in their best interest to recognize those who are far above them in order to avoid unnecessary and costly competition with them. Thus, the group-stabilizing consequences of dominance hiearchies are indirect byproducts of individual selfishness.

Ultimate Goals Are Not Necessarily Conscious or "Rational"

It is important to note that evolutionary psychologists do not assume that people, or other organisms, are conscious of the ultimate goals of their behavior. A woman, for instance, does not have to be aware of choosing a dominant man for his genetic potential. In fact, evolutionary theorists have considered a variety of circumstances under which "self-deception" about one's ulterior motives would be adaptive (e.g., Lockard & Paulhus, 1988; Trivers, 1985). Just because humans are capable of some degree of self-awareness, it is not any more necessary to assume that humans are fully aware of the ultimate motivations underlying their behaviors than it is to assume that caterpillars or planarians are.

It is also important to note that the evolved mechanisms are not designed to confer omniscience about the adaptive consequences of every choice. Rather, they are blindly calibrated to the average consequences of a given behavior for our ancestors. A good example is the human preference for sugar, which assisted our ancestors in identifying ripe fruit (Lumsden & Wilson, 1981). This preference was helpful for millions of years and is still strong, even in those who are safe from

starvation within modern society and those who have stored several months' worth of calories in the form of fat. In the same way, the comment "Our romance is based on a shared interest in Beethoven, and we have no interest in reproducing" may reflect on the depth of human self-awareness, but it does not negate the evolutionary significance of the mate choice mechanisms.

Empirical Findings From Evolutionary Psychology

Evolutionary hypotheses have generated a number of empirical findings in recent years. We first review findings on universals in interpersonal communication. Next we consider findings on sexuality, mating, and mate preferences, many of which follow directly from evolutionary models of sexual selection and parental investment. These same models have led to predictions regarding intrasexual competition, jealousy, and deception, discussions of which are followed by a review of evolution-inspired research on aggression and child abuse. Finally, we consider the less extensive literatures on kinship and friendship.

Universals in Communication

The first research in the field of evolutionary psychology was conducted by Charles Darwin (1872), who surveyed early anthropologists and missionaries for evidence of universals in emotional expression. His conclusion that certain aspects of human emotional expression are universal has received corroboration from a series of studies by Ekman and his colleagues (e.g., Ekman, 1992; Ekman & Friesen, 1971; Ekman et al., 1987). In general, they have found that expressions indicating basic emotional states such as anger and happiness are recognized world-wide; and, although they can be suppressed in public or partially masked when necessary, the expressions do not appear to depend on shared cultural exposure.

Eibl-Eibesfeldt unobtrusively filmed women's responses to flirtation across a wide range of Western and non-Western cultures, and found certain universalities in the sequences of their movements. The patterns were too subtle to have been trained, and they agreed in microscopic detail from Samoa to Papua, France, Japan, Africa, and in South American Indian tribes (Eibl-Eibesfeldt, 1975). Women's flirtation gestures include "proceptive" cues (Beach, 1976; Perper & Weis, 1987), such as smiling and maintaining mutual gaze a bit longer than usual, that invite advances from selected men (Givens, 1978; Moore, 1985).

Sexuality

Because of inherent differences in parental investment, males and females face a different matrix of costs and benefits in casual sexual relationships. A male faces an opportunity to replicate genes with relatively low cost. A female faces the danger of impregnation by a male who has made little commitment to invest in the offspring. If she has an existing partner, there is much less marginal genetic gain from an additional partner, and the danger of abandonment or intense jealousy from her current partner can be extremely costly.

There is abundant evidence that women are less eager than are men to engage in promiscuous sex. Clark and Hatfield (1989) had confederates approach opposite-sex students with one of three invitations, to: "Go out tonight?", "Come over to my apartment?", or "Go to bed with me?" Approximately half of the women said yes to the date, but only 3% were receptive to going to the man's apartment, and not one said yes to the invitation to go to bed. When men were approached with the same questions, about half of them also responded favorably to the confederate's invitation for a date, almost 70% were willing to go to her apartment, and over 70% were willing to go to bed with her. Buss and Schmitt (1993) also found that college men desired to have sex much sooner in a relationship than did women.

Besides being more willing to have sex, men also want to have sex with more partners than do women. Buss and Schmitt (1993) asked college students how many sexual partners they would ideally like to have during the rest of their lives. Men wanted, on average, over 18 sex partners in their lifetimes, whereas women desired, on aver-

age, fewer than five. Consistent findings are also found in research on erotica, with males generally indicating more interest in erotica and more fantasies involving strangers (Ellis & Symons, 1990; Kenrick et al., 1980). Men have somewhat more extramarital affairs than women. If not for the scarcity of willing women, the sex difference in partners would likely be even more pronounced, as indicated by the very large difference in sexual experience between male and female homosexuals (Daly & Wilson, 1983; Symons, 1979).

Men are also less selective about casual sexual partners. Kenrick et al. (1990) asked male and female college students about their minimum criteria in a member of the opposite sex for a date, a sexual partner, a steady dating relationship, or a marriage. The two sexes differed most noticeably in their criteria for a sexual partner, with males willing to have sex with someone who did not meet their minimum criteria for a date.

Are these gender differences simply a reflection of an American or Western "double standard" of sexual behavior for men and women? Although there are clear cross-cultural variations in the norms involving premarital and extramarital sex, early anthropological reports of societies in which women were as interested in casual sex as men do not bear up under examination (Freeman, 1983). In reviewing the cross-cultural data on gender differences in sexuality, anthropologist Donald Symons concludes: "Everywhere sex is understood to be something females have that males want" (1979, p. 253). One of the unfortunate consequences of the inherent gender differences in selectivity for sexual partners is that males are much more likely to be the perpetrators, and females to be the victims, of sexual harassment (Studd & Gattiker, 1991). As noted by Clark and Hatfield (1989), males are likely to be receptive to, or at worst flattered by, sexual advances, whereas females are more likely to respond with some degree of aversion.

Love and Marriage

Anthropologists have observed cultural variations in mating relationships: Some societies allow polyandry, some allow polygyny but not polyandry, and some allow only monogamy. However, the mix of possibilities is neither random nor arbitrary. First, all human societies have some form of marriage (Daly & Wilson, 1983). This is only surprising when one notes that pair-bonding is relatively rare among other mammals. If human mating patterns were completely arbitrary, one would see whole societies in which people were completely promiscuous, as in the Bonobo chimp, or arena mating patterns such as those found in the Uganda kob (in which females select highly dominant males, but males make no investment in the offspring beyond insemination). On the other hand, pair-bonding is more commonly found in bird species that, like ours, have helpless offspring who require intensive parental care. Evolutionary theorists have argued that forming a strong bond serves the same function in humans as it does in birds—to ensure cooperation in caring for their helpless offspring (e.g., Kenrick & Trost, 1987; Mellen, 1981).

If humans are designed to bond together to facilitate caring for their young, one would assume romantic love to be a universal feature of our species. That assumption was seemingly contradicted by social scientists' common wisdom that romantic love is a recent phenomenon, traceable to the idle, courtly classes of Medieval Europe (e.g., Stone, 1988). In a recent review of reports from 166 societies, however, Jankowiak and Fischer (1992) found only one in which the anthropologist explicitly stated that there was no romantic love (and the supplementary evidence was insufficient to confirm or deny the report). There was evidence of sexual affairs in another 18 cultures, but ethnographers had not asked about romantic love, and Jankowiak and Fischer were unable to establish that the participants felt love. For the remaining 147 cultures, however, they found clear, positive evidence of romantic love.

Although romantic love is a prevalent human bonding pattern, most societies do not require that it occur within a monogamous relationship. Daly and Wilson (1983) reviewed evidence from 849 cultures and found that only 137 were supposedly "strictly" monogamous—although even in those societies men were likely to engage in more extra-pair

copulations than were women. Most (708) cultures allowed polygyny (one man with several wives), whereas only four allowed polyandry (one woman with several husbands). Moreover, whenever polyandry was allowed, so was polygyny. For instance, Pahari brothers in India pool resources to secure a wife, whom they share. If they accumulate more wealth, however, they add wives. The tendency toward polygyny over polyandry is consistent with the parental investment model. Women select men for their resources, and men with great wealth or power, such as Roman emperors, can attract multiple women because the benefits of sharing a wealthy husband may outweigh the advantages of having a poorer man all to oneself (Betzig, 1992). However, the reverse is not true. Because men select women for direct reproductive potential, a man sharing a woman, even a very desirable one, suffers a disadvantage over a man having a less attractive woman to himself. Also, a woman married to multiple husbands gains resources, but does not increase her own reproductive output substantially enough to compensate for the additional costs, such as male jealousy (Daly & Wilson, 1983, 1988a).

Mate Selection Criteria

Studies of characteristics requested and offered in singles' advertisements support predictions from the parental investment model—men seek youth and attractiveness in partners, and promise economic and emotional resources; women are more likely to seek resources and offer attractiveness (e.g., Harrison & Saeed, 1977; Rajecki, Bledsoe, & Rasmussen, 1991; Thiessen, Young, & Burroughs, 1993; Wiederman, 1993). Although one could argue that such criteria reflect norms of American society, an extensive cross-cultural study of marriage preferences (Buss, 1989) indicated that men in diverse cultures place greater value than do women on youth and beauty in potential spouses, whereas women place greater value on characteristics associated with resource potential. There is also substantial cross-cultural agreement in judgments of female attractiveness, which cannot be explained by exposure to Western standards of beauty through the media (Cunningham et al., 1995).

Age Preferences in Mates

Researchers studying singles' advertisements have been struck by a consistent contradiction to the powerful similarity-attraction principle: Women generally prefer older men and men prefer younger women (Harrison & Saeed, 1977; Bolig, Stein, & McKenry, 1984; Cameron, Oskamp, & Sparks, 1977). Explanations for this irregularity typically rely upon the influence of cultural norms (Brehm, 1985; Cameron, Oskamp, & Sparks, 1977; Deutsch, Zalenski, & Clark, 1986; Presser, 1975), such as the "norm" specifying that a husband should be older and taller so as to appear "mentally and physically superior" to his wife (Presser, 1975). An alternative evolutionary explanation focuses on inherent sex differences in resources that men and women bring to relationships (e.g., Buss, 1989; Symons, 1979). Men's indirect resources (e.g., food, money, protection, security) may actually increase over the lifespan, whereas the direct reproductive potential contributed by women decreases as they age, and ends with menopause around age 50.

Although both perspectives could predict the average 2–3-year difference in desired ages across all advertisers, their predictions differ if the preferences are broken down across the lifespan. A societal norm should operate the same for everyone in that society, regardless of age. This slavish desire to do what is regarded as societally "normal" should be most pronounced among younger people, who are especially sensitive to gender-role norms (Deutsch et al., 1986). In fact, the difference in ages should be most pronounced among teenage males, who are most concerned with gender-role-appropriate behavior. An evolutionary perspective, however, suggests that the reproductive value of men and women, not societal norms, underlies gender differences in age preference. Female fertility peaks around age 24, and then declines more rapidly than does male fertility. In fact, men can father children until very late in life. Therefore, a man's preferred age for a partner should, as he ages, get progressively younger than

his own age. For a man in his forties, a woman of similar age would have few reproductive years left, but a younger woman would have many.

According to this view, teenage males should also be concerned with their partner's reproductive capabilities. A similarly-aged female would maximize the remaining reproductive years, but her fertility is lower. Contrary to the normative account, this reproductive exchange emphasis would predict that young males should not discriminate against women who are actually a few years older than they. Women, on the other hand, are looking for signs of status and wealth. Even though older males may lose physical resources (such as health and sexual arousability), they may gain indirect resources and social status.

Kenrick and Keefe (1992) conducted a series of archival analyses of age preferences in mates, and found results consistent with an evolutionary life-history model. Women's preferences, even when broken down by decade, were surprisingly consistent: Women of all ages specified men who were, on average, a few years younger to approximately 5 years older. When men's preferences were broken down by decade, however, they did not reflect the supposed normative pressure to marry someone several years younger. Men in their twenties were equally attracted to older and younger women, and older males expressed increasingly divergent age preferences. Men in their fifties and sixties showed a strong interest in younger partners. This same sex-differentiated pattern was found in singles advertisements from different regions of the United States (even those placed by "relatively wealthy" East Coast men and women) and in advertisements in Holland, Germany, and India. It was also found in marriage records from a Philippine island during the early years of this century (Kenrick & Keefe, 1992), as well as records from several traditional African cultures (Broude, 1992; Harpending, 1992). The body of evidence makes it difficult to argue that these preferences are due to the arbitrary norms of modern American society.

Even more problematic for a normative explanation are the preferences of younger men. Not only are men in their twenties interested in both younger and older women, but adolescent males (aged 12–18) indicated a range of ages extending much further above than below their own age (Kenrick et al., 1996). Moreover, their "ideal" partner was several years older than their own age. The norm to prefer slightly younger women is obviously not shaping their preferences, but they are perfectly consistent with the reproductive exchange model, as the most fertile females will be older, not younger, than a teenage male.

Intrasexual Competition

As described earlier, human evolution is also subject to intrasexual selection-competition among members of the same sex for mating opportunities (Darwin, 1859). Within most species, intrasexual competition occurs mainly among males, manifested as (1) aggressive behaviors designed to limit other males' access to females; (2) competition to range more widely in search of females; or (3) competition in courtship for females (Trivers, 1985). Intrasexual selection plays out somewhat differently for humans because both men and women contribute substantial resources to their offspring. Human males, for instance, do not typically engage in direct combat for access to females, as do elephant seals or bighorn sheep; neither do they display anything similar to the bright plumage of the peacock in order to entice discriminating women. In addition, an ill-fated mating is disproportionately costly for women, so women should be just as eager to attract a man who is willing and able to invest in the offspring as men should be to attract a healthy and fertile woman.

Human intrasexual competition is more likely to be waged by both men and women through differential skills at (1) locating mates; (2) demonstrating interest or availability; (3) acquiring resources desired by the opposite sex; or (4) altering appearance to look more attractive (Buss, 1988a). The most effective tactics for mate attraction should emphasize the characteristics most valued by the opposite sex. Buss asked subjects to describe the behaviors that people use to make themselves attractive to the opposite sex. Men and women expressed a high degree of similarity not only in their alluring behaviors, but also in the

rated effectiveness of those behaviors. For instance, having a good sense of humor and being sympathetic, well-mannered, and well-groomed were the most effective behaviors for both sexes. Buss also found results consistent with the predictions of a resource exchange perspective. Men were significantly more likely to engage in tactics related to the display of resources (e.g., flashing money to impress a partner), tactics that were also judged to be more effective than a woman's displaying resources. Women, on the other hand, were more likely to engage in tactics related to enhancing their appearance (e.g., wearing flattering make-up or dieting), tactics that were also judged to be more effective than men doing the same. In general, tactics of intrasexual competition are closely linked to characteristics desired in long-term partners (Buss & Barnes, 1986; Kenrick et al., 1990, 1993).

Jealousy

Selecting an appropriate mate is an essential element in successful reproduction. However, maintaining that relationship was also important to our ancestors, as a child with two devoted parents would be more likely to reach adulthood than a child with only one. Although we tend to associate jealousy with a variety of negative personal characteristics (cf., White & Mullen, 1989), it may also have had an adaptive function as a mate retention mechanism (Buss, 1988b; Daly & Wilson, 1983). Jealousy is both a pervasive (Buunk & Hupka, 1987) and potentially lethal reaction (Daly, Wilson, & Weghorst, 1982). Women and men from Hungary, Ireland, Mexico, The Netherlands, the Soviet Union, and the United States all express strong, negative reactions to thoughts that their partner might flirt or have sex with another (Buunk & Hupka, 1987). In addition, anthropological evidence indicates that jealous outbursts result in wife-beating and spousal homicide across a wide variety of cultures (Buss, 1994; Daly, Wilson, & Weghorst, 1982). Although jealousy is usually described as undesirable, its adaptiveness for our ancestors may have contributed to its widespread occurrence.

Both sexes can gain genetic fitness if their jealousy prevents a partner from being successfully courted by a rival: Women can prevent the loss of resources required to raise children and men can avoid threats to paternal certainty. Because fertilization occurs inside the woman's body, men risk investing valuable resources in another man's offspring, and any behaviors reducing this possibility would have been selected (Daly, Wilson, & Weghorst, 1982). Ancestral women were always certain of their genetic relatedness to their offspring, but had difficulty raising their highly dependent children without support. Women who could defend against threats to their relationship would thus be better able to raise their offspring to adulthood (Daly, Wilson, & Weghorst, 1982). So, both men and women lose when a relationship is torn apart, and jealousy may be one of the psychological mechanisms that activates mate-guarding strategies (Buss, 1994).

Given the differences in the relational threats experienced by men and women, the circumstances that elicit jealousy should differ between the sexes. Even though both men and women report similar *levels* of jealousy (Wiederman & Allgeier, 1993), men report more intense jealousy to a scenario describing their partners' sexual indiscretions (exaggerating concerns about paternity); and women report more jealousy to a scenario describing their partners' emotional attachment to a rival (which could cause the man to redirect his resources). This pattern was found not only in the United States (Buss et al., 1992; Wiederman & Allgeier, 1993), but also in Holland and Germany (Buunk et al., in press). Moreover, the sex differences were most dramatic when imagining an infidelity before it had occurred (Wiederman & Allgeier, 1993). Once an infidelity *has* occurred, it may be most adaptive to end the tainted relationship and find a new, potentially monogamous partner, especially for men. Cross-cultural evidence indicates that wives' infidelity is cited more frequently as a cause for divorce than husbands' infidelity (Betzig, 1989), even though men are more likely to have extra-marital relationships. Moreover, consistent with the general tendency for men to be more violent, men are significantly more likely to murder their partners during a jealous rage than are women (Daly, Wilson, & Weghorst, 1982). Assuming that

a couple's offspring were conceived before an infidelity occurred, this tendency to flee an unfaithful partner might be attenuated in couples who have children because, for most of our evolutionary history, children with both parents would have had a survival advantage over single-parent children.

Deceptive Strategies in Mating and Acquiring Resources

Animals have evolved a variety of elaborate systems of deception (Trivers, 1985). These mechanisms tend to take the form of either deceiving predators or deceiving competitors for valued resources, such as food or mates. As an example of a physical characteristic designed to deceive predators, the brightly colored bands of the non-poisonous shovelnose snake mimic those of the highly poisonous coral snake. Another approach to avoiding predators is to develop deceptive behavioral strategies. For example, female pronghorn antelope routinely distance themselves from their fawns, presumably to decrease predation by coyotes (Byers & Byers, 1983). Deceiving the competition to gain access to valued resources, such as food or the opposite sex, can also enhance genetic fitness. For instance, male scorpionflies mimic female courtship behaviors in order to lure other males into handing over their nuptial gift of food, intended to woo a real female. This single act has the double benefit of disadvantaging the competitor while increasing the deceptive male's likelihood of attracting a mate (cf. Trivers, 1985). As these examples illustrate, successful deceit can provide a survival advantage.

Although modern humans may not need to "change our stripes" to repel predators, our mating strategies often involve deceiving both competitors and potential partners (Tooke & Camire, 1991). Moreover, the types of deception exhibited in intrasexual competition and intersexual relations take a familiar pattern: Men and women deceive others about those characteristics that are most desired by the opposite sex. Women tend to enhance their bodily appearance through behaviors such as wearing perfume, suntanning, and walking with a greater swing than normal when around men. Men exaggerate their dominance or resources (e.g., wearing expensive "label" clothing they cannot really afford or misleading the partner about their career) and exaggerate their commitment (e.g., their sincerity, trust, vulnerability, and kindness). Men also engage in more intrasexual deception to create the illusion that they are more desirable to women than their competitors. For example, in their interactions with other men, men tend to elaborate on their superiority (e.g., intelligence, toughness), and to exaggerate their level of sexual activity, sexual intensity, and sexual popularity. Moreover, women use relatively passive deceptive techniques whereas men use active deception, in line with the notion that female choice limits male reproductive success and escalates the intensity of male–male competition.

Because hunter-gatherer groups were highly interdependent, the ability to detect violations of reciprocity in social exchange would be highly adaptive (Axelrod & Hamilton, 1981). Cosmides and Tooby (1989) argue that we may have evolved "social contract algorithms" allowing quick and effective detection of cheating. In line with this reasoning, Cosmides and Tooby (1989) found that students had great difficulty with an exercise in formal logic (called the Wason task) unless the content of the problem related to a standard social contract (costs vs. benefits). When the problem was framed in terms of "looking for a cheater", people easily solved the traditionally difficult logical problem. Cosmides and Tooby (1989) argue that, rather than having a brain that operates as a "general-purpose learning mechanism", the human brain is equipped with specialized algorithms that facilitate reasoning about social exchange problems with very little learning.

Violence in Relationships

Criminologists have frequently noted the high prevalence of homicide among family members. Gelles and Straus (1985) observed that: "With the exception of the police and the military, the family is perhaps the most violent social group, and the home the most violent social setting, in our society" (p. 88). Indeed, one of the classic studies

of homicide found that almost one-quarter of victims were "relatives" (Wolfgang, 1958). From the standpoint of models of kin selection and inclusive fitness, family violence seemed to pose a puzzle for evolutionary views of human behavior. However, a closer examination of the classic statistics indicated that most homicide victims labeled as "relatives" were not blood relatives, but spouses (Daly & Wilson, 1988b; Kenrick, Dantchik, & MacFarlane, 1983). Many were also step-relatives, who do not share common genes, but may compete for common resources. Children living with a step- or foster parent in two samples were 70–100 times more likely to be fatally abused than children living with both natural parents (Daly & Wilson, 1988b; Daly & Wilson, 1994). Relatives also spend more time together, providing more opportunities for conflict; however, the risk of homicide for unrelated co-residents is 11 times greater than the risk for related co-residents (Daly & Wilson, 1988b).

Daly & Wilson (1988a, 1989) have criticized prevailing cultural determinist explanations of homicide. The prominent criminologist Marvin Wolfgang, for instance, attributed the enormous gender difference in homicide he found to the "theme of masculinity in American culture" and the cultural expectation that females not engage in violence. Indeed, an examination of homicide statistics from the FBI's uniform crime reports indicates that, every year and despite changes in the overall rate of homicide, men commit over 80% of all homicides. However, to attribute any phenomenon to a particular culture requires cross-cultural comparisons (Daly & Wilson, 1989; Kenrick & Trost, 1993). In the case of homicide, Daly and Wilson note that the same gender difference appeared in every culture for which they found records and during every period of history they examined. In fact, the gender difference is somewhat less pronounced in American society than in other cultures—men never commit less than 80% of homicides in any society, and often commit closer to 100%. The universality of the gender difference fits with the parental investment and sexual selection models. Given that humans are mildly polygynous and that women select high-status men, it follows that men should be more competitive with one another everywhere. Further, male violence is particularly pronounced among males who are young, unmated, and resource-poor (Wilson & Daly, 1985). Homicide case reports show that male-male violence is most often precipitated by an encounter between acquaintances, one of whom challenges the other's position in the local dominance hierarchy by attempting to humiliate him (Wilson & Daly, 1985).

Examination of spousal homicides reveals that they tend to occur when the reproductive interests of men and women conflict. As we noted above, men, not women, face the danger of cuckoldry. Consequently, jealousy is the predominant reason for a man to kill a woman across cultures (Daly & Wilson, 1988a, 1988b). When a woman kills a man, she is less likely to be jealous of another woman and more likely to be protecting herself from the man's jealous threats (Daly & Wilson, 1988a). Daly and Wilson (1994) also found that, in the rare instances in which a father kills his own children, it is likely to be accompanied by suicide and/or uxoricide (wife-killing). Step-fathers who kill children are unlikely to commit suicide or kill their wives, but they are more likely to be brutal (beating the child to death). The authors suggest that step-fathers' murders seem to reflect feelings of antipathy towards their victims, whereas killings by genetic fathers indicate very different underlying motivations (accompanying suicide notes, for instance, often claim the motivation to "rescue" the children from a hopeless situation). Thus, the differential prevalence of step-parental murder, and the different means used, suggest different underlying conflicts that are consistent with inclusive fitness theory.

Rather than viewing homicide in terms of individual psychopathology, evolutionary theorists view it as the tip of the iceberg, revealing evolved coercive impulses in genetically important situations. Presumably, all humans possess the same cognitive mechanisms designed to elicit competitiveness and hostility in situations where survival or reproductive interests are challenged. Kenrick and Sheets (1994) asked people if they had ever had a homicidal fantasy, and if so, who and what caused it. Most men (75%) and women (62%) reported having had at least one homicidal fantasy.

Men's fantasies were more frequent, longer, and more detailed. Only 13% of the respondents had lived with a step-parent, and of those who had lived with a step-parent for over 6 years, 59% had at least one fantasy about killing that parent (compared to 25% for natural fathers and 31% for natural mothers). Thus, per unit of time spent together, homicidal fantasies were more likely to be provoked by step-parents, providing a complement to the statistics on step-parental abuse of children (Daly & Wilson, 1988b; Lenington, 1981).

Kinship, Friendship, and Altruism

Although there has been less work conducted on kinship, the theory of inclusive fitness leads to a number of predictions about the preferential treatment of relatives. Rushton (1989a) reviewed human and animal evidence linking genetic similarity with altruism, family relations, and friendship. Experimental research suggests that animals can recognize their kin, and are likely to treat them preferentially (Greenberg, 1979; Holmes & Sherman, 1983). For instance, rhesus monkeys are promiscuous, and it would be difficult for a male to know which offspring are his own. Nevertheless, blood tests matching adult males with the troop's young show that males treat their own offspring better than others (Suomi, 1982). Because of random variation and overlap between parents' genes, it is possible for children to have more genetic similarity to one parent than to another (Rushton, 1989a). There is evidence that human children who share more genes with their parents are perceived to be more similar to the parent than children who share fewer genes; to be seen as "taking after" the genetically-related parent more than the other. When a child dies, parents who perceive that the child "takes after" their side grieve more for the loss (Littlefield & Rushton, 1986). Compared with dizygotic twins, monozygotic twins are more altruistic, and more affectionate, towards one another (Segal, 1988). Finally, there is evidence that people choose friends who are genetically similar to them, and that the similarity cannot be fully explained as due to the tendency to choose friends who look like oneself (Rushton, 1989b).

Burnstein, Crandall, and Kitayama (1994) asked people about their inclination to help others who varied in genetic relatedness, age, and health. People were more inclined to help someone with whom they were more related (e.g., a nephew before a cousin of the same age). Most interestingly, helping genetic kin increased markedly in life-or-death situations and was linked to their reproductive capability. In everyday situations, people did the socially appropriate behavior–helping a grandmother in preference to a teenage sister, or a sick relative in preference to a healthy one. In life-or-death situations, however, helping was more likely to be directed towards those who would pass on shared genes–the teenage sister in preference to grandmother, and the healthy relative in preference to the sick one. These experimental findings, which indicate that kinship has a strong influence on life-or-death helping, are corroborated by studies of actual disasters, in which kin are helped first (e.g., Form & Nosow, 1958).

Shared genetic interests also influence the stability of romantic relationships. For instance, marriages with children from former unions have elevated divorce rates, but marriages in which the couple shares children are less likely to end in divorce (Daly & Wilson, 1988b). The importance of shared genetic interests is underlined by the fact that sharing children increases marital stability even though it decreases marital satisfaction.

The Cohesiveness of the Evolutionary Approach

The evolutionary approach is appealing for its intellectual cohesiveness and comprehensiveness. Although we have ranged over a wide variety of topics, from jealousy and violence through parenting and love, they are all closely connected.

The basic concepts of evolutionary psychology can be used to generate empirical questions about many topics. Consider, for instance, community psychology and social support. An evolutionary perspective could make predictions about the role of kinship networks in social support. As people are more likely to help kin in highly threatening situations, it might be hypothesized that, controlling

for degree of stress, psychological disorder might be lower for those surrounded by kin as opposed to non-kin. Depression has increased dramatically during this century. Is its incidence inversely related to the decrease in contact with kin that accompanies urbanization and the modern work environment? If so, depression would be less prevalent in those who have maintained close relationships with kin. Interesting questions can also be asked about evolutionarily important issues in life stress. For instance, the most stressful life events include events such as divorce, death of a spouse, and loss of a job (Holmes & Rahe, 1967), events that are directly connected to reproductive ability. Evolutionary hypotheses could be generated about the influence of gender, kinship networks, and the stage of life cycle on the stressfulness of these events. For example, Thornhill and Thornhill (1989) review evidence and theory on psychological distress from an evolutionary perspective.

Likewise, we might ask about the role of kinship and shared reproductive interests in Aron and Aron's (1986) measures of overlap between self and others, or the effect of concerns about "face" in dominance hierarchies. For example, Wilson and Daly (1985) noted that "saving face" was a central concern in homicides committed by young males, and Hogan (1982) considered evolutionary constraints on self-presentation in social groups. The evolutionary life history perspective assumes changes in reproductive behaviors at different ages that interact with variations in the social and physical environment (Belsky, Steinberg, & Draper, 1991; Kenrick & Keefe, 1992). For instance, we noted that some fish change from a small drab male into a large colorful male if a territory becomes available, and even a female in a harem may change sex if the male dies. Do analogous processes apply to humans? For instance, is the onset of puberty influenced by the availability of attractive members of the opposite sex (signalled by a favorable sex ratio or feedback from the opposite sex about a pre-adolescent's relative attractiveness)? Is the onset of menopause influenced by the existence of nearby healthy children and grandchildren? These questions are not necessarily meant to be exhaustive. However, all living beings, including contemporary humans, are conglomerations of mechanisms designed by millions of years of natural selection. Our task is to identify those mechanisms and how they interact with the social and physical environment. Humans are in many ways unique as a species, but so are kinkajous, vampire bats, and carpenter ants. An evolutionary perspective does not suggest that we ignore the unique adaptations of our species, only that we consider how they may be elucidated by the light of the most powerful set of principles applying to all living things.

An evolutionary perspective is completely compatible with an interest in cultural determinants of behavior (e.g., Barkow, Cosmides, & Tooby, 1992; Lumsden & Wilson, 1981). However, researchers considering culture should also consider regularities across cultures, in addition to some of the seemingly bizarre differences between "us" and "them". Emerging evidence of cross-cultural universals, such as those regarding love and marriage, flirtation, aggression, and mate criteria, suggest that underneath the surface variability there may be a similar core to human nature. Even cross-cultural differences, as in the case of marriage patterns, may reflect flexible underlying mechanisms. For instance, in cultures where there is a reasonable degree of promiscuity, paternal certainty is more problematic than in cultures with stronger norms of monogamy. In those cultures, maternal uncles may show relatively more interest in their sisters' children and relatively less interest in their wives' children (Daly & Wilson, 1983). This response makes sense from an evolutionary perspective because maternal uncles can be certain they share genes with their sisters' children. Considering culture through an evolutionary lens goes beyond cross-cultural universals, then, to consider how cultural practices reflect an interaction between ecological demands and the evolved cognitive and emotional mechanisms of our species.

Adaptively "Irrational" Mate Preferences

Researchers using an evolutionary framework are often confronted with questions stemming from false assumptions (cf., Buss, 1995; Kenrick, 1994; Kenrick & Trost, 1987; Tooby & Cosmides, 1992). However, one recurring question is still unanswered: What about homosexuality? Homosexuality results in a failure to reproduce, making it appear to be genetically maladaptive. However, the involvement of genetic proclivities, hormones, and neural structures contribute further to the puzzling biological status of homosexuality (e.g., Bailey & Pillard, 1991; Whitam, Diamond, & Martin, 1993; Ellis & Ames, 1987; LeVay, 1993). A variety of hypotheses have addressed the potential adaptiveness of homosexuality (c.f., Kenrick et al., 1995), and it is premature to assume that it is either solely a result of environmental influences or uninformative about evolved adaptive mechanisms.

Bailey et al. (1994) suggested that homosexual preference might actually be informative about heterosexual mechanisms. They found that homosexual women, like heterosexual women, were relatively uninterested in casual sex (c.f., Buss & Schmitt, 1993; Kenrick et al., 1990, 1993). Obviously, this avoidance is not due to a conscious analysis of the relative costs of pregnancy, or lesbians would be more favorable toward casual sex than heterosexual women. Bailey et al. also found gay men to be as interested in physical attractiveness as heterosexual men, suggesting that heterosexual men's interest in attractiveness may not simply be a by-product of media emphasis on female beauty. In general, Bailey et al. found the biological sex differences to be stronger than the effects of sexual orientation. In addition, the life span pattern of age preferences in homosexual males is exactly the same as that shown by heterosexual males: Young males want slightly older or younger partners, whereas older males prefer increasingly younger partners (Kenrick et al., 1995). These findings are difficult to explain in terms of either market-based rationality or cultural norms. Older homosexual males are not desirable to their preferred partners, for instance. Moreover, if media projections of the ideal member of the opposite sex determine preferences, homosexual men should, like heterosexual women, prefer relatively older partners. Instead, these data are more consistent with the notion that sexual attraction, like other adaptive systems, is a multi-faceted set of proximate mechanisms, each under the control of independent developmental processes (e.g., Buss, 1995; Tooby & Cosmides, 1992).

Modern evolutionary theorists assume that natural selection operates on specific environmentally triggered mechanisms, rather than producing individuals designed to think, feel and act in ways that are "generally adaptive". A generally adaptive organism is somehow presumed to be omniscient: to have prior knowledge about the particular genetic advantages likely to be gained from using each mechanism in each particular set of circumstances. The fallacy of that assumption can be demonstrated by considering a few mechanisms that appear to have evolved because of their past adaptive consequences. We have already mentioned the evolved preference for sweet tastes which, in the modern environment of abundant sugary foods, can lead to obesity and diabetes. However, this preference was selected under circumstances where it had, on average, a positive effect on survival. In the arena of sexual attraction, Shepher (1971) found that unrelated children raised in the same family-like kibbutz pods later showed a surprising lack of sexual and romantic attraction. Shepher argued that the unusual conditions of raising children together triggered a mechanism designed to dampen romantic attraction between siblings (thereby decreasing the danger of recessive gene combinations from incest). Again, the incest mechanism seems somewhat "irrational" when considered in isolation and in a novel, modern context.

From the modularity perspective, it becomes easier to understand how homosexual and heterosexual men can be alike in so many ways. By analogy, consider the case of vision, where we do not simply have a mechanism for "seeing" in general but a number of different structures for analyzing color, shape, movement, depth and other complex features of visual stimuli (Livingstone & Hubel, 1988). Given the central importance of reproduction to evolution, it would be surprising if the human brain had a single mechanism that controlled "reproducing like a male" vs. "reproducing like a female". Reproduction involves a series of very different tasks, including choosing a mate (weighing the relative importance of physical health, status, beauty and faithfulness), evaluating one's ability to attract a mate, making oneself attractive to a potential mate, competing with members of one's own sex for that mate, establishing an ongoing relationship, and so on (Buss, 1995; Kenrick & Trost, 1989). If these different processes, like the processes underlying vision or language, are controlled by independent mechanisms, we would not expect a change in one mechanism to be accompanied by reversals in all related mechanisms. If there is a biological mechanism that controls direction of sexual preference, it need not be accompanied by a complete reversal of other biological sex-typing mechanisms. Homosexual males clearly do not develop physically feminine secondary sex characteristics, such as wider hips and breasts, for instance. Hence, any biological mechanism involved in homosexual choice reflects not a global change in the "general" reproductive biology of the organism, but a much narrower change in one or a few specific cognitive mechanisms. Considered more broadly, this line of research suggests that even behaviors that seem anomalous may lead to interesting insights when considered in light of the emerging interdisciplinary synthesis of cognitive science and evolutionary biology.

Conclusion

The evolutionary perspective provides a comprehensive model of relationships, with the potential for elucidating and integrating all areas of relationship research. Beyond that, the model connects our work with cognitive science, anthropology and other areas of social science, as well as ecology, genetics, zoology and other sciences concerned with living organisms.

REFERENCES

Alcock, J. (1993). *Animal Behavior* (5th Ed). Sunderland, MA: Sinauer.

Aron, A. & Aron, E.N. (1986). *Love and the Expansion of Self: Understanding Attraction and Satisfaction* (pp. 19–67). Washington: Hemisphere.

Axelrod, R. & Hamilton, W.D. (1981). The evolution of cooperation. *Science*, **211**, 1390–96.

Bailey, J.M. & Pillard, R.C. (1991). A genetic study of male sexual orientation. *Archives of General Psychiatry*, **48**, 1089–96.

Bailey, J.M., Gaulin, S., Agyei, Y. & Gladue, B.A. (1994). Effects of gender and sexual orientation on evolutionarily relevant aspects of human mating psychology. *Journal of Personality and Social Psychology*, **66**, 1074–80.

Barkow, J.H., Cosmides, L. & Tooby, J. (1992). *The Adapted Mind: Evolutionary Psychology and the Generation of Culture*. New York: Oxford University Press.

Beach, F.A. (1976). Sexual attractivity, proceptivity and receptivity in female mammals. *Hormones and Behavior*, **7**, 105–38.

Belsky, J., Steinberg, L. & Draper, P. (1991). Childhood experience, interpersonal development, and reproductive strategy: an evolutionary theory of socialization. *Child Development*, **62**, 647–70.

Betzig, L. (1989). Causes of conjugal dissolution: a cross-cultural study. *Current Anthropology*, **30**, 654–76.

Betzig, L. (1992). Roman polygyny. *Ethology and Sociobiology*, **13**, 309–49.

Bolig, R., Stein, P.J. & McKenry, P.C. (1984). The self-advertisement approach to dating: male–female differences. *Family Relations*, **33**, 587–92.

Brehm, S.S. (1985). *Intimate Relationships*. New York: Random House.

Broude, G.J. (1992). The May–September algorithm meets the 20th century actuarial table. *Behavioral and Brain Sciences*, **15**, 94–5.

Brown, D.E. (1991). *Human Universals*. New York: McGraw-Hill.

Burnstein, E., Crandall, C. & Kitayama, S. (1994). Some neo-Darwinian rules for altruism: weighing cues for inclusive fitness as a function of the biological importance of the decision. *Journal of Personality and Social Psychology*, **67**, 773–89.

Buss, D.M. (1988a). The evolution of human intrasexual competition: tactics of mate attraction. *Journal of Personality and Social Psychology*, **54**, 616–28.

Buss, D.M. (1988b). From vigilence to violence: tactics of mate retention in American undergraduates. *Ethology and Sociobiology*, **9**, 291–317.

Buss, D.M. (1989). Sex differences in human mate preferences: evolutionary hypotheses tested in 37 cultures. *Behavioral and Brain Sciences*, **12**, 1–49.

Buss, D.M. (1994). *The Evolution of Desire: Strategies of Human Mating*. New York: Basic Books.

Buss, D.M. (1995). Evolutionary psychology: a new paradigm for psychological science. *Psychological Inquiry*, **6**, 1–30.

Buss, D.M. & Barnes, M.F. (1986). Preferences in human mate selection. *Journal of Personality and Social Psychology*, **50**, 559–70.

Buss, D.M. & Kenrick, D.T. (in press). Evolutionary social psychology. In D. Gilbert, S. Fiske & G. Lindzey (Eds), *Handbook of Social Psychology* (4th Edn). New York: McGraw-Hill.

Buss, D.M. & Schmitt, D.P. (1993). Sexual strategies theory: an evolutionary perspective on human mating. *Psychological Review*, **100**, 204–32.

Buss, D.M., Larsen, R., Westen, D. & Semmelroth, J. (1992). Sex differences in jealousy: evolution, physiology, and psychology. *Psychological Science*, **3**, 251–5.

Buunk, A.P. & Hupka, R.B. (1987). Cross-cultural differences in the elicitation of sexual jealousy. *Journal of Sex Research*, **23**, 12–22.

Buunk, A.P, Angleitner, A., Oubaid, V. & Buss, D.M. (in press). Sexual and cultural differences in jealousy: tests from The Netherlands, Germany, and the United States. *Psychological Science*.

Byers, J.A. & Byers, K.Z. (1983). Do pronghorn mothers reveal the locations of their hidden fawns? *Behavioral Ecology and Sociobiology*, **13**, 147–56.

Cameron, C., Oskamp, S. & Sparks, W. (1977). Courtship American style—newspaper ads. *Family Coordinator*, **26**, 27–30.

Clark, M.S. & Mills, J. (1979). Interpersonal attraction in exchange and communal relationships. *Journal of Personality and Social Psychology*, **37**, 12–24.

Clark, R.D. & Hatfield, E. (1989). Gender differences in receptivity to sexual offers. *Journal of Psychology and Human Sexuality*, **2**, 39–55.

Cosmides, L. & Tooby, J. (1989). Evolutionary psychology and the generation of culture. II. Case study: a computational theory of social exchange. *Ethology and Sociobiology*, **10**, 51–97.

Crawford, C.B. & Anderson, J.L. (1989). Sociobiology: an environmentalist discipline. *American Psychologist*, **44**, 1449–59.

Cunningham, M.R., Roberts, A.R., Barbee, A.P., Druen, P.B. & Wu, C. (1995). "Their ideas of beauty are, on the whole, the same as ours": consistency and variability in the cross-cultural perception of female physical attractiveness. *Journal of Personality and Social Psychology*, **68**, 261–79.

Daly, M. & Wilson, M. (1983). *Sex, Evolution, and Behavior* (2nd Edn). Belmont, CA: Wadsworth.

Daly, M. & Wilson, M. (1988a). *Homicide*. New York: Aldine de Gruyter.

Daly, M. & Wilson, M. (1988b). Evolutionary social psychology and family homicide. *Science*, **242** (October), 519–24.

Daly, M. & Wilson, M. (1989). Homicide and cultural evolution. *Ethology and Sociobiology*, **10**, 99–110.

Daly, M. & Wilson, M.I. (1994). Some differential attributes of lethal assaults on small children by stepfathers versus genetic fathers. *Ethology and Sociobiology*, **15**, 207–17.

Daly, M., Wilson, M. & Weghorst, S.J. (1982). Male sexual jealousy. *Ethology and Sociobiology*, **3**, 11–27.

Darwin, C. (1859). *The Origin of Species*. London: Murray.

Darwin, C. (1872). *The Expression of the Emotions in Man and Animals*. London: Murray.

Deutsch, F.M., Zalenski, C.M. & Clark, M.E. (1986). Is there a double standard of aging? *Journal of Applied Social Psychology*, **16**, 771–5.

deWaal, F. (1989). *Chimpanzee Politics*. Baltimore: Johns Hopkins University Press.

Eibl-Eibesfeldt, I. (1975). *Ethology: the Biology of Behavior* (2nd Edn). New York: Holt, Rinehart & Winston.

Ekman, P. (1992). An argument for basic emotions. *Cognition and Emotion*, **6**, 169–200.

Ekman, P. & Friesen, W.V. (1971). Constants across cultures in the face and emotion. *Journal of Personality and Social Psychology*, **17**, 124–9.

Ekman, P., Friesen, W.V., O'Sullivan, M., Chan, A., Diacoyanni-Tarlatzis, I., Heider, K., Krause, R., LeCompte, W.A., Pitcairn, T., Ricci-Bitti, P.E., Scherer, K., Tomita, M. & Tzavaras, A. (1987). Universals and cultural differences in the judgments of facial expressions of emotion. *Journal of Personality and Social Psychology*, **53**, 712–17.

Ellis, B. J. & Symons, D. (1990). Sex differences in sexual fantasy: an evolutionary psychological approach. *Journal of Sex Research*, **27**, 527–56.

Ellis, L. & Ames, M.A. (1987). Neurohormonal functioning and sexual orientation: a theory of homosexuality–heterosexuality. *Psychological Bulletin*, **101**, 233–58.

Form, W.H. & Nosow, S. (1958). *Community in Disaster*. New York: Harper.

Freeman, D. (1983). *Margaret Mead and Samoa*. Cambridge, MA: Harvard University Press.

Gelles, R.J. & Straus, M.A. (1985). Violence in the American family. In A.J. Lincoln & M.A. Straus (Eds), *Crime and the Family* (pp. 88–110). Springfield, IL: Thomas.

Givens, D.B. (1978). The nonverbal basis of attraction: flirtation, courtship, and seduction. *Psychiatry*, **41**, 346–59.

Greenberg, L. (1979). Genetic component of bee odor in kin recognition. *Science*, **206**, 1095–7.

Gross, M. (1984). Sunfish, salmon, and the evolution of alternative reproductive strategies and tactics in fishes. In G. Potts & R. Wootton (Eds), *Fish Reproduction: Strategies and Tactics* (pp. 55–75). New York: Academic Press.

Hamilton, W.D. (1964). The genetical evolution of social behavior. *Journal of Theoretical Biology*, **7**, 1–32.

Harpending, H. (1992). Age differences between mates in southern African pastoralists. *Behavioral and Brain Sciences*, **15**, 102–3.

Harrison, A.A. & Saeed, L. (1977). Let's make a deal: analysis of revelations and stipulations in lonely hearts advertisements. *Journal of Personality and Social Psychology*, **35**, 257–64.

Hill, K. & Hurtado, M. (1989). Hunter-gatherers of the new world. *American Scientist*, **77**, 437–43.

Hogan, R. (1982). A socioanalytic theory of personality. In M. Page (Ed.), *Nebraska Symposium on Motivation* (pp. 55–89). Lincoln, NE: University of Nebraska Press.

Holmes, T.H. & Rahe, R.H. (1967). The social readjustment scale. *Journal of Psychosomatic Research*, **11**, 213–18.

Holmes, W.G. & Sherman, P.W. (1983). Kin recognition in animals. *American Scientist*, **71**, 46–55.

James, W. (1890). *The Principles of Psychology*. New York: Holt.

Jankowiak, W.R. & Fischer, E.F. (1992). A cross-cultural perspective on romantic love. *Ethnology*, **31**, 149–55.

Kenrick, D.T. (1987). Gender, genes, and the social environment: a biosocial interactionist perspective. In P. Shaver & C. Hendrick (Eds), *Review of Personality and Social Psychology*, Vol. 7 (pp. 14–43). Newbury Park, CA: Sage.

Kenrick, D.T. (1994). Evolutionary social psychology: from sexual selection to social cognition. In M.P. Zanna (Ed.), *Advances in Experimental Social Psychology*, Vol. 26 (pp. 75–122). San Diego, CA: Academic Press.

Kenrick, D.T. & Keefe, R.C. (1992). Age preferences in mates reflect sex differences in reproductive strategies. *Behavioral and Brain Sciences*, **15**, 75–133.

Kenrick, D.T. & Sheets, V. (1994). Homicidal fantasies. *Ethology and Sociobiology*, **14**, 231–46.

Kenrick, D.T. & Trost, M.R. (1987). A biosocial model of relationship formation. In K. Kelley (Ed.), *Females, Males and Sexuality: Theories and Research* (pp. 58–100). Albany: SUNY Press.

Kenrick, D.T. & Trost, M.R. (1989). A reproductive exchange model of heterosexual relationships: putting proximate economics in ultimate perspective. In C. Hendrick (Ed.), *Review of Personality and Social Psychology*, Vol. 10. *Close Relationships* (pp. 92–118). Newbury Park: Sage.

Kenrick, D.T. & Trost, M.R. (1993). The evolutionary perspective. In A.E. Beall & R.J. Sternberg (Eds), *Perspectives on the Psychology of Gender* (pp. 148–72). New York: Guilford.

Kenrick, D.T., Dantchik, A. & MacFarlane, S. (1983). Personality, environment, and criminal behavior: an evolutionary perspective. In W.S. Laufer & J.M. Day (Eds), *Personality Theory, Moral Development and Criminal Behavior* (pp. 201–34). Lexington, MA: D.C. Heath & Co.

Kenrick, D.T., Gabrielidis, C., Keefe, R.C. & Cornelius, J.S. (1996). Adolescents' age preferences for dating partners: support for an evolutionary model of life-history strategies. *Child Development*, **67**, 1499–1511.

Kenrick, D.T., Groth, G.E., Trost, M.R. & Sadalla, E.K. (1993). Integrating evolutionary and social exchange perspectives on relationships: effects of gender, self-appraisal, and involvement level on mate selection. *Journal of Personality and Social Psychology*, **64**, 951–69.

Kenrick, D.T., Keefe, R.C., Bryan, A., Barr, A. & Brown, S. (1995). Age preferences and mate choice among homosexuals and heterosexuals: a case for modular psychological mechanisms. *Journal of Personality and Social Psychology*, **69**, 1166–72.

Kenrick, D.T., Sadalla, E.K., Groth, G. & Trost, M.R. (1990). Evolution, traits, and the stages of human courtship: qualifying the parental investment model. *Journal of Personality*, **58**, 97–116.

Kenrick, D.T., Stringfield, D.O., Wagenhals, W.L., Dahl, R.H. & Ransdell, H.J. (1980). Sex differences, androgyny, and approach responses to erotica: a new variation on the old volunteer problem. *Journal of Personality and Social Psychology*, **38**, 517–24.

Lenington, S. (1981). Child abuse: the limits of sociobiology. *Ethology and Sociobiology*, **2**, 17–29.

LeVay, S. (1993). *The Sexual Brain*. Cambridge, MA: MIT Press.

Littlefield, C.H. & Rushton, J.P. (1986). When a child dies: the sociobiology of bereavement. *Journal of Personality and Social Psychology*, **51**, 797–802.

Livingstone, M. & Hubel, D. (1988). Segregation of form, color, movement, and depth: Anatomy, physiology, and perception. *Science*, **240**, 740–49.

Lockard, J.S. & Paulhus, D.L. (1988). *Self-deception: an Adaptive Mechanism?* Englewood Cliffs, NJ: Prentice-Hall.

Lumsden, C.J. & Wilson, E.O. (1981). *Genes, Mind, and Culture: the Coevolutionary Process.* Cambridge, MA: Harvard University Press.

McDougall, W. (1908). *Social Psychology: an Introduction.* London: Methuen.

Mellen, S.L.W. (1981). *The Evolution of Love.* Oxford: W.H. Freeman.

Moghaddam, F.M., Taylor, D.M. & Wright, S.C. (1993). *Social Psychology in Cross-cultural Perspective.* New York: W.H. Freeman.

Moore, M.M. (1985). Nonverbal courtship patterns in women. *Ethology and Sociobiology*, **6**, 237–47.

Morris, D. (1972). *Intimate Behavior.* New York: Bantam.

Perper, T. & Weis, D.L. (1987). Proceptive and rejective strategies of U.S. and Canadian women. *Journal of Sex Research*, **23**, 455–80.

Pinker, S. (1994). *The Language Instinct.* New York: William Morrow.

Presser, H.B. (1975). Age differences between spouses: trends, patterns, and social implications. *American Behavioral Scientist*, **19**, 190–205.

Rajecki, D.W., Bledsoe, S.B. & Rasmussen, J.L. (1991). Successful personal ads: gender differences and similarities in offers, stipulations, and outcomes. *Basic and Applied Social Psychology*, **12**, 457–69.

Rushton, J.P. (1989a). Genetic similarity, human altruism, and group selection. *Behavioral and Brain Sciences*, **12**, 503–59.

Rushton, J.P. (1989b). Genetic similarity in male friendships. *Ethology and Sociobiology*, **10**, 361–373.

Sadalla, E.K., Kenrick, D.T. & Vershure, B. (1987). Dominance and heterosexual attraction. *Journal of Personality and Social Psychology*, **52**, 730–38.

Segal, N. (1988). Cooperation, competition, and altruism in human twinships: a sociobiological approach. In K.B. MacDonald (Ed.), *Sociobiological Perspectives on Human Development* (pp. 168–206). New York: Springer-Verlag.

Shepher, J. (1971). Mate selection among second generation kibbutz adolescents and adults: incest avoidance and negative imprinting. *Archives of Sexual Behavior*, **1**, 293–307.

Singh, D. (1993). Adaptive significance of female physical attractiveness: role of waist-to-hip ratio. *Journal of Personality and Social Psychology*, **65**, 293–307.

Stone, L. (1988). Passionate attachments in the West in historical perspective. In W. Gaylin & E. Person (Eds), *Passionate Attachments* (pp. 15–26). New York: Free Press.

Studd, M.V. & Gattiker, U.E. (1991). The evolutionary psychology of sexual harassment in organizations. *Ethology and Sociobiology*, **12**, 247–90.

Suomi, S.J. (1982). Sibling relationships in nonhuman primates. In M.E. Lamb & B. Sutton-Smith (Eds), *Sibling Relationships.* Hillsdale, NJ: Erlbaum.

Symons, D. (1979). *The Evolution of Human Sexuality.* New York: Oxford University Press.

Thiessen, D., Young, R.K. & Burroughs, R. (1993). Lonely hearts advertisments reflect sexually dimorphic mating strategies. *Ethology and Sociobiology*, **14**, 209–29.

Thornhill, R. & Thornhill, N.W. (1989). The evolution of psychological pain. In R.W. Bell & N.J. Bell (Eds), *Sociobiology and the Social Sciences* (pp. 73–103). Lubbock: Texas Tech University Press.

Thornhill, R. & Gangestad, S.W. (1994). Human fluctuating asymmetry and sexual behavior. *Psychological Science*, **5**, 297–302.

Tooby, J. & Cosmides, L. (1990). On the universality of human nature and the uniqueness of the individual: the role of genetics and adaptation. *Journal of Personality*, **58**, 17–67.

Tooby, J. & Cosmides, L. (1992). The psychological foundations of culture. In J.H. Barkow, L. Cosmides & J. Tooby (Eds), *The Adapted Mind: Evolutionary Psychology and the Generation of Culture* (pp. 19–136). New York: Oxford University Press.

Tooke, J. & Camire, L. (1991). Patterns of deception in intersexual and intrasexual mating strategies. *Ethology and sociobiology*, **12**, 345–64.

Trivers, R. (1985). *Social Evolution.* Menlo Park, CA: Benjamin/Cummings Publishing.

Trivers, R.L. (1972). Parental investment and sexual selection. In B. Campbell (Ed.), *Sexual Selection and the Descent of Man 1871–1971* (pp. 136–79). Chicago: Aldine.

Warner, R.R. (1984). Mating behavior and hermaphroditism in coral reef fishes. *American Scientist*, **72**, 128–34.

Whitam, F.L., Diamond, M. & Martin, J. (1993). Homosexual orientation in twins: a report on 61 pairs and three triplet sets. *Archives of Sexual Behavior*, **22**, 187–206.

White, G.L. & Mullen, P.E. (1989). *Jealousy: Theory, Research, and Clinical Strategies.* New York: Guilford.

Wiederman, M.W. (1993). Evolved gender differences in mate preferences: evidence from personal advertisements. *Ethology and Sociobiology*, **14**, 331–52.

Wiederman, M.W. & Allgeier, E.R. (1993). Gender differences in sexual jealousy: adaptionist or social learning explanation? *Ethology and Sociobiology*, **14**, 115–40.

Wilkinson, G.S. (1988). Reciprical altruism in bats and other mammals. *Ethology and Sociobiology*, **9**, 85–100.

Wilkinson, G.S. (1990). Food sharing in vampire bats. *Scientific American*, **February**, 76–82.

Wilson, E.O. (1975). *Sociobiology: the New Synthesis.* Cambridge, MA: Harvard University Press.

Wilson, M. & Daly, M. (1985). Competitiveness, risk taking, and violence: the young male syndrome. *Ethology and Sociobiology*, **6**, 59–73.

Wolfgang, M.E. (1958). *Patterns in Criminal Homicide.* Philadelphia: University of Pennsylvania Press.

Sex Differences in Human Mate Preferences: Evolutionary Hypotheses Tested in 37 Cultures

David M. Buss • University of Texas

Electronic mail: *dbuss@psy.utexas.edu*

Contemporary mate preferences can provide important clues to human reproductive history. Little is known about which characteristics people value in potential mates. Five predictions were made about sex differences in human mate preferences based on evolutionary conceptions of parental investment, sexual selection, human reproductive capacity, and sexual asymmetries regarding certainty of paternity versus maternity. The predictions centered on how each sex valued earning capacity, ambition–industriousness, youth, physical attractiveness, and chastity. Predictions were tested in data from 37 samples drawn from 33 countries located on six continents and five islands (total $N = 10{,}047$). For 27 countries, demographic data on actual age at marriage provided a validity check on questionnaire data. Females were found to value cues to *resource acquisition* in potential mates more highly than males. Characteristics signaling *reproductive capacity* were valued more by males than by females. These sex differences may reflect different evolutionary selection pressures on human males and females; they provide powerful cross-cultural evidence of current sex differences in reproductive strategies. Discussion focuses on proximate mechanisms underlying mate preferences, consequences for human intrasexual competition, and the limitations of this study.

Keywords: assortative mating; cultural differences; evolution; mate preferences; reproductive strategy; sex differences; sexual selection; sociobiology

Introduction

Mate preferences acquire importance in at least three scientific contexts. First, they can affect the *current direction* of sexual selection by influencing who is differentially excluded from and included in mating (Darwin 1871). Favored mate characteristics that show some heritability will typically be represented more frequently in subsequent generations. Individuals lacking favored characteristics tend to become no one's ancestors (Thornhill & Thornhill 1983). Second, current mate preferences may reflect *prior* selection pressures, thus providing important clues to a species' reproductive history. Third, mate preferences can exert selective pressures on other components of the mating system. In the context of intrasexual competition, for example, tactics used to attract and retain mates should be strongly influenced by the mate preferences expressed by members of the opposite sex (Buss 1988). Because of the powerful reproductive consequences of preferential mating, it is reasonable to assume that mate preferences will depart from randomness and evolve through sexual selection (Darwin 1859; 1871; Fisher 1930). This assumption, first advanced by Darwin, has been documented empirically for a variety of nonhuman species (e.g., Bateson 1983; Majerus 1986).

In spite of the importance of mate preferences, little is known about precisely which characteristics in potential mates are valued by human males and females (Buss 1985; Thiessen & Gregg 1980). Particularly lacking are good cross-cultural data. Cross-cultural studies become crucial for testing evolution-based hypotheses that posit species-typical or sex-typical mate preferences. Recent theoretical work by Trivers (1972), Williams (1975), Symons (1979), and Buss (1987) provides a foundation from which specific evolutionary hypotheses about mate preferences can be derived.

Predictions from Parental Investment and Sexual Selection Theory

Trivers (1972) posits that sexual selection is driven in part by different levels of investment by males and females in their offspring (Bateman 1948). In humans and other mammals, male parental investment tends to be less than female parental investment (Fisher 1930; Trivers 1972; Williams 1975). Mammalian fertilization occurs internally within females, as does gestation. A copulation that requires minimal male investment can produce a 9-month investment by the female that is substantial in terms of time, energy, resources, and foreclosed alternatives.

Investment, of course, does not begin with fertilization, nor does it end with parturition. Trivers describes several forms of male investment. Males may provide mates with food, find or defend territories, defend the female against aggressors, and feed and protect the young. Human males may also provide opportunities for learning, they may transfer status, power, or resources, and they may aid their offspring in forming reciprocal alliances. These forms of male investment, when provided, tend to decrease the investment disparities between males and females (Trivers 1972, p. 142).

Trivers's theory proposes that the sex investing more in offspring (typically the female) will be selected to exert stronger preferences about mating partners. This greater choosiness by the more heavily investing sex exists because greater reproductive costs are associated with indiscriminate mating and greater benefits are associated with exerting a choice. The costs of less discriminating mating will be lower for the sex investing less and the benefits will be greater. In species where investment in offspring by males and females is equivalent, the sexes are expected to be equally discriminating in their choice of mating partners (Trivers 1985).

What mate characteristics might be predicted on theoretical grounds in the selection preferences of females? In species with male parental investment, such as *Homo sapiens* (Alexander & Noonan 1979), females should seek to mate with males who have the ability and willingness to provide resources related to parental investment such as food, shelter, territory, and protection. Trivers's prediction should apply only in contexts where resources can be accrued, monopolized, and defended, where males tend to control such resources, and where male variance in resource acquisition is sufficiently high (Trivers 1972). The hypothesis that females will mate preferentially with males bearing greater gifts, holding better territories, or displaying higher rank has been confirmed empirically in many nonhuman species (Calder 1967; Lack 1940; Trivers 1985).

These resources can provide (a) immediate material advantage to the female and her offspring, (b) enhanced reproductive advantage for offspring through acquired social and economic benefits, and (c) genetic reproductive advantage for the female and her offspring if variation in the qualities that lead to resource acquisition is partly heritable.

Among humans, resources typically translate into earning capacity. This suggests that females will value characteristics in potential mates that are associated with increased earning capacity, such as ambition and industriousness (Barron 1963; Willerman 1979). These premises, combined with conditions of resource defensibility and high variance in male resource acquisition, produce a specific prediction: Females, more than males, should value attributes in potential mates such as ambition, industriousness, and earning capacity that signal the possession or likely acquisition of resources.

Predictions Based on Fertility and Reproductive Value

For males more than for females, reproduction is limited by access to reproductively valuable or fertile mates (Symons 1979; Trivers 1972; Williams 1975). *Reproductive value* is defined actuarially in units of expected future reproduction—the extent to which persons of a given age and sex will contribute, on average, to the ancestry of future generations (Fisher 1930). *Fertility* is defined as the probability of present reproduction. In human females, reproductive value typically peaks in the mid-teens and declines monotonically thereafter with age. Fertility typically peaks in the early 20s and shows a similar decrement with age (Thornhill & Thornhill 1983). The difference between fertility and reproductive value may be illustrated by contrasting two females, aged 13 and 23. The younger female would have higher reproductive value than the older one because, actuarially, her *future* reproduction is expected to be higher. In contrast, the 23-year-old female would be more fertile than the

13-year-old because the current probability of reproduction is higher for the 23-year-old.

Both fertility and reproductive value differ across cultures and are affected by factors such as cultural norms, contraceptive practices, and differences in age-specific mortality. In all cultures, however, female fertility and reproductive value are strongly age-dependent (Williams 1975). Thus, age provides a powerful cue to female reproductive capacity—a cue that can be inferred through physical and behavioral attributes or with veridical use of counting systems.

Males should prefer attributes in potential mates associated with reproductive value *or* fertility, depending on whether males in human evolutionary history have tended to seek long-term or short-term mating partners (Buss 1987; Symons 1979; Williams 1975). Specifically, if males in our evolutionary past have tended to seek short-term mating partners, selection should have favored male preferences for females in their early 20s who show cues that are positively correlated with fertility. If males in our evolutionary past have tended to seek long-term mating partners, selection should have favored preferences for females in their mid-teens who show cues indicative of high reproductive value. Evolutionary theorists differ on which of these hypotheses they judge to be most likely. Symons (1979) argues that males have been selected to find most attractive those females of high reproductive value. Williams (1975), in contrast, predicts a compromise preference between reproductive value and fertility due to the existence of both long-term mating bonds *and* some possibility of divorce and extrapair matings.

Features of physical appearance associated with youth—such as smooth skin, good muscle tone, lustrous hair, and full lips—and behavioral indicators of youth—such as high energy level and sprightly gait—have been hypothesized to provide the strongest cues to female reproductive capacity (Symons 1979; Williams 1975). Sexual attraction and standards of beauty are hypothesized to have evolved to correspond to these features. On this account, males *failing* to prefer females possessing attributes that signal high reproductive capacity would, on average, leave fewer offspring than would males who do prefer to mate with females displaying these attributes.

Female reproductive success, in contrast to male reproductive success, is not as closely linked with obtaining fertile mates. Male fertility, to the degree that it is valued by females, is less steeply age-graded from puberty on than is female fertility and therefore cannot be assessed as accurately from physical appearance. Physical appearance, therefore, should be less central to female mate preferences than to male mate preferences. These premises lead to specific predictions: Males, more than females, will value relative *youth* and *physical attractiveness* in potential mates because of their links with fertility and reproductive value.

Predicting that males will value physical attractiveness in females because of its association with reproductive capacity does not negate or deny the existence of cultural and other determinants of standards for attractiveness. Ford and Beach (1951) have documented cultural variability in standards for female attractiveness along the dimensions of plump versus slim body build, light versus dark skin, and emphasis on particular features such as the eyes, ears, or genitals. Symons (1979) suggested that regularity of features, proximity to the population average, and association with status might also have an important influence on attractiveness standards (see also Buss 1987).

The predicted sex differences in mate preferences for youth and physical attractiveness, however, are expected to transcend cultural variations and other determinants of beauty standards. The physical and behavioral cues that signal youth and health and are regarded as attractive should be linked with reproductive capacity among human females in all cultures. These sex differences are predicted to be species-typical among *Homo sapiens*, despite cross-cultural variations in absolute age preferences, the presence or absence of counting systems to mark age, or culture-specific criteria for female attractiveness that are not linked with reproductive capacity.

Prediction Based on Paternity Probability

In mating systems where males invest parentally, selection should favor males who act to insure

that their investment is directed toward their own offspring and not the offspring of another male. Sexual jealousy is one mechanism that has been proposed to increase paternity probability (Daly et al. 1982). Male sexual jealousy presumably functions to guard a mate and to dissuade intrasexual competitors, thus lowering the likelihood of alien insemination. Daly et al. (1982) and Daly & Wilson (1988) present compelling evidence that many homicides and much male violence stem from male sexual jealousy.

Another possible paternity probability mechanism is valuation of *chastity* in a potential mate (Dickemann 1981). Males who preferred chaste females in our environment of evolutionary adaptedness, *ceteris paribus*, presumably enjoyed greater reproductive success than males who were indifferent to the sexual contact that a potential mate had with other males. Prior to the use of modern contraceptive devices, chastity of a potential mate would provide a cue to paternity confidence. Assuming some temporal stability to behavioral proclivities, chastity would also provide a cue to the *future* fidelity of a selected mate. A male failing to express such a preference would risk wasting the time and effort involved in courtship and would risk investing in offspring that were not his (Daly & Wilson 1983; Dickemann 1981).

The association between chastity and probability of parenthood, however, shows a sexual asymmetry. In our environment of evolutionary adaptedness, maternity was never in doubt. A female could be sure that her putative children were her own, regardless of the prior sexual experiences of her mate. This sexual asymmetry yields a specific prediction: Males will value chastity in a potential mate more than will females. Evidence limited to a few cultures exists regarding the importance of a mate's lack of prior sexual experience in mate preferences (Borgerhoff Mulder 1988; Dickemann 1981).

It should be noted that this predicted sex difference would be compromised if prior sexual experience by a male provided a cue that signaled diversion of resources away from the female and her offspring. To the degree that prior sexual experience by males provides this cue, females should also value chastity in a potential mate.

In sum, three clusters of sex differences in mate preferences were predicted, based on an evolutionary account of differing male and female reproductive strategies. A woman's "mate value" (Symons 1987) should be determined more by her reproductive capacity. Youth and physical appearance, as powerful cues to this capacity, should be more highly valued by men. Chastity should also be valued because it functions to increase a male's probability of paternity. A man's "mate value" is determined less by fertility and more by the external resources he can provide. Characteristics indicative of one's potential to provide resources, such as earning capacity, ambition, and industriousness, should receive more emphasis in female mate preferences. The following study was designed to test these hypotheses in 37 cultures differing widely in ecology, location, racial and ethnic composition, religious orientation, political inclination, and nature of mating system.

Methods

Samples

Thirty-seven samples were obtained from 33 countries located on six continents and five islands, with a total N of 10,047. The samples range in mean age from 16.96 (New Zealand) to 28.71 (West Germany), with an overall unit-weighted mean of 23.05. Sample sizes vary from a low of 55 (Iran) to highs of 500 (mainland China), 566 (Taiwan, Republic of China), 630 (Brazil), 1,083 (West Germany), and 1,491 (mainland United States). All samples but one have Ns exceeding 100. The mean sample size for the 37 samples is 272. Obviously, greater confidence can be placed in the results from the large samples; results from all samples are presented for completeness.

The samples obtained cannot be viewed as representative of the populations in each country. In general, rural, less-educated, and lower levels of socioeconomic status are underrepresented, although there are many exceptions, such as the Soviet Estonian, Gujarati Indian, South African Zulu, Venezuelan, and Santa Catarina Brazilian samples. The 37 samples do represent a tremendous diversity of geographic, cultural, political, ethnic, religious, racial, and economic groups; combined, they are the largest ever obtained on mate preferences.

Sampling techniques varied widely across countries. In Estonia, for example, one subsample consisted of all couples applying for a marriage license at a certain location within a given time span, whereas another Estonian subsample consisted of 200 high school students. The Venezuelan sample was obtained by contacting every fifth house within each of a series of neighborhoods that varied in socioeconomic class. The South African Zulu sample was rural, and questions were read aloud to some subjects. The West German sample was obtained by mail through newspaper advertisements. The New Zealand samples were drawn from three public high schools, two urban and one rural, with subjects differing widely in socioeconomic level. Many were samples of convenience (e.g., university students) and cannot be viewed as representative. The wide variety of sampling techniques used tends to increase the generality of consistent results that do emerge by minimizing the biasing effects of any particular sampling procedure.

Problems were encountered, and data collection proved difficult and time consuming. In Sweden, many couples do not get married, but instead live together without the official marriage certificate. The instruments had to be modified to reflect this cultural difference. In Nigeria, polygyny is practiced, and so questions had to be added to reflect the possibility of multiple wives. In South Africa, data collection was described as "a rather frightening experience" due to the political turmoil and its violent ramifications. In several countries, mailing the data was delayed for many months, pending approval of central government committees. In one country, after data collection was nearly completed, the study had to be terminated because of a failure to obtain official sanction. Data from this country were never received.

In most cases, data were collected by native residents within each country and mailed to the United States for statistical analysis.

Measures

Factors in choosing a mate. This instrument consisted of three parts. The first part requested biographical data, including age, sex, religion, marital status, number of brothers, and number of sisters. The second section requested information on the age at which the respondent preferred to marry, the age difference the respondent preferred to have between self and spouse, who the respondent preferred to be older (self or spouse), and how many children were desired.

The third section requested subjects to *rate* each of 18 characteristics (e.g., dependable character, sociability, chastity, intelligence) on how important or desirable it would be in choosing a mate. A four-point scale was used, ranging from "3" (indispensable) to "0" (irrelevant or unimportant). The 18 characteristics were drawn from a previously developed instrument used widely within the United States over the past 50 years (Hill 1945; Hudson & Henze 1969; McGinnis 1958). Interspersed among the 18 characteristics were the target variables "good financial prospect," "good looks," "chastity: no previous sexual intercourse," and "ambition and industriousness."

Preferences concerning potential mates. The second instrument was developed from the factor analysis (Buss & Barnes 1986) of an expanded 76-item instrument (Gough 1973). The highest loading items from this factor analysis were included (e.g., religious, kind and understanding, exciting personality), along with several items to test the specific hypotheses about sex differences in mate preferences. Interspersed among the 13 characteristics were the target variables "good earning capacity" and "physically attractive."

In contrast to the rating procedure used in the first instrument, subjects were requested to *rank* each characteristic on its desirability in a mate. The instructional set was as follows:

> Below are listed a set of characteristics. Please *rank* them on their desirability in someone you might marry. Give a "1" to the most desirable characteristic in a potential mate; a "2" to the second most desirable characteristic in a potential mate; a "3" to the third most desirable characteristic, and

so on down to "13" for the 13th most desirable characteristic in a potential mate.

In sum, two instruments were used, each containing target variables to test the key predictions. They differed in context (presence of other items) and scaling procedure (rating vs. ranking), permitting a partial test of the generality of the findings across methods.

Translations. Instructions were provided to each research collaborator for translating the two instruments into the appropriate language for their sample. These included the use of three bilingual speakers who, respectively, (a) translated from English to the native language, (b) back-translated from the native language to English, and (c) resolved discrepancies between the first two translators. Instructions were provided to make all terms "sex neutral" in the sense of being equally applicable to males and females. The phrase "physically attractive," for example, could be applied to either sex, whereas "handsome" and "beautiful" were considered sex-linked and were therefore not used.

Results

Earning Potential and Ambition–Industriousness

Table 8.1 shows the means, standard deviations, *t*-tests for sex differences, and significance levels for valuation of the rated variable "good financial prospect" for each of the 37 samples. Samples vary considerably in how much this mate characteristic is valued, ranging from quite high (Indonesia, Nigeria, Zambia) to quite low (South African Zulu, Netherlands, Great Britain). In general, South American, North American, Asian, and African samples valued earning capacity more than did Western European samples, although there are important variations among samples within each continent.

In 36 of 37 samples, the predicted sex difference emerged—females valued "good financial prospect" in a potential mate more highly than males did. The sole exception was the sample from Spain, which showed the predicted direction

TABLE 8.1. Good Financial Prospect

Sample	Males Mean	SD	Females Mean	SD	t-test	Sig.
African						
Nigeria	1.37	0.82	2.30	0.76	−7.00	.000
S. Africa (whites)	0.94	0.78	1.73	0.78	−5.58	.000
S. Africa (Zulu)	0.70	0.87	1.14	0.80	−2.61	.006
Zambia	1.46	0.90	2.33	0.62	−6.35	.000
Asian						
China	1.10	0.98	1.56	0.94	−5.34	.000
India	1.60	0.96	2.00	0.69	−3.63	.000
Indonesia	1.42	0.87	2.55	0.57	−9.46	.000
Iran	1.25	1.04	2.04	0.85	−3.06	.002
Israel (Jewish)	1.31	1.01	1.82	0.87	−5.58	.000
Israel (Palestinian)	1.28	1.05	1.67	0.92	−2.05	.023
Japan	0.92	0.75	2.29	0.58	−15.97	.000
Taiwan	1.25	0.81	2.21	0.70	−15.16	.000
European–Eastern						
Bulgaria	1.16	0.94	1.64	0.91	−4.29	.000
Estonian S.S.R.	1.31	0.86	1.51	0.85	−2.06	.025
Poland	1.09	0.82	1.74	0.80	−6.18	.000
Yugoslavia	1.27	0.76	1.66	0.75	−3.07	.002
European–Western						
Belgium	0.95	0.87	1.36	0.88	−2.74	.004
France	1.22	0.97	1.68	0.92	−3.35	.001
Finland	0.65	0.76	1.18	0.84	−4.10	.000
Germany–West	1.14	0.88	1.81	0.93	−10.19	.000
Great Britain	0.67	0.63	1.16	0.78	−3.65	.000
Greece	1.16	0.95	1.92	0.78	−4.97	.000
Ireland	0.82	0.95	1.67	0.77	−5.51	.000
Italy	0.87	0.69	1.33	0.80	−3.06	.002
Netherlands	0.69	0.81	0.94	0.84	−3.00	.002
Norway	1.10	0.84	1.42	0.97	−2.03	.023
Spain	1.25	0.94	1.39	0.89	−0.80	ns
Sweden	1.18	0.90	1.75	0.75	−4.44	.000
North American						
Canada (English)	1.02	0.82	1.91	0.76	−5.61	.000
Canada (French)	1.47	0.83	1.94	0.63	−3.25	.001
USA (Mainland)	1.08	0.88	1.96	0.82	−20.00	.000
USA (Hawaii)	1.50	0.81	2.10	0.72	−5.10	.000
Oceanian						
Australia	0.69	0.73	1.54	0.80	−8.47	.000
New Zealand	1.35	0.97	1.63	0.75	−2.03	.022
South American						
Brazil	1.24	0.89	1.91	0.78	−9.91	.000
Colombia	1.72	0.90	2.21	0.75	−3.47	.001
Venezuela	1.66	0.96	2.26	0.78	−4.72	.000

Note. Potential mean values can range from 0 (unimportant) to 3 (indispensable).
Sig. = significance; ns = not significant.

of the sex difference, but not significantly so. The ranked variable "good earning capacity" similarly did not show a significant sex difference for the Spanish sample. Whether this lack of significant sex difference is due to particulars of the Spanish mating system, features of the broader socioecol-ogy, or chance sample fluctuation must await replication. In sum, with the exception of the Spanish sample, the predicted sex difference in preferences for mates with good earning potential was found across widely varying cultures, typically at a high level of statistical significance.

Table 8.2 shows analogous results for valuation of "ambition and industriousness." Across both sexes, the Nigerian, Zulu, Chinese, Taiwanese, Estonian, Palestinian, Colombian, and Venezuelan samples placed particularly high value on this mate characteristic. In no sample was ambition–industriousness rated low. Samples from the Netherlands, Great Britain, West Germany, and Finland, however, expressed less preference for this mate characteristic than did other samples.

Thirty-four of the 37 samples (92%) for ambition–industriousness were in the predicted direction, with females expressing a higher valuation than males. In 29 samples (78%), the sex difference was

TABLE 8.2. Ambition and Industriousness

Sample	Males		Females		t-test	Sig.
	Mean	SD	Mean	SD		
African						
Nigeria	2.25	0.68	2.61	0.56	−3.49	.001
S. Africa (whites)	1.73	0.84	2.16	0.70	−3.14	.001
S. Africa (Zulu)	2.41	0.81	2.10	0.73	2.02	.023
Zambia	1.97	0.92	2.14	0.75	−1.06	ns
Asian						
China	2.22	0.85	2.63	0.59	−6.41	.000
India	1.79	0.86	2.44	0.76	−6.31	.000
Indonesia	1.97	0.73	2.29	0.62	−2.70	.004
Iran	2.68	0.55	2.81	0.48	−0.98	ns
Israel (Jewish)	1.78	0.99	2.43	0.71	−7.66	.000
Israel (Palestinian)	2.28	0.76	2.58	0.71	−2.15	.017
Japan	1.92	0.71	2.37	0.62	−5.53	.000
Taiwan	2.24	0.73	2.81	0.42	−11.31	.000
European–Eastern						
Bulgaria	1.67	0.91	2.15	0.81	−4.63	.000
Estonian S.S.R.	2.31	0.68	2.46	0.64	−2.06	.020
Poland	1.93	0.84	2.29	0.72	−3.49	.001
Yugoslavia	1.82	0.72	2.24	0.74	−3.44	.001
European–Western						
Belgium	1.67	0.82	1.97	0.87	−2.01	.023
France	1.75	1.02	2.00	0.90	−1.79	.037
Finland	1.44	0.83	1.56	0.73	−1.07	ns
Germany–West	1.40	0.81	1.66	0.87	−4.23	.000
Great Britain	1.15	0.70	1.59	0.90	−2.84	.003
Greece	1.96	0.94	2.25	0.90	−1.81	.037
Ireland	1.44	0.88	1.76	0.81	−2.10	.019
Italy	1.63	0.85	2.07	0.94	−2.46	.008
Netherlands	1.28	0.97	1.41	0.93	−1.35	ns
Norway	1.60	0.80	1.70	0.87	−0.72	ns
Spain	1.73	0.90	1.69	0.98	0.22	ns
Sweden	1.97	0.78	2.04	0.76	−0.60	ns
North American						
Canada (English)	1.82	0.69	2.32	0.71	−3.53	.001
Canada (French)	1.79	0.85	2.08	0.75	−1.78	.039
USA (Mainland)	1.84	0.76	2.45	0.61	−16.66	.000
USA (Hawaii)	1.95	0.76	2.24	0.65	−2.66	.005
Oceanian						
Australia	1.38	0.92	1.82	0.77	−3.69	.000
New Zealand	1.57	0.76	1.86	0.53	−2.64	.005
South American						
Brazil	1.70	0.90	2.21	0.82	−7.25	.000
Colombia	2.36	0.80	2.24	0.90	0.80	ns
Venezuela	2.18	0.89	2.42	0.75	−2.03	.022

Note. Potential mean values can range from 0 (unimportant) to 3 (indispensable).

statistically significant beyond the .05 level. Three samples—Colombian, Spanish, and South African Zulu—show the opposite sex difference, significant only in the Zulu sample. According to the research collaborator who collected the Zulu data, it is considered women's work to build the house, fetch water, and perform other arduous physical tasks, whereas men often travel from their rural homes to urban centers for work. This local division of labor might account for the sex difference reversal among the Zulu. In sum, moderate support was found for the hypothesized sex difference in this cue to resource acquisition, although this difference cannot be considered universal.

Age Differences

Table 8.3 shows the age differences preferred between self and mate. In each of the 37 samples, males prefer mates who are younger, which is consistent with the hypothesis that males value mates with higher reproductive capacity. These sex differences are the largest ones found in this study, showing statistical significance beyond the .0001 level in each of the 37 samples. Do the age preferences males express for females correspond more closely to peak reproductive value (mid-teens) or to peak fertility (early 20s)? By subtracting the mean age difference preferred between males and their mates (2.66 years) from the age at which males prefer to marry (27.49 years), it can be inferred that males in these samples prefer to marry females who are approximately 24.83 years old. This age preference is closer to peak female fertility than to peak reproductive value.

Not specifically predicted, but also consistent across all countries, females prefer mates who are older than they are. Indeed, females appear to prefer a larger age difference (3.42 years older) than do males (2.66 years younger). Adding the mean age difference preferred by females to the age at which females prefer to marry (25.39 years) yields a preferred mate age of 28.81 years.

The samples vary strikingly in age difference preferences. Nigeria and Zambia are the two countries in which males prefer the largest age difference between self and mate, 6.45 and 7.38 years younger, respectively. These are the only two countries in this study that practice substantial polygyny. In polygynous mating systems, males are typically older when they acquire wives than is the case in monogamous mating systems (Hart & Pilling 1960; Murdock 1967).

Actual Age Differences at Marriage—A Validity Check

Two crucial questions can be posed about the validity of the methods and the reality of the preferences indicated by this study: Are self-reported preferences accurate indices of actual preferences? Are mate preferences reflected in actual mating decisions? To begin to address these questions, data were obtained from the most recent *Demographic Yearbook* (United Nations 1988) and the *Demographic Fact Book* on actual age at marriage. Demographic statistics were obtained for 27 of the 33 countries sampled in this study.

Actual age at marriage is not the same variable as preferred age at marriage or preferred mate age. Actual age at marriage is undoubtedly determined by many factors, including personal preferences, parental preferences, preferences exerted by members of the opposite sex, sex ratio, local availability of mates, and perhaps current resource holdings. Nonetheless, personal preferences, if they are to bear the conceptual importance ascribed to them in this study, should be reflected to some degree in actual mating decisions.

Actual age at marriage was estimated from the data presented for each country in the *Demographic Yearbook* and the *Demographic Fact Book*. Data in the *Yearbook* are broken down by age of bride and age of groom within each of a series of 5-year age brackets (e.g., 15–19; 20–24; 25–29). An estimated mean age of marriage was obtained by taking the mid-point of each of these age ranges and weighting this by the actual number of brides or grooms falling within the range. This must be regarded as an estimate or approximation of actual marriage age.

Several validity checks can be conducted by comparing these data with the preferred age at marriage, the age difference desired between self and mate, and the preferred mate age derived from these variables. Perhaps most central to this article are the comparisons between the age difference

TABLE 8.3. Age Difference Preferred Between Self and Spouse

Sample	Males		Females		t-test	Sig.	Actual age diff.
	Mean	SD	Mean	SD			
African							
Nigeria	−6.45	5.04	4.90	2.17	21.99	.000	—
S. Africa (whites)	−2.30	2.19	3.50	2.23	13.38	.000	3.13
S. Africa (Zulu)	−3.33	2.31	3.76	3.68	10.80	.000	2.38
Zambia	−7.38	6.39	4.14	1.99	12.22	.000	—
Asian							
China	−2.05	2.47	3.45	1.73	29.06	.000	—
India	−3.06	2.55	3.29	1.96	19.07	.000	—
Indonesia	−2.72	4.41	4.69	1.87	13.29	.000	—
Iran	−4.02	1.62	5.10	1.79	17.98	.000	—
Israel (Jewish)	−2.88	3.82	3.95	4.90	14.13	.000	3.57
Israel (Palestinian)	−3.75	1.99	3.71	1.86	6.66	.000	3.57
Japan	−2.37	2.29	3.05	1.62	20.98	.000	2.92
Taiwan	−3.13	2.29	3.78	1.98	36.76	.000	3.50
European–Eastern							
Bulgaria	−3.13	2.87	4.18	2.61	21.35	.000	3.54
Estonian S.S.R.	−2.19	2.58	2.85	1.52	22.69	.000	2.49
Poland	−2.85	2.94	3.38	3.02	14.66	.000	2.10
Yugoslavia	−2.47	2.29	3.61	1.98	16.29	.000	3.55
European–Western							
Belgium	−2.53	5.15	2.46	2.49	5.49	.000	2.37
France	−1.94	2.47	4.00	3.17	12.97	.000	2.28
Finland	−0.38	3.22	2.83	2.35	5.57	.000	2.30
Germany–West	−2.52	3.87	3.70	3.67	20.18	.000	3.19
Great Britain	−1.92	3.78	2.26	2.58	6.02	.000	2.61
Greece	−3.36	3.20	4.54	2.55	14.98	.000	4.92
Ireland	−2.07	1.93	2.78	1.91	12.79	.000	2.17
Italy	−2.76	2.77	3.24	2.41	10.85	.000	3.68
Netherlands	−1.01	2.51	2.72	3.01	9.82	.000	2.58
Norway	−1.91	4.14	3.12	2.36	7.80	.000	2.87
Spain	−1.46	2.43	2.60	4.25	5.92	.000	2.45
Sweden	−2.34	4.87	2.91	2.79	8.08	.000	2.97
North American							
Canada (English)	−1.53	1.93	2.72	2.01	10.15	.000	2.51
Canada (French)	−1.22	1.69	1.82	1.83	7.43	.000	2.51
USA (Mainland)	−1.65	2.62	2.54	1.90	31.76	.000	2.71
USA (Hawaii)	−1.92	2.46	3.30	3.25	11.57	.000	—
Oceanian							
Australia	−1.77	2.34	2.86	2.72	12.16	.000	2.73
New Zealand	−1.59	2.47	2.91	1.85	11.66	.000	2.78
South American							
Brazil	−2.94	3.35	3.94	3.23	22.06	.000	3.52
Colombia	−4.45	3.01	4.51	2.85	16.88	.000	4.53
Venezuela	−2.99	3.05	3.62	3.25	13.63	.000	3.47
Mean	−2.66		3.42				2.99

Note. Negative values signify preference for a *younger* mate; positive values signify preference for an *older* mate.

desired between self and mate and the actual age difference between marriage partners. These data are shown in Table 8.3 along with data on preferred age differences.

Across the 27 countries, the actual age differences between men and women at marriage range from 2.17 years (Ireland) to 4.92 years (Greece), all showing the wives to be younger on average than their husbands. The unit-weighted average age difference between husbands and wives across countries is 2.99 years. The present study found that males prefer their marriage partners to be 2.66 years younger on average, whereas females prefer mates to be 3.42 years older. Averaging across the sexes yields a mean preferred age difference of 3.04 years, which corresponds closely to the actual age difference of 2.99 years between spouses. Thus, preferred age differences between spouses are indeed reflected in actual age differences at marriage.

Physical Attractiveness

Table 8.4 shows the results for the rated variable "good looks." All 37 samples show sex differences in the predicted direction, with 34 significant

TABLE 8.4. Good Looks

Sample	Males		Females		t-test	Sig.
	Mean	SD	Mean	SD		
African						
Nigeria	2.24	0.67	1.82	0.72	3.65	.000
S. Africa (whites)	1.58	0.65	1.22	0.65	3.05	.002
S. Africa (Zulu)	1.17	0.80	0.88	0.68	1.94	.027
Zambia	2.23	0.85	1.65	0.84	3.72	.000
Asian						
China	2.06	0.62	1.59	0.68	8.17	.000
India	2.03	0.73	1.97	0.75	0.59	ns*
Indonesia	1.81	0.81	1.36	0.62	3.76	.000
Iran	2.07	0.73	1.69	0.68	1.97	.027
Israel (Jewish)	1.77	0.93	1.56	0.75	2.52	.006
Israel (Palestinian)	2.38	0.60	1.47	0.81	6.72	.000
Japan	1.50	0.75	1.09	0.74	4.36	.000
Taiwan	1.76	0.77	1.28	0.66	8.07	.000
European–Eastern						
Bulgaria	2.39	0.68	1.95	0.84	4.70	.000
Estonian S.S.R.	2.27	0.69	1.63	0.70	8.10	.000
Poland	1.93	0.83	1.77	0.76	1.57	ns*
Yugoslavia	2.20	0.66	1.74	0.72	3.86	.000
European–Western						
Belgium	1.78	0.84	1.28	0.79	3.58	.000
France	2.08	0.81	1.76	0.77	2.78	.003
Finland	1.56	0.81	0.99	0.73	4.79	.000
Germany–West	1.92	0.74	1.32	0.72	11.37	.000
Great Britain	1.96	0.60	1.36	0.72	4.76	.000
Greece	2.22	0.69	1.94	0.77	2.14	.018
Ireland	1.87	0.64	1.22	0.69	5.33	.000
Italy	2.00	0.70	1.64	0.83	2.36	.010
Netherlands	1.76	0.72	1.21	0.72	7.81	.000
Norway	1.87	0.83	1.32	0.83	3.85	.000
Spain	1.91	0.68	1.24	0.82	4.65	.000
Sweden	1.65	0.77	1.46	0.83	1.55	ns*
North American						
Canada (English)	1.96	0.50	1.64	0.71	2.55	.007
Canada (French)	1.68	0.64	1.41	0.65	2.00	.024
USA (Mainland)	2.11	0.69	1.67	0.69	12.19	.000
USA (Hawaii)	2.06	0.75	1.49	0.81	4.67	.000
Oceanian						
Australia	1.65	0.74	1.24	0.73	4.20	.000
New Zealand	1.99	0.69	1.29	0.73	5.98	.000
South American						
Brazil	1.89	0.75	1.68	0.86	3.25	.001
Colombia	1.56	0.79	1.22	0.75	2.63	.005
Venezuela	1.76	0.90	1.27	0.98	3.64	.000

Note. *indicates significant in predicted direction on the ranking procedure for variable "physically attractive."

beyond the .05 level. For those three countries (India, Poland, and Sweden) in which the difference was not significant for "good looks," the sex difference was significant in the predicted direction for the ranked variable "physically attractive." Thus, the hypothesis that males value physical attractiveness in potential mates more than females do is strongly supported by these cross-cultural data.

Chastity: No Previous Sexual Intercourse

Table 8.5 shows the results for the variable of "chastity: no previous experience in sexual intercourse."

TABLE 8.5. Chastiy: No Previous Experience in Sexual Intercourse

	Males		Females			
Sample	Mean	SD	Mean	SD	*t*-test	Sig.
African						
Nigeria	1.22	1.10	0.51	0.72	4.97	.000
S. Africa (whites)	1.06	1.05	0.84	1.12	1.13	ns
S. Africa (Zulu)	1.17	1.06	0.31	0.62	4.82	.000
Zambia	1.66	1.03	0.98	1.03	3.29	.001
Asian						
China	2.54	0.82	2.61	0.77	−1.03	ns
India	2.44	0.98	2.17	1.11	1.95	.027
Indonesia	2.06	1.10	1.98	1.18	0.39	ns
Iran	2.67	0.88	2.23	0.99	1.70	.049
Israel (Jewish)	0.93	1.12	0.58	0.97	3.46	.001
Israel (Palestinian)	2.24	1.10	0.96	1.18	5.81	.000
Japan	1.42	1.09	0.78	0.86	5.17	.000
Taiwan	2.32	0.85	2.20	0.91	1.71	.040
European–Eastern						
Bulgaria	0.69	0.90	0.44	0.86	2.31	.011
Estonian S.S.R.	1.25	1.04	0.84	0.98	3.51	.001
Poland	1.23	1.03	0.99	1.03	1.80	.031
Yugoslavia	0.47	0.81	0.08	0.36	3.60	.001
European–Western						
Belgium	0.67	1.02	0.38	0.72	1.89	.031
France	0.45	0.88	0.41	0.81	0.30	ns
Finland	0.27	0.59	0.29	0.67	−0.17	ns
Germany–West	0.34	0.73	0.17	0.52	3.61	.000
Great Britain	0.46	0.75	0.49	0.93	−0.20	ns
Greece	0.48	0.85	0.40	0.88	0.51	ns
Ireland	1.49	1.03	1.47	1.08	0.11	ns
Italy	0.65	0.92	0.27	0.53	2.47	.008
Netherlands	0.29	0.69	0.29	0.69	−0.01	ns
Norway	0.31	0.72	0.30	0.74	0.08	ns
Spain	0.66	0.96	0.36	0.73	1.92	.029
Sweden	0.25	0.53	0.28	0.67	−0.32	ns
North American						
Canada (English)	0.55	0.76	0.33	0.80	1.41	ns
Canada (French)	0.62	0.95	0.33	0.68	1.58	ns
USA (Mainland)	0.85	0.96	0.52	0.85	6.88	.000
USA (Hawaii)	0.91	0.94	0.58	0.87	2.33	.011
Oceanian						
Australia	0.73	0.93	0.45	0.86	2.40	.009
New Zealand	0.88	1.07	0.72	1.04	0.91	ns
South American						
Brazil	0.93	1.08	0.36	0.78	7.32	.000
Colombia	1.27	1.06	0.30	0.61	6.33	.000
Venezuela	0.93	1.07	0.59	0.97	2.35	.010

Cultures in this study vary tremendously in the value placed on this mate characteristic. The samples from China, India, Indonesia, Iran, Taiwan, and Israel (Palestinian Arabs only) attach high value to chastity in a potential mate. At the opposite extreme, samples from Sweden, Norway, Finland, the Netherlands, West Germany, and France indicate that prior sexual experience is irrelevant or unimportant in a potential mate. A few subjects even indicated in writing that chastity was *undesirable* in a potential mate. The Irish sample departs from the other Western European samples in placing moderate emphasis on chastity. Also showing moderate valuation of chastity are samples from Africa, Japan, Poland, and the Soviet republic of Estonia. It is noteworthy that chastity shows greater cross-cultural variability than any other rated variable in this study.

In contrast to the strong cross-cultural consistency of sex differences found with the previous four variables, only 23 (62%) of the samples show significant sex differences in the predicted direction. The remaining 14 samples (38%) show no significant sex differences in valuation of chastity. These results provide only moderate support for the evolution-based paternity probability hypothesis. They also yield equally powerful evidence of proximate cultural influences on the degree of importance placed on lack of prior sexual intercourse in a potential mate.

Conclusions

Each of the five evolution-based predictions received some empirical support from these data. Females value the financial capacity of potential mates more than males do. Ambition and industriousness, cues to resource acquisition, also tend to be valued more heavily by females than by males across cultures. Support was strong for the financial capacity prediction (36 of 37 samples), and moderate for the ambition–industriousness prediction (29 of 37 samples).

Although these results give powerful support to the evolution-based hypothesis about female preference for males with high providing capacity,

the precise functions of this preference remain obscure. By way of comparison, the male arctic tern's ability to bring food to the female during courtship is a good predictor of his ability to feed chicks (Nisbet 1973). Does earning potential provide a similar cue in humans? Or does it provide a cue to increased status, protection, and perhaps even "good genes" (Trivers 1972) that pass to the female's offspring? Future research is needed to identify these functions and to examine characteristics that signal not just the capacity to acquire resources, but the male's *willingness* to devote those resources to a female and her offspring.

Males value physical attractiveness and relative youth in potential mates more than do females— sex differences that show remarkable generality across cultures. Our demographic data corroborate the preference data, showing that females are younger than males at actual age of marriage. The greater male preference for relative youth and physical attractiveness supports the evolution-based hypothesis about male preference for females showing cues to high reproductive capacity. These findings are especially noteworthy in that they reverse a general trend in these data suggesting that females in a majority of cultures tend to be more exacting in mate preferences across many characteristics. Although cultural variations exist with respect to standards of beauty, these variations apparently do not override sex differences in the importance attached to physical attractiveness.

The male age preference for females of just under 25 years implies that *fertility* has been a stronger ultimate cause of mate preferences than reproductive value. Not specifically predicted was the finding that *females prefer somewhat older mates* in all 37 cultures. This finding, in conjunction with the known positive correlation between age and income among males (Jencks 1979; Willerman 1979), provides additional circumstantial evidence for the hypothesis that females prefer mates who show characteristics associated with having a high providing capacity. Older male age also could provide a cue to longevity, maturity, prowess, confidence, judgment, or experience (cf. Ellis, in preparation; Symons 1979). Further research is needed to uncover the functions of this cross-culturally robust female preference for older males.

The fifth evolution-based prediction, that males would value *chastity* in potential mates more than would females, was supported in 23 out of the 37 samples. In the remaining 14 samples, no significant sex differences emerged. Samples from Africa, the Middle East, South America, and Eastern Europe generally show the predicted sex differences in preferences for chastity in a potential mate. Many of the samples indicating no sex differences were concentrated in Western Europe, Canada, New Zealand, China, and Indonesia. These results provide modest support for the evolutionary hypothesis based on paternity probability. The wide variation in preference for chastity suggests that cultural differences, ecological differences, or mating system differences exert powerful effects on the value attached to chastity.

In sum, three of the five predictions—those involving mate preferences for earning potential, relative youth, and physical attractiveness—were strongly confirmed across cultures. The prediction regarding ambition–industriousness was confirmed only in 29 samples, and showed a significant reversal among the Zulu. The chastity prediction received still less empirical support, with only 23 of the 37 samples showing significant sex differences.

Qualifications and Limitations

Several important qualifications must attend the interpretation of these findings. First, the samples cannot be viewed as representative of the populations of each country; rural and less-educated individuals are underrepresented, although the samples of such individuals in this study indicate no departure from the primary predicted sex differences. Second, male and female preference distributions overlap considerably, in spite of mean differences. Third, neither earning potential nor physical appearance emerged as the highest rated or ranked characteristic for either sex, even though these characteristics showed large sex differences. *Both* sexes ranked the characteristics "kind–understanding" and "intelligent" higher than earning power and attractiveness in all samples, suggesting that species-typical mate preferences may be more potent than sex-linked preferences.

Other limitations surround the instruments, data sources, and operationalizations of the key constructs. Self-report contains obvious limitations and should be supplemented by alternative data sources in future studies. The close correspondence between the demographic data showing actual age at marriage data and the expressed mate preference data, however, suggests that we need not be pessimistic about the capacity of individuals to report preferences that are reflected in their actual mating decisions. Another limitation is that the single items used here may underestimate the magnitudes of the present sex differences, as they tend to be less reliable than composite clusters of items (Nunally 1978). And the set of characteristics representing each construct could be expanded to assess other mate characteristics such as the willingness of a male to invest resources, the willingness of a female to devote reproductive capacity to a given male, and behavioral cues associated with both proclivities.

A potential limitation involves the particular cultures selected for study. These samples are biased toward urbanized, cash-economy cultures. Less urbanized, non-cash cultures obviously must be studied to circumvent this bias. The tremendous cultural variability with respect to chastity, however, belies the notion that these 37 samples might somehow be culturally homogeneous and gives greater credibility to the empirical sex differences that transcend this cultural diversity.

Arranged marriages in some cultures pose another potential problem. If parents and other kin arrange marriages, how could mate preferences evolve or be expressed? We lack knowledge about the prevalence of arranged marriages in our environment of evolutionary adaptedness. Nonetheless, two factors mitigate this potential problem. First, if parents do arrange the marriages of their children, there is no reason to assume that they would not express preferences reflecting the reproductive considerations on which the central hypotheses here have been based. Research on parents' preferences for the mates of their sons and daughters is needed to confirm or falsify this speculation. Second, even in societies with arranged marriages, sons and daughters do exert choice. Offspring influence their parents' choices, carry on clandestine affairs, defy their parents' wishes, make threats of various sorts, and sometimes simply elope with a preferred mate (O'Kelly & Carney 1986). Personal preferences appear to be expressed even under socially constrained conditions.

Finally, these results yield little information about the proximate (social, psychological, physiological, ontogenetic) mechanisms directly responsible for their existence. Possible candidates include genetic differences between the sexes, sensory preferences analogous to food preferences, socialization differences during development, and structural effects at a societal level such as those that limit female access to economic resources (Buss & Barnes 1986). Although the evolutionary hypotheses presented here are largely supported by the results, research on proximate mechanisms is needed to develop a more complete explanatory account of observed sex differences in mate preferences.

Implications

This is the first study to examine human mate preferences across cultures on a broad scale (cf. Kurian 1979). It exceeds prior studies in geographic, cultural, political, economic, ethnic, religious, and racial diversity. However, many questions remain unanswered. Currently unknown are the cultural and ecological causes of variation from country to country in (1) the magnitudes of obtained sex differences, and (2) the absolute levels of valuing reproductively relevant mate characteristics. The internationally consistent sex differences in mate preferences found here, however, yield insight into human reproductive history, provide hypotheses about current sexual selection, and are among the most robust psychological sex

differences of any kind ever documented across cultures (cf. Willerman 1979).

What do these results reveal about human reproductive history? They support the hypothesis that males and females have faced different constraints on reproductive success in our evolutionary past. Females appear to have been limited in reproductive success by access to resources for self and offspring. Males appear to have been limited by access to fertile females. These different selection pressures have presumably produced different male and female reproductive strategies. The greater female preference for mates displaying cues to high resource potential and the greater male preference for mates displaying cues to high reproductive capacity appear to represent adaptations to sex-differentiated reproductive constraints in our evolutionary past.

What do these results reveal about current sexual selection? No definitive answer can be provided, as we lack data on reproductive differences associated with the expression of mate preferences. The findings, however, have strong implications for human intrasexual competition—a key component of Darwin's theory of sexual selection. Mate preferences should influence intrasexual competition such that males compete with each other to display the resources that females desire in mates; females should compete with each other to display the reproductively linked cues that males desire in mates (Buss 1988). Furthermore, mate preferences should affect opposite sex intrasexual maneuvers, such as tactics used to guard or retain mates (Flinn 1988), tactics used for mate poaching, and perhaps tactics used to derogate intrasexual competitors (Buss & Dedden, 1988). These now established sex differences in mate preferences across 37 cultures provide a foundation for testing hypotheses about human intrasexual competition on an international scale.

ACKNOWLEDGMENTS

Special thanks go to research collaborators of the International Mate Selection Project: M. Abbott, A. Angleitner, A. Asherian, A. Biaggio, A. Blanco, H.Y. Ch'u, B. Ekehammar, J. Czapinski, B. DeRaad, M. Fioravanti, J. Georgas, P. Gjerde, R. Guttman, F. Hazan, S. Iwawaki, N. Janakiramaiah, F. Khosroshahi,

S. Kreitler, L. Lachenicht, M. Lee, K. Liik, S. Makim, S. Mika, M. Moadel-Shahidi, G. Moane, A. Mundy-Castle, B. Little, M. Montero, E. Nsenduluka, T. Niit, R. Pienkowski, A. Pirttila-Backman, J. Ponce de Leon, J. Rousseau, M. Runco, M. Safir, C. Samuels, R. Sanitioso, B. Schweitzer, R. Serpell, N. Smid, C. Spencer, M. Tadinac, E. Todorova, K. Troland, L. Van den Brande, G. Van Heck, L. Van Langenhove, and K. S. Yang.

REFERENCES

Alexander, R.D., & Noonan, K.M. (1979). Concealment of ovulation, parental care, and human social evolution. In Chagnon, N.A., & Irons, E.G. (Eds.), *Evolutionary Biology and Human Social Behavior: An Anthropological Perspective*. MA: Duxbury Press.

Barron, F. (1963). *Creativity and Psychological Health*. New York: Van Nostrand.

Bateman, A.J. (1948). Intrasexual selection in Drosophila. *Heredity, 2*, 349–368.

Bateson, P. (1983). *Mate Choice*. Cambridge: Cambridge University Press.

Borgerhoff Mulder, M. (1988). Kipsigis bridewealth payments. In Betzig, L.L., Borgerhoff Mulder, M., & P.W. Turke (Eds.), *Human Reproductive Behavior: A Darwinian Perspective*. Cambridge: Cambridge University Press, pp. 65–82.

Buss, D.M. (1985). Human mate selection. *American Scientist, 73*, 47–51.

Buss, D.M. (1987). Sex differences in human mate selection criteria: An evolutionary perspective. In Crawford, C., Smith, M., & Krebs, D. (Eds.), *Sociobiology and Psychology: Ideas, Issues, and Applications*. Hillsdale, NJ.: Erlbaum.

Buss, D.M. (1988). The evolution of human intrasexual competition: Tactics of mate attraction. *Journal of Personality and Social Psychology, 54*, 616–628.

Buss, D.M. (in press). From vigilance to violence: Tactics of mate retention in American undergraduates. *Ethology and Sociobiology, 9*.

Buss, D.M., & Barnes, M.F. (1986). Preferences in human mate selection. *Journal of Personality and Social Psychology, 50*, 559–570.

Buss, D.M., & Dedden, L. (1988). *Derogation of competitors*. Manuscript under editorial review.

Calder, C. (1967). Breeding behavior of the roadrunner *Geococcyx Californianus. Aux, 84*, 597–598.

Daly, M., & Wilson, M. (1983). *Sex, Evolution, and Behavior*. Boston: Willard Grant Press.

Daly, M., & Wilson, M. (1988). *Homicide*. New York: Aldine de Gruyter.

Daly, M., Wilson, M., & Weghorst, S.J. (1982). Male sexual jealousy. *Ethology and Sociobiology, 3*, 11–27.

Darwin, C. (1859). *On the Origin of the Species by Means of Natural Selection, or Preservation of Favoured Races in the Struggle for Life*. London: Murray.

Darwin, C. (1871). *The Descent of Man and Selection in Relation to Sex*. London: Murray.

Dickemann, M. (1981). Paternal confidence and dowry competition: A biocultural analysis or purdah. In Alexander, R.D., & Tinkle, D.W. (Eds.), *Natural Selection and Social Behavior*. New York: Chiron Press.

Ellis, B. (in preparation). *The Evolution of Sexual Attraction: Evaluative Mechanisms in Men and Women*. Unpublished manuscript.

Fisher, R.A. (1930). *The Genetical Theory of Natural Selection*. Oxford: Clarendon Press.

Flinn, M. (1988). Mate guarding in a Trinidadian village. *Ethology and Sociobiology*.

Ford, C.S., & Beach, F.A. (1951). *Patterns of Sexual Behavior*. New York: Harper & Row.

Gough, H.G. (1973). Personality assessment in the study of population. In Fawcett, J.T. (Ed.). *Psychological Perspectives on Population*, pp. 329–353. New York: Basic Books.

Hart, C.W., & Pilling, A.R. (1960). *The Tiwi of North Australia*. New York: Holt, Rinehart, & Winston.

Hill, R. (1945). Campus values in mate selection. *Journal of Home Economics, 37*, 554–558.

Hudson, J.W., & Henze, L.F. (1969). Campus values in mate selection: A replication. *Journal of Marriage and the Family, 31*, 772–775.

Jencks, C. (1979). Who gets ahead? *The Determinants of Economic Success in America*. New York: Basic Books.

Kurian, G. (1979). *Cross-cultural Perspectives of Mate-Selection and Marriage*. Kurian, G. (Ed.). Westport, CT: Greenwood.

Lack, D. (1940). Pair formation in birds. *Condor, 42*, 269–286.

Majerus, M. (1986). The genetics and evolution of female choice. *Trends in Ecology and Evolution, 1*, 1–7.

McGinnis, R. (1958). Campus values in mate selection. *Social Forces, 35*, 368–373.

Ministry of the Interior. (1987). *1986 Taiwan-Fukien Demographic Fact Book: Republic of China*. Taipei, Taiwan, China.

Murdock, G.P. (1967). *Ethnographic Atlas*. Pittsburgh: University Press.

Murstein, B.I. (1986). *Paths to Marriage*. Beverly Hills: Sage Publications.

Nisbet, I.C.T. (1973). Courtship feeding, egg-size and breeding success in common terns. *Nature, 241*, 141–142.

Nunally, J. (1978). *Psychometric Theory*. New York: McGraw-Hill.

O'Kelly, C.G., & Carney, L.S. (1986). *Women and Men in Society: Cross-cultural Perspectives on Gender Stratification*. Belmont, CA: Wadsworth Publishing Company.

Symons, D. (1979). *The Evolution of Human Sexuality*. New York: Oxford University Press.

Symons, D. (1987). Can Darwin's view of life shed light on human sexuality? In Geer, J.H., and O'Donohue, W.T. (Eds.), *Approaches and Paradigms in Human Sexuality*. New York: Plenum.

Thiessen, D.D., & Gregg, B. (1980). Human assortative mating and genetic equilibrium. *Ethology and Sociobiology, 1,* 111–114.

Thornhill, R., & Thornhill, N.W. (1983). Human rape: An evolutionary analysis. *Ethology and Sociobiology. 4,* 63–99.

Trivers, R.L. (1972). Parental investment and sexual selection. In Campbell, B. (Ed.), *Sexual Selection and the Descent of Man*, pp. 1871–1971. Chicago: Aldine.

Trivers, R. (1985). *Social Evolution*. Menlo Park, CA: Benjamin/Cummings.

United Nations. (1988). *1986 Demographic Yearbook*. New York: United Nations.

Willerman, L. (1979). *The Psychology of Individual and Group Differences*. San Francisco: Freeman.

Williams, G.C. (1975). *Sex and Evolution*. Princeton, NJ: University Press.

Attachment as an Organizational Framework for Research on Close Relationships

Cindy Hazan • Cornell University

Phillip R. Shaver • University of California, Davis

Recent years have witnessed a proliferation of research on close relationships and the emergence of a new relationship subdiscipline within the social sciences. To date, the new science of relationships has been dominated by data. This article is based on the conviction that progress now hinges on the development of theory to organize and interpret extant findings and to guide future investigations. Through a selective but extensive review of the major bodies of empirical literature, we attempt to show that attachment theory can incorporate a broad range of findings on adult relationships. In addition, attachment theory addresses an impressive array of research questions concerning the functions, emotional dynamics, evolutionary origins, and developmental pathways of human affectional bonds. We conclude that a comprehensive theory of close relationships is both desirable and, with the integration of existing theories and concepts, currently achievable.

In 1958, Harry Harlow wrote:

Our assigned mission as psychologists is to analyze all facets of human and animal behavior into their component variables. So far as love or affection is concerned, psychologists have failed in their mission. The little we know about love does not transcend simple observation and the little we write about it has been written better by poets and novelists. (Harlow, 1958, p. 673)

Today, more than 30 years later, there is an international network of researchers whose investigative efforts are devoted entirely to the study of personal relationships. Have we made any progress in understanding love and affection? Most definitely, we have.

Many have argued that what is needed in the field of personal relationships is what every new science requires, a descriptive base of knowledge from which to derive principles and construct theory (e.g., Hinde, 1979; Rubin, 1984). This article is based on the conviction that, after more than three decades of research on close relationships, there is ample data to justify a search for meaningful patterns and organizing principles. In what follows, we draw on attachment theory (Bowlby, 1973, 1980, 1969/1982, 1988) to propose a generative theoretical framework for organizing extant data and for making predictions beyond what can be currently documented. What we seek is a comprehensive theory of close relationships, and what we propose here is the outline of such a theory.

In searching for a theory of relationships, we are led to ask what, ideally, one would want from such a theory. What questions should it answer? We believe that, at a minimum, it should address the following: What makes a potential relationship partner appealing? How is a relationship formed, and how does it develop? How are relationships maintained, and what makes them satisfying or enduring? Why and how are relationships dissolved? What are the reactions to relationship breakup?

Beyond these basics, a comprehensive theory of relationships should offer models of both normative and individual-difference phenomena and account for the role of relationships in a person's overall adaptation and functioning throughout life. It should be able to explain the universal human tendency to form close relationships and the similarities and differences in affectional bonds from infancy through adulthood. Perhaps most important, a theory of close relationships must be consistent and compatible with existing empirical findings. And, as with any theory that earns its keep, it must be parsimonious, testable, and generative.

The challenge awaiting a comprehensive theory of close relationships is formidable. Consider the diversity of findings and phenomena to be incorporated: Frequency of mutual gazing is a good indicator of the amount of love that partners feel for each other (Rubin, 1973). We tend to fall in love with people who seem especially responsive to our needs (A. P. Aron, Dutton, E. N. Aron, & Iverson, 1989; Berscheid, 1984). Inadequate care during infancy is predictive of later troubled relations with peers (Arend, Gove, & Sroufe, 1979). Children who are anxiety prone are more inclined to develop romantic crushes (Hatfield & Rapson, 1987). Within the context of laboratory marital interaction, physiological arousal predicts the

eventual demise of the marriage (Levenson & Gottman, 1985). Fear of intimacy is associated with workaholism (Hazan & Shaver, 1990). Adolescents who idealize their parents are judged as hostile by their peers (Kobak & Sceery, 1988). The typical initial reaction to the ending of a close relationship is anxiety (Weiss, 1988). Obstacles tend to enhance romantic passion (Driscoll, K. W. Davis, & Lipetz, 1972). Parental divorce during childhood is associated with chronic loneliness in adulthood (Shaver & Rubenstein, 1980). People tend to overlook the faults and limitations of a new partner (Tennov, 1979). Relationship satisfaction typically declines in the early years (Spanier, Lewis, & Cole, 1975). And so on.

Is it possible to detect laws of relationship structure and process that lend coherence to these and other relationship facts? We believe that a parsimonious explanation of much of the existing data is both desirable and possible, and we think attachment theory is a good place to start. We are not ready to claim that, in its current form, attachment theory tells us all we would ever want or need to know in order to understand close relationships. Some shortcomings of attachment theory can be handled nicely by interdependence theory (Kelley et al., 1983; Thibaut & Kelley, 1959) and theories that stress the mutual construction of relationship narratives (e.g., Duck, 1991). At the end of this article, we say more about how we see the alternative theories fitting together.

Attachment Theory

In 1950, John Bowlby was invited by the World Health Organization (WHO) to report on the mental health of London's many homeless children. The invitation followed his publication (Bowlby, 1944) of an article entitled "Forty-Four Juvenile Thieves: Their Characters and Home Life," which reported a strong association between early maternal separations and subsequent delinquency among boys. The WHO report (Bowlby, 1951) asserted that maternal deprivation, especially during the first 3 years of life, puts children at increased risk for physical and mental illness. Although influential and well received, the report was deficient in one important respect: It failed to explain why or how early maternal deprivation has such deleterious effects.

Bowlby had been trained in the psychoanalytic tradition but, almost as soon as he began to practice child therapy, he found himself troubled by what he perceived to be inadequacies in psychoanalytic theory. Most objectionable was its exclusive focus on fantasy and the internal life; a child's real-life experiences were of little interest relative to intrapsychic events. Bowlby was also troubled by inconsistencies between psychoanalytic theory and his own observations. That institutionalized children suffered extreme distress and even sometimes failed to thrive despite being fed and cared for by staff did not follow from psychoanalytic notions that children love their mother simply because they associate her with the satisfaction of a hunger drive. Bowlby's growing dissatisfaction with psychoanalytic theory helped launch a search for answers to questions raised in his WHO report.

The search took him through the literatures of several disciplines, but it was in ethology that he found what he believed to be an important part of the answer. Research on the bonding behavior of birds and mammals was particularly influential in his thinking, gradually leading to the insight that maternal deprivation is developmentally harmful because it thwarts the satisfaction of an inborn need. Further, the work of ethologists like Lorenz and Tinbergen provided dramatic examples of how even inborn, instinctual tendencies can become distorted or fail to develop in non-optimal environments. Almost 20 years later, Bowlby published the first of three major volumes on attachment theory. For obvious reasons, we cannot review all the supporting evidence on which the theory is based; we will settle instead for an explication of the theory itself. (For a more extensive review of the evidence, see Bowlby, 1973, 1980, 1969/1982.)

The Attachment System

A basic assumption of attachment theory is that, because of their extreme immaturity at birth, human infants can survive only if an adult is willing to provide protection and care. As a result of selection pressures, infants evolve behaviors that function to maintain proximity to a protector/caregiver. Adult caregiving is regulated by a complementary behavioral system. Babies smile, and parents find the smiles rewarding. Babies cry, and parents are motivated to soothe them. Parents move away, and babies follow visually or physically. These two systems conspire to create the kind of relationship that fosters the infant's survival.

A behavioral system consists of a set of behaviors that serve the same function, although they may be morphologically dissimilar (e.g., crying, smiling, following). The attachment system is similar in some respects to the physiological systems that regulate body temperature, blood pressure, and the like. Any real or perceived obstacle to proximity maintenance results in anxiety, which in turn triggers attachment behaviors designed to reestablish proximity. Such behaviors persist until the "set goal" for proximity has been achieved. The degree of proximity required to keep anxiety at bay is related to a variety of endogenous and exogenous factors, including the child's age, emotional and physical state, and perceived environmental threat. The establishment and maintenance of proximity engender feelings of security and love, whereas disruptions in the relationship typically beget anxiety and sometimes anger or sadness (depending on particular appraisals). Hence, Bowlby argued that an attachment is an emotional bond.

Attachment is one of several distinct but interlocking behavioral systems, including exploration, caregiving, affiliation, and sexual mating. Each system serves unique functions and responds to different environmental cues. At least during infancy and childhood, attachment is the preeminent system, and its full activation precludes activation of other systems. As long as the child experiences "felt security" (Sroufe & Waters, 1977), the attachment system is quiescent, and other behavioral systems become available for activation, although periodic checking of the attachment figure's availability continues to occur. In evolutionary terms, it has been adaptive for human young to feel safe enough to engage in play and exploration only as long as a familiar protector is available to respond if needed. The safest reaction to any threat or strong uncertainty is to devote all energy and attention to reestablishing proximity. (See Figure 9.1 for a model of the attachment system.)

Attachment Formation

Children could conceivably direct their attachment behaviors to any available person. In reality, however, by the sixth or seventh month of life, all normal infants selectively direct these behaviors to one person, with whom they also seek proximity and from whom they object to being separated (Schaffer & Emerson, 1964). How is this person "selected"? Of definite significance to infants is *who* usually responds to their signals of distress. Also of significance is the *quality* of the response. Thus, familiarity and responsiveness dictate preferences and influence the selection of an attachment figure.

The functions of attachment are apparent in the infant's behavior. Proximity to the attachment figure is especially likely to be sought when the infant is fearful or distressed for any reason. The caregiver serves as a haven of safety to which the infant can retreat for comfort and reassurance during such times. In addition, the caregiver serves as a base from which to engage in nonattachment behaviors, such as exploration. According to Bowlby, *proximity maintenance* (including proximity seeking and separation protest), *safe haven*, and *secure base* are the three defining features of attachment and the functions of an attachment relationship (see Figure 9.2).

The process of attachment formation takes an average of 2 or 3 years (Bowlby, 1979, 1969/1982). The endpoint of the process is referred to as a *goal-corrected partnership*, in which the goal of proximity maintenance is adjusted for the child's ability to delay gratification and to mentally represent the caregiver's availability. At this point, caregiver and child can begin to negotiate the terms of their relationship and verbally

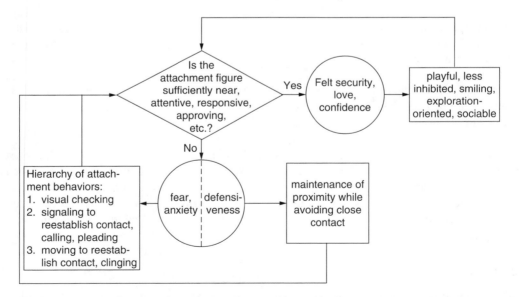

FIGURE 9.1 ■ The attachment behavioral system. In the diamond is the test question (G. A. Miller, Galanter, & Pribram, 1960). The circles represent emotions triggered by the appraisals that answer the test question, and the boxes represent behaviors that follow from the appraisals and emotions.

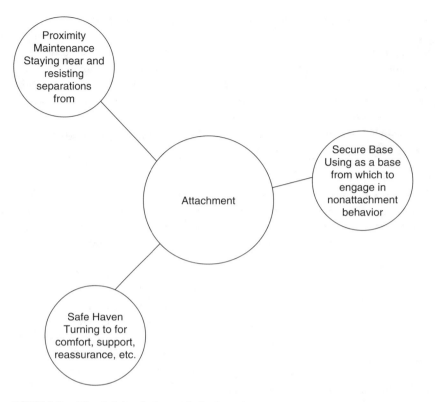

FIGURE 9.2 ■ The defining features of attachment.

communicate about and coordinate their respective goals.

Attachment Disruption and Dissolution

Bowlby's investigations of attachment stemmed from his interest in the effects of maternal deprivation. He observed infants and young children who were being housed in residential nurseries, separated from their familiar caregivers for extended periods of time—in some cases, forever. Bowlby was struck by two aspects of the children's responses. First, there was a remarkable degree of similarity across children in the way they responded to the separations, gradually revealing a predictable and invariant sequence of emotional reactions. The first was *protest*, which involves crying, active searching, and resistance to others' soothing efforts. This is followed by *despair*, characterized by passivity and obvious sadness. The third and final phase is *emotional detachment*.

The second striking aspect of the children's responses was that even short-term separations seemed to have prolonged effects. Children who were reunited with their caregivers while still in the protest phase exhibited heightened anxiety over abandonment and an excessive need for physical contact and reassurance. This insecurity continued, in some cases, for months after the separation had ended. Those reunited after passing through the phase of despair tended initially to avoid contact with their mothers, as if they had coped with the separation by emotionally detaching. However, in time they resumed seeking contact and comfort.

According to Bowlby, reactions of anxiety and protest, even detachment, are highly adaptive responses to separation from one's primary protector. A child expresses distress because it usually brings the caregiver around. If, however, there appears to be no hope of reestablishing proximity, continued expressions of distress not only risk attracting the attention of predators (a very real threat in earlier periods of human evolution), but also physically exhaust the child. The characteristic inactivity of the despair phase keeps the child quiet and still, allowing for recuperation. Detachment makes possible the resumption of normal activity, possibly even the search for a new attachment figure. Just as with routine proximity maintenance, reactions to prolonged separation reflect the functioning of the attachment system.

Internal Working Models

The attachment system is an organism-level system that is organized and regulated by social input, specifically by primary caregiver responsiveness to distress signals. On the basis of repeated interactions with the caregiver, infants learn what to expect, and they adjust their behavior accordingly. These expectations form the basis of mental representations (or, to use Bowlby's term, *internal working models*) that can be used to forecast caregiver availability and responsiveness and that include interrelated models of self and attachment figure.

> Confidence that an attachment figure is, apart from being accessible, likely to be responsive can be seen to turn on at least two variables: (a) whether or not the attachment figure is judged to be the sort of person who in general responds to calls for support and protection; [and] (b) whether or not the self is judged to be the sort of person towards whom anyone, and the attachment figure in particular, is likely to respond in a helpful way. Logically these variables are independent. In practice they are apt to be confounded. As a result, the model of the attachment figure and the model of the self are likely to develop so as to be complementary and mutually confirming. (Bowlby, 1973, p. 238)

Attachment theory thus implies that beliefs and feelings about the self, especially social and global self-esteem, are determined in part by the responsiveness of the caregiving environment to individual needs for comfort and security (Cassidy, 1988). According to Bowlby, these models guide thoughts, feelings, and behavior in subsequent close relationships.

Individual Differences

Theoretically and logically speaking, there is no limit to the amount and kind of variability that could exist in models of the caregiving environment. In reality, however, infants parse the flow of information about caregiver behaviors into a limited number of categories corresponding to responses to the following question: "Can I count on my attachment figure to be available and responsive when needed?" There are three possible answers to this question: yes, no, and maybe. That is, as concerns the internal working model, a caregiver is consistently responsive, consistently unresponsive, or inconsistent. In fact, these three types of caregiver responsiveness have been empirically linked to three major patterns of infant–caregiver attachment (Ainsworth, Blehar, Waters, & Wall, 1978).

The procedure that Ainsworth developed for assessing attachment quality—the Strange Situation—was designed to activate an infant's attachment system through repeated separations from the caregiver in an unfamiliar environment. It was also meant to activate the exploration system through the availability of attractive toys. Ainsworth was especially interested in whether and when infants sought proximity and contact, to what degree they accepted and were comforted by such contact, and whether their exploratory behavior was facilitated by the caregiver's presence. In other words, she was interested in observing proximity-maintenance, safe-haven, and secure-base behaviors. Infant behavior in the laboratory setting was assumed to reflect expectations (internal working models) based on the caregiver's past responsiveness to the infant's bids for contact and comfort. The models themselves were assumed to be founded on a history of actual interactions. Home observations confirmed the link between daily caregiver responsiveness and infant laboratory behavior. The following paragraphs, based on passages in Ainsworth et al. (1978), describe the three major patterns.

Secure. The behavior of securely attached infants matched Bowlby's conception of nature's prototype, in terms of proximity maintenance, comfort seeking, and the ability to use the caregiver as a secure base for exploration. In the laboratory, the typical securely attached infant was distressed when the mother left the room, was comforted by her return, and engaged in active exploration as long as she was present. During home observations made before the laboratory visits, caregivers were judged to be consistently available and responsive. This is the most commonly observed pattern, averaging about 60% in American samples (Campos, Barrett, Lamb, Goldsmith, & Stenberg, 1983).

Anxious/Ambivalent. The typical caregiver of an anxious/ambivalently attached infant, observed in the home, exhibited inconsistent responsiveness to the infant's signals, being sometimes unavailable or unresponsive and at other times intrusive. In the laboratory, anxious/ambivalently attached infants appeared both anxious and angry and were preoccupied with their caregivers to such a degree that it precluded exploration. This is the most uncommon pattern, averaging about 15% in American samples (Campos et al., 1983).

Anxious/Avoidant. At home, caregivers of avoidantly attached infants consistently rebuffed or deflected their infants' bids for comfort, especially for close bodily contact. In the laboratory setting, these infants appeared not to be distressed by separations, avoided contact with their caregivers, and kept their attention directed toward the toys (although with less apparent interest and enthusiasm than the securely attached infants). On average, about 25% of American infants are classified as avoidantly attached (Campos et al., 1983).

Note that the effects of psychological availability of the caregiver are remarkably similar to the effects observed for physical availability. Inconsistent responsiveness is functionally equivalent to short-term separations, and the corresponding attachment pattern—anxious/ambivalence—is characterized by the same protest behaviors. Consistent caregiver unresponsiveness, like long-term absence, results in avoidance and apparent emotional detachment. Again, the behaviors are traceable to the organization and functioning of the attachment behavioral system.

In recent years, researchers have identified a fourth pattern, *disorganized/disoriented attachment* (Main & Solomon, 1990), that is distinguishable by the absence of a coherent strategy for managing anxiety and that is manifested in a mixture of avoidant and ambivalent behaviors. Research suggests that this pattern arises in infancy, when the infant's primary caregiver is depressed, disturbed, or abusive in some way (e.g., Crittenden, 1988; Main & Hesse, 1990).

Source and Stability of Individual Differences

Perhaps the two most controversial claims of attachment theory are that caregiver responsiveness largely determines the quality of the attachment relationship and that working models of attachment tend to be stable. Many writers have criticized attachment theory for its apparent failure to acknowledge the importance of infant characteristics, especially temperament (e.g., Campos et al., 1983; Lamb, Thompson, Gardner, Charnov, & Estes, 1984), and the theory's seemingly deterministic view of development, which some see as allowing little room for growth and change. The debate over temperament is by no means settled, but there is mounting evidence that both temperament and caregiver responsiveness are important influences on attachment quality. For example, one temperamental characteristic—distress proneness—has been linked in anxious/ambivalent attachment (Goldsmith & Alansky, 1987). On the other hand, responsiveness training for the caregivers of distress-prone infants appears to override the risks for later insecure attachment (van den Boom, 1990). At least one study (Crockenberg, 1981) has suggested that the relationship between temperament and attachment may be mediated by maternal social support. To date, no investigation has shown temperament to be better than caregiver responsiveness at predicting attachment classification, and no reported findings would lead to the conclusion that the consistency and quality of caregiver responsiveness are not important determinants of infant attachment behavior. (See Colin, 1991, for a comprehensive review.)

In some ways, the debate over whether individual differences are stable is even murkier. Research subsequent to Ainsworth's identification of the three patterns (e.g., K. E. Grossmann & K. Grossmann, 1991; Main, Kaplan, & Cassidy, 1985; Sroufe, 1983; Waters, 1978) has indicated that the patterns are generally stable over the first several years of life if family conditions are stable, but can change if a child's social circumstances change (Egeland & Farber, 1984; Vaughn, Egeland, Sroufe, & Waters, 1979). Attachment theory does not dictate absolute stability of individual differences induced during infancy. Nevertheless, as with any cognitive construction, internal working models are resistant to change, in part because they tend to be overlearned and operate out of awareness, and in part because the default strategy for processing incoming information is to assimilate it to existing schemes rather than modify the schemes to accommodate the information (Fiske & Taylor, 1991; Piaget, 1952).

When defensive emotional processes are intertwined with overlearned cognitive and behavioral patterns, as is hypothesized to be the case with insecure-attachment models, change can be difficult. It seems more sensible to ask not whether working models are stable or unstable but under what conditions they are most and least likely to change. Bowlby has suggested several possible routes to change, including (a) the capacity to think about and reflect upon one's own working models and (b) "corrective" relationship experience. Both come into play in good therapeutic relationships (Bowlby, 1988). In light of what is known about the dynamics of the attachment system and the inborn need for security, change would seem more likely to be in the direction of secure than insecure attachment. The attachment system's "primary strategy" (Main, 1990) should always be to seek security if security is perceived as possible. Consistent with this, secure attachments

have been found to be more stable (Egeland & Farber, 1984).

Attachment patterns set in infancy need not be fixed for life. As with cognitive structures in general, internal working models of attachment face the stability–plasticity dilemma (Grossberg, 1980). Mental models strive for stability, but have to remain plastic if they are to continue to be adaptive and useful. To date, longitudinal studies have indicated significant but not perfect continuity of attachment patterns over the first several months and years of life (Cassidy, 1988; Owen, Easterbrooks, Chase-Lansdale, & Goldberg, 1984; Waters, 1978). Ultimately, the degree of continuity from infancy through adulthood and the circumstances under which change is facilitated must be determined empirically.

Attachment Beyond Infancy

Attachment is an integral part of human behavior "from the cradle to the grave" (Bowlby, 1979). The functions and dynamics of the attachment behavioral system are hypothesized to be virtually the same across the life span. Presumably, this is because the neural foundation of the attachment system remains largely unchanged. As Konner (1982) put it, "The evolution of the brain would have to be considered unparsimonious if it were not able to draw upon the same basic capacities of emotion and action in the various settings where strong attachment is called for" (p. 298).

Despite some basic similarities, adult attachment differs from infant attachment in important ways (Weiss, 1982). First, childhood attachments are typically complementary. An attachment figure provides but does not receive care; an infant or child seeks but does not normally provide security. In contrast, adult attachment relationships are typically reciprocal, with each partner being both a provider and a recipient of care. In addition, the attachment relationship moves from the level of external, observable interactions to internally represented beliefs and expectations (Main et al., 1985). Whereas infants and young children may require physical contact with an attachment figure to feel completely secure, older children and adults are often able to derive comfort from the mere knowledge that their attachment figures can be contacted if needed (although the need for physical-contact comfort probably never disappears entirely). What matters is "felt security" (Sroufe & Waters, 1977), and adults have more options for achieving it than do infants.

Another difference is that a child's primary attachment figure is usually a parent, whereas an adult's primary attachment figure is most commonly a peer, usually a sexual partner. Prototypical adult attachment relationships thus involve the integration of three behavioral systems—attachment, caregiving, and sexual mating (Shaver, Hazan, & Bradshaw, 1988; Weiss, 1982).

Related to this are differences in what motivates proximity seeking. Anxiety and distress appear to be primary motivators in people of all ages. However, adult proximity-seeking can also result from a desire to protect or offer comfort (caregiving) or to engage in sexual activity (sexual mating). Attachments are hypothesized to form in the context of physical closeness, but the forces promoting such closeness may change with development.

If adult peers begin to serve similar functions and satisfy the same needs for emotional support and security for which parents are primarily responsible during infancy and childhood, then at some point attachment will be transferred from parents to peers. The timing of this transfer and the processes involved are not specified within the theory. However, from both the theory and the empirical literature on parent–child and peer relations (e.g., Furman & Buhmester, 1985; Gottman, 1983; Hartup, 1983; G. Levinger & A. C. Levinger, 1986; Rubin, 1980; Steinberg & Silverberg, 1986), a process model can be derived. The model (Hazan, Hutt, Sturgeon, & Bricker, 1991) is based on the assumption that, rather than being shifted in concert, all attachment functions are gradually transferred, one by one. According to this model, attachments begin with proximity seeking (motivated by security needs when directed toward parents and by exploratory and affiliative needs when directed toward peers). In late childhood and early adolescence, close proximity provides the context

that eventually fosters support-seeking (i.e., safe-haven) behavior. Repeated interactions in which comfort is sought and provided or distress is expressed and alleviated may lead to reliance on the responder as a base of security. Parents are never completely relinquished as attachment figures, but their place in a hierarchy of attachment figures, relative to that of the place of peers, naturally changes by adulthood.

An Attachment Perspective on Relationship Data

Having outlined attachment theory, we now briefly review some of the major bodies of data on close relationships in order to show how each could be organized and explained by the theory. We have tried to preserve the fundamental theoretical constructs and processes, but we have not hesitated to extend or mold the theory wherever warranted. In our opinion, the real strength of attachment theory lies in its ability to explain findings derived from other approaches and other theories in terms of the same limited number of proximal processes and evolved tendencies as it uses to explain infant–caregiver bonds. The degree to which attachment theory and we succeed in this endeavor reflects on the generative power of the theory. It is conceivable that each new finding in the field of personal relationships would necessitate the addition of a new theoretical construct. However, we attempt to show that attachment theory is able to incorporate a vast range of such findings without significant alteration or addition. And, when additions are required, they follow naturally from the principles established for relationship functioning during infancy.

Our focus here is on close relationships of the attachment variety—which adults prototypically form with a romantic or sexual partner—but much of what we say is also applicable to other types of close relationships. Our review of the literature is necessarily selective, but it is extensive enough to illustrate both the diversity of available findings and the integrative capacity of attachment theory. The review is organized around what traditionally have been considered fundamental questions in the study of close relationships.

What Makes a Potential Relationship Partner Appealing?

From an attachment perspective, humans possess basic needs that are naturally satisfied by social relationships, such as the needs for emotional support, care, and sexual gratification. Theoretically, each need is regulated by a distinct behavioral system designed to respond to specific social cues. We should, therefore, be attracted to people who display these cues. Given that the most basic need (for felt security) is regulated by the attachment system, and given that this system is assumed to function similarly across the life span, among the most important characteristics of a potential partner should be the very characteristics shown to be centrally important in the selection of an attachment figure during infancy and childhood—namely, familiarity and responsiveness.

Interpersonal attraction is not only the first stage of many relationships, it is also the topic with which the field of close relationships began, in the pioneering work of Berscheid and Hatfield (Berscheid & E. Walster, 1974) and Rubin (1973). The list of features and characteristics that have been shown to be determinants of attraction is long and heterogeneous (for reviews, see Aronson, 1988; Berscheid, 1984). For example, we are attracted to people whose values, attitudes, opinions, and even physical features are similar to our own (Hinsz, 1989; Rubin, 1973). Unless we dislike someone to begin with, increased exposure is associated with increased liking (Zajonc, 1968). Socially responsive children are more attractive to their peers (Rubin, 1980). Among all the people with whom we could socialize, we typically choose those who live or work nearby (Festinger, Schachter, & Back, 1950; Newcomb, 1961). We have a predilection for people who smile frequently, who are good-humored, and who make us laugh (Folkes & Sears, 1977). We are especially attracted to people we know find us appealing (A. P. Aron et al., 1989). Anxiety tends to enhance attraction (Dutton & A. P. Aron, 1974; Hatfield &

Rapson, 1987) and the desire to affiliate (Schachter, 1959).

These data indicate that attraction to another person tends to increase with familiarity and the likelihood of a positive response. Anyone who is like us (in appearance, attitude, etc.) or who likes us, is smiling, or makes us smile is more likely than an unfamiliar or unresponsive person to be viewed as safe, approachable, and thus attractive. Anxiety apparently intensifies the need to be near another person or makes that person's security-promoting potential more salient. Within attachment theory, anxiety is a signal to get closer.

However, attachment is not the only behavioral system motivating interpersonal attraction. As stated earlier, adult love can be conceptualized as a joint function of the attachment, caregiving, and sexual mating systems (Shaver et al., 1988), so, theoretically, attraction can result from one person's seeing the possibility of another person's meeting attachment, caregiving, or sexual needs. Another's attractiveness is thus determined by the type of relationship that is sought and the kinds of needs or desires that are likely to be satisfied. From an attachment perspective, the multiform features of attractiveness are reducible to a small number of conceptual categories that correspond to the behavioral systems relevant to close relationships, each of which is triggered by different and distinct cues.

The caregiving system, for example, responds to babyish features, distress, and vulnerability—which in the case of adults may include self-disclosures of fear or weakness, or the vulnerability inherent in the letting down of defenses. A person who wants to provide care should logically be attracted to someone who seems to need such care. Cues associated with targets of caregiving constitute one interpersonal-attraction category that has been understudied, perhaps due to the lack of a theory that would encourage such investigations. Also, many studies of interpersonal attraction involve adolescents and young adults, for whom caregiving may be a relatively undeveloped or less salient need. There are, in fact, age-related changes in the relevance of such cues. One study (Fullard & Reiling, 1976) documented a

developmental shift in preference for infant relative to adult faces. Before puberty, both males and
females preferred photographs of adult faces; after puberty, they spent more time looking at infant
faces.

A person who seeks gratification of sexual
needs should be attracted to someone who displays
cues of sexual availability and value. In sexual relationships, an attractive physical appearance can
be remarkably important (e.g., E. Walster, Aronson,
Abrahams, & Rottmann, 1966). Also, there appears to be considerable cross-cultural and cross-
age consistency in what is viewed as physically
attractive, including characteristics associated
with youth and/or health—smooth skin, clear
eyes, white teeth, a lively gait. Also desirable in a
potential sexual partner—especially in a male being evaluated by a female—is evidence of social
status and resources, such as popularity, material
wealth, physical strength, intelligence, and wit
(Buss, 1985).

To say that we are attracted to someone is to
say that we would like to be physically and/or
psychologically close to that person. Within an attachment framework, what motivates such proximity seeking depends on which social-behavioral
system is activated. Conceptualizing interpersonal attraction in this way makes it possible to
reduce the many interpersonal-attraction factors
to a few conceptually meaningful categories.

How Is a Relationship Formed, and How Does It Develop?

Some attractions develop into relationships, and
some do not. Also, it is generally assumed and
well documented that relationships, after being
formed, tend to change over time (e.g., Berscheid
& E. Walster, 1974; Huston, Surra, Fitzgerald, &
Cate, 1981; G. Levinger, 1983; G. Levinger &
Snoek, 1972; Lewis & Spanier, 1979; Taylor &
Altman, 1987; E. Walster & G. W. Walster, 1978).
A nascent relationship is obviously different from
an established relationship, and discovering just
what changes and why is an important task for relationship researchers and has been the focus of
much study (Altman & Taylor, 1973; Kerckhoff &

K. E. Davis, 1962; G. Levinger, 1983; Lewis, 1973;
Murstein, 1976; Reiss, 1960). In general, efforts
to identify a uniform sequence of stages for all
close relationships have met with great difficulty
(e.g., Huston et al., 1981).

From an attachment perspective, the formation
of a close relationship between two individuals of
any age typically forms in the context of close
physical proximity. In other words, for an attachment to form there must be a strong force promoting closeness. In infancy, proximity is regulated
by the attachment system and the infant's need for
security. In adult romantic relationships, the sexual mating system (sexual attraction) is hypothesized to be another primary instigator for the
proximity seeking that is the first step toward
attachment formation.

Even though the motivation to seek closeness is
hypothesized to be somewhat different and more
complex for adults than for infants, the first phase
in what may eventually become an attachment relationship is remarkably similar (Shaver et al.,
1988). Like an adult in love, the infant is preoccupied with and notably vigilant for signs of the target person's responsiveness. Further, for infants
as well as adults, one's emotional state hinges on
the target person's behavior, with responsiveness
generally leading to feelings of security and joy
and unresponsiveness evoking anxiety and distress (Ainsworth et al., 1978; Tennov, 1979). In
both kinds of relationships—between infant and
caregiver and between adult lovers—strong
forces attract the individuals to each other and, in
some cases, hold them together long enough for
an emotional bond to develop. In both, the formation of such a bond is facilitated by close physical
contact. Only between parents and children or between adult lovers is prolonged bodily contact
considered normal. It is noteworthy that laypersons
judge these two types of relationships to be the
"closest" (Berscheid & Graziano, 1979). For good
or ill, the intensity of the need for close contact
eventually diminishes (Fisher, 1992; Traupmann
& Hatfield, 1981)—an important fact that needs
to be explained.

Logically, the safe-haven component of attachment would be expected to develop within the

context of closeness. Consistent with this, researchers have found that mutual attraction and sexual passion are most important early in a relationship, but the degree to which a partner provides comfort and emotional support becomes increasingly important over time (Reedy, Birren, & Schaie, 1981). In attachment terms, what eventually comes to matter most is whether the partner serves as a reliable haven of safety. Mutual attraction and sexual interest can get couples together, but, if partners fail to satisfy each other's needs for comfort and security, dissatisfaction will likely result. Kotler (1985) found that sensitive and responsive care, not sexual attraction, was the most accurate predictor of marital strength.

When does a relationship become a base of security? It is relatively safe to assume that parents are committed to their offspring for life. This commitment is not typically questioned or broken. Commitments between peers, however, tend to be less robust and more susceptible to both internal and external influences (G. Levinger, 1976). It is likely that, only after an extended period of time and/or after an explicit commitment has been made, a peer relationship can serve as a secure base with a degree of certainty approaching that of the base provided by parents. Marriage, for example, is usually accompanied by a legally binding, public promise to care for the partner until death.

In terms of the three defining attachment features described earlier (see Figure 9.2), the process of attachment formation, at any age, is hypothesized to involve the same sequence: proximity seeking followed by safe-haven behavior followed by the establishment of a secure base. In some cases, of course, the process will not be completed. As suggested earlier, the major difference between infant–caregiver and adult-pair bonds is in the motivation for seeking closeness in the first place.

An attachment perspective adds to our understanding of how close relationships develop and change over time and helps explain some of the phenomena that have been repeatedly documented and described. The attachment view of

relationship development helps account for some important characteristics of the time course of close relationships. It also makes implicit predictions concerning both the nature and timing of important milestones and transitions in developing relationships. The three components of a prototypical pair bond, each corresponding to a separate behavioral system—attachment, caregiving, and sexual mating—gradually become integrated.

What Makes Relationships Satisfying and/or Enduring?

As the wording of this question implies and as the data confirm, an enduring relationship may not be a satisfying one. Therefore, it is essential that a theory of close relationships specify and explain the factors that predict each.

According to attachment theory, a relationship is satisfying to the extent that it meets basic needs. At any age, attachment quality turns in large part on the answer to the question, "Can I trust my partner to be available and responsive to my needs?" Trust promotes self-disclosure and the development of intimacy (Reis & Shaver, 1988). Trust is also associated with open communication about and the "voicing" of needs (Holmes & Rempel, 1989; Rusbult & Zembrodt, 1983). Satisfying relationships are not conflict free, but they involve the kind of trust that allows couples to argue constructively (Rands, G. Levinger, & Mellinger, 1981) and to engage in effective problem-solving behaviors (Kobak & Hazan, 1991). The "hidden agendas" that interfere with successful conflict resolution are often about unmet needs (Gottman, Notarius, Gonso, & Markman, 1976). Attachment theory tells us what the needs are likely to be and explains why trust in a partner's responsiveness to these needs is critical.

Many unsatisfying relationships endure, and these are among the most challenging for researchers. What makes a partner decide to leave? The belief that important needs could be better met in another relationship—what has been called *comparison level for alternatives*—is influential in decisions to continue or end a relationship (Kelley, 1983; Rusbult, 1980, 1983). In defining relationship commitment, it is helpful to distinguish between the desire to continue a relationship because it is satisfying and the tendency to stay simply because the constraints against breakup seem too great to overcome (Stanley, 1986). External constraints to break up include joint ownership of property, poverty, children, and a relative absence of alternatives (G. Levinger, 1976).

Attachment theory suggests an additional factor that may contribute to the maintenance of an unsatisfying relationship—the emotional bond of attachment. Recall that an attachment is typically formed in the context of close proximity. Weiss (1982) argued that proximity alone can maintain the bond. Often couples are unaware of the bond between them until it is disrupted or threatened in some way (Berscheid, 1983). Even a burdensome and unsatisfying relationship can contribute to one's sense of security. Perhaps the best evidence for the security-promoting function of an unhappy relationship is the intense anxiety that typically accompanies separation (Weiss, 1975). Bowlby (1973) theorized that separation from an attachment figure is one of many natural cues to potential danger and, as such, triggers a fear response and, in turn, attachment behaviors.

To summarize, from an attachment perspective, relationship satisfaction depends largely on the satisfaction of basic needs for comfort, care, and sexual gratification. Trust in a partner's willingness and ability to meet needs is determined in part by the partner's actual behavior and in part by the expectations or comparison levels (Kelley, 1983; Rusbult, 1983) each person brings to the relationship. A history of close relationships lacking in trust, for example, might be expected to result in the kind of minimal expectations that could lead one to stay in an unsatisfying relationship. Thus, relationship longevity may be influenced by relationship history. After an emotional bond has developed, it can act as a psychological tether that provides some security and holds two people together regardless of whether they still enjoy being together. Anxiety resulting from contemplation of or attempted separation can activate attachment behaviors that lead one back to the relationship, unless there is an available and willing alternative.

What Are the Precursors and Reactions to Relationship Dissolution?

Just as research has uncovered multiple correlates of relationship satisfaction, scores of studies have been directed at revealing the causes of breakup (e.g., Felmlee, Sprecher, & Bassin, 1990; Gottman, Markman, & Notarius, 1977; G. Levinger, 1966; Lund, 1985; Simpson, 1990). At the risk of sounding glib, one can conclude from this research that failure to engage in behaviors that enhance relationship satisfaction and longevity renders dissolution more likely. If partners lack trust in each other and, as a result, do not openly and clearly communicate their thoughts and feelings, do not engage in effective strategies of conflict resolution, or are not committed to remaining together, the probability that the relationship will endure is lessened. Structural factors of the sort mentioned earlier—children, limited financial resources, and religious or societal prohibitions—also figure prominently in a couple's decision to end or maintain their relationship. As long as each member of a pair has confidence (i.e., trust) in the other's ability and willingness to supply essential relational provisions, each will be motivated to maintain the relationship. In G. Levinger's (1976) terms, internal attractions will be so strong that external barriers and alternative attractions will be of little practical importance.

The desire to leave a relationship necessarily comes after the relationship has been formed. The question, then, is what changes between the time a person decides to enter a relationship and the time a decision is made to leave. The answer, we believe, lies in a process model of attachment formation. Relationship satisfaction always reduces to whether needs are being satisfied or not (Shaver & Hazan, 1984). The problem is that the relative importance of various needs changes over time. In fact, what gets two people into a relationship may be what matters least in the long run. If sexual passion is indeed the initial motivating force in the formation of many adult pair bonds, a decline in satisfaction is inevitable unless the relationship meets other needs after they have become important. Unfortunately, people in the throes of romantic passion may give relatively little thought to whether the people to whom they are attracted will make reliable long-term providers of care and support—which in time will come to dominate their feelings about the relationship. Dissatisfaction would be expected to peak around the time that intense attraction has faded and the partner's competence as a haven of safety and secure base assumes relatively greater importance. It should be at this point in a relationship that expectations, alternatives, and constraints come into play in a major way.

Attachment theory has much to say about how people respond when a relationship ends. Response to separation and loss, after all, was the topic with which Bowlby began his inquiries. It is difficult to discuss the function of attachment without considering disruptions and separations, because the system that regulates attachment feelings and behaviors includes "built-in" responses to disruption. Even though there is tremendous cultural variation in associated rituals and customs, the human response to the breaking of an attachment bond hardly varies (Gorer, 1973; Marris, 1958; S. I. Miller & Schoenfeld, 1973; Palgi, 1973). Moreover, the way in which adults respond to attachment disruption is not essentially different from the way infants and children respond (Bowlby, 1980; Hazan & Shaver, 1992; Heinicke & Westheimer, 1966; Parkes & Weiss, 1983).

The first reaction to the disruption of an attachment relationship, whether due to death or voluntary separation, is intense separation-protest behavior. Individuals report feeling agitated, anxious, and preoccupied with thoughts of the lost partner, coupled with a compulsion to search for him or her, as though trying to undo the loss even if it is consciously known to be irreversible. Eventually, with the realization that the loss cannot be recovered, there comes a period of deep sadness, during which intense activity and rumination give way to depression and despair. Many individuals experience an unusual and marked lack of concern about or interest in life and other people.

Gradually, the sadness subsides, and most people achieve an adaptive degree of emotional detachment from the lost partner and return to ordinary living. In adults especially, constructing a causal account of the loss helps bring about acceptance and detachment (Harvey, Orbuch, & Weber, 1990).

When the attachment system is activated—for example, by the sudden unavailability of the primary attachment—the natural response is to seek proximity to the attachment figure, and this seems to happen whether or not establishing proximity is possible or even rationally desirable. That an estranged partner may still be attainable can foster not only hope but also protracted protest (Weiss, 1975, 1988). In some cases, chronic activation of the attachment system in the absence of the former partner may result in premature attachment to another person. Likely candidates would include individuals providing support and care during the difficult postseparation period. By the time a couple decides to separate, all former fondness and affection may have eroded. For this reason, many newly separated individuals, especially the ones who initiate separation, are surprised when they begin to experience a compulsion to be near the former partner. Weiss (1975) argued that this very common feeling is due to the persistence of attachment and suggested that an attachment bond can be broken only by an extended period of separation. The same sequence of responses would not be expected unless an attachment had been fully formed, which may take several years. Weiss (1988) noted that responses to divorce are distinctly different in individuals married for fewer than 2 years.

Most of what attachment theory has to say about separation and loss applies equally well to loneliness (Peplau & Perlman, 1982), which seems to take two major forms—emotional and social isolation (Weiss, 1973). Emotional isolation is the kind of loneliness associated with the lack of an intimate companion, whereas feelings of social isolation result from the lack of a social network or sense of community. The two forms of loneliness correspond well to Bowlby's distinction between the attachment and affiliation behavioral systems, which are thought to have different functions. In addition, the two types of loneliness have different symptoms, causes, and cures (Rubenstein & Shaver, 1982). Weiss (1973) viewed loneliness as an adaptive if uncomfortable emotional state because it serves as a reminder that important social needs are not being met, and it tends to continue until corrective action is taken. Again, reactions to the loss or absence of an emotional bond are hypothesized to be the direct result of the functioning of the attachment behavioral system.

How and Why Do Individuals Differ in the Way They Think, Feel, and Behave in Relationships?

Up to this point, we have emphasized normative aspects of close relationships. However, one cannot ignore the immense variability in the ways people relate to one another. Some people fear intimacy, whereas others embrace it (Hatfield, 1984). Some self-disclose to an excessive degree, whereas others disclose little or not at all (Altman & Taylor, 1973). Attitudes about romantic involvements range from game playing to pragmatism (C. Hendrick & S. Hendrick, 1986). Relationships can involve commitment without passion or passion without intimacy (Sternberg, 1986). Partners may attribute each other's problematic behavior to character flaws or explain it in terms of situational factors (Fincham, Beach, & Nelson, 1987). In response to conflict, partners may withdraw or accommodate (Rusbult, Zembrodt, & Gunn, 1982). Communication may be open and coherent or defensive and disorganized (Bretherton, 1990). Relationships appear to be as diverse as the individuals involved.

Ideally, the multitude of differences could be reduced to a more manageable number of conceptual categories. If we accept that confidence and trust in the responsiveness of others are central issues in close relationships, then a few broad categories of individual differences naturally follow. As Main et al. (1985) saw it, the social environment can be perceived as consistently responsive, inconsistently responsive, or consistently unresponsive

to an individual's attempts to establish security-promoting closeness. Given that this important issue appears to be the same in infancy and adulthood, we assume that the important individual-difference categories will also be essentially the same. One would not expect to see the exact same behaviors but rather the same basic strategies for maintaining felt security. In emphasizing normative attachment, we have actually been describing security or the secure attachment type. In this section on individual differences, we focus instead on the other end of the dimension—insecurity.

The strategy associated with inconsistent responsiveness—*anxious/ambivalent (preoccupied) attachment*—is characterized by a lack of confidence in the reliable responsiveness of others. The proximal goal of all attachment behavior is to achieve a state of felt security. In the case of anxious/ambivalent attachment, this is attempted and at times accomplished by devoting immense mental energy and behavioral effort to keeping others close by and engaged. It is manifested in intensified expressions of distress and anger and diminished exploratory activity.

In studies of adult attachment, anxious/ambivalent attachment is associated with obsessive preoccupation with a romantic partner's responsiveness; falling in love easily; being extremely jealous; being subject to fear, anxiety, and loneliness (even when involved in a relationship); having low self-esteem (Collins & Read, 1990; Feeney & Noller, 1990); and experiencing a higher rate of relationship dissolution (Hazan & Shaver, 1987). The anxious/ambivalently attached also tend to view partners as reluctant to commit and as inadequate or insufficiently attentive caregivers (Kunce & Shaver, 1991). They engage in indiscriminant and overly intimate self-disclosure (Mikulincer & Nachshon, 1991) and assert their own feelings and needs without adequate regard for the partner's feelings and needs (Daniels & Shaver, 1991). In laboratory problem-solving tasks with their partners, anxious/ambivalent subjects tended to express dysfunctional anger (Kobak & Hazan, 1991). They also reported more physical and psychological symptoms (Fiala, 1991; Hazan & Shaver, 1990) and had greater difficulty making friends in a new setting (Hazan & Hutt, 1991b). At work, anxious/ambivalence is associated with distraction, procrastination, and suboptimal performance (Hazan & Shaver, 1990) and, in discussions of attachment history, with overly effusive and poorly organized discourse (Main et al., 1985). (For a review of additional correlates of anxious/ambivalent attachment, see Shaver & Hazan, 1993.)

In contrast, avoidant attachment is believed to result from consistent unresponsiveness. The avoidant strategy for maintaining felt security involves avoidance of intimate social contact, especially in stressful or distressing circumstances, and compensatory engagement in nonsocial activities. According to research on adult attachment, avoidance is manifested in fear of intimacy and a tendency to maintain distance in "close" relationships, with pessimistic views of relationships and a relatively high rate of relationship dissolution (Hazan & Shaver, 1987). When answering interview questions concerning childhood relationships with parents, avoidantly attached adults (a) use idealized descriptors, but are unable to provide supporting examples (Main et al., 1985) and (b) show spikes in skin conductance when probed for such examples (Dozier & Kobak, in press). They avoid self-disclosure and experience discomfort with relationship partners who do self-disclose (Mikulincer & Nachshon, 1991). They are more susceptible to sudden religious conversion (Kirkpatrick & Shaver, 1990). They are judged by their peers to be hostile (Kobak & Sceery, 1988). They tend to use work to avoid social interaction (Hazan & Shaver, 1990) and are prone to engaging in uncommitted sexual relations and using alcohol and other substances to reduce tension (Brennan, Shaver, & Tobey, 1991). (For additional findings on avoidant attachment, see Shaver & Hazan, 1993.)

Theoretically, these two major patterns of insecurity are based on internal working models constructed from actual attachment experience, beginning with parents. The anxious/ambivalent strategy is "logical" in the sense that it reflects a history of inconsistent responsiveness. Expecting close relationship partners to be somewhat unreliable may lead to heightened vigilance and fears of abandonment and neglect, both of which can interfere with nonattachment activities. The avoidant strategy is equally logical in light of a history of frequent rejection or inhibitions on physical affection and intimate emotional expression. Such experiences can lead to an avoidance of closeness, extreme self-reliance, and a habit of regulating anxiety by keeping oneself distracted. In line with social psychological research showing that actions often follow from beliefs and interpersonal schemes in a way that encourages repeated confirmation (e.g., Snyder & Swann, 1978), internal working models may have self-fulfilling effects on social behavior and social-information processing. For example, there is evidence that mates are selected for their ability to confirm attachment-related expectations, even if the expectations are negative (Kirkpatrick & K. E. Davis, in press; Swann, Hixon, & De La Ronde, 1992). We believe that individual differences in attachment, mediated by internal working models, may underlie many of the interpersonal differences that have been discovered by researchers working from other theoretical bases. Further, insecure attachment might be at the root of many dysfunctional behaviors contributing to relationship dissatisfaction and dissolution.

Despite forces favoring the stability of individual differences in attachment, change is always possible. For example, the experience of just one important relationship that disconfirms insecure expectations of unreliability or rejection increases the likelihood of forming a secure attachment in adulthood (Hazan & Hutt, 1991a). In most cases, these disconfirming relationship experiences were formed with nonparental adults (e.g., teachers, relatives) during childhood or with romantic partners during late adolescence or early adulthood. Consistent with studies of change in infancy and childhood, secure attachment is the most stable pattern.

The distribution of adults across attachment categories—55% secure, 25% avoidant, and 20% anxious/ambivalent—has been replicated in many studies in several different countries (e.g., Feeney & Noller, 1990; Hazan & Shaver, 1987; Mikulincer, Florian, & Tolmacz, 1990). The proportions are similar to those found in infant studies using Ainsworth's Strange Situation procedure (Campos et al., 1983). To date, there have been no reliable gender differences reported in the distribution of subjects across the three categories.

Gender Differences

No treatment of close relationships would be complete without some discussion of gender differences. Males and females differ significantly in their styles of communication (Tannen, 1990), in their tendency to engage in extra-relationship affairs (Skolnick, 1978), and in their skill at reading nonverbal cues (Hall, 1978). They differ as well in their likelihood of initiating breakups (Hill, Rubin, & Peplau, 1976) and in their subsequent adjustment (Wallerstein & Kelly, 1980). They also differ in the degree to which they value physical attractiveness (Berscheid, Dion, E. Walster, & G. W. Walster, 1971) and material resources (Buss & Barnes, 1986) in a potential mate.

The measure we developed for assessing individual differences in adult attachment (Hazan & Shaver, 1987) might have been expected to show gender differences. The anxious/ambivalent pattern sounds very much like the clingy, dependent aspects of the female stereotype, and the avoidant pattern strongly resembles the stereotypical intimacy-evading male. That males and females do not fall disproportionately into either category lends support to Bowlby's claim that all human beings have an inborn need for felt security.

Informal examination of the data suggests that gender differences lie primarily in the domains of caregiving and sexuality, rather than attachment. In general, females are more oriented toward caregiving, and males are more oriented toward sex. Some of the major differences between lesbian and gay male relationships seem to support this view (Peplau & Gordon, 1983). Buss (1985) developed a sociobiological theory of human male selection that is also consistent with this conceptualization of gender differences. However, within an attachment framework, gender differences do not entail a biological explanation. Because the caregiving and sexual mating systems develop later than the attachment system, it is likely that they are more subject to sex-role socialization pressures. The extent of biological versus social causation is still a legitimate matter for dispute and further research.

Concluding Remarks

Our review of the literature has necessarily been selective, and there are many additional facts that we have not attempted to integrate, although many seem amenable to explanation within an attachment framework. Even so, we do not believe that the framework we have proposed will be able to explain all important relationship phenomena. Each theory has its boundaries, and attachment theory is no exception. In fairness to Bowlby, he was not attempting to explain every aspect or type of close relationship. His aim was simply to explain the structure and functions of attachment, and it took him three volumes to do it. Even in beginning to extend his theory to adult attachments, we have taken great liberties.

At the outset, we said that we see attachment and interdependence as largely complementary theories. We asked what a good theory of close relationships should be able to do. A reasonable response is that it should offer a precise and operational definition of *close* and should emphasize relationships more than individual relationship partners. Interdependence theory is superior to attachment theory in both regards, and, in its models of interaction and types of transformations that occur over the course of an interaction, interdependence theory is unparalleled. Attachment theory, in contrast, emphasizes what of psychological value individuals will try to accomplish in their interactions. Attachment is a motivated model, and the motives on which it focuses are based in biology. We are active, biological organisms that build internal structures. As with other behavioristic models in psychology, the strength of interdependence theory rests with its operational definitions and measurement of observables. However, it would be a mistake to believe that all important relationship phenomena can be reduced to observable ones.

The theories that emphasize socially constructed, shared meanings and narratives also add something important to attachment theory, which, because of its roots in ethology, does not stress the unique properties of human verbal communication. Nevertheless, attachment theory may provide some of the themes of and constraints on interpersonal story construction, whereas communication-oriented theories add to attachment theory's conceptualization of the ways in which internal working models of self, relationships, and relationship partners get constructed. A complete integration of attachment, interdependence, and communication theories would require more space and expertise than we have at present, but we firmly believe that such a union would be fruitful.

It is common to hear attachment theory described as a theory about three (or maybe four) types of babies. Such emphasis on individual differences does not reflect the main thrust of attachment theory, which is first and foremost a normative theory. An added strength is that it can also account for the nature and form of individual differences. Ainsworth's creation of an innovative paradigm for assessing attachment quality in infancy focused attention on individual differences. By creating a simple self-report measure of adult attachment styles, we inadvertently helped extend the individual-differences approach to the study of adult relationships. The normative implications of attachment theory have rarely been spelled out or tested.

We imagine that Harlow would be pleased to see that researchers are finally grappling with love and affection and are analyzing these important facets of human behavior into their component variables. Such a bottom-up approach and the construction of a descriptive base constitute a useful first phase in the development of our science, but it is not the ultimate goal. Eventually, the accumulation of facts in the absence of theory becomes inefficient. Without theory as a guide, research is difficult to plan, and findings are difficult to interpret. Our goal here has been to persuade the reader that a theoretical integration of research findings on close relationships is neither premature nor impossible and that attachment theory

can provide the core constructs of such an integrative framework. If we have failed to be persuasive, we hope we have at least been provocative enough to inspire the kind of integrative thought and conceptual debate that will help advance the science of close relationships.

NOTES

Preparation of this target article was facilitated by a Special Projects Grant from Cornell University to Cindy Hazan and by National Science Foundation Grant BSN-8808736 to Cindy Hazan and Phillip R. Shaver.

We thank Rick Canfield, Robert Turgeon, and Joanne Sturgeon for their helpful comments on drafts of this target article.

Cindy Hazan, Department of Human Development and Family Studies, Van Rensselaer Hall, Cornell University, Ithaca, NY 14853–4401.

REFERENCES

Ainsworth, M. D. S., Blehar, M. C., Waters, E., & Wall, S. (1978). *Patterns of attachment: A psychological study of the Strange Situation*. Hillsdale, NJ: Lawrence Erlbaum Associates, Inc.

Altman, I., & Taylor, D. A. (1973). *Social penetration: The development of interpersonal relationships*. New York: Holt, Rinehart & Winston.

Arend, R., Gove, F., & Sroufe, L. A. (1979). Continuity of individual adaptation from infancy to kindergarten: A predictive study of ego resiliency and curiosity in preschoolers. *Child Development, 50,* 950–959.

Aron, A. P., Dutton, D. G., Aron, E. N., & Iverson, A. (1989). Experiences of falling in love. *Journal of Social and Personal Relationships, 6,* 243–257.

Aronson, E. (1988). *The social animal* (5th ed.). New York: Freeman.

Berscheid, E. (1983). Emotion. In H. H. Kelley, E. Berscheid, A. Christensen, J. H. Harvey, T. L. Huston, G. Levinger, E. McClintock, L. A. Peplau, & D. R. Peterson (Eds.), *Close relationships* (pp. 110–168). New York: Freeman.

Berscheid, E. (1984). Interpersonal attraction. In G. Lindzey & E. Aronson (Eds.), *Handbook of social psychology* (3rd ed., pp. 413–484). Reading, MA: Addison-Wesley.

Berscheid, E., Dion, K., Walster, E., & Walster, G. W. (1971). Physical attractiveness and dating choice: A test of the matching hypothesis. *Journal of Experimental Social Psychology, 7,* 173–189.

Berscheid, E., & Graziano, W. (1979). The initiation of social relationships and social attraction. In R. L. Burgess & T. L. Huston (Eds.), *Social exchange in developing relationships*. New York: Academic.

Berscheid, E., & Walster, E. (1974). A little bit about love. In T. L. Huston (Ed.), *Foundations of interpersonal attraction* (pp. 355–381). New York: Academic.

Bowlby, J. (1944). Forty-four juvenile thieves: Their characters and home life. *International Journal of Psycho-Analysis, 25*, 19–52, 107–127.

Bowlby, J. (1951). *Maternal care and mental health*. Geneva: World Health Organization.

Bowlby, J. (1973). *Attachment and loss: Vol. 2. Separation: Anxiety and anger*. New York: Basic.

Bowlby, J. (1979). *The making and breaking of affectional bonds*. London: Tavistock.

Bowlby, J. (1980). *Attachment and loss: Vol. 3. Loss: Sadness and depression*. New York: Basic.

Bowlby, J. (1982). *Attachment and loss: Vol. 1. Attachment* (2nd ed.). New York: Basic. (Original work published 1969.)

Bowlby, J. (1988). *A secure base: Parent–child attachment and healthy human development*. New York: Basic.

Brennan, K., Shaver, P. R., & Tobey, A. E. (1991). Attachment styles, gender, and parental problem drinking. *Journal of Social and Personal Relationships, 8*, 451–466.

Bretherton, I. (1990). Open communication and internal working models: Their role in the development of attachment relationships. In R. A. Thompson (Ed.), *Nebraska Symposium on Motivation: Vol. 36. Socioemotional development* (pp. 57–113). Lincoln: University of Nebraska Press.

Buss, D. M. (1985). Human mate selection. *American Scientist, 73*, 47–54.

Buss, D. M., & Barnes, M. (1986). Preferences in human mate selection. *Journal of Personality and Social Psychology, 50*, 559–570.

Campos, J. J., Barrett, K., Lamb, M. E., Goldsmith, H. H., & Stenberg, C. (1983). Socioemotional development. In P. H. Mussen (Ed.), *Handbook of child psychology: Vol. 2. Infancy and developmental psychobiology* (pp. 783–915). New York: Wiley.

Cassidy, J. (1988). Child–mother attachment and the self in six-year-olds. *Child Development, 59*, 121–134.

Colin, V. L. (1991). *Human attachment: What we know now*. Chevy Chase, MD: U.S. Department of Health and Human Services.

Collins, N. L., & Read, S. J. (1990). Adult attachment, working models, and relationship quality in dating couples. *Journal of Personality and Social Psychology, 58*, 644–663.

Crittenden, P. M. (1988). Relationships at risk. In J. Belsky & T. Nezworski (Eds.), *Clinical implications of attachment* (pp. 136–174). Hillsdale, NJ: Lawrence Erlbaum Associates, Inc.

Crockenberg, S. B. (1981). Infant irritability, mother responsiveness, and social support influences on the security of infant–mother attachment. *Child Development, 52*, 857–869.

Daniels, T., & Shaver, P. R. (1991). *Attachment styles and power strategies in romantic relationships*. Unpublished manuscript, State University of New York at Buffalo, Department of Psychology.

Dozier, M., & Kobak, R. R. (in press). Psychophysiology and adolescent attachment interviews: Converging evidence for repressing strategies. *Child Development*.

Driscoll, R., Davis, K. W., & Lipetz, M. E. (1972). Parental interference and romantic love. *Journal of Personality and Social Psychology, 24*, 1–10.

Duck, S. W. (1991, May). *New lamps for old: A new theory of relationships and a fresh look at some old research*. Paper presented at the meeting of the International Network on Personal Relationships, Normal, IL.

Dutton, D. G., & Aron, A. P. (1974). Some evidence for heightened sexual attraction under conditions of high anxiety. *Journal of Personality and Social Psychology, 30*, 510–517.

Egeland, B., & Farber, E. A. (1984). Infant–mother attachment: Factors related to its development and changes over time. *Child Development, 55*, 753–771.

Feeney, J., & Noller, P. (1990). Attachment style as a predictor of adult romantic relationships. *Journal of Personality and Social Psychology, 58*, 281–291.

Felmlee, D., Sprecher, S., & Bassin, E. (1990). The dissolution of intimate relationships: A hazard model. *Social Psychology Quarterly, 52*, 13–30.

Festinger, L., Schachter, S., & Back, K. W. (1950). *Social pressures in informal groups: A study of human factors in housing*. New York: Harper.

Fiala, K. B. (1991). *Attachment and psychosocial functioning of depressed, remitted depressed, and nondepressed women and their partners*. Unpublished doctoral dissertation, University of Massachusetts, Amherst.

Fincham, F. D., Beach, S., & Nelson, G. (1987). Attribution processes in distressed and non-distressed couples: Self–partner attribution for spouse behavior. *Cognitive Therapy and Research, 11*, 71–86.

Fisher, H. E. (1992). *Anatomy of love*. New York: Norton.

Fiske, S. T., & Taylor, S. E. (1991). *Social cognition*. New York: Random House.

Folkes, V. S., & Sears, D. O. (1977). Does everybody like a liker? *Journal of Experimental Social Psychology, 13*, 505–519.

Fullard, W., & Reiling, A. M. (1976). An investigation of Lorenz's "babyness." *Child Development, 47*, 1191–1193.

Furman, W., & Buhmester, D. (1985). Children's perceptions of the personal relationships in their social networks. *Developmental Psychology, 21*, 1016–1024.

Goldsmith, H. H., & Alansky, J. A. (1987). Maternal and infant temperamental predictors of attachment: A meta-analytic review. *Journal of Consulting and Clinical Psychology, 55*, 805–816.

Gorer, G. (1973). Death, grief and mourning in Britain. In E. J. Anthony & C. Koupernik (Eds.), *The child in his family: The impact of disease and death*. New York: Wiley.

Gottman, J. M. (1983). How children become friends. *Monographs of the Society for Research in Child Development, 48* (3, Serial No. 201).

Gottman, J., Markman, H., & Notarius, C. (1977). The topography of marital conflict: A sequential analysis of verbal and nonverbal behavior. *Journal of Marriage and the Family, 39*, 461–477.

Gottman, J., Notarius, C., Gonso, J., & Markman, H. J. (1976). *A couple's guide to communication.* Champaign, IL: Research Press.

Grossberg, S. (1980). How does a brain build a cognitive code? *Psychological Review, 87*, 1–51.

Grossmann, K. E., & Grossmann, K. (1991). Attachment quality as an organizer of emotional and behavioral responses in a longitudinal perspective. In C. M. Parkes, J. Stevenson-Hinde, & P. Marris (Eds.), *Attachment across the life cycle* (pp. 93–114). London: Tavistock/ Routledge.

Hall, J. A. (1978). Gender effects in decoding nonverbal cues. *Psychological Bulletin, 85*, 845–857.

Harlow, H. (1958). The nature of love. *American Psychologist, 13*, 673–685.

Hartup, W. (1983). Peer relations. In E. M. Hetherington (Vol. Ed.) & P. H. Mussen (Series Ed.), *Handbook of child psychology: Vol. 4. Socialization, personality, and social development* (pp. 103–196). New York: Wiley.

Harvey, J. H., Orbuch, T. L., & Weber, A. L. (1990). A social psychological model of account-making: In response to severe stress. *Journal of Language and Social Psychology, 9*, 191–207.

Hatfield, E. (1984). The dangers of intimacy. In V. J. Derlega (Ed.), *Communication, intimacy and close relationships* (pp. 207–220). New York: Academic.

Hatfield, E., & Rapson, R. L. (1987). Passionate love: New directions in research. In W. H. Jones & D. Perlman (Eds.), *Advances in personal relationships* (Vol. 1, pp. 109–140). Greenwich, CT: JAI.

Hazan, C., & Hutt, M. J. (1991a). *Continuity and change in internal working models of attachment.* Unpublished manuscript, Cornell University, Department of Human Development and Family Studies.

Hazan, C., & Hutt, M. J. (1991b). *From parents to peers: Transitions in attachment.* Unpublished manuscript, Cornell University, Department of Human Development and Family Studies.

Hazan, C., Hutt, M. J., Sturgeon, J., & Bricker, T. (1991, April). *The process of relinquishing parents as attachment figures.* Paper presented at the meeting of the Society for Research in Child Development, Seattle.

Hazan, C., & Shaver, P. R. (1987). Romantic love conceptualized as an attachment process. *Journal of Personality and Social Psychology, 52*, 511–524.

Hazan, C., & Shaver, P. R. (1990). Love and work: An attachment-theoretical perspective. *Journal of Personality and Social Psychology, 59*, 270–280.

Hazan, C., & Shaver, P. R. (1992). Broken attachments. In T. L. Orbuch (Ed.), *Close relationship loss: Theoretical approaches* (pp. 90–108). Hillsdale, NJ: Lawrence Erlbaum Associates, Inc.

Heinicke, C., & Westheimer, I. (1966). *Brief separations.* New York: International Universities Press.

Hendrick, C., & Hendrick, S. (1986). A theory and method of love. *Journal of Personality and Social Psychology, 50*, 392–402.

Hill, C. T., Rubin, Z., & Peplau, L. A. (1976). Breakups before marriage: The end of 103 affairs. *Journal of Social Issues, 32*, 147–168.

Hinde, R. (1979). *Towards understanding relationships.* London: Academic.

Hinsz, V. B. (1989). Facial resemblance in engaged and married couples. *Journal of Social and Personal Relationships, 6*, 223–229.

Holmes, J. G., & Rempel, J. K. (1989). Trust in close relationships. In C. Hendrick (Ed.), *Close relationships* (pp. 187–220). Newbury Park, CA: Sage.

Huston, T. L., Surra, C. A., Fitzgerald, N. M., & Cate, R. M. (1981). From courtship to marriage: Mate selection as an interpersonal process. In S. Duck & R. Gilmour (Eds.), *Personal relationships: Vol. 2. Developing personal relationships* (pp. 53–88). New York: Academic.

Kelley, H. H. (1983). Love and commitment. In H. H. Kelley, E. Berscheid, A. Christensen, J. H. Harvey, T. L. Huston, G. Levinger, E. McClintock, L. A. Peplau, & D. R. Peterson (Eds.), *Close relationships* (pp. 265–314). New York: Freeman.

Kelley, H. H., Berscheid, E., Christensen, A., Harvey, J. H., Huston, T. L., Levinger, G., McClintock, E., Peplau, L. A., & Peterson, D. R. (Eds.). (1983). *Close relationships.* New York: Freeman.

Kerckhoff, A. C., & Davis, K. E. (1962). Value consensus and need complementarity in mate selection. *American Sociological Review, 27*, 295–303.

Kirkpatrick, L. A., & Davis, K. E. (in press). Attachment style, gender, and relationship stability: A longitudinal analysis. *Journal of Personality and Social Psychology.*

Kirkpatrick, L., & Shaver, P. R. (1990). Attachment theory and religion: Childhood attachments, religious beliefs, and conversion. *Journal for the Scientific Study of Religion, 29*, 315–334.

Kobak, R. R., & Hazan, C. (1991). Attachment in marriage: Effects of security and accuracy of working models. *Journal of Personality and Social Psychology, 60*, 861–869.

Kobak, R. R., & Sceery, A. (1988). The transition to college: Working models of attachment, affect regulation, and perceptions of self and others. *Child Development, 88*, 135–146.

Konner, M. (1982). *The tangled wing: Biological constraints on the human spirit.* New York: Holt, Rinehart & Winston.

Kotler, T. (1985). Security and autonomy within marriage. *Human Relations, 38*, 299–321.

Kunce, L. J., & Shaver, P. R. (1991). *An attachment-theoretical approach to caregiving in romantic relationships.* Unpublished manuscript, State University of New York at Buffalo, Department of Psychology.

Lamb, M. E., Thompson, R. A., Gardner, W. P., Charnov, E. L., & Estes, D. (1984). Security of infantile attachment as assessed in the Strange Situation: Its study and biological interpretation. *Behavioral and Brain Sciences, 7*, 127–171.

Levenson, R. W., & Gottman, J. M. (1985). Six physiological and affective predictors of change in relationship satisfaction. *Journal of Personality and Social Psychology, 49*, 85–94.

Levinger, G. (1966). Systematic distortion in spouses' reports of preferred and actual sexual behavior. *Sociometry, 29*, 291–299.

Levinger, G. (1976). A social psychological perspective on marital dissolution. *Journal of Social Issues, 32*(1), 21–47.

Levinger, G. (1983). Development and change. In H. H. Kelley, E. Berscheid, A. Christensen, J. H. Harvey, T. L. Huston, G. Levinger, E. McClintock, L. A. Peplau, & D. R. Peterson (Eds.), *Close relationships* (pp. 315–359). New York: Freeman.

Levinger, G., & Levinger, A. C. (1986). The temporal course of close relationships: Some thoughts about the development of children's ties. In W. W. Hartup & Z. Rubin (Eds.), *Relationships and development* (pp. 111–134). Hillsdale, NJ: Lawrence Erlbaum Associates, Inc.

Levinger, G., & Snoek, J. D. (1972). *Attraction in relationship: A new look at interpersonal attraction*. Morristown, NJ: General Learning Press.

Lewis, R. A. (1973). A longitudinal test of a developmental framework for premarital dyadic formation. *Journal of Marriage and the Family, 35*, 16–25.

Lewis, R. A., & Spanier, G. B. (1979). Theorizing about the quality and stability of marriage. In W. R. Burr, R. Hill, F. I. Nye, & I. L. Reiss (Eds.), *Contemporary theories about the family* (Vol. 1). New York: Free Press.

Lund, M. (1985). The development of investment and commitment scales for predicting continuity of personal relationships. *Journal of Social and Personal Relationships, 2*, 3–23.

Main, M. (1990). Parental aversion to infant-initiated contact is correlated with the parent's own rejection during childhood: The effects of experience on signals of security with respect to attachment. In K. E. Barnard & T. B. Brazelton (Eds.), *Touch: The foundation of experience* (pp. 461–495). Madison, CT: International Universities Press.

Main, M., & Hesse, E. (1990). Parents' unresolved traumatic experiences are related to infant disorganized status: Is frightened and/or frightening parental behavior the linking mechanism? In M. T. Greenberg, D. Cicchetti, & E. M. Cummings (Eds.), *Attachment in the preschool years* (pp. 161–184). Chicago: University of Chicago Press.

Main, M., Kaplan, N., & Cassidy, J. (1985). Security in infancy, childhood, and adulthood: A move to the level of representation. *Monographs of the Society for Research in Child Development, 50*(1–2, Serial No. 209), 66–104.

Main, M., & Solomon, J. (1990). Procedures for identifying infants as disorganized/disoriented during the Ainsworth Strange Situation. In M. T. Greenberg, D. Cicchetti, & E. M. Cummings (Eds.), *Attachment in the preschool years* (pp. 121–160). Chicago: University of Chicago Press.

Marris, P. (1958). *Widows and their families*. London: Routledge & Kegan Paul.

Mikulincer, M., Florian, V., & Tolmacz, R. (1990). Attachment styles and fear of personal death: A case study of affect regulation. *Journal of Personality and Social Psychology, 58*, 273–280.

Mikulincer, M., & Nachshon, O. (1991). Attachment styles and patterns of self-disclosure. *Journal of Personality and Social Psychology, 61*, 321–331.

Miller, G. A., Galanter, E., & Pribram, K. H. (1960). *Plans and the structure of behavior*. New York: Holt, Rinehart & Winston.

Miller, S. I., & Schoenfeld, L. (1973). Grief in the Navajo: Psychodynamics and culture. *International Journal of Psychiatry, 19*, 187–191.

Murstein, B. I. (1976). *Who will marry whom?* New York: Springer.

Newcomb, T. M. (1961). *The acquaintance process*. New York: Holt, Rinehart & Winston.

Owen, M. T., Easterbrooks, M. A., Chase-Lansdale, L., & Goldberg, W. A. (1984). The relation between maternal employment status and the stability of attachments to mother and father. *Child Development, 55*, 1894–1901.

Palgi, P. (1973). The socio-cultural expressions and implications of death, mourning and bereavement arising out of the war situation in Israel. *Israel Annals of Psychiatry, 11*, 301–329.

Parkes, C. M., & Weiss, R. S. (1983). *Recovery from bereavement*. New York: Basic.

Peplau, L. A., & Gordon, S. L. (1983). The intimate relationships of lesbians and gay men. In E. R. Allgeier & N. B. McCormick (Eds.), *The changing boundaries: Gender roles and sexual behavior* (pp. 226–244). Palo Alto, CA: Mayfield.

Peplau, L. A., & Perlman, D. (Eds.). (1982). *Loneliness: A sourcebook of current theory, research and therapy*. New York: Wiley-Interscience.

Piaget, J. (1952). *The origins of intelligence in children*. New York: International Universities Press.

Rands, M., Levinger, G., & Mellinger, G. D. (1981). Patterns of conflict resolution and marital satisfaction. *Journal of Family Issues, 2*, 297–321.

Reedy, M. N., Birren, J. E., & Schaie, K. W. (1981). Age and sex differences in satisfying love relationships across the adult life span. *Human Development, 24*, 52–66.

Reis, H. T., & Shaver, P. R. (1988). Intimacy as an interpersonal process. In S. Duck (Ed.), *Handbook of research in personal relationships* (pp. 367–389). London: Wiley.

Reiss, I. L. (1960). Toward a sociology of the heterosexual love relationship. *Marriage and Family Living, 22*, 139–145.

Rubenstein, C., & Shaver, P. R. (1982). *In search of intimacy*. New York: Delacorte.

Rubin, Z. (1973). *Liking and loving*. New York: Holt, Rinehart & Winston.

Rubin, Z. (1980). *Children's friendships*. Cambridge: Harvard University Press.

Rubin, Z. (1984). Toward a science of relationships. *Contemporary Psychology, 29*, 856–858.

Rusbult, C. E. (1980). Commitment and satisfaction in romantic associations: A test of the investment model. *Journal of Experimental Social Psychology, 16*, 172–186.

Rusbult, C. E. (1983). A longitudinal test of the investment model: The development (and deterioration) of satisfaction and commitment in heterosexual involvements. *Journal of Personality and Social Psychology, 45,* 101–117.

Rusbult, C. E., & Zembrodt, I. M. (1983). Responses to dissatisfaction in romantic involvement: A multidimensional scaling analysis. *Journal of Experimental Social Psychology, 19,* 274–293.

Rusbult, C. E., Zembrodt, I. M., & Gunn, L. K. (1982). Exit, voice, loyalty, and neglect: Responses to dissatisfaction in romantic involvements. *Journal of Personality and Social Psychology, 43,* 1230–1242.

Schachter, S. (1959). *The psychology of affiliation: Experimental studies of the sources of gregariousness.* Stanford, CA: Stanford University Press.

Schaffer, H. R., & Emerson, P. E. (1964). The development of social attachments in infancy. *Monographs of the Society for Research in Child Development, 29* (3, Serial No. 94).

Shaver, P. R., & Hazan, C. (1984). Incompatibility, loneliness, and "limerence." In W. Ickes (Ed.), *Compatible and incompatible relationships* (pp. 163–184). New York: Springer-Verlag.

Shaver, P. R., & Hazan, C. (1993). Adult romantic attachment: Theory and evidence. In D. Perlman & W. Jones (Eds.), *Advances in personal relationships* (Vol. 4, pp. 29–70). Greenwich, CT: JAI.

Shaver, P. R., Hazan, C., & Bradshaw, D. (1988). Love as attachment: The integration of three behavioral systems. In R. J. Sternberg & M. L. Barnes (Eds.), *The psychology of love* (pp. 68–99). New Haven, CT: Yale University Press.

Shaver, P. R., & Rubenstein, C. (1980). Childhood attachment experience and adult loneliness. In L. Wheeler (Ed.), *Review of personality and social psychology* (Vol. 1, pp. 42–73). Beverly Hills, CA: Sage.

Simpson, J. A. (1990). The influence of attachment styles on romantic relationships. *Journal of Personality and Social Psychology, 59,* 971–980.

Skolnick, A. (1978). *The intimate environment: Exploring marriage and the family* (2nd ed.). Boston: Little, Brown.

Snyder, M., & Swann, W. B., Jr. (1978). Behavioral confirmation in social interaction: From social perception to social reality. *Journal of Experimental Social Psychology, 14,* 148–162.

Spanier, G. B., Lewis, R. A., & Cole, C. L. (1975). Marital adjustment over the family life cycle: The issue of curvilinearity. *Journal of Marriage and the Family, 37,* 263–275.

Sroufe, L. A. (1983). Infant-caregiver attachment and patterns of adaptation in preschool: The roots of maladaptation and competence. In M. Perlmutter (Ed.), *Minnesota Symposium on Child Psychology* (Vol. 16, pp. 41–83). Hillsdale, NJ: Lawrence Erlbaum Associates, Inc.

Sroufe, L. A., & Waters, E. (1977). Attachment as an organizational construct. *Child Development, 48,* 1184–1199.

Stanley, S. M. (1986). *Commitment and the maintenance and enhancement of relationships.* Unpublished doctoral dissertation, University of Denver.

Steinberg, L., & Silverberg, S. B. (1986). The vicissitudes of autonomy in early adolescence. *Child Development, 57,* 841–851.

Sternberg, R. J. (1986). A triangular theory of love. *Psychological Review, 93,* 119–135.

Swann, W. B., Jr., Hixon, J. G., & De La Ronde, C. (1992). Embracing the bitter "truth": Negative self-concepts and marital commitment. *Psychological Science, 3,* 118–121.

Tannen, D. (1990). *You just don't understand: Women and men in conversation.* New York: Morrow.

Taylor, D. A., & Altman, I. (1987). Communication in interpersonal relationships: Social penetration processes. In M. Roloff & G. Miller (Eds.), *Interpersonal processes: New directions in communication research* (pp. 257–277). Newbury Park, CA: Sage.

Tennov, D. (1979). *Love and limerence: The experience of being in love.* New York: Stein & Day.

Thibaut, J. W., & Kelley, H. H. (1959). *The social psychology of groups.* New York: Wiley.

Traupmann, J., & Hatfield, E. (1981). Love: Its effects on mental and physical health. In J. March, S. Kiesler, R. Fogel, E. Hatfield, & E. Shana (Eds.), *Aging: Stability and change in the family.* New York: Academic.

van den Boom, D. (1990). Preventive intervention and the quality of mother–infant interaction and infant exploration in irritable infants. In W. Koops, H. J. G. Soppe, J. L. van der Linden, P. C. M. Molenaar, & J. J. F. Schroots (Eds.), *Developmental psychology behind the dikes: An outline of developmental psychology research in The Netherlands.* The Netherlands: Uitgeverij Eburon.

Vaughn, B., Egeland, B., Sroufe, L. A., & Waters, E. (1979). Individual differences in infant–mother attachment at 12 and 18 months: Stability and change in families under stress. *Child Development, 50,* 971–975.

Wallerstein, J. B., & Kelly, J. B. (1980). *Surviving the breakup: How children and parents cope with divorce.* New York: Basic.

Walster, E., Aronson, E., Abrahams, D., & Rottmann, L. (1966). The importance of physical attractiveness in dating behavior. *Journal of Personality and Social Psychology, 4,* 508–516.

Walster, E., & Walster, G. W. (1978). *A new look at love.* Reading, MA: Addison-Wesley.

Waters, E. (1978). The reliability and stability of individual differences in infant–mother attachment. *Child Development, 49,* 483–494.

Weiss, R. S. (1973). *Loneliness: The experience of emotional and social isolation.* Cambridge, MA: MIT Press.

Weiss, R. S. (1975). *Marital separation.* New York: Basic.

Weiss, R. S. (1982). Attachment in adults. In C. M. Parkes & J. Stevenson-Hinde (Eds.), *The place of attachment in human behavior* (pp. 171–184). New York: Basic.

Weiss, R. S. (1988). Loss and recovery. *Journal of Social Issues, 44,* 37–52.

Zajonc, R. B. (1968). Attitudinal effects of mere exposure. *Journal of Personality and Social Psychology Monograph Supplement, 9*(2, Pt. 2), 1–27.

READING 10

Attachment Working Models and the Sense of Trust: An Exploration of Interaction Goals and Affect Regulation

Mario Mikulincer • Bar-Ilan University

Three studies examined the association between adult attachment style and the sense of trust in close relationships. Study 1 focused on the accessibility of trust-related memories. Studies 2–3 focused on trust-related goals and coping strategies, while using different data collection techniques (open-ended probes, lexical decision task). Findings showed that secure persons felt more trust toward partners, showed higher accessibility of positive trust-related memories, and adopted more constructive strategies in coping with the violation of trust than insecure persons. In addition, whereas intimacy attainment was the main trust-related goal for all the attachment groups, security attainment was an additional goal of anxious–ambivalent persons, and control attainment was an additional goal of avoidant persons. Findings are discussed in terms of attachment working models.

During the last three decades, social psychologists have attempted to understand how adult relationships function and to delineate the source of individual differences in the way people relate to others. In the present study, I focus on one source of individual differences—adult attachment style—and examine its association with an important relational process—the experience of trust in a relationship. The study of the attachment–trust link is highly significant, because it brings together two important processes in relationships, each with its own well-developed body of research and theory. Moreover, it provides a theoretical framework to understand how people appraise and react to partner behaviors that reinforce or violate the trust they feel toward him or her, and thereby to explain the construction of the sense of trust in a relationship—what would seem to be a necessary condition for the development of secure, intimate, and satisfactory relationships.

Adult Attachment Style and the Sense of Trust

Attachment theory (Bowlby, 1973) proposes that mental representations of self and others ("attachment working models") formed throughout interactions with attachment figures organize cognitions, affect, and behavior in close relationships. Hazan and Shaver (1987) examined this hypothesis in adult love relationships, using Ainsworth, Blehar, Waters, and Wall's (1978) typology of attachment style. The secure style, defined by comfort with closeness and interdependence and by confidence in others' love, was associated with happy, intimate, and friendly love relationships. The avoidant style, defined by insecurity in others' intentions and preference for distance, was associated with fear of intimacy and difficulty depending on partners. The anxious–ambivalent style, defined by a strong desire for intimacy together with insecurity about others' responses, was associated with love addiction, passionate love, and fear of being unloved. These findings were replicated in other studies (see Shaver & Hazan, 1993, for a review).

The current study further explores the implications of attachment working models in adult love by focusing on the individual's sense of trust. Trust is one of the most desired qualities in love relationships (Holmes & Rempel, 1989). It is a definitional element of the intimacy component of love (Sternberg, 1986) and a necessary condition for the development of commitment and feelings of security (Holmes & Rempel, 1989). In fact, lack of trust may produce distress, reduce relational rewards, and lead to relationship dissolution (Holmes & Rempel, 1989).

Several definitions of interpersonal trust have been proposed (e.g., Deutsch, 1973; Rotter, 1980; Scanzoni, 1979). Rempel, Holmes, and Zanna (1985) reviewed these definitions and concluded that trust involves (a) the appraisal of partners as reliable and predictable, (b) the belief that partners are concerned with one's needs and can be counted on in times of need, and (c) feelings of confidence in the strength of the relationship. Rempel et al. (1985) labeled these components partner's predictability, partner's dependability,

and faith in the future of the relationship. With the development of theory and research, trust is now defined only on the basis of dependability and faith (Holmes & Rempel, 1989; Murray & Holmes, 1993; Sorrentino, Holmes, Hanna, & Sharp, 1995).

The above definition of trust implies that trust is an integral part of secure attachment. The dependability component of trust refers to the confidence one has that a partner in a close relationship will be concerned about and responsive to one's needs, goals, and desires. Thus, this component of trust includes positive expectations about partner availability as well as about his or her responsiveness and caring. All of these expectations are the core components of secure persons' working models of others (Shaver & Hazan, 1993). These persons believe in the availability, sensitivity, and responsiveness of others and thereby may experience high levels of trust toward them.

In support of this view, studies have found that a secure attachment style is positively related to the level of trust a person feels in love relationships (e.g., Brennan & Shaver, 1995; Feeney & Noller, 1990; Hazan & Shaver, 1987; Levy & Davis, 1988; Mikulincer & Erev, 1991; Simpson, 1990), to the trust felt by his or her partner, and to his or her generalized sense of interpersonal trust (Collins & Read, 1990). In addition, secure persons have been found to maintain high levels of trust over time, whereas insecure persons have been found to show a deterioration of trust over time (Keelan, Dion, & Dion, 1994). Beyond stylistic differences, persons from the three attachment styles report having experienced more trust in particular relationships wherein they feel securely attached than in "insecure" relationships (Baldwin, Keelan, Fehr, Enns, & Koh-Rangarajoo, 1996).

The problem with the above studies is that they do not tap the complex and multifaceted nature of the sense of trust. In fact, people may differ not only in the level of "felt trust," but also in the meanings they attach to trust, the emotions they experience in trust-related episodes, and their cognitive and behavioral reactions to these episodes. Furthermore, a narrow focus of research does not take into account that working models of attachment contain, at least, four components (Collins & Read, 1994): (a) autobiographical memories of social interactions, (b) expectations about self or others in interpersonal situations, (c) goals that guide one's responses in social situations, and (d) strategies aimed at attaining these goals and at regulating the distress produced by lack of goal attainment (Collins & Read, 1994; Shaver, Collins, & Clark, 1996). These components may be relevant to the appraisal, processing, and reactions to trust-related experiences and might underlie attachment-style differences in the sense of trust.

With regard to the expectation component of working models, Baldwin, Fehr, Keedian, Seidel, and Thompson (1993) reported attachment-style differences in the outcomes expected in response to trusting a partner. In the first study, secure persons expected a hypothetical partner to respond more positively to situations in which they trust that partner than insecure persons. In the second study, reaction times in a lexical decision task revealed attachment-style differences in the outcomes that are automatically activated in the working memory upon the priming of a trust-related context. Whereas secure persons reacted more quickly to a positive outcome word (*care*), insecure persons reacted more quickly to a negative outcome word (*hurt*). These findings were replicated and extended by Baldwin et al. (1996) in their analysis of relationships that people chose as exemplars of secure and insecure patterns.

To date, there is no published study that examined the manifestations of the memory, goal, and strategy components of attachment working models in the sense of trust. This is the original contribution of the current study. Instead of asking whether people differing in attachment style differ in the level of trust they feel in a relationship, I asked whether they differ in the processing of trust-related memories, the goals they attach to trust-related experiences, and the strategies they use in dealing with betrayal of trust. This is the first systematic study that adopts a multifaceted approach in assessing the manifestations of attachment working model

components in trust-relevant memories, goals, and strategies.

Trust-Related Memories

The first set of hypotheses concerns trust-related memories. Collins and Read (1994) and Main, Kaplan, and Cassidy (1985) claimed that people differing in attachment style differ in their memories of attachment-related episodes. According to Collins and Read, secure persons should recall more positive and less negative relationship episodes than insecure persons. Indeed, Baldwin et al. (1996) found that positive exemplars of relationships were more available and accessible for secure persons, whereas negative exemplars were more available and accessible for avoidant and anxious–ambivalent persons.

On this basis, I hypothesized that attachment groups would differ in the accessibility (the easiness with which a memory is retrieved) of trust-related autobiographical memories. For secure persons, their positive working model of others (Shaver & Hazan, 1993) would promote a clear-cut pattern of memories. These persons would have more accessibility to memories of positive trust-related experiences (episodes in which they felt that partners were responsive and caring) than to memories of negative trust-related experiences (episodes in which they felt a betrayal of trust).

For insecure persons, however, one cannot make simple predictions. On the one hand, the fact that both avoidant and anxious–ambivalent persons hold negative working models of others (Shaver & Hazan, 1993) may bias their memories and make episodes of betrayal of trust more accessible and positive trust-related episodes less accessible.

On the other hand, there are some findings that complicated this prediction. First, although the uncertainty inherent in the working models of anxious–ambivalent persons (Collins & Read, 1994; Main et al., 1985) may lead to mistrust and accessibility of negative trust-related memories, it could also increase the accessibility of positive memories. These persons may be uncertain about the extent to which partners are available and responsive and then may be able to access both negative and positive trust-related memories. Second, avoidant people tend to repress negative memories (Main et al., 1985; Mikulincer & Orbach, 1995), which, in turn, may reduce the accessibility to negative trust-related memories. Thus, one can predict that avoidant persons would have low accessibility to both negative and positive trust-related memories and anxious–ambivalent persons would have high accessibility to these two types of memories.

Trust-Related Goals

The second set of hypotheses concerns the interaction goals that may be related to the sense of trust. According to Collins and Read (1994), people differing in attachment style differ in the goals they pursue in social interactions. Secure persons' experiences with caring and responsive attachment figures teach them that attachment behaviors are rewarding, that they can rely on the attachment system during social interactions, and that they can organize interpersonal behaviors around the basic goal of the attachment system: proximity maintenance (Shaver & Hazan, 1993). On this basis, Collins and Read (1994) claimed that secure persons construe their interaction goals around the search for intimacy and closeness to significant others. The positive feelings of secure persons that they are loved by significant others led them to the conviction that intimate relationships are rewarding and foster the desire to become intimate with people (Mikulincer & Erev, 1991).

Insecure persons' experiences with nonresponsive others teach them that attachment behaviors are painful (Shaver & Hazan, 1993) and that other interaction goals and behaviors should be developed as defenses against the distress caused by attachment experiences (Bowlby, 1988). In response to this distress, anxious–ambivalent persons seem to construe their interaction goals around the hyperactivation of the attachment system and the unfulfilled need for security (Collins & Read, 1994; Mikulincer & Nachshon, 1991). These persons attempt to minimize distance from attachment figures and fight for conquering "felt security"

through clinging and hypervigilant responses (Main et al., 1985; Mikulincer, Florian, & Tolmacz, 1990). They desire intimate relationships, but their hyperactivation of the attachment system may lead them to seek enmeshed love as a way of increasing felt security (Collins & Read, 1994). In contrast, avoidant persons seem to react to attachment distress by organizing their interaction goals around the deactivation of the attachment system and the search for autonomy and control (Collins & Read, 1994). These persons take distance from attachment figures and attempt to attain a sense of self-reliance as a means for compensating their reluctance to rely on their partners (Bowlby, 1988).

I hypothesize that the above attachment-style differences in interactions goals would be directly reflected in the sense of trust. Specifically, the intimacy goal would be related to secure persons' sense of trust. These persons hold a positive sense of trust (Shaver & Hazan, 1993), which may encourage them to actualize their desire for intimacy in a particular relationship. Their sense of trust may act as an internalized "secure base" from which they can confidently take the risks associated with the expression of personal information (e.g., feelings, fantasies). For secure persons, episodes that validate their sense of trust would thus contribute to the formation and maintenance of intimacy in close relationships, whereas betrayal of trust may raise concerns about the personal vulnerability inherent in intimacy.

For anxious–ambivalent persons, security seeking would be a central component of their sense of trust. These persons hold a negative sense of trust (Shaver & Hazan, 1993), which can reactivate their attachment insecurity and their defensive hyperactivation of the attachment system. That is, anxious–ambivalent persons' negative trust-related memories and expectations may activate concerns about security and security-seeking behaviors. Then, episodes in which partners behave in a responsive way may be appraised as contributing to security feelings, whereas betrayal of trust may be appraised as a threat to these feelings.

For avoidant persons, concerns about control would be central components of their sense of trust. These persons also hold a negative sense of trust (Shaver & Hazan, 1993), which may reactivate their attachment insecurity and their defensive deactivation of the attachment system and may lead them to search for personal control. For these persons, this pursuit of control seems to be necessary to validate their sense of self-reliance. Moreover, this pursuit seems to be necessary to ensure the attainment of desired outcomes in the absence of confidence that the partner will voluntarily respond to their needs. On this basis, avoidant persons may perceive each episode in which a partner is responsive as a validation of the control they exert over partner behaviors, whereas betrayal of trust may raise doubts about the control they have in the relationship.

Coping With the Violation of Trust

The third set of hypotheses concerns the ways by which people deal with negative trust-related experiences. Attachment theory and research suggest that attachment groups differ in the way they manage distress (e.g., Collins & Read, 1994; Mikulincer et al., 1990). Secure persons' interactions with supportive and caring attachment figures teach them that the attachment system is an effective device for attaining comfort and relief (Mikulincer & Florian, 1998). That is, secure persons seem to learn to manage distress through the basic guidelines of the attachment system: acknowledgment of distress, engagement in constructive actions, and turning to others for support (Bowlby, 1988; Mikulincer & Florian, 1998).

In contrast, insecure persons learn that attachment behaviors are ineffective regulatory devices and that other defensive strategies should be developed (Bowlby, 1988). According to Bowlby, the strategies developed in response to attachment-related distress (hyperactivation or deactivation of the attachment system) are generalized to the management of other sources of distress, of which the negative infant–caregiver interaction is a prototypical situation. In this way, anxious–ambivalent persons' hyperactivation of their attachment to painful others and their excessive focus on attachment-related distress (Bowlby, 1988) may result in a hyperactivation of distress cues. These

persons seem to direct attention to distress in a hypervigilant manner, to mentally ruminate on its causes and meanings, and to deliberate on related negative thoughts (Shaver & Hazan, 1993). Accordingly, avoidant persons' tendency to detach from attachment distress may result in behavioral and cognitive distancing from distress cues. Specifically, avoidant people seem to deal with distress by suppressing bad thoughts, inhibiting display of distress, repressing painful memories, and escaping from any confrontation with problems (Shaver & Hazan, 1993).

These patterns of coping have been found in response to (a) missile attacks during the Gulf War (Mikulincer, Florian, & Weller, 1993), (b) a demanding military training (Mikulincer & Florian, 1995), (c) the process of divorce (Birnbaum, Orr, Mikulincer, & Florian, 1998), and (d) parenthood-related problems (Mikulincer & Florian, 1998). More important, they have been found in the ways people deal with relationship conflict and negative partner behavior (e.g., Levy & Davis, 1988; Pistole, 1989; Scharfe & Bartholomew, 1995).

In my terms, the violation of the sense of trust is an interpersonal stressor, an exemplar of what Scharfe and Bartholomew (1995) called "potentially destructive acts committed by romantic partners." As such, it may produce distress and activate habitual ways of coping. On this basis, I hypothesized that people differing in attachment style would deal with negative trust-related experiences in the same way they deal with other stressors. Whereas secure persons would rely on constructive strategies (e.g., talking with partner), avoidant persons would rely on distancing strategies (e.g., ignoring the problem, taking distance from partner), and anxious–ambivalent persons would engage in ruminative worry about the future of the relationship and their bad destiny.

The Current Study

The current series of studies examined the associations between attachment style and trust-related memories, goals, and strategies. In examining these issues, I used newly developed, nonobvious measures and cross-validated the findings through different research techniques. Study 1 examined attachment-style differences in the accessibility of trust-related memories. Studies 2–3 focused on attachment-style differences in trust-related goals and strategies. Whereas Study 2 used open-ended probes, Study 3 used a lexical decision task. The hypotheses were as follows:

1. Secure persons would have more accessibility to positive trust-related memories than to negative trust-related memories; avoidant persons would have relatively low accessibility to both negative and positive trust-related memories; and anxious–ambivalent persons would have relatively high accessibility to these two types of memories.
2. Secure persons' sense of trust would be more related to the intimacy goal, anxious–ambivalent persons' sense of trust to the security goal, and avoidant persons' sense of trust to the control goal.
3. Secure persons would deal with negative trust-related experiences by talking with partner, anxious–ambivalent persons by engaging in ruminative worry, and avoidant persons by taking distance from partner.

Study 1

Study 1 examined the hypothesis concerning attachment-style differences in the accessibility of trust-related memories. For this purpose, participants were asked to recall positive and negative trust-related memories. The response time (RT) for the retrieval of a memory was recorded as a measure of cognitive accessibility (Davis, 1987). Participants also rated the emotions that a memory aroused in order to explore the affective quality of trust-related memories.

Method

Participants. Seventy undergraduate students from Bar-Ilan University (46 women and 24 men, ranging in age from 21 to 34, *mdn* = 23) participated in the study without any monetary reward.

Materials and procedure. Participants were tested individually. They were told that they would participate in a study on social cognitions. The questionnaires were given in a random order.

Attachment style was assessed by asking participants to read Hazan and Shaver's (1987) three descriptions of attachment styles and to endorse the one that best described their feelings. Fifty-five percent of the participants (*n* = 39) classified themselves as securely attached, 32% as avoidant (*n* = 22), and 13% as anxious–ambivalent (*n* = 9).[1]

In the memory task, the experimenter, who was blind to participant attachment style, told participants that they would be asked to recall six well-defined personal experiences and that when an experience came to mind, they should simply press a button and describe that experience briefly in writing. The six to-be-recalled experiences consisted of three positive trust-related episodes (trust validation) and three negative trust-related episodes (trust violation). Each of the experiences consisted of an episode in which either the father, the mother, or a romantic partner was involved. Instructions for each of the three positive memories were worded as follows: "Try to recall an episode in which your [father/mother/romantic partner] behaved in such a way that [he/she] increased the trust you felt toward [him/her]." Instructions for each of the three negative memories were worded as follows: "Try to recall an episode in which your [father/mother/romantic partner] behaved in such a way that [he/she] violated the trust you felt toward [him/her]." The order of the six requested memories was randomized across participants.

Each experience was preceded by the instruction to "think of an episode in which ——." The experimenter started an electronic timer immediately after the targeted episode was presented; the timer was stopped when the participant pressed the

---

[1]No gender difference in the distribution of attachment styles was found in any of the studies. ANOVAs revealed no significant interaction between gender and attachment style. Results of no study changed when gender was introduced as a covariate.

TABLE 10.1. Means and Standard Deviations of Retrieval Time and Emotional Reactions According to Valence of Trust-Related Memories and Attachment Style (Study 1)

Measure	Secure		Avoidant		Anxious–ambivalent	
	M	SD	M	SD	M	SD
Retrieval time (in s)						
Positive memories	9.41$_a$	7.06	18.38$_b$	10.43	14.24$_b$	11.98
Negative memories	14.93$_a$	8.76	9.54$_b$	7.91	9.67$_b$	11.29
Strength of positive emotions						
Positive memories	3.53$_a$	1.08	1.92$_b$	0.75	3.78$_a$	1.34
Negative memories	1.18$_a$	0.28	1.12$_a$	0.26	1.15$_a$	0.24
Strength of negative emotions						
Positive memories	1.23$_a$	0.36	1.20$_a$	0.37	1.18$_a$	0.24
Negative memories	2.01$_a$	0.86	1.89$_a$	0.85	2.74$_b$	0.81

Note. Within each row, means with different subscripts are significantly different.

button. As with Davis's procedure (1987, Experiment 3), participants were given 60 s to retrieve a personal experience. If there was no response in the time available, a missing response was recorded for the episode. In fact, participants had no problem in retrieving trust-related memories.

On completing the memory task, participants were told to rate the extent to which they felt happy, satisfied, hopeful, sad, worried, and angry in each recalled episode. These emotions were rated on 6-point bipolar scales, ranging from *not at all* (1) to *very much* (6). A factor analysis of the six emotions revealed two main factors, which explained 73% of the variance. The first factor consisted of the three negative emotions (Cronbach's α = .72); the second included the three positive emotions (Cronbach's α = .75). On this basis, two scores were computed for each memory by averaging items that loaded high in a factor. A significant, but moderate, inverse correlation was found between these two scores, $r(68)$ = −.32, p <.05.

For each participant, two accessibility scores were computed by separately averaging RTs of positive and negative memories. Pearson correlations were high between the three positive memories (from .45 to .59) as well as between the three negative memories (from .51 to .62). Four emotion scores were computed by separately averaging the two emotion scores across positive and negative memories. Correlations were high for positive memories (from .41 to .55 for positive

emotions; from .43 to .50 for negative emotions) and for negative memories (from .57 to .60 for positive emotions; from .54 to .58 for negative emotions).

Results and Discussion

Data were analyzed by two-way analyses of variance (ANOVAs) for attachment style (secure, avoidant, anxious–ambivalent) and valence of trust-related memories (positive, negative). The last variable was a within-subject repeated measurement. Cognitive accessibility, positive emotion, and negative emotion were the dependent variables. Relevant means and standard deviations are presented in Table 10.1.[2]

The ANOVA for cognitive accessibility revealed a significant interaction between attachment style and valence of memories, $F(2, 67)$ = 12.13, p < .01. Tests for simple main effects for repeated measures revealed that secure persons were the quickest to retrieve positive trust-related memories, and that avoidant and anxious–ambivalent retrieved negative memories quicker than secure persons (see Table 10.1). In addition, whereas secure

---

[2]Similar patterns of findings were found when analyses were separately performed for each of the six recalled events and when the order of the questionnaires was entered as a factor. No significant order effect and no significant interaction between order and attachment style was found, implying that participants' memories were not influenced by answering the attachment style scale.

persons showed higher accessibility of positive than negative memories, the two insecure groups retrieved negative memories quicker than positive memories.

The ANOVA for positive emotion revealed an expected significant main effect for valence of memories, $F(1, 67) = 226.22, p < .01$, with positive trust-related memories promoting more intense positive affect ($M = 3.06$) than negative memories ($M = 1.16$). The interaction effect was significant, $F(2, 67) = 17.58, p < .01$. Tests for simple main effects for repeated measures revealed no difference for negative memories. However, secure and anxious–ambivalent persons reported more intense positive affect than avoidant persons when retrieving positive memories (see Table 10.1).

The ANOVA for negative emotion also revealed an expected significant main effect for valence of memories, $F(1, 67) = 54.91, p < .01$, with negative trust-related memories promoting more intense negative affect ($M = 2.06$) than positive memories ($M = 1.21$). In addition, the interaction effect approximated significance, $F(2, 67) = 2.81, p = .06$. No meaningful attachment-style difference was found for positive trust-related memories. However, anxious–ambivalent persons reported having experienced more intense negative emotions than secure and avoidant persons upon the retrieval of negative memories (see Table 10.1).

To assess whether cognitive accessibility accounted for the observed attachment-style differences in emotion scores, two-way ANOVAs were performed on negative and positive emotions with accessibility as a covariate. Findings indicated that the introduction of accessibility did not change the pattern of attachment-style differences in emotion scores observed in the original ANOVAs. That is, the data did not provide any support for a cognitive mediation of these differences.

The findings revealed attachment-style differences in the cognitive accessibility of trust-related memories. Whereas secure persons had more accessible memories of trust-validation episodes, avoidant and anxious–ambivalent persons showed more accessibility of memories of trust-violation episodes. The findings also qualified the affective nature of these memories. Whereas secure persons

reacted emotionally mainly to positive trust-related memories, anxious–ambivalent persons showed relatively strong emotions in response to both positive and negative memories, and avoidant persons displayed weak emotional reactions to any type of memory. These differences fit Mikulincer and Orbach's (1995) findings on the emotional architecture of attachment groups.

Taken as a whole, the findings reflect an integration of the alternative predictions presented in the introduction. On the one hand, accessibility findings may reflect the underlying action of working model of others, which might have biased secure persons' memories toward positive trust-related episodes and insecure persons' memories toward negative trust-related episodes. On the other hand, findings on affective ratings reflect the action of other components of attachment working model. For avoidant persons, their tendency to deactivate distress-related cues might have counteracted the arousal of negative trust memories by suppressing the distressing emotions related to these memories. For anxious–ambivalent persons, their dependence on others and wish for security might have led them to react with intense emotions not only to negative trust memories but also to positive trust memories. It seems that these components fail to affect the cognitive accessibility to trust memories, but make an important contribution to the affective reactions of insecure people to these memories.

Study 2

Study 2 examined the hypotheses concerning attachment-style differences in trust-related goals and strategies. Participants freely reported on the benefits they attached to trusting a romantic partner as well as on their reactions to betrayal of trust. Secure persons were predicted to report more on intimacy-related gains; avoidant persons, on control-related gains; and anxious–ambivalent persons, on security-related gains. In addition, secure persons were predicted to react to betrayal of trust with attempts to talk with partner; avoidant persons, with attempts to take distance from partner; and anxious–ambivalent persons, with engagement in ruminative worry. Study 2 also attempted to replicate previous findings on the association between attachment style and level of trust in love relationships.

Method

Participants. Seventy-four students from Bar-Ilan University (43 women and 31 men, ranging in age from 21 to 45, *mdn* = 23) participated in the study without any monetary reward. All the participants reported that they were involved at the time of the study in a serious (at least 6 months) love relationship (26% were married).[3]

Materials and procedure. Participants were tested in groups of 15–20 individuals and received the questionnaires in a random order. Attachment style was assessed using the scale described in Study 1. Fifty percent of the participants (*n* = 37) classified themselves as securely attached, 34% as avoidant (*n* = 25), and 16% as anxious–ambivalent (*n* = 12).

Level of trust in love relationships was assessed by a Hebrew version of Rempel et al.'s (1985) Trust Scale. This self-report scale consisted of 16 items designed to tap three domains of trust in love relationships: predictability, dependability, and faith. Four items assess the perceived predictability of partner behavior. Five items focus on the belief in partner availability in times of need. Seven items tap the perceived strength of the relationship. Participants answered how much each item described their current love relationship in a bipolar 6-point scale, ranging from *not at all* (1) to *very much* (6). In the current sample, alpha coefficients for the trust subscales were adequate (ranging from .72 to .79). On this basis, three scores were computed by averaging items from each subscale.

The experience of trust was assessed by a semistructured interview. Participants were asked to freely respond, in writing, to two open-ended probes: (a) Describe what are the gains and benefits related to the experience of trust in close relationships, and (b) describe your responses when your partner violates the trust you give to him or her. Participants were told to write until they felt they had completely described their beliefs, feelings, and behaviors. Participants were given no definition of trust, and no data were collected on personal definitions of this construct.

Answers were categorized by two psychology students (unaware of participants' attachment style), who were trained on the coding system and the meaning of the coded categories. These judges read professional literature on trust, interpersonal goals, and coping behaviors. Then, they participated in a focus group, wherein they discussed, together with me and other psychology students, the personal concerns and goals related to trust and the possible responses to betrayal of trust. Finally, they coded, together with me, responses written by students who did not participate in the study until they were confident about how to classify responses in the various categories.

Judges independently read participants' descriptions and recorded verbatim every statement. Then, for the trust-related gains probe, they coded whether participants referred in their answers to goals of intimacy, security, or control. For the trust-violation probe, judges coded whether participants mentioned responses of denial, distancing from partner, rationalization of partner behavior, talking with partner about the situation, and engagement in ruminative worry. For each participant, judges coded whether he or she mentioned or not (1 or 0) a given category. The percentage of items that judges congruently allocated into the same category ranged from 86% to 95% (kappa coefficients ranged from .60 to .67). Disagreements were easily resolved.

Results and Discussion

Trust level. A one-way multivariate analysis of variance (MANOVA) on the three trust subscales yielded a significant effect for attachment style, $F(4, 142) = 4.77, p < .01$. ANOVAs revealed that this effect was significant in the dependability, $F(2, 71) = 4.44, p < .05$, and faith subscales, $F(2, 71) = 10.94, p < .01$. As predicted, Scheffé post hoc tests indicated that secure participants scored higher in the dependability ($M = 4.65$) and faith subscales ($M = 4.85$) than anxious–ambivalent

---

[3]No significant effect was found for marital status.

($M = 4.05$, $M = 4.08$) and avoidant participants ($M = 4.07$, $M = 4.20$).

Trust-related gains. A log-linear two-way ANOVA (SAS FUNCAT procedure) for attachment and gain category revealed a significant interaction, $\chi^2(4, N = 74) = 12.25, p < .01$. Chi-square tests revealed that all the coded trust-related gains were significantly related to attachment style (see Table 10.2). Whereas increase of intimacy was most frequently mentioned by secure persons as a trust-related gain, control attainment was most frequently mentioned by avoidant persons, and security attainment was most frequently mentioned by anxious–ambivalent persons (see frequencies in Table 10.2).

Trust-related coping strategies. A log-linear two-way ANOVA (SAS FUNCAT procedure) for attachment and strategy category revealed a significant interaction, $\chi^2(8, N = 74) = 9.74, p < .05$. Chi-square tests revealed that the categories of talking, distancing, and worrying were significantly related to attachment style (see Table 10.2). No significant association was found between attachment style and categories of denial and rationalization. Table 10.2 shows that talking with partner was most frequently reported by secure persons, taking distance from partner was most frequently mentioned by avoidant persons, and ruminative worry was most frequently reported by anxious–ambivalent persons.

Trust level and trust-related gains and coping strategies. Because the above attachment-style differences may have resulted from differences in the level of trust, it is important to examine the association between level of trust and trust-related gains and coping strategies. For this purpose, the sample was divided in three groups according to the thirds of the distribution of each trust variable (predictability, dependability, and faith), and chi-square tests were computed between each of these variables and the endorsement of each category of trust-related gains and coping strategies. Chi-square tests revealed no significant association between level of trust and endorsement of specific trust-related gains and coping strategies. That is, although the level of trust was related to attachment style, it was not directly related to the goals people attach to trust and the way they cope with trust violation.

Conclusions. The findings delineated the link between attachment style and the sense of trust. First, in a replication of past results, secure persons reported more trust in their relationships than insecure persons. Second, the gains related to the experience of trust seemed to fit the goal component of their working models: Secure persons focused on intimacy increase, anxious–ambivalent persons emphasized security seeking, and avoidant persons were more concerned with control attainment. Third, the ways by which people cope with trust-violation episodes seemed to fit the strategy component of their working models. People relied on their habitual ways of coping when dealing with trust-violation events: Secure persons adopted a constructive attitude (talking with partner),

TABLE 10.2. Frequencies of Response Categories According to Attachment Style (Study 2)

Response category	Secure		Avoidant		Anxious–ambivalent		$\chi^2(2, N = 74)$
	n	%	n	%	n	%	
Trust-related gains							
Increase of intimacy	28	75	11	44	4	33	9.76**
Increase of security	19	51	19	76	11	92	11.01**
Attainment of control	3	8	15	60	1	8	23.30**
Reactions to the violation of trust							
Denial	14	37	10	40	5	42	0.07
Rationalization	16	42	6	24	4	33	1.24
Talking with partner	29	78	9	36	6	48	11.28**
Ruminative worry	5	14	9	36	8	67	12.97**
Distancing from partner	3	8	17	68	2	17	26.79**

*$p < .05$. **$p < .01$.

avoidant persons tended to take distance from partner, and anxious–ambivalent persons engaged in ruminative worry.

Study 3

Study 3 assessed attachment-style differences in trust-related goals. Participants performed a lexical decision task (Meyer & Schvaneveldt, 1971). They read a string of letters and tried to identify as quickly as possible whether it was a word or not. In this study, the target words were trust-related goals (*intimacy, security*, and *control*) and they were embedded within trust-relevant or trust-irrelevant context sentences.

Two past findings highlight the suitability of a lexical decision task for exploring the cognitive structure underlying a person's sense of trust. First, research found a context-relatedness effect: RTs for identifying target words are quicker when these words are primed by semantically related context sentences (e.g., Stanovich & West, 1983). Second, this RT facilitation has been found mainly when the target word is the most available association that a person can produce for the context sentence (e.g., Fischler & Bloom, 1979). In this way, individual differences in RTs reflect the extent to which a word is congruent with the person's own concerns and cognitions (e.g., Baldwin et al., 1993).

Given the above findings, I made the following predictions: First, a context-relatedness effect would be found for words reflecting trust-related goals. That is, placing the words *intimacy, security*, and *control* in a trust-relevant context would lead to faster RTs overall. Second, this context-relatedness effect would be the strongest when a target word matches the goal component of a person's working model. That is, secure persons would show the greatest context effect (quickest RTs) for the word *intimacy*, avoidant persons for the word *control*, and anxious–ambivalent persons for the word *security*.

Method

Participants. Thirty participants (10 secure, 10 avoidant, and 10 anxious) were randomly chosen

from the pool of 250 students. The sample consisted of 18 women and 12 men ranging in age from 20 to 34 (*mdn* = 23).

Materials and procedure. The lexical decision task was performed on an individual basis, and it was described as a social cognition task. The task was programmed on the basis of apparatus, procedure, and stimuli used by Baldwin et al. (1993). It was run on a 386-SX computer, with an SVGA color monitor. Brightness and contrasts were set somewhat low, and the target stimuli were displayed in light gray letters. The context sentences were displayed in white lettering on a black background.

For the current study, four context sentences and eight target stimuli were constructed. Two of the sentences were trust-relevant sentences and were adapted from Rempel et al.'s (1985) Trust Scale ("I count on my partner to be concerned with things that are important to me" and "I rely on my partner to keep the promises that my partner makes to me"). The other two sentences were trust-irrelevant sentences, which were matched for number of words and length with the trust-relevant sentences ("I buy a book that received good critiques in yesterday's newspaper"). The eight target stimuli were constructed as follows: Three stimuli were Hebrew words that reflect trust-related goals (*intimacy, security*, and *control*). One stimulus was a noninterpersonal, neutral Hebrew word (*operation*) and served as a control for the time required to identify a word stimulus. Finally, four nonwords were generated by taking common Hebrew verbs and nouns (e.g., *thinking*) and changing one letter (e.g., *tlinking*). These nonwords were matched for number of characters with target words. In this way, there were 32 context sentence–target pairs, which were presented twice, for a total of 64 trials. Trials were randomly ordered across participants.[4]

Participants worked at their own pace. They were first given nine practice trials with different

---

[4]The Hebrew words used in the lexical decision task in Study 3 were *kirva*, which means closeness; *shlita*, which means control; and *bitahon*, which means security.

words and nonwords from those of the experimental trials. In each trial, a letter string was displayed on the computer screen and participants were asked to judge as quickly as possible whether it was a word or nonword. They initiated each trial by pressing the space bar and responded by pressing the "1" on the keyboard number pad if they thought that the letter string was a word or the "2" if they thought that the letter string was a nonword.

Before beginning the experimental trials, participants were told that "to make this task a little more difficult" they would do a second task at the same time. This second task involved reading some sentences and trying to remember them for later. Then, each trial consisted of a rapid presentation of the context sentence followed by the presentation of a letter string. Each context sentence was displayed one word at a time on the computer screen at a rate of 600 ms per word. After a 1,000-ms pause, the sentence was followed by one of the target letter strings, presented for 1,500 ms, which participants were to identify as either a word or a nonword. After participants pressed either "1" or "2" on the number pad, the letter string vanished and, after a 5-sec pause, the next trial began.

Results and Discussion

For each person, RTs were averaged according to type of sentence (trust-relevant or -irrelevant) and type of target stimuli (trust-related goals, neutral word, or nonword). RTs for trust-related goals (only correct responses) were analyzed by a three-way ANOVA for attachment style, type of sentence, and type of goal. The two last variables were within-subject repeated variables. The RTs for nonwords and neutral words in each context sentence were introduced as covariates in the analyses.[5]

The ANOVA revealed a significant main effect for type of context sentence, $F(1, 27) = 32.34$,

_____
[5]The covariates were included to control for individual differences in overall RT. ANOVAs revealed no significant effects for attachment style and type of context sentence on RTs for neutral words as well as on RTs for nonwords.

$p < .01$, with quicker RTs for trust-relevant sentences ($M = 621.66$) than for trust-irrelevant ones ($M = 667.87$). This difference implies the existence of a context-relatedness effect, by which RTs for trust-related goal words were facilitated by sentences that placed these words in a meaningful trust context.

The ANOVA also revealed that the interaction for type of context sentence and type of goal word approximated statistical significance, $F(2, 54) = 2.92$, $p < .10$. Tests for simple main effects for repeated measures revealed that under trust-irrelevant sentences, no significant difference was found in RTs among the three goal words ($M = 668.99$ for intimacy; $M = 663.70$ for security; $M = 667.92$ for control). However, under trust-relevant sentences, RTs for intimacy were quicker ($M = 592.96$) than for security ($M = 639.66$) and control ($M = 635.37$). This effect suggests that intimacy was the most available trust-related goal.

Attachment style, however, qualified the above effects, as shown in the three-way interaction that approximated significance, $F(4, 54) = 2.01$, $p < .10$. Tests for simple main effects for repeated measures revealed no significant effect under a trust-irrelevant context (see Table 10.3). Under a trust-relevant context, however, a significant interaction for attachment and target word was found, $F(4, 54) = 4.32, p < .01$.

Simple main effects tests across attachment styles revealed that (a) anxious–ambivalent persons reacted quicker to the word *security* than secure and avoidant persons, $F(2, 54) = 4.30, p < .05$, and (b) avoidant persons reacted quicker to the word *control* than secure and anxious–ambivalent persons, $F(2, 54) = 3.22, p < .05$ (see means in Table 10.3). No significant attachment effect was found in RTs for the word *intimacy*. Additional simple main effects tests across target words revealed that (a) secure persons reacted quickest to the word *intimacy*, (b) avoidant persons reacted quicker to the words *intimacy* and *control* than to *security*, and (c) anxious–ambivalent persons reacted quicker to the words *intimacy* and *security*. The goal of secure persons in trust-related contexts was defined by intimacy, the goal of anxious–ambivalent persons by intimacy and

TABLE 10.3. Means and Standard Deviations of Lexical Decision Response Times by Attachment Style, Type of Context Sentence, and Type of Trust-Related Goal Word (Study 3)

Context and word type	Secure		Avoidant		Anxious–ambivalent	
	M	SD	M	SD	M	SD
Trust-related context						
Intimacy	595.07$_a$	66.67	590.09$_a$	70.75	593.72$_a$	73.90
Security	658.72$_a$	66.42	666.05$_a$	73.15	585.22$_b$	64.60
Control	661.48$_a$	70.84	588.55$_b$	76.20	656.07$_a$	67.48
Trust-unrelated context						
Intimacy	668.73$_a$	73.54	672.82$_a$	76.16	662.25$_a$	56.40
Security	665.51$_a$	73.23	661.02$_a$	76.71	666.57$_a$	69.75
Control	669.75$_a$	69.83	665.27$_a$	79.86	674.95$_a$	67.53

Note. Within each row, means with different subscripts are significantly different.

security, and the goal of avoidant persons by intimacy and control.

General Discussion

Taken as a whole, the findings demonstrate the usefulness of a multifaceted approach for the study of the sense of trust in close relationships. They clearly show that attachment groups differed in the level of trust they felt toward romantic partners, the accessibility and affective quality of trust-related memories, the appraisal of trust-related experiences, the interaction goals related to the sense of trust, and the strategies used in coping with trust-violation events. These differences were found in self-reports and in the cognitive structure underlying a person's sense of trust. Theoretically, the findings might imply that attachment working models are closely related to the way people construe and process trust-related memories, experiences, goals, and coping strategies.

For secure persons, the sense of trust was found to be exclusively related to the goal of intimacy in a relationship. Together with past findings (Mikulincer & Nachshon, 1991), the data seem to emphasize the prevalence of the relational goal of intimacy over more intrapersonal goals of security and control. It may be that the attainment of a secure base satisfies these latter intrapersonal needs and frees cognitive and emotional resources to the regulation of relationship quality. On this basis, secure persons could develop a more open, selfless, and caring attitude toward their partners.

They could become an active agent responsible for partner well-being and relationship quality rather than a passive recipient of caring and comfort and thus could move from egocentric to more reciprocal relationships. This is particularly important in the realm of adult relationships, wherein the attachment and caregiving systems are combined, and both partners are equally responsible for the development of an atmosphere of closeness and the maintenance of the relationship (Berman & Sperling, 1994).

The findings seem to emphasize the importance of attachment security for the development of a positive attitude toward trust. Secure persons have been found to be confident in others' benevolence (e.g., Shaver & Hazan, 1993) and to believe that a partner would not hurt or abandon them if they trust him or her (Baldwin et al., 1993). On this basis, secure persons can develop trusting relationships and feel confident in their partners' trustworthiness. In the current studies, this positive attitude can be seen in the high level of trust secure persons felt toward partners as well as in the way they processed trust-related episodes.

Attachment security also appears to be associated with constructive coping. The most direct expression of this coping strategy was found in the tendency of secure persons to openly talk with their partners in response to a trust-violation episode. It is possible to view these findings as manifestations of the cognitive and affective maneuvers secure persons make to minimize the distressing impact of negative partner behaviors. These maneuvers may include the suppression of memories that raise doubts about a partner's goodwill, the suppression of negative affect related to these memories, and the dismissal of trust-violation events.

Although secure persons' pattern of memories and appraisals can be interpreted as a manifestation of coping strategies, it may also reflect secure persons' actual relationships. It may be that secure people are involved in more rewarding relationships (Shaver & Hazan, 1993) and then may have a smaller proportion of negative memories to recall. Further research should explore this alternative and examine the interactive effects of stable working models and ongoing relationships on the sense of trust.

The association between attachment security and the sense of trust is further highlighted by the trust-related memories, goals, and coping strategies of insecure persons. The sense of trust of these persons was found to be negative and maladaptive. Specifically, both avoidant and anxious–ambivalent persons reported low levels of trust toward partners, showed high accessibility of negative trust-related memories, and dealt with them by relying on strategies that would seem to be maladaptive for relationship maintenance (Shaver & Hazan, 1993).

Despite the above similarities, avoidant and anxious–ambivalent persons differed in several aspects of the sense of trust. First, they differed in trust-related goals: Whereas avoidant persons put emphasis in control attainment, anxious–ambivalent persons emphasized security attainment. Second, differences were found in coping strategies with a trust-violation event. On the one hand, avoidant persons usually tended to distance from partners. On the other hand, anxious–ambivalent people usually engaged in ruminative worry, though the lexical decision task showed additional activation of the "talking with partner" strategy. Third, differences were found in the affective and cognitive configuration of trust-related experiences. Anxious–ambivalent persons reacted to these experiences with stronger affect than avoidant persons. In my terms, these differences reflect the rules that guide each insecure group in regulating distress.

Avoidant persons cope with their insecurity by suppressing painful attachment-related thoughts and affects, striving for autonomy and control, dismissing the importance of attachment episodes, and distancing from attachment figures (Bowlby, 1988; Shaver & Hazan, 1993). Though these strategies may reduce overt expressions of distress, they are unable to mitigate inner insecurity, as manifested in below-level-of-awareness measures and physiological recordings (Feeney & Kirpatrick, 1996; Mikulincer et al., 1990). These strategies are seen in current findings showing that avoidant persons' sense of trust was related to control attainment and that these persons reported weak negative trust-related affect and coped with trust-violation events by distancing from partners.

The most original finding with regard to avoidant persons' sense of trust was their endorsement of control as a trust-related goal. Although the idea of control as a theme for avoidants is implicit in Bowlby's (1988) theory, it did not receive sufficient theoretical attention in recent attachment literature and it was not empirically examined in adult attachment research. It seems to me that this idea sheds light on avoidant persons' way of relating to others and expands our knowledge of avoidant persons' working models. Future studies should examine more in depth the ways by which the control theme pervades avoidant persons' cognitions, emotions, and behaviors.

Anxious–ambivalent persons deal with insecurity by obsessively searching for security in any relationship (Shaver & Hazan, 1993). In this way, they are unable or unwilling to end frustrating relationships. Rather, they attach high importance to these relationships, excessively ruminate on problems and frustrations, and tend to be overwhelmed by negative affect, all of which divert mental resources away from instrumental actions. In my terms, these strategies are seen in current findings showing that anxious–ambivalent persons tended to link trust with security attainment, experienced high levels of negative trust-related affect, attached high importance to negative trust-related events, and coped with these events by engaging in ruminative worry.

Although the above reasoning can explain the current findings, an alternative line of thinking can be proposed. Unlike many stressors, a betrayal of trust is a direct attack on attachment working models. Consequently, a person's ways of coping with this betrayal may be a direct reflection, if not the product, of their level of trust. Secure persons may talk with their partner because they need to understand an unexpected violation. They have the confidence that confronting their partner does not represent an untenable risk and it can result in a productive outcome. Anxious–ambivalent persons' basic doubts about a partner's responsiveness could lead them to feel greater levels of anxiety in response to a betrayal of trust and to engage in rumination about the conditions that can predict partner's future responses. Finally, avoidant persons may distance from their partner because they are not at all confident that he or she will respond in a positive way if discussion about the betrayal episode is raised.

As this discussion indicates, levels of trust may underlie attachment-style differences in coping with betrayal of trust. Although trust has often been conceptualized as a relationship-specific process, people are still likely to have a more stable trust orientation that may be activated and applied in close relationships. It is possible that this trust orientation is central to the attachment working model of others. Moreover, it may determine the way people differing in attachment style cope with the betrayal of trust.

Findings of Study 2 deal with the above possibility. Although secure attachment was significantly related to positive trust orientation, this orientation was not significantly related to trust-related goals and to the way people cope with trust-violation episodes. This pattern of findings sorts out the extent to which trust and attachment differ or reflect the same underlying process. On the one hand, level of trust was found to differentiate between secure and insecure attachment. On the other hand, it did not differentiate between avoidant and anxious–ambivalent persons and failed to explain the way these persons construct the meaning of trust and the way they deal with

trust violation. On this basis, one can argue that the observed differences between avoidant and anxious–ambivalent persons may result from their habitual way of affect regulation rather than from their trust orientation. Although both of them hold a similar negative trust orientation, their habitual ways of affect regulation lead them to react to trust-related episodes in different ways.

The findings enrich our knowledge on the meaning of trust among young adults. Regardless of a person's attachment style, trusting a partner was more strongly associated with the search for intimacy than with the attainment of security or control. This primacy of intimacy is far from surprising. A sense of trust may be a prerequisite to taking risks in a relationship and to openly sharing one's feelings and thoughts with partners. It may strengthen a partner's commitment to the relationship and his or her willingness to initiate intimate interactions.

The question here concerns the directional sequence of the above relational events: Is trust a means for strengthening intimacy, or is intimacy a precondition for trusting a partner? I think that the answer is simple and complex at the same time. Like other personality and social psychology phenomena, trust and intimacy may be reciprocally related. Trust may promote intimacy, and intimacy, in turn, may increase trust. Further research should conduct a prospective follow-up of the trust–intimacy link throughout the different stages of a relationship and attempt to increase the internal validity of the findings by experimentally manipulating key variables.

The current findings can be viewed as a further contribution to the understanding of the role attachment working models play in adult relationships. Specifically, they delineate the manifestations of the memory, goal, and strategy components of these models in a basic relationship phenomenon. Moreover, the current findings enrich our knowledge on the experience of trust and contribute to a multifaceted conceptualization of the sense of interpersonal trust. In this way, the current study opens a new avenue of research for studying specific relationship processes and phenomena from an attachment perspective.

NOTES

I would like to thank Hadar Lans and Zunio Crystal for their assistance in data collection, and Aron Weller for his comments on a draft of this article.

Correspondence concerning this article should be addressed to Mario Mikulincer, Department of Psychology, Bar-Ilan University, Ramat Gan 52900, Israel. Electronic mail may be sent to mikulm@mail.biu.ac.il

REFERENCES

Ainsworth, M. D. S., Blehar, M. C., Waters, E., & Wall, S. (1978). *Patterns of attachment: A psychological study of the strange situation.* Hillsdale, NJ: Erlbaum.

Baldwin, M. W., Fehr, B., Keedian, E., Seidel, M., & Thompson, D. W. (1993). An exploration of the relational schemata underlying attachment styles: Self report and lexical decision approaches. *Personality and Social Psychology Bulletin, 19,* 746–754.

Baldwin, M. W., Keelan, J. P. R., Fehr, B., Enns, V., & Koh-Rangarajoo, E. (1996). Social-cognitive conceptualization of attachment working models: Availability and accessibility effects. *Journal of Personality and Social Psychology, 71,* 94–109.

Berman, W. H., & Sperling, M. B. (1994). The structure and function of adult attachment. In M. B. Sperling & W. H. Berman (Eds.), *Attachment in adults: Clinical and developmental perspectives* (pp. 3–29). New York: Guilford Press.

Birnbaum, G., Orr, I., Mikulincer, M., & Florian, V. (1998). When marriage breaks up—Does attachment style contribute to coping and mental health? *Journal of Social and Personal Relationships, 14,* 643–645.

Bowlby, J. (1973). *Attachment and loss: Separation, anxiety and anger.* New York: Basic Books.

Bowlby, J. (1988). *A secure base: Clinical applications of attachment theory.* London: Routledge.

Brennan, K. A., & Shaver, P. R. (1995). Dimensions of adult attachment, affect regulation, and romantic relationship functioning. *Personality and Social Psychology Bulletin, 21,* 267–283.

Collins, N. L., & Read, S. J. (1990). Adult attachment, working models, and relationship quality in dating couples. *Journal of Personality and Social Psychology, 58,* 644–663.

Collins, N. L., & Read, S. J. (1994). Cognitive representations of attachment: The structure and function of working models. In K. Bartholomew & D. Perlman (Eds.), *Attachment processes in adulthood* (pp. 53–92). London: Jessica Kingsley.

Davis, P. J. (1987). Repression and the inaccessibility of affective memories. *Journal of Personality and Social Psychology, 53,* 585–593.

Deutsch, M. (1973). *The resolution of conflict: Constructive and destructive processes.* New Haven, CT: Yale University Press.

Feeney, B. C., & Kirpatrick, L. A. (1996). Effects of adult attachment and presence of romantic partners on physiological responses to stress. *Journal of Personality and Social Psychology, 70,* 255–270.

Feeney, J. A., & Noller, P. (1990). Attachment style as a predictor of adult romantic relationships. *Journal of Personality and Social Psychology, 58,* 281–291.

Fischler, I. S., & Bloom. P. A. (1979). Automatic and attentional processes in the effects of sentence contexts on word recognition. *Journal of Verbal Learning and Verbal Behavior, 18,* 1–20.

Hazan, C., & Shaver, P. (1987). Romantic love conceptualized as an attachment process. *Journal of Personality and Social Psychology, 52,* 511–524.

Holmes, J. G., & Rempel, J. K. (1989). Trust in close relationships. In C. Hendrick (Ed.), *Review of personality and social relationships* (Vol. 10, pp. 187–219). Newbury Park, CA: Sage.

Keelan, J. P. R., Dion, K. L., & Dion, K. K. (1994). Attachment style and heterosexual relationships among young adults: A short term panel study. *Journal of Social and Personal Relationships, 11,* 201–214.

Levy, M. B., & Davis, K. E. (1988). Lovestyles and attachment styles compared: Their relations to each other and to various relationship characteristics. *Journal of Social and Personal Relationships, 5,* 439–471.

Main, M., Kaplan, N., & Cassidy, J. (1985). Security in infancy, childhood, and adulthood: A move to the level of representation. *Monographs of the Society for Research in Child Development, 50,* 66–104.

Meyer, D., & Schvaneveldt, R. W. (1971). Facilitation in recognizing pairs of words: Evidence of a dependence between retrieval operations. *Journal of Experimental Psychology, 90,* 227–234.

Mikulincer, M. (1995). Attachment style and the mental representation of the self. *Journal of Personality and Social Psychology, 69,* 1203–1215.

Mikulincer, M., & Erev, I. (1991). Attachment style and the structure of romantic love. *British Journal of Social Psychology, 30,* 273–291.

Mikulincer, M., & Florian, V. (1995). Appraisal of and coping with a real life stressful situation: The contribution of attachment styles. *Personality and Social Psychology Bulletin, 21,* 406–414.

Mikulincer, M., & Florian, V. (1998). The relationship between adult attachment styles and emotional and cognitive reactions to stressful events. In J. A. Simpson & W. S. Rholes (Eds.), *Attachment theory and close relationships* (pp. 143–165). New York: Guilford Press.

Mikulincer, M., Florian, V., & Tolmacz, R. (1990). Attachment styles and fear of personal death: A case study of affect regulation. *Journal of Personality and Social Psychology, 58,* 273–280.

Mikulincer, M., Florian, V., & Weller, A. (1993). Attachment styles, coping strategies, and post-traumatic psychological distress: The impact of the Gulf War in Israel. *Journal of Personality and Social Psychology, 64,* 817–826.

Attachment Working Models and the Sense of Trust ■ 191

Mikulincer, M., & Nachshon, O. (1991). Attachment styles and patterns of self disclosure. *Journal of Personality and Social Psychology, 61*, 321–331.

Mikulincer, M., & Orbach, I. (1995). Attachment styles and repressive defensiveness: The accessibility and architecture of affective memories. *Journal of Personality and Social Psychology, 68*, 917–925.

Murray, E. L., & Holmes, J. G. (1993). Seeing virtues as faults: The transformation of interpersonal narratives in close relationships. *Journal of Personality and Social Psychology, 65*, 707–722.

Pistole, M. C. (1989). Attachment in adult romantic relationships: Style of conflict resolution and relationship satisfaction. *Journal of Social and Personal Relationships, 6*, 505–510.

Rempel, J. K., Holmes, J. G., & Zanna, M. P. (1985). Trust in close relationships. *Journal of Personality and Social Psychology, 49*, 95–112.

Rotter, J. B. (1980). Interpersonal trust, trustworthiness, and gullibility. *American Psychologist, 35*, 1–7.

Scanzoni, J. (1979). Social exchange and behavioral interdependence. In R. L. Burgess & T. L. Huston (Eds.), *Social exchange in developing relationships* (pp. 133–159). New York: Academic Press.

Scharfe, E., & Bartholomew, K. (1995). Accommodation and attachment representations in young couples. *Journal of Social and Personal Relationships, 12*, 389–401.

Shaver, P. R., Collins, N., & Clark, C. L. (1996). Attachment styles and internal working models of self and relationship partners. In G. Fletcher & J. Fitness (Eds.), *Knowledge structures in close relationships: A social psychological approach*. Hillsdale, NJ: Erlbaum.

Shaver, P. R., & Hazan, C. (1993). Adult romantic attachment: Theory and evidence. In D. Perlman & W. Jones (Eds.), *Advances in personal relationships* (Vol. 4, pp. 29–70). London: Jessica Kingsley.

Simpson, J. A. (1990). Influence of attachment styles on romantic relationships. *Journal of Personality and Social Psychology, 59*, 971–980.

Sorrentino, R. M., Holmes, J. G., Hanna, S. E., & Sharp, A. (1995). Uncertainty orientation and trust in close relationships: Individual differences in cognitive styles. *Journal of Personality and Social Psychology, 68*, 314–327.

Stanovich, K. E., & West, R. F. (1983). On priming by a sentence context. *Journal of Experimental Psychology: General, 112*, 1–36.

Sternberg, R. J. (1986). A triangular theory of love. *Psychological Review, 93*, 119–135.

SECTION 4

Developing Relationships

Man, as you know, is one of the most pathetic creatures on earth, condemned to a desire that contradicts all the laws of nature—to close the gap between two human beings . . . Nevertheless, I would like to delude myself one more time—to feel intrigued, hopeful, enthusiastic.

— Carlos Fuentes

When two people are under the influence of the most violent, most insane, most delusive, and most transient of passions, they are required to swear that they will remain in that excited, abnormal, and exhausting condition continuously until death do them part.

— George Bernard Shaw

Why do some people we meet develop into long-term close friends whereas others remain acquaintances or disappear entirely from our social lives? Over the years, the answer to this seemingly simple question has remained surprisingly elusive. Early research, including a few papers reprinted in this reader, examined the qualities of one person that predict another person's attraction and initial interest, as though the only thing necessary to progress from first contact to established friendship was to combine the correct ingredients, step out of the way, and let them mix around for a while. Of course, the process of developing a relationship is more complex than this. In everyday life we come into contact with many different people, most of whom are potential friends and lovers. Yet few become more than casual acquaintances.

Most researchers today would agree at least in principle that advancing from passing familiarity to close friendship depends less on two people's personal characteristics and more on the nature of their interaction with each other (Reis, Capobianco, & Tsai, 2002; Rusbult & Van Lange, 2003). The earliest research, spurred by Sidney Jourard's (1964) theorizing and the seminal studies of Irwin Altman and Dalmas Taylor (1973), focused exclusively on the act of self-disclosure—the ways in which we reveal private information about ourselves to new partners. More recent work recognizes that the processes involved in developing a relationship are many and diverse. Over the course of the past two decades, researchers have turned their attention to intimacy, love, commitment, trust, empathy, helping, and communication, to name only a few prominent examples.

The articles reproduced in this section concern two of these processes, intimacy and love. In the first paper, Laurenceau, Barrett, and Pietromonaco use a diary study to evaluate Reis and Shaver's (1988) "interpersonal process" model of intimacy. Reis and Shaver were among the first theorists to propose that intimacy involves not only Dave's willingness to open up to Anna, as demonstrated in self-disclosure research, but *also* Anna's inclination to respond positively to such disclosure. Laurenceau et al.'s research supported this hypothesis, revealing that ordinary social interactions are more likely to engender feelings of intimacy when people express their emotions to each other and when they feel that their partners respond in an understanding, accepting, and caring manner. A natural conclusion—one that links the results of this study to a good deal of other research—is that the

development of an intimate relationship depends importantly on the perception of support and acceptance by a partner who is well aware of one's innermost thoughts and feelings.

Robert Sternberg is interested in another popular process, love. Although love has consumed the attention of lay people, poets, philosophers, songwriters, and scholars throughout history, researchers have found it difficult to sort out its varying manifestations, features, and varieties of expression. For example, consider the differences among the following: falling in love, motherly love, love for humanity, love of God, and the love that long-term teammates, soldiers, and coworkers often feel for each other. In his widely cited paper, Sternberg suggests that the general term "love" subsumes three distinct processes—intimacy, passion, and commitment. He proceeds to describe how different combinations of these three components create distinctive types of love relationship. Sternberg's tripartite categorical scheme has been confirmed in subsequent, more sophisticated psychometric studies (e.g., Aron & Westbay, 1996; Fehr & Russell, 1991), which have helped researchers better understand the role of love in the development of certain types of relationship.

Robert Levine and his colleagues ask whether the role of one particular kind of love—romantic love—in one particular kind of relationship—marriage—varies across time and culture. Although there is strong evidence that romantic love is a universal emotion (e.g., Fisher, 1998), norms and practices about the relevance of romantic love to courtship and divorce vary markedly across historical periods (as suggested by temporal trends in divorce rates), cultures, and religious beliefs. In their research,

Levine and his colleagues tackled this fundamental issue by asking college students in 11 cultures whether they would marry someone they didn't love, as well as whether the absence of love is sufficient reason for a married couple to divorce. The trends they identify raise important questions about the influence of cultural values that researchers have only begun to address.

REFERENCES

Altman, I., & Taylor, D. A. (1973). *Social penetration: The development of interpersonal relationships.* New York: Holt, Rinehart, & Winston.

Aron, A., & Westbay, L. (1996). Dimensions of the prototype of love. *Journal of Personality and Social Psychology, 70,* 535–551.

Fehr, B., & Russell, J. A. (1991). The concept of love viewed from a prototype perspective. *Journal of Personality and Social Psychology, 60,* 425–438.

Fisher, H. E. (1998). Lust, attraction, and attachment in mammalian reproduction. *Human Nature, 9,* 23–52.

Jourard, S. M. (1964). *The transparent self.* New York: Van Nostrand.

Reis, H. T., Capobianco, A. E., & Tsai, F. F. (2002). Finding the person in personal relationships. *Journal of Personality, 70,* 813–850.

Reis, H. T., & Shaver, P. R. (1988). Intimacy as an interpersonal process. In S. Duck (Ed.), *Handbook of personal relationships* (pp. 367–389). Chichester, U.K.: John Wiley and Sons, Ltd.

Rusbult, C. E., & Van Lange, P. A. M. (2003). Interdependence, interaction, and relationships. *Annual Review of Psychology, 54,* 351–375.

Suggestions for Further Reading

Aron, A., & Aron, E. N. (1986). *Love as the expansion of self: Understanding attraction and satisfaction.* New York: Hemisphere. A comprehensive theoretical statement of the self-expansion theory of romantic love.

Baumeister, R. (1999). Passion, intimacy, and time: Passionate love as a function of change in intimacy. *Personality and Social Psychology Review, 3,* 49–68. This paper discusses the ways in which passion and intimacy may be interrelated, emphasizing the development of relationships over time.

Baumeister, R. F., Wotman, S. R., & Stillwell, A. M. (1993). Unrequited love: On heartbreak, anger, guilt, scriptlessness, and humiliation. *Journal of Personality and Social Psychology, 64,* 377–394. Sometimes love can be distressing, as revealed in this research regarding unrequited love.

Berscheid, E. (1988). Some comments on love's anatomy: Or, whatever happened to old-fashioned lust? In R. J. Sternberg & M. L. Barnes (Eds.), *The psychology of love* (pp. 359–374). New Haven, CT: Yale University Press. Ellen Berscheid, a pioneer in the social psychological study of love (and one of the field's best writers), gives us an insightful and engaging commentary on current research.

Derlega, V. J., Metts, S., Petronio, S., & Margulis, S. T. (1993). *Self-disclosure.* Newbury Park, CA: Sage. A thoroughly readable and comprehensive review of self-disclosure research.

Fisher, H. E. (1998). Lust, attraction, and attachment in mammalian reproduction. *Human Nature, 9,* 23–52. One of the best treatments of the anthropological and biological bases of love.

Hatfield, E., & Rapson, R. L. (1993). *Love, sex, and intimacy: Their psychology, biology, and history.* New York: Harper Collins. A comprehensive and accessible review of relevant theories and research.

McAdams, D. P. (1989). *Intimacy: The need to be close.* New York: Doubleday. A thoughtful overview of the importance of intimacy to human well-being.

Miller, L. C., & Kenny, D. A. (1986). Reciprocity of self-disclosure at the individual and dyadic levels: A social relations analysis. *Journal of Personality and Social Psychology, 50,* 713–719. This research utilizes Kenny's Social Relations Model for untangling actor, partner, and relationship effects in a mathematically precise manner. It demonstrates clearly that self-disclosure rests less on characteristics of the sender (actor) or recipient (partner) of disclosure than on the relationship *between* two individuals.

Reis, H. T., & Patrick, B. C. (1996). Attachment and intimacy: Component processes. In A. Kruglanski & E. T. Higgins (Eds.), *Social psychology: Handbook of basic principles* (pp. 523–563). New York: Guilford. An update and literature review regarding the Reis and Shaver model.

Yovetich, N. A., & Drigotas, S. M. (1999). Secret transmission: A relative intimacy hypothesis. *Personality and Social Psychology Bulletin, 25,* 1135–1146. A theory and empirical demonstration of the norms governing secret-telling and secret-keeping.

Discussion Questions

1. Looking back over your relationships, what differences do you see in your interactions with people who became close friends in comparison to others with whom friendship never quite jelled?

2. What is the difference between disclosing facts about oneself and disclosing emotions? Can the same general content be disclosed in either way? Is this distinction important? If so, why?

3. There are many ways in which a listener can convey responsiveness to a partner's self-disclosures. What are some of these ways? Moreover, some authors have described responsiveness as the most important social skill. How might people learn to exhibit greater responsiveness?

4. Discuss the relative contributions of intimacy, passion, and commitment to romantic relationships in three films or books that you have recently seen or read. In your opinion, which component is most important in a romantic relationship, and why?

5. What exactly *is* love? Although social scientists have developed many theories to explain the causes of love, there is less agreement about precisely how to define the experience of love. What are the essential components of this phenomenon? Does love entail acceptance of a partner, "warts and all"? Does it entail willingness to place another's needs above one's own, or the desire to share oneself and one's life with another? Or is love ultimately indefinable? How would you define love?

6. Do you think that the rising U.S. divorce rate may have contributed to the temporal changes discussed by Levine and his colleagues? What differences would you predict if their survey were conducted today at your college?

7. What do the words "individualism" and "collectivism" mean, and how do these concepts help explain cross-cultural differences in young adults' beliefs about the importance of love in marriage?

8. Relationships researchers generally agree that attraction to another rests on "reward value." Thus, when you meet a person who possesses several qualities that you greatly value, you will probably find that you *like* that person. At the same time, over the course of a lifetime, most of you will encounter many people who possess several qualities that you value—for example, physical attractiveness, intelligence, sense of humor, and the like—yet you will come to *love* very few of those people. Why is this so? What is the difference between liking and loving?

Intimacy as an Interpersonal Process: The Importance of Self-Disclosure, Partner Disclosure, and Perceived Partner Responsiveness in Interpersonal Exchanges

Jean-Philippe Laurenceau • University of Miami
Lisa Feldman Barrett • Boston College
Paula R. Pietromonaco • University of Massachusetts at Amherst

H. T. Reis and P. Shaver's (1988) interpersonal process model of intimacy suggests that both self-disclosure and partner responsiveness contribute to the experience of intimacy in interactions. Two studies tested this model using an event-contingent diary methodology in which participants provided information immediately after their social interactions over 2 weeks. For each interaction, participants reported on their self-disclosures, partner disclosures, perceived partner responsiveness, and degree of intimacy experienced in the interaction. Overall, the findings strongly supported the conceptualization of intimacy as a combination of self-disclosure and partner disclosure at the level of individual interactions with partner responsiveness as a partial mediator in this process. Additionally, self-disclosure of emotion emerged as a more important predictor of intimacy than did self-disclosure of facts and information.

Most theorists and researchers agree that intimacy is an essential aspect of many interpersonal relationships (e.g., Bartholomew, 1990; Clark & Reis, 1988; McAdams & Constantian, 1983; Prager, 1995; Reis, 1990; Sullivan, 1953; Waring, 1984). Nevertheless, considerable variability exists in conceptualizations of intimacy (Perlman & Fehr, 1987). Some theorists have defined intimacy as a quality of interactions between persons: Individuals emit reciprocal behaviors that are designed to maintain a comfortable level of closeness (e.g., Argyle & Dean, 1965; Patterson, 1976, 1982).

Other theorists have focused on the motivation to seek intimate experiences: People vary considerably in the strength of their need or desire for warm, close, and validating experiences with other people (e.g., McAdams, 1985; Sullivan, 1953). Variations also exist in assumptions about the way in which intimacy develops and is sustained in relationships. Some theorists propose that intimacy develops primarily through self-disclosure (e.g., Derlega, Metts, Petronio, & Margulis, 1993; Jourard, 1971; Perlman & Fehr, 1987), whereas others have suggested that additional components, such as a partner's level of responsiveness, contribute significantly to the development of intimacy in relationships (e.g., Berg, 1987; Davis, 1982). Furthermore, intimacy has been conceptualized both as a state or end product of a relationship and as a moment-to-moment outcome of a process reflecting movement or fluctuation through time (Duck & Sants, 1983).

A recently developed model of intimacy (Reis & Patrick, 1996; Reis & Shaver, 1988) integrates these multiple perspectives by describing intimacy as the product of a transactional, interpersonal process in which self-disclosure and partner responsiveness are key components. In this view, intimacy develops through a dynamic process whereby an individual discloses personal information, thoughts, and feelings to a partner; receives a response from the partner; and interprets that response as understanding, validating, and caring. Although the Reis and Shaver (1988) model provides a rich description of how intimacy develops on an interaction-by-interaction basis, some of the hypothesized links have yet to be directly tested in empirical work. In the present investigation, we test several components of the interpersonal process model of intimacy within the context of naturally occurring daily social interactions, thus allowing for an examination of the intimacy process on an interaction-by-interaction basis.

The Interpersonal Process Model of Intimacy

According to Reis and Shaver (1988), intimacy results from a process that is initiated when one person (the speaker) communicates personally relevant and revealing information to another person (the listener). The speaker discloses factual information, thoughts, or feelings and may further communicate emotions through nonverbal behaviors (e.g., gaze, touch, body orientation; see Patterson, 1984). As the intimacy process continues, the listener must respond to the speaker by disclosing personally relevant information, expressing emotion, and emitting various behaviors. For the speaker to interpret the listener's communication as responsive, the listener must convey that he or she understands the content of the speaker's disclosure, accepts or validates the speaker, and feels positively toward the speaker. At each stage of this process, personal qualities and individual differences, including motives, needs, and goals, can influence each person's behaviors and their interpretation of a partner's behavior (Reis & Patrick, 1996). Although Reis and Shaver largely focused on what occurs in any given interaction, they explicitly acknowledge that intimacy accrues across repeated interactions over time. As individuals interpret and assimilate their experiences in these interactions, they form general perceptions that reflect the degree to which the relationship is intimate and meaningful (Reis, 1994). Although these generalized perceptions of intimacy in the relationship develop over the course of repeated interactions, over time, they may take on an emergent property that goes beyond experiences in each individual interaction (Chelune, Robison, & Kommor, 1984).

The model emphasizes two fundamental components of intimacy: self-disclosure and partner responsiveness (Reis & Patrick, 1996; Reis & Shaver, 1988). Many definitions suggest that intimacy is a feeling of closeness that develops from personal disclosures between people (Perlman & Fehr, 1987). Self-disclosure refers to the verbal communication of personally relevant information, thoughts, and feelings to another; research in this area has often relied on degree or depth of self-disclosure as an index of intimacy (Altman & Taylor, 1973; Derlega et al., 1993; Jourard, 1971). Some theorists (Morton, 1978; Reis & Patrick, 1996; Reis & Shaver, 1988) have suggested that particular types of self-disclosure (i.e., those revealing the core self) are more closely linked to the experience of intimacy than others.

Researchers have distinguished between factual (i.e., descriptive) and emotional (i.e., evaluative) disclosure when examining the impact of disclosing the self in intimate relationships (Morton, 1978; Reis & Shaver, 1988). Factual self-disclosures are those that reveal personal facts and information (e.g., "I've had three romantic partners in my life"). Emotional self-disclosures are those that reveal one's private feelings, opinions, and judgments (e.g., "The last breakup was so painful that I'm not sure if I can love someone again"). Although both types of disclosures reveal private aspects of the self to others, disclosures involving emotions and feelings lie most closely at the core of one's self-definition (Greenberg & Safran, 1987; Reis & Patrick, 1996). Self-disclosures that involve emotions are believed to generate greater intimacy than those that are merely factual because such disclosures open the way for the listener to support and confirm core aspects of the discloser's view of self (Reis & Shaver, 1988; Sullivan, 1953).

Partner responsiveness is the other key component in the development of intimacy (Berg, 1987; Berg & Archer, 1982; Davis, 1982; Kelley et al., 1983). Partners are responsive when their behaviors (e.g., disclosures, expressions of emotion) address the communications, needs, wishes, or actions of the person with whom they are interacting (Miller & Berg, 1984). According to Reis and Shaver (1988), speakers are more likely to experience an interaction as intimate if they perceive their partner's response as understanding (i.e., accurately capturing the speaker's needs, feelings, and situation), validating (i.e., confirming that the speaker is an accepted and valued individual), and caring (i.e., showing affection and concern for the speaker). Reis and Shaver regard the speaker's interpretation of the listener's communication as more important for the development of intimacy than a speaker's disclosure or the listener's actual response. Although a partner may make a genuine attempt to be responsive to a disclosure, the speaker may not perceive the partner's behavior as responsive to his or her needs. This reasoning

suggests that the degree to which a listener's actual communication (what we will call partner disclosure) is associated with intimacy in the interaction should depend heavily on the nature of the speaker's perceptions of and feelings about the partner's response (what we will call perceived partner responsiveness). Thus, the extent to which the speaker perceives the partner as responsive should mediate the association between the partner's disclosure and level of intimacy in the interaction.

Despite the conceptual appeal of Reis and Shaver's (1988) interpersonal process model of intimacy, little empirical research has addressed its validity. One unpublished investigation of the model (Lin, 1992), however, suggests that both self-disclosure and partner responsiveness contribute to perceptions of intimacy at the level of the relationship. In this study, college students reported on their level of self-disclosure and perceptions of their partner's responsiveness after every social interaction over a 10-day period and, in a later interview, indicated the degree of relationship intimacy with each interaction partner. Both self-disclosure and perceived partner responsiveness, aggregated across daily interactions, predicted overall relationship intimacy: People who, on average, disclosed more and perceived a partner to be responsive reported greater intimacy in their relationship with that partner. In addition, there was some evidence that emotional disclosures were more important to relationship intimacy than were disclosures about facts. Although this study provided initial evidence that both self-disclosure and partner responsiveness are central components of intimacy at the level of the relationship, other important aspects of the model remain to be validated. In the present work, we sought to test the Reis and Shaver model by examining the links among several components of the intimacy process (i.e., self-disclosure, partner disclosure, partner responsiveness) on an interaction-by-interaction basis. It is particularly important to investigate these links at the level of interactions to determine whether feelings of intimacy in a given interaction are associated with the perception that self-disclosure has occurred and the perception that the partner returned the disclosure and was responsive.

Overview

The overarching goal of the present work was to test Reis and Shaver's (1988) interpersonal process model of intimacy at the level of individual social interactions. We examined three key tenets of the Reis and Shaver model: (a) self-disclosure and partner disclosure will contribute to feelings of intimacy on an interaction-by-interaction basis; (b) this process will be mediated by the degree to which a partner is perceived as responsive; and (c) emotional disclosures will contribute more to intimacy in the interaction than will factual disclosures.

We examined these aspects of the model by having participants complete a version of the Rochester Interaction Record (RIR; Reis & Wheeler, 1991). The RIR is an event-contingent diary that participants complete immediately following their social interactions over a specified period of time. In our studies, after every interaction, participants provided detailed information about their degree of self-disclosure, their perceptions of partner's disclosure, the degree to which they perceived their partners as responsive toward them, and their feelings of intimacy over a 2-week period. The RIR methodology allowed us to examine the hypothesized relationships among self-disclosure, partner disclosure, partner responsiveness, and intimacy on an interaction-by-interaction basis.

We tested two basic hypotheses following from the Reis and Shaver (1988) model. First, we tested the hypothesis that both self-disclosure and partner disclosure predict feelings of intimacy. Figure 11.1A shows the path model representing the hypothesized links among self-disclosure, partner disclosure, and intimacy. The degree to which individuals self-disclose should contribute to their feelings of intimacy, after controlling for their perceptions of the partner's disclosure (path p_{31}). The degree to which individuals view the partner's disclosing in turn also should contribute to feelings of intimacy, after controlling for self-disclosure (path p_{32}).

Second, we tested the hypothesis that individuals will experience intimacy in an interaction when self-disclosure and partner disclosure are linked to feelings that the partner is being responsive. Reis and Shaver (1988) emphasized the potential mediating role of partner responsiveness in the relationship between partner disclosure and intimacy. In addition, it is possible that partner responsiveness might also mediate the link between self-disclosure and intimacy, and for completeness, we tested this possibility. The mediational model, shown in Figure 11.1B, includes paths representing (a) the effect of self-disclosure (p_{31}) and partner disclosure (p_{32}) on perceived partner responsiveness and (b) the effect of each variable (i.e., self-disclosure, partner disclosure, and perceived partner responsiveness) on intimacy, while controlling for the effect of the others (paths p_{41}, p_{42}, and p_{43}). For a partial mediation effect, perceived partner responsiveness should be related significantly to ratings of self-disclosure and to partner disclosure (paths p_{31} and p_{32}), as well as to ratings of intimacy (path p_{43}; Kenny, Kashy, & Bolger, 1997). For a full mediation effect (Baron & Kenny, 1986; Kenny et al., 1997), there is an additional requirement that self-disclosure, partner disclosure, or both no longer have a significant direct effect on intimacy (i.e., path p_{41}, p_{42}, or both should not be significantly different from zero).

We measured self-disclosure with items that distinguished descriptive self-disclosures (disclosures of facts) from evaluative self-disclosures (disclosures of feelings) to allow for a finer grained analysis of the relative contributions of different types of self-disclosure. This refined measure allowed us to follow up on previous work (i.e., Lin, 1992; Morton, 1978) that has suggested that emotional self-disclosure would be more strongly related to intimacy than would factual self-disclosure.

Method

Participants

The study began with 244 participants who were selected from a larger undergraduate subject pool,

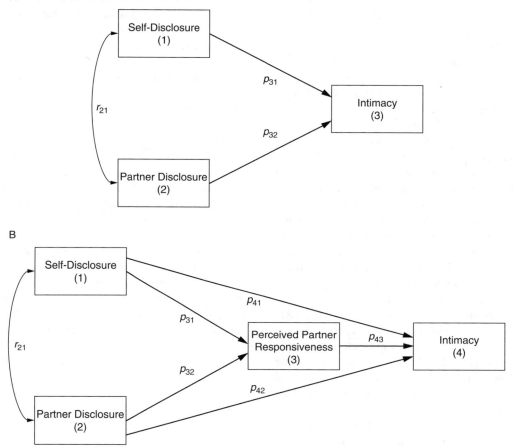

FIGURE 11.1 ■ Models containing the disclosure components of the intimacy process (A) and perceived partner responsiveness as a mediator of the intimacy process (B).

158 sampled from the University of Massachusetts and 86 sampled from the Pennsylvania State University. Twenty percent of the sample (48 participants) did not complete the study. Thirty-nine percent of the remaining sample (77 participants) reported having used their memory to complete more than 25% of the interaction records. We removed these participants' data from the analysis to minimize the influence of recall bias on participants' reports. Twenty-five percent (30 participants) of the remaining sample (119 participants) reported no dyadic relationships; that is, all of the interactions that they recorded involved more than

one person. We suspect that many participants who appeared to have had no dyadic interactions actually made recording errors in reporting the number of interactions partners present (i.e., counting both themselves and the interaction partner rather than the interaction partner alone). Given that it was not possible to determine when such errors were made, we used a conservative approach and removed all such individuals' data from the analyses. The final sample consisted of 89 participants (51 women, 38 men) who reported a total of 3,955 dyadic interactions (68% of all interactions recorded). All participants received extra credit for their participation and had a chance to win $50 in a lottery at the end of the semester.

Interaction Record

We adapted the RIR to assess self-disclosure, partner disclosure, feeling accepted by a partner, and intimacy experienced during social interactions. Participants completed the fixed-format interaction record after every interaction lasting 10 min or longer (Reis & Wheeler, 1991) for a 2-week (i.e., 14-days) period. We defined an interaction as any encounter with another person(s) in which the individuals attended to one another and possibly adjusted their behavior in response to one another (Reis & Wheeler, 1991). We called the interactions "social" because they involved at least one other person, but the interactions included more than situations in which the participants socialized for entertainment purposes (e.g., we sampled interactions at work, over the telephone, during classes, on errands). Using the RIR, participants provided information about the number of interaction partners present, the initials of partners for each interaction, and who initiated the interaction. We analyzed only dyadic interactions, because theories of intimacy focus primarily on dyadic exchanges.

Participants completed a version of the RIR after each social interaction lasting 10 min or longer and rated their interactions using 5-point scales (1 = *very little*, 5 = *a great deal*). Only the RIR items of interest for this report are presented here (see Appendix A for exact wording of RIR items).

Self-disclosure. Participants rated the degree to which they disclosed facts (one item), how much they expressed their thoughts (one item), and how much they expressed their emotions (one item) to their partner in the interaction. An overall summary variable for self-disclosure was created using the average of these three items. Descriptive self-disclosure was operationalized using the disclosure-of-facts item; evaluative self-disclosure was operationalized using the expression-of-emotions item.

Partner disclosure. Participants rated the degree to which the interaction partner disclosed thoughts and emotions (one item).

Perceived partner responsiveness. Participants rated the degree to which they felt accepted by their interaction partner (one item), how much they felt understood by their interaction partner (one item), and how much they felt cared for by their interaction partner (one item) during each social interaction. A summary variable was created using the average of these three items.

Intimacy. Participants rated the amount of closeness that they experienced in the interaction. We chose the term *closeness* rather than *intimacy* to ensure that participants understood that we were referring to psychological proximity and not to sexual intimacy.

Using HLM, we calculated the average within-subject correlations for items within all composite variables. These correlations are presented in Table 11.1.

Procedure

Participants attended three laboratory sessions. During the first session, the experimenter explained that the study concerned how people think and feel about their social interactions with others and that participants would keep records of all of their social interactions for 14 days. To preserve confidentiality, participants selected a code name to write on all of their study materials. Participants

TABLE 11.1. Average Within-Subject Correlations for Items Used in Composite Variables

Variable	1	2	3	4	5	6
1. Self-disclosure of facts	—					
2. Self-disclosure of thoughts	.20	—				
3. Self-disclosure of emotions	.10	.70	—			
4. Understanding by partner	.14	.33	.29	—		
5. Acceptance by partner	.08	.24	.22	.81	—	
6. Cared for by partner	.02[a]	.33	.40	.46	.42	—

Note. All correlations are significant at $p < .005$, except as noted. Variables 1, 2, and 3 constitute the self-disclosure composite. Variables 4, 5, and 6 constitute the partner responsiveness composite. [a]*ns.*

also completed several questionnaires during the first session (for a complete description, see Pietromonaco & Feldman Barrett, 1997). Afterward, the experimenter explained the procedure for completing the interaction records and carefully defined all items on the interaction record form. The experimenter emphasized the importance of answering honestly when using the interaction records and of completing a record as soon as possible (within 15 min) after each interaction. In addition to oral instructions, participants received written instructions to which they could refer during the course of the study. Prior to leaving the first laboratory session, participants received several interaction records with which to practice.

During the second laboratory session, participants reviewed their practice interaction records with the experimenter. The experimenter answered any questions and gave participants a final written set of instructions for completing 14 days of interaction records. Participants returned their interaction records three times during each recording week, and they received extra lottery tickets for returning their forms on time. The experimenter phoned, within 24 hr, any participants who did not return their forms on time and reminded them to return the forms.

During the third laboratory session, the experimenter interviewed participants about their reactions to the study. Participants estimated how difficult they found the study, how accurate their recording was, and how much their social patterns changed as a result of being in the study. To ensure that participants followed all instructions, the experimenter asked several specific questions about the accuracy with which participants had recorded their interactions, including (a) whether they had recorded all of their interactions and, if they had not, what percentage they had not recorded (percentage not recorded: $M = 15.4\%$, $SD = 14.8$) and (b) whether they had completed any interaction records from memory (i.e., more than 1 hr later) and, if they had, the percentage of interaction forms that they had completed from memory. The experimenter stressed that participants would not be penalized in any way (i.e., they would still receive credit and lottery tickets) if they had not followed instructions and that we were simply interested in obtaining an accurate picture of their data.

Results

Data Analytic Strategy

The interaction data in this study conformed to a multilevel data structure (Goldstein, 1987; Kenny et al., 1997). A defining feature of multilevel data is the existence of a hierarchy of observations in which multiple lower level observations are grouped within upper level units. In this research, the lower level data consisted of participants' ratings of self-disclosure, partner disclosure, partner responsiveness, and intimacy experienced during social interactions. Each lower level variable was measured on an interaction-by-interaction basis and, therefore, consisted of multiple data points for each individual. These lower level data were nested within upper level units, or participants. Hierarchical linear modeling (HLM; Bryk & Raudenbush, 1987, 1992; Bryk, Raudenbush, & Congdon, 1996) is a statistical program designed for use with multilevel data sets. HLM was used to analyze the interaction data because it allowed us to analyze within-subject (lower level) and between-subject (upper level) variation simultaneously, thus enabling us to model each source of variation while taking the statistical characteristics of the other level into account. HLM first computes a regression equation for each participant in which a lower level outcome variable is regressed on lower level predictors; the individual regression parameters for these predictors are then used to estimate the average parameter estimates for all participants as well as the amount of individual variation around this average. Standardized HLM regression coefficients were used to estimate paths.

Self-Disclosure and Partner Disclosure in the Intimacy Process

Using HLM, we computed the average correlations across individuals for the RIR variables. These values are reported in Table 11.2.

TABLE 11.2. Average Within-Subject Correlations of Rochester Interaction Record Variables

Variable	1	2	3	4
1. Self-disclosure	—			
2. Partner disclosure	.60	—		
3. Partner responsiveness	.41	.39	—	
4. Intimacy	.55	.57	.59	—

Note: All correlations are significant at $p < .001$.

A

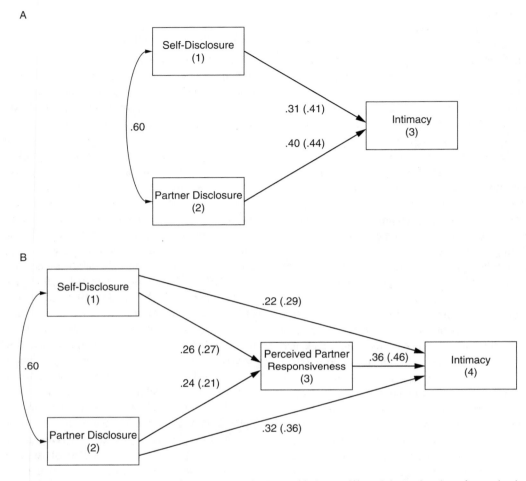

FIGURE 11.2 ■ The relationship of disclosure to feelings of intimacy (A) and the estimation of perceived partner responsiveness as a mediator in the intimacy process (B). Unstandardized coefficients are presented in parentheses. All paths were statistically significant.

Next, we estimated the path relationships among self-disclosure, partner disclosure, and feelings of intimacy. The results, presented in Figure 11.2A, indicated that on average, both self-disclosure and partner disclosure demonstrated significant predictive effects on ratings of intimacy across a range of social interactions. Self-disclosure and partner disclosure were significantly correlated with each other on average ($r = .60, p < .001$) and were significantly correlated with intimacy ($r = .55, p < .001$, and $r = .57, p < .001$, respectively). Intimacy was uniquely predicted by both self-disclosure, $p_{31} = .31, t = 10.71$, $p < .001$, and partner disclosure, $p_{32} = .40, t = 13.27, p < .001$.

The Role of Partner Responsiveness in the Intimacy Process

Next, we examined whether perceived partner responsiveness acted as a mediator of the intimacy process. The results, presented in Figure 11.2B, revealed that self-disclosure was significantly correlated with perceived partner responsiveness ($r = .41, p < .001$) and demonstrated a unique predictive relationship, $p_{31} = .26, t = 9.35, p < .001$. Partner disclosure was also significantly correlated with perceived partner responsiveness ($r = .39$, $p < .001$) and demonstrated a unique predictive relationship, $p_{32} = .24$, $t = 8.53$, $p < .001$. Moreover, perceived partner responsiveness correlated significantly with intimacy ($r = .59$, $p < .001$) and was uniquely related to intimacy, $p_{43} = .36$, $t = 15.07$, $p < .001$. Perceived partner responsiveness partially mediated the intimacy process because both self-disclosure and partner disclosure demonstrated decreased, yet still significant, direct effects on intimacy, $p_{41} = .22$, $t = 8.69$, $p < .001$, and $p_{42} = .32$, $t = 11.26$, $p < .001$, respectively. The reduction in the direct effect of self-disclosure on intimacy (from .31 to .22) was significant ($z = 8.06$, $p < .001$), indicating that perceived partner responsiveness partially mediated the effect of self-disclosure on intimacy. Similarly, the reduction in the direct effect of partner disclosure on intimacy (from .40 to .32) was significant ($z = 9.82$, $p < .001$), indicating that perceived partner responsiveness partially mediated the effect of partner disclosure on intimacy.

The Importance of Emotional Self-Disclosure

To test the prediction that emotional self-disclosure would contribute more to intimacy than would factual disclosure, we separated these two types of self-disclosure in the same HLM analysis by using both variables as predictors of intimacy in addition to partner disclosure and partner responsiveness. We first replaced the overall self-disclosure variable, shown in Figure 11.1A, with two self-disclosure variables: one for disclosure of facts and one for disclosure of emotion. In this set of analyses, we use β to refer to standardized path coefficients and b to refer to unstandardized coefficients. Self-disclosure of emotion significantly predicted intimacy after controlling for effects of self-disclosure of facts and partner disclosure, $\beta = .37$ ($b = .33$), $t = 12.53$, $p < .001$, but self-disclosure of facts was not a significant predictor, $\beta = -.01$ ($b = -.01$), $t = -0.32$, ns; in addition, self-disclosure of emotion was statistically more important to the prediction of felt intimacy than was self-disclosure of facts, $\chi^2(1, N = 85) =$

98.22, $p < .001$. Because the path between self-disclosure of facts and intimacy was not significantly different from zero in this analysis, we dropped factual self-disclosure from future analyses.

Next, we tested a model in which perceived partner responsiveness mediated the relationship between self-disclosure of emotion and intimacy (i.e., we replaced the overall self-disclosure variable, shown in Figure 11.1B, with self-disclosure of emotion). Self-disclosure of emotion was significantly related to perceived partner responsiveness, $\beta = .25$ ($b = .17$), $t = 8.27$, $p < .001$, and perceived partner responsiveness, in turn, was significantly related to intimacy, $\beta = .33$ ($b = .42$), $t = 13.83$, $p < .001$. The direct path from self-disclosure of emotion to intimacy significantly differed from zero, $\beta = .30$ ($b = .27$), $t = 12.22$, $p < .001$, but is decreased in magnitude from the corresponding path in the model without perceived partner responsiveness as a mediator. These results suggest that the disclosure of emotion was more important to the experience of intimacy in interactions than was the disclosure of mere facts or information. Furthermore, perceived partner responsiveness partially mediated the relationship between emotional self-disclosure and intimacy. The partial mediating role of partner responsiveness is consistent with the contention that emotional self-disclosures provide opportunities for listeners to support and validate the discloser, thereby furthering the intimacy process.

Discussion

This experience-sampling study provides the first direct test of Reis and Shaver's (1988) interpersonal process model of intimacy. Overall, the findings provide strong support for the basic tenets of the model. Self-disclosure and partner disclosure emerged as significant predictors of intimacy on an interaction-by-interaction basis. We found support for the hypothesis that self-disclosure and partner disclosure are associated with feelings of intimacy in part because this process takes place within the context of a partner being responsive. These findings indicate that mere behaviors (or perceptions of behaviors) may not be sufficient for strong feelings of intimacy to develop. The experience of intimacy in interactions was related to feeling understood, accepted, and cared for by an interaction partner. Thus, intimate interactions are those that are self-revealing and impart the feeling that one is known, validated, and valued by one's partner (Reis, 1990; Sullivan, 1953).

Also, emotional self-disclosures are more predictive of intimacy than are factual self-disclosures. These findings lend support to the notion that disclosures of emotion are more important to the development of intimacy in social interactions than are disclosures of personal facts or information (Lin, 1992; Reis & Shaver, 1988). Self-disclosures of emotion allow for core aspects of the self to be revealed and provide the opportunity for disclosers to be understood and validated, thus facilitating the experience of intimacy. These findings are confined, however, to global ratings of affective and factual disclosures and may not reflect the contribution of specific emotions or the content of the emotional or factual expression in the intimacy process.

Of course, these interpretations of our findings are limited in several respects. First, although the findings are consistent with the directional hypotheses following from Reis and Shaver's (1988) model, our correlational data cannot determine the causal direction of the effects. That is, reverse causal effects (i.e., intimacy causing partner responsiveness) cannot be ruled out (see Kenny et al., 1997, for a discussion of specification errors). Our data also cannot determine whether "third" variables associated with intimacy or partner responsiveness might account for the observed effects. Second, we did not explicitly test the transactional aspect of the interpersonal process model of intimacy. Our data did not include responses from both participants in the interaction or take into account the contingencies between partners' responses. Instead, our studies captured the subjective experiences of one individual and thus examined the interpersonal process model from one person's perspective. Although this methodology brings us closer to the transactional

process envisioned by Reis and Shaver, it does not capture all of the complex interpersonal contingencies inherent in the model. Third, the degree to which these findings, based on the responses of U.S. college students, can be generalized to other kinds of individuals remains unclear. For example, it will be important to investigate the nature of intimacy processes in older adults in longer term, committed relationships (i.e., married spouses), and in non-Western cultures in which the self is more embedded in the social context and defined by relationships (Kitayama & Markus, 1995).

Implications and Future Directions

The present research not only provides strong support for the Reis and Shaver (1988) model of intimacy, but also suggests some ways in which the model should be elaborated or modified.

Individual Variation in the Relationships Between Intimacy Components

Additional analyses (not reported in the *Results* section) indicated that significant variability existed in the size of the lower level relationships between intimacy components across different individuals. The existence of significant individual variation around estimates of lower level path coefficients indicates that the strength (and in some cases, the direction) of the relationships among self-disclosure, partner disclosure, partner responsiveness, and intimacy varies from person to person. This variation may be a function of measurable individual differences (Reis & Patrick, 1996). For example, individuals can vary in their motivation for engaging in intimate interactions and establishing intimate relationships. Individuals possess skills, goals, concerns, and other personality characteristics that affect how much they disclose to others, how they respond to others, and how they interpret disclosures and responses from others (Davis, 1982; Mikulincer & Nachshon, 1991; Miller, Berg, & Archer, 1983; Reis & Shaver, 1988). Indeed, significant individual variation existed around the estimates of the average path coefficients presented for all models; some participants had larger coefficients and some had smaller coefficients than the average coefficients for the entire sample. Some of this between-subjects variation around the average path coefficients may be due to sampling. Some of this between-subjects variation may represent meaningful differences in the path coefficients across different groups of people.

We attempted to model the variation in the lower level estimates by including between-subjects (upper level) variables in the HLM models tested. For example, we used HLM procedures to test whether sex of participant accounted for any of the observed individual variation, but found that men and women did not differ significantly in the size of their path coefficients. In addition, attachment style was used as a between-subjects predictor of lower level variation. Attachment style, whether measured as set of categorical (e.g., Bartholomew & Horowitz, 1991) or as continuous (Brennan & Shaver, 1995), resulted in few and inconsistent differences from average path relationships. It will be important for future work to examine whether other individual-differences variables account for predictable variations in the size of the associations between intimacy components.

Practical Applications of Reis and Shaver's (1988) Intimacy Model

The interpersonal process model not only explains how intimacy develops and is maintained across time, but may also provide a way of understanding how to intervene when the intimacy process goes awry. For example, we found that self-disclosure and responsive behaviors from an interaction partner (i.e., partner disclosure) are linked to feelings of intimacy in part through their ability to make the participant feel understood, accepted, and cared for in an interaction. Recently, strategies that promote acceptance and validation have been added to traditional behavioral interventions used in the treatment of couple difficulties because they are thought to enhance intimacy (Christensen, Jacobson, & Babcock, 1995; Jacobson, 1992). Our findings are consistent with the developing trend that places acceptance as a central construct in the development of intimacy in couples, and they suggest that interventions should target all components of the intimacy

process when attempting to enhance intimacy. Our results suggest that acceptance of a partner is best understood in theoretically broader terms, incorporating both a sense of understanding and caring for a partner. This finding is reflected in the basic strategies of traditional behavioral couples therapy in which couples are guided to communicate effectively and establish positive reciprocity (Gottman, Notarius, Gonso, & Markman, 1976; Jacobson & Margolin, 1979). Effective communication requires the acquisition of speaker and listener skills that avoid mutual blaming and sidetracking, resulting in mutual understanding; increasing positive reciprocity consists of partners increasing and enhancing positive verbal and nonverbal behaviors, resulting in a sense of caring. Although social psychologists and clinical psychologists often approach the study of personal relationships from different perspectives, the findings in support of the Reis and Shaver model of intimacy may help to bridge the gap between these two overlapping fields. The study of personal relationships is one that lies at the interface of clinical and social psychology and calls for the integration of different, but related, perspectives (Acitelli, 1995).

Conclusion

This investigation provided direct empirical support for the interpersonal process model of intimacy. Self-disclosure, partner disclosure, and partner responsiveness were all significant components of the intimacy process at an interaction-by-interaction level. Moreover, emotional self-disclosure was found to be more strongly linked to intimacy than factual self-disclosure. Furthermore, this investigation suggested possible elaborations of the model: Perceived partner responsiveness was found to mediate the predictive effects of self-disclosure and partner disclosure on intimacy. Future work should attempt to expand the empirical support of the model to studies of long-term, committed relationships and to model the individual variation found across participants in the component process. Such research endeavors will contribute to our understanding of the richness and complexity inherent in the interpersonal process that shapes the experience of intimacy in relationships over time.

NOTES

Jean-Philippe Laurenceau, Department of Psychology, Pennsylvania State University; Lisa Feldman Barrett, Department of Psychology, Boston College; Paula R. Pietromonaco, Department of Psychology, University of Massachusetts at Amherst.

We are grateful to Niall Bolger, Dave Kenny, and Aline Sayer for their statistical input. We would also like to thank George Levinger for his comments on a draft of this article.

Correspondence concerning this article should be addressed to either Jean-Philippe Laurenceau, Department of Psychology, University of Miami, Coral Gables, Florida 33124 or Lisa Feldman Barrett, Department of Psychology, Boston College, Chestnut Hill, Massachusetts 02167. Electronic mail may be sent to jlaurenceau@miami.edu or barretli@bc.edu.

REFERENCES

Acitelli, L. K. (1995). Disciplines at parallel play. *Journal of Social and Personal Relationships, 12,* 589–596.

Altman, I., & Taylor, D. A. (1973). *Social penetration: The development of interpersonal relationships.* New York: Holt, Rinehart & Winston.

Argyle, M., & Dean, J. (1965). Eye contact, distance, and affiliation. *Sociometry, 28,* 289–304.

Baron, R. M., & Kenny, D. A. (1986). The moderator–mediator distinction in social psychological research: Conceptual, strategic, and statistical considerations. *Journal of Personality and Social Psychology, 51,* 1173–1182.

Bartholomew, K. (1990). Avoidance of intimacy: An attachment perspective. *Journal of Social and Personal Relationships, 7,* 147–178.

Bartholomew, K., & Horowitz, L. M. (1991). Attachment styles among young adults: A test of a model. *Journal of Personality and Social Psychology, 61,* 226–244.

Berg, J. H. (1987). Responsiveness and self-disclosure. In V. J. Derlega & J. H. Berg (Eds.), *Self-disclosure: Theory, research, and therapy* (pp. 101–130). New York: Plenum Press.

Berg, J. H., & Archer, R. L. (1982). Responses to self-disclosure and interaction goals. *Journal of Experimental Social Psychology, 18,* 501–512.

Brennan, K. A., & Shaver, P. R. (1995). Dimensions of adult attachment, affect regulation, and romantic attachment. *Personality and Social Psychology Bulletin, 21,* 267–283.

Bryk, A. S., & Raudenbush, S. W. (1987). Application of hierarchical linear models to assessing change. *Psychological Bulletin, 101,* 147–158.

Bryk, A. S., & Raudenbush, S. W. (1992). *Hierarchical linear models: Applications and data analysis methods.* Newbury Park, CA: Sage.

Bryk, A. S., Raudenbush, S. W., & Congdon, R. T. (1996). *Hierarchical linear modeling with the HLM/2L and HLM/3L programs.* Chicago: Scientific Software.

Chelune, G. J., Robison, J. T., & Kommor, M. J. (1984). A cognitive interaction model of intimate relationships. In V. J. Derlega (Ed.), *Communication, intimacy, and close relationships* (pp. 11–40). Orlando, FL: Academic Press.

Christensen, A., Jacobson, N. S., & Babcock, J. C. (1995). Integrative behavioral couples therapy. In N. S. Jacobson & A. S. Gurman (Eds.), *Clinical handbook of couples therapy* (2nd ed., pp. 31–64). New York: Guilford Press.

Clark, M. S., & Reis, H. T. (1988). Interpersonal processes in close relationships. *Annual Review of Psychology, 39,* 609–672.

Davis, D. (1982). Determinants of responsiveness in dyadic interaction. In W. Ickes & E. S. Knowles (Eds.), *Personality, roles, and social behavior* (pp. 85–139). New York: Springer-Verlag.

Derlega, V. J., Metts, S., Petronio, S., & Margulis, S. T. (1993). *Self-disclosure.* Newbury Park, CA: Sage.

Duck, S. W., & Sants, H. K. A. (1983). On the origins of the specious: Are personal relationships really interpersonal states? *Journal of Clinical and Social Psychology, 1,* 27–41.

Goldstein, H. (1987). *Multilevel models in educational and social research.* New York: Oxford University Press.

Gottman, J. M., Notarius, C., Gonso, J., & Markman, H. J. (1976). *A couple's guide to communication.* Champaign, IL: Research Press.

Greenberg, L. S., & Safran, J. D. (1987). *Emotion in psychotherapy.* New York: Guilford Press.

Jacobson, N. S. (1992). Behavioral couple therapy: A new beginning. *Behavior Therapy, 23,* 493–506.

Jacobson, N. S., & Margolin, G. (1979). *Marital therapy: Strategies based on social learning and behavior exchange principles.* New York: Brunner/Mazel.

Jourard, S. M. (1971). *Self-disclosure: An experimental analysis of the transparent self.* New York: Wiley.

Kelley, H. H., Berscheid, E., Christensen, A., Harvey, J. H., Huston, T. L., Levinger, G., McClintock, E., Peplau, L. A., & Peterson, D. (1983). Analyzing close relationships. In Kelley, H. H., Berscheid, E., Christensen, A., Harvey, J. H., Huston, T. L., Levinger, G., McClintock, E., Peplau, L. A., & Peterson, D. (Eds.), *Close relationships: Development and change.* New York: Freeman.

Kenny, D. A., Kashy, D., & Bolger, N. (1997). Data analysis in social psychology. In D. Gilbert, S. Fiske, & G. Lindzey (Eds.), *Handbook of social psychology* (4th ed., pp. 233–265). New York: McGraw-Hill.

Kitayama, S., & Markus, H. R. (1995). Culture and self: Implications for internationalizing psychology. In N. R. Goldberger & J. B. Veroff (Eds.), *The culture and psychology reader* (pp. 366–383). New York: New York University Press.

Lin, Y. C. (1992). *The construction of the sense of intimacy from everyday social interactions.* Unpublished doctoral dissertation, University of Rochester, Rochester, New York.

McAdams, D. P. (1985). Motivation and friendship. In S. Duck & D. Perlman (Eds.), *Understanding personal relationships* (pp. 85–105). London: Sage.

McAdams, D. P., & Constantian, C. A. (1983). Intimacy and affiliation motives in daily living: An experience sampling analysis. *Journal of Personality and Social Psychology, 45,* 851–861.

Mikulincer, M., & Nachshon, O. (1991). Attachment styles and patterns of self-disclosure. *Journal of Personality and Social Psychology, 61,* 321–331.

Miller, L. C., & Berg, J. (1984). Selectivity and urgency in interpersonal exchange. In V. J. Derlega (Ed.), *Communication, intimacy, and close relationships* (pp. 161–206). Orlando, FL: Academic Press.

Miller, L. C., Berg, J. H., & Archer, R. L. (1983). Openers: Individuals who elicit intimate self-disclosure. *Journal of Personality and Social Psychology, 44,* 1234–1244.

Morton, T. L. (1978). Intimacy and reciprocity of exchange: A comparison of spouses and strangers. *Journal of Personality and Social Psychology, 36,* 72–81.

Patterson, M. L. (1976). An arousal model of interpersonal intimacy. *Psychological Review, 83,* 235–245.

Patterson, M. L. (1982). A sequential functional model of nonverbal exchange. *Psychological Review, 89,* 231–249.

Patterson, M. L. (1984). Intimacy, social control, and nonverbal involvement: A functional approach. In V. J. Derlega (Ed.), *Communication, intimacy, and close relationships* (pp. 13–42). New York: Academic Press.

Perlman, D., & Fehr, B. (1987). The development of intimate relationships. In D. Perlman & S. W. Duck (Eds.), *Intimate relationships: Development, dynamics and deterioration* (pp. 13–42). Beverly Hills, CA: Sage.

Pietromonaco, P. R., & Feldman Barrett, L. (1997). Working models of attachment and daily social interactions. *Journal of Personality and Social Psychology, 73,* 1409–1423.

Prager, K. J. (1995). *The psychology of intimacy.* New York: Guilford Press.

Reis, H. T. (1990). The role of intimacy in interpersonal relationships. *Journal of Social and Clinical Psychology, 9,* 15–30.

Reis, H. T. (1994). Domains of experience: Investigating relationship processes from three perspectives. In R. Erber & R. Gilmore (Eds.), *Theoretical frameworks in personal relationships* (pp. 87–110). Hillsdale, NJ: Erlbaum.

Reis, H. T., & Patrick, B. C. (1996). Attachment and intimacy: Component processes. In E. T. Higgins & A. W. Kruglanski (Eds.), *Social psychology: Handbook of basic principles* (pp. 523–563). New York: Guilford Press.

Reis, H. T., & Shaver, P. (1988). Intimacy as an interpersonal process. In S. Duck (Ed.), *Handbook of personal relationships* (pp. 367–389). Chichester, England: Wiley.

Reis, H. T., & Wheeler, L. (1991). Studying social interaction with the Rochester Interaction Record. In M. P. Zanna (Ed.), *Advances in experimental social psychology* (Vol. 24, pp. 269–318). San Diego, CA: Academic Press.

Sullivan, H. S. (1953). *The interpersonal theory of psychiatry.* New York: Norton.

Waring, E. M. (1984). The measurement of marital intimacy. *Journal of Marital and Family Therapy, 10,* 185–192.

Appendix A

Exact Wording for Rochester Interaction Record Items

Self-disclosure: I disclosed my emotions . . . .
I disclosed my thoughts . . . .
I disclosed my facts . . . .

Partner disclosure: My interaction partner disclosed thoughts and feelings . . . .

Partner responsiveness: How much did your interaction partner understand you?
How much did you feel cared for?
Did the other person see you as acceptable?

Intimacy: How close was the interaction?

A Triangular Theory of Love

Robert J. Sternberg • Yale University

This article presents a triangular theory of love. According to the theory, love has three components: (a) *intimacy*, which encompasses the feelings of closeness, connectedness, and bondedness one experiences in loving relationships; (b) *passion*, which encompasses the drives that lead to romance, physical attraction, and sexual consummation; and (c) *decision/commitment*, which encompasses, in the short term, the decision that one loves another, and in the long term, the commitment to maintain that love. The amount of love one experiences depends on the absolute strength of these three components, and the kind of love one experiences depends on their strengths relative to each other. The three components interact with each other and with the actions that they produce and that produce them so as to form a number of different kinds of loving experiences. The triangular theory of love subsumes certain other theories and can account for a number of empirical findings in the research literature, as well as for a number of experiences with which many are familiar firsthand. It is proposed that the triangular theory provides a rather comprehensive basis for understanding many aspects of the love that underlies close relationships.

What does it mean "to love" someone? Does it always mean the same thing, and if not, in what ways do loves differ from each other? Why do certain loves seem to last, whereas others disappear almost as quickly as they are formed? This article seeks to answer these and other questions through a triangular theory of love. This tripartite theory deals both with the nature of love and with loves in various kinds of relationships.

The presentation of the theory will be divided into two main parts. In the first part, the main tenets of the theory will be explained and discussed, and the theory will be compared with other theories of love. In the second part, the theory will be shown to account for many of the empirical phenomena that have been observed with regard to love.

The Triangle of Love

Three Components

The triangular theory of love holds that love can be understood in terms of three components that together can be viewed as forming the vertices

213

of a triangle. These three components are inti-macy (the top vertex of the triangle), passion (the left-hand vertex of the triangle), and decision/commitment (the right-hand vertex of the triangle). (The assignment of components to vertices is arbitrary.) Each of these three terms can be used in many different ways, so it is important at the outset to clarify their meanings in the context of the present theory.

The intimacy component refers to feelings of closeness, connectedness, and bondedness in loving relationships. It thus includes within its purview those feelings that give rise, essentially, to the experience of warmth in a loving relationship.

The passion component refers to the drives that lead to romance, physical attraction, sexual consummation, and related phenomena in loving relationships. The passion component thus includes within its purview those sources of motivational and other forms of arousal that lead to the experience of passion in a loving relationship.

The decision/commitment component refers to, in the short term, the decision that one loves someone else, and in the long term, the commitment to maintain that love. The decision/commitment component thus includes within its purview the cognitive elements that are involved in decision making about the existence of and potential long-term commitment to a loving relationship.

In general, the intimacy component might be viewed as largely, but not exclusively, deriving from emotional investment in the relationship; the passion component as deriving largely, although not exclusively, from motivational involvement in the relationship; and the decision/commitment component as deriving largely, although not exclusively, from cognitive decision in and commitment to the relationship. From one point of view, the intimacy component might be viewed as a "warm" one, the passion component as a "hot" one, and the decision/commitment component as a "cold" one.

The experience of love can be partitioned in a number of ways, and so it is important to note at the outset that the present partitioning into intimacy, passion, and decision/commitment is not the only one possible, nor is it even valid for all possible purposes. Nevertheless, the argument will be made that the proposed partitioning is particularly useful for understanding the elements of love, and how they function in close relationships.

Although love, like other psychological phenomena, can be partitioned into various kinds of components, it is important not to lose sight of the whole in the analysis of its parts. Love is a complex whole that appears to derive in part from genetically transmitted instincts and drives, but probably in larger part from socially learned role modeling that, through observation, comes to be defined as love. To a large extent, then, love is prototypically organized (Rosch, 1978), such that certain feelings, drives, thoughts, and behaviors appear as more highly characteristic of love as it is socially defined, whereas others appear as less characteristic. Indeed, one way to study love would be through the examination of people's conceptions or implicit theories of love (Barnes & Sternberg, 1986, are currently involved in such an investigation). Such an investigation capitalizes on principles of descriptive psychology in order to provide a framework for love-related phenomena (Davis & Roberts, 1985; Ossorio, 1985). A theory of love, therefore, can help one understand the range and composition of the phenomenon of love, but should not result in the whole's being lost in its parts.

The similarities and differences among the three components of love may be better understood by examining their respective properties, some of which are summarized in Table 12.1.

Properties of the Components of Love

The three components of love differ with respect to a number of their properties. For example, the emotional and other involvement of the intimacy component and the cognitive commitment of the decision/commitment component seem to be relatively stable in close relationships, whereas the motivational and other arousal of the passion component tends to be relatively unstable and to come and go on a somewhat unpredictable basis. One has some degree of conscious control over the feelings of the intimacy component that one experiences (if one is aware of them), a high degree

TABLE 12.1. Properties of Triangle Vertices

Property	Component		
	Intimacy	Passion	Decision/commitment
Stability	Moderately high	Low	Moderately high
Conscious controllability	Moderate	Low	High
Experiential salience	Variable	High	Variable
Typical importance in short-term relationships	Moderate	High	Low
Typical importance in long-term relationships	High	Moderate	High
Commonality across loving relationships	High	Low	Moderate
Psychophysiological involvement	Moderate	High	Low
Susceptibility to conscious awareness	Moderately low	High	Moderately high

of control over the commitment of the decision/commitment component that one invests in the relationship (again, assuming awareness), but very little control over the amount of motivational and other arousal of the passion component one experiences as a result of being with or even looking at another person. One is usually quite aware and conscious of the passion component, but one's awareness of the intimacy and decision/commitment components can be highly variable. Sometimes one experiences warm feelings of intimacy without being aware of them or without being able to label them. Similarly, one is often not certain of how committed one is to a relationship until people or events intervene to challenge that commitment.

The importance of each of the three components of love differs, on the average, as a function of whether a loving relationship is short-term or long-term. In short-term involvements, and especially romantic ones, the passion component tends to play a large part. The intimacy component may play only a moderate part, and the decision/commitment component may play hardly any part at all. In contrast, the intimacy component and the decision/commitment component typically play relatively large parts in a long-term close relationship. Indeed, it is difficult to sustain such a relationship without at least some degree of involvement and commitment. In contrast, the passion component typically plays only a moderate part, and its role may decline somewhat over time.

The three components of love also differ in their commonality across loving relationships.

The intimacy component appears to be at the core of many loving relationships (Sternberg & Grajek, 1984), whether that relationship is toward a parent, a sibling, a lover, or a close friend. The passion component tends to be limited to just certain kinds of loving relationships, especially romantic ones, whereas the decision/commitment component can be highly variable across the different kinds of loving relationships. For example, commitment tends to be very high in one's love for one's children, but relatively low in one's love for those friends that come and go throughout the span of one's lifetime.

The three components also differ in the amount of psychophysiological involvement they offer. The passion component is highly dependent on psychophysiological involvement, whereas the decision/commitment component appears to involve only a modest amount of psychophysiological response. The intimacy component involves an intermediate amount of psychophysiological involvement.

In sum, the three components of love have somewhat different properties, which tend to highlight some of the ways in which they function in the experiences of love as they occur in various kinds of close relationships.

Composition of the Triangle

The intimacy component. In the context of the triangular theory, the intimacy component refers to those feelings in a relationship that promote closeness, bondedness, and connectedness. Our research indicates that it includes, among other things, feelings of (a) desire to promote the welfare of the loved one, (b) experienced happiness with the loved one, (c) high regard for the loved one, (d) being able to count on the loved one in times of need, (e) mutual understanding with the loved one, (f) sharing of one's self and one's possessions with the loved one, (g) receipt of emotional support from the loved one, (h) giving of emotional support to the loved one, (i) intimate communication with the loved one, and (j) valuing the loved one in one's life (Sternberg & Grajek, 1984). These feelings form only a subset of the possible ones that can be experienced in the intimacy component of love, and moreover, it is not necessary to experience all of these feelings in order to experience love. To the contrary, our research indicates that one experiences the intimacy component of love when one samples a sufficient number of these feelings, with the number that is sufficient probably differing from one person to another. The feelings are usually not experienced independently; to the contrary, they may be experienced as one overall feeling. Nevertheless, they appear to be at least partially decomposable, as in the listing here.

Sternberg and Grajek (1984) actually tested three alternative theories of the nature of love, focusing upon its intimacy component. They referred to the three theories as Spearmanian, Thomsonian, and Thurstonian. The nature of the three theories is illustrated in Figure 12.1. All three theories are based on structural models of intelligence.

The Spearmanian theory is based on Spearman's (1927) theory of general intelligence (*g*). In terms of a structural model of love, one might conceptualize love partly in terms of a single *g*, which would be an undifferentiated "glob" of highly positive feelings that is essentially nondecomposable. To experience love would be to experience this glob of highly positive feelings.

The Thomsonian model is based on Thomson's (1939) theory of the "bonds" of intelligence. In terms of a structural model of love, one might conceptualize love partly in terms of feelings that, when sampled together, yield the composite experience that we label *love*. On this view, though, the composite is not an undifferentiated unity; rather,

it can be decomposed into a large number of underlying bonds that tend to co-occur in certain close relationships and that in combination result in the global experience that we view as love.

The Thurstonian theory is based on Thurstone's (1938) theory of primary factors. In terms of a structural model of love, one would emerge with a theory viewing love partly in terms of a small, consistent set of feelings that have approximately equal importance and salience in the overall experience we describe as love. Love is not one main thing, whether decomposable (Thomsonian model) or not (Spearmanian model). Rather, it is a set of primary structures that are best understood separately rather than as an integrated whole. All contribute simultaneously to the experience of love. According to this notion, global experiences such as love can be decomposed into multiple

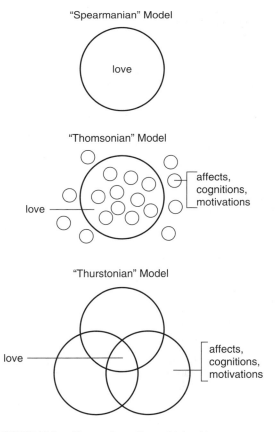

FIGURE 12.1 ■ Three alternative models of love.

overlapping (correlated) factors, and one could essentially combine factor scores to obtain an overall index of the strength of the love.

Sternberg and Grajek (1984) used factor- and cluster-analytic methods to distinguish among these three theories. These methods were applied to the Rubin Loving and Liking Scales as well as to the Scale of Interpersonal Involvement used by Levinger, Rands, and Talaber (1977). The data were analyzed not only for the measures of loving and liking for one's lover, but also for measures of loving and liking for one's mother, father, sibling closest in age, and best friend of the same sex. Subjects in the study were 35 men and 50 women in southern Connecticut, ranging in age from 18 to 70 years, with a mean of 32 years.

Factor analysis of the data of these subjects for each of the close relationships supported a Thomsonian model: A general factor emerged even after varimax rotation of the principal-axis solution (which tends to obscure rather than to highlight a general factor), but the general factor proved to be decomposable through hierarchical cluster analysis. In other words, the factor analysis supported either the Spearmanian model or the Thomsonian model, both of which are consistent with a general factor, but not the Thurstonian model, which is not consistent with a general factor (at least at the first order of analysis). The decomposability of the general factor supported the Thomsonian model but not the Spearmanian one, in that Spearman's model does not allow for the decomposability of the general factor.

An interesting and, to some extent, surprising finding of the Sternberg-Grajek (1984) study was that the structure of intimacy in love does not appear to differ consequentially from one loving relationship to another. In other words, the general factor and ensuing clusters that were obtained for each relationship were about the same. This finding suggests that the intimacy component of love forms a common core in loving relationships. In other words, whereas the passion and decision/commitment components appear to be unique to loving relationships with certain classes of individuals, the intimacy component does not appear to be limited to just certain loving relationships.

Consider, for example, loves for a mother, a father, a sibling, a best friend of the same sex, and a lover. According to the present point of view, the intimacy component forms a common core in each of these loving relationships. However, the passion and decision/commitment components are experienced more selectively. For example, the passion component probably plays a major part in love for a lover, but only a minor part, if any at all, in love for a parent, especially a same-sex parent. Similarly, the decision/commitment component is likely to play an important role in certain loving relationships, especially those with members of one's nuclear family (e.g., the mother, father, and siblings, if any). However, commitment over the long term need not play an important role, or any role at all, in love for a lover. Indeed, many romantic loves are short term and are never intended to be anything else. (Note that the term *commitment* is used here and elsewhere in this article to refer to long-term investment in a loving relationship, not to refer to the degree of responsibility one feels for another in a loving relationship.)

Although the structure of the intimacy component of love may be roughly the same from one loving relationship to another, the amounts of love one feels toward various individuals may differ considerably. For example, in the Sternberg-Grajek (1984) study, we found that men tend both to love and to like their lover more than their mother, father, sibling closest in age, or best friend. Women, on the other hand, were found to love their lover and their best friend of the same sex about equally, but to like their best friend of the same sex somewhat more than they like their lover. For the women, as for the men, loving and liking of the lover and best friend exceeded that of the mother, father, and sibling closest in age. For both men and women, the sibling closest in age was loved and liked least of all from among this group of individuals. Our pattern of results is generally comparable to that of Swensen (1972), who used a different set of measures in order to obtain his results. Thus, both of these sets of results suggest that there are consistent differences in typical amounts of love across different close relationships.

Sternberg and Grajek (1984) also found that the predictability of the amount of love one feels for one individual from the amount of love one feels for other individuals differs across relationships. In particular, they found that the amount of love one experiences for one member of one's nuclear family (mother, father, sibling closest in age) tends to be predictable from the amount of love one feels for another member of that nuclear family. However, amounts of love experienced toward members of the nuclear family do not predict amounts of love one experiences for individuals outside the nuclear family. In other words, whereas the amount of love one experiences for one's mother, father, and sibling closest in age are mutually predictive, these amounts of love are not predictive of the amount of love one feels for one's lover or one's best friend of the same sex. Nor is the amount of love one experiences for one's lover predictable from the amount of love one experiences for one's best friend of the same sex. In other words, amounts of love tend to be predictable within but not outside of the nuclear family.

As noted above, the Sternberg-Grajek (1984) study focused on the intimacy component of love. However, there is more to love than just the intimacy component. Consider in turn the passion and decision/commitment components.

The passion component. The passion component of love comprises those motivational and other sources of arousal that lead to the experience of passion. It includes what Hatfield and Walster (1981) refer to as "a state of intense longing *for union* with the other" (p. 9). In a loving relationship, sexual needs may well predominate in this experience. However, other needs, such as those for self-esteem, succorance, nurturance, affiliation, dominance, submission, and self-actualization, may also contribute to the experiencing of passion. The strengths of these various needs will almost certainly vary across persons, situations, and kinds of loving relationships. For example, sexual fulfillment is likely to be a strong need in romantic relationships but not in filial ones. The manifestations of these needs are through psychological arousal and physiological arousal, although these two kinds of arousal are not easily separable. Indeed, psychological arousal will almost inevitably interact with physiological arousal, with arousal of one kind leading to arousal of the other kind.

The passion component of love will almost certainly be highly and reciprocally interactive with intimacy. One will feel, for example, intimacy in a relationship in large part as a function of the extent to which the relationship meets one's needs for passion. Conversely, passion may be aroused by intimacy. In some close relationships with members of the opposite sex, for example, the passion component develops almost immediately, and it is only after a while that the intimacy component develops. The passion component is what may draw the individual to the relationship in the first place, but the intimacy component helps sustain closeness in the relationship. In other close relationships, however, the passion component, especially as it applies to physical attraction, develops only after the intimacy one. Two close friends of the opposite sex may find themselves developing a physical attraction for each other that did not develop immediately, and indeed did not develop until they achieved a certain level of intimacy with each other.

The intimacy and passion components need not always covary positively. In certain kinds of relationships, for example, those with prostitutes, individuals may seek out another who maximizes fulfillment of needs for passion while purposefully minimizing intimacy. Negative covariation between the intimacy and passion components can be a function of person as well as of situation: Some people find that the attainment of emotional closeness and intimacy actually interferes with their attainment of sexual fulfillment. The point to be made, quite simply, is that although the form of interaction between the intimacy and passion components will vary across persons and situations, the two components of love will almost certainly interact in close relationships, in one way or another.

The decision/commitment component. The decision/commitment component of love consists of two aspects, a short-term one and a long-term one. The short-term one is the decision that one loves a certain other. The long-term aspect is the commitment to maintain that love. These two aspects of the decision/commitment component of love do not necessarily go together. The decision to love does not necessarily imply a commitment to love. Oddly enough, commitment does not necessarily imply decision. Many people are committed to the love of another without necessarily even admitting that they love or are in love with the other. Most often, however, decision will precede commitment both temporally and logically. Indeed, the institution of marriage represents a legalization of the commitment to a decision to love another throughout one's life.

It is important not to neglect the decision/commitment component of love just because it does not have the "heat" or "charge" of the intimacy and passion components of love. Loving relationships almost inevitably have their ups and downs, and there may be times in such relationships when the decision/commitment component is all or almost all that keeps the relationship going. This component can be essential for getting through hard times and for returning to better ones. In ignoring it or separating it from love, one may be missing exactly that component of loving relationships that enables one to get through the hard times as well as the easy ones.

The decision/commitment component of love interacts with both the intimacy and the passion components. For most people, it results from emotional and other involvement of the intimacy component or the motivational and other arousal of the passion component. However, intimate involvement or passionate arousal can follow from commitment, as would be the case in certain arranged marriages or in close relationships in which one does not have a choice of partners. For example, one does not get to choose one's mother, father, siblings, aunts, uncles, cousins, or the like. In at least some of these close relationships, one is likely to find that whatever intimacy or passion one experiences results from one's cognitive commitment to the relationship, rather than the other way around. Thus, love can start off as a decision, and whatever else follows may follow from that decision.

The decision is not always one that promotes involvement or arousal. For example, a married individual may meet another with whom he or she falls in love. Whereas it can be difficult to control the intimacy component of love and exceedingly difficult to control passion, the decision/commitment component is one over which one has considerable control, and this control may prevent the further development of the relationship into a full-fledged romance. Of course, the decision can also go the other way. The point to be made, simply, is that the decisional aspect can control the other aspects of the relationship. It is important to distinguish the decisional aspect from the commitment aspect, however. In the example of the married individual who meets another with whom he or she falls in love, the decision to pursue that relationship does not necessarily imply a commitment to it. Husbands and wives who discover that their spouses are having affairs often leap immediately to conclusions on the basis of this knowledge about the decision of the spouse to have an affair. The more important information, however, might be the commitment of the spouse to that affair and to the relationship that generated it.

In sum, the three components are all important parts of loving relationships, although their importance differs from one relationship to another. Moreover, the importance of these components of love may differ over time within a relationship as well as across relationships at a given time.

Kinds of Love

The components of love and their interrelationships can better be understood by considering the kinds of love to which they may give rise in different combinations. These various kinds of love are summarized in Table 12.2.

There are eight possible subsets of the various components of love. Each of these subsets differs in the kind of loving experience to which it gives rise. Consider the limiting cases.

1. *Nonlove.* Nonlove refers simply to the absence of all three components of love. Nonlove characterizes the large majority of our personal relationships, which are simply casual interactions that do not partake of love at all.

TABLE 12.2. Taxonomy of Kinds of Love

Kind of love	Component		
	Intimacy	Passion	Decision/commitment
Nonlove	−	−	−
Liking	+	−	−
Infatuated love	−	+	−
Empty love	−	−	+
Romantic love	+	+	−
Companionate love	+	−	+
Fatuous love	−	+	+
Consummate love	+	+	+

Note. + = component present; − = component absent. These kinds of love represent limiting cases based on the triangular theory. Most loving relationships will fit between categories, because the various components of love are expressed along continua, not discretely.

2. *Liking.* Liking results when one experiences only the intimacy component of love in the absence of passion and decision/commitment. The term *liking* is used here in a nontrivial sense, not merely to describe the feelings one has toward casual acquaintances and passers-by in one's life. Rather, it refers to the set of feelings one experiences in relationships that can truly be characterized as friendships. One feels closeness, bondedness, and warmth toward the other, without feelings of intense passion or long-term commitment. Stated in another way, one feels emotionally close to the friend, but the friend does not "turn one on," nor does the friend arouse the thought that "one loves the friend" or that one plans to love the friend for the rest of one's life.

It is possible for friendships to have elements of passionate arousal or long-term commitment, but in such cases, the friendship goes beyond mere liking and is best classified in one of the categories below. A test that can distinguish mere liking from love that goes beyond liking is the absence test. If a typical friend whom one likes goes away, even for an extended period of time, one may miss the friend, but one does not tend to dwell on the loss. One can pick up the friendship some years later, often in a different form, without even having thought much about the friendship during the intervening years. When a close relationship goes beyond liking, however, one's reaction to the absence test is quite different. One actively misses the other person and tends to dwell on or be preoccupied with that person's absence. The other is actively rather than passively missed, and the absence has a substantial and fairly long-term effect both on one's life and on one's reactions to one's life. When the absence of the other arouses strong feelings of intimacy, passion, or commitment, it is best to classify the relationship as going beyond liking; thus, to classify it in one of the categories described below is appropriate.

3. *Infatuated love.* Infatuated love is "love at first sight." Infatuated love, or simply, infatuation, results from the experiencing of passionate arousal in the absence of the intimacy and decision/commitment components of love. Infatuations are usually rather easy to spot, although they tend to be somewhat easier for others to spot than for the individual who is experiencing the infatuation. Infatuations can arise almost instantaneously and dissipate as quickly under the right circumstances. They tend to be characterized by a high degree of psychophysiological arousal, manifested in somatic symptoms such as increased heartbeat or even palpitations of the heart, increased hormonal secretions, erection of genitals (penis or clitoris), and so on. Infatuation is essentially the same as what

Tennov (1979) calls "limerence," and like Tennov's limerence, it can be quite lasting in duration under certain circumstances.

4. *Empty love*. This kind of love emanates from the decision that one loves another and has commitment to that love in the absence of both the intimacy and passion components of love. It is the kind of love one sometimes finds in stagnant relationships that have been going on for years, but that have lost both the mutual emotional involvement and physical attraction that once characterized them. Unless the commitment to the love is very strong, such love can be close to none at all, because commitment can be so susceptible to conscious modification. Although in our society we are most accustomed to empty love as it occurs as a final or near-final stage of a long-term relationship, in other societies, empty love may be the first stage of a long-term relationship. For example, in societies where marriages are arranged, the marital partners may start with the commitment to love each other, or to try to love each other, and not much more. Such relationships point out how empty love need not be the terminal state of a long-term relationship. Indeed, it can be the beginning rather than the end!

5. *Romantic love*. This kind of love derives from a combination of the intimacy and passion components of love. In essence, it is liking with an added element, namely, the arousal brought about by physical attraction and its concomitants. According to this view, then, romantic lovers are not only drawn physically to each other but are also bonded emotionally. This view of romantic love seems to be similar to that found in classic works of literature, such as *Romeo and Juliet* and *Tristan and Isolde*. This view of romantic love differs, however, from that of Hatfield and Walster (1981), who argue that romantic love does not differ from infatuation.

6. *Companionate love*. This kind of love evolves from a combination of the intimacy and decision/commitment components of love. It is essentially a long-term, committed friendship, the kind that frequently occurs in marriages in which the physical attraction (a major source of passion) has died down. This view is captured in the title of Duck's (1983) book, *Friends for Life*. This view of companionate love is also essentially the same as that of Berscheid and Walster (1978).

7. *Fatuous love*. Fatuous love results from the combination of the passion and decision/commitment components in the absence of the intimacy component. It is the kind of love we sometimes associate with Hollywood, or with whirlwind courtships, in which a couple meets on Day *X*, gets engaged two weeks later, and marries the next month. It is fatuous in the sense that a commitment is made on the basis of passion without the stabilizing element of intimate involvement. Although the passion component can develop almost instantaneously, the intimacy component cannot, and hence relationships based on fatuous love are at risk for termination and, in the case of shot-gun marriages, for divorce.

8. *Consummate love*. Consummate, or complete, love results from the full combination of the three components. It is a kind of love toward which many of us strive, especially in romantic relationships. Attaining consummate love can be analogous in at least one respect to meeting one's target in a weight-reduction program: Reaching the goal is often easier than maintaining it. The attainment of consummate love is no guarantee that it will last. Indeed, its loss is sometimes analogous to the gain of weight after a weight-reduction program: One is often not aware of the loss of the goal until it is far gone.

I do not believe that all manifestations of consummate love are necessarily difficult either to develop or maintain. For example, one's love for one's children often carries with it the deep emotional involvement of the intimacy component, the satisfaction of motivational needs (e.g., nurturance, self-esteem, self-actualization) of the passion component, and the firm commitment of the decision/commitment component. For many but not all parents, formation and maintenance of this love is nonproblematical. Perhaps the bonding between parents and children at birth renders this love relatively easier to maintain, or perhaps evolutionary forces are at work to ensure that parent–child bonding survives at least those formative years in which the child must depend very heavily on the parent's love and support. Whichever of these may be the case (and it may be more than one), consummate love can be easier or more difficult to form and maintain, depending on the relationship and the situation in which it is developed and maintained.

Relations of Triangular Theory to Other Theories of Love

The framework for understanding love generated by the triangular theory seems to make intuitive sense in terms of people's everyday experience and also seems to capture some of the kinds of love that are perhaps missed by frameworks that are not theoretically generated. For example, the Berscheid-Walster (1978) distinction between romantic and companionate love is useful, but according to the present framework, it is incomplete and not quite correct in that it does not distinguish between infatuated and romantic love. Similarly, Maslow's (1962) distinction between D-love (Deficiency love) and B-love (Being love) seems incomplete in light of the framework presented above. D-love is closest to what is referred to here as infatuated love, whereas B-love is closest to consummate love. However, there seem to be many other kinds of love as well. As noted earlier, Tennov's (1979) concept of limerence deals only with what is referred to here as infatuated love. Concepts similar to Maslow's D-love and Tennov's limerence derive from other clinical psychologists such as Reik (1944), who viewed love as the search for salvation, and Freud (1922), who viewed love largely in terms of striving for an ego ideal.

According to the present framework, though, love in at least some of its forms is much more than the search for salvation or an ego ideal. Similarly, it potentially comprises more than the decisional and commitment aspects emphasized by Peck (1978).

The taxonomy above also differs in spirit from some recent theories that have emanated from or at least have been closely associated with questionnaire studies. For example, Rubin (1970, 1973) has used psychometric methods to derive what he has called a Love Scale, which he has distinguished from a Liking Scale. The Love Scale is based on a three-component theory of love: affiliation or dependent need, predisposition to help, and exclusiveness and absorption. Rubin's Love Scale measures some elements of all three vertices of the love triangle, but probably measures most reliably and validly the vertex of the intimacy component. It is perhaps because of this concentration on the measurement of this vertex that scores on the Rubin Liking and Loving Scales are fairly highly correlated. In our own data, we have obtained a correlation of .72 between the two scales for liking and loving of a lover and higher correlations for liking and loving of a mother (.73), father (.81), and sibling (.80), but a slightly lower correlation for liking and loving of a best friend (.66; Sternberg & Grajek, 1984). Rubin (1970) obtained somewhat lower correlations between the two scales for lovers, but his lower correlations were based on a college-student sample of couples who answered a newspaper advertisement directed at "dating couples." This sample was probably somewhat restricted in range in a number of respects. Our own sample consisted of adults (not necessarily tested in couples) ranging in age from 18 to 70 years, with a mean age of 32, all of whom were presently or recently involved in love relationships. Thus, it is proposed that the Rubin Love Scale is differentiated from the Rubin Liking Scale to the extent that it measures the passion and decision/commitment components of love as well as intimacy.

Another recent theory, that of Davis (1985), is logically rather than factor analytically derived, but has been tested using questionnaire data. Davis has proposed that love differs from liking by the addition of two clusters, a physical attraction cluster and a caring cluster. Whereas the triangular theory would view physical attraction as separating infatuated or romantic love from liking, it would not separate caring from the liking involved in a friendship. According to the triangular theory, caring is typically a part of the liking in a friendship, and indeed, Davis's own data may not clearly support his separation of the caring cluster from the liking involved in good friendships.

A taxonomy that is related in spirit, although perhaps not in content, to that generated by the triangular theory is that of Lee (1977), who has proposed what he refers to as "a typology of styles of loving." His taxonomy includes (a) *eros*, the love style characterized by the search for a beloved whose physical presentation of self embodies an image already held in the mind of the lover; (b) *ludus*, which is Ovid's term for playful or gamelike love; (c) *storge*, a style based on slowly developing affection and companionship; (d) *mania*, a love style characterized by obsession, jealousy, and great emotional intensity; (e) *agape*, which is altruistic love in which the lover views it as his or her duty to love without expectation of reciprocation; and (f) *pragma*, a practical style involving conscious consideration of the demographic characteristics of the loved one. Although Lee's theory is related to the triangular theory in spirit, its content is quite different. For example, eros would be regarded in the triangular theory as fairly close to infatuated love, whereas mania would be regarded as infatuated love gone berserk. Ludus would not be viewed as a kind of love but rather as a style of interrelating that people can use in various kinds of loving relationships. For example, infatuated lovers, romantic lovers, and companionate lovers, as well as lovers of the other kinds, are all capable of playing games with one another. Storge would be viewed as quite close to companionate love. Agape would be viewed as a concomitant to the love that characterizes the loving relationships of persons with an altruistic disposition in their personalities. Finally, pragma would not be viewed as a kind of love at all but rather as a pragmatic style of search for a lover, as its name implies. Indeed, an overly pragmatic style can get in the way of ever

finding any kind of love at all. Those who exhibit pragma may be searching for physical, financial, or other forms of comfort rather than love.

Lasswell and Lobsenz (1980) used Lee's theory as the basis for the construction of a Love Scale Questionnaire. Their questionnaire was designed to measure each of the six kinds of love in Lee's theory. We administered the Lasswell-Lobsenz questionnaire to the 85 subjects in our own experiment on the nature of love, but our factor-analytic results failed to uphold the typology proposed by Lee. However, the triangular theory has never been tested against Lee's theory, and so the issue of the relative empirical validities of the two theories remains an open question. Indeed, the triangular theory is at present being tested as a whole for the first time (Sternberg, 1986).

Whereas the triangular theory seeks an integration of a number of relationship-based phenomena into love, other theories seek more of a separation. For example, some would view infatuation as wholly distinct from love (e.g., Peck, 1978). Others would view commitment as distinct from love (e.g., Kelley, 1983; Lund, 1985). Yet, both clinical and empirical data suggest the difficulties of making clean separations. Exhaustive reviews of the literature (e.g., Brehm, 1985; Duck, 1983; Hinde, 1979) show how intricately woven together are concepts and feelings of love and romance, or infatuation, in contemporary western civilization, and how difficult it is statistically even to separate romantic love from love in general. Moreover, the data of Lund indicate a high correlation between measures of love and commitment, even after items with very high correlations have been weeded out of a commitment scale. As Kelley (1983) notes, even though he "has drawn a distinction between love and commitment, . . . [he] has recognized the considerable overlap between the two" (p. 312). The data of those who have studied the various phenomena of close relationships strongly suggest the wisdom of retaining conceptual distinctions among these phenomena (as in the three components of the triangular theory), while at the same time recognizing their strong correlation in loving relationships. Although pure, limiting cases of separation among components of love can be conceptualized and identified, it is perhaps better to view these components as interactive aspects of love rather than as independent phenomena to be conceived of and studied in isolation from each other.

Empirical Phenomena as Viewed Through the Lens of the Triangular Theory

The triangular theory of love can account for a number of the main empirical phenomena in the literature on love and close relationships. It is possible to provide here only a brief review of findings and their interface with the triangular theory. Nevertheless, such a review helps show how the theory can be used to understand various kinds of data in the literature and in people's experiences.

Some of the main empirical and anecdotal data have already been dealt with in one way or another in this article. For example, the range in kinds of love that one can experience is dealt with in theory primarily by the different possible combinations of intimacy, passion, and decision/commitment, as shown in Table 12.2. There are a number of other phenomena, not discussed above, that can also be understood in terms of the triangular theory.

One such phenomenon is the finding by Walster, Aronson, Abrahams, and Rottman (1966) that on initial dates, physical attractiveness is about all that matters for satisfaction with the date. According to the triangular theory, the passion component of love is the quickest to recruit; the other two components take more time. As a result, there may be relatively little basis for judgment of a partner as suitable for a loving relationship—after a first date—other than passion criteria, such as physical attractiveness.

Yet another related finding is that of Dutton and Aron (1974), who found that individuals who are physiologically aroused are more likely to take a romantic interest in a member of the opposite sex whom they meet during the period of that arousal than are individuals who are not so aroused. In particular, these investigators had their subjects walk across either a bridge that swayed from side to side as one walked across it or a bridge that was more stable and closer to the ground. Men who walked across the unstable bridge were more likely to be romantically interested in a confederate who was at the scene of the crossing.

One of the most common observations in everyday life is that people want what they cannot have. In the domain of interpersonal relationships, the phenomenon is simply that of the attraction of the individual who is "hard to get." The status of the hard-to-get phenomenon is not totally clear. For example, Walster, Walster, Piliavin, and Schmidt (1973) found that people tended to be attracted not to those who were hard to get, in general, but to those who were hard to get for others but relatively easier to get for themselves. However, the interpretation of this study appears to be open to at least some question (Wright & Contrada, 1983). The Walster et al. (1973) findings notwithstanding, the hard-to-get phenomenon appears to be one that is well entrenched in people's experience as well as in literature and even in a musical, *The Fantasticks*. In the psychological literature, there is a theory—reactance theory—that seeks to explain psychologically why people should want what they have difficulty getting (Brehm, 1966; Brehm & Brehm, 1981).

In terms of the triangular theory, the locus of reactance in interpersonal relationships would be in the passion component of love. The inability to attain a desired goal state coupled with the belief that the desired goal state is not beyond attainment would lead to increasing the level of the passion component and, usually, behavioral attempts to attain that goal state. After a certain point, these attempts can start to feed on themselves and to persist, even in the absence of realism regarding the likelihood that the goal state will be attained.

One of the most robust findings in the literature on attraction in close relationships is the finding that similarity works in close relationships. In other words, people are more likely to form relationships with and later marry people who are more similar to themselves, and also to be happier in relationships with such people (Burgess & Wallin, 1953; Byrne, 1971). In the triangular theory, greater similarity in each of the three components of love will lead to triangles with more overlapping area and correspondingly less nonoverlapping area. Such relationships are predicted to be more satisfactory. Hence, to the extent that greater similarity in background, attitudes about life, and attitudes about the particular relationship affect the love triangles of the two individuals so as to make them more similar, the couple is more likely to be happy in their relationship.

One of the odder findings in the literature is what is sometimes referred to as the "exposure effect" (Saegert, Swap, & Zajonc, 1973). It has been found that mere exposure to another individual can foster liking, although it is much less clear that mere exposure fosters loving. This finding fits in with the triangular theory. Whereas mere exposure is not likely to generate physical attraction in and of itself, it is likely to generate at least some elements of emotional connectedness. It is difficult to be with a person over an extended period of time and not to form some kind of emotional bond. And it is the emotional bond that is responsible for liking in the triangular theory. Hence, the exposure effect is likely to promote liking, but not passionate or necessarily committed love.

One aspect of development in virtually all successful relationships will be what Altman and Taylor (1973) refer to as "social penetration." Social penetration refers to the increasing depth and breadth that characterize relationships as people get to know each other over time. In the triangular theory, social penetration has its most immediate effects on the intimacy component of a relationship. Indeed, the results of the Sternberg-Grajek (1984) study suggest that ability to communicate effectively is almost a sine qua non of a successful loving relationship. In traditional conceptions of sex roles, women tend to stress intimacy and social penetration more in their lives than do men, and one might speculate that the Sternberg-Grajek (1984) finding that women like their best friend of the same sex more than they like their lover stems from the women's success in finding greater communicational intimacy in closeness with other women than with men.

The divorce rate today is approaching 50% in the United States, and it seems fitting to conclude this article with some comments on what kinds of things can sustain each of the three components of love in close relationships.

First, consider the intimacy component of love. If we accept Berscheid's (1983) view that emotion in close relationships is felt when there is some kind of interruption or disruption of a paired behavioral chain between two people, then it would appear that the worst enemy of the intimacy component of love is stagnation. Although people want some predictability from a loving relationship, too much predictability can probably undermine the amount of intimacy experienced in a close relationship. Hence, it is necessary always to introduce some elements of change and variation—to keep the relationship growing. Obviously, there will be different ways in which change and growth might take place. For some people, the elements of change will be through vacations. For others, it will be through developing new mutual interests. For still others, it will be through experimenting with new behavioral patterns in the relationship. The means of growth and change must be individualized to the relationship, but the need for these two elements is probably common across long-term relationships.

Second, consider the passion component of love. In some sense, this component is probably the most difficult to sustain, because it is least subject to conscious control and most subject to habituation. It is well known from conditioning theory that intermittent reinforcement is probably the best maintainer of behavior that results from acquired motivation. However, intermittent reinforcement in the context of a long-term close relationship can potentially take on a rather sinister character. In some cases, the administration of intermittent reinforcement can border on the manipulative or actually become manipulative. Perhaps the best way to maximize the passion component of love over the long term is, first, to analyze the needs the relationship is fulfilling and to do what one can to make sure that these needs continue to be fulfilled and, second, to analyze what needs the relationship is not fulfilling and to try to develop the relationship so that it can meet these needs as well. Again, the particular set of needs and the ways in which they are best met will probably differ somewhat from one relationship to another.

Third, consider the decision/commitment component of love. This is the component in which intervention is easiest because it is most subject to conscious control. The best way to maintain commitment in a relationship is probably both to maintain the importance of the relationship in the couple's lives and to maximize the happiness one achieves through the relationship. Doing these things entails working on the intimacy and passion components of love, and especially expressing these components as well as one's commitment to the relationship through action. If one can attain the consummate love that results from high degrees of the three components in a loving relationship, then under suitable situational circumstances, that relationship seems likely to be one that will last and thrive.

To conclude, a triangular theory of love has been presented that attempts to explain and characterize a variety of love-related phenomena. The theory analyzes love in terms of three components—intimacy, passion, and decision/commitment—attempting to provide at the same time both a descriptive and an explanatory framework for how these components can combine into different forms of love (see Ossorio, 1985; also Shweder & Miller, 1985). Although the theory remains at this point an incomplete statement, it provides at least one step toward understanding the nature of love in everyday life.

NOTES

I am grateful to Michael Barnes, Susan Grajek, and Sandra Wright for their collaborations in my empirical research on love, and to Ellen Berscheid, Keith Davis, Elaine Hatfield, Martin Hoffman, and George Levinger for their excellent comments on an earlier version of this article.

Correspondence concerning this article should be addressed to Robert J. Sternberg, Department of Psychology, Yale University, Box 11A Yale Station, New Haven, Connecticut 06520.

REFERENCES

Altman, I., & Taylor, D. A. (1973). *Social penetration: The development of interpersonal relationships*. New York: Holt, Rinehart & Winston.

Barnes, M., & Sternberg, R. J. (1986). *Implicit theories of love*. Manuscript in preparation.

Bem, D. J. (1972). Self-perception theory. *Advances in Experimental Social Psychology, 6*, 1–62.

Berscheid, E. (1983). Emotion. In H. H. Kelley et al. (Eds.), *Close relationships* (pp. 110–168). New York: Freeman.

Berscheid, E., & Walster, E. H. (1978). *Interpersonal attraction* (2nd ed.). Reading, MA: Addison-Wesley.

Brehm, J. W. (1966). *A theory of psychological reactance*. New York: Academic Press.

Brehm, S. S. (1985). *Intimate relationships*. New York: Random House.

Brehm, S. S., & Brehm, J. W. (1981). *Psychological reactance: A theory of freedom and control*. New York: Academic Press.

Burgess, E. W., & Wallin, P. (1953). *Engagement and marriage*. Philadelphia: Lippincott.

Byrne, D. (1971). *The attraction paradigm*. New York: Academic Press.

Davis, K. E. (1985, February). Near and dear: Friendship and love compared. *Psychology Today*, pp. 22–30.

Davis, K. E., & Roberts, M. K. (1985). Relationships in the real world: The descriptive approach to personal relationships. In K. J. Gergen & K. E. Davis (Eds.), *The social construction of the person* (pp. 145–163). New York: Springer-Verlag.

Duck, S. (1983). *Friends for life*. New York: St. Martin's.

Dutton, D. G., & Aron, A. P. (1974). Some evidence for heightened sexual attraction under conditions of high anxiety. *Journal of Personality and Social Psychology, 30*, 510–517.

Freud, S. (1922). Certain neurotic mechanisms in jealousy, paranoia, and homosexuality. In *Collected Papers* (Vol. 2). London: Hogarth.

Hatfield, E., & Walster, G. W. (1981). *A new look at love*. Reading, MA: Addison-Wesley.

Hinde, R. A. (1979). *Towards understanding relationships*. London: Academic Press.

Kelley, H. H. (1983). Love and commitment. In H. H. Kelley et al. (Eds.), *Close relationships* (pp. 265–314). New York: Freeman.

Kerchoff, A. C., & Davis, K. E. (1962). Value consensus and need complementarity in mate selection. *American Sociological Review, 27*, 295–303.

Lasswell, M., & Lobsenz, N. M. (1980). *Styles of loving*. New York: Ballantine.

Lee, J. A. (1977). A typology of styles of loving. *Personality and Social Psychology Bulletin, 3*, 173–182.

Levinger, G. (1983). Development and change. In H. H. Kelley et al. (Eds.), *Close relationships* (pp. 315–359). New York: Freeman.

Levinger, G., Rands, M., & Talaber, R. (1977). *The assessment of involvement and rewardingness in close and casual pair relationships* (National Science Foundation Tech. Rep. DK). Amherst: University of Massachusetts.

Lund, M. (1985). The development of investment and commitment scales for predicting continuity of personal relationships. *Journal of Social and Personal Relationships, 2*, 3–23.

Maslow, A. H. (1962). *Toward a psychology of being*. Princeton, NJ: Van Nostrand.

Murstein, B. I. (1976). *Who will marry whom? Theories and research in marital choice*. New York: Springer.

Ossorio, P. G. (1985). An overview of descriptive psychology. In K. J. Gergen & K. E. Davis (Eds.), *The social construction of the person* (pp. 19–40). New York: Springer-Verlag.

Peck, M. S. (1978). *The road less traveled: A new psychology of love, traditional values and spiritual growth*. New York: Simon & Schuster.

Reik, T. (1944). *A psychologist looks at love*. New York: Farrar & Rinehart.

Reiss, I. L. (1960). *Premarital sexual standards in America*. New York: Free Press.

Rosch, E. (1978). Principles of categorization. In E. Rosch & B. B. Lloyd (Eds.), *Cognition and categorization* (pp. 27–48). Hillsdale, NJ: Erlbaum.

Rubin, Z. (1970). Measurement of romantic love. *Journal of Personality and Social Psychology, 16*, 265–273.

Rubin, Z. (1973). *Liking and loving: An invitation to social psychology*. New York: Holt, Rinehart & Winston.

Saegert, S. C., Swap, W., & Zajonc, R. (1973). Exposure, context, and interpersonal attraction. *Journal of Personality and Social Psychology, 25*, 234–242.

Shweder, R. A., & Miller, J. G. (1985). The social construction of the person: How is it possible? In K. J. Gergen & K. E. Davis (Eds.), *The social construction of the person* (pp. 41–69). New York: Springer-Verlag.

Spearman, C. (1927). *The abilities of man*. New York: Macmillan.

Sternberg, R. J. (1985). *Beyond IQ: A triarchic theory of human intelligence*. New York: Cambridge University Press.

Sternberg, R. J. (1986). *Construct validation of a triangular theory of love*. Manuscript in preparation.

Sternberg, R. J., & Grajek, S. (1984). The nature of love. *Journal of Personality and Social Psychology, 47*, 312–329.

Swensen, C. H. (1972). The behavior of love. In H. A. Otto (Ed.), *Love today* (pp. 86–101). New York: Association Press.

Tennov, D. (1979). *Love and limerence*. New York: Stein & Day.

Thomson, G. H. (1939). *The factorial analysis of human ability*. London: University of London Press.

Thurstone, L. L. (1938). *Primary mental abilities*. Chicago: University of Chicago Press.

Walster, E., Aronson, V., Abrahams, D., & Rottman, L. (1966). Importance of physical attractiveness in dating behavior. *Journal of Personality and Social Psychology, 4*, 508–516.

Walster, E., Walster, G., Piliavin, J., & Schmidt, L. (1973). "Playing hard-to-get": Understanding an elusive phenomenon. *Journal of Personality and Social Psychology, 26*, 113–121.

Wright, R. A., & Contrada, R. J. (1983). *Dating selectivity and interpersonal attractiveness: Support for a "common sense" analysis*. Unpublished manuscript, University of Texas, Austin.

Love and Marriage in Eleven Cultures

Robert Levine • California State University, Fresno
Suguru Sato • Sapporo Medical University
Tsukasa Hashimoto • Doshisha University, Kyoto
Jyoti Verma • Patna University

College students from secondary population centers in India, Pakistan, Thailand, Mexico, Brazil, Japan, Hong Kong, the Philippines, Australia, England, and the United States were asked to rate the importance of love for both the establishment and the maintenance of a marriage. Love tended to receive greatest importance in the Western and Westernized nations and least importance in the underdeveloped Eastern nations. These differences were stronger and clearer for decisions regarding the establishment of a marriage than for the maintenance and dissolution of a marriage. There were few significant sex differences, either across or within countries. Individualistic cultures, as opposed to collective cultures, assigned much greater importance to love in marriage decisions. Respondents assigning greater importance to love also tended to come from nations with higher economic standards of living, higher marriage rates and divorce rates, and lower fertility rates.

Cultural stereotype has long asserted that Americans consider love a necessary precondition for marriage. As Burgess and Wallin (1953) wrote more than 40 years ago, "The expected, approved, and sanctioned precondition to marriage in American society is falling in love. According to our mores, love is the only right basis for marriage."

The few studies that have empirically tested this assumption indicate that Americans do, indeed, tend to perceive love as an essential precondition to marriage—and that this belief is even more widespread today than it was when Burgess and Wallin made their observation. The strongest evidence comes from Simpson, Campbell, and Berscheid (1986), who asked U.S. college students their opinions about the necessity of love as both a precondition for marriage and for remaining in a marriage. The authors asked these questions, both in 1976 and 1984, and compared their data to those obtained earlier by Kephart (1967) from a similar survey of college students (see Table 13.1).

TABLE 13.1. Distribution of Responses to Kephart/Simpson et al. Questions in 1967, 1976, 1984, and Present Study

		Study							
		Kephart (in 1967)[a,b]		Simpson et al. (in 1976)[c]		Simpson et al. (in 1984)[d]		Present Study[e]	
Question	Response	Male	Female	Male	Female	Male	Female	Male	Female
1. If a man (woman) had all the other qualities you desired, would you marry this person if you were not in love with him (her)?	No	64.6	24.3	86.2	80.0	85.6	84.9	79.2	80.0
	Yes	11.7	4.0	1.7	4.6	1.7	3.6	2.1	13.3
	Undecided	23.7	71.7	12.1	15.4	12.7	11.5	18.8	6.7
2. If love has completely disappeared from a marriage, I think it is probably best for the couple to make a clean break and start new lives.	Agree			57.0	61.9	46.2	44.3	35.4	35.4
	Disagree			26.3	24.4	26.7	33.3	27.1	38.5
	Neutral			16.7	13.7	27.2	22.4	37.5	26.0
3. In my opinion, the disappearance of love is not a sufficient reason for ending a marriage, and should not be viewed as such.	Agree			27.2	20.6	30.8	30.9	35.4	37.5
	Disagree			60.5	64.9	42.6	44.9	37.5	41.7
	Neutral			12.3	14.5	26.6	24.2	27.1	20.8

Note. Figures given are in percentages.
a. Kephart's wording of Question 1 used "boy (girl)" instead of "man (woman)."
b. N = 503 males and 576 females.
c. N = 116 males and 130 females for Question 1, N = 114 males and 130 females for Questions 2 and 3.
d. N = 173 males and 166 females for Question 1, N = 169 males and 165 females for Questions 2 and 3.
e. N = 48 males and 96 females.

In the 1967 survey, Kephart reported that 64.6% of all males and 24.3% of all females answered no to the question: "If a boy (girl) had all the other qualities you desired, would you marry this person if you were not in love with him (her)?" In the Simpson et al. 1976 and 1984 surveys, more than 80% of both males and females answered no to virtually the same question. It may also be seen that only about one quarter of all men and women in 1976, and slightly more in 1984, absolutely disagreed with the statement that the disappearance of love is a sufficient reason for ending a marriage. (Questions concerning reasons for ending a marriage were not asked in Kephart's survey.) Simpson et al. concluded that Americans—at least, American college students—do mostly regard romantic love as a necessary precondition for marriage. This was true for men in 1967, and by 1984 was now true for both men and women.

Our culture's belief in the importance of love for marriage, however, appears to be far from universally accepted (e.g., Beach & Tesser, 1988; Branden, 1980). In the majority of the world's cultures, marriages are arranged by family members—not by the bride and groom (Skolnick, 1987). Within marriage, our conception of love also diverges sharply from those of many other cultures. In India, for example, romantic love and intense emotional attachment is typically seen as a threat to the family structure. Far from bolstering the joint family, it often disrupts it (Nyrop, 1985).

Virtually all empirical studies of romantic love, however, have been unicultural. The vast majority have focused on the United States, sometimes offering passing acknowledgment that their findings may be culture specific (see Simmons, vom Kolke, & Shimizu, 1986, and Buss, 1989, for some notable exceptions to this criticism). More pertinent, there are no empirical data systematically comparing cultures or nations concerning their beliefs about the importance of love for marriage. The main purpose of the present study was to collect these data. More specifically, we compared the responses of college students from 11 developed and underdeveloped Eastern and Western countries—India, Pakistan, Thailand, Mexico, Brazil, Japan, Hong Kong, Republic of the

Philippines, Australia, England, and the United States—on the questions about love and marriage posed in Simpson et al.'s U.S. surveys.

What might we predict? Theoretical discussion of romantic love has also tended to focus on the United States. In an early article, however, Goode (1959) presented a theory of love that makes predictions about the relationship of love and marriage across cultures. He argued that the importance of romantic love varies inversely with the strength of extended-family ties. In cultures with strong kinship networks and extended-family ties, romantic love relationships are viewed as irrelevant or even disastrous for marriages, because they disrupt the tradition of family-approved, often arranged, marriage choices. Romantic love in these cultures must be "controlled," through social disapproval, to maintain the strength of kinship networks.

Two studies offer support for some predictions of Goode's thesis. Rosenblatt (1967), using the Human Relations Area File, found that love was more important for marriage in cultures where economic interdependence between spouses was weak. The study by Simmons et al. (1986) also provided tangential support for the theory. They compared attitudes toward love among college students in Japan, where they assumed a priori that extended-family ties are stronger, to those of college students in the United States and in Germany. Consistent with Goode's prediction, romantic love was least highly valued in the Japanese sample.

Hofstede's (1980) massive 40-nation study of work-related values provides a database for more clearly testing Goode's theory, or at least an extension of his theory. Hofstede's study identified four main dimensions along which the dominant value systems of nations could be ordered and compared. One of these dimensions—individualism-collectivism—appears to be directly related to Goode's extended-family theory.

In societies characterized by individualism, the main concern is with one's own interests and that of one's immediate family. In collective societies, people identify with and conform to the expectations of more extended groups—their relatives, clan, or other in-group—who look after their interests in return for their loyalty.

Triandis and his colleagues, who have extended Hofstede's work, believe that individualism-collectivism is one of the most important sources of cultural differences in social behavior. In collective societies, the individual goes along with the in-group even when the demands are costly. One important feature of this process that Triandis has identified is an emphasis on social norms and duty as defined by the in-group over the pursuit of personal pleasure (e.g., Triandis, 1988; Triandis, Bontempo, Villareal, Asai, & Lucca, 1988).

According to Goode (1959), individual freedom of choice must be controlled in societies where the interests of the extended family predominate. Hofstede and Triandis's notion of individualism-collectivism is more general, but should lead to the same prediction: Societies where the interests of the group predominate over those of the individual should be characterized by less individual freedom of choice. Love, which is clearly associated with freedom of choice, should be viewed as less important in marriage decisions in collective cultures.

The study had two main goals: first, to examine the cross-cultural generality of the importance placed on romantic love in marriage decisions; and, second, to identify predictors and consequences of these differences. For this second goal, we extracted several social and economic characteristics of each nation from the literature. Our main hypothesis concerned collectivism, which we predicted would be negatively related to the importance placed on romantic love.

Method

Participants

A total of 497 males and 673 females enrolled in undergraduate liberal arts classes completed the questionnaire. Samples were drawn from universities in cities from 11 countries (including Hong Kong, which is technically a colony):

Patna, India (58 males, 46 females, mean age = 22.2)

Peshawar, Pakistan (47 males, 68 females, mean age = 21.6)

Chiangmai, Thailand (33 males, 48 females, mean age = 19.2)

Irapuato, Mexico (52 males, 67 females, mean age = 22.5)

Fresno, California, United States (48 males, 96 females, mean age = 21.9)

Birmingham, England (15 males, 41 females, mean age = 21.8)

Kyoto, Japan (56 males, 73 females, mean age = 20.1)

Uberlandia, Brazil (36 males, 35 females, mean age = 24.0)

Darwin, Australia (49 males, 57 females, mean age = 26.2)

Tacloban City, Republic of the Philippines (40 males, 48 females, mean age = 19.3)

Shatin, Hong Kong (63 males, 93 females, mean age = 18.9)

Each of these cities is a secondary population center in its country.

Besides providing easy access, college students were chosen with the intention of maximizing equivalence across cultures. Although age and educational level were controlled, it should be noted that the 11 groups do not necessarily represent the same subpopulations in each culture, as different proportions of these cultures attend universities. Students were sampled from secondary—in most cases, remote—population centers under the assumption that they would reflect more traditional values of their culture than students in larger cities.

Measures of the Importance of Romantic Love

Participants were asked the same three questions about their beliefs about the importance of love in marriage that were originally asked in the Kephart and Simpson et al. studies described earlier:

1. If a man (woman) had all the other qualities you desired, would you marry this

person if you were not in love with him (her) (yes, no, or undecided)?

2. If love has completely disappeared from a marriage, I think it is probably best for the couple to make a clean break and start new lives (agree, disagree, or neutral).

3. In my opinion, the disappearance of love is not a sufficient reason for ending a marriage and should not be viewed as such (agree, disagree, or neutral).

The questions were administered in English to participants in India, Pakistan, Thailand, England, the Philippines, Australia, Hong Kong, and the United States. For some of these countries— Thailand and Hong Kong, in particular—the decision to administer the questionnaires in English only was based on the judgment of a native professor that the participant sample was relatively fluent in English. It was felt that any potential problems in understanding the questions were less than potential problems in the translation process. However, it should be pointed out that the word *love* might have different meanings depending on the language used. The questionnaires were back-translated into Spanish for the Mexican sample, Portuguese for the Brazilian sample, and Japanese for the Japanese sample.

Predictors and Consequences of Romantic love

The relationships of several social and economic characteristics of nations to beliefs about the importance of romantic love were examined:

Collectivism-individualism. National scores and ranks on collectivism-individualism (described earlier) were taken from Hofstede's (1980) data for his 40-nation study of work-related values.

Economic status. Estimates of per capita wealth were based on per capita gross domestic product (GDP) corrected for living costs, or purchasing power parity (PPP), for 1988 (from Samuelson, 1990).

Marriage and family statistics. Fertility, marriage (available for nine countries), and divorce (available for eight countries) rates for the latest available year were taken from Samuelson (1990).

Results

The United States: The Present Data Versus Kephart's 1967 Data and Simpson et al.'s 1976 and 1984 Data

Table 13.1 presents the present data for U.S. participants compared to the findings from the earlier Kephart and Simpson et al. studies. A series of chi-square analyses indicated that the distribution of responses obtained in the present study did not differ significantly from the distributions obtained by Simpson et al. in 1986 for either men or for women on any of the three questions (Question 1: both χ^2s < 1.66, n.s.; Question 2: both χ^2s < 3.08; Question 3: both χ^2s < 1.03, n.s.; $df = 2$ in all cases). Also, as in 1976 and 1984, the overall distribution of responses for men versus women did not significantly differ on any of the three questions, all χ^2s ($df = 2$) < 1.81, n.s.

Romantic Love as a Prerequisite for Establishing a Marriage

The percentages of participants from each country who responded yes, no, and undecided to Kephart's original question are presented in Table 13.2. Initial chi-square analyses indicated that the overall distributions for males versus females were not

TABLE 13.2. Responses to Question 1: "If a man (woman) had all the other qualities you desired, would you marry this person if you were not in love with him (her)?"

Response	India	Pakistan	Thailand	United States	England	Japan	Philippines	Mexico	Brazil	Hong Kong	Australia
Yes	49.0	50.4	18.8	3.5	7.3	2.3	11.4	10.2	4.3	5.8	4.8
No	24.0	39.1	33.8	85.9	83.6	62.0	63.6	80.5	85.7	77.6	80.0
Undecided	26.9	10.4	47.5	10.6	9.1	35.7	25.0	9.3	10.0	16.7	15.2

Note. Figures given are in percentages.

significantly different, χ^2 ($df = 2$) = 1.36, n.s.; nor were the distributions for males versus females within any one country, all χ^2s ($df = 2$) < 5.61, n.s.; nor were the distributions for males versus females within any single response category, χ^2s ($df = 1$) < 1.29, n.s. Thus, data for males and females were collapsed for Table 13.2 and for further analyses.

The overall across-country chi-square, simultaneously comparing all three responses, was highly significant, χ^2 ($df = 20$) = 389.3, $p < .0000$. To better identify the source of these between-country differences, we also performed across-country chi-square analyses for each response option separately. These data indicated significant between-country differences for each of the three response options, all χ^2s ($df = 10$) > 99.5, $p < .0001$. Overall, participants from India and Pakistan were most likely to say they would marry without love, followed by Thailand. Participants from the remaining countries were considerably less likely to agree to marriage without love. Of the remaining countries, the Japanese and Philippine respondents were less likely than the others to answer "no" and more likely than the others to answer "undecided." The response patterns of Brazil, Hong Kong, Australia, the United States, and England were difficult to distinguish. (See summary below for further across-country comparisons.)

Romantic Love as a Prerequisite for Maintaining a Marriage

The percentages of men and women from each country who responded agree, disagree, and neutral to the two Simpson et al. questions assessing the role that love should assume in maintaining a marital relationship are presented in Tables 13.3 and 13.4. The overall distributions for men versus women were again not significantly different for either question, both χ^2s ($df = 2$) < 1.68, n.s. Further, the distribution of responses for men versus women did not significantly differ within any single country, all χ^2s ($df = 2$) < 4.52, n.s.; nor did the distributions for males versus females within any single response category, all χ^2s ($df = 1$) < 1.94, n.s. Thus, data for men and women were, again, collapsed for these two questions.

For Question 2 ("If love has completely disappeared from . . ."), the overall across-country chi-square, simultaneously comparing all three responses, was highly significant, χ^2 ($df = 20$) = 107.2, $p < .0000$. Taking each response option separately, all three between-country differences were significant, all χ^2s ($df = 10$) > 52.3, $p < .0001$. As seen in Table 13.3, Brazilians were most likely to agree that the disappearance of love warranted divorce. Pakistani and Philippine respondents were most likely to disagree. Disagreement was least frequent among the Brazilians and Japanese. Japanese and Australian respondents were most likely, and Brazilians were least likely, to respond "neutral."

For Question 3 ("In my opinion, the disappearance of love . . ."), the overall distribution of responses across countries was again significantly different, χ^2 ($df = 20$) = 163.1, $p < .0000$. Taking each response option separately, all three between-country differences were again significant, all χ^2s ($df = 10$) > 64.7, $p < .0001$. As seen in Table 13.4, response trends were generally similar to those for Question 2. Again, Brazilians were most likely to believe that the absence of love was sufficient reason for ending a marriage. Philippine participants were least likely to believe that the absence of love warranted divorce. The Japanese were, again, most likely

TABLE 13.3. Responses to Question 2: "If love has completely disappeared from a marriage, I think it is probably best for the couple to make a clean break and start new lives."

Response	India	Pakistan	Thailand	United States	England	Japan	Philippines	Mexico	Brazil	Hong Kong	Australia
Agree	46.2	33.0	46.9	35.4	44.6	41.1	45.5	51.7	77.5	47.1	29.3
Disagree	26.0	49.6	32.1	34.7	23.2	17.1	40.9	28.0	12.7	25.5	31.1
Neutral	27.9	17.4	21.0	29.9	32.1	41.9	13.6	20.3	9.9	27.4	39.6

Note. Figures given are in percentages.

TABLE 13.4. Response to Question 3: "In my opinion, the disappearance of love is not a sufficient reason for ending a marriage and should not be viewed as such."

Response	India	Pakistan	Thailand	United States	England	Japan	Philippines	Mexico	Brazil	Hong Kong	Australia
Agree	47.1	54.8	50.6	36.8	26.8	26.4	71.6	34.8	26.8	51.6	39.6
Disagree	34.6	35.7	34.2	40.3	46.4	27.9	23.9	50.9	63.4	24.8	22.6
Neutral	18.3	9.6	15.2	22.9	26.8	45.7	4.6	14.4	9.9	23.6	37.7

Note. Figures given are in percentages.

to respond "neutral." Pakistanis were least likely to be neutral.

Cross-National Differences on the Kephart/Simpson et al. Questions

To more clearly describe across-country differences on the original Kephart/Simpson questions, we next converted these responses to an ordinal scale from 1 to 3. Responses indicating greatest importance for love were assigned a 3 (no, agree, and disagree responses to Questions 1, 2 and 3, respectively); undecided and neutral responses were assigned a 2; and responses ascribing least importance to love were assigned a 1 (yes, disagree, and agree responses for Questions 1, 2 and 3, respectively). This scaling makes assumptions about the distance between response categories that are, of course, technically questionable. However, this method appeared preferable to other possible approaches for comparing countries' beliefs.

Each country was treated as an individual participant ($N = 11$ participants), with 9 participants for birth rates and 8 participants for divorce rates. The small sample size requires treating these statistics with caution. Because of the small sample

size, Spearman rank correlations were calculated as well as Pearson's. The resulting sets of correlation coefficients were relatively similar. The Spearman coefficients are presented in Table 13.5.

It may be seen that each of the social and economic variables was significantly related to beliefs about the importance of love. Overall, these correlations were strongest for Question 1, regarding the establishment of a marriage.

Collectivism-individualism, it may be seen, was highly correlated with beliefs about love on Questions 1 and 3. Respondents from individualist countries were much more likely to rate love as essential for the establishment of a marriage, and somewhat less likely to agree that the disappearance of love is not a sufficient reason for ending a marriage.

Economic health was even more strongly related to the importance placed on romantic love—particularly, once again, concerning the establishment of a marriage. As for collectivism, there was also a tendency for economically stronger nations to express disagreement on Question 3.

Countries assigning greater importance to romantic love for the establishment of a relationship had significantly higher marriage rates, significantly lower fertility rates, and somewhat higher divorce

TABLE 13.5. Spearman Correlations Between the Love/Marriage Questions and Social and Economic Variables

Love/Marriage Questions[a]	Social and Economic Variable				
	Collectivism-Individualism (n = 11)	Gross Domestic Product/Living Costs (n = 11)	Marriage Rates (n = 9)	Fertility Rates (n = 11)	Divorce Rates (n = 8)
1. If a man (woman) had all the other qualities . . .	0.56*	0.75**	0.70*	−0.56*	0.35
2. If love has completely disappeared . . .	−0.06	0.13	−0.03	−0.30	−0.74*
3. In my opinion, the disappearance of love . . .	0.41	0.33	0.16	−0.15	−0.17

a. For love questions, higher scores indicate greater importance assigned to love.
*$p < .05$. **$p < .01$.

rates. Divorce rates were also highly correlated with the belief that the disappearance of love warrants dissolution of the marriage (Question 2).

Discussion

Several main findings emerged. First, as predicted, there were strong cross-cultural differences in the perceived importance of love as a prerequisite for *establishing* a marriage. Love tended to receive greatest importance in the Western and Westernized nations (the United States, followed by Brazil, England, and Australia) and least importance in the four underdeveloped Eastern nations (India, Pakistan, Thailand, and the Philippines). The two most economically developed of the Eastern nations—Japan and Hong Kong—fell between these two groups.

Second, there were also significant cross-cultural differences in beliefs about love as a prerequisite for *maintaining* a marriage. Again, the Western and Westernized nations tended to assign greatest importance, and the underdeveloped Eastern nations tended to assign least importance to love. These differences, however, were neither as strong nor as clear as the above differences pertaining to the establishment of a marriage. Cultural norms concerning the import of love for establishing a marriage, it appears, do not necessarily coincide with those regarding the maintenance and dissolution of a marriage. Future studies may need to treat these issues separately. The present data for U.S. participants provides the sharpest case in point. U.S. participants were highest in beliefs about the importance of love for establishing a marriage, but were closer to the median in their beliefs about love as a necessity for maintaining a marriage.

Third, there were few significant sex differences, either across or within countries, on any of the questions. It appears that Simpson et al.'s (1986) findings for the United States, indicating relatively few sex differences in beliefs about the necessity of romantic love for marriage, are also true for many other cultures.

Although the general lack of sex differences is consistent with Simpson et al.'s findings for U.S. participants, they are not necessarily what would be predicted in many of the countries in the current sample. There are considerable differences in sex roles within many of these countries, and the extent of these differences varies greatly from country to country. In Buss's (1989) study of human mate preferences in a similarly heterogeneous group of cultures, strong sex differences did emerge, with females more highly valuing cues to resource acquisition and males more highly valuing cues to reproductive capacity. Although neither of these two categories would necessarily imply preference for romantic love, it is certainly possible that the lack of sex differences in the current study needs further exploration. It is possible, for example, that the lack of differences may reflect sampling biases within countries. We would expect sex differences to be minimized in student samples, especially in underdeveloped countries, where women who go to college are more likely to be less restricted by traditional sex role expectations.

Fourth, our main hypothesis, concerning the relationship of individualism-collectivism to beliefs about the importance of love, was strongly supported. The high correlation (.56) between individualism and the necessity of love for the establishment of a marriage (Question 1) was particularly impressive.

Further, it should be recognized that these high correlations were based on data from different subpopulations within each country. Hofstede's (1980) collectivism sample consisted of employees in business settings, whereas our "love" sample consisted of college students. Each of our samples also came from different locations in each country. Given these differences, it would appear that the nation-level relationship between collectivism and beliefs about love for establishing a marriage is quite robust. To some degree, at least, it appears to cut across age, regional, and educational groups at the level of nations.

Fifth, economic standards of living were very strongly related to beliefs about love—particularly, again, concerning the establishment of a marriage ($r = .76$). Because the present data are correlational, it would be speculative to infer causality between economic conditions, collectivism, and beliefs about love. One possible explanation, however, is that industrial growth produces pressures toward individualism and away from collectivism. As argued earlier, the endorsement of individualism allows the freedom of choice that is inherent in marriages based on freedom of choice.

Certainly, this hypothesis is consistent with the United States' movement from collectivist values, where pragmatic marriage decisions predominated, to individualist values, where romantic love became the guiding force in marriage decisions. This change, most historians agree, coincided with the Industrial Revolution in the 19th century. Until that time, marriage in the United States was primarily an economic arrangement between two families. The Industrial Revolution, however, required that work move outside the home, eventually resulting in an escalation of individualist values, particularly those concerning marriage and the nuclear family (Leslie & Korman, 1989).

Japan and Hong Kong, it has been argued, are currently undergoing this same transition. Both have achieved economic prosperity out of traditionally collectivist value systems. Both, however, now appear to be moving closer to Western style individualism (Iwao, 1989). Consistent with our hypothesis, their scores on our romantic love questions tended to fall between those of the developed Western nations and the underdeveloped Eastern nations.

Sixth, it appears that beliefs about the importance of love have behavioral consequences for marital decisions. Respondents assigning greater importance to love, particularly for decisions about the formation of a marriage, tended to come from nations with higher marriage rates, lower fertility rates, and higher divorce rates. The U.S. sample, for example, which put greatest emphasis on love in decisions about getting married, had the highest marriage and divorce rates and the third lowest fertility rates in our sample.

Once again, these data are correlational. However, it is interesting to speculate about possible causative relations. It might be argued that designating romantic love as the decisive criterion for marital decisions results in less inhibition toward getting married. There may, for example, be less

pressure to consider long-term consequences when potential spouses feel responsibility only toward each other, rather than knowing that their decisions will affect many others in their collective families.

After marriage, it is not surprising that fertility rates are lower in love marriages. After all, the primary reason for marriage in traditional collectivist cultures is, often, to have children, who will then take part in the larger collective.

Finally, we found that divorce rates were much higher in countries where respondents agreed with the statement that the disappearance of love warrants making a clean break from the marriage. Given that "staying in love" is a difficult proposition, it is not surprising that marriages made in cultures that place great importance on love would be less likely to endure. Also, the fact that love-marriages are less likely to produce children may reduce the pressure to remain together after love disappears.

These arguments are post hoc and speculative. They are, however, consistent with the present findings and identify potential interdisciplinary directions for future research on the role and consequences of romantic love in family life. These issues may be particularly worthy of study in the United States, where divorce rates continue at frighteningly high levels—recent statistics indicate that about two thirds of U.S. marriages made today will end in divorce or permanent separation (Martin & Bumpass, 1989).

As noted earlier, we must be extremely cautious when generalizing the beliefs of college students to the general population. First, college students represent a biased sample of the overall population. Second, they do not necessarily represent the same subpopulations in each country, as different proportions of these countries attend university.

In some ways, however, the fact that any cross-national differences emerged in college student samples is all the more impressive. One would expect these groups to be considerably less traditional than their countries as a whole—particularly in the Eastern and the less affluent countries. The fact that clear cross-cultural differences emerged, particularly on the question of love's importance in the establishment of a marriage, demonstrates the perseverance and pervasiveness of cultural values.

Finally, it is important to consider Bond's (1988) distinction between "cultural-level" and "individual-level" relationships. Are a culture's norms about love and marriage, and their consequences for marital quality, more closely paralleled at the individual level in some cultures than in others? What are the consequences of marrying for love in a culture that discourages individual choice, or of marrying for pragmatic reasons in a culture that values marrying for love? Is there, as Dion and Dion (1988) have argued, an inherent conflict between individualistic values and the interdependence demanded by romantic love? These are difficult questions. Given the importance of the marital relationship, however, and the difficulties it currently faces, they warrant further study.

NOTES

We wish to thank Alay Ahmad (Pakistan), Michael Bond (Hong Kong), Siriperm Chowsilpa (Thailand), Jose and Maria Dela Coleta (Brazil), Purificacion Flores (Philippines), Linda Hantrais and Nicola Hodgson (England), and David Richards (Australia) for their generosity in collecting data in their respective countries. Thanks to Michael Bond, Michael Botwin, David Buss, Harry Reis, and two anonymous reviewers for their comments on an earlier version of this article. Requests for reprints should be sent to the first author at the Department of Psychology, California State University–Fresno, Fresno, CA 94740–0011.

REFERENCES

Beach, S., & Tesser, A. (1988). Love and marriage: A cognitive account. In R. S. Sternberg & M. L. Barnes (Eds.), *The psychology of love* (pp. 330–355). New Haven, CT: Yale University Press.

Bond, M. H. (1988). Finding universal dimensions of individual variation in multicultural studies of values: The Rokeach and Chinese value surveys. *Journal of Personality and Social Psychology, 55*, 1009–1015.

Branden, N. (1980). *The psychology of romantic love.* New York: Bantam.

Burgess, E. W., & Wallin, P. (1953). *Engagement and marriage.* Philadelphia: Lippincott.

Buss, D. M. (1989). Sex differences in human mate preferences: Evolutionary hypotheses tested in 37 cultures. *Behavioral and Brain Sciences, 12*, 1–49.

Dion, K. L., & Dion, K. K. (1988). Romantic love: Individual and cultural perspectives. In R. S. Sternberg & M. L. Barnes (Eds.), *The psychology of love* (pp. 264–289). New Haven: Yale University Press.

Goode, W. J. (1959). The theoretical importance of love. *American Sociological Review, 24*, 38–47.

Hofstede, G. (1980). *Culture's consequences: International differences in work-related values.* Beverly Hills, CA: Sage.

Iwao, S. (1989). Changing lives and social consciousness. In Nippon Steel Corporation, *Contemporary Japan: Self-portraits* (pp. 51–62). Tokyo: Gakuseisha.

Kephart, W. M. (1967). Some correlates of romantic love. *Journal of Marriage and the Family, 29*, 470–474.

Leslie, G. R., & Korman, S. K. (1989). *The family in social context.* New York: Oxford University Press.

Martin, T., & Bumpass, L. (1989). Recent trends in marital disruption. *Demography, 26*, 37–51.

Nyrop, R. E. (1985). *India: A country study.* Washington, DC: U.S. Government Printing Office.

Rosenblatt, P. C. (1967). Marital residence and the functions of romantic love. *Ethnology, 6*, 471–480.

Samuelson, R. J. (1990). *The economist book of vital world statistics.* New York: Times Books.

Skolnick, A. S. (1987). *The intimate environment: Exploring marriage and the family.* Boston: Little, Brown.

Simmons, C. H., vom Kolke, A., & Shimizu, H. (1986). Attitudes toward romantic love among American, German, and Japanese students. *Journal of Social Psychology, 126*, 327–336.

Simpson, J., Campbell, B., & Berscheid, E. (1986). The association between romantic love and marriage: Kephart (1967) twice revisited. *Personality and Social Psychology Bulletin, 12*, 363–372.

Triandis, H. C. (1988). Collectivism vs. individualism: A reconceptualization of a basic concept in cross-cultural social psychology. In G. K. Verma & C. Bagley (Eds.), *Personality, cognition and values: Cross-cultural perspectives of childhood and adolescence* (pp. 60–96). London: Macmillan.

Triandis, H. C., Bontempo, R., Villareal, M. J., Asai, M., & Lucca, N. (1988). Individualism and collectivism: Cross-cultural perspectives on self-ingroup relationships. *Journal of Personality and Social Psychology, 54*, 323–338.

Interdependence in Relationships

I'm beginning to think that maybe it's not just how much you love someone; maybe what matters is who you are when you're with them.

— Anne Tyler

"He's my friend," said Mark. "We don't meddle in each others' lives." "Of course we do," I said, "we meddle constantly. That's what true friendship is about."

— Nora Ephron

What makes the association between Dave and Anna a "relationship"? Several theorists have argued that interdependence is the key—that interdependent partners, in contrast to independent individuals, exert causal effects on each other's motives, preferences, behaviors, and outcomes (Rusbult & Van Lange, 1996). By causal influence, we mean that Anna's thoughts, feelings, or actions bring about changes in Dave's thoughts, feelings, or actions, and vice versa. Some researchers, in fact, believe that closeness should be defined as the degree of such interdependence—in other words, that their relationship is close to the extent that they exert frequent, strong effects on each other for a relatively long duration of time and across diverse kinds of activities (e.g., Berscheid, Snyder, & Omoto, 1989). In highly interdependent relationships, then, partners influence each other often, substantially, variously, and for extended periods of time; in superficial relationships, the behavior of one person has minimal impact on the other.

One of the most important qualities of an interdependence-based analysis is the assumption that the nature of the bond *between* two people is as important in shaping their behavior as are the attributes of the two people themselves. For example, Dave and Anna will behave quite differently when they initially become acquainted (having no history with each other and no expectation of future involvement) than after they have become highly interdependent, even though Dave and Anna themselves are identical in the two instances. Thus, this orientation is clearly distinguishable from work that attempts to explain behavior solely by reference to individual traits or personal histories. Interdependence is not only a question of "how much," but also of "what kind"—relationships differ not only in the degree of influence that partners exert on each other, but also in the nature of that influence. For example, Anna and Dave may exert mutual influence over each other or Anna may have much greater power than Dave; Dave may need the relationship much more than Anna does; Dave's and Anna's preferences and interests may be compatible or incompatible. The field's understanding of these issues has been shaped by the seminal contributions of interdependence theory, a theory conceived and articulated by John Thibaut and Harold Kelley (Thibaut & Kelley, 1959; Kelley & Thibaut, 1978). Interdependence theory was intended to help identify the patterns of outcome interdependence that underlie any and all situations involving interaction. In a 1979 book, Kelley described the implications of this theory for personal relationships. Since that time, interdependence principles have been prominent themes in research and theory regarding relationships.

In an interdependent relationship, each person's behavior has consequences for the other, so the partners cannot act as solitary individuals. Instead,

they must adapt to each other. For example, to spend Saturday night together, Dave and Anna must decide how to reconcile their differing preferences about which film to see. There are numerous possibilities, each of which to some degree is revealing of their personalities and their relationship: Anna might demand Dave's acquiescence; they might take turns from one week to the next; Anna might sacrifice her preference and accede to Dave's inclination; or they might go their separate ways and meet at the end of the evening. Because the need to adapt to our partners permeates nearly all aspects of relationships, in certain respects, all of the articles reprinted in this book (especially those in Sections 6 and 7) illustrate the operation of interdependence processes. Interdependence is particularly evident when individuals modify their behavior to take into account the preferences, expectations, actions, wishes, needs, or talents of a partner. We have chosen to include in this section three articles that describe interesting examples of the basic concept of interdependence.

One way in which patterns of interdependence may differ from one relationship to another concerns the rules that characterize the giving and receiving of benefits. Clark and Mills have theorized extensively about the important distinction between communal and exchange relationships. In communal relationships, partners are concerned first and foremost with each other's welfare, and provide benefits (e.g., assistance, emotional support) to help fulfill each other's needs. In exchange relationships, on the other hand, each partner benefits the other either to repay a past benefit or in expectation of a comparable future benefit. In the research reprinted here, Clark and Mills demonstrate that attraction to a new acquaintance is greater when the provision of benefits is consistent with the type of relationship expected. Similar findings have been obtained in subsequent studies using alternative manipulations of relationship type, as well as in work examining existing communal and exchange relationships.

The second article in this section, by Schlenker and Britt, examines impression management. The importance of strategic self-presentation is well known: People usually try to put their "best foot forward" when describing themselves to strangers, especially when they care about what the strangers think of them. This study demonstrates that we also extend the benefit of strategic self-presentation to our close friends, describing them to a desirable stranger, but not to an undesirable stranger, in such a manner as to maximize the likelihood that the stranger will find our friend appealing. This is one of the more clever and benevolent ways in which partners in interdependent relationships seek to influence each other's outcomes.

Interdependence can also affect how relationship partners manage an intangible entity, information. Wegner, Erber, and Raymond's research examines a process they term transactive memory, which describes the degree to which partners rely on each other for encoding, storing, and retrieving information. Transactive memory exemplifies a distributed information system, a common means by which organizations deal with complex information: Difficult, multifaceted tasks are divided into more manageable components and distributed among individuals with specialized expertise. Wegner and his colleagues' research suggests that to the degree that Dave and Anna are close, they may operate similarly, thereby enhancing their overall memory for specialized information. However, there's a catch: Coordination of this sort appears to enhance collaborative memory only when the organizational scheme maps onto a couple's natural patterns of expertise.

REFERENCES

Berscheid, E., Snyder, M., & Omoto, A. M. (1989). Issues in studying close relationships: Conceptualizing and measuring closeness. In C. Hendrick (Ed.), *Review of personality and social psychology, Vol. 10: Close relationships* (pp. 63–91). Newbury Park: Sage.

Kelley, H. H. (1979). *Personal relationships: Their structures and processes.* Hillsdale, NJ: Erlbaum.

Kelley, H. H., & Thibaut, J. W. (1978). *Interpersonal relations: A theory of interdependence.* New York: Wiley.

Rusbult, C. E., & Van Lange, P. A. M. (1996). Interdependence processes. In E. T. Higgins & A. Kruglanski (Eds.), *Social psychology: Handbook of basic mechanisms and processes* (pp. 564–596). New York: Guilford.

Thibaut, J. W., & Kelley, H. H. (1959). *The social psychology of groups.* New York: Wiley.

Suggestions for Further Reading

Agnew, C. R., Van Lange, P. A. M., Rusbult, C. E., & Langston, C. A. (1998). Cognitive interdependence: Commitment and the mental representation of close relationships. *Journal of Personality and Social Psychology, 74,* 939–954. An interesting demonstration of the cognitive side of interdependence.

Beach, S. R. H., Tesser, A., Fincham, F., Jones, D. J., Johnson, D., & Whitaker, D. J. (1998). Pleasure and pain in doing well, together: An investigation of performance-related affect in close relationships. *Journal of Personality and Social Psychology, 74,* 923–938. A partner's success may pose a dilemma: When do we react with jealousy, and when do we react with pride?

Drigotas, S. M., Rusbult, C. E., Wieselquist, J., & Whitton, S. (1999). Close partner as sculptor of the ideal self: Behavioral affirmation and the Michelangelo phenomenon. *Journal of Personality and Social Psychology, 77,* 293–323. This research not only demonstrates that close partners shape one another's traits, values, and behavioral tendencies, but also reveals that relationships are enhanced to the extent that such "sculpting" moves each person closer to his or her ideal self.

Fiske, A. P. (1992). The four elementary forms of sociality: Framework for a unified theory of social relations. *Psychological Review, 99,* 689–723. In this paper, Fiske describes four elementary types of social relationship, which can be construed as differing in their predominant patterns of interdependence.

Hardin, C. D., & Higgins, E. T. (1996). Shared reality: How social verification makes the subjective objective. In R. M. Sorrentino & E. T. Higgins (Eds.), *Handbook of motivation and cognition, Vol. 3: The interpersonal context.* New York: Guilford. Transactive memory is one interesting form of cognitive interdependence in close relationships. Shared reality, discussed in this thought-provoking article, is another.

Holmes, J. G. (2000). Social relationships: The nature and function of relational schemas. *European Journal of Social Psychology, 30,* 447–495. This broad-reaching paper reviews developments in the field of close relationships from an interdependence theory perspective, focusing on the relational, dyadic aspects of closeness that have led to a much better understanding of social cognition and interpersonal processes.

Kelley, H. H., Berscheid, E., Christensen, A., Harvey, J. H., Huston, T. L., Levinger, G., McClintock, E., Peplau, L. A., & Peterson, D. (1983). *Close relationships.* New York: Freeman. A classic. Written by leading scholars in the field, this book provides a comprehensive conceptual analysis of close relationships from an interdependence perspective.

Kelley, H. H., Holmes, J. G., Kerr, N. L., Reis, H. T., Rusbult, C. E., & Van Lange, P. A. M. (2003). *An atlas of interpersonal situations.* New York: Cambridge University Press. Written in clear language, this book provides a systematic analysis of how patterns of interdependence underlie the most common situations that people encounter in everyday life.

Mills, J., & Clark, M. S. (2001). Viewing close romantic relationships as communal relationships: Implications for maintenance and enhancement. In J. H. Harvey & A. E. Wenzel (Eds.), *Relationship maintenance and enhancement* (pp. 13–25). Mahwah, NJ: Erlbaum. A comprehensive review of research and theory on the distinction between communal and exchange relationships.

Tice, D. M., Butler, J. L., Muraven, M. B., & Stillwell, A. M. (1995). When modesty prevails: Differential favorability of self-presentation to friends and strangers. *Journal of Personality and Social Psychology, 69,* 1120–1138. The inclination to "put one's best foot forward" is much stronger in interactions with strangers than in interactions with friends.

Discussion Questions

1. Explain the key differences between communal and exchange relationships.
2. Think of one friend with whom you have an exchange relationship and one friend with whom you have a communal relationship. Then, imagine trying to select a birthday present for each. How do your thoughts about this differ?
3. Some research regarding relationships has emphasized the importance of equity, or sustaining "fair exchange" in ongoing close relationships. How does this notion square with research by Clark and Mills regarding the character of communal relationships?
4. Schlenker and Britt propose that "identity management" is a process in which close friends may strategically collaborate. Discuss several ways in which friends might do this.
5. Often, the goals of strategic self-presentation conflict with the goal of honesty. When does this occur? How might people reconcile these conflicting tendencies?
6. Discuss an example of transactive memory from your own relationships. What factors help determine which partner will adopt which particular areas of expertise?
7. Suggest some cognitive tasks other than memory that partners might divide between them. Explain how this might be beneficial for a couple.
8. The three primary theoretical orientations reviewed thus far—the evolutionary, attachment, and interdependence orientations—present alternative models of motivation and behavior in relationships. Explain how a theorist from each of these orientations would construe the experience of trust (versus mistrust) in a partner.

Interpersonal Attraction in Exchange and Communal Relationships

Margaret S. Clark • Carnegie-Mellon University

Judson Mills • University of Maryland

Communal relationships, in which the giving of a benefit in response to a need for the benefit is appropriate, are distinguished from exchange relationships, in which the giving of a benefit in response to the receipt of a benefit is appropriate. Based on this distinction, it was hypothesized that the receipt of a benefit after the person has been benefited leads to greater attraction when an exchange relationship is preferred and decreases attraction when a communal relationship is desired. These hypotheses were supported in Experiment 1, which used male subjects. Experiment 2, which used a different manipulation of exchange versus communal relationships and female subjects, supported the hypotheses that (a) a request for a benefit after the person is aided by the other leads to greater attraction when an exchange relationship is expected and decreases attraction when a communal relationship is expected, and (b) a request for a benefit in the absence of prior aid from the other decreases attraction when an exchange relationship is expected.

This research is concerned with how the effects of receiving a benefit and a request for a benefit differ depending on the type of relationship one has with the other person. Two kinds of relationships in which persons give benefits to one another are distinguished, exchange relationships and communal relationships. The stimulus for this distinction was Erving Goffman's (1961, pp. 275–276) differentiation between social and economic exchange.

In the present theorizing, the term *exchange relationship* is used in place of Goffman's term *economic exchange* because many of the benefits that people give and receive do not involve money or things for which a monetary value can be calculated. A benefit can be anything a person can choose to give to another person that is of use to the person receiving it.[1]

In an exchange relationship, members assume that benefits are given with the expectation of receiving a benefit in return. The receipt of a benefit incurs a debt or obligation to return a comparable benefit. Each person is concerned with how much he or she receives in exchange for benefiting the other and how much is owed the other for the benefits received.

Since all relationships in which persons give and receive benefits are social, another term is needed to describe relationships in which each person has a concern for the welfare of the other. The term *communal* seems to be the most appropriate. The typical relationship between family members exemplifies this type of relationship. Although it might appear to an observer that there is an exchange of benefits in communal relationships, the rules concerning giving and receiving benefits are different than in exchange relationships.

Members of a communal relationship assume that each is concerned about the welfare of the other. They have a positive attitude toward benefiting the other when a need for the benefit exists. They follow what Pruitt (1972) has labeled "the norm of mutual responsiveness." This rule may create what appears to an observer to be an exchange of benefits, but it is distinct from the rule that governs exchange relationships, whereby the receipt of a benefit must be reciprocated by the giving of a comparable benefit. The rules concerning the giving and receiving of benefits are what distinguish communal and exchange relationships, rather than the specific benefits that are given and received.

---

[1]Benefits are not the same as rewards, when the term *rewards* refers to "the pleasures, satisfactions, and gratifications the person enjoys" (Thibaut & Kelley, 1959, p. 12). The receipt of a benefit usually constitutes a reward, however rewards occur for reasons other than the receipt of a benefit. For example, the rewards that a parent receives from a newborn infant would not fall within the definition of a benefit, since the infant does not choose to give them to the parent. The present theorizing is not concerned with "dependent" relationships in which one person receives benefits from another but does not give benefits to the other.

From the perspective of the participants in a communal relationship, the benefits given and received are not part of an exchange. The attribution of motivation for the giving of benefits is different from that in an exchange relationship. In a communal relationship, the receipt of a benefit does not create a specific debt or obligation to return a comparable benefit, nor does it alter the general obligation that the members have to aid the other when the other has a need. In a communal relationship, the idea that a benefit is given in response to a benefit that was received is compromising, because it calls into question the assumption that each member responds to the needs of the other.

Experiment 1

If two people have an exchange relationship and one person benefits the other, it is appropriate for the other to give the person a comparable benefit. The receipt of a benefit under these circumstances should lead to greater attraction. On the other hand, if two people have a communal relationship and one person benefits the other, it is inappropriate for the other to give the person a comparable benefit, since it leaves the impression that the benefit was given in response to the benefit received previously. The other is treating the relationship in terms of exchange, which is inappropriate in a communal relationship.

When a communal relationship does not yet exist but is desired, the receipt of a benefit should have the same effect as when a communal relationship is assumed to exist. A benefit from the other after the other has been benefited should reduce attraction if there is a desire for a communal relationship with the other. If an exchange relationship is preferred, the receipt of a benefit after the other is benefited should result in greater attraction. Experiment 1 was conducted to test these hypotheses.

The predictions concerning communal relationships might seem contrary to what would be expected from equity theory (Adams, 1963). On the basis of equity theory, one might expect that a benefit from another following aid to that other would increase liking in *any* relationship, because it would reduce inequity. However, the predictions are not inconsistent with a recent discussion of equity theory (Walster, Walster, & Berscheid, 1978). According to Walster, Walster, and Berscheid:

> Another characteristic of intimate relationships, which may add complexity, is that intimates, through identification with and empathy for their partners, come to define themselves as a *unit*; as *one* couple. They see themselves not merely as individuals interacting with others, but also as part of a partnership, interacting with other individuals, partnerships, and groups. This characteristic may have a dramatic impact on intimates' perceptions of what is and is not equitable. (pp. 152–153)

In Experiment 1, the desire for a communal relationship was manipulated by using unmarried males as the subjects and having the part of the other played by an attractive woman, who was described as either married or unmarried. It was assumed that people desire communal relationships with attractive others, but only with those available for such relationships. It was further assumed that the unmarried woman would be considered available for a communal relationship, whereas the married woman would not. Thus, it was assumed that the male subjects would desire a communal relationship with the attractive, unmarried woman, but would prefer an exchange relationship with the attractive, married woman.

Method

Overview. Under the guise of a study of task performance, unmarried male college students worked on a task while a television monitor showed an attractive woman working on a similar task in another room. When the subject completed the task, he was awarded 1 point toward extra credit for finishing on time and given the opportunity to send some of his excess materials to the other, who supposedly had a more difficult task. Following receipt of the aid, the other completed her task and was awarded 4 points. Some of the subjects received a note from the other that thanked them (no-benefit conditions), whereas some received a note from the other that thanked them and gave them one of her points (benefit conditions). After receiving the note, the subjects were given information indicating that the other was either married (exchange conditions) or unmarried (communal conditions). Shortly thereafter, liking for the other and expectations concerning a future discussion with the other were assessed.

Subjects. The subjects were 96 unmarried, male students in introductory psychology courses who participated in order to earn extra course credit. They were randomly assigned to one of the four experimental conditions: exchange–benefit, exchange–no benefit, communal–benefit, communal–no benefit.

Procedure. Upon arriving for the experiment, the subject was greeted by the experimenter and told that another subject had already arrived and was in an adjacent room. The subject was seated so that he could see a video monitor that showed an attractive female. The experimenter mentioned that the person appearing on the monitor was the other subject, Tricia. The experimenter told the subject that before starting she would explain some things about the studies in which the subject would be participating, which she had already mentioned to Tricia.

The experimenter said that the first study was actually one of two she would ask them to participate in that day. Each of the two studies took less than half an hour. Although the studies were unrelated, she was asking people to participate in both of them during one session. The first study involved having both subjects work on a vocabulary task. She suspected that people's approaches to solving this task varied when certain conditions were changed. In the condition to which he and Tricia had been randomly assigned, they would be able to see each other over closed-circuit television, but not be able to talk to each other directly. To enhance credibility, there was a portable television camera in the room pointing at the subject. Through the use of videotape, what appeared on the monitor was the same for every subject. When the subject asked why he was watching the other person on the monitor, which typically happened, he was told that in the past it had been found that when people worked separately on these tasks in the same room their performance was often affected by the presence of the other person. This might have happened because people could talk to one another or because they could see one another, and the experiment was designed to separate those variables.

The experimenter explained that the second study would be quite different from the first, since it would involve much more contact with the other person. She would bring both participants into one room and ask them to talk over things that they had in common. She was interested in the way in which holding common interests helped people to get to know one another. The experimenter mentioned that in the past, people who had participated had sometimes gotten to know each other quite well.

Vocabulary task. The experimenter next pointed to a batch of letters printed on small cards in front of the subject and said that his task in the first study was to form 10 different four-letter words from the letters. She went on to say that there were two versions of this task and one was more difficult than the other. She had flipped a coin to determine which task each of them would be working on, and the subject would have the easier one, while Tricia would have the more difficult one. The subject's task was easier because he had 55 letters ranging from A to Z, whereas Tricia had only 45 letters ranging from A to L. The subject was to time himself on the task with a stopwatch. Although he and Tricia were not permitted to speak to each other directly, one type of communication was permitted: They would be allowed to send and request letters. Simple forms were available for this purpose. The experimenter would come into the room from time to time to see if the subject had any messages he wanted to send and would deliver them for him.

The experimenter explained that time was a factor in the first study and that an individual's motivation to do well on a task would obviously affect the time taken to complete the task. Therefore, she was taking precautions to insure that motivation to do well was kept at a high level. She would award points toward a possible extra credit for finishing the task in a minimum amount of time. The subjects were not told exactly what that

amount of time would be or how the conversion to credit would be made, but just to finish as quickly as they could. The experimenter mentioned that the awarding of points to maintain motivation would obviously not be necessary in the second study.

The subject was told to start his stopwatch, begin working, and stop the watch when he had finished. The experimenter picked up another stopwatch and left, saying she would give Tricia the watch and start her on her task. The 55 letters that the subject had to work with allowed him to complete the task within 10 minutes. When approximately 10 minutes had elapsed, the experimenter returned and asked if the subject had any letters he wanted to send to Tricia. All subjects gave the experimenter some letters for Tricia. At this point, the experimenter looked at the subject's stopwatch and told him that he had finished the task in time to get 1 point toward extra credit. As she did so, she also filled out a form indicating the time the subject had taken to complete the task and that he had earned 1 point. She explained that if Tricia finished her task in time she would earn 4 points, since her task was more difficult. The experimenter went on to say that since she allowed participants in the study to send and request letters, she also allowed them to share points they earned. Thus, Tricia could send the subject some of her points if she wanted to do so. The experimenter left the room saying she would give Tricia the letters. Tricia continued to work on her task for about 5 minutes and then finished. The experimenter handed Tricia a form similar to that given the subject earlier. Tricia smiled, wrote a note on a slip of paper, folded it, and gave it to the experimenter.

Benefit manipulation. Within a few moments, the experimenter returned to the subject's room and turned off the monitor. She mentioned that Tricia had completed her task within the necessary time and had received 4 points. She handed the subject a folded note that she said Tricia had asked be given to him. In the no benefit condition, the note said, "Thanks for sending the letters." In the benefit conditions, the note said, "Thanks for sending the letters. The experimenter said it would be OK to give you one of my points. She said she would add it onto the points you've already earned before the end of today's session." Which message the note contained was unknown to the experimenter at the time she handed it to the subject. This was accomplished by having the experimenter pick the note out of a container of folded notes of both types.

Relationship manipulation. The experimenter told the subject that there was one more thing to be done before getting on to the next study. She said she was going to give Tricia some questionnaires to fill out and would then get some more forms for the subject. In the exchange conditions, the experimenter said:

> Tricia is anxious to get on to the next part of the study, since she thinks it will be interesting. Her husband is coming to pick her up in about half an hour and she wants to finish before then.

In the communal conditions, she said:

> Tricia is anxious to get on to the next part of the study, since she thinks it will be interesting. She's new at the university and doesn't know many people. She has to be at the administration building in about half an hour and she wants to finish before then.

Dependent measures. The experimenter then left the room for approximately 5 minutes. When she reappeared she brought two forms, mentioning that these were the forms she had told the subject about. She reminded the subject that the second study involved having the participants talk over things they had in common with each other. She said that before starting it was necessary to get some idea of what their expectations were in order to control for them, since they would vary from person to person. The subject was asked to fill out a form indicating what his first impressions of the other person were. The experimenter said that these forms would be kept completely confidential and left the room while they were filled out.

The first-impressions form, which was given to the subject on top of the form concerning expectations about the discussion, asked him to rate how well 11 traits applied to the other, on a scale from 0 (extremely inappropriate) to 20 (extremely

appropriate). The traits were *considerate, friendly, insincere, intelligent, irritating, kind, open-minded, sympathetic, understanding, unpleasant*, and *warm*. The subject was also asked to indicate his degree of liking for the other, on a scale from 0 (dislike very much) to 20 (like very much).

Suspicion check. After the subject had completed both forms, the experimenter casually mentioned that there was something more to the study and asked whether the subject had any idea what it might be. The responses of eight persons indicated suspicion of the instructions, and they were not included as subjects.

Finally, the true purpose of the experiment was fully explained, and the subject promised not to discuss it with anyone.

Results

A measure of liking for the other was calculated by summing the scores for each of the 11 traits and the direct measure of liking on the impressions questionnaire. The scores for the favorable traits and for the direct rating of liking were the same as the subject's ratings. The scores for the unfavorable traits were obtained by subtracting the subject's ratings for those characteristics from 20. The means for the experimental conditions for the measure of liking are presented in Table 14.1.

From the hypotheses, it would be expected that the scores on the measure of liking would be greater in the exchange–benefit condition than in the exchange–no-benefit condition and would be lower in the communal–benefit condition than in the communal–no-benefit condition. From Table 14.1 it can be seen that the results are in line with the predictions. An analysis of variance of the measure

TABLE 14.1. Means for the Measure of Liking in Experiment 1

Relationship	Benefit from the other	
	Benefit	No benefit
Exchange	193	176
Communal	177	194

Note. The higher the score, the greater the liking. Scores could range from 0 to 240. *n* = 24 per cell.

of liking revealed that the interaction between type of relationship and benefit was significant, $F(1, 92) = 8.35, p < .01$. Neither of the main effects approached significance. A planned comparison indicated that the difference between the exchange–benefit condition and the exchange–no-benefit condition was significant, $F(1, 92) = 4.17, p < .05$. A second planned comparison indicated that the difference between the communal–benefit condition and the communal–no-benefit condition was also significant, $F(1, 92) = 4.37, p < .05$.

Discussion

The results of Experiment 1 provide support for the hypothesis that when a communal relationship is desired, a benefit following prior aid decreases attraction. When the attractive woman they had aided was unmarried (communal conditions), the unmarried male subjects liked her less when she gave them a benefit than when she did not. When the attractive woman who was aided turned out to be married (exchange conditions), she was liked more when she gave the subject a benefit than when she did not. The results for the married woman are consistent with the hypothesis that the receipt of a benefit after the other is benefited leads to greater attraction when an exchange relationship is preferred.

It might be thought that the lower liking of the unmarried woman in the benefit condition than in the no-benefit condition could be explained by a difference in the anticipation of future interaction, a variable which has been shown to influence liking in previous research (Darley & Berscheid, 1967; Mirels & Mills, 1964). Such an interpretation would make the assumption that the repayment by the unmarried woman with whom the subject wished to interact suggested that she did not wish to interact with him. However, this assumption is reasonable only if the future interaction is of the kind referred to here as a communal relationship. If the future interaction involved an explicit exchange of benefits, there is no reason the repayment would have suggested that the unmarried women did not wish to interact with the subject. Since an interpretation in terms of the anticipation of future

interaction requires a distinction between different types of interaction similar to the distinction between communal and exchange relationships, it is not an alternative explanation, but essentially the same interpretation in somewhat different language.

A different interpretation might be suggested that has to do with the role relationships of males and females. It might be argued that the male subjects subscribed to a "traditional" rule that males should give gifts to females, who should gracefully accept them and not attempt to repay their benefactor, and the unmarried woman who gave them a point violated this rule. Such an interpretation would assume that the males did not apply the same rule to their relationships with a woman who is married, which does not seem consistent with traditional values concerning the role of men vis-à-vis women. If the interpretation is restricted to the relation of men and women in romantic relationships, then it is not an alternative explanation, since romantic relationships are communal relationships.

That the desire for a communal relationship was induced by creating a situation in which there was a possibility of a romantic relationship with an attractive member of the opposite sex was not fortuitous. A romantic relationship that might lead to the development of a family relationship through marriage is a particularly appropriate situation for the study of communal relationships, since relationships between family members are the most typical kind of communal relationships. However, the distinction between communal and exchange relationships is not restricted to romantic relationships with members of the opposite sex. The same effect should occur in situations in which a communal relationship, such as friendship, is desired or expected with a member of the same sex.

It was assumed not only that the other was perceived as available for a communal relationship in the communal conditions, but also that she was regarded as an attractive partner for such a relationship. If the other is unattractive, a communal relationship with her should not be desired even if she is available for such a relationship. People do not desire communal relationships with people they dislike. An exchange relationship should be preferred with an unattractive other, and thus a benefit from such a person after he or she has been aided should lead to greater attraction.

Since the effect found in the first study involves the assumption that the benefit that the person received from the other is perceived as a response to the previous benefit that the other received, it should not occur if the other had not received something of value from the person. The receipt of a benefit when the other has not been aided previously should lead to greater liking when a communal relationship is expected or desired. The rule in communal relationships is to respond to a need rather than to reciprocate benefits. The giving of a benefit when no prior help has been received is appropriate for a communal relationship if there is or might be a need for the benefit.

Experiment 2

The distinction between communal and exchange relationships also has implications for reactions to a request for a benefit. If it is true that in an exchange relationship any benefit given by one member to the other creates a debt or obligation to return a comparable benefit, a request for a benefit from another after one has been given aid by that other creates an opportunity to repay the debt. Thus, such a request following aid should be appropriate in an exchange relationship. Since it provides an opportunity to eliminate any tension caused by the presence of the debt, it should increase liking for the other.

The idea that the recipient of a benefit will like his or her benefactor more if he or she can return the benefit has been expressed before (Mauss, 1954). Several studies have shown that recipients of benefits like the donor more if they are able to repay the benefit than if they are not able to repay, whether the opportunity is provided by the donor's specifically requesting that the other repay the benefit (Gergen, Ellsworth, Maslach, & Seipel, 1975) or whether the opportunity to repay is provided, but repayment is not specifically asked for (Castro, 1974; Gross & Latané, 1974).

In a communal relationship, to request a benefit after having given another person aid is inappropriate. It may imply that the original aid was not

given with the intent of satisfying a need but rather with the expectation of receiving something in return, which may be taken as an indication that the other does not desire involvement in a communal relationship. Assuming that beginning or maintaining a communal relationship with another is desirable, such an implication should be frustrating and therefore result in decreased liking.

If one has not been previously aided by another and there is no opportunity to aid the other in the future, a request from that other is inappropriate in an exchange relationship. In an exchange relationship, a person who has not been aided by another should like the other more when he or she does not ask for a benefit than when he or she does ask for a benefit.

However, requesting a benefit in the absence of prior aid is appropriate in a communal relationship. Such a request implies that the other desires a communal relationship and, assuming that beginning or maintaining such a relationship is desirable, it should result in increased liking. Jones and Wortman (1973) suggest that asking another for a benefit is a way of conveying that we think highly of them. They say, "This tactic is likely to convey that we feel good about our relationship with the target person, since it is not customary to ask people to do favors for us unless our relationship is a relatively good one" (Jones & Wortman, 1973, p. 13).

The implications of the distinction between communal and exchange relationships for reactions to requests for a benefit in the context of prior aid or lack of prior aid were investigated in Experiment 2. A situation was arranged in which aid could be given to the subject and, later, a different benefit requested from the subject. The anticipation of a communal relationship was created by leading the subject to believe that the other wanted to meet people and that she would be discussing common interests with the other. The anticipation of an exchange relationship was created by not mentioning anything about the other wanting to meet people, implying that the other was very busy and leading the subject to believe that she would be discussing differences in interests with the other.

The following hypotheses were tested in the second experiment:

1. A request for a benefit from another after the person is aided by the other leads to greater attraction when an exchange relationship is expected.
2. When a communal relationship is expected, a request for a benefit after the person is aided by the other decreases attraction.
3. A request for a benefit in the absence of aid from the other decreases attraction when an exchange relationship is expected.
4. When a communal relationship is expected, a request for a benefit in the absence of aid from the other increases attraction.

Method

Overview. Under the guise of a study of task performance, female college students worked on a task while a television monitor showed another female working on a similar task in another room. Some of the subjects were told that the other was married, had a child, and lived far from the university, and that she and the subject would be discussing differences in interests in a second study (exchange conditions). Other subjects were told that the other was new at the university and did not know many people, and that she and the subject would be discussing common interests in a second study (communal conditions). The other female finished the task, received 1 point, and gave the subject aid on her supposedly more difficult task or did not give the subject aid. The other female then requested a point from the subject or did not request a point. Finally, the subject's liking for the other and expectations concerning the future discussion with the other were assessed.

Subjects. The subjects were 80 female, introductory psychology students who received extra credit toward their course grade for their participation. They were randomly assigned to one of the eight experimental conditions: exchange–aid–request, exchange–aid–no request, exchange–no aid–request, exchange–no aid–no request, communal–aid–request, communal–aid–no request, communal–no aid–request, and communal–no aid–no request.

Procedure. Upon arriving for the study, the subject was greeted by the experimenter and told

that the other subject scheduled to participate at the same time had already arrived and was waiting in another room for the experiment to begin. The experimenter explained that it would take a little time for the equipment to warm up before the experiment could begin.

Relationship manipulation. In the communal conditions, the experimenter casually stated that the other person was anxious to begin because:

> She thinks it will be interesting. She's new at the university, doesn't know many people, and she's interested in getting to know people.

In the exchange conditions, the experimenter casually said:

> She wants to finish soon. Her husband is coming by to pick her up, then they have to pick up her child and go home to Columbia (a city some distance from the university).

The experimenter said that the first study was actually one of two short, unrelated studies they would be asked to participate in that day. The rationale for the first study was the same as in Experiment 1. The experimenter went on to say that the second study would be quite different from the first. In the communal conditions she continued:

> What we're going to do is bring you both into one room. We want you to talk over common interests. We're interested in finding out how people get to know one another. We try to create a relaxed atmosphere, and actually, in the past we've found that some of the people have gotten to know one another quite well.

In the exchange conditions she continued:

> What we're going to do is bring you both into one room. We want you to talk over differences in interests. We're doing this because most people avoid talking about differences in interests and we're interested in getting people's reactions to doing so.

Vocabulary task. After the subject had signed an experimental consent form, the procedure for the vocabulary task was explained in the same manner as in Experiment 1, except that the subject was told that she would be performing the more difficult task while the other person would be performing the easier task. The experimenter pointed out that since the subject's task was the more difficult one, she would have a chance to earn 4 points toward the extra credit, whereas the other person, Tricia, only had a chance to earn 1 point, since she had the easier task. As in Experiment 1, the experimenter mentioned that the awarding of points to maintain motivation obviously would not be necessary in the second study.

After the same instructions concerning the stopwatches as in Experiment 1, the subject was left alone to work on the task for a short time. With the 45 letters the subject had it was impossible for her to finish the task in that time. Subjects typically finished between five and seven words. During the time the subject was working, the experimenter, who always wore a lab coat so that changes in clothing over days could not be detected, could be seen on the monitor starting Tricia on her task and then leaving the room. Tricia finished her task easily. After a short time, the experimenter reentered the other room, and Tricia could be seen pushing some extra letters to the front of the table. At this point, the experimenter stepped in front of the camera, blocking the subject's view of the other so that the subject could not see whether the other handed the letters to the experimenter. Finally, the experimenter could be seen leaving the room, and Tricia sat back in her chair.

Aid manipulation. Shortly thereafter, the experimenter reentered the subject's room and said that Tricia had finished her task and received 1 point. The experimenter turned off the monitor, commenting that it wouldn't be needed any more. In the aid conditions, she said, "Tricia asked me to give you these letters," and handed the subject some letters. In the no-aid conditions, there was no mention of the letters. The experimenter then left the room, telling the subject she would be back shortly. In approximately 3 minutes, she returned, and regardless of whether the subject had finished (none in the no-aid conditions did, whereas most in the aid conditions did), she told the subject she had done well enough to receive the 4 points toward extra credit. She filled out a form indicating this and handed it to the subject. The experimenter said that was all there was to the first study, except for filling out a form if the subject

wanted to request any points from Tricia. Before the subject had an opportunity to look at the form, the experimenter said she would check with Tricia and see if she wanted to fill out a form and left the room for approximately 2 minutes.

Request manipulation. When she appeared, the experimenter handed the subject a folded note, supposedly from Tricia, in which a box was checked indicating either that she wished to request 1 point from the subject (request conditions) or that she did not wish to request any points (no-request conditions). The experimenter was unaware of how the form was checked, having drawn it from a container of folded forms checked in both ways. If the subject wished to fill out a form to request points from the other, the experimenter took it.

Dependent measures. Next, the experimenter reminded the subject that the second study would involve having both subjects talk over common interests (communal conditions) or differences in interests (exchange conditions). Before starting the study it was necessary to get some idea of what their expectations were about the forthcoming interaction in order to control for those expectations, since they might vary from person to person. Therefore, she was asking the subject to fill out two forms indicating what her first impressions of the other person were and also what she expected the discussion to be like. The subject was told that these forms would be kept completely confidential.

The first-impressions form, which was given the subject on top of the form concerning expectations about this discussion, was the same as the first-impression form used in Experiment 1.

Suspicion check. The experimenter left and watched through a one-way mirror until she could see that the subject had finished the forms. She then waited approximately 30 additional sec and reentered the room. As she picked up the forms, she casually said that there was something more to the study than she had mentioned before and asked the subject if she had any idea of what it might be. The responses of eight persons indicated suspicion of the instructions, and they were not included as subjects.

Finally, the true purpose of the experiment was fully explained, and the subject promised not to discuss it with anyone.

Results

A measure of liking for the other was calculated in the same way as in Experiment 1. The means for the experimental conditions for the measure of liking are presented in Table 14.2. An analysis of variance of the measure of liking revealed that the main effect of type of relationship was significant, $F(1, 72) = 6.21$, $p < .05$. Neither of the other main effects nor any of the two-way interactions were significant. The three-way interaction between type of relationship, aid, and request was significant, $F(1, 72) = 12.73$, $p < .001$.

From the first hypothesis, it would be expected that scores on the measure of liking would be greater in the exchange–aid–request condition than in the exchange–aid–no-request condition. As can be seen in Table 14.2, the difference was in the predicted direction. A planned comparison indicated that this difference was significant, $F(1, 72) = 4.03$, $p < .05$.

From the second hypothesis, it would be expected that liking would be less in the communal–aid–request condition than in the communal–aid–no-request condition. As can be seen in Table 14.2, the difference was as predicted. A planned comparison indicated that this difference was significant, $F(1, 72) = 8.60$, $p < .01$.

From the third hypothesis, it would be expected that liking would be less in the exchange–no-aid–request condition than in the exchange–no-aid–no-request condition. As can be seen in Table 14.2, the difference was as predicted. A planned comparison indicated that this difference was significant, $F(1, 72) = 4.07$, $p < .05$.

From the fourth hypothesis, it would be expected that liking would be greater in the communal–no-aid–request condition than in the communal–no-aid–no-request condition. As can be seen in Table 14.2, the means for these two conditions were very similar. A planned comparison indicated that the difference between these two means was not significant.

Another way of looking at the results is to compare the aid and the no-aid conditions. It would be expected that liking would be greater in the exchange–aid–request condition than in the exchange–no-aid–request condition. As can be seen in Table 14.2, this expected difference was obtained. A planned comparison indicated that the difference was significant, $F(1, 72) = 3.99$, $p < .05$. It would be expected that liking would be less in the communal–aid–request condition than in the communal–no-aid–request condition. As can be seen in Table 14.2, this expected difference was obtained. A planned comparison indicated that the difference was marginally significant, $F(1, 72) = 3.93$, $p < .06$. It would be expected that liking would be less in the exchange–aid–no-request condition than in the exchange–no-aid–no-request condition. As can be seen in Table 14.2, this expected difference was obtained. A planned comparison indicated that it was significant, $F(1, 72) = 4.10$, $p < .05$. Finally, it would be expected that liking would be greater in the communal–aid–no-request condition than in the communal–no-aid–no-request condition. Although the means were in the expected direction, the planned comparison indicated that this difference was not significant.

Discussion

In general, the results supported the hypotheses concerning reactions to a request for a benefit based on the distinction between communal and exchange relationships. As expected from the hypothesis that a request for a benefit after the person

TABLE 14.2. Means for the Measure of Liking in Experiment 2

| Relationship | Aid from & request for benefit from the other | | | |
	Aid–request	Aid–no request	No aid–request	No aid–no request
Exchange	173	149	149	173
Communal	156	191	179	177

Note. The higher the score, the greater the liking. Scores could range from 0 to 240. $n = 10$ per cell.

is aided by the other leads to greater attraction when an exchange relationship is expected, it was found that liking for the other was higher in the exchange–aid–request condition than in the exchange–aid–no-request condition. As predicted from the hypothesis that a request for a benefit after the person is aided decreases attraction when a communal relationship is expected, liking was lower in the communal–aid–request condition than in the communal–aid–no-request condition. In line with the hypothesis that a request for a benefit in the absence of aid from the other decreases attraction when an exchange relationship is expected, liking for the other was lower in the exchange–no-aid–request condition than in the exchange–no-aid–no-request condition.

The hypothesis that a request for a benefit in the absence of aid from the other increases attraction when a communal relationship is expected was not supported; there was no difference in liking between the communal–no-aid–request condition and the communal–no-aid–no-request condition. The subjects in the communal–no-aid–request condition may have been somewhat uncertain about the intentions of the other. Although the request may have indicated to the subject that the other wanted a communal relationship with her and consequently led the subject to expect such a relationship, it also may have reminded the subject that the other had not given her aid earlier. This reminder may have raised doubt about whether the other would behave in an appropriate way for a communal relationship. This could explain why the request did not result in increased liking for the other in the communal–no-aid–request condition.

As would be expected from the distinction between communal and exchange relationships, liking was greater in the exchange–aid–request condition than in the exchange–no-aid–request condition, marginally less in the communal–aid–request condition than in the communal–no-aid–request condition, and less in the exchange–aid–no-request condition than in the exchange–no-aid–no-request condition. The greater liking in the exchange–aid–request condition than in the exchange–no-aid–request condition could be due to a general tendency for aid to increase liking, as well as to the appro-

priateness of the request. However, the fact that liking was less in the exchange–aid–no-request condition than in the exchange–no-aid–no-request condition is opposite to what would be expected from a general tendency for aid to increase liking, but follows from the idea that differences in liking are due to the appropriateness of the other's behavior for the type of relationship. That liking was less in the communal–aid–request condition than in the communal–no-aid–request condition is also opposite to the tendency for aid to increase liking and consistent with the effect on liking of the appropriateness of the other's behavior for the type of relationship.

Since the focus was on the interactive effects of type of relationship, a main effect of type of relationship was not specifically predicted. However, the significant main effect that was obtained for liking is understandable in view of the operations used to manipulate type of relationship. Among other things, subjects in the communal conditions may have expected the other to be more similar than did subjects in the exchange conditions.

General Discussion

While it is assumed that the distinction between communal and exchange relationships is made implicitly by most people in their interactions with others, it is not assumed that they are explicitly aware of the distinction or are able to describe how it affects their reactions. Certainly they do not use the terms *communal* and *exchange relationships*. It is also not assumed that everyone makes the distinction in the same way. Some people restrict their communal relationships to only a very few persons, whereas others have communal relationships with a wide circle of others. There are some people who do not make the distinction at all. Some people treat every relationship, even relationships with members of their own immediate family, in terms of exchange.

It is possible for a person to have both a communal relationship and an exchange relationship with the same other, for example, when a person sells something to a friend or hires a family member as an employee. In such instances, a distinction is typically made between what is appropriate for the business (exchange) relationship and what is appropriate for the family or friendship (communal) relationship. Exchange relationships sometimes can develop into communal relationships, such as when a merchant and a customer become close friends or when an employer and an employee marry.

The lack of attention paid to communal relationships in previous research on interpersonal attraction may be accounted for by the fact that almost all of the past research has involved attraction toward persons who are not only previously unknown to the subject but who are not expected by the subject ever to be known in the future. Communal relationships involve an expectation of a long-term relationship, whereas exchange relationships need not be long-term. However, the variables of communal versus exchange relationship and expected length of the relationship are conceptually independent. Exchange relationships may be expected to continue over a long period.

If it is true that treating a communal relationship in terms of exchange compromises the relationship, then exchange theories of interpersonal attraction (e.g., Secord & Backman, 1974, chapter 7) may create a misleading impression about the development and breakup of intimate relationships. The idea that exchange is the basis of intimate relationships may actually have the effect of impairing such relationships. For example, the recommendation, which seems to be growing in popularity, that prior to marriage a marriage contract be drawn up that specifies in detail what each partner expects from the other, should, if followed, tend to undermine the relationship.

If the theoretical viewpoint of this research is correct, a communal relationship will be strained by dickering about what each of the partners will do for the other. Of course, if one of the partners in a communal relationship is convinced that he or she is being exploited by the other because that person is concerned about the other's welfare while the other is not concerned about his or her welfare, the communal relationship has disintegrated. If this happens in a marriage, there may be attempts to preserve the marriage by changing it into an exchange relationship through dickering.

NOTES

This research was supported by a grant from the National Science Foundation.

Requests for reprints should be sent to Margaret S. Clark, Department of Psychology, Carnegie-Mellon University, Pittsburgh, Pennsylvania 15213.

REFERENCES

Adams, J. S. Toward an understanding of inequity. *Journal of Abnormal and Social Psychology*, 1963, *67*, 422–436.

Castro, M. A. C. Reactions to receiving aid as a function of cost to donor and opportunity to aid. *Journal of Applied Social Psychology*, 1974, *4*, 194–209.

Darley, J. M., & Berscheid, E. Increased liking as a result of the anticipation of personal contact. *Human Relations*, 1967, *20*, 29–40.

Gergen, K. J., Ellsworth, P., Maslach, C., & Seipel, M. Obligation, donor resources, and reactions to aid in three cultures. *Journal of Personality and Social Psychology*, 1975, *31*, 390–400.

Goffman, E. *Asylums*. Garden City, N.Y.: Anchor Books, 1961.

Gross, A. E., & Latané, J. G. Receiving help, reciprocation, and interpersonal attraction. *Journal of Applied Social Psychology*, 1974, *4*, 210–223.

Jones, E. E., & Wortman, C. *Ingratiation: An attributional approach*. Morristown, N.J.: General Learning Press, 1973.

Keisler, S. B. The effect of perceived role requirements on reactions to favor doing. *Journal of Experimental Social Psychology*, 1966, *2*, 198–210.

Mauss, M. *The gift: Forms and functions of exchange in archaic societies*. Glencoe, Ill.: Free Press, 1954.

Mirels, H., & Mills, J. Perception of the pleasantness and competence of a partner. *Journal of Abnormal and Social Psychology*, 1964, *68*, 456–459.

Pruitt, D. G. Methods for resolving differences of interest: A theoretical analysis. *Journal of Social Issues*, 1972, *28*, 133–154.

Secord, P. F., & Backman, C. W. *Social psychology* (2nd ed.). New York: McGraw-Hill, 1974.

Thibaut, J. W., & Kelley, H. H. *The social psychology of groups*. N.Y.: Wiley, 1959.

Walster, E., Walster, G. W., & Berscheid, E. *Equity: Theory and research*. Boston: Allyn & Bacon, 1978.

READING 15

Beneficial Impression Management: Strategically Controlling Information to Help Friends

Barry R. Schlenker • University of Florida

Thomas W. Britt • Walter Reed Army Institute of Research

It was hypothesized that people will strategically regulate information about the identities of friends to help them create desired impressions on audiences. We demonstrated that participants described a friend consistently with the qualities preferred by an attractive, opposite-sex individual, but inconsistently with the qualities preferred by an unattractive, opposite-sex individual. Impression management to benefit friends by promoting and protecting their desired identities may be one of the more common and pleasant forms of help giving in everyday life.

Jennie Jerome Churchill, the charming, *bon viveur* mother of Winston Churchill, once shared one of her insights into friendship: "Treat your friends as you do your pictures, and place them in their best light" (Churchill, 1916). Her advice is a sage reminder of the importance of social support in relationships, especially support that affirms and enhances the desired images of close others. Through private and public displays of appreciation, approval, respect, and encouragement, people cement their relationships and provide one another with an array of immediate and long-range benefits. Such support can benefit recipients by boosting their confidence, self-efficacy, and self-esteem; by creating positive moods or dispelling negative ones; by inspiring them to tackle and accomplish desirable new challenges; by enhancing or protecting their public image and reputation; and, ultimately, by making it easier for them to achieve their goals in business and social life. People often can provide as much or more help by regulating and controlling beneficial information about others as by delivering some tangible material or physical good. The strategic provision of social support may be one of the more important and frequently used types of interpersonal help that occur in daily life. In this article, we examine the strategic control of information as a way to benefit close others. The research aims to open the door to future integration of work on helping behavior, social support, and impression management.

Consider a few examples:

1. A high school ballplayer buoys the spirits of a teammate who struck out at a key moment by emphasizing the latter's game-winning hit last week and noting that even the greatest big-league hitters fail about 7 times out of 10. He may privately suspect his teammate has only mediocre baseball talent, but by putting the best side to his comments and not sharing his doubts, he makes the teammate feel better, builds his confidence so he can face tomorrow's game in a more optimistic frame of mind, and boosts the teammate's image in front of the other players who can hear his reassuring words.

2. At a party, a college student describes her roommate to a potential date she knows her friend finds extremely attractive. She stresses her friend's intelligence, attractiveness, and common interests, but fails to mention that her friend can also be quite arrogant.

3. A woman is fired from her job. At a gathering of friends later that night, her husband suppresses his private concerns about the state of the local job market and cheers her up by joking that her boss is an uninsightful jerk, the job was holding her back and not allowing her to get the most out of her numerous talents, and they can certainly manage to get by financially until she finds a job in which her many special skills are appreciated.

What do these examples have in common? In each case, an individual is actively trying to regulate the image of a close other. Communications are used strategically to accomplish a goal that goes beyond simply describing someone or expressing one's feelings. The individual's efforts are centered on trying to present the close other's identity in the best possible light, that is, on trying to craft a desirable image of that person. Such images are not necessarily false, although they sometimes can be. They usually represent a "packaged" or edited interpretation of available

information that aims to accomplish a goal while remaining reasonably faithful to the evidence (Schlenker, Britt, & Pennington, 1996; Schlenker & Weigold, 1989, 1992). *Strategic* activities are defined as ones that deal with a pattern of decisions that attempt to accomplish certain goals, thereby trying to bring about specific outcomes and to avoid others (see Higgins, 1997). In social life, people are constantly helping one another to achieve identity-relevant goals. In close relationships involving family, romantic partners, and friends, people are inextricably enmeshed in mutual identity regulation. Often, though certainly not always, one goal of such strategic communication is to affirm and protect a desirable identity for the other. Even in nonclose relationships, such as in encounters between strangers or acquaintances, people usually follow rules that call for mutual consideration, politeness, and civility, whereby the parties act in ways that respect the image projected by the other and help one another save face when confronted by threats (Goffman, 1959).

Despite the pervasiveness and importance of these types of phenomena, virtually no research has been devoted to examining how people strategically regulate the identities of those who are close to them. However, a great deal of research has focused on how people regulate their own identities (e.g., Baumeister, 1982; Jones & Pittman, 1982; Leary, 1995: Rosenfeld, Giacalone, & Riordan, 1995; Schlenker, 1980; Schlenker et al., 1996; Schlenker & Weigold, 1989, 1992; Tedeschi & Norman, 1985; Tetlock & Manstead, 1985). This research falls under the headings of impression management and self-presentation, which are often treated synonymously even though, as the preceding examples illustrate, it is common for people to regulate information about other individuals and not just themselves. *Impression management* refers to the goal-directed activity of influencing the impressions that audiences form of some person, group, object, or event (Schlenker, 1980; Schlenker et al., 1996; Schlenker & Weigold, 1992). *Self-presentation* is a subcategory that deals with the control of self-relevant information.

Some theoretical analyses presume that impression management is guided by selfish and often illicit motives, such as the desire to augment one's own power, enhance one's image, and manipulate others into providing personally satisfying outcomes. People who engage in impression management are portrayed as Machiavellian manipulators who are concerned with appearance over substance, who lack authenticity in their behavior, and who are focused on promoting their own interests at the expense of others (Buss & Briggs, 1984; Jones & Pittman, 1982). In our view, however, impression management is like any other social activity in that it can be guided by a variety of goals. In the helping literature, distinctions can be drawn between aid that appears to be motivated by concerns about self versus concerns about others who are in need (Batson, 1995). There is no reason to think that the strategic provision of social support through impression management would be more restricted in its motivation. Indeed, we propose that impression-management activities are often influenced by the potential consequences for the identities of others, and not just one's own identity (Schlenker et al., 1996; Schlenker & Weigold, 1992). Schlenker (1984) argued that a key task for those who are involved in long-term relationships is to help their partners attain desired identity images and that the success of a close relationship is linked to the effective use of other-benefitting impression management.

Studying beneficial impression management may yield new insights into the nature of social support by focusing on how it is strategically provided. Social support is widely regarded as a vital ingredient for psychological well-being and interpersonal success. Social support can provide a buffer against stress; is inversely related to negative affect, depression, and psychological distress (L. A. Clark & Watson, 1991; Cohen & Wills, 1985; Coyne, Burchill, & Stiles, 1991; Sarason, Sarason, & Pierce, 1990); and can enhance the recipient's positive affect, self-esteem, and well-being (Cohen & Hoberman, 1983; Major, Testa, & Blysma, 1991). Although support can take many forms, including companionship, informational problem solving, and tangible assistance (Rook, 1987), identity support is a form that has a demonstrable impact on the recipient. Feedback

that affirms and enhances desired identities tends to be sought after, better remembered, and mood boosting (Brown, 1997). In close relationships, partners who compliment and encourage one another report greater satisfaction with their relationship and remain closer than those who do not (Gottman, 1994; Noller & Fitzpatrick, 1990). People are more satisfied in relationships when they idealize their partners and their partners idealize them (Murray, Holmes, & Griffen, 1996). In contrast, being preoccupied with self, rather than other-oriented, is associated with problems in relationships. Bragging out of proportion to one's own accomplishments; slighting the positive qualities of the partner; blaming the partner for problems; and criticizing, nagging, and complaining about the partner are all associated with troubled relationships characterized by less satisfaction and a greater likelihood of breakup or divorce (Bradbury & Fincham, 1990; M. S. Clark & Reis, 1988; Karney, Bradbury, Fincham, & Sullivan, 1994; Levinger, 1976; Markham, 1979).

Expanding the Domain of Impression Management

Studying beneficial impression management also may offer new insights into the nature of impression management itself. Prior research has shown that people will use impression management to enhance the identities of others, but this benefit has always been instrumental to achieving the actor's primary goal of achieving some selfish, personal objective, such as procuring social or material advantages like approval and pay raises, boosting self-esteem, or maintaining a desirable public identity. In this traditional view, there is no concern for the welfare of the other independent of what it means for personal profit.

By focusing on the potential consequences for others, not for the actor, research that examines beneficial impression management represents a significant departure from the existing literature. Such research can build on prior work, but with a major reemphasis: The social conditions that are investigated should be designed to have an impact on the identity and outcomes of another person who can be benefited by the participants, and not the participants' themselves. For example, instead of manipulating whether the target audience is attractive or unattractive to the participant, or whether the target audience will or will not deliver an important face-to-face evaluation of the participant, research can focus on the impact such factors will have on another person. Research has identified a variety of situational and target factors that affect strategic self-presentation, including the audience's power or attractiveness, the audience's preferences, and the importance of the performance (e.g., Leary, 1995; Rosenfeld et al., 1995; Schlenker, 1980; Schlenker & Weigold, 1992), and these factors can be readily adapted to the study of beneficial impression management.

Beneficial Impression Management Among Friends

Friends should be especially likely to receive assistance through beneficial impression management. People in close relationships exhibit a genuine concern for each other's welfare (M. S. Clark & Mills, 1979; M. S. Clark & Reis, 1988). Further, close others become an extension of one's own identity, as people define themselves partly in terms of these relationships (Aron, Aron, Tudor, & Nelson, 1991). As a result, relationship closeness is associated with systematic changes in cognitive, affective, and behavioral patterns toward the other (Aron et al., 1991).

First, close relationships are characterized by a change in resource allocations as people shift from trying to maximize their own resources to trying to maximize joint resources (Aron et al., 1991; Rusbult & Arriaga, 1997). Close relationships have a communal character in which concerns about immediate reciprocity and exchange are replaced by concerns about the needs of the other (M. S. Clark & Mills, 1979).

Second, close relationships are characterized by greater vicarious participation in which partners are more likely to share one another's joys

and sorrows (Aron et al., 1991). People experience heightened pleasure at the success of close others, provided they are not competing with the others on the task, and relationship closeness permits people to bask in the reflected glory of the other's accomplishments (Brown, Novick, Lord, & Richards, 1992; Cialdini et al., 1990; Tesser, 1988). Further, friends evoke greater empathy for one another and exhibit greater helping (M. S. Clark, 1983; Krebs, 1970).

Third, close relationships are characterized by a change in cognitive perspective. Instead of exhibiting traditional actor–observer differences, people in close relationships tend to make attributions about their partner more like they do about themselves (Aron et al., 1991) and sometimes are even more generous in their treatment of their partners than themselves (Hall & Taylor, 1976; Taylor & Koivumaki, 1976). Even new relationships, created in the lab through a self-disclosure induction, are characterized by minimal self-serving biases on interdependent-outcome tasks (Sedikides, Campbell, Reeder, & Elliot, 1998).

We examined whether people will strategically vary their descriptions of a friend to help that friend make a good impression on an attractive other. The study was partly inspired by the work of Zanna and Pack (1975), who found that women varied their own self-presentations in order to fulfill the role expectations of an attractive man, but showed little change in self-presentations for an unattractive man. It was hypothesized that people will provide strategic social support to help a friend impress a member of the opposite sex whom their friend finds attractive. If the attractive target audience prefers someone who is outgoing and sociable as an ideal date, they will describe their friend as relatively outgoing and sociable. If the attractive target prefers someone who is more reflective, understanding, and quiet, their friend will be described as relatively high on these qualities. In contrast, if they believe their friend finds the target to be unattractive, they will not shape their friend's image in line with the target's preferences. If the target is sufficiently unattractive, they may even go out of their way to show that their friend is the opposite of the target's preferences as a way to help the friend avoid any uncomfortable entanglements.

Method

Overview and Design

Participants reported to the lab with a same-sex friend, were taken to separate rooms, and were told they would be participating in a study examining the development of acquaintanceships and the role that friends and associates play in the process. All participants believed their friend would meet and interact with someone of the opposite sex, who was one of another pair of friends supposedly participating during the same session. They also believed they would provide information to the other pair to simulate the role that third parties might play in the acquaintanceship process.

Participants received bogus information that supposedly described the reactions of their friend and the other after a brief get-acquainted meeting. A questionnaire, ostensibly completed by the other person, described his or her "ideal date" as someone who was either extraverted (outgoing, loves to party) or introverted (reflective, prefers a quiet evening at home to a boisterous social gathering).

Participants then completed a questionnaire that asked for their honest descriptions of their friend's personality and preferences on qualities relevant to extraversion or introversion. This questionnaire supposedly would be delivered to the other person prior to a second meeting with their friend and thus had the potential to influence his or her impressions of their friend. They were assured the questionnaire would not be seen by their friend at any time, nor would they ever meet directly with any of the other participants or discuss their role. It was also made clear at the outset that the length of the session permitted only one pair to get to know one another, so there could be no opportunity to reverse roles (e.g., the participant would not get acquainted with either member of the other pair) and no possibility of reciprocation in the session. The design thus was a 2 (attractiveness of other to friend: attractive or unattractive) × 2 (other's ideal: prefers extravert or prefers introvert) between-groups factorial.

Participants

Participants were recruited from introductory psychology classes and offered credit toward a course research requirement. Participants were instructed to report with a friend of the same sex. One hundred seventy-two students participated (152 women and 20 men).

Procedure

On arriving, participants were greeted and taken to separate rooms in the laboratory complex. From this point forward, they did not see or communicate with one another; they were treated independently and separately assigned to different conditions in the design. The written instructions explained that the study was examining the role of communications in the development of acquaintanceships, with a focus on what happens when people initially begin to get acquainted with one another.

Participants read that one of them would be randomly assigned to the role of a "discussant," who would meet and interact face-to-face with someone of the opposite sex whom he or she did not previously know. The other would be assigned to the role of an "associate," who would supply information to one or both of the discussants at key points during their interaction. Supposedly, comparable assignments would occur for a second pair of participants who were also scheduled for the session: One would be a discussant and the other would be an associate. It was made clear that the associates for each pair would communicate written information, but they would not be physically present during the discussants' interactions; this was justified by explaining that this procedure ensured a high degree of experimental control. Further, participants read that, because the research was systematically investigating communication and acquaintanceship, different communication conditions were being created, with some participants communicating with everyone and others communicating with fewer people. Also, different types and amounts of information would be exchanged in different conditions. These instructions provided justifications for structuring the session with limited communications.

All participants then learned that they were assigned to be an associate and the person who came with them would be a discussant. They read the following description of what the sequence of events would be:

1. The two discussants will have a preliminary "get acquainted" meeting.
2. The two discussants will complete "first impression" questionnaires.
3. You will have a chance to look over some of these questionnaires from the discussants. You will then be asked to complete questionnaires that will be delivered to one or both of the discussants.
4. The discussants will look over the associates' questionnaires. The discussants will then have another face-to-face meeting to form a "second impression."

The instructions made clear that the associates would not meet face-to-face with the others nor discuss their written feedback with the others. After waiting an appropriate amount of time, the researcher told participants that the two discussants had had their initial meeting and had completed the initial questionnaires. Supposedly on the basis of a randomly generated condition assignment, they received only two of these questionnaires to examine: (a) a first impression questionnaire, describing their friend's reactions to the other discussant, that was supposedly completed by their friend and (b) a preferences questionnaire, describing the type of person one of the discussants most prefers in a member of the opposite sex, that was allegedly completed by the other discussant.

Attractiveness manipulation. The first impression questionnaire supposedly described their friend's reaction to the opposite-sex discussant. The instructions atop the questionnaire asked for honest opinions and indicated that their answers would not be shown to the other discussant at any time, although they might be shown to "your associate." Answers to eight items, indicated by checks on 7-point rating scales, indicated that their friend found the other person to be either highly attractive or unattractive. The items included attribute ratings of how friendly–aloof, interesting–boring, intelligent–unintelligent, pleasant–unpleasant, and physically attractive–physically unattractive the other was, along with items asking how good a first impression the other made, how much they wanted to make a good first impression on the other, and how much they would like to get to know the other. In the attractive condition, the other was described in highly positive terms on the attributes ($M = 6.6$ on the 7-point scale) and the friend supposedly indicated the other created an excellent first impression, they wanted to make a very good first impression on the other, and they very much wanted to get to know the other (scores of 7, 6, and 7, respectively). In the unattractive condition, the other was described in generally negative terms ($M = 3.0$ on the 7-point scale) and the friend supposedly indicated that the other created a poor first impression, they did not care about making a good first impression, and they had little interest in getting to know the other (scores of 2, 2, and 2, respectively).

Other's preference manipulation. The second questionnaire supposedly contained the other discussant's preferences for an ideal date. Seven items each described two types of reactions in everyday situations, one of which was an extraverted type of response and the other of which was an introverted type of response. For example, one item stated, "I prefer someone who would rather: (a) take a long, quiet walk through the woods; (b) go to a sports bar and have a great time with friends watching a game." A second item stated, "With regard to partying, I am more attracted to someone who feels: (a) the more the merrier (25 or more people present); (b) it is nicest to be in a small group of intimate friends (6 or 8 people at most)," and a third item stated, "I am more attracted to someone who: (a) is kind, sensitive, and compassionate; (b) is outgoing and the life of the party." Circled answers indicated that the other discussant consistently preferred either an outgoing, sociable date (extraverted condition) or a more quiet, compassionate, thoughtful one (introverted condition).

Presentations of friend. After looking over this material, participants were given a questionnaire that asked them to describe their friend and constituted the measure of beneficial impression management. The written instructions atop the questionnaire, which the experimenter verbally repeated for emphasis, asked for their honest opinions about their friend and assured them that their friend would not see or learn of their answers at any time; the questionnaire would be seen by the other discussant only. Participants were asked to describe how characteristic each of 25 attributes was of their friend on a 5-point scale (1 = *not at all characteristic*, 5 = *perfectly characteristic*) and to indicate whether their friend would agree or disagree with each of six statements that described his or her behavioral tendencies on 5-point scales (1 = *strongly disagree*, 5 = *strongly agree*). Most of these items were selected to represent the types of qualities that were preferred (or not preferred) by the other discussant; for ease of exposition, we call these groupings *extraversion* and *introversion*. Extraversion was represented by seven attributes (outgoing, talkative, sociable, extraverted, life of the party, socializer, boisterous) and three behavioral tendencies ("If I had more time, I would more often go out with my friends," "I like exciting, noisy places with plenty of crowd activity, like a nightclub," and "I am happiest when I have other people around me").

Introversion was represented by a different set of seven attributes (introspective, sentimental, reflective, serene, sensitive, thoughtful, romantic) and three behavioral tendencies ("If I had more time, I would spend more evenings at home doing things I'd like to do," "I like quiet, romantic spots, like sitting by a lake with my friends," and "On a cold winter night, I like to curl up and watch a favorite movie on the VCR"). The remaining attributes were filler items that seemed to be largely irrelevant to extraversion and introversion (e.g., generous, helpful, loyal, cheerful, selfish). Finally, participants completed a sheet containing manipulation checks, were probed for suspicions, and were debriefed. None of the participants voiced any suspicions that their friend was not meeting another person or that the feedback sheets were bogus.

Results

Manipulation Checks

Written checks completed prior to the debriefing indicated that the manipulations were effective. When asked how positive or negative a first impression the other person made on their friend, participants indicated that a very positive impression was created in the attractive condition and a negative impression was created in the unattractive condition (Ms = 6.55 and 2.37, respectively), $F(1, 166) = 1,144.97$, $p < .0001$. When asked whether the other person preferred someone who is more introspective or extraverted, participants correctly indicated that the other preferred someone who is introspective in the introverted condition and extraverted in the extraverted condition (Ms = 6.69 and 1.91, respectively), $F(1, 166) = 1,771.83$, $p < .0001$. These were the only effects obtained on these items.

Presentations of Friends

The questionnaire on which participants described their friend to the other discussant contained items selected to exemplify sociable, extraverted individuals versus reflective, introverted individuals. The items in each grouping were highly intercorrelated (αs = .89 and .83 for the extraversion and introversion ratings, respectively). Therefore, summed scores across the 10 items in each grouping were calculated and constituted the measures of relevant presentations of the friend.

A 2 (attractiveness of other) × 2 (other's ideal) × 2 (presented trait: extraversion or introversion) mixed-model analysis of variance (ANOVA) was conducted; the first two factors were between-groups variables and the last factor was a within-subjects variable.[1] The analysis revealed a main effect of presented trait, $F(1, 168) = 13.15, p < .001$,

---

[1] Initial analyses also included sex of participant as a factor. The only finding was a main effect of sex on the total evaluation of the other, $F(1, 164) = 6.74, p < .02$, with women giving their friend higher ratings on both extraversion and introversion than men (Ms = 35.4 and 34.4, respectively). No other effects even approached significance. Further, the patterns of means for the interaction of attractiveness by other's ideal by trait were very similar for men and women. Sex was therefore dropped as a factor.

TABLE 15.1. Presentations of One's Friend on Extraverted and Introverted Qualities: Means for the Attractiveness by Ideal by Trait Interaction

	Presented trait	
Condition	Extraverted qualities	Introverted qualities
Attractive other		
Prefers extraverts	$39.9_{a,b,c}$	$32.3_{a,d,e}$
Prefers introverts	$32.7_{b,f,g}$	$36.8_{d,f,h}$
Unattractive other		
Prefers extraverts	$35.5_{c,i}$	$35.1_{e,j}$
Prefers introverts	$38.5_{g,l,k}$	$30.5_{h,j,k}$

Note. Higher numbers indicate greater amounts of the presented trait (i.e., greater extraverted or introverted qualities). Means that share subscripts differ at $p < .05$ in tests of simple effects.

as participants described their friend more highly overall on extraversion than introversion ($Ms = 36.6$ and 33.7), qualified by a three-way interaction of attractiveness by ideal by trait, $F(1, 168) = 35.56, p < .001$. Means for the interaction are shown in Table 15.1. Attractiveness by ideal interactions were obtained on both the extraverted traits, $F(1, 168) = 21.99, p < .001$, and introverted traits, $F(1, 168) = 26.03, p < .001$.

Participants' presentations of their friend followed the predicted pattern of strategic and beneficial impression management. Participants described their friend in ways that fulfilled the attractive other's ideal. When the other was attractive, there was a significant simple interaction of other's ideal by presented trait, $F(1, 168) = 28.12, p < .001$. When describing their friend to an attractive other who preferred extraverts, participants emphasized that their friend was higher on extraversion than introversion, $F(1, 168) = 24.01, p < .001$, but when describing their friend to an attractive other who preferred introverts, they portrayed their friend as higher on introversion than extraversion, $F(1, 168) = 6.89, p < .02$. In their portrayals, their friend thus became the type of person who was desired by a highly attractive other.

When their friend found the other to be very unattractive, participants offered quite different portraits. These seemed designed to emphasize that their friend was "not your type." When the other was unattractive, there was a significant simple interaction of other's ideal by presented trait, $F(1, 168) = 10.30, p < .01$. When describing their friend to an unattractive other who preferred introverts, they emphasized that their friend was higher on extraversion than introversion, $F(1, 168) = 22.04, p < .001$, but when describing their friend to an unattractive other who preferred extraverts, they presented their friend as about equally high on introversion and extraversion ($F < 1$). Thus, when presenting their friend to an unattractive other, participants did not remain neutral or unbiased in their portraits or ignore the other's ideal. Instead, they shifted their descriptions of their friend to reduce the match with the other's preferences.

The questionnaire also contained attribute items that were designed to be largely irrelevant to introversion and extraversion—for example, generous, helpful, loyal, cheerful, selfish (reverse scored). These items seemed to tap a general positivity factor, emerged as a separate factor in a factor analysis, and were moderately correlated with one another ($\alpha = .75$). Participants described their friends very positively on these items ($M = 4.22$ on a 5-point scale, where 5 was the most positive possible rating), and differences between conditions may have been muted by ceiling effects. No significant effects were found. Thus, participants seemed to confine their strategic efforts to the dimensions that seemed to count most in the eyes of the audience.

Discussion

The results strongly supported the hypotheses. People's descriptions of their friends followed the patterns one would expect if they were using strategic impression management to benefit friends. Although participants were encouraged to describe their friends honestly, their communications appeared to be optimized to produce a desired impact on the audience. If their friend thought the target audience was very attractive, they described their friend consistently with the target's preferences for an ideal date; their friend "became" extraverted if the other's ideal was of an extravert and introverted if the other's ideal was of an introvert.

It is worth noting that it was never explicitly stated that the target preferred an "introvert" over an "extravert" or vice versa. The manipulation of the other's preference was accomplished more subtly by indicating the types of activities that he or she preferred in an ideal date (e.g., curling up with a good book in front of a fire vs. going to a party where there would be lots of people). From these preferences, participants readily inferred the types of qualities that the target admired and then crafted their portrait of their friend to be consistent. Further, these were not merely subtle shifts, with slightly greater ratings in one condition than another, but relative positioning remaining the same (such as always rating their friend as more extraverted than introverted, with this difference being larger in one condition than another). These were more profound changes in description, with their friend rated higher on extraversion than introversion to impress the attractive target who preferred an extravert and higher on introversion than extraversion to impress the attractive target who preferred an introvert.

In contrast to how they portrayed their friend when the other person was attractive, they helped in a different way when their friend supposedly thought the other was very unattractive. They then described their friend in ways that indicated he or she was "not your type." If the unattractive other preferred introverts, their friend "became" quite extraverted; if the unattractive other preferred extraverts, their friend acquired introverted qualities to balance extraverted ones. By so doing, participants may have been aiming to cool any potential interest the other person had in their friend. This "you-wouldn't-be-interested" tactic could serve to protect the friend from unappreciated and unwanted attention.

These results suggest that people may play an important role in regulating the contact their friends have with specific others by influencing how appealing or unappealing their friends appear to be. By describing friends in a way that is consistent with the preferences of desirable others, people increase the likelihood that their friends might affiliate with those others and perhaps form enduring relationships. Conversely, by describing friends in a way that is inconsistent with the preferences of undesirable others, people reduce the likelihood that their friends might affiliate with those others and form enduring relationships. Such regulatory effects have not been previously examined in the relationship literature.

The pattern in the unattractive other condition would appear to weaken an alternative interpretation of the findings based on biased scanning. It might be argued that the other's preferences for an ideal date produced biased scanning in memory of the friend's qualities, yielding descriptions that were consistent with the other's ideal. One also might argue that this process is more likely to occur when the other is attractive than unattractive, in that "birds of a feather flock together" and the friend was obviously attracted to the other. However, the fact that participants went out of their way to reduce the match between their friend's qualities and the unattractive other's preferences seems counter to a biased scanning interpretation. It is more consistent with a motivated, strategic shift designed to benefit the friend. This type of shift has not, to our knowledge, been previously reported in the support or relationship literatures.

Why were friends favored for such helpful treatment? In close relationships, people tend to exhibit a greater concern for each other's welfare and come to define themselves partly in terms of their relationship with the other (Aron et al., 1991; M. S. Clark & Reis, 1988). Such changes could lead to help in the form of social support for several reasons. These include (a) egoistic reasons—because of increased self–other overlap, helping friends produces benefits for self such as positive affect (Cialdini, Brown, Lewis, Luce, & Neuberg, 1997); (b) altruistic reasons—because friends evoke greater empathy and empathy produces greater concern for the welfare of others, people may help in order to increase their friends' well-being (Batson, 1995); (c) collective or mutual gain reasons (Batson, 1995)—helping the other maximizes joint gain, which is a valued objective in close relationships; and (d) reasons of principle (Batson, 1995)—because friends have a duty to help one another, aid is offered as a matter of principle. The present studies were not designed to dissect the relative contributions of each of these reasons: doing so remains a job for future research. In any case, the helping literature shows that friends are helped more than strangers (Krebs, 1970), and the same is true for help given by means of beneficial impression management.

The strategic shifts in descriptions of friends seemed to be guided by differences in the social needs of the friends and not by any obvious or salient differences between conditions in personal gains or losses. Participants' descriptions were equally public vis-à-vis the target audience and equally confidential vis-à-vis the friend regardless of the condition of the friend's social need. Further, participants believed they would not have to go through any meeting, interview, or other form of public questioning that involved showing what they had done (or failed to do). Under these conditions of confidentiality, people still responded to the social need of their friend by providing help when their friend could most use it. Those needs initiated the activity and guided the form it took.

This is not to say, of course, that there are no personal benefits that follow from providing social support. The literature on prosocial behavior (e.g., Batson, 1995; Cialdini et al., 1997) attests to the beneficial personal consequences that can accrue from helping those in need, including increases in the helper's positive mood, self-esteem, and sense of self-efficacy, as well as potential punishments avoided, including guilt and recriminations from failure to help. Further, people who are known to do good deeds for others are usually admired and respected. We suggest that people who are proficient at helping others through beneficial impression management are greatly admired for their social skills and are sought out as

friends. Successful leaders may be especially likely to be skilled in the art of beneficial impression management.

The concept of impression management is broadened by the recognition that it can be used to benefit others as well as for selfish, exploitative purposes. Impression management is the goal-directed activity of editing, packaging, and communicating information to audiences (Schlenker et al., 1996; Schlenker & Weigold, 1992). Such packaging is omnipresent when people describe and explain themselves, other people, and events; it occurs in people's own minds as well as in their communications to others and is an inherent property of how information is treated. Phrased differently, impression management is the regulation of information that takes into account the objectives of the actor in relation to particular audiences, both real and imagined. Thoughts and communications are inherently goal directed (Kunda, 1990; Schlenker, 1980; Schlenker & Weigold, 1989).

Some people react to the term *packaging* as if it must represent superficial, pretentious, or deceitful conduct. In contrast, we argue that packaging is not necessarily false or untruthful, although it certainly can be. More often, it represents a justifiable construction of reality that is shaped by the actor's agenda (goals and plans). When people contemplate themselves or others, they simply cannot bring all relevant information to mind at once nor describe all relevant information to others. People cannot do a "mind dump" of everything that might pertain to what they are describing. Even if it could be done, it would be an unintelligible mess. Information must be edited (categorized, weighted, evaluated) to fit the appropriate circumstances, making it relevant to the topic and to the interests of the others who may be present (Higgins, 1992; Schlenker, 1980; Schlenker et al., 1996). During the editing process, people's goals intervene to filter information and shape it in advantageous but usually justifiable ways. Such packaging usually seems to take place routinely or automatically, without conscious effort or awareness. During socialization, people learn what looks and sounds best to significant audiences and later shape their communications accordingly, shading their interpretations in ways that increase the odds of having a desired impact. During the flow of daily events, it is probably unusual for people to think that their actions are deceitful or even biased, despite the types of strategic shifts in communications that can be demonstrated under controlled conditions. Although people are often willing to point out how others' communications are biased in favor of those others' agendas, people prefer to see their own communications as objective and truthful; this, too, serves the actors' agenda to see self as discerning, fair, and unbiased.

Research on beneficial impression management opens the door to the investigation of factors that influence the strategic provision of social support. Prior research clearly demonstrates the importance of social support for the recipient's social and psychological well-being. However, past research has not examined social support as an interpersonal, goal-oriented strategy. Relatively little is known about why, when, and how people regulate information in order to support others. Research on helping behavior has provided insights into how and why people help someone in need, but has not examined the control of information as a type of help. The provision of social support, either directly to the target or indirectly through communications about the target to third parties, involves strategic, goal-directed behavior, in that alternative behavioral paths must be evaluated and selected for their perceived likelihood of leading to goal achievement. We suggest that the regulation of information designed to benefit others—by building their confidence, boosting their moods, and enhancing their identities—may be one of the more frequently encountered and appreciated types of help in everyday life.

NOTES

Barry R. Schlenker, Department of Psychology, University of Florida; and Thomas W. Britt, Department of Operational Stress Research, Division of Neuropsychiatry, Walter Reed Army Institute of Research, Washington, DC.

We thank Andrew Christopher and Margarethe Uglum for their helpful comments and assistance and Benjamin Karney for his insights into the relationship literature. The views expressed in this article do not necessarily reflect those of the Department of the Army or the Department of Defense.

Correspondence concerning this article should be addressed to Barry R. Schlenker, Department of Psychology, University of Florida, Gainesville, Florida 32611. Electronic mail may be sent to schlenkr@psych.ufl.edu.

REFERENCES

Aron, A., Aron, E. N., Tudor, M., & Nelson, G. (1991). Close relationships as including other in the self. *Journal of Personality and Social Psychology, 60*, 241–253.

Batson, C. D. (1995). Prosocial motivation: Why do we help others? In A. Tesser (Ed.), *Advanced social psychology* (pp. 333–381). New York: McGraw-Hill.

Baumeister, R. F. (1982). A self-presentational view of social phenomena. *Psychological Bulletin, 91*, 3–26.

Bradbury, T. N., & Fincham, F. D. (1990). Attributions in marriage: Review and critique. *Psychological Bulletin, 107*, 3–33.

Brown, J. D. (1997). *The self*. New York: McGraw-Hill.

Brown, J. D., Novick, N. J., Lord, K. A., & Richards, J. M. (1992). When Gulliver travels: Social context, psychological closeness, and self-appraisals. *Journal of Personality and Social Psychology, 62*, 717–727.

Buss, A. H., & Briggs, S. R. (1984). Drama and the self in social interaction. *Journal of Personality and Social Psychology, 47*, 1310–1324.

Churchill, J. J. (1916). *Small talks on big subjects*. London: Pearson.

Cialdini, R. B., Brown, S. L., Lewis, B. P., Luce, C., & Neuberg, S. L. (1997). Reinterpreting the empathy-altruism relationship: When one into one equals oneness. *Journal of Personality and Social Psychology, 73*, 481–494.

Cialdini, R. B., Finch, J. F., & De Nicholas, M. E. (1990). Strategic self-presentation: The indirect route. In M. J. Cody & M. L. McLaughlin (Eds.), *The psychology of tactical communication* (pp. 194–206). Bristol, PA: Multilingual Matters.

Clark, L. A., & Watson, D. (1991). General affective dispositions in physical and psychological health. In C. R. Snyder & D. R. Forsyth (Eds.), *Handbook of social and clinical psychology: The health perspective* (pp. 221–245). New York: Pergamon Press.

Clark, M. S. (1983). Reactions to aid in communal and exchange relationships. In J. D. Fisher, A. Nadler, & B. M. DePaulo (Eds.), *New directions in helping* (Vol. 1, pp. 281–304). San Diego: Academic Press.

Clark, M. S., & Mills, J. (1979). Interpersonal attraction in exchange and communal relationships. *Journal of Personality and Social Psychology, 37*, 12–24.

Clark, M. S., & Reis, H. T. (1988). Interpersonal processes in close relationships. *Annual Review of Psychology, 39*, 609–672.

Cohen, S., & Hoberman, H. (1983). Positive events and social supports as buffers of life change stress. *Journal of Applied Social Psychology, 13*, 99–125.

Cohen, S., & Wills, T. A. (1985). Stress, social support, and the buffering hypothesis. *Psychological Bulletin, 98*, 310–357.

Coyne, J. C., Burchill, S. A. L., & Stiles, W. B. (1991). An interactional perspective on depression. In C. R. Snyder & D. R. Forsyth (Eds.), *Handbook of social and clinical psychology: The health perspective* (pp. 327–349). New York: Pergamon Press.

Goffman, E. (1959). *The presentation of self in everyday life*. New York: Simon & Schuster.

Gottman, J. (with Silver, N.). (1994). *Why marriages succeed or fail*. New York: Simon & Schuster.

Hall, J. A., & Taylor, S. E. (1976). When love is blind: Maintaining idealized images of one's spouse. *Human Relations, 29*, 751–761.

Higgins, E. T. (1992). Achieving "shared reality" in the communication game: A social action that creates meaning. *Journal of Language and Social Psychology, 11*, 107–131.

Higgins, E. T. (1997). Beyond pleasure and pain. *American Psychologist, 52*, 1280–1300.

Jones, E. E., & Pittman, T. S. (1982). Toward a general theory of strategic self-presentation. In J. Suls (Eds.), *Psychological perspectives on the self* (Vol. 1, pp. 231–262). Hillsdale, NJ: Erlbaum.

Karney, B. R., Bradbury, T. N., Fincham, F. D., & Sullivan, K. T. (1994). The role of negative affectivity in the association between attributions and marital satisfaction. *Journal of Personality and Social Psychology, 66*, 413–424.

Krebs, D. (1970). Altruism—An examination of the concept and a review of the literature. *Psychological Bulletin, 73*, 258–302.

Kunda, Z. (1990). The case for motivated reasoning. *Psychological Bulletin, 108*, 480–498.

Leary, M. R. (1995). *Self-presentation: Impression management and interpersonal behavior*. Madison, WI: Brown & Benchmark.

Levinger, G. (1976). A social psychological perspective on marital dissolution. *Journal of Social Issues, 32*, 21–47.

Major, B., Testa, M., & Blysma, W. H. (1991). Response to upward and downward comparisons: The impact of esteem relevance and perceived control. In J. Suls & T. A. Wills (Eds.), *Social comparison: Contemporary theory and research* (pp. 237–260). Hillsdale, NJ: Erlbaum.

Markham, H. J. (1979). Application of a behavioral model of marriage in predicting relationship satisfaction of couples planning marriage. *Journal of Consulting and Clinical Psychology, 47*, 743–749.

Murray, S. L., Holmes, J. G., & Griffen, D. W. (1996). The benefits of positive illusions: Idealization and the construction of satisfaction in close relationships. *Journal of Personality and Social Psychology, 70*, 79–98.

Noller, P., & Fitzpatrick, M. A. (1990). Marital communication in the eighties. *Journal of Marriage and the Family, 52*, 832–843.

Rook, K. S. (1987). Social support versus companionship: Effects on life stress, loneliness, and evaluations by others. *Journal of Personality and Social Psychology, 52*, 1132–1147.

Rosenfeld, P., Giacalone, R. A., & Riordan, C. A. (1995). *Impression management in organizations*. New York: Routledge.

Rusbult, C. E., & Arriaga, X. B. (1997). Interdependence theory. In S. Duck (Ed.), *Handbook of personal relationships: Theory, research and intervention* (2nd ed., pp. 221–250). Chichester, England: Wiley.

Sarason, B. R., Sarason, I. G., & Pierce, G. R. (Eds.). (1990). *Social support: An interactional view*. New York: Wiley.

Schlenker, B. R. (1980). *Impression management: The self-concept, social identity, and interpersonal relations*. Monterey, CA: Brooks/Cole.

Schlenker, B. R. (1984). Identities, identifications, and relationships. In V. Derlega (Ed.), *Communication, intimacy, and close relationships* (pp. 71–104). New York: Academic Press.

Schlenker, B. R., Britt, T. W., & Pennington, J. W. (1996). Impression regulation and management: A theory of self-identification. In R. M. Sorrentino & E. T. Higgins (Eds.), *Handbook of motivation and cognition: The interpersonal context* (Vol. 3, pp. 118–147). New York: Guilford Press.

Schlenker, B. R., & Weigold, M. F. (1989). Goals and the self-identification process: Constructing desired identities. In L. Pervin (Ed.), *Goals concept in personality and social psychology* (pp. 243–290). Hillsdale, NJ: Erlbaum.

Schlenker, B. R., & Weigold, M. F. (1992). Interpersonal processes involving impression regulation and management. *Annual Review of Psychology, 43*, 133–168.

Sedikides, C., Campbell, W. K., Reeder, G. D., & Elliot, A. J. (1998). The self-serving bias in relational context. *Journal of Personality and Social Psychology, 74*, 378–386.

Taylor, S. E., & Koivumaki, J. H. (1976). The perception of self and others: Acquaintanceship, affect, and actor–observer differences. *Journal of Personality and Social Psychology, 33*, 403–408.

Tedeschi, J. T., & Norman, N. (1985). Social power, self-presentation, and the self. In B. R. Schlenker (Ed.), *The self and social life* (pp. 293–321). New York: McGraw-Hill.

Tesser, A. (1988). Toward a self-evaluation maintenance model of social behavior. In L. Berkowitz (Ed.), *Advances in experimental social psychology* (Vol. 21, pp. 181–227). New York: Academic Press.

Tetlock, P. E., & Manstead, A. R. S. (1985). Impression management versus intrapsychic explanations in social psychology: A useful dichotomy? *Psychological Review, 92*, 59–77.

Zanna, M. P., & Pack, S. J. (1975). On the self-fulfilling nature of apparent sex differences in behavior. *Journal of Experimental Social Psychology, 11*, 583–591.

READING 16

Transactive Memory in Close Relationships

Daniel M. Wegner • Harvard University
Ralph Erber • DePaul University
Paula Raymond • New York University

Memory performance of 118 individuals who had been in close dating relationships for at least 3 months was studied. For a memory task ostensibly to be performed by pairs, some Ss were paired with their partners and some were paired with an opposite-sex partner from another couple. For some pairs a memory structure was assigned (e.g., 1 partner should remember food items, another should remember history items, etc.), whereas for others no structure was mentioned. Pairs studied together without communication, and recall was tested in individuals. Memory performance of the natural pairs was better than that of impromptu pairs without assigned structure, whereas the performance of natural pairs was inferior to that of impromptu pairs when structure was assigned.

Knowledge is of two kinds: we know a subject ourselves, or we know where we can find information upon it.

— Samuel Johnson

People in close relationships know many things about each other's memories. One partner may not know where to find candles around the house, for instance, but may still be able to find them in a blackout by asking the other partner where the candles are. Each partner can enjoy the benefits of the pair's memory by assuming responsibility for remembering just those items that fall clearly to him or to her and then by attending to the categories of knowledge encoded by the partner so that items within those categories can be retrieved from the partner when they are needed. Such knowledge of one another's memory areas takes time and practice to develop, but the result is that close couples have an implicit structure for carrying out the pair's memory tasks. With this structure in place, couples in close relationships have a *transactive memory* that is greater than either of their individual memories.

Transactive memory is a shared system for encoding, storing, and retrieving information (Wegner, 1986; Wegner, Giuliano, & Hertel, 1985).

269

This research was designed to examine transactive memory by introducing new structures for memory organization in the couple. We expected that couples formed on an impromptu basis in the laboratory might gain in group memory performance as a result of an imposed organizational strategy, as such a plan would help them to focus their individual memory efforts to the pair's benefit. Because close couples already have an understood structure in place, however, we expected that an imposed organizational strategy might interfere with their implicit arrangement and thus undermine their memory performance.

Formation of Transactive Memory Structure

Our analysis begins with the observation that close relationships normally foster the development of shared memory schemes. Wegner et al. (1985) and Wegner (1986) viewed this development in terms of early theories of the group mind. By this account, individual memory systems can become involved in larger, organized social memory systems that have emergent group mind properties not traceable to the individuals. Dyads or groups of strangers do not start out with any sort of group mind, of course, as they have no shared system for knowledge storage and access. Without such a system, social memory performance among strangers is dependent primarily on the combination processes whereby individuals' retrievals are assembled into a group retrieval (see, e.g., Clark, Stephenson, & Rutter, 1986; Hartwick, Sheppard, & Davis, 1982; Hintz, 1990; Stasser, Taylor, & Hanna, 1989; Stephenson, Brandstatter, & Wagner, 1982). However, very different features of group memory become important if a system for both encoding and retrieval develops over time.

One way to understand such transactive memory systems is by analogy to memory sharing in computer systems. Some computers perform memory sharing very simply: They read from and write to the same electronic memory storage area. The luxury of a single memory bank that is shared in this way is not possible for humans, of course, as humans' brains are not connected. This means

that humans must share memory as do the computer systems that begin as separate computers and later develop memory-sharing capacities. When computers have physically separate memory systems, they can be programmed to share memory through the creation of a directory within each isolated memory system that contains an abbreviated record of the contents of other memory systems (Mason, 1987).

Physically isolated memory systems can be accessed reliably from the different computer processors linked to each system to the degree that each memory system contains an up-to-date record of the organization and general contents of the other systems. The analogy to humans is simple: If each person learns in some general way what the other person may know in detail, the two can share the detailed memories enjoyed by both. The development of a transactive memory in the pair, then, involves the communication and updating of information each has about the areas of the other's knowledge. In essence, each partner cultivates the other as an external memory aid (Engestrom, Brown, Engestrom, & Koistinen, 1990; Harris, 1978; Norman, 1988) and in so doing becomes part of a larger system.

Directories to others' knowledge are developed in a variety of ways. At the outset, simple information about the other's social categorization (sex, age, etc.) serves through stereotyping to inform a person of the other's likely areas of knowledge. One expects different areas of memory storage from a woman than from a man, for instance (Ross & Holmberg, 1988). These default settings allow a person to estimate the memory items available from even a stranger. The key to the formation of a more advanced transactive memory structure, however, is directory updating that moves beyond the defaults.

One way to move beyond defaults is through negotiated entries in the directory. That is, if one partner agrees to accept the responsibility for certain domains of knowledge, this partner will thereafter be known as the repository of relevant items. When one partner agrees to perform particular tasks (Atkinson & Huston, 1984) or to make particular decisions (Davis, 1976), this person will then be the pair's expert in that domain. The one who agrees to do the bills, for instance, will become the source and repository of financial data for the couple. Couples may negotiate systems for the allocation of memory that parallel the more formal systems often codified in working groups (e.g., Mullen, Copper, & Johnson, 1990).

A second general method of updating one's directory for a partner's knowledge is through perceptions of the relative expertise of self and partner in different knowledge domains. These perceptions can be expected to develop in the self-disclosure process that characterizes relationship formation (see, e.g., Archer, 1980). Self-disclosure involves the mutual revelation of traits, past activities, emotions, and preferences, many of which serve as plausible bases for inferences about relative expertise. Learning that one's partner likes the zoo, for instance, suggests that he or she might know about animals or nature in general. Relative expertise might also be judged, of course, from awareness of deficiencies in one's own stock of knowledge. In this case, the partner is judged as more expert because almost anyone might be judged as more expert than self in a particular area.

A third general source of directory updates comes from knowledge of the partner's access to information. Knowing that the partner accessed some information first (e.g., he or she got the initial call about a party this weekend), accessed it for a longer time (e.g., he or she talked at length with others about the party), or accessed it most recently (e.g., he or she just talked to the party host again) could all serve as bases for inferences about the partner's knowledge. In each case, one will assume that the partner knows more than self about this topic and so will defer to the partner in this area. A good example of these bases for inference about knowledge can be found in the pages of this or any scientific journal: The typical citations suggesting relevant knowledge to the reader come from the first researcher to discover something, from the researcher who has studied it longest, or from the one reporting on it most recently. Like scientific citations, signs of access to information can inform the person in a close

relationship of the partner's likelihood of holding knowledge in a variety of domains.

There are surely other sources of information people use in fashioning directories of one another's knowledge (e.g., Ickes, Stinson, Bissonnette, & Garcia, 1990). The key point for the present analysis is that the most complete and current directories are likely to be formed in relationships that are close. In particular, relationships in which partners are highly interdependent (cf. Kelley et al., 1983) are likely to have had many occasions for updating directory information and for using such information to solve the problems of successful coaction and interaction. Knowledge will commonly be stored and accessed in a transactive system rather than by some random scheme. Couples who are able to remember things transactively offer their constituent individuals storage for and access to a far wider array of information than they would otherwise command.

Structural Interference

The existence of an organized system for knowledge in the couple holds with it the potential for disorganization. This means that unlike a pair of strangers who have no transactive memory, close partners are open to special sorts of disruption. When one partner in a close couple always remembers directions on trips, for instance, it would be disruptive if the other suddenly began to store and access such information. Unless a clear transition of responsibility for travel directions could be negotiated and then successfully maintained, the stage would be set for frequent duplication of efforts and for lapses in which each partner mistakenly refrained from storing an item in the expectation that the other would hold it for the pair. Over time, of course, the new arrangement could be learned, but the interim confusion might leave the couple doing lots of unexpected sightseeing.

These complications resemble the difficulties that occur when a new knowledge organization system is imposed on an individual who has previously been using another system (see, e.g.,

Thorndyke & Hayes-Roth, 1979). There is commonly interference between organization systems so that retrieval of the previously organized information is undermined, and the encoding of new information is impaired. Interference resulting from the imposition of an organizational scheme can be used, in fact, as a measure of the degree to which information was previously organized in memory (e.g., Crouse, 1971). It was with this idea in mind that the present experiment was designed.

We gave couples a memory task that would prompt the use of their transactive system. Individuals working in pairs either with their partner or with someone else were exposed to items from various categories of knowledge. Some of these pairs were instructed to share the memory task by means of an explicit assignment of categories, whereas others were not given this structure. In all cases, however, pairs working together were led to expect that they would retrieve the items together and be scored for recall as a pair. We expected that explicit assignment of categories to individuals during encoding might help unacquainted pairs, but that it would inhibit the memory performance of close couples. The close couple would follow the new assignment plan only on occasion during encoding, with each partner at times reverting to his or her version of the couple's implicit organization. Such haphazard dissent from the new plan would yield only haphazard adherence to the old plan as well and so would produce a general deficit in retrieval, measurable as a setback both for the individual and for the couple.

Method

Overview and Design

Subjects in ongoing dating relationships were asked to memorize items from seven everyday categories either with their partner or with a stranger. These *natural* or *impromptu* pairs were asked to remember items as a pair under one of two conditions. For some, an arbitrary *assignment of expertise* was made such that one partner was given responsibility for remembering items from some of the categories and the other partner was given responsibility for remembering items from

the remaining categories. For other pairs, *no assignment of expertise* was made. After pairs were exposed to items (words or phrases embedded in sentences that made their category membership clear), they performed a filler task and then were separated to complete a measure of individual recall.

Subjects

Subjects were 59 heterosexual dating couples who had been seeing each other exclusively for at least 3 months. They were recruited through posters on the campus of Trinity University in San Antonio, Texas, for an experiment on memory in close relationships. Each couple received $7 for participation. Couples participated two at a time whenever possible. Either before or after the key task of the experiment, the dyadic memory task, subjects were separated for privacy and filled out individual questionnaires about their relationships. This before/after variation allowed the assessment of any effects of prior questionnaire administration on memory task performance.

The responses indicated that, on average, subjects had known their partners for 28.7 months and had been close for 19.6 months. They saw each other for an average of 6.53 days a week; they reported spending 5.68 hours together on weekdays and 11.08 hours together on weekend days. Some 52.5% of subjects expected their relationship to last forever, 31.4% thought it would last for some time, and 16.1% expected it to end soon. On a 1- to 9-point scale, subjects rated themselves as highly satisfied with their relationship ($M = 8.12$) and reported that the relationship fulfilled their expectations ($M = 7.93$). Also, when asked to rate their group memory ability on a 1- to 9-point scale, subjects reported that they generally remembered well as a couple ($M = 6.92$).

We were concerned about whether typical college dating relationships would promote enough different shared activities so that a transactive memory structure would have a good chance to develop. Thus, we asked subjects to check a list of 90 activities in which couples can engage (Giuliano, 1983). The responses indicated a wide range of shared activity. According to at least one member of each couple, for example, 97% had watched television together, 95% had gone shopping together, 96% had slept in the same bed together, 89% had eaten together regularly, 66% had done laundry together, 84% had cooked meals together, 72% had gone on vacation together, 80% had had sex together, and 97% had met the other's family. Still, only 19% of the sample couples were engaged to be married and only 21% were living together, so these couples were still in the formative stages of their relationships.

Procedure

In addition to being asked questions about their relationship, subjects were asked individually about their relative expertise in a number of categories of knowledge. As in the case of the relationship questionnaires, these questionnaires were completed either before or after the memory task. Subjects who remained together as natural couples for the memory task filled out a Knowledge Organization Questionnaire, in which each partner was asked to make forced choices as to whether self or partner was more expert in the areas of science, food, spelling, alcohol, history, television, and psychology. Subjects who were paired with a stranger filled out a similar Knowledge Estimation Questionnaire, in which they were asked to indicate their areas of expertise relative to a typical other of the opposite sex.

For the dyadic memory task, subjects were randomly assigned either to remain with their partner (natural couple condition) or to be paired with a person of the opposite sex from another couple (impromptu couple condition). The resulting pairs were then randomly selected to encode the items either with assigned expertise for categories of items or with no assignment instructions. Assignment of expertise was determined for each pair by random selection of a previous subject's pattern of expertise judgments from the Knowledge Organization Questionnaire or Knowledge Estimation Questionnaire. These patterns typically assigned three categories to one partner and four to another; some, however, assigned categories at a 2:5 ratio, and a very few did so at a 1:6 ratio. We yoked our imposed assignments to the actual assignments from natural couples on the assumption that any standardized assignment patterns we might invent could depart from natural assignments in ways that could cloud the interpretation of the effects of assignment per se.

The instruction to assign expertise was as follows:

> Now just for today, let's assume that you (one participant) are the expert in _____ (categories of items), and that you (the other participant) are the expert in _____ (the remaining categories of items). Please try to remember the items for which you are the expert.

Cards labeling the categories were placed in front of the pair on a table for both to see, with each person's assigned categories nearer to that person.

The memory stimuli consisted of 64 different sentences typed 4 at a time on index cards. Each sentence offered a context for an underlined word or phrase, such that the category membership of the underlined item was made clear. So, for example, the category of alcohol was represented by items such as "Midori is a Japanese melon liqueur," the category of television was represented by items such as "Luke and Laura got married on 'General Hospital,'" and the category of science was represented by items such as "Yeasts reproduce by budding." Each category was represented by 9 or 10 items in the set. All pairs were told

> I'd like you to try to remember the underlined items on these cards together, as a pair. Later you will be tested together. At a prerecorded tone, turn over the top card on the stack in front of you and study it. Every 30 seconds when you hear the tone, turn over the next card until you're through with the entire stack. Please don't discuss this as you do it.

When the study session was complete, each pair was asked to step over to a table containing a jigsaw puzzle. They were asked to try to see how many pieces they could put together in 5 min. After this filler task, subjects were separated and asked to write down all the underlined items that they could remember from the index cards. Following the experiment, subjects were debriefed in detail, thanked, and given chocolate kisses.

Results

Natural couples were in substantial agreement on which partner in the pair was more expert for each of the seven categories of memory items. Those natural couples completing the Knowledge Organization Questionnaire agreed in their assessments of relative expertise on a mean of 5.52 of the 7 possible categories. This value was significantly greater than the comparison mean of 4.04 agreements found between impromptu couples whose responses to the Knowledge Estimation Questionnaire were examined for agreement, $t(57) = 4.60, p < .001$.

The natural couples thus seemed to have in place a shared assessment of who would be more inclined to know about each of several topics in the pair, even through these topics were an arbitrarily selected sample of everyday and academic knowledge areas. (Agreement might have been even stronger if areas had been selected to reflect the natural array of topics for which transactive memory is commonly used.) At any rate, natural couples' level of agreement was greater than the one that impromptu couples derived from minimal information—only the general knowledge of what comparative expertise might exist in self and an unknown opposite-sex partner. It is worth noting, however, that even impromptu opposite-sex couples did have a slight edge over chance in their judgments of relative expertise in the pair. The agreement observed for impromptu opposite-sex pairs ($M = 4.04$) was significantly greater than the chance agreement rate of 3.5 of seven possible categories, $t(29) = 2.32, p < .05$.

Couple Recall

As a first step in the analysis of couples' memory performance, we examined the total number of items correctly recalled by each couple (i.e., recalled by either partner). In this and subsequent analyses, order of administration of the questionnaires (before or after the memory session) was included in a preliminary analysis and did not account for any significant effects. A 2 (natural vs. impromptu couple) × 2 (assigned expertise vs. no assignment) analysis of variance (ANOVA)

revealed a significant interaction effect, $F(1, 55) = 10.00, p < .003$, and no significant main effects (see Figure 16.1).

A follow-up analysis consisted of a set of planned comparisons testing differences between specific means; the directions of comparisons were predicted, so one-tailed tests were used. The first comparison involved the recall of natural couples versus impromptu couples without memory assignment. As predicted, in the absence of assignment, natural couples remembered more items ($M = 31.40$) than impromptu couples ($M = 27.64$), $t(55) = 1.69, p < .05$. Although this result is not particularly robust, it does attest to the advantage of natural couples over impromptu couples in a group memory task and so indicates the possible operation of a transactive memory structure in the natural couples.

The advantage of natural couples over impromptu couples was entirely reversed, however, when couples were provided with an explicit memory assignment. Natural couples with assignments remembered fewer items ($M = 23.75$) than did impromptu couples with assignments ($M = 30.14$), $t(55) = 2.90, p < .005$. The interference with natural couples' memory that was introduced by the assignment was also evident in a comparison with natural couples working without assignment. Natural couples with assignment recalled

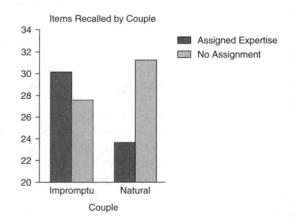

FIGURE 16.1 ■ Couple recall as a function of couple type (natural vs. impromptu) and assignment (assigned expertise vs. no assignment).

fewer items ($M = 23.75$) than did natural couples without assignment ($M = 31.40$), $t(55) = 3.54$, $p < .001$. Finally, it is worth noting that impromptu couples did not benefit significantly from the assignment of expertise in this research. Although they recalled more items when provided with assignment ($M = 30.78$) than they did without assignment ($M = 25.43$), the difference was nonsignificant, $t(55) = 1.19$.

To investigate the degree to which couples' memory performance might reflect overlapping rather than independent efforts of the partners, we divided each couple's memory performance into two scores: overlapping performance (number of items both members recalled) and nonoverlapping performance (number of items one member but not both members recalled). This overlap versus nonoverlap variable was then included as a repeated measure in an ANOVA corresponding to the study design. The analysis indicated a significant main effect: Overlapping memory performance for couples ($M = 5.28$) was far less than nonoverlapping performance ($M = 22.88$), $F(1, 55) = 710.48$, $p < .0001$. In general, then, individuals within pairs tended to recall somewhat independent portions of the list of items.

The significant interaction of couple type and assignment was again observed in this analysis, $F(1, 55) = 10.00$, $p < .003$, and no other effects approached significance. The patterns for overlapping and nonoverlapping recall thus followed the pattern for total couple recall quite faithfully. It appears that the assignment variable may not have its effect on couple recall, then, by influencing the way in which individual patterns combine into a group pattern. One way for assignment to influence memory in natural couples, after all, might be to increase the overlap between partners. Their transactive structure could commonly lead them to attend to different areas, and assignment might be disruptive of such differentiation. However, the observations for overlapping and nonoverlapping recall suggest that assignment did not interfere with natural couples' memory in this way. Rather than increasing overlap, assignment significantly undermined the degree to which both overlapping and nonoverlapping memories were constructed.

These findings suggest that assigned expertise may influence the overall memory performance of a couple by affecting individual memory performance. Instead of influencing the way in which individual memories combine, assignment may make certain individual memory strategies more or less operative and so influence group performance secondarily. This was examined through the analysis of individual recall.

Individual Recall

For the analysis of individual recall, an ANOVA was performed on individual recall scores within couples, treating sex of partner as a repeated measure. The results of this analysis paralleled the results of the analysis of couple recall. A significant interaction of assignment and couple type occurred, $F(1, 55) = 10.92$, $p < .002$, and no other effects were significant. Planned comparisons indicated that mean recall for individuals in natural couples who were not assigned expertise ($M = 18.90$) was significantly greater than recall for individuals in impromptu couples without assignment ($M = 16.31$), $t(55) = 1.69$, $p < .05$. Thus, it was advantageous for individuals' memory performance if they were paired with their natural partner.

Once again, however, this pattern was reversed when expertise was assigned. Individuals in natural couples who were assigned expertise remembered fewer items ($M = 13.66$) than did those in impromptu couples who were assigned expertise ($M = 18.21$), $t(55) = 2.14$, $p < .025$. Individuals in natural couples remembered fewer items when they were assigned expertise ($M = 13.66$) than when they were not given an assignment ($M = 18.90$), $t(55) = 3.15$, $p < .005$. On the other hand, individuals in impromptu couples did not benefit significantly from the assignment of expertise. Although they remembered more items when assigned expertise ($M = 18.21$) than without assignment of expertise ($M = 16.31$), the difference was nonsignificant ($t < 1$).

An auxiliary analysis of individual recall was conducted to establish whether the observed effects were memory effects or the effects of motivated confabulation. If the effects stemmed from simple motivation to respond (right or wrong), a pattern of incorrect responses mirroring the observed pattern would be expected. To check on this, we conducted a parallel ANOVA on the number of incorrect responses in the recalled items. Overall, the intrusion rate was low ($M = 1.45$), and this rate did not differ significantly among conditions (all $Fs < 1$). Thus, the individual recall findings do not seem attributable to variation in motivation to report answers for the recall test.

We also examined the impact of relationship duration on memory performance. Reports of the number of months the natural couples had been close were added as a continuous independent variable in the overall ANOVA, and no significant main effect or interaction for this variable was observed. Individuals from couples who had been together longer performed no differently on the memory task than did individuals who had been together a shorter time.

Individual Recall by Reported and Assigned Expertise

The analyses of individual recall suggest that the conflict between transactive memory structure and imposed memory assignments may indeed operate at the level of individual memory. Assignment of memory tasks appears to interfere with individual performance in the context of the natural couple working together. A more fine-grained analysis was undertaken, therefore, to examine the possibility that some clues to the operation of transactive memory might be found in the specific items recalled by individuals.

For this purpose, items were sorted into four groups for each individual in the assigned expertise condition. First, items were sorted according to whether they had been assigned (by category) to that subject for recall. Second, items were sorted by reported expertise; for each individual, the items were divided into those from the categories chosen in the Knowledge Organization Questionnaire or Knowledge Estimation Questionnaire as more likely to fall in areas of own expertise versus those from categories more likely to fall in areas of the other's expertise.

Our intent was to survey the protocols of individuals in the natural and impromptu conditions for any differential recall among the four item sets constructed by the crossing of assigned and reported expertise. The study was not designed, of course, with the systematic distribution of items to these sets in mind. Thus, the random combination of individual differences in reported expertise and experimental variations in assigned expertise necessarily resulted in several individuals for whom no items existed in one or more of these sets. With complete data contributed by only 21 couples from the assigned expertise condition, the proportion of items recalled within sets was examined in an ANOVA with couple type (natural vs. impromptu) and questionnaire order (before vs. after memory task) as between-subjects variables and partner sex (male vs. female), reported expertise on item set (self vs. other), and assigned expertise on item set (self vs. other) as within-subjects variables.

We anticipated that the implicit assignment structures of natural couples were leading them to respond poorly to our experimental assignments, and a marginally reliable interaction was observed in the analysis that reflected precisely these variables. Couple type, assigned expertise, and reported expertise tended to interact, $F(1, 17) = 2.61, p < .16$, and tests of simple main effects between natural and impromptu couples indicated that this interaction took an interesting form. Among the four item sets created by the crossing of reported and assigned expertise, individuals in natural couples showed a significant inferiority to those in impromptu couples on only one: items assigned to self that were also reported to be within the self's area of expertise. Individuals in natural couples recalled a significantly smaller proportion of these ($M = 0.17$) than did individuals in impromptu couples ($M = 0.28$), $F(1, 17) = 4.86, p < .05$. Recall for items in the other sets (i.e., those reported to be in self's expertise that were assigned to other, those reported to be in other's expertise that were assigned to self, and those reported to be in other's expertise that were assigned to other) showed no parallel difference between natural and impromptu couples. Although there was a slight deficit for natural couples in all item sets, this difference was not significant (all simple effect $Fs < 1$).

These results indicate, albeit in a preliminary way, that individuals in natural couples were particularly inclined to forget items that they felt were in their own area of expertise when those items were assigned to them by the experimenter. In essence, when their implicit memory assignment was made explicit, their fulfillment of the assignment deteriorated markedly. It is as though individuals in close relationships who normally and naturally step forward to perform their memory function for the couple suddenly decline to do so when their function is pointed out and explicitly required.

Discussion

Close couples attempting to remember information together were handicapped in this effort when they were given an organizational scheme for sharing the memory task. The imposition of the scheme did not handicap the performance of pairs of strangers in the same way. Under the conditions imposed by this experiment, then, it is oddly detrimental to be a member of a close relationship. It actually hurts task performance to get a new plan for sharing the memory task. In settings outside this study, however, the impairment observed here implies that close couples have their own transactive memory schemes in place that may be widely beneficial to the individuals and to the dyad in everyday life. Indeed, when assignments were not imposed on natural couples, their memory performance exceeded that of pairs of strangers given the same task.

These results provide several clues as to how the assignment of expertise hampered close couples' memory ability. It seems, first, to be an individual phenomenon. The analyses of overlapping recall and nonoverlapping recall, as well as the general parallelism found between couple recall and individual recall, combine to suggest that the impact of assigned expertise occurred primarily at the level of the individual. No greater or lesser overlap in memory coverage was observed when natural couples were given assignments, so their group memory did not depart from an average of their individual memories.

In searching for the locus of the effect of assignment on natural couples' memory, it also seems reasonable to rule out couple closeness as a factor. The length of the relationship did not moderate the observed effect of assignment. It may be that some minimal level of transactive memory—at least for the domains of memory items used in this study—is achieved rather rapidly in a relationship, and that within the limited range of closeness available in this sample, strong influences of closeness would not be observed. It is of interest, of course, just how fast and over what course a transactive memory develops, and for this reason, inclusion of a wider range of close and distant relationships is an agenda for further research.

Our results also appear to rule out any simple motivational interpretation of the effect of assignment on natural couples' memory. Although it seems reasonable to suggest that assignment might be somehow more disruptive, exciting, or distracting for natural couples than for impromptu couples, a parallel measure of puzzle performance was included in the analyses to test for such broad motivational effects. Puzzle performance did not differ among experimental conditions, and its inclusion as a covariate in the analysis of memory performance did not alter the experimental conclusions.

Our strongest clues with regard to how assignment disturbed natural couples' memory come from the analysis of individual recall for the various classes of items. It was found that individuals in natural couples failed to recall the items from their own reported area of normal expertise in the couple when they were assigned those items to recall. So, for instance, a female subject who reported knowing more than her partner about psychology later failed to recall psychology items, particularly when such items had been assigned to her. So, it seems that the effect of assignment may have had to do with forgetting one's normal role in the natural couple. This conclusion must be viewed as preliminary, however, as the present experiment was not designed to emphasize the measurement of these processes, and the effect was not predicted in advance.

Our account of the influence of imposed assignment on memory in natural couples at this time, then, is as follows: Individuals in a close couple responded to the conflict between their implicit assignment plan and our imposed assignment plan only on occasion during encoding. When they encountered items that their implicit assignment usually allocated to their partner, they paid no special attention to our explicit plan—memorizing items explicitly assigned to self no more often than those explicitly assigned to their partner. The imposed assignment made them no more inclined to remember anything they were assigned and instead prompted a specific flaw in their pattern of recall. Items normally assumed to fall within the individual's own domain were given less than the usual attention when they were explicitly assigned. This strategy yielded a general deficit in retrieval both for the individual and for the couple.

Why would the explicit assignment of one's own areas of expertise to self impair memory for the natural couple? Several possibilities might explain this effect, each of which suggests avenues for further inquiry. It may be, for instance, that the explicit assignment of tasks that were once implicit introduces new uncertainty about task assignment or perhaps instills over-confidence that leads to a tendency to ignore the task at hand. Alternatively, it may be that making this implicit task explicit has the effect of cognitively disrupting the flow of an otherwise fluid performance (cf. Vallacher, Wegner, & Somoza, 1989). Like the tennis stroke that falters when it is analyzed, the transactive memory performance of the partner in a close relationship suffers when the partner is explicitly reminded of it. It makes sense, in short, that assignment affects individuals by making them fail to do their normal part in the task, but just how this failure occurs is a matter of interest.

One other result of this study should be discussed. In this experiment, although assigned expertise had some slight influence on the memory performance of impromptu pairs, it did not lead to a significant improvement. If imposed assignment was not effective here, how is it effective when it occurs implicitly in a transactive memory structure?

We suspect that imposed assignments may take some time and practice to get right, not just in close couples, but in impromptu couples as well. Even impromptu couples had access to a rudimentary transactive memory in this study—one based on the perception of sex role stereotypes as well as their partner's physical appearance. Their performance may have slightly faltered because they experienced a bit of the interference from assignment that was felt more profoundly by close couples. For assignment to improve the memory performance of any couple, it would appear to require some study and practice. These were not provided in the experiment, and the trifling advantage introduced by assignment to impromptu couples seems understandable as a result.

As a final comment on these findings, we can consider how they may illustrate memory processes that occur at transitions in relationships. Although memory reassignments may happen frequently—and apparently with ill effects—in an ongoing relationship, perhaps the most jarring reassignment of expertise of all occurs when a relationship ends. Suddenly, the individual becomes the de facto expert on a multiplicity of topics that were previously in the partner's domain. Beyond the sheer loss of all that the partner knew, there will now be further difficulties that emerge from the disruption of the transactive system. New information about items in the partner's areas is likely to be handled very poorly at first and perhaps for a while. Items in one's own areas of expertise may also be missed in the confusion. And even if a new partner is found and life as a member of a couple is resumed, the new transactive memory will not only be in its infancy compared with the old one, it may frequently and unfortunately afford new assignments that conflict with earlier habits. Ultimately, it may take time and effort for the new couple to know even a small part of what the old couple took for granted.

NOTES

We thank Julie Aniol for assisting in the conduct of the research and Toni Wegner for helpful comments on an earlier draft.

Correspondence concerning this article should be addressed to Daniel M. Wegner, Department of Psychology, Harvard University, Cambridge, Massachusetts 02138. Electronic mail may be sent to wegner@wjh.harvard.edu.

REFERENCES

Archer, R. L. (1980). Self-disclosure. In D. M. Wegner & R. R. Vallacher (Eds.), *The self in social psychology* (pp. 183–205). New York: Oxford University Press.

Atkinson, J., & Huston, T. (1984). Sex role orientation and division of labor early in marriage. *Journal of Personality and Social Psychology 46*, 330–345.

Clark, N. K., Stephenson, G. M., & Rutter, D. R. (1986). Memory for complex social discourse: The analysis and prediction of individual and group recall. *Journal of Memory and Language, 25*, 295–313.

Crouse, J. (1971). Retroactive interference in reading prose materials. *Journal of Educational Psychology, 62*, 39–44.

Davis, H. L. (1976). Decision making within the household. *Journal of Consumer Research, 2*, 241–260.

Engestrom, Y., Brown, K., Engestrom, R., & Koistinen, K. (1990). Organizational forgetting: An activity-theoretical perspective. In D. Middleton & D. Edwards (Eds.), *Collective remembering* (pp. 137–168). Newbury Park, CA: Sage.

Giuliano, T. (1983). *Group and individual identities in intimate relations*. Unpublished doctoral dissertation, University of Texas at Austin.

Harris, J. E. (1978). External memory aids. In M. M. Gruneberg, P. E. Morris, & R. N. Sykes (Eds.), *Practical aspects of memory* (pp. 172–180). San Diego, CA: Academic Press.

Hartwick, J., Sheppard, B. H., & Davis, J. H. (1982). Group remembering: Research and implications. In R. A. Guzzo (Ed.), *Improving group decision making in organizations* (pp. 41–72). San Diego, CA: Academic Press.

Hintz, V. B. (1990). Cognitive and consensus processes in group recognition memory performance. *Journal of Personality and Social Psychology, 59*, 707–718.

Ickes, W., Stinson, L., Bissonnette, V., & Garcia, S. (1990). Naturalistic social cognition: Empathic accuracy in mixed-sex dyads. *Journal of Personality and Social Psychology, 59*, 730–742.

Kelley, H. H., Berscheid, E., Christensen, A., Harvey, J. H., Houston, T., Levinger, G., McClintock, E., Peplau, L. A., & Peterson, D. R. (Eds.). (1983). *Close relationships*. New York: Freeman.

Mason, W. A. (1987, November). Distributed processing: The state of the art. *Byte*, pp. 291–297.

Mullen, B., Copper, C., & Johnson, C. (1990, July). *Memory structures in working groups*. Paper presented at the meeting of the International Society for the Study of Personal Relationships, Oxford, England.

Norman, D. A. (1988). *The psychology of everyday things*. New York: Basic Books.

Ross, M., & Holmberg, D. (1988). Recounting the past: Gender differences in the recall of events in the history of a close relationship. In J. M. Olson & M. P. Zanna (Eds.), *Self-inference processes: The Ontario Symposium* (Vol. 6, pp. 135–152). Hillsdale, NJ: Erlbaum.

Stasser, G., Taylor, L. A., & Hanna, C. (1989). Information sampling in structured and unstructured discussions of three- and six-person groups. *Journal of Personality and Social Psychology, 57*, 67–78.

Stephenson, G. M., Brandstatter, H., & Wagner, W. (1982). An experimental study of social performance and delay on the testimonial validity of story telling. *European Journal of Social Psychology, 13*, 175–191.

Thorndyke, P. W., & Hayes-Roth, B. (1979). The use of schemata in the acquisition and transfer of knowledge. *Cognitive Psychology, 11*, 82–106.

Vallacher, R. R., Wegner, D. M., & Somoza, M. (1989). That's easy for you to say: Action identification and speech fluency. *Journal of Personality and Social Psychology, 56*, 199–208.

Wegner, D. M. (1986). Transactive memory: A contemporary analysis of the group mind. In B. Mullen & G. R. Goethals (Eds.), *Theories of group behavior* (pp. 185–208). New York: Springer-Verlag.

Wegner, D. M., Giuliano, T., & Hertel, P. (1985). Cognitive interdependence in close relationships. In W. J. Ickes (Ed.), *Compatible and incompatible relationships* (pp. 253–276). New York: Springer-Verlag.

Maintaining Relationships

Virtue consists, not in abstaining from vice, but in not desiring it.

— George Bernard Shaw

And in the end, the love you get is equal to the love you give.

— The Beatles

Things happen to you when you're single. You meet new men, you travel alone, you learn new tricks, you read Trollope, you try sushi, you buy nightgowns, you shave your legs. Then you get married, and the hair grows in.

— Nora Ephron

For many years, relationship research concentrated almost exclusively on beginnings—initial attraction and the development of acquaintance—and endings—divorce and other breakups. Surprisingly little attention was devoted to what happens in between, perhaps because it was assumed that nothing much of substantive interest was occurring during those "steady as she goes," in-between periods. We now know that this assumption was misguided: Relationship maintenance—the mechanisms by which partners conserve, protect, and enhance the health of their important relationships, once those relationships have achieved some degree of closeness—is both psychologically interesting and essential to the longevity of a relationship. That the topic of relationship maintenance warrants scrutiny in its own right is underscored by the high rates of divorce and marital dissatisfaction in most Western nations. (We hasten to add that the findings of relationship maintenance research are believed to apply across most types of close relationships and in most cultures, although they have been investigated predominantly in romantic relationships in North America.) At the same time, many close relationships, marital and otherwise, endure and thrive over long periods of time. What processes contribute to their stability and longevity?

As researchers began to look closely at relationship maintenance processes—a trend that took hold in the 1990s—it became apparent that the factors that predict the success of long-term relationships differ from those that attract us to these relationships in the first place. That is, whereas initial attraction tends to be oriented toward assessing the qualities of a new acquaintance and the possibilities afforded by a close relationship with him or her, as shown by the articles reprinted in earlier sections of this volume, maintenance is more directly oriented toward managing the realities of interdependence in daily life, as well as with promoting continued pleasurable interaction and growth. A further complexity is added when we recognize that in ongoing relationships, the individuals themselves develop and change over time and across varying life circumstances. Partners must find ways of adapting to these changes in each other.

The catalog of relationship maintenance strategies is extensive. Some maintenance activities involve joint planning for the future, based on the assumption that a given relationship will persist into the future; others pertain to behaviors that make social interaction rewarding. Thus, under the broad topic of relationship maintenance, researchers have studied such diverse phenomena as politeness, social support, shared recreation, communication patterns, the distribution of household activities, openness, expressions of affection, and engaging as a couple with wider social networks (i.e., friends and family). For this section, we have bypassed research that addresses specific behaviors, and instead selected three articles that examine general processes that facilitate relationship maintenance. In other words, the processes described in these papers are thought to underlie any and all of the myriad specific behaviors that individuals may enact in order to enhance the well-being and continuity of their ongoing relationships.

One important process is commitment, which Rusbult and her colleagues describe as a "sense of allegiance" and an expectation of continuity that fosters a variety of "prorelationship" processes—that is, behavioral and cognitive mechanisms that support and sustain the well-being and stability of a relationship. These mechanisms are particularly important when Dave's and Anna's goals, needs, and preferences do not coincide. Under such circumstances, what is optimal for Dave clashes with what is optimal for Anna or their relationship, requiring some sort of resolution. To the extent that Dave is committed to Anna, he is more likely to choose resolutions that in the long run are good for their relationship. These include behavioral strategies such as the willingness to sacrifice, along with cognitive strategies such as thinking about the relationship in "we" terms. Rusbult et al.'s model of relationship maintenance is theoretically rich, identifying the functional roots of these processes and providing a framework in which numerous other specific strategies might be proposed (for examples, see the reprinted articles in Sections 5, 7, and 8).

One mechanism Rusbult and her colleagues discuss is "positive illusion," a concept that Murray, Holmes, and Griffin explore in greater detail. "Positive illusion" describes Dave's tendency to perceive Anna in an especially positive light—even more positively than she perceives herself—emphasizing her virtues while downplaying her faults. (Other research by these authors has shown that such positively toned partner perceptions are also more positive than the perceptions of mutual friends, thereby demonstrating the depth of partners' "myth-making" regarding each other.) Murray and her colleagues argue that idealization on the part of Dave and Anna is beneficial for their relationship because it provides a buffer that psychologically "protects" them from the conflicts and threats to security that are inevitable in a close relationship, simultaneously fostering their feelings of satisfaction, commitment, and love. (A brief word of caution: This paper includes complex statistics. We suggest that readers unfamiliar with these methods skip some of the more difficult data analytic details and focus instead on the figures and conceptual argument.)

The final paper in this section, by Simpson, Gangestad, and Lerma, provides evidence for a phenomenon known as "derogation of alternatives." The availability of alternative partners is an ever-present potential threat to ongoing romantic relationships, especially in a college environment. By cognitively diminishing the attractiveness of tempting alternatives, it becomes easier for Anna to maintain—and to feel comfortable in—her committed relationship with Dave. This process is a good example of what social psychologists call "motivated social cognition"—cognition that helps Anna fulfill important psychological goals and needs, in this instance, the need to sustain her conviction that Dave is a more desirable partner than any alternative partner would be. Simpson and his colleagues report two clever experiments that illustrate the operation of this process, while simultaneously ruling out key alternative explanations for the phenomenon.

Suggestions for Further Reading

Canary, D. J., & Stafford, L. (Eds.). (1994). *Communication and relational maintenance.* New York: Academic Press. A useful overview of many different strategies for relationship maintenance, with an emphasis on communication.

Harvey, J. H., & Omarzu, J. (1997). Minding the close relationship. *Personality and Social Psychology Review, 1,* 224–240. Their concept of "minding the relationship" suggests a particularly helpful strategy for engaging in relationship maintenance.

Harvey, J. H., & Wenzel, A. E. (Eds.). (2001). *Close romantic relationships: Mainte-nance and enhancement.* Mahwah, NJ: Erlbaum. An excellent and timely collection of chapters by leading researchers in the field, in which they discuss implications of their work for relationship maintenance.

Holmes, J. G., & Rempel, J. K. (1989). Trust in close relationships. In C. Hendrick (Ed.), *Review of personality and social psychology, Vol. 10: Close relationships* (pp. 187–220). London: Sage. Trust is an important component of relationship maintenance, and this paper nicely illustrates how an interdependence perspective can be informative.

Murray, S. L. (1999). The quest for conviction: Motivated cognition in romantic relationships. *Psychological Inquiry, 10*, 23–34. A more extensive conceptual analysis of positive illusion, with additional empirical examples, followed by the commentaries of other scholars.

Noller, P., & Feeney, A. (Eds.). (2002). *Understanding marriage.* New York: Cambridge University Press. Relationship maintenance from the perspective of marriage.

Salovey, P. (Ed.). (1991). *The psychology of jealousy and envy.* New York: Guilford. When jealousy and envy are unwarranted by objective circumstances, these emotions can be regarded as failures in relationship maintenance. This collection of essays discusses contemporary theory and research on these important emotions.

Sedikides, C., Campbell, W. K., Reeder, G. D., & Elliot, A. J. (1998). The self-serving bias in relational context. *Journal of Personality and Social Psychology, 74*, 378–386. This research demonstrates that self-serving bias—that is, the inclination to accept responsibility for successes and deny responsibility for failures—is considerably stronger in interactions with strangers than in interactions with close partners.

Swann, W. B., Jr., DeLaRonde, C., & Hixon, J. G. (1994). Authenticity and positivity strivings in marriage and courtship. *Journal of Personality and Social Psychology, 66*, 857–869. These authors predict, and find, that in dating relationships we prefer partners who enhance us (perceive us in an exceedingly positive light), whereas in marital relationships we prefer partners who verify us (perceive us as we really are).

Wieselquist, J., Rusbult, C. E., Foster, C. A., & Agnew, C. R. (1999). Commitment, pro-relationship behavior, and trust in close relationships. *Journal of Personality and Social Psychology, 77*, 942–966. This paper presents a model of "mutual cyclical growth," whereby trust in a partner serves as a monitor of the strength of the partner's commitment and pro-relationship orientation.

Discussion Questions

1. Describe the operation of one of the behavioral or cognitive maintenance strategies discussed by Rusbult and her colleagues. Discuss an instance from your personal experience in which you or a partner exhibited this strategy.

2. Propose an additional behavioral or cognitive maintenance mechanism not discussed by Rusbult and her colleagues. Explain how and why this mechanism might promote couple well-being.

3. Explain the concept of "positive illusion," suggesting how it might foster long-term satisfaction and stability in close romantic relationships.

4. Discuss an example of "positive illusion" from a relationship other than a romantic relationship (e.g., best friends, parents-and-children, teammates). Do the mechanisms proposed by Murray, Holmes, and Griffin still apply? If so, explain how.

5. Explain how "derogation of alternatives" by one partner in a relationship may contribute to *both* partners' feelings of security in the relationship.

6. Following the logic suggested by Simpson, Gangestad, and Lerma, what might the same principles predict about the social cognition of an individual who is thinking about ending a relationship?

7. Cognitive maintenance activities such as positive illusion and derogation of alternatives are described as "motivated phenomena," in that they help people cope with psychological threats and reduce feelings of insecurity. What sorts of experiences might stimulate the psychological need for motivated cognition?

8. The phrase "maintenance strategy" seems to imply that maintenance activities are conscious and deliberate. Can you think of instances in which such activities might be relatively unconscious and automatic? What might account for such unconscious and automatic tendencies?

Commitment and Relationship Maintenance Mechanisms

Caryl E. Rusbult, Nils Olsen, Jody L. Davis and
Peggy A. Hannon • University of North Carolina at Chapel Hill

Sometimes involvement with a close partner is simple. When partners' goals correspond and their preferences are compatible, partners can readily achieve desirable outcomes such as security, companionship, and sexual fulfillment. When circumstances of interdependence are congenial, it is relatively easy for partners to gratify one another's most important needs. The real test of a relationship arises when circumstances are not so congenial—when partners encounter dilemmas involving conflicted interaction, incompatible preferences, extrarelationship temptation, or experience of betrayal. In dilemmas of this sort, the well-being of each person is incompatible with the well-being of the relationship and something must give. Thus, sometimes it is not so easy to maintain a healthy and vital ongoing relationship.

Over the past two decades, we have conducted a program of research that explores the means by which close partners manage to sustain healthy, long-term relationships. Our model of persistence and couple well-being employs the principles and constructs of interdependence theory (Kelley & Thibaut, 1978; Thibaut & Kelley, 1959). This chapter describes the main propositions and findings from our ongoing research program. First, we review the interdependence theoretic principles that underlie our work, describing interdependence dilemmas, discussing partners' adaptations to such dilemmas, and outlining the manner in which partners' adaptations become embodied in personal dispositions, relationship-specific motives, and normative prescriptions. Second, we discuss three primary bases for dependence on a relationship, introduce the concept of commitment, and describe the role of commitment in promoting persistence and maintenance behaviors. Third, we review research regarding each of several relationship maintenance phenomena, including both (a) behavioral maintenance mechanisms (accommodative behavior, willingness to sacrifice, and forgiveness of betrayal), and (b) cognitive maintenance mechanisms (cognitive interdependence, positive illusion, and the derogation of tempting alternatives). Fourth, we describe recent work regarding mutual cyclical growth, discussing the manner in which one person's dependence, commitment, and enactment of maintenance behaviors affects the partner's trust and willingness to become increasingly dependent on the relationship. We conclude with a discussion of the benefits of an interdependence theoretic analysis of behavior in ongoing close relationships.

An Interdependence Theoretic Analysis of Relationship Maintenance

Interdependence Dilemmas in Ongoing Relationships

As noted earlier, the real test of a relationship arises when partners encounter dilemmas involving conflicted interaction, incompatible preferences, and the like. An interdependence dilemma is termed a *dilemma* because it involves noncorrespondent outcomes (Kelley & Thibaut, 1978). Interdependence dilemmas are situations in which the immediate well-being of one person is incompatible with the immediate well-being of the partner and relationship. Interdependence dilemmas involve conflicting motives. On the one hand, there may be compelling reasons for the individual to pursue immediate self-interest. On the other hand, there may be compelling reasons to promote the interests of one's relationship. Resolving interdependence dilemmas therefore entails some degree of effort or personal cost.

For example, if Mary enacts a rude or hostile behavior, John's immediate impulse may be to behave rudely in return. John may feel demeaned, wish to defend his dignity, or seek to gain some measure of revenge. The impulse to reciprocate negativity—to defend oneself in the face of attack—appears to be quite strong (Rusbult, Verette, Whitney, Slovik, & Lipkus, 1991; Yovetich & Rusbult, 1994). However, a retaliative act on John's part is likely to escalate conflict, producing a hostile interaction that could harm his relationship. Thus, John's direct, self-interested impulses are at odds with the interests of his relationship.

From a strictly personal point of view, the loss of pride John would endure if he were to quietly suffer Mary's insult may seem more unpleasant than the unpleasantness associated with retaliating, further irritating Mary, and harming their relationship. If John is to behave in such a manner as to benefit his relationship, he must swallow his pride, control his impulse toward retaliation, and find it in himself to behave in a conciliatory manner. Thus, interdependence dilemmas require individuals to reveal their priorities; such situations provide us with opportunities to demonstrate whether our motives are self-oriented or relationship-oriented.

Adaptation to Interdependence Dilemmas

Transformation of motivation. The interdependence theory distinction between the given situation and the effective situation provides a framework for understanding what leads some partners to "behave well" in interdependence dilemmas, enduring cost or exerting effort to ensure the well-being of their relationships (Kelley & Thibaut, 1978). As illustrated in Figure 17.1, the *given situation* refers to each partner's immediate well-being in a specific situation, describing what we assume to be each person's gut-level, self-centered preferences (e.g., the impulse to retaliate when Mary behaves in a hostile manner). Hedonistic motivation is the default option in interaction. We assume that, at some level, individuals recognize that which is in their self-interest, and we assume that departures from this default baseline to some degree are costly or effortful (and therefore meaningful).

It should be clear that we do not always pursue our self-oriented given preferences. (Indeed, we could not sustain ongoing relationships if we were consistently governed by our default, hedonistic impulses.) Frequently behavior is shaped by broader concerns, including strategic considerations, long-term goals, or desire to promote both one's own and a partner's well-being. Frequently we act on the basis of desire to create or sustain ongoing involvements. Movement away from given preferences results from transformation of motivation—a process that leads individuals to relinquish hedonistic preferences based on

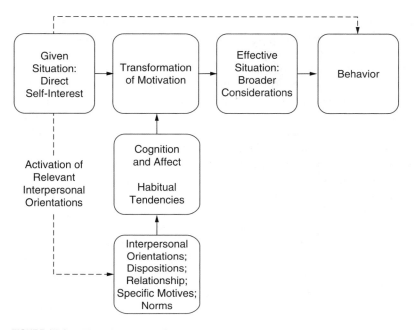

FIGURE 17.1 ■ Transformation of motivation.

immediate self-interest and instead act on the basis of broader considerations. The effective situation describes the modified preferences that are assumed to result from the transformation process—reconceptualized, effective preferences guide behavior (e.g., accommodating rather than retaliating when Mary behaves rudely).

The transformation process may produce any of a variety of goals (Kelley & Thibaut, 1978; McClintock, 1972). In well-functioning relationships, the transformation process frequently yields prorelationship motives, producing a shift from desire to maximize one's immediate self-interest (MaxOwn) toward prorelationship orientations such as desire to maximize the partner's interests (MaxOther) or joint interests (MaxJoint). At the same time, antirelationship transformation is also possible (e.g., desire to maximize the difference between one's own and the partner's interests [MaxRel]).

In light of the variety of transformational tendencies that partners might display in the context of a specific interaction, interdependence dilemmas can be construed as diagnostic situations (Holmes

& Rempel, 1989). Interdependence dilemmas are diagnostic in the sense that behavior in such situations is revealing of the individual's broader goals, values, and motives. Does John resolve a specific dilemma by pursuing his immediate self-interest, or does he set aside self-interest for the good of the relationship? If John reacts to Mary's rudeness by swallowing his pride and accommodating, such a departure from his gut-level self-interest demonstrates his benevolent feelings for Mary and his constructive goals for their relationship.

Stable transformational tendencies and interpersonal orientations. Relatively stable transformational tendencies are argued to emerge as a result of adaptation to ongoing circumstances of interdependence. How so? Specific interdependence dilemmas initially are experienced as unique problems or opportunities. Reactions to novel situations sometimes rest on conscious thought. John may deliberately review his behavioral options, take account of his feelings for Mary and his goals for their future, and actively decide whether to behave selfishly or benevolently ("Mary hurt me, but I'm concerned about our future, so I'll inhibit my impulse to be hostile"). Alternatively, reactions may involve little conscious thought. John may react impulsively, automatically experiencing sympathy and reacting in a benevolent manner. In either event, the unique dilemma has been dealt with and experience is acquired.

Over time, some types of interdependence dilemmas will be experienced repeatedly. Through the process of adaptation, we develop habitual tendencies to react to specific patterns in specific ways—that is, we develop habitual transformational tendencies (Kelley, 1983b). At critical choice points, we may continue to engage in active decision making, but just as often transformation may be guided by habit. Habitual transformational tendencies are guided by *interpersonal orientations*, defined as relatively stable pattern-contingent and partner-contingent solutions to specific interdependence patterns (Rusbult & Van Lange, 1996). That is, tendencies toward one type of transformation rather than another are guided by the habitual solutions we acquire over the course of adaptation to a variety of interdependence situations. These solutions frequently are specific to a particular type of interdependence situation and frequently are specific to a particular interaction partner. Interpersonal orientations may be embodied in: (a) personal dispositions, or actor-specific inclinations to respond to particular interdependence situations in a specific manner across numerous interaction partners (e.g., secure attachment, dispositional competitiveness); (b) relationship-specific motives or dyad-specific inclinations to respond to particular interdependence situations in a specific manner (e.g., commitment, trust); and (c) social norms or group-based inclinations to respond to particular interdependence situations in a specific manner, either across numerous interaction partners or within the context of a given relationship (e.g., the Golden Rule, the social contract).

The transformation process. How does transformation of motivation come about? Human intelligence is highly interpersonal: We can identify key features of interactions insofar as such features are relevant to personal well-being, recognizing that some interaction situations resemble previously encountered situations. That is, we respond to specific interdependence dilemmas as instances of general patterns rather than perceiving and responding to each situation de novo (Kelley, 1984). Thus, as represented in Figure 17.1, the transformation process begins when the individual recognizes the given situation as either a novel situation or as a situation similar to previous interactions sharing the same general pattern.

If the pattern of the given situation is unfamiliar, the individual may actively consider its structure and implications; if the pattern is familiar, its structure and implications may be readily apparent. The pattern perceived to exist in the given situation may be one for which the solution rests on broader considerations (i.e., interpersonal orientations) or may be one for which no broader considerations are relevant. If the pattern is one for which no broader considerations are relevant, the individual will simply act on the basis of immediate self-interest (MaxOwn). No transformation occurs, and the effective situation is equivalent to the given situation— that is, the pattern of outcomes in the given situation governs overt behavior.

However, if the given pattern is more complex, any of a variety of interpersonal orientations may be activated. The dispositions, motives, or norms that are activated influence motivation via either (a) cognitively or affectively mediated transformation, or (b) automatic transformation. In the mediated case, orientations color meaning analysis or the cognitions and affective responses that accompany interaction (Kelley, 1979, 1984). For example, if John is strongly committed, rather than experiencing indignation when Mary behaves rudely, he may feel concerned about Mary's well-being and form benign interpretations of her actions. These thoughts and feelings lead him to place high value on both his own and Mary's well-being, yielding prorelationship motives. Alternatively, the individual may automatically exhibit prorelationship transformation with little or no internal mediation. For example, if John and Mary have a history of commitment and have encountered many noncorrespondent interactions, John may automatically exhibit concern for Mary's well-being and prorelationship transformation may come about in a rather habitual and unmediated manner.

Whether the transformation process is mediated by meaning analysis or comes about automatically, the process produces a shift in motivation from the pursuit of direct self-interest to an alternative motive. This shift yields an effective situation that reflects the modified preferences dictated by the governing interpersonal orientation. For example, in a given situation involving noncorrespondent preferences, John's strong commitment will yield a set of effective preferences in which prorelationship behavior takes on greater value. As a consequence, John will behave in a constructive and benevolent manner.

Transformation of motivation reflects the influence of important social psychological causes of behavior. If we conceptualize human behavior in terms of person-by-situation interactions, the transformation process is the juncture at which the "rubber meets the road"—the juncture at which the person meets the situation. Transformation describes the process during which (a) characteristics of a specific person (a given individual's dispositions, relationship-specific motives, and norms) combine with (b) characteristics of a specific situation (properties of a given situation, characterized in terms of that which is dictated by immediate self-interest), to yield (c) individual action. Accordingly, to understand behavior in interdependence dilemmas, it becomes important to ask what it is that leads some individuals to react on the basis of immediate self-interest (the situation per se), whereas other individuals exhibit prorelationship transformation and behavior. In the following section, we propose that, among the several interpersonal orientations that affect the transformation process, commitment to a relationship plays a key role in inducing prorelationship motivation.

Dependence, Commitment, and Persistence

Interdependence theory suggests that dependence is a fundamental property of relationships (Kelley & Thibaut, 1978). *Dependence level* describes the

degree to which an individual needs his or her relationship or the extent to which the individual's personal well-being is influenced by involvement in the relationship. What are the primary bases of dependence, and what are its consequences? In the following section, we describe the investment model of commitment processes.

Bases of Dependence

Consistent with interdependence theory tenets, and as illustrated in Figure 17.2, we suggest that individuals become increasingly dependent on their relationships to the degree that: (a) satisfaction level is high, or the relationship fulfills the individual's most important needs (e.g., needs for intimacy, companionship, sexuality); (b) quality of alternatives is poor, or the individual's most important needs could not be fulfilled independent of the relationship (e.g., in alternative romantic involvements, through independent action, by friends or kin); and (c) investment size is high, or many important resources have become attached to the relationship, including resources that would be lost or decline in value if the relationship were to end (e.g., time and effort, material possessions, shared friendship network; Rusbult, 1983; Rusbult, Drigotas, & Verette, 1994).

FIGURE 17.2 ■ Dependence, commitment, and persistence.

What is Commitment?

Consistent with other major models of the commitment process (cf. M. Johnson, 1991; Levinger, 1979), the investment model suggests that as individuals become dependent on their relationships, they develop increasingly strong commitment (Rusbult, 1983; Rusbult et al., 1994). *Commitment level* is defined in terms of three interrelated components, including conative, affective, and cognitive properties. The conative component of commitment is intent to persist—with increasing dependence, we become intrinsically motivated to persist with our partners. The affective component is psychological attachment—with increasing dependence, we come to experience life in dyadic terms, such that our emotional well-being is influenced by our partners and relationships. The cognitive component is long-term orientation—with increasing dependence, we increasingly envision ourselves as involved in our relationships for the foreseeable future, considering the implications of current action for future outcomes.

Commitment, Persistence, and Adjustment

Much of the existing literature regarding close involvement implicitly or explicitly assumes that individuals persist because they are satisfied with their relationships (for a review of the literature, see Berscheid & Reis, 1998). In contrast, the investment model suggests that feeling good—liking, attraction, satisfaction, and the like—is not sufficient to predict persistence and willingness to go the extra mile on behalf of a relationship. Granted, satisfaction level is one basis for dependence. However, satisfaction alone is not sufficient to induce strong dependence or commitment. Moreover, the psychological experience of commitment reflects more than the bases of dependence out of which it arises. Dependence is a fundamental property of relationships—a structural property describing the additive effects of wanting to persist (feeling satisfied), needing to persist (having high investments), and having no choice but to persist (possessing poor alternatives). In contrast, commitment can be construed as the sense of allegiance that is established with

regard to the source of one's dependence. Because John is dependent on his relationship with Mary, John develops an inclination to persist with Mary, he comes to think of himself as part of John and Mary, and he considers the broader implications of his actions—implications extending beyond his immediate self-interest, including effects on the relationship next week, next month, and next year.

The empirical literature provides consistent support for investment model claims, demonstrating that: (a) commitment is positively associated with satisfaction and investment size and negatively associated with quality of alternatives; (b) each of these variables contributes unique variance to predicting commitment; (c) compared with less committed individuals, highly committed individuals are substantially more likely to persist in their relationships; and (d) commitment is the most direct and powerful predictor of persistence, partially or wholly mediating the effects of satisfaction, alternatives, and investments on decisions to remain in versus end a relationship. Such findings have been observed in several cultures (e.g., the United States, the Netherlands, Taiwan), in research employing diverse methods, and a variety of participant populations (e.g., marital and nonmarital relationships, heterosexual and gay or lesbian relationships, abusive relationships; e.g., Drigotas & Rusbult, 1992; Felmlee, Sprecher, & Bassin, 1990; Kurdek, 1993; Lin & Rusbult, 1995; Rusbult, 1980, 1983; Rusbult & Martz, 1995; Rusbult, Martz, & Agnew, 1998; Simpson, 1987; South & Lloyd, 1995; Van Lange et al., 1997). For example, compelling support for the investment model was observed in a 15-year longitudinal test of the investment model—an empirical test demonstrating that (a) the investment model predicts persistence in relationships over a 15-year time period; and (b) satisfaction, alternatives, and investments account for substantial variance in strength of commitment (Bui, Peplau, & Hill, 1996).

Maintenance Mechanisms in Ongoing Relationships

In addition to promoting persistence, we suggest that strong commitment encourages a variety of *relationship maintenance mechanisms*, defined as the specific means by which partners manage to sustain long-term, well-functioning relationships. Maintenance acts serve a positive function for relationships, helping couples persist despite threats such as uncertainty, noncorrespondent outcomes, and tempting alternatives. At the same time, maintenance acts are not necessarily unambiguously positive for individuals—particularly in terms of the individual's immediate self-interest—in that they involve the enactment of otherwise undesirable behaviors, the modification of existing cognitive representations, or other forms of cost or effort. Some maintenance acts involve trivial inconvenience, whereas others entail considerable cost. Therefore, it is useful to construe maintenance mechanisms as solutions to problematic situations—solutions that rest on prorelationship transformation.

Why should commitment promote prorelationship motives and behavior? As noted earlier, committed individuals experience high satisfaction, perceive their alternatives to be poor, and have invested heavily. They are also psychologically attached to their relationships and think about their relationships over the long run rather than in the here and now. The implications of this combination of conditions should be clear: Committed individuals have a considerable stake in their relationships and wish to ensure that they persist and exhibit good adjustment. If John is strongly committed to his relationship, he has a variety of reasons to put the interests of the relationship before his own needs on those occasions when it is necessary to do so. First, because John is dependent, he literally needs his relationship; the more he stands to lose, the more effort he is likely to exert to hold on to what he has got (cf. Holmes, 1981). Second, because John is oriented toward long-term outcomes, he recognizes that it is in his long-term interest to develop patterns of reciprocal prorelationship behavior. Also, the costs of foregoing self-interest are aggregated over a longer time perspective and in light of the partner's reciprocal departures from self-interest (cf. Kelley, 1983a). Third, because John is psychologically attached to his relationship, he may come to experience himself and Mary as *merged* (i.e., the line separating

self-interest from partner interests may become blurred), such that departures from self-interest benefiting Mary may not be experienced as costly (cf. Aron & Aron, 1997). Fourth, strong commitment may yield collectivistic orientation, including inclinations to respond to Mary's needs in a relatively unconditional manner—John may endure cost and exert effort without calculating what he will receive in return (cf. Clark & Mills, 1979).

Over the past decade, we have identified a handful of mechanisms by which committed individuals sustain long-term involvements; additional mechanisms are likely to be identified in the future. In the following section, and as illustrated in Figure 17.3, we review (a) behavioral maintenance acts, which involve shifts in behavior toward the goal of enhancing couple well-being; and (b) cognitive maintenance acts, which involve cognitive restructuring toward the goal of enhancing couple well-being.

Behavioral Maintenance Mechanisms

As noted earlier, the real test of a relationship arises when circumstances of interdependence are problematic—when the well-being of one or both partners is incompatible with the well-being of the relationship. Behavioral maintenance mechanisms are the positive, prorelationship acts that close partners exhibit in problematic interdependence dilemmas of this sort. That is, behavioral maintenance acts involve shifts in behavior toward the goal of enhancing couple well-being.

Accommodative behavior. Work regarding accommodative behavior emerged out of research using the exit–voice–loyalty–neglect typology to examine responses to dissatisfaction in everyday interaction (Rusbult & Zembrodt, 1983; Rusbult, Zembrodt, & Gunn, 1982). This typology identifies four possible reactions to accommodative dilemmas—responses that differ in terms of constructiveness versus destructiveness and activity versus passivity. Exit reactions are actively destructive (e.g., screaming at the partner), voice reactions are actively constructive (e.g., suggesting that the partners discuss matters), loyalty reactions are passively constructive (e.g., patiently waiting for improvement), and neglect reactions are passively

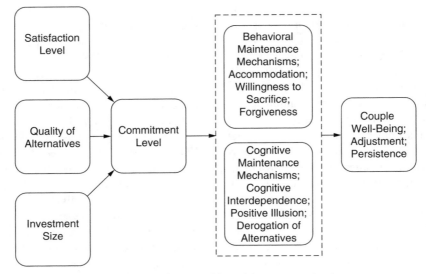

FIGURE 17.3 ■ Commitment and relationship maintenance mechanisms.

destructive (e.g., giving one's partner the "cold shoulder"). Research regarding the functional value of exit, voice, loyalty, and neglect behaviors reveals support for a *good manners* model of conflicted interaction: It is less important that partners enact constructive behaviors than that they *not* enact destructive behaviors because the harmful effects of negative acts are substantially stronger than the beneficial effects of positive acts (e.g., Drigotas, Whitney, & Rusbult, 1995; Rusbult, Johnson, & Morrow, 1986).

Unfortunately, it is nearly inevitable that, at some point, one or both partners will engage in destructive acts. *Accommodation* describes the willingness, when a partner enacts a potentially destructive behavior, to (a) inhibit the impulse to react destructively in turn, and (b) instead react in a constructive manner (Rusbult et al., 1991). (Operationally, accommodation describes the willingness, when a partner enacts exit or neglect behaviors, to inhibit the impulse toward reciprocal exit and neglect, instead enacting voice or loyalty behaviors.) For example, after a bad day at work, Mary may snap at John with no provocation. John's gut-level response may be to snap back. Based on the clinical literature regarding negative reciprocity, it is apparent that John's reaction will

yield escalating hostility (for reviews of the literature, see Gottman, 1994; Jacobson & Margolin, 1979): Mary says something thoughtless, John reacts with a snide comment, Mary makes a nasty retort, and so on. Resolving such a chain of increasingly hostile interaction requires the ability to avoid destructive reciprocity, moving toward reconciliation rather than escalation. To reduce tension and soothe heated feelings, John must inhibit the impulse to fight fire with fire, instead reacting in a constructive manner. For example, John might ask Mary how her day went or might simply ignore the incident.

Does accommodation indeed result from prorelationship transformation? Is destructive reciprocity the impulsive reaction to accommodative dilemmas? Does accommodation represent a departure from the individual's immediate, gut-level impulses? In short, yes. Prior research has demonstrated that when confronted with accommodative dilemmas, individuals given plentiful response time (time for transformation) exhibit greater inclinations to accommodate than do those given limited response time (no time for transformation; Yovetich & Rusbult, 1994). Also, in reacting to accommodative dilemmas, compared with the behaviors individuals consider enacting (given preferences), the behaviors they actually enact (effective preferences) are considerably more constructive and less destructive (Yovetich & Rusbult, 1994). Moreover, compared with individuals' inclinations under conditions of reduced social concern (eliminating concern for the partner's well-being, broader social norms, and the like; given preferences), preferences under conditions of normal social concern (effective preferences) are considerably more constructive and less destructive (Rusbult et al., 1991).

Does strong commitment motivate accommodative behavior? Several cross-sectional survey studies of dating partners—along with a longitudinal study of marital relationships—have revealed that self-reported accommodation is more likely among individuals with strong commitment (Rusbult, Bissonnette, Arriaga, & Cox, 1998; Rusbult et al., 1991). Accommodation is positively associated with satisfaction level, negatively associated with quality of alternatives, and positively associated with investment size. Also, self-report measures of accommodation appear to be reasonably valid in that individuals' self-reports of accommodation are associated with (a) partners' descriptions of the individual's accommodative acts, and (b) a variety of behavioral measures of accommodation, including measures obtained from videotaped recordings of partners' conflicted interactions (Rusbult, Bissonnette et al., 1998; Rusbult et al., 1991).

Of course, commitment is not the only variable that promotes inclinations to accommodate rather than retaliate when a partner behaves badly. Prior research has demonstrated that individuals are more likely to accommodate to the degree that they exhibit secure attachment style, are more psychologically feminine, and engage in partner perspective-taking (Arriaga & Rusbult, 1998; Gaines et al., 1997; Kilpatrick, Bissonnette, & Rusbult, 2000; Rusbult et al., 1991; Scharfe & Bartholomew, 1995). Also, the inclination to accommodate is predictable based on the nature of the internal events accompanying accommodative dilemmas. For example, the impact of commitment on accommodation has been shown to be mediated by internal events such as (a) benevolent

meaning analysis, or the tendency to experience benign emotions and develop benevolent interpretations of the partner's actions during the course of accommodative dilemmas (Arriaga & Rusbult, 1998); and (b) empathic accuracy, or the tendency to accurately perceive the partner's cognitions and affect during the course of conflicted interaction (Kilpatrick et al., 2000).

Given that accommodation is a costly and effortful departure from immediate self-interest, it is important to ask whether accommodation is truly beneficial. If John turns the other cheek every time Mary behaves badly, is their relationship benefited? Will Mary simply learn that she can get away with outrageous behavior? One way to answer these questions is to examine the association of accommodation with quality of couple functioning. High levels of accommodation consistently have been shown to be associated with indexes of couple well-being, including persistence and dyadic adjustment (Rusbult, Bissonnette et al., 1998; Rusbult et al., 1986, 1991). At the same time, it appears that couple functioning is greatest in relationships exhibiting mutually high levels of accommodation—that is, couple well-being is enhanced when partners take turns exhibiting strong and equal inclinations to behave constructively in accommodative dilemmas (Rusbult et al., 1991). Thus, although accommodation involves personal cost, the tendency of committed individuals to accommodate clearly is beneficial to ongoing relationships.

Willingness to sacrifice. Although partners in ongoing relationships may experience many interactions in which their preferences are compatible, it is inevitable that, at some time, they will be forced to deal with noncorrespondent situations. For example, on Friday night, John may wish to attend a hockey game, whereas Mary would rather spend the evening at home. John may receive a desirable job offer in Chicago, whereas Mary's most desirable offer may be in New York. When partners encounter such noncorrespondent situations, it becomes necessary that one or both persons exhibit *willingness to sacrifice*, defined as the tendency to forego immediate self-interest to promote the well-being of the partner and relationship

(Van Lange et al., 1997). Sacrifice may entail foregoing behaviors that otherwise would be desirable (passive sacrifice), enacting behaviors that otherwise would not be desirable (active sacrifice), or both. Acts of sacrifice may be minor and transitory (e.g., John may attend an opera that Mary wants to see) or substantial and lasting (e.g., John may agree to live in an undesirable locale for the sake of Mary's career).

Noncorrespondent situations are quite common, yet such situations are potentially disruptive to a relationship—partners may expend a good deal of energy working to resolve conflicts of interest, they may become aggravated at one another's differing preferences, and they may feel hurt when one or both partners ignore the other's preferences in the pursuit of self-interest. Thus, there is reason to wonder whether commitment indeed promotes willingness to sacrifice and whether the willingness to do so is beneficial to relationships.

We have examined willingness to sacrifice in six studies that used diverse methods, employed both self-report and behavioral measures, and examined both dating relationships and marital relationships (Van Lange et al., 1997). This research revealed that (a) commitment is positively associated with willingness to sacrifice; (b) willingness to sacrifice is greater among individuals who exhibit high satisfaction, poor alternatives, and high investments; and (c) the associations of satisfaction, alternatives, and investments with willingness to sacrifice are largely accounted for by the associations of these variables with commitment (i.e., commitment largely mediates the association of the bases of dependence with sacrifice). Also, willingness to sacrifice is positively associated with dyadic adjustment and probability of persisting, and sacrifice partially mediates the association of commitment with adjustment—that is, the enhanced adjustment characterizing committed couples is partially attributable to the fact that committed partners exhibit greater willingness to sacrifice and therefore enjoy greater adjustment. Thus, although sacrificial behavior necessitates foregoing immediate self-interest, the willingness of committed individuals to sacrifice—when it

becomes necessary to do so—yields clear benefits in ongoing relationships.

Forgiveness of betrayal. One of the most serious threats to a relationship involves the experience of betrayal or the violation of an implicit or explicit relationship-relevant norm. How do betrayal incidents differ from accommodative dilemmas and dilemmas involving sacrifice? Whereas dilemmas involving sacrifice arise when partners' preferences are incompatible (through no necessary fault of either person), and whereas accommodative dilemmas are instigated when a partner enacts a potentially destructive behavior, dilemmas relevant to forgiveness arise when a partner breaks the rules governing the relationship. Because acts of betrayal violate relationship-relevant norms, such incidents possess a uniquely moral character. It is the moral dimension of betrayal that gives such incidents their power, producing righteous indignation and hostile behavioral tendencies.

Betrayal incidents vary in severity (telling a white lie vs. sexual infidelity), but to a greater or lesser degree such incidents yield a signature constellation of negative feelings, thoughts, and behavioral tendencies (for a review of the literature, see McCullough, Sandage, & Worthington, 1997). Victims of betrayal frequently react with anger, confusion, and demands for atonement. Perpetrators often experience guilt or shame and may show remorse or apologize for the harm they have caused. If victims continue to express outrage, perpetrators may become angry and may seek to defend themselves or minimize the severity of the betrayal. Thus, the aftermath of betrayal is complex, and such incidents are difficult to resolve.

Recovery from betrayal rests on *forgiveness*, defined as the victim's willingness to forego desire for retribution and demands for atonement, instead reacting in a less judgmental, more constructive manner. Complete forgiveness may be difficult, in that it rests on the resumption of pre-betrayal patterns of interaction—the victim no longer obsessively reviews the betrayal, reminds the perpetrator of the incident, demands apology, or exhibits any residue of the incident. In the case of complete forgiveness, the victim experiences a *change of heart* and fully relegates the incident to the past. Consistent with researchers operating in the clinical tradition, we assume that it may be useful to distinguish between forgiveness (an individual act) and reconciliation (a joint act; Enright & the Human Development Study Group, 1996). For example, although John may forgive Mary for a heinous act of betrayal, he may find that he cannot find his way to reconciliation with her.

Does forgiveness result from prorelationship transformation—is vengeance indeed the impulsive reaction to betrayal incidents, and does forgiveness represent a departure from the individual's immediate, gut-level impulses? Following the research strategy reviewed earlier for accommodation, we have found that when confronted with betrayal incidents, individuals given plentiful response time (time for transformation) exhibit greater inclinations toward forgiveness than do those given limited response time (no time for transformation; Rusbult, Davis, Finkel, Hannon, & Olsen, 2000). Also, when describing reactions to betrayal incidents, the responses people consider enacting (given preferences) are considerably more vengeful and less forgiving than the responses they actually enact (effective preferences; Rusbult, Davis et al., 2000). Thus, it is by no means easy for the victims of betrayal to forgive their partners.

We anticipated that forgiveness of betrayal would be more probable to the extent that individuals are more highly committed. We conducted four studies to test this prediction: (a) a cross-sectional survey study examining betrayal incidents in ongoing relationships; (b) a diary study examining everyday betrayal incidents occurring over the course of a 2-week period; (c) an experiment in which we manipulated commitment level in interactions between strangers, examining reactions to betrayal in the context of an experimental game; and (d) a priming experiment in which we manipulated commitment by temporarily activating low versus high commitment (Rusbult, Finkel, Hannon, Kumashiro, & Childs, 2000). Consistent with expectations, the four studies revealed good evidence that victims of betrayal are more forgiving to the degree that they are more committed to their partners; the commitment–forgiveness association

is evident even controlling for the recency and severity of betrayal. Thus—and parallel to prorelationship acts such as accommodation and willingness to sacrifice—although forgiveness is a complex phenomenon that in many respects defies individuals' gut-level impulses, forgiveness arguably is beneficial to ongoing relationships.

Cognitive Maintenance Mechanisms

It is difficult to consistently feel thankful and sustain conviction in the desirability of one's relationship. Interdependence dilemmas not only pit individual interests against the interests of the relationship, but also threaten the stability of an involvement, creating uncertainty and challenging partners' convictions. Cognitive maintenance mechanisms involve mental restructuring toward the goal of enhancing couple well-being. Prior to discussing these mechanisms, it is important to note that, although individuals may sometimes consciously and deliberately engage in such activities, cognitive maintenance acts typically are relatively automatic products of strong commitment.

Cognitive interdependence. Prior research has demonstrated that, in perceiving and recalling information about other individuals, we tend to spontaneously categorize information using relationship categories (Sedikides, Olsen, & Reis, 1993). In research designed to determine whether involvement in a relationship produces parallel shifts in cognitions regarding the self, we have found that strong commitment produces a prorelationship restructuring of the actor's representation of self. Cognitive interdependence involves movement from a largely individual-based internal representation of the self to a collective representation of self and partner. For example, compared with less committed individuals, highly committed individuals exhibit a greater rate of plural pronoun usage (*we, us, our* rather than *I, me, mine*; Agnew, Van Lange, Rusbult, & Langston, 1998). In addition, compared with less committed individuals, highly committed individuals perceive greater overlap between the self and the partner and describe their relationships as more central in bringing meaning to life. These constructs exist in a congenial, mutually sustaining pattern—strong commitment predicts increases over time in cognitive interdependence, and strong cognitive interdependence predicts increases over time in commitment.

Positive illusion. Over time in a relationship, we tend to develop idealized beliefs regarding our partners and relationships, constructing storylike narratives and cognitive representations that diffuse feelings of uncertainty and dampen doubts regarding our relationships. We sustain idealized beliefs via several mechanisms, including: (a) cognitive filters, whereby we screen out negative information regarding our own relationships; (b) downward social comparison, whereby we compare our relationships to other relationships that are less well-off; and (c) dimensional comparison, whereby we evaluate our own relationships in comparison to other relationships with regard to dimensions on which our relationships truly do excel (Van Lange & Rusbult, 1995).

Individuals sustain idealized beliefs in part by translating their partners' faults into virtues, reinterpreting qualities that might otherwise be regarded in a negative light ("he slurps coffee in an adorable way"; Murray & Holmes, 1993). Interestingly, actors possess more positive beliefs regarding their partners than their partners hold regarding themselves. Also, idealized beliefs represent more than simple in-the-head illusion, in that the tendency to idealize one's partner is associated with two sorts of positive consequence: (a) increases over time in love, satisfaction, and trust, as well as decreases over time in uncertainty and conflict; and (b) increases over time in the partner's positive regard for self (Murray, Holmes, & Griffin, 1996a , 1996b).

The inclination to develop idealized beliefs in response to psychological threat appears to be particularly characteristic of individuals with high self-esteem (Murray, Holmes, MacDonald, & Ellsworth, 1998). For example, when individuals with high self-esteem are confronted with a threat to their feelings of self-worth (e.g., guilt about a transgression), they bring to mind numerous thoughts emphasizing the partner's acceptance of the self, deflecting potentially damaging self-doubts. In contrast, when individuals with low

self-esteem are confronted with such a threat, they respond with increased uncertainty regarding the partner's acceptance of the self, which in turn leads them to perceive the partner in a less positive light.

Prior research has also examined social comparison of one's own to others' relationships. Research regarding perceived superiority reveals that people tend to: (a) hold a greater number of positive thoughts about their own relationships than other relationships; and (b) hold fewer negative thoughts about their own than other relationships (Rusbult, Van Lange, Wildschut, Yovetich, & Verette, in press; Van Lange & Rusbult, 1995). We not only exhibit: (a) *perceived superiority*—perceiving a greater number of positive attributes in our own relationships than in others' relationships; but also (b) *excessive optimism*—perceiving that our relationships have rosier futures than other relationships; and (c) *unrealistic perceptions of control*—perceiving that we possess greater control over our relationships than others do (Martz, Verette, Arriaga, Slovik, Cox, & Rusbult, 1998).

The tendency toward positive illusion is more pronounced among people who are highly committed (Martz et al., 1998; Rusbult et al., in press). Also, positive illusion appears to be a motivated phenomenon. For example, emotionally threatening manipulations (e.g., "college students' relationships exhibit poor adjustment") yield enhanced levels of perceived superiority, suggesting that committed individuals exhibit this tendency in part because they "need to do so"—because doing so reduces anxiety and doubt (Murray & Holmes, 1993; Rusbult et al., in press). Moreover, the inclination toward positive illusion is driven more by commitment to a relationship than by self-esteem—that is, in the relationships context, positive illusion is a relationship-driven phenomenon, not simply another mechanism by which individuals sustain positive self-regard (Martz et al., 1998; Rusbult et al., in press). Finally, positive illusion is positively associated with dyadic adjustment and probability of persistence (Martz et al., 1998; Rusbult et al., in press).

Derogation of tempting alternatives. Tempting alternatives may threaten ongoing relationships.

How do we deal with such threats? First, alternative partners may become more scarce over the course of an ongoing relationship. Potentially tempting alternatives may "take themselves out of the running" when they know that an individual is committed, or committed individuals may drive away alternatives by displaying conspicuous symbols of their involvement (e.g., a wedding ring; cf. Kelley, 1983a). At the same time, alternatives typically do not completely disappear—attractive alternatives continue to represent a threat to many relationships.

Research regarding derogation of alternatives reveals that involved individuals cognitively disparage alternative partners—for example, they subtly minimize alternative partners' abilities or attributes ("I bet he has no sense of humor"). The tendency to derogate alternatives is greater among highly committed individuals (D. Johnson & Rusbult, 1989; Simpson, Gangestad, & Lerma, 1990), as is the tendency to exhibit defensive perceptual maneuvers—compared with less committed people, those with high commitment spend less time attending to tempting alternatives (Miller, 1997).

Mutual Cyclical Growth in Ongoing Relationships

Given that commitment plays a central role in relationships, it would be adaptive for partners to implicitly or explicitly attend to one another's commitment levels. Why so? First, commitment and dependence make individuals vulnerable; such vulnerability is reduced when the partner is equally vulnerable (equal vulnerability represents balance of power; Drigotas, Rusbult, & Verette, 1999). Second, couple well-being has been shown to rest on both level of commitment and mutuality of commitment (Drigotas et al., 1999). Third, maintenance acts follow the principle of reciprocity—we are more willing to enact prorelationship behaviors to the degree that the partner is expected to do so (Van Lange et al., 1997). To the extent that achieving and sustaining equal dependence, mutual commitment, and reciprocity of prorelationship acts rest on knowledge of a partner's commitment, an implicit gauge of the partner's

commitment would seem to have considerable functional value. We suggest that relationship-specific trust is such a gauge.

Most theory and research concerning trust has examined this phenomenon as a relatively enduring personal disposition that is assumed to yield considerable stability in cognition, affect, and behavior across a variety of situations and across a variety of interaction partners. For example, Rotter (1980) described trust as a personality trait, and attachment theory emphasizes the ways in which early attachment experiences influence mental models of attachment, which in turn shape later inclinations to trust close partners (for a review of this literature, see Hazan & Shaver, 1994).

In the present context, it is suitable to describe trust as an interpersonal phenomenon, constructing trust not as a stable trait, but as a quality that is specific to a particular relationship with a particular partner. Toward this goal, Holmes and his colleagues have conceptualized trust as a relationship-specific phenomenon, defining *trust level* as the expectation that a given partner can be relied on to behave in a benevolent manner and be responsive to one's needs (Holmes, 1989; Rempel, Holmes, & Zanna, 1985). Trust is said to include three components (Holmes & Rempel, 1989): (a) predictability, or belief that the partner's behavior is consistent; (b) dependability, or belief that the partner can be counted on to be honest, reliable, and benevolent; and (c) faith, or conviction that the partner is intrinsically motivated to be responsive and caring—belief that the partner's motives go beyond instrumental bases for benevolence.

How do we develop conviction that our partners are predictable and dependable; how do we develop faith that our partners consistently will be responsive to our needs? Over the course of extended involvement, partners inevitably confront situations in which personal interests are pitted against the interests of the relationship—that is, individuals encounter the sorts of interdependence dilemmas described earlier. In such situations, individuals implicitly make a choice: Should I do what's good for me, or should I put my partner's needs before my own? Holmes and Rempel

(1989) suggested that the emergence of trust rests on the manner in which individuals are perceived to behave during such episodes. Episodes of this sort are diagnostic, in that behavior in such situations is diagnostic of the individual's broader goals, values, and motives.

Commitment-inspired maintenance acts are diagnostic of prorelationship orientation. Accommodation and sacrifice provide particularly unambiguous evidence of benevolent motives, in that when individuals accommodate rather than retaliate—and when they sacrifice otherwise desirable activities to solve problems of noncorrespondence—they demonstrate that they are willing to behave in a generous and giving manner. To some extent, cognitive maintenance tendencies may provide parallel evidence, especially insofar as such tendencies involve exceptional effort or cost. If it is true that the benevolent acts promoted by commitment provide evidence regarding strength of prorelationship orientation, then trust can be construed as a mirror reflecting the strength of a partner's commitment.

As partners develop increased trust in one another, they are likely to become increasingly dependent on one another—that is, they are likely to become increasingly satisfied, increasingly willing to forego alternatives, and increasingly willing to invest in the relationship (Holmes & Rempel, 1989). As John becomes confident that Mary will be responsive to his needs, he is likely to experience enhanced satisfaction with their relationship. Moreover, as John's trust grows, he should be more willing to make himself vulnerable by cognitively or behaviorally driving away alternatives, and he should be more willing to throw in his lot with Mary by investing in their relationship, emotionally or behaviorally. Such increased dependence will yield strengthened commitment, which in turn should produce increased willingness to engage in generous, prorelationship acts.

Conclusions

What do we gain by adopting an interdependence theoretic analysis of maintenance process in close relationships? First, although social psychologists frequently allude to person-by-situation interactions, we devote little attention to understanding situations per se. For example, the most prominent model of couples therapy is cognitive–behavioral therapy, which emphasizes the role of poor social skills and attributional tendencies in causing marital distress. From the point of view of interdependence theory, distress may rest at least in part on the situation—that is, on problematic interdependence structure. To help couples achieve harmonious interaction, we should exert as much effort modifying the couple's circumstances of interdependence as we exert modifying each person's social skills and thought processes.

Second, some theories emphasize the disappearance of self-interest in close relationships, suggesting that with increasing closeness, self-interest and partner interests become merged (Aron & Aron, 1997), or arguing that in communal relationships, individuals depart from their self-interest simply because the partner needs them to do so (Clark & Mills, 1979). In contrast, interdependence theory proposes that self-interest continues to make itself known in ongoing relationships. Indeed, the fact that close partners frequently engage in positive yet personally costly acts is precisely what communicates their prorelationship motives. The fact that we engage in positive acts, despite awareness that such behavior frequently is antithetical to our self-interest, is precisely what makes positive behavior meaningful.

Finally, some theories of close relationships emphasize individual-level processes, explaining behavior by reference to properties that reside within actors—by reference to individual-level cognition, dispositions, or motives. In contrast, interdependence theory explains behavior by reference to properties that reside both within and between actors, highlighting the importance of interdependence structure in shaping the course of ongoing involvements. By calling attention to truly dyadic features of closeness (e.g., by calling attention to the importance of dependence and the existence of noncorrespondent outcomes), an interdependence theoretic analysis provides the field with a much-needed social psychological analysis of human behavior.

ACKNOWLEDGMENT

The work reported in this chapter was supported in part by grants to the first author from the NIMH (No. BSR-1-R01-MH-45417), the NSF (No. BNS-9023817), and the Templeton Foundation (Grant No. 5158).

REFERENCES

Agnew, C. R., Van Lange, P. A. M., Rusbult, C. E., & Langston, C. A. (1998). Cognitive interdependence: Commitment and the mental representation of close relationships. *Journal of Personality and Social Psychology, 74,* 939–954.

Aron, A., & Aron, E. N. (1997). Self-expansion motivation and including other in the self. In S. Duck (Ed.), *Handbook of personal relationships: Theory, research, and interventions* (2nd ed., pp. 251–270). Chichester: Wiley.

Arriaga, X. B., & Rusbult, C. E. (1998). Standing in my partner's shoes: Partner perspective-taking and reactions to accommodative dilemmas. *Personality and Social Psychology Bulletin, 9,* 927–948.

Berscheid, E., & Reis, H. T. (1998). Attraction and close relationships. In D. T. Gilbert, S. T. Fiske, & G. Lindzey (Eds.), *Handbook of social psychology* (4th ed., Vol. 2, pp. 193–281). New York: Random House.

Bui, K. T., Peplau, L. A., & Hill, C. T. (1996). Testing the Rusbult model of relationship commitment and stability in a 15-year study of heterosexual couples. *Personality and Social Psychology Bulletin, 22,* 1244–1257.

Clark, M. S., & Mills, J. (1979). Interpersonal attraction in exchange and communal relationships. *Journal of Personality and Social Psychology, 37,* 12–24.

Drigotas, S. M., & Rusbult, C. E. (1992). Should I stay or should I go?: A dependence model of breakups. *Journal of Personality and Social Psychology, 62,* 62–87.

Drigotas, S. M., Rusbult, C. E., & Verette, J. (1999). Level of commitment, mutuality of commitment, and couple well-being. *Personal Relationships, 6,* 389–409.

Drigotas, S. M., Whitney, G. A., & Rusbult, C. E. (1995). On the peculiarities of loyalty: A diary study of responses to dissatisfaction in everyday life. *Personality and Social Psychology Bulletin, 21,* 596–609.

Enright, R. D., & the Human Development Study Group. (1996). Counseling within the forgiveness triad: On forgiving, receiving forgiveness, and self-forgiveness. *Counseling and Values, 40,* 107–122.

Felmlee, D., Sprecher, S., & Bassin, E. (1990). The dissolution of intimate relationships: A hazard model. *Social Psychology Quarterly, 53,* 13–30.

Gaines, S. O., Jr., Reis, H. T., Summers, S., Rusbult, C. E., Cox, C. L., Wexler, M. O., Marelich, W. D., & Kurland, G. J. (1997). Impact of attachment style on reactions to accommodative dilemmas in close relationships. *Personal Relationships, 4,* 93–113.

Gottman, J. M. (1994). *What predicts divorce?: The relationship between marital processes and marital outcomes.* Hillsdale, NJ: Lawrence Erlbaum Associates.

Hazan, C., & Shaver, P. R. (1994). Attachment as an organizational framework for research on close relationships. *Psychological Inquiry, 5,* 1–22.

Holmes, J. G. (1981). The exchange process in close relationships: Microbehavior and macromotives. In M. J. Lerner & S. C. Lerner (Eds.), *The justice motive in social behavior* (pp. 261–284). New York: Plenum.

Holmes, J. G. (1989). Trust and the appraisal process in close relationships. In W. H. Jones & D. Perlman (Eds.), *Advances in personal relationships* (Vol. 2, pp. 57–104). London: Jessica Kingsley.

Holmes, J. G., & Rempel, J. K. (1989). Trust in close relationships. In C. Hendrick (Ed.), *Review of personality and social psychology* (Vol. 10, pp. 187–220). London: Sage.

Jacobson, M. S., & Margolin, G. (1979). *Marital therapy: Strategies based on social learning and behavior exchange principles.* New York: Brunner-Mazel.

Johnson, D. J., & Rusbult, C. E. (1989). Resisting temptation: Devaluation of alternative partners as a means of maintaining commitment in close relationships. *Journal of Personality and Social Psychology, 57,* 967–980.

Johnson, M. P. (1991). Commitment to personal relationships. In W. H. Jones & D. W. Perlman (Eds.), *Advances in personal relationships* (Vol. 3, pp. 117–143). London: Jessica Kingsley.

Kelley, H. H. (1979). *Personal relationships: Their structures and processes.* Hillsdale, NJ: Lawrence Erlbaum Associates.

Kelley, H. H. (1983a). Love and commitment. In H. H. Kelley, E. Berscheid, A. Christensen, J. H. Harvey, T. L. Huston, G. Levinger, E. McClintock, L. A. Peplau, & D. R. Peterson (Eds.), *Close relationships* (pp. 265–314). New York: W. H. Freeman.

Kelley, H. H. (1983b). The situational origins of human tendencies: A further reason for the formal analysis of structures. *Personality and Social Psychology Bulletin, 9,* 8–30.

Kelley, H. H. (1984). Affect in interpersonal relations. In P. Shaver (Ed.), *Review of personality and social psychology* (Vol. 5, pp. 89–115). Newbury Park, CA: Sage.

Kelley, H. H., & Thibaut, J. W. (1978). *Interpersonal relations: A theory of interdependence.* New York: Wiley.

Kilpatrick, S. D., Bissonnette, V. L., & Rusbult, C. E. (2000). *Empathic accuracy among newly married couples.* Unpublished manuscript, University of North Carolina at Chapel Hill, Chapel Hill, NC.

Kurdek, L. A. (1993). Predicting marital dissolution: A five year prospective longitudinal study of newlywed couples. *Journal of Personality and Social Psychology, 64,* 221–242.

Levinger, G. (1979). A social exchange view on the dissolution of pair relationships. In R. L. Burgess & T. L. Huston (Eds.), *Social exchange in developing relationships* (pp. 169–193). New York: Academic Press.

Lin, Y. H. W., & Rusbult, C. E. (1995). Commitment to dating relationships and cross-sex friendships in America and

China: The impact of centrality of relationship, normative support, and investment model variables. *Journal of Social and Personal Relationships, 12*, 7–26.

Martz, J. M., Verette, J., Arriaga, X. B., Slovik, L. F., Cox, C. L., & Rusbult, C. E. (1998). Positive illusion in close relationships. *Personal Relationships, 5*, 159–181.

McClintock, C. G. (1972). Social motivation—a set of propositions. *Behavioral Science, 17*, 438–454.

McCullough, M. E., Sandage, S. J., & Worthington, E. L., Jr. (1997). *To forgive is human.* Downers Grove, IL: Inter Varsity.

Miller, R. S. (1997). Inattentive and contented: Relationship commitment and attention to alternatives. *Journal of Personality and Social Psychology, 73*, 758–766.

Murray, S. L., & Holmes, J. G. (1993). Seeing virtues in faults: Negativity and the transformation of interpersonal narratives in close relationships. *Journal of Personality and Social Psychology, 65*, 707–722.

Murray, S. L., Holmes, J. G., & Griffin, D. W. (1996a). The benefits of positive illusions: Idealization and the construction of satisfaction in close relationships. *Journal of Personality and Social Psychology, 70*, 79–98.

Murray, S. L., Holmes, J. G., & Griffin, D. W. (1996b). The self-fulfilling nature of positive illusions in romantic relationships: Love is not blind, but prescient. *Journal of Personality and Social Psychology, 71*, 1155–1180.

Murray, S. L., Holmes, J. G., MacDonald, G., & Ellsworth, P. C. (1998). Through the looking glass darkly?: When self-doubts turn into relationship insecurities. *Journal of Personality and Social Psychology, 75*, 1459–1480.

Rempel, J. K., Holmes, J. G., & Zanna, M. P. (1985). Trust in close relationships. *Journal of Personality and Social Psychology, 49*, 95–112.

Rotter, J. B. (1980). Interpersonal trust, trustworthiness, and gullibility. *American Psychologist, 35*, 1–7.

Rusbult, C. E. (1980). Commitment and satisfaction in romantic associations: A test of the investment model. *Journal of Experimental Social Psychology, 16*, 172–186.

Rusbult, C. E. (1983). A longitudinal test of the investment model: The development (and deterioration) of satisfaction and commitment in heterosexual involvements. *Journal of Personality and Social Psychology, 45*, 101–117.

Rusbult, C. E., Bissonnette, V. L., Arriaga, X. B., & Cox, C. L. (1998). Accommodation processes during the early years of marriage. In T. N. Bradbury (Ed.), *The developmental course of marital dysfunction* (pp. 74–113). New York: Cambridge.

Rusbult, C. E., Davis, J. L., Finkel, E. J., Hannon, M. A., & Olsen, N. (2000). *Forgiveness of betrayal in close relationships: Does it rest on transformation of motivation?* Unpublished manuscript, University of North Carolina at Chapel Hill, Chapel Hill, NC.

Rusbult, C. E., Drigotas, S. M., & Verette, J. (1994). The investment model: An interdependence analysis of commitment processes and relationship maintenance phenomena. In D. Canary & L. Stafford (Eds.), *Communication and relational maintenance* (pp. 115–139). New York: Academic Press.

Rusbult, C. E., Finkel, E. J., Hannon, M. A., Kumashiro, M., & Childs, N. M. (2000). *Dealing with betrayal in close relationships: Does commitment promote forgiveness?* Unpublished manuscript, University of North Carolina at Chapel Hill, Chapel Hill, NC.

Rusbult, C. E., Johnson, D. J., & Morrow, G. D. (1986). Impact of couple patterns of problem solving on distress and nondistress in dating relationships. *Journal of Personality and Social Psychology, 50*, 744–753.

Rusbult, C. E., & Martz, J. M. (1995). Remaining in an abusive relationship: An investment model analysis of nonvoluntary commitment. *Personality and Social Psychology Bulletin, 21*, 558–571.

Rusbult, C. E., Martz, J. M., & Agnew, C. R. (1998). The investment model scale: Measuring commitment level, satisfaction level, quality of alternatives, and investment size. *Personal Relationships, 5*, 357–391.

Rusbult, C. E., & Van Lange, P. A. M. (1996). Interdependence processes. In E. T. Higgins & A. Kruglanski (Eds.), *Social psychology: Handbook of basic principles* (pp. 564–596). New York: Guilford.

Rusbult, C. E., Van Lange, P. A. M., Wildschut, T., Yovetich, N. A., & Verette, J. (in press). Perceived superiority in close relationships: Why it exists and persists. *Journal of Personality and Social Psychology.*

Rusbult, C. E., Verette, J., Whitney, G. A., Slovik, L. F., & Lipkus, I. (1991). Accommodation processes in close relationships: Theory and preliminary empirical evidence. *Journal of Personality and Social Psychology, 60*, 53–78.

Rusbult, C. E., & Zembrodt, I. M. (1983). Responses to dissatisfaction in romantic involvements: A multidimensional scaling analysis. *Journal of Experimental Social Psychology, 19*, 274–293.

Rusbult, C. E., Zembrodt, I. M., & Gunn, L. K. (1982). Exit, voice, loyalty, and neglect: Responses to dissatisfaction in romantic involvements. *Journal of Personality and Social Psychology, 43*, 1230–1242.

Scharfe, E., & Bartholomew, K. (1995). Accommodation and attachment representations in young couples. *Journal of Social and Personal Relationships, 12*, 389–401.

Sedikides, C., Olsen, N., & Reis, H. T. (1993). Relationships as natural categories. *Journal of Personality and Social Psychology, 64*, 71–82.

Simpson, J. A. (1987). The dissolution of romantic relationships: Factors involved in relationship stability and emotional distress. *Journal of Personality and Social Psychology, 53*, 683–692.

Simpson, J. A., Gangestad, S. W., & Lerma, M. (1990). Perception of physical attractiveness: Mechanisms involved in the maintenance of romantic relationships. *Journal of Personality and Social Psychology, 59*, 1192–1201.

South, S. J., & Lloyd, K. M. (1995). Spousal alternatives and marital dissolution. *American Sociological Review, 60*, 21–35.

Thibaut, J. W., & Kelley, H. H. (1959). *The social psychology of groups.* New York: Wiley.

Van Lange, P. A. M., & Rusbult, C. E. (1995). My relationship is better than—and not as bad as—yours is: The perception of superiority in close relationships. *Personality and Social Psychology Bulletin, 21*, 32–44.

Van Lange, P. A. M., Rusbult, C. E., Drigotas, S. M., Arriaga, X. B., Witcher, B. S., & Cox, C. L. (1997). Willingness to sacrifice in close relationships. *Journal of Personality and Social Psychology, 72*, 1373–1395.

Wieselquist, J., Rusbult, C. E., Foster, C. A., & Agnew, C. R. (1999). Commitment, prorelationship behavior, and trust in close relationships. *Journal of Personality and Social Psychology, 77*, 942–966.

Yovetich, N. A., & Rusbult, C. E. (1994). Accommodative behavior in close relationships: Exploring transformation of motivation. *Journal of Experimental Social Psychology, 30*, 138–164.

Perception of Physical Attractiveness: Mechanisms Involved in the Maintenance of Romantic Relationships

Jeffry A. Simpson • Texas A&M University
Steven W. Gangestad • University of New Mexico
Margaret Lerma • Corpus Christi State University

In 2 studies, factors involved in the perception of attractiveness of opposite-sex persons were examined. Investigation 1 revealed that individuals involved in dating relationships, relative to those not involved in them, tend to perceive opposite-sex persons as less physically and sexually attractive. Investigation 2 revealed that this dating status effect was not attributable to differences in physical attractiveness, self-esteem, empathy, self-monitoring, or altruism between individuals who were and those who were not involved in exclusive dating relationships. Moreover, both groups perceived young/same-sex and older/opposite-sex persons as equally attractive, suggesting that the effect is specific to young/opposite-sex persons. Results are discussed in terms of possible proximate and ultimate explanations underlying relationship maintenance processes.

Research on romantic relationships traditionally has focused on processes underlying either relationship initiation (e.g., Berscheid, 1985; Byrne, 1971; Duck & Gilmour, 1981; Newcomb, 1961) or, more recently, relationship dissolution (e.g., Baxter, 1984; Berg & McQuinn, 1986; Duck, 1982; Simpson, 1987). Somewhat less attention has been devoted to examining processes that may serve relationship-maintenance functions (Byrne & Murnen, 1988; for exceptions, see Dindia & Baxter, 1987; Johnson & Rusbult, 1989; Rusbult, 1983).

Despite this state of affairs, a variety of cognitive and perceptual phenomena have been presumed to promote the maintenance of romantic relationships. Selective memory for relationship-relevant events (Beach & Tesser, 1988), biased attributional accounts of relationship-relevant outcomes

(Harvey, Wells, & Alvarez, 1978; Fincham, Beach, & Nelson, 1987), and biased perceptions of partner attributes and abilities (Graziano & Musser, 1982) all have been conjectured to directly or indirectly promote relationship maintenance. Some of the most in-depth theoretical speculation, however, has centered on the perception of attractive, opposite-sex persons, particularly those external to the current relationship. Indeed, researchers adopting several different theoretical perspectives, including interdependence theories (e.g., Berscheid, 1986; Thibaut & Kelley, 1959), attachment theories (e.g., Bowlby, 1979), and evolutionary biological theories (e.g., Mellen, 1981; Symons, 1979), all have suggested that the stability of a relationship may be enhanced by the subtle perceptual derogation of attractive, opposite-sex persons.[1]

Relatively little empirical research, however, has directly addressed this topic. Johnson and Rusbult (1989) recently have demonstrated that individuals who are highly committed to their relationships actively and perhaps consciously derogate attractive, ostensibly available alternative partners on several interpersonal dimensions (e.g., intelligence, sense of humor, similarity of attitudes, dependability, and faithfulness). Derogation appears to be particularly pronounced when available alternatives are attractive and pose a clear threat to ongoing relationships. Aside from these findings, however, little is known about whether, how, and under what conditions perceptual derogation processes might promote relationship maintenance.

Needless to say, attractive alternatives can be evaluated and derogated within many different interpersonal domains (see Johnson & Rusbult, 1989). One of the most important dimensions ought to involve perceptions of physical and sexual attractiveness. Relative to other interpersonal attributes, an alternative's physical and sexual attractiveness is unique in that it often acts as the first and sometimes *only* dimension on which interpersonal evaluations are based (Berscheid &

Walster, 1974). As such, derogation of it may serve as the first and perhaps primary line of defense in relationship-maintenance processes. Moreover, initial evaluations of attractiveness can strongly affect judgments concerning a host of other interpersonal characteristics (Dion, Berscheid, & Walster, 1972), most of which require considerably more time to evaluate. Despite these considerations, derogation processes involving the perception of attractiveness per se have not been examined.

Dating Status

Highly attractive opposite-sex persons can constitute one of the greatest potential threats to the stability of an existing relationship (Levinger, 1979; Rusbult, 1980, 1983; Thibaut & Kelley, 1959). If alternative partners are perceived to be extremely attractive, they frequently may draw individuals away from established relationships, particularly if such alternatives are readily available. Past theory (e.g., Thibaut & Kelley, 1959) and research (e.g., Berg & McQuinn, 1986; Rusbult, 1983) on alternatives typically have focused on whether and how attractive, available opposite-sex persons influence the stability or internal functioning of established relationships. Attractive opposite-sex persons, however, need not necessarily be realistic or accessible to have negative, deleterious effects on existing relationships. Brief exposure to highly attractive opposite-sex individuals (e.g., media figures), for example, is known to attenuate evaluations of opposite-sex acquaintances (Kenrick & Gutierres, 1980) and, in some situations, current romantic partners (Kenrick, Gutierres, & Goldberg, 1989). To the extent that current partners routinely pale in comparison to highly attractive others, such persons—even if they are neither realistic nor accessible alternatives—may subtly undermine the satisfaction and perhaps stability of established relationships (cf. Weiss, 1975).

Given the considerable impact that close, ongoing relationships can have on promoting an individual's physical health (Bloom, Asher, & White, 1978) and psychological well-being (Campbell, Converse, & Rodgers, 1976), and in light of the

---

[1]Throughout this article, the term *derogation* is used to connote relative derogation.

myriad of factors that can precipitate the demise of an existing relationship (Levinger, 1979), it seems reasonable to conjecture that psychological processes designed to buffer established relationships from the lure of highly attractive persons might exist. When individuals enter a romantic relationship, psychological processes geared toward maintaining and perhaps promoting relationship stability should begin to operate. These processes, whether motivational or purely perceptual in origin, are likely to operate covertly, possibly outside of conscious awareness. Highly attractive individuals, who are most likely to indirectly undermine or threaten the permanence of established relationships, ought to be subtly derogated and seen as less desirable. Accordingly, we hypothesize that individuals involved in ongoing dating relationships (daters), relative to those not involved in relationships (nondaters), should perceive highly desirable opposite-sex persons as less physically and sexually attractive.

Investigation 1

Method

Participants

A total of 204 Texas A&M University undergraduates (101 men and 103 women) participated in a study on "psychology and advertising" for introductory psychology course credit. Their median age was 19.3 years.

Procedure

Participants reported to the study in same-sex groups of 10 to 20. Upon arrival, they were informed that a large advertising company, in cooperation with local psychologists, was interested in college students' reactions to several current magazine advertisements. Participants were told they would view and rate a series of magazine ads and then provide some background information about themselves. This cover story was used to deflect participants' attention away from the central hypotheses of the investigation in order to negate potential subject awareness biases (Aronson, Brewer, & Carlsmith, 1985).

Participants then viewed and rated 16 slides. Each slide depicted an advertisement taken from one of several popular magazines (e.g., *Cosmopolitan*, *Gentlemen's Quarterly*, and *Time*). The ads promoted a wide variety of products, including clothes, shoes, life insurance, food products, jewelry, liquor, cologne, soft drinks, and cigarettes.

By design, only 6 of the 16 ads featured opposite-sex persons. Male participants saw 6 ads featuring women and female participants saw 6 featuring men. These 6 opposite-sex ads served as the primary stimulus materials for male and female participants, respectively. The remaining 10 filler ads, which were viewed by both men and women, contained either no persons or mixed-sex groups of individuals. These filler ads were included to camouflage the true purpose of the study. To further minimize possible awareness biases, relationship measures were collected after the attractiveness measures. This ensured that participants' current dating status was not overly salient when the attractiveness ratings were made.

As they viewed each ad, participants first responded to four Likert-type filler items that inquired about their liking for, and the persuasiveness of, each ad. For ads featuring opposite-sex persons, they also responded to two additional questions that served as measures of physical and sexual attractiveness.

Once participants had evaluated all 16 ads, they completed measures that assessed their attractiveness, the frequency of their sexual activity in the preceding month, and their current dating status.

Measures

Physical and sexual attractiveness index. For each of the six ads containing an opposite-sex person, participants responded to two items: "How attractive do you find the person in the ad?" (rated on a 7-point scale, where 1 = *not at all* and 7 = *extremely*) and "From your perspective, how much sex appeal does the person in this ad possess?" (rated on a 7-point scale, where 1 = *none at all* and 7 = *a great deal*). These two items were highly correlated across the six opposite-sex stimulus

TABLE 18.1 Investigation 1: Means and Standard Deviations for the Physical and Sexual Attractiveness Index

Status	Men			Women		
	n	M	SD	n	M	SD
Dating	46	55.37	13.51	66	61.34	11.81
Not dating	55	61.40	10.18	37	67.49	11.97

Note. The possible range on the physical and sexual attractiveness index was from 12 (*minimal attractiveness*) to 84 (*maximal attractiveness*).

persons viewed by men and the six viewed by women (*r*s ranged from .58 to .90 and from .81 to .89 for men and women, respectively). To construct a more reliable index of physical and sexual attractiveness, we aggregated participants' responses to these two items across all six opposite-sex stimulus persons separately for men and women. Participants' scores on this global index could range from 12 (indicating opposite-sex persons were seen as minimally attractive) to 84 (indicating such persons were seen as maximally attractive). This index was internally consistent (Cronbach's alpha = .87).

Physical attractiveness. Participants' self-reported physical attractiveness was assessed by the question "How attractive do you consider yourself to be, relative to other people your age?" (answered on a 7-point scale, where 1 = *very unattractive* and 7 = *very attractive*).

Frequency of sex in the previous month. The frequency with which participants recently had engaged in sex was assessed by the item "How many times have you had sex (intercourse) in the past month?"

Current dating status. Participants' current dating status was assessed by the item "Are you currently dating someone?" (answered "yes" or "no"). Among daters (*n* = 106), men and women reported having dated their current partner for a median of 17 and 15 months, respectively.

Results and Discussion

Dating Status

To determine whether involvement in a dating relationship has effects on the perceived attractiveness of opposite-sex persons, we conducted

a 2 (dating status: dating vs. not dating) × 2 (sex: male vs. female) between-subjects analysis of variance (ANOVA), treating the physical and sexual attractiveness index as the dependent measure. As is evident in Table 18.1, individuals involved in ongoing dating relationships found the opposite-sex persons to be significantly less physically and sexually attractive than did individuals not involved in dating relationships, $F(1, 197) = 11.28$, $p < .001$. Simple effects analyses revealed that this result was reliable for both men, $F(1, 197) = 6.34$, $p < .02$, and women, $F(1, 197) = 6.59$, $p < .02$. A reliable Dating Status × Sex interaction failed to emerge, $F(1, 197) = .03$, *ns*.[2]

Participants' ratings of the persons depicted in the ads could have been influenced by their own level of physical attractiveness. Individuals who perceive themselves to be highly attractive relative to their peers may possess higher standards for attractiveness when evaluating the appearance of other people. Because attractive individuals are more likely to be involved in dating relationships (Berscheid, Dion, Walster, & Walster, 1971), the dating status effect might be attributable to this potentially confounding variable.

To determine whether participants' self-reported physical attractiveness did account for this effect, we conducted a 2 (dating status: dating vs. not dating) × 2 (sex: male vs. female) between-subjects analysis of covariance (ANCOVA), treating the physical and sexual attractiveness index as the dependent measure and participants'

---

[2]In this analysis and subsequent analyses involving the perception of opposite-sex persons, main effects for sex are not reported. Given that men and women viewed different stimulus persons, the results of such analyses are not informative.

perceived attractiveness as a covariate. When the effects of self-rated attractiveness were statistically removed, the dating status effect still emerged. Specifically, individuals involved in dating relationships found the opposite-sex persons to be less attractive than did those not involved in them, $F(1, 196) = 11.25$, $p < .001$. In fact, self-rated attractiveness did not covary with scores on the physical and sexual attractiveness index for either men ($r = .04$, ns) or women ($r = .12$, ns).

It also might be argued that the dating status effect could be mediated by "new look" perceptual processes in individuals who are not dating someone (cf. Bruner & Goodman, 1947). Many individuals who are *not* involved in dating relationships may be deprived of certain important, rewarding activities and outcomes that typically can be secured within ongoing relationships. If individuals who are not dating anyone experience greater deprivation on these important relationship-contingent dimensions, they may be motivated to perceive opposite-sex persons who theoretically could redress their deprivation as more attractive.

One of the most important relationship-contingent dimensions that might influence the perception of attractiveness in others is the sexual one (cf. Stephan, Berscheid, & Walster, 1971). Because recurrent sexual activity requires the presence and cooperation of a consenting partner, individuals who are not involved in a relationship, relative to those who are, theoretically should engage in sex less frequently. As a result, they may experience higher levels of sexual deprivation. Individuals not involved in a relationship did report having had sex significantly less often during the preceding month compared with those involved in one ($Ms = .56$ and 5.29 for nondaters and daters, respectively), $t(202) = 3.64$, $p < .001$. To control for this potentially confounding variable, we covaried the effects of participants' frequency of sex out of their scores on the physical and sexual attractiveness index. When these effects were statistically removed, a significant main effect for dating status still emerged, $F(1, 196) = 10.45$, $p < .001$. In sum,

sexual deprivation per se does not appear to account for the dating status effect.

Investigation 2

Although Investigation 1 provides preliminary support for our initial hypothesis, it does not address several alternate explanations for the dating status effect. First, Investigation 1 does not reveal whether the effect is confined to persons who theoretically could undermine the stability of an ongoing relationship (e.g., young, opposite-sex persons) or whether it extends to persons not likely to do so (e.g., young, same-sex persons and older, opposite-sex persons). If psychological processes designed to maintain established relationships do in fact exist, their effects should be specific to the perception of young, opposite-sex persons rather than persons in general.

Second, the first investigation did not control for variables that past research suggests may distinguish daters from nondaters. If the dating status effect predominately serves relationship-maintenance functions, involvement in an exclusive relationship per se, and not individual differences that differentiate daters from nondaters, should principally account for it. Previous research suggests that individuals who are more physically attractive (Berscheid et al., 1971) and who exhibit higher self-esteem (Morse, Reis, Gruzen, & Wolff, 1974) are more likely to be dating someone at any given point in time. Moreover, individuals who possess interpersonal skills or dispositions that may facilitate the development of relationships (e.g., empathy: Mehrabian & Epstein, 1972; altruism: Rushton, Chrisjohn, & Fekken, 1981; and self-monitoring: Ickes & Barnes, 1977) also might be more inclined to be involved in relationships. If any of these potentially confounding variables systematically predispose individuals to evaluate the appearance of opposite-sex persons either more or less favorably, a relationship-maintenance interpretation for the dating status effect would be rendered less plausible.

Third, in controlling for the effects of participants' physical attractiveness, Investigation 1 relied on self-reported attractiveness rather than more objective ratings provided by independent observers. Because self-reports of physical attractiveness do not always correlate highly with observer ratings (Berscheid & Walster, 1974), the physical attractiveness analyses reported in Investigation 1 may underestimate the extent to which participants' physical attractiveness systematically influenced their evaluations of opposite-sex persons.

Given our initial predictions, Investigation 1 also used a rather imprecise measure of current dating status. If psychological processes that serve to buffer established relationships from dissolution do exist, such processes should operate most strongly for individuals involved in *exclusive* dating relationships (i.e., those in which only one partner is being dated). They should operate less strongly, if at all, for individuals involved in nonexclusive relationships (i.e., those in which more than one partner is being dated simultaneously). In fact, nonexclusive daters ought to be more similar to nondaters in that neither group has a single, established relationship to maintain. Perceptual derogation processes, therefore, should not be evident within either of these groups. In view of these considerations, the dating status measure used in Investigation 2 distinguished between individuals involved in exclusive dating relationships (exclusive daters) and those not involved in exclusive relationships (nonexclusive daters and nondaters).

Method

Participants

A total of 197 Texas A&M University undergraduates (96 men and 101 women) participated in a study on "psychology and advertising" for introductory psychology course credit. Their median age was 19.4 years.

Procedure

The procedures and cover story were the same as those reported in Investigation 1. Participants viewed and rated a series of 15 *new* slides. Each slide depicted an advertisement taken from one of several popular magazines. Five of the slides depicted young/opposite-sex persons, five depicted older/opposite-sex persons, and five depicted young/same-sex persons.

As they viewed each ad, participants first answered four Likert-type filler items that inquired about their liking for, and the persuasiveness of, each ad. They then responded to two additional questions that served as measures of physical and sexual attractiveness. Once participants had rated the ads, they reported on the nature of their current dating status and responded to several individual difference measures. As participants returned their questionnaire packets, they were unobtrusively rated on their physical and sexual attractiveness by two independent raters. Following this, participants were thanked and debriefed.

Measures

Physical and sexual attractiveness index. For each ad, participants responded to two items: "How attractive do you find the person in this ad?" (rated on a 7-point scale, where $1 = not at all$ and $7 = extremely$) and "From your perspective, how much sex appeal does the person in this ad possess?" (rated on a 7-point scale, where $1 = none at all$ and $7 = a great deal$). These two items were highly correlated within the five slides depicting young/opposite-sex persons, the five depicting older/opposite-sex persons, and the five depicting young/same-sex ones (rs ranged from .60 to .93 for both men and women). To construct reliable indices of physical and sexual attractiveness, we aggregated participants' responses to these two items across the subsets of five slides depicting young/opposite-sex persons, older/opposite-sex persons, and young/same-sex persons separately for men and women. Participants' scores on these three global indices could range from 10 (indicating minimal attractiveness) to 70 (indicating maximal attractiveness). These indices were internally consistent (Cronbach's alphas = .69, .81, and .93 for men, respectively, and .77, .85, and .81 for women, respectively).

For each ad depicting a young/opposite-sex person, participants also responded to the question

"To what extent do you think you could find and actually date someone who is as attractive as the person in this ad?" (anchored 1 = *I definitely could not* and 7 = *I definitely could*). When their responses were averaged across all five stimulus persons, most individuals thought they could date someone of similar attractiveness (*M*s = 4.99 for men and 4.41 for women).

Exclusivity of dating status. The exclusivity of participants' dating status was assessed by two items: "Are you currently dating someone?" (answered "yes" or "no") and "If yes, what is your current dating status: dating my current partner and others/engaged or dating my current partner and no one else." Individuals who indicated they were dating someone exclusively (*n* = 88) were designated as belonging to the "exclusive" category. Those who indicated they either were not dating anyone or were dating more than one person (*n* = 109) were classified as belonging to the "nonexclusive" category. Among exclusive daters, men and women reported having dated their current partner for a median of 15 and 13 months, respectively.

Individual difference measures. Participants then responded to several individual difference measures designed to assess self-esteem (the Texas Social Behavior Inventory; Helmreich, Stapp, & Ervin, 1972) as well as various interpersonal skills and dispositions (altruism: Rushton et al., 1981; empathy: Mehrabian & Epstein, 1972; and self-monitoring: Gangestad & Snyder, 1985).

Physical and sexual attractiveness ratings. As they returned their materials, participants were unobtrusively rated according to their physical and sexual attractiveness by two independent observers (one male and one female) who posed as experimental assistants. Observers rated each participant (relative to his or her peers) on two 7-point Likert-type scales, each anchored 1 = *very unattractive* and 7 = *very attractive*. Raters' physical and sexual attractiveness ratings were added together and their composite ratings were then aggregated to form a more reliable index of observer-rated attractiveness. Given that this index was composed of only two composite ratings, it

possessed reasonably good internal consistency (Cronbach's alpha = .56).

Results and Discussion
Dating Status

Data were analyzed within a 3 (person type: young/same-sex, young/opposite-sex, or older/opposite-sex) × 2 (dating status: exclusive vs. not exclusive) × 2 (sex: female vs. male) ANOVA framework in which person type was treated as a within-subjects variable and dating status and sex were treated as between-subjects variables. To discern whether the dating status effect was limited to young /opposite-sex persons, we performed two orthogonal, planned contrasts with respect to the person type variable. The first contrast tested whether the predicted Dating Status (exclusive vs. not exclusive) × Person Type (young/opposite-sex vs. young/same-sex and older/opposite-sex) interaction emerged (see Cohen & Cohen, 1983). As expected, this contrast produced a marginally reliable effect, $F(1, 190) = 3.03, p < .09$. Specifically, exclusive daters perceived young/opposite-sex persons as being less attractive than did nonexclusive daters, whereas the two groups did not differ in their evaluations of either young/same-sex or older/opposite-sex persons. No residual variance was accounted for by person type. The second contrast tested whether a second Dating Status (exclusive vs. not exclusive) × Person Type (young/same-sex vs. older/opposite-sex) interaction emerged. As anticipated, this contrast was not reliable, $F(1, 190) < 1, ns$.

Following this, we performed a 2 (dating status: exclusive vs. not exclusive) × 2 (sex: female vs. male) simple effects ANOVA, treating participants' scores on the physical and sexual attractiveness index for young/opposite-sex persons as the dependent variable. As revealed in Table 18.2, individuals involved in exclusive dating relationships perceived the young/opposite-sex persons to be reliably less attractive than did those who were not, $F(1, 193) = 8.16, p < .005$. Additional simple effects analyses indicated that this finding was reliable for women, $F(1, 193) = 10.82, p < .001$.

TABLE 18.2 Investigation 2: Means and Standard Deviations for the Physical and Sexual Attractiveness Indexes of Young/Opposite-Sex Persons, Young/Same-Sex Persons, and Older/Opposite-Sex Persons

| Sex/dating status | n | Physical and sexual attractiveness index | | | | | |
| | | Young/opposite-sex | | Young/same-sex | | Older/opposite-sex | |
		M	SD	M	SD	M	SD
Female/exclusive	50	49.80	11.03	49.54	9.51	19.52	7.64
Male/exclusive	38	56.05	7.49	30.03	13.70	16.41	6.96
Female/not exclusive	51	55.35	8.01	49.12	9.10	20.50	8.42
Male/not exclusive	58	57.31	5.87	34.95	16.04	16.70	7.40

Note. The possible range on each index was from 10 (*minimal attractiveness*) to 70 (*maximal attractiveness*).

Although the effect was in the predicted direction, it was not reliable for men, $F(1, 193) < 1$, *ns*. A marginally reliable Dating Status × Sex interaction emerged, $F(1, 193) = 3.24, p < .08$.

We then conducted two additional 2 (Dating Status) × 2 (Sex) simple effects analyses, one treating participants' scores on the physical and sexual attractiveness index for young/same-sex persons as the dependent measure and the other treating scores on the attractiveness index for older/opposite-sex persons as the dependent measure. Table 18.2 reveals that both individuals who were and those who were not involved in exclusive relationships perceived young/same-sex persons and older/opposite-sex persons to be equally attractive: for young/same-sex persons, $F(1, 192) = 1.56$, *ns*; for older/opposite-sex persons, $F(1, 190) = .33$, *ns*. No Dating Status × Sex interaction emerged for either analysis: for young/same-sex persons, $F(1, 192) = 2.20$, *ns*; for older/opposite-sex persons, $F(1, 190) = .09$, *ns*.

We next examined the extent to which various measures presumed to covary with dating status actually were associated with it. A series of point-biserial correlations (with exclusivity of dating status serving as the dichotomously coded variable) revealed that none of the five individual difference measures—altruism, empathy, self-esteem, self-monitoring, and observer-rated physical attractiveness—were reliably correlated with dating status (all *rs* < .10, *ns*). To ensure that none of these five variables accounted for the dating status effect, we conducted a series of five 2 (dating status: exclusive vs. not exclusive) × 2 (sex: female

vs. male) ANCOVAs, treating participants' scores on the attractiveness index for young/opposite-sex persons as the dependent measure and their scores on each of the five individual difference measures as covariates. When the effects of observer-rated attractiveness, altruism, empathy, self-esteem, and self-monitoring were individually controlled for, reliable effects for dating status still emerged (all five $Fs > 5, p < .03$). Hence, individual differences on these dimensions do not appear to account for the dating status effect.

Combined Analyses

Although the dating status effect was reliable for both sexes in Investigation 1, it emerged only for women in Investigation 2. To arrive at a better and more reliable estimate of the overall magnitude of this effect, we combined the data from Investigations 1 and 2, classified individuals according to the one measure common to both studies (i.e., dating status: daters vs. non-daters), and conducted an omnibus analysis. Specifically, we performed a 2 (dating status: dating vs. not dating) × 2 (sex: female vs. male) × 2 (investigation: 1 vs. 2) ANOVA, treating scores on the indices of young/opposite-sex persons within each study as the dependent variable. This combined analysis revealed a highly reliable main effect for dating status, $F(1, 393) = 20.95, p < .001$. All two- and three-way interactions were nonsignificant (all *Fs* < 1.50), including the Sex × Dating Status interaction, $F(1, 393) = 1.40$, *ns*. Moreover, simple effects analyses indicated that an overall reliable effect for dating status emerged for *both* women, $F(1, 393) = 16.94, p < .001$, and men, $F(1, 393) = 5.75, p < .02$. Thus, when data from both studies are pooled, the dating status effect is robust for both sexes, although it tends to be somewhat larger for women ($\eta^2 = .08$) than for men ($\eta^2 = .03$).

General Discussion

Viewed together, these investigations suggest that individuals involved in dating relationships, relative to those not involved in them, perceive young, opposite-sex persons as less physically and sexually attractive. Investigation 1 revealed that this dating status effect is not attributable to differences between daters and nondaters in frequency of recent sexual activity, suggesting that the effect may not be attributable to perceptual accentuation of opposite-sex attractiveness on the part of nondaters due to sexual deprivation. Investigation 2 documented that this effect is confined to the perception of young, opposite-sex persons and that several additional variables likely to differentiate exclusive daters from nonexclusive daters do not account for it. Although results vary somewhat across the two studies, combined analyses indicated that the effect is reliable for both sexes. Moreover, neither objective nor subjective measures of emotional bonding strongly moderate the extent to which young, opposite-sex persons were viewed as being attractive, particularly in the case of women.

These findings extend our understanding of perceptual derogation processes in several different ways. First, by demonstrating that the dating status effect is specific to young/opposite-sex persons, these investigations provide compelling evidence that the effect may operate expressly to promote relationship maintenance. Second, contrary to past research (e.g., Johnson & Rusbult, 1989), the current findings provide evidence for perceptual derogation of attractive yet *unavailable* persons (i.e., models). These results are noteworthy because they indicate that attractive, opposite-sex individuals need not necessarily be accessible in order to be derogated. Perceptual derogation, therefore, may be a much more generalized and

pervasive mechanism through which relationship stability might be enhanced than previously has been presumed. Third, past research (e.g., Johnson & Rusbult, 1989) has explored derogation as a function of subjective commitment to relationships. By using a more objective indicator of relationship involvement (i.e., current dating status) and by ruling out several different alternate explanations, the present research provides some of the strongest evidence to date that relationship involvement actually may cause perceptual derogation.

Dating Status

What psychological processes might underlie the dating status effect and, more generally, why does it exist? Although definitive answers to these questions cannot be provided, the effect can be understood at both proximate and ultimate levels of explanation.

At a proximate level, individuals involved in dating relationships may be motivated to derogate attractive, opposite-sex persons in order to justify their involvement in the current relationship (Festinger, 1957). Because of effort justification processes (Aronson & Mills, 1959), individuals involved in relationships may be motivated to perceive opposite-sex persons as less attractive.

How might this effect be accounted for at an ultimate level of explanation? Involvement in an exclusive, stable relationship is known to have strong, positive effects on individuals' physical health (Bloom et al., 1978). Moreover, the pair bonding that occurs between partners in a relationship is believed to have assumed a critical role in promoting individuals' reproductive success and in fostering adequate parental care at one time in evolutionary history (Mellen, 1981). In fact, some theorists have suggested that pair bonding might have evolved precisely because it fulfills these vital biological functions (Hinde, 1984; Symons, 1979). Given the diversity of factors that can precipitate the demise of enduring relationships, it seems reasonable to conjecture that psychological mechanisms designed to promote relationship stability might have emerged during evolutionary history (see Mellen, 1981). Because attractive, opposite-sex persons can present serious threats to the permanence of an established relationship, it is conceivable that relationship-maintenance mechanisms may have evolved—and may still operate—to reduce the appeal of attractive persons. One such mechanism might produce a perceptual effect whereby individuals who are involved in an exclusive relationship are inclined to perceive opposite-sex persons as less attractive than those who are not.

These conjectures, of course, are highly speculative. We cannot unequivocally demonstrate that this perceptual effect reflects psychological processes that have evolved and exist explicitly for purposes of promoting relationship maintenance. The dating status effect may exist because it serves entirely different functions. Moreover, it is possible that effort justification processes may serve as the proximate psychological process that mediates this ultimate, evolutionary-based account. Nevertheless, when one considers the importance that stable relationships assume in enhancing individuals' welfare and reproductive fitness, it seems reasonable to surmise that the psychological processes that produce the dating status effect might have evolved primarily to enhance relationship permanence. Future research must discern whether this effect stems from general dissonance reduction processes or whether it operates according to other, more idiosyncratic psychological processes (cf. Cosmides & Tooby, 1987).

Conclusions

It is conceivable that two distinct yet related psychological mechanisms serving relationship-maintenance functions through perceptual derogation may exist. The more subtle, less conscious mechanism may involve perceptual derogation with respect to global attractiveness, one of the first, most salient, and most readily discernible dimensions on which initial impressions of others typically are based. Once involved in a relationship, individuals may possess perceptual "blinders" that effectively insulate them from the distracting and tempting lure of highly attractive persons whom they regularly may encounter. The less

subtle, more conscious mechanism may entail overt and perhaps premeditated derogation of alternatives who pose a direct and real threat to established relationships. This second psychological mechanism, which might involve derogation on a variety of different interpersonal dimensions, may serve to further shield current relationships from challenges posed by accessible, real-life alternatives.

Perceptual derogation represents only one of several possible domains in which psychological mechanisms designed to promote relationship maintenance might be evident. Maintenance processes specific to other domains—including perceptions of and attributions about both one's current romantic partner and the relationship in general—also might exist. Fincham et al. (1987), for instance, have shown that nondistressed marital couples often exhibit a positive bias when generating attributions for both their partner's actions and events that commonly occur in the relationship. Although findings such as these typically have not been interpreted in the context of relationship-maintenance processes, they may reflect them. Future research should identify additional domains in which relationship-maintenance processes may operate and determine how these domains interact to facilitate relationship stability.

NOTES

This research was supported by a grant from the Computing Services Center at Texas A&M University.

We would like to thank Scott Culpepper, Mystel Johnson, and Melinda Jones for their assistance with Investigation 1. We thank William Ickes, Douglas Kenrick, Caryl Rusbult, and several anonymous reviewers for their helpful feedback on earlier versions of this article.

Correspondence concerning this article should be addressed to either Jeffry A. Simpson, Department of Psychology, Texas A&M University, College Station, Texas 77843, or Steven W. Gangestad, Department of Psychology, University of New Mexico, Albuquerque, New Mexico 87131.

REFERENCES

Aronson, E., Brewer, M., & Carlsmith, M. J. (1985). Experimentation in social psychology. In G. Lindzey & E. Aronson (Eds.), *The handbook of social psychology* (pp. 441–486). New York: Random House.

Aronson, E., & Mills, J. (1959). The effect of severity of initiation on liking for a group. *Journal of Abnormal and Social Psychology, 59*, 177–181.

Baxter, L. A. (1984). Trajectories of relationship disengagement. *Journal of Social and Personal Relationships, 1*, 29–48.

Beach, S. R. H., & Tesser, A. (1988). Love in marriage: A cognitive account. In R. J. Sternberg & M. L. Barnes (Eds.), *The psychology of love* (pp. 330–335). New Haven, CT: Yale University Press.

Berg, J. H., & McQuinn, R. D. (1986). Attraction and exchange in continuing and noncontinuing dating relationships. *Journal of Personality and Social Psychology, 50*, 942–952.

Berscheid, E. (1985). Interpersonal attraction. In G. Lindzey & E. Aronson (Eds.), *The handbook of social psychology* (pp. 413–484). New York: Random House.

Berscheid, E. (1986). Emotional experience in close relationships: Some implications for child development. In W. Hartup & Z. Rubin (Eds.), *Relationships and development* (pp. 135–166). Hillsdale, NJ: Erlbaum.

Berscheid, E., Dion, K., Walster, E., & Walster, G. W. (1971). Physical attractiveness and dating choice: A test of the matching hypothesis. *Journal of Experimental Social Psychology, 7*, 173–189.

Berscheid, E., & Walster, E. (1974). Physical attractiveness. In L. Berkowitz (Ed.), *Advances in experimental social psychology* (Vol. 7, pp. 157–215). New York: Academic Press.

Bloom, B. L., Asher, S. J., & White, S. W. (1978). Marital disruption as a stressor: A review and analysis. *Psychological Bulletin, 85*, 867–894.

Bowlby, J. (1979). *The making and breaking of affectional bonds*. London: Tavistock.

Bruner, J. S., & Goodman, C. D. (1947). Value and need as organizing factors in perception. *Journal of Abnormal and Social Psychology, 42*, 33–44.

Byrne, D. (1971). *The attraction paradigm*. New York: Academic Press.

Byrne, D., & Murnen, S. K. (1988). Maintaining loving relationships. In R. J. Sternberg & M. L. Barnes (Eds.), *The psychology of love* (pp. 293–310). New Haven, CT: Yale University Press.

Campbell, A., Converse, P. E., & Rodgers, W. L. (1976). *The quality of American life*. New York: Russell Sage Foundation.

Cohen, J., & Cohen, P. (1983). *Applied multiple regression/correlation analysis for the behavioral sciences*. Hillsdale, NJ: Erlbaum.

Cosmides, L., & Tooby, J. (1987). From evolution to behavior: Evolutionary psychology as the missing link. In J. Dupre (Ed.), *The latest on the best: Essays on evolution and optimality* (pp. 277–306). Cambridge, MA: MIT Press.

Dindia, K., & Baxter, L. A. (1987). Strategies for maintaining and repairing marital relationships. *Journal of Social and Personal Relationships, 4*, 143–158.

Dion, K. K., Berscheid, E., & Walster, E. (1972). What is beautiful is good. *Journal of Personality and Social Psychology, 24*, 285–290.

Duck, S. W. (Ed.). (1982). *Personal relationships 4: Dissolving personal relationships*. London: Academic Press.

Duck, S. W., & Gilmour, R. (Eds.). (1981). *Personal relationships 2: Developing personal relationships*. London: Academic Press.

Festinger, L. (1957). *A theory of cognitive dissonance*. Stanford, CA: Stanford University Press.

Fincham, F., Beach, S. R. H., & Nelson, G. (1987). Attribution process in distressed and nondistressed couples: 3. Casual and responsibility attributions for spouse behavior. *Cognitive Therapy and Research, 11*, 71–86.

Gangestad, S., & Snyder, M. (1985). To carve nature at its joints: On the existence of discrete classes in personality. *Psychological Review, 92*, 317–349.

Graziano, W. G., & Musser, L. M. (1982). The joining and parting of ways. In S. Duck (Ed.), *Personal relationships 4: Dissolving personal relationships* (pp. 75–106). London: Academic Press.

Harvey, J. H., Wells, G. L., & Alvarez, M. D. (1978). Attribution in the context of conflict and separation in close relationships. In J. H. Harvey, W. Ickes, & R. F. Kidd (Eds.), *New directions in attribution research* (Vol. 2, pp. 235–260). Hillsdale, NJ: Erlbaum.

Helmreich, R., Stapp, J., & Ervin, C. (1972). The Texas Social Behavior Inventory (TSBI): An objective measure of self-esteem or social competence. *Journal Supplement Abstract Service Catalog of Selected Documents in Psychology, 4*, 79.

Hinde, R. A. (1984). Why do the sexes behave differently in close relationships? *Journal of Social and Personal Relationships, 1*, 471–501.

Ickes, W. J., & Barnes, R. D. (1977). The role of sex and self-monitoring in unstructured dyadic interactions. *Journal of Personality and Social Psychology, 35*, 315–330.

Johnson, D. J., & Rusbult, C. E. (1989). Resisting temptation: Devaluation of alternative partners as a means of maintaining commitment in close relationships. *Journal of Personality and Social Psychology, 57*, 967–980.

Kelley, H. H., Berscheid, E., Christensen, A., Harvey, J. H., Huston, T. L., Levinger, G., McClintock, E., Peplau, L. A., & Peterson, D. R. (1983). *Close relationships*. San Francisco: Freeman.

Kenrick, D. T., & Gutierres, S. E. (1980). Contrast effects and judgments of physical attractiveness: When beauty becomes a social problem. *Journal of Personality and Social Psychology, 38*, 131–140.

Kenrick, D. T., Gutierres, S. E., & Goldberg, L. L. (1989). Influence of popular erotica on judgments of strangers and mates. *Journal of Experimental Social Psychology, 25*, 159–167.

Levinger, G. (1979). A social exchange view on the dissolution of pair relationships. In R. L. Burgess & T. L. Huston (Eds.), *Social exchange in developing relationships* (pp. 169–193). New York: Academic Press.

Mehrabian, A., & Epstein, N. (1972). A measure of emotional empathy. *Journal of Personality, 40*, 525–543.

Mellen, S. L. W. (1981). *The evolution of love*. Oxford, England: Freeman.

Morse, S. J., Reis, H. T., Gruzen, J., & Wolff, E. (1974). The "eye of the beholder": Determinants of physical attractiveness judgements in the U.S. and South Africa. *Journal of Personality, 42*, 528–542.

Newcomb, T. M. (1961). *The acquaintance process.* New York: Holt, Rinehart, & Winston.

Rusbult, C. E. (1980). A longitudinal test of the investment model: The development (and deterioration) of satisfaction and commitment in heterosexual involvements. *Journal of Personality and Social Psychology, 45*, 101–117.

Rusbult, C. E. (1983). Commitment and satisfaction in romantic associations: A test of the investment model. *Journal of Experimental Social Psychology, 16*, 172–186.

Rushton, J. P., Chrisjohn, R. D., & Fekken, G. C. (1981). The altruistic personality and the self-report Altruism Scale. *Personality and Individual Differences, 2*, 293–302.

Simpson, J. A. (1987). The dissolution of romantic relationships: Factors involved in relationship stability and emotional distress. *Journal of Personality and Social Psychology, 53*, 683–692.

Stephan, W. E., Berscheid, E., & Walster, E. (1971). Sexual arousal and heterosexual attraction. *Journal of Personality and Social Psychology, 20*, 93–101.

Symons, D. (1979). *The evolution of human sexuality.* New York: Oxford University Press.

Thibaut, J. W., & Kelley, H. H. (1959). *The social psychology of groups.* New York: Wiley.

Weiss, R. S. (1975). *Marital separation.* New York: Basic Books.

READING 19

The Benefits of Positive Illusions: Idealization and the Construction of Satisfaction in Close Relationships

Sandra L. Murray, John G. Holmes, and
Dale W. Griffin • University of Waterloo

In the case of love, realities model themselves enthusiastically on one's
desires . . . it is the passion in which violent desire is most completely satisfied.

—Beyle Stendhal, *De L'Amour*

It is proposed that satisfaction is associated with idealistic, rather than realistic, perceptions of one's partner. To provide baselines for assessing relationship illusions, both members of married and dating heterosexual couples were asked to rate themselves and their partners on a variety of interpersonal attributes. Participants also rated the typical and ideal partner on these attributes. Path analyses revealed that individuals' impressions of their partners were more a mirror of their self-images and ideals than a reflection of their partners' self-reported attributes. Overall, intimates saw their partners in a more positive light than their partners saw themselves. Furthermore, these idealized constructions predicted greater satisfaction. Individuals were happier in their relationships when they idealized their partners and their partners idealized them. Taken together, these results suggest that a certain degree of idealization or illusion may be a critical feature of satisfying dating and even marital relationships.

As Stendhal's musings in *De L'Amour* illustrate, people immersed in the experience of romantic love often appear to bend reality to the will of their hopes and desires. Rather than being constrained by the sometimes-disappointing reality of their partners' actual attributes, individuals may view their partners through the rosy filters provided by images of ideal partners. Within such idealized constructions, intimates may even see virtues in one another's apparent faults. For example, individuals may preserve feelings of confidence in their romantic relationships—in the face of the doubts posed by a partner's failings—by weaving stories that depict such faults in the best possible light (Murray & Holmes, 1993, 1994).

But is idealization the key to enduring happiness, or does it only leave people vulnerable to inevitable disappointments and disillusionment? Psychologists often depict idealization as a dangerous malady associated only with the early infatuation period (e.g., Brickman, 1987). After all, because few individuals are perfect, increased interdependence should reveal the many ways in which an intimate falls short of one's hopes and ideals (e.g., Brehm, 1992). Continuing to idealize one's partner in the face of negative evidence should then impede adjustment, particularly if intimates love only the idealized image they construct. In this light, understanding the reality of a partner's virtues and faults may prove to be the key to enduring satisfaction, whereas idealization may leave intimates vulnerable to dashed hopes and expectations.

Despite such arguments, growing evidence suggests that "positive illusions" about the self are critical for adjustment and mental health (e.g., Taylor & Brown, 1988; Weinstein, 1980). In this article, we propose a related perspective on relationship illusions, arguing that a certain degree of idealization is critical for satisfying dating and even marital relationships.

The Idealization Process: Seeing What One Wants to See

Love to faults is always blind,

Always is to joy inclined,

Lawless, winged, and unconfined,

And breaks all chains from every mind. (William Blake, 1971)

Early on in romantic relationships, intimates' absorption in their partners' virtues fuels their hopes for their relationship's success (Holmes & Boon, 1990; Weiss, 1980). Self-presentation, interaction across restricted, positive domains, and intimates'

desire not to perceive negativity all likely strengthen the perception that the partner really is the "right" person (e.g., Brehm, 1988; Brickman, 1987). Intimates' models of the ideal relationship also may help them fill in the gaps in their limited knowledge about their partners, a process of wish fulfillment in which realities become a reflection of their desires (e.g., Murstein, 1971). The allure of a partner's apparent virtues draws individuals into their relationships, creating feelings of confidence and hope that belie the lack of more representative experiences.

As interdependence increases, individuals begin interacting across broader, more conflictual domains, and the potential for partners to exhibit negative behaviors increases (e.g., Braiker & Kelley, 1979; Levinger, 1983). Even in marriage, intimates may continue to uncover new sources of conflict as new demands surface, such as balancing a career and children (e.g., Hackel & Ruble, 1992). In fact, the potential for recurrent negativity may be greatest in marriage because of the strength and diversity of the bonds connecting husbands and wives. Discovering such harsh realities may then threaten intimates' hopes and idealized perceptions by raising the disturbing possibility that one's partner really is not the "right" person after all.

In the face of existing commitments, such competing hopes and doubts likely intensify intimates' need to reach confident, unequivocal conclusions about their partners (Brehm, 1988; Brickman, 1987; Fletcher, Fincham, Cramer, & Heron, 1987; Holmes & Rempel, 1989). Paradoxically, then, suffering the inevitable disappointments of romantic life might actually strengthen idealized perceptions rather than tarnishing them. For instance, Hillary might quell her disappointment in Bill's stubbornness during conflicts by interpreting it as integrity rather than as egocentrism. Alternatively, she might try to excuse this fault by embellishing Bill's generally tolerant nature. As these examples illustrate, sustaining confidence in an intimate partner may necessitate weaving an elaborate story (or fiction) that both embellishes a partner's virtues and minimizes faults (Murray & Holmes, 1993, 1994).

This argument rests on the general assumption that a partner's qualities cannot be directly perceived. Instead, behavior must be interpreted and given meaning, motives for that behavior must be inferred, and, most indirectly of all, impressions of a partner's personal characteristics must be constructed (e.g., Gergen, Hepburn, & Fisher, 1986; Griffin & Ross, 1991). As a result, intimates need not be bound by only one possible interpretation of one another's virtues and faults as dictated by some stern objective reality. Instead, given the license in the storytelling process, individuals may come to see their partners in highly idealized ways (e.g., Hall & Taylor, 1976; Johnson & Rusbult, 1989; Murray & Holmes, 1993, 1994; Van Lange & Rusbult, 1995).

Constraining Desire: A Role for Reality?

Even from a social constructionist perspective, one must admit that "objective" reality constrains and structures an individual's interpretation of the social world. If intimates are even reasonably accurate social perceivers, their representations should at least partially reflect their partners' actual virtues and faults. After all, only characters in fairy tales can turn frogs into princes or princesses. Some mixture of social construction and reality must underlie people's images of their partners. These representations might best be conceptualized in terms of an additive model that apportions part of the variance in perceptions to "construction" and part to "reality," as the following conceptual equation illustrates: actor's perception = reality of partner + actor's construction.

But given the difficulty of pinpointing "objective" truths, we're faced with a dilemma: How can we measure the actor's constructions without knowledge of the partner's "real" qualities or "true" nature? In the absence of a gold standard for reality, we turned to partners' own perspective on their virtues and faults. Investigators typically use such self-ratings as indexes of individuals' personality traits, despite the necessary caveats associated with using self-reports to estimate reality. Using this subjective reality baseline allows the separation of the reality-based and the constructed aspects of individuals' representations of

their partners, as this adaptation of our initial model illustrates: actor's perception = partner's reality + actor's construction.

For example, Hillary's perception of Bill may partly reflect Bill's own reality, as defined by his self-perceptions, and partly reflect her construction. In our thinking, Hillary's perceptions may diverge from Bill's reality for both cognitive and motivational reasons. From a more cognitive perspective, Hillary's idiosyncratic theories about which traits cluster together in most people may guide her construction. Alternatively, Hillary might come to see Bill in much different ways than he sees himself if she relies on different contexts and experiences as her information base. From a more motivational perspective, Hillary's desire to see Bill in a particular way, perhaps as her own ideal partner, may also structure the nature of her constructions.

In contemplating our index of partners' realities, it is critical to note that we are not arguing that individuals possess true insight into the actual nature of their own attributes. In fact, there is every reason to believe that individuals' self-perceptions are in part constructions. For instance, individuals typically see themselves in much more positive, idealized ways than their actual attributes appear to warrant (Alicke, 1985; Brown, 1986; Greenwald, 1980; Taylor & Brown, 1988). But given this evidence of self-aggrandizement, individuals' self-views may provide a conservative benchmark for indexing the idealized nature of their partners' perceptions (i.e., Hillary's illusions about Bill must surpass his own illusions about himself).

In this article, we explore three separate questions concerning the nature of intimates' representations of reality. First, do actors' impressions of their partners mirror their partners' self-perceptions? This is the question of convergence, or "reality matching." Or do actors' impressions of their partners diverge systematically from their partners' self-perceptions? This is the related question of projection. Second, do intimates tend to view their partners more positively than their partners view themselves? This is the question of distortion in perceptions. Finally, do intimates' unique, idealized constructions of one another's attributes predict greater satisfaction? This is the question of function.

Individuals' perceptions of their partners' attributes should mirror their partners' self-perceptions to the extent that they both reflect a shared social reality. Indeed, considerable evidence suggests that social perceivers often agree on one another's attributes (e.g., Kenny & DePaulo, 1993). Such convergence, or "reality matching" is reflected in the shaded area of Figure 19.1. In the domain of romantic relationships, such evidence of mutual understanding may be an integral part of the intimacy process (McCall, 1974; Reis & Shaver, 1988).

But if idiosyncratic construal also plays a preeminent role in shaping representations, as we expect, such realities may diverge and individuals may see their partners in much different ways than their partners see themselves. Such constructions are reflected in the hatched area of Figure 19.1. We believe that individuals' desire to see their partners in the best possible light biases the nature of their constructions. In particular, we expect actors to see their partners in a more positive, idealized way than their partners see themselves. In the current research, we explored how self- and relationship schemas might structure impressions

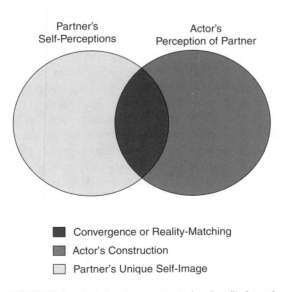

Partner's
Self-Perceptions

Actor's
Perception of Partner

■ Convergence or Reality-Matching

■ Actor's Construction

□ Partner's Unique Self-Image

FIGURE 19.1 ■ Isolating the constructed and reality-based components of actors' representations of their partners.

in such ways that sometimes harsh relationship realities become reflections of intimates' wishes.

The Projection of Self and Ideals

In terms of self-schemas (e.g., Markus & Zajonc, 1985), intimates might project their own virtues onto their partners, including their partners in their own illusory self-views. Seeing oneself in one's partner is even thought to be a sign of a close, interdependent relationship (Aron, Aron, Tudor, & Nelson, 1991). Such projection may occur because traits that are schematic for the self represent a general "value system" that guides perception. More purely motivational biases may also underlie projection. Seeing oneself in one's partner may foster a sense of predictability that is critical for feelings of security (Holmes & Rempel, 1989). Also, individuals might affirm their own self-images by assuming that their partners are just like them, only slightly better (e.g., Berscheid & Walster, 1978).

As an even more direct path to wish fulfillment, intimates may see one another's attributes through the rosy filter provided by their images of the ideal partner (e.g., Murstein, 1967, 1971). Such ideals represent individuals' working models of the attributes they hope and perhaps need to find in an intimate partner if they are to feel secure in their commitment (e.g., Bowlby, 1977). Like other relationship schemas, ideals may provide a template for shaping intimates' construal of their partners' attributes (Baldwin, 1992).

Beginning with Bowlby (1982), attachment theorists have argued that models of self and other are intricately related. This suggests that individuals' idiosyncratic models of the ideal partner should be conditional on their own sense of self-worth. Individuals with a stronger sense of self-worth should set higher ideals, whereas individuals with a weaker sense of self-worth should expect less from an intimate partner. If self- and ideal models are tied in this way, ideals may mediate the hypothesized link between self-perceptions and impressions of a romantic partner.

In summary, by using partners' self-impressions as "reality" benchmarks, we will explore whether actors project their self-images and ideals onto their partners, thereby seeing them differently, even more positively, than their partners see themselves. We hope to show that individuals' impressions of their partners are as much a mirror of their own self-images and ideals as a reflection of their partners' actual, or at least self-perceived, attributes.

Illusion, Idealization, and Satisfaction

An illusion which makes me happy is worth a verity which drags me to the ground. (Christoph Martin Wieland, *Idris und Zemde, canto III*)

Sharing Wieland's sentiment, we believe that idealized constructions or positive illusions are a critical feature of satisfying dating and even marital relationships. Taylor and Brown (1988) have been the staunchest advocates of such a perspective on illusion, arguing that illusions about the self promote healthy functioning. Such "positive illusions," including idealized self-perceptions, exaggerated perceptions of control, and unrealistic optimism, appear to function as buffers, protecting self-esteem in the face of the threats posed by negative information about the self. Also, individuals' perhaps illusory assumption that the world is in fact benevolent and meaningful may provide a sense of security in the face of uncertainty (Janoff-Bulman, 1989). From these perspectives, happiness and contentment depend not on individuals' acceptance of a stern reality, but on their ability to see themselves and their worlds in the best possible light.

In this article, we argue that feelings of satisfaction reflect intimates' ability to see imperfect partners in idealized ways (cf. Van Lange & Rusbult, 1995). If illusions predict satisfaction, individuals should be happier in their relationships to the extent that they see their partners in an even more positive light than their partners' self-perceptions justify: a *projected illusions hypothesis*. These idealized constructions may prove to be just as important for feelings of satisfaction as the reality of the partner's actual, or at least self-perceived, attributes. We also expected individuals to be happier in their relationships to the extent that their partners idealize them: a *reflected illusions hypothesis*. Such unconditional positive regard—a sense of being valued and accepted in spite of one's faults and imperfections—may prove to be the key to satisfying romantic relationships (Reis & Shaver, 1988). From this perspective, satisfied couples may appear to be living a shared illusion, colluding to see the best in one another (Gurman, 1978).

Our emphasis on shared illusions, however, contrasts with the compelling notion that understanding the reality of a partner's attributes is the key to continued relationship satisfaction (e.g., Kobak & Hazan, 1991). In this light, recognizing truths, even harsh truths, provides the foundation for satisfying romantic relationships by facilitating interpersonal adjustment and accommodation. Individuals should therefore be happier to the extent that they see their partners as they "really" are, rather than as a reflection of their own hopes and ideals. Furthermore, being idealized may only detract from feelings of satisfaction if individuals really want their partners to see them as they see themselves (Swann, Hixon, & De La Ronde, 1992). For example, in a sample of married respondents, Swann and his colleagues (1992) found that individuals were more committed to their relationships to the extent that their partners verified their self-perceptions, even when this involved confirming a negative self-concept. From this perspective, satisfaction depends on converging realities: actors' impressions mirroring or verifying their partners' self-perceptions.

The purpose of this research was to contrast the roles of converging realities and idealized constructions in predicting feelings of satisfaction. Although intimates' accurate understanding of one another's attributes may well be an important aspect of satisfying relationships, we believe that intimates' idealized constructions or "positive illusions" may have an even greater bearing on satisfaction. In satisfying relationships, the pleasure principle may overwhelm the reality principle.

Method

Overview

This research was designed to examine the role of "positive illusions" in dating and marital relationships. To explore our hypotheses, we asked our respondents to describe themselves and their partners on a variety of positive and negative attributes. These individuals also described the typical and ideal partner on these attributes as further benchmarks for assessing idealized constructions. A global measure of relationship satisfaction served as our criterion. We administered these scales to both partners in samples of 98 heterosexual dating couples and 82 heterosexual married couples.

Participants

Married sample. Sixty-nine couples volunteered to participate in a study on thoughts and feelings in close relationships at the Ontario Science Centre in Toronto, Ontario, Canada. Thirteen additional couples from introductory psychology classes at the University of Waterloo also participated, creating a total sample of 82 couples. Of the total sample, 60 couples were married, 11 couples were cohabiting, and 11 couples were engaged.[1] The mean age was 30.5 years. The average duration of their relationships was 6.5 years. The average number of children was 2.1 among the 33 couples who had children. Our science center respondents received a paper on constructive problem-solving skills as a token of our appreciation for their participation. Our University of Waterloo respondents received either course credit or $5.

Dating sample. Ninety-eight dating couples volunteered to participate in a study on thoughts and feelings in dating relationships held at the University of Waterloo. Five of these couples described themselves as casually dating; the remaining couples described themselves as exclusively dating. The mean age was 19.5 years, and they had been dating 19.0 months on average. Participants received course credit or payment for participating.

Procedure

Married sample. In recruiting our married sample, we posted a sign promoting the study in the main hall of the Ontario Science Centre. This sign

---

[1] All of the results we present remained consistent whether we based our analyses solely on the married couples or on the combined sample of married, cohabiting, and engaged couples.

invited married, cohabiting, or engaged couples to participate in a questionnaire study on thoughts and feelings in close relationships. The experimenter first introduced the study to the volunteers and then gave them packets containing the questionnaires and the instruction sheets. In her instructions, the experimenter cautioned couples to complete the measures without comparing their responses with their partners'. On completion of the measures, participants placed their questionnaires within sealed envelopes and returned them to the experimenter. She then thanked the participants and gave them the short feedback paper on constructive problem-solving skills.

Dating sample. We invited introductory psychology students who were currently involved in dating relationships to participate in a questionnaire study on thoughts and feelings in close relationships. On their arrival at the laboratory, the experimenter first gave a brief introduction to the study and then asked participants to complete the questionnaires. If both members of the couple were present in the laboratory session, we placed them at separate tables and asked them to complete their questionnaires independently. Once the participants finished, the experimenter explained the purpose of the study and answered any questions.

If only one member of the couple could attend the laboratory session, we asked these participants if their partners might also be willing to complete the questionnaires. If the participants agreed, we then sent their partners the questionnaire and a letter inviting them to participate in the study. Again, we cautioned these participants to complete the questionnaire without discussing their responses with their partners. On receiving their completed questionnaires, we sent these participants an explanation of the study and a check for $5.

Measures

The questionnaires for both the married and dating couples included (a) our interpersonal qualities scales, tapping individuals' perceptions of themselves, their partner, their ideal partner, and the typical partner; (b) a measure of self-esteem; and

(c) a global index of relationship satisfaction. The first page of each questionnaire asked respondents for the following demographic information: gender, age, relationship status (i.e., married, cohabiting, engaged, dating), relationship length, and number of children (if applicable).

Interpersonal qualities scale. In developing our 21-item measure of interpersonal qualities, we selected positive and negative attributes from the interpersonal circle (e.g., Leary, 1957; Wiggins, 1979), a model based on the primary dimensions of warmth–hostility and dominance–submissiveness. These traits were as follows: kind and affectionate, open and disclosing, patient, understanding, responsive to my needs, tolerant and accepting, critical and judgmental, lazy, controlling and dominant, emotional, moody, thoughtless, irrational, distant, complaining, and childish. We also selected a number of attributes often considered to represent commodities in the social exchange process (e.g., Rubin, 1973), including self-assured, sociable or extraverted, intelligent, witty, and traditional. For both married and dating samples, principal-components analyses (varimax rotation) on both self- and partner ratings yielded parallel three-factor solutions consistent with our expectations. These three factors largely reflected virtues (e.g., understanding), faults (e.g., complaining), and social commodities (e.g., intelligent and witty).

To provide a number of different baselines for assessing positive constructions, we asked participants to describe themselves, their own partner, the ideal partner, and the typical partner on this attribute measure. In defining the "ideal partner," we attempted to ensure that participants described their own idiosyncratic hopes for an ideal partner rather than some cultural ideal or standard. Therefore, we asked them to describe their own unique standard for the ideal partner in terms of their perceptions of how they would most prefer their current partner to be. We defined the "typical partner" as possessing those traits or attributes that participants believed to be most descriptive of the general population of partners. Participants rated how well each of the traits described the target (e.g., self, partner, typical, ideal) on a 9-point scale (1 = *not at all*

characteristic, 9 = *completely characteristic*). The order of the attribute ratings for the different targets was partially counterbalanced across subjects.

Self-esteem. Rosenberg's (1965) 10-item measure assessed participants' global self-evaluation (e.g., "I feel that I am a person of worth, at least on an equal basis with others"). Participants responded to such items on a 4-point scale (1 = *strongly disagree*, 4 = *strongly agree*).

Satisfaction. We designed the three-item satisfaction scale to assess participants' global evaluation of their relationships. These items were (a) "I am extremely happy with my relationship," (b) "I have a very strong relationship with my partner," and (c) "I do not feel that my relationship is successful" (reverse scored). Participants responded to these items on a 9-point scale (1 = *not at all true*, 9 = *completely true*).

Personal Attributes Questionnaire. A subset of our dating respondents (*n* = 56) completed Pelham and Swann's (1989) 10-item Personal Attributes Questionnaire (e.g., musical ability, physical attractiveness, athletic ability). Participants rated both themselves and their partners on a 10-point scale, indicating where they (or their partner) stood on the qualities relative to others (i.e., bottom 5% of the population through top 5% of the population).

Results

In exploring our hypotheses, we first discuss the question of convergence or reality matching (i.e., whether individuals see their partners as their partners see themselves). We then explore whether individuals project their self-images and ideals onto their intimates, essentially constructing impressions of the partner they most hope to see. Finally, we examine the potential benefits and liabilities of these idealized constructions. Do positive illusions predict greater satisfaction? Or are the most satisfied individuals those who validate one another's self-concepts, seeing one another as they "really" are? Before we turn to our results, we first debate possible methods for statistically indexing the "constructed" and "reality-based" aspects of intimates' impressions of their partners.

Analytic Strategy: Providing Estimates for "Reality" and "Illusion"

Earlier, we described intimates' representations in terms of an additive model that apportioned part of the variance in their perceptions to "reality" and part to "construction" (i.e., actor's perception = partner's reality + actor's construction). Following a difference score approach, we could subtract the partner's reality from the actor's perceptions to obtain an index of construction or illusion. Unfortunately, creating these difference scores confounds, rather than separates, these two perceptions (e.g., Cohen & Cohen, 1983; Humphreys, 1990; Johns, 1981). However, we can unconfound these factors by using path-analytic models to examine the constructed and reality-based components of intimates' representations of their partners.

Structural equations modeling, using a maximum-likelihood program such as LISREL, EQS, or CALIS (covariance analysis of linear structural equations) allows the simultaneous estimation of the path coefficients in a number of different equations. For instance, we could define the man's perception of the woman as part reality, part projection, and part unexplained variance or error. This model of actors' perceptions of their partners is represented by the following equations:

man's perception of woman

$$= B_1 \text{ female self} + B_2 \text{ male self} + \text{Error 1}$$

woman's perception of man

$$= B_3 \text{ male self} + B_4 \text{ female self} + \text{Error 2}$$

In this structural model, B_1 indexes the reality component of the male's perceptions (i.e., whether he sees his partner as she sees herself, holding the man's self-image constant). More simply, B_1 assesses the male's understanding of his partner's self-perceptions. B_2 indexes one possible projection component of the man's perceptions (i.e., whether he tends to see himself in his partner, holding the reality of her attributes constant). That is, do aspects of the man's construction or "illusion" reflect his projection of his own attributes onto his partner?

As this example illustrates, we can index intimates' illusions statistically by partialing the effects of the partner's reality out of the actor's perceptions (i.e., by controlling for the partner's self-reports; e.g., B_1 or the shaded area in Figure 19.1). Actors' constructions, or "illusions," then refer to their idiosyncratic perceptions of their partners, what they see in their partners that their partners do not see in themselves (i.e., the hatched area in Figure 19.1). We can then explore whether the projection of self (e.g., B_2), for example, predicts the nature of these illusions.

Because of its ability to test the fit of competing models, structural equation modeling also allows one to test for gender differences in the path models. For example, one interesting question is whether men and women are equally attuned to the reality of their partners' attributes. We could test this hypothesis by comparing the fit of a model that estimates common "reality" coefficients for men and women to the fit of a model that estimates separate "reality" coefficients. If men and women do differ in their accuracy, the goodness of fit for the model estimating separate "reality" coefficients should be significantly better (i.e., a smaller chi-square) than the goodness of fit for the model estimating common "reality" coefficients (a 1-df test).

The Nature of Intimates' Representations: Reality or Illusion?

In the following analyses, individuals' mean ratings of themselves and their partners on the interpersonal qualities scale indexed the overall positivity of partners' realities and actors' impressions, respectively. In computing this trait perceptions index, negative traits were reverse scored, such that higher scores represented more favorable perceptions.

Estimating convergence or "reality matching." Do individuals' impressions of their partners mirror their partners' self-perceptions? First, at the level of zero-order correlations, we found significant but modest levels of convergence. In the married sample, men's impressions of their partners did reflect their partners' self-perceptions,

$r(73) = .31, p < .01$, as did women's impressions, $r(73) = .35, p < .01$. In the dating sample, we found similar levels of "reality matching": Both men's, $r(96) = .45, p < .001$, and women's, $r(96) = .41, p < .001$, impressions reflected their partners' self-perceptions.

Clearly, individuals' global representations of their partners are not just a direct reflection of their partners' self-perceptions. Instead, there is still variance left to be explained in actors' impressions once we have accounted for the "reality" of partners' self-perceived attributes. Such evidence of diverging realities leaves open the possibility that projection and idiosyncratic construal play a role in shaping the nature of intimates' constructions. In particular, we predict that actors' constructions are shaped by their own self-perceptions and by their ideals.

Projecting the self. Figure 19.2 shows our most basic model of projection in romantic relationships. First, the double-arrowed line connecting male and female self-perceptions represents the zero-order correlation indexing the similarity between partners' self-perceptions. Paths b and c represent social reality, or convergence, effects. In other words, these paths index the extent to which people's representations of their partners mirror their partners' self-perceptions. Finally, Paths a and d index the role of projection, assessing the extent to which individuals see themselves in their partners. Note that each path in this model reflects a partial or unique effect. For example, Path a represents one source of the female's "illusion"—how much she tends to see herself in her partner, holding the reality of his actual attributes (Path b) constant.

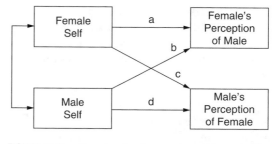

FIGURE 19.2 ■ Constructing impressions: The projection of self.

To test this (and all subsequent) models, we used the structural equation modeling program within the CALIS procedure of SAS. As a general analytic strategy in examining this (and all subsequent) models, we first fit models estimating separate path coefficients for men and women. In the preceding model, for example, we first allowed the "reality" and "projection" paths for men and women to differ. However, in this (and all other) cases, the size of these paths were strikingly similar for both men and women. As a result, we collapsed across gender in our analyses, presenting pooled (i.e., common) path coefficients for men and women.

Table 19.1 shows the pooled coefficients (standardized path coefficients) for the basic projection model for both married and dating couples. First, the pooled reality Paths b and c were significant for both samples, indicating that individuals' impressions of their partners were in part a reflection of their partners' "real," or at least self-perceived, attributes. More important, the pooled construction

TABLE 19.1. Constructing Impressions: The Projection of Self

Predicting actor's perception of partner	Married sample		Dating sample	
	Coefficient	t	Coefficient	t
Reality paths				
b and c: Reflection of partner's self-image	.304	4.22*	.240	3.99*
Construction paths				
a and d: Projection of actor's self-image	.315	4.33*	.456	7.63*

Note. $GFI_{(married)} = .99$, $\chi^2 (2, N = 75) = 0.67$, *ns.* $GFI_{(dating)} = .98$, $\chi^2 (2, N = 98) = 4.19$, *ns.* GFI = goodness-of-fit index.
*$p < .001$.

Paths a and d were at least as large as the reality paths for both married and dating couples. Individuals who saw themselves in a positive light projected their rosy self-images onto their partners, whereas individuals with more negative self-images were less generous in their depictions. Finally, the similarity between partners' self-images, as indexed by the zero-order correlation, was minimal: $r(73) = .05$, *ns*, for married couples, and $r(96) = .24$, $p < .05$, for dating couples.

The results presented in Table 19.1 support our prediction that actors' impressions are in part constructions that reflect their projection of their own virtues and vices onto their partners. We also hypothesized that intimates might see their partners through the rosy filter provided by their ideals and hopes. Intimates' ideals may even mediate the link between self-perceptions and perceptions of others, as we suggested earlier.

Projecting ideals. Figure 19.3 shows the theoretical model derived from this prediction. As in Figure 19.2, Paths g and h represent social reality or convergence effects. New to this model, Paths a and d tap whether intimates' ideals reflect their own self-perceptions. Paths b and c assess whether ideals are also attuned to the "reality" of their partners' self-perceptions. Turning to our construction paths, Paths f and i index intimates' tendency to see their partners through the filters provided by their ideals, essentially seeing them, not as they are, but as they wish to see them. Finally, Paths e and j are direct projection paths, indexing whether actors see themselves in their partners, even when we control for the impact of their ideals.

Table 19.2 illustrates that married and dating couples' ideals were strongly related to their own self-perceptions (i.e., pooled Paths a and d were both highly significant). The better, or more positively, individuals felt about themselves, the higher were their hopes or expectations for the ideal partner. In contrast, the partner's actual qualities had little bearing on the ideal standards actors set; pooled Paths b and c were nonsignificant in both samples.

Also consistent with our predictions, married couples projected their ideals onto their partners, apparently seeing them through the filter provided by these working models, as the significant pooled projection Paths f and i illustrate. Self-perceptions had no significant direct effect on actors' perceptions once their ideals were included in the model (Paths e and j). Therefore, among married couples, ideals completely mediated the link between self-perceptions and representations of a romantic partner. In contrast, ideals only partially mediated this relation for dating couples. For dating men and women, actors' self-perceptions structured their impressions of their partners both directly, as the significant pooled Paths e and j illustrate, as well as indirectly, through the projection of their ideals (Paths f and i).

Evidence for projection? The constructed aspects of intimates' representations—what they

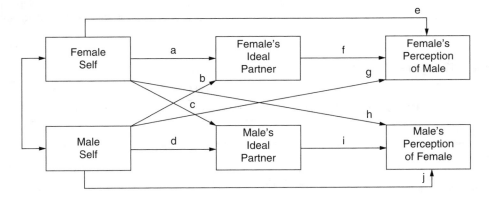

FIGURE 19.3 ■ Constructing impressions: The projection of ideals.

TABLE 19.2. Constructing Impressions: The Projection of Self and Ideals

	Married sample		Dating sample	
	Coefficient	t	Coefficient	t
Predicting actor's ideal partner				
Paths b and c: Reflection of partner's self-image	.043	ns	.097	ns
Paths a and d: Projection of actor's self-image	.500	7.13*	.436	6.78*
Predicting actor's perceptions of partner				
Reality paths				
g and h: Reflection of partner's self-image	.285	4.39*	.210	3.73*
Construction paths				
e and j: Projection of actor's self-image	.087	ns	.307	4.98*
f and i: Projection of actor's ideals	.454	5.95*	.332	5.36*

Note. $GFI_{(married)} = .95$, χ^2 (7, $N = 75$) = 10.52, ns. $GFI_{(dating)} = .98$, χ^2 (7, $N = 98$) = 5.11, ns.
GFI = goodness-of-fit index.
*$p < .001$.

saw in their partners that their partners did not see in themselves—appear to reflect actors' tendency to see their partners through the filters provided by their hopes and ideals (Paths f and i). Higher hopes and ideals predicted rosier, more idealized impressions of an intimate partner. Among dating couples, more positive self-images also predicted more idealized impressions (Paths e and j). However, possible alternative interpretations of these results should be considered.

First, individuals might see themselves in their partners simply because they truly are alike. According to this logic, the apparent evidence for projection might simply be an artifact of actual similarity. However, the degree of actual similarity between partners' self-ratings was minimal. Furthermore, we controlled for this limited degree of similarity within our path models. Therefore, the "projection of self," or perceived similarity, paths we report were completely independent of the effects of actual similarity.

Second, our evidence for projected perceptions could simply be an artifact of method variance. Individuals rated their self-perceptions, ideals, and partners on the same attributes using the same response scales. In addition, our construction paths reflect within-person correlations (e.g., the female's ideals and her perception of her partner), whereas our reality paths reflect between-person correlations (e.g., the female's self-perceptions and the male's perception of her). As a result,

shared variance may have artificially inflated the magnitude of the projection paths. Alternatively, our evidence for projection might be a result of global positivity. Individuals who see themselves and their partners in idealized ways may see almost everything in their worlds in idealized ways, a Pollyanna effect. If this is the case, intimates' seemingly illusory perceptions may not speak to their specific idealization of their partners. Their impressions of the typical partner, for example, may be just as positive.

To explore these possibilities, we included both perceptions of the typical partner and global self-esteem as control variables within our model. Including typical ratings controls for method variance (as individuals made their self-, partner, ideal, and typical partner ratings on scales with identical traits and formats) as well as within-person variance. In addition to controlling for more mundane response biases, self-esteem and perceptions of the typical partner also control for individuals' general tendency to see themselves and their worlds in positive ways. Importantly, neither control variable changed the observed pattern of results. Our projection paths remained strong and significant when we controlled for perceptions of the typical partner and global self-esteem. Therefore, actors' apparent tendency to see their partners through the filters provided by their self-perceptions and ideals reflects something more than just method variance or global positivity. Instead, these idealized constructions are specific to actors' perceptions of their romantic partners.

More generally, perceptions of the typical partner provide yet another benchmark for assessing the idealized, perhaps illusory, nature of intimates' representations. Some authors have defined *illusory perceptions* as the tendency for people to see themselves or their partners in a more positive light than they see the typical or average person (e.g., Buunk & Van Yperen, 1991; Taylor & Brown, 1988; Van Lange & Rusbult, 1995). By controlling for actors' perceptions of the typical partner, we indexed the virtues individuals ascribed to their own partners, above and beyond any tendency to embellish their partners' qualities through downward social comparison.

Bias or positive distortion. We hypothesized that individuals' general desire to see the best in their intimates may lead them to see their partners in more positive ways than their partners see themselves. The models we have presented so far suggest that individuals' ideals shape their perceptions of their partners' attributes. However, these models cannot address whether actors' impressions are in fact systematically more positive than their partners' self-impressions. Nor can they address whether actors generally do see their partners more positively than they see other potential partners. Finding evidence of such distortions would provide complementary evidence that intimates' perceptions are generally idealized constructions.

To explore these hypotheses, we conducted a number of repeated measures analyses of variance (ANOVAs), treating the couple as the unit of analysis. Our within-subject variables were target (e.g., self vs. partner or partner vs. typical) and gender (male or female intimate). The results indicate that married individuals evaluated their partners ($M = 6.51$) even more positively than their partners evaluated themselves ($M = 6.24$), $F(1, 74) = 12.46$, $p < .001$. Not surprisingly, married individuals also rated their own partners' attributes ($M = 6.51$) more positively than the typical partner's attributes ($M = 5.62$), $F(1, 75) = 65.85, p < .001$.

Dating couples' perceptions were slightly more complicated. Parallel to married couples, partner evaluations ($M = 6.70$) were again more favorable than self-evaluations ($M = 6.30$), $F(1, 97) = 58.38$, $p < .001$. However, this main effect was qualified by a significant Target (self vs. partner) × Gender interaction, $F(1, 97) = 28.30, p < .001$. Dating women were more likely to idealize their partners relative to their partners' self-perceptions (a discrepancy of 0.84), $F(1, 97) = 6.67, p < .01$, than were dating men (a discrepancy of -0.04), $F(1, 97) < 1$. This finding does not seem to reflect men's lack of idealization but dating women's extremely high self-regard. Also, parallel to married couples, dating intimates saw their partners ($M = 6.70$) in a more favorable light than they saw the typical partner ($M = 5.81$), $F(1, 97) = 140.54$, $p < .001$. Finally, married and dating women's perceptions tended to be more favorable than men's independent of target: $Ms = 6.20$ and 6.05, $F(1, 74) = 3.52, p < .07$, for married women and men, respectively; $Ms = 6.46$ and 6.09, $F(1, 97) = 28.68$, $p < .001$, for dating women and men, respectively.

Evidence for positive illusions? Taken together, our evidence for both projection and distortion supports the notion that many intimates' representations are idealized constructions. The results suggest that many actors' impressions of their partners are more a mirror of their own positive illusions and ideals than a reflection of their partners' reported realities (see Tables 19.1 and 19.2). In fact, actors' representations are even more positive than their partners believe their attributes merit. This apparent distortion is particularly striking considering that most individuals already idealize their own attributes (e.g., Taylor & Brown, 1988). For example, married and dating individuals rated their own attributes far more favorably than the typical partner's attributes: married, $Ms = 6.12$ vs. 5.57, $F(1, 75) = 42.83, p < .001$; dating, $Ms = 6.18$ vs. 5.69, $F(1, 97) = 68.56, p < .001$. Thus, actors' constructions even transcended their partners' own rosy self-perceptions. In summary, individuals' representations generally appear to be "positive illusions," particularly when they are considered in light of their partners' own realities.

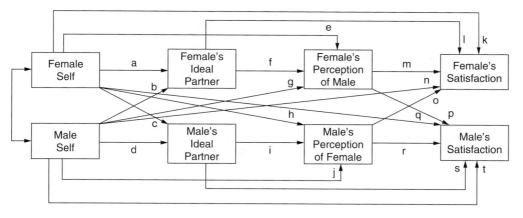

FIGURE 19.4 ■ Projected and reflected illusions and satisfaction.

Seeing What One Wants to See: The Benefits of Positive Illusions

Love is a gross exaggeration of the difference between one person and everybody else. (George Bernard Shaw)

Heeding Shaw's intuitions, we hypothesized that the realities intimates constructed would be intricately tied to feelings of satisfaction. We expected individuals to be happier in their relationships to the extent that they idealized their partners: the projected illusions hypothesis. To translate this hypothesis into path-analytic terms, actors' illusions should predict their own feelings of satisfaction, controlling for the "reality" of their partners' attributes. We also hypothesized that intimates would be happier with partners who idealized them: the reflected illusions hypothesis. In path-analytic terms, individuals should be happier when their partners see positive qualities in them that they do not see in themselves.

Figure 19.4 shows the theoretical model derived to test these predictions. New to this model, Paths n and q index social reality effects, tapping whether the partner's self-perceived attributes predict the actor's satisfaction. Paths k and t index whether actors' self-evaluations directly relate to their own satisfaction. The ideal Paths l and s index whether ideals directly relate to satisfaction. The projected illusion paths m and r index whether actors are happier when they idealize their partners,

seeing virtues in them that their partners do not see in themselves. The reflected illusion Paths o and p index the effects of being idealized on satisfaction.

Before turning to our results, note that each path in this model reflects a partial or unique effect. For example, Path n represents the direct effect of the male's "reality" on the female's satisfaction, controlling for any degree of "reality-matching" (Path g). In other words, do the qualities that men see in themselves—but women fail to see in them—relate to women's satisfaction? The projected illusions Paths m and r tap whether actors' illusions predict their satisfaction, controlling for the reality of their partners' attributes. Paths l and s represent the direct effect of the actors' ideals on his or her satisfaction; that is, do the qualities that individuals desire—but fail to see in their partners—relate to actors' satisfaction?

As Table 19.3 illustrates, we found considerable support for the benefits of positive illusions.[2] Both dating and married intimates were happier in their relationships when they idealized their partners, as the significant pooled projected illusion Paths m and r illustrate. The more positive, the more

---

[2]All paths in Figure 19.4 were included in the estimation of the model (including Paths a through j). We only report the path coefficients predicting satisfaction in Table 19.3 because the remaining coefficients are identical to those presented in Table 19.2.

TABLE 19.3. Positive Illusions and Satisfaction

Predicting actor's satisfaction	Married sample		Dating sample	
	Coefficient	t	Coefficient	t
Reality paths				
k and t: Actor's self-image	.007	ns	−.060	ns
n and q: Partner's self-image	.086	ns	−1.660	−2.37*
Construction paths				
l and s: Actor's ideals	.230	2.89**	.012	ns
m and r: Actor's idealized constructions	.339	4.47***	.526	6.95***
o and p: Partner's idealized constructions	.203	2.90**	.242	3.45***

Note. $GFI_{(married)}$ = .95, χ^2 (14, N = 75) = 15.18, *ns.* $GFI_{(dating)}$ = .97, χ^2 (14, N = 98) = 13.83, *ns.*
GFI = goodness-of-fit index.
*p < .05. **p < .01. ***p < .001.

idealized their constructions—controlling for the partner's actual attributes—the happier actors were in their relationships. Being idealized also predicted greater satisfaction for both dating and married couples. That is, intimates were happier in their relationships when their partners looked beyond their actual attributes and saw the best in them, as the significant pooled reflected illusion Paths o and p illustrate.

Turning to the ideal paths, even high (but unmet) ideals predicted greater satisfaction for married men and women, as the significant pooled Paths l and s illustrate. However, the direct effect of ideals was nonsignificant for dating couples. Turning to the "reality" paths, the partner's self-perceived attributes had little impact on married couples' satisfaction. The pooled effects of the partner's own reality (Paths n and q) were nonsignificant. For dating couples, however, the pooled "reality" paths were significant and negative, suggesting that dating individuals were less happy when their partners claimed virtues in themselves that the individuals failed to see in them.

To ensure that the illusions–satisfaction relation was not attributable to Pollyannaism, we included individuals' perceptions of the typical partner as a control variable within the model. Even in this model, the projected and reflected illusion paths remained strong and significant, suggesting that the relation between illusions and satisfaction was not a global positivity effect. Similarly, the illusion–satisfaction relations persisted even when we controlled for actors' own rosy self-perceptions

(Paths k and t) as well as their global self-esteem, suggesting that relationship-specific illusions are indeed critical for satisfaction.

Seeing What One's Partner Sees: The Benefits of Shared Realities?

Our evidence for the importance of positive illusions contrasts with the notion that understanding a partner's "true" qualities is the key to continued satisfaction. From this perspective, actors should be happier to the extent that their impressions of their partners match their partners' self-perceptions. Similarly, individuals should be happiest when their partners see them as they see themselves, even if this involves confirming a negative self-view (e.g., Kobak & Hazan, 1991; Swann et al., 1992). To this point, we have not found any strong support for the importance of such validation processes. However, the path models do not explicitly test this self-verification hypothesis.

To explore the relationship benefits of understanding, we conducted a series of regression analyses predicting satisfaction from the actor's perceptions of the partner, the partner's self-ratings, and their interaction. If self-verification promotes satisfaction, we should find a significant interaction in the regression analyses. Understanding (i.e., seeing what one's partner sees) should predict greater satisfaction, whereas misunderstandings should predict less satisfaction. But if unconditional admiration is all that matters, we should find a main effect only for the actor's perceptions. Intimates should simply be happier

TABLE 19.4. The Relation Between Self-Verification (or Understanding) and Satisfaction

	Married sample		Dating sample	
	β	t	β	t
Predicting actor's satisfaction				
Female partner's reality	.115	ns	−.076	ns
Male actor's perception	.510	5.13****	.526	5.43****
Interaction (men's understanding)	−.207	−2.25**	−.007	ns
Male partner's reality	.060	ns	−.034	ns
Female actor's perception	.552	5.62****	.567	6.35****
Interaction (women's understanding)	.077	ns	−.065	ns
Predicting partner's satisfaction				
Male partner's reality	.211	1.94*	.072	ns
Female actor's perception	.301	2.77***	.310	3.07***
Interaction (women's understanding)	.052	ns	−.105	ns
Female partner's reality	.177	1.68*	.305	2.99***
Male actor's perception	.383	3.63****	.184	1.81*
Interaction (men's understanding)	−.017	ns	−.274	−2.92***

*p < .10.   **p < .05.   ***p < .01.   ****p < .0001.

to the extent that they see one another in a positive, idealized light.

Table 19.4 shows the results of the regression analyses on the interpersonal qualities scale. For married couples, projected illusions, as indexed by the significant main effects for actors' perceptions (in predicting actors' satisfaction), again predicted greater satisfaction. Men and women were both happier the more positive their images of their spouse. Unexpectedly, men's understanding of women's self-concepts also predicted men's satisfaction, as the significant interaction illustrates. Inspection of the means in a 2 × 2 ANOVA revealed that married men were the least satisfied when their impressions matched their partners' relatively negative self-views. Such understanding should predict greater satisfaction in a self-verification framework.

Parallel to our reflected illusions findings, married intimates were also happier when their partners saw the best in them, as reflected in the significant main effects for actors' perceptions (in predicting partners' satisfaction). We did not find any evidence of an interaction, suggesting that misunderstandings did not detract from partners' satisfaction. Instead, married individuals were happier to the extent that their partners saw the best in them, regardless of whether such idealized impressions were consistent with their self-perceptions.

Among dating couples, projected illusions again predicted greater satisfaction. Both men and women were happier the more positive their impressions of their partners, as the significant main effects for actors' perceptions illustrate (in predicting actors' satisfaction). Actors' understanding of their partners' self-concepts (i.e., the interaction term) did not predict their happiness. Turning to reflected illusions, dating men were also happier to the extent that their partners idealized them. We again found no evidence of an interaction (in predicting partners' satisfaction): These men were simply happier if they were idealized, regardless of whether such rosy constructions validated their own self-perceptions. Unexpectedly, dating women's satisfaction was predicted by men's understanding of them, as the significant interaction illustrates. In contrast, the main effect for actors' perceptions was marginal.

To further explore this interaction, we first plotted the residualized cross-product term against dating women's level of satisfaction. On inspecting this plot, we noticed that one respondent had an extremely low satisfaction score. This woman's satisfaction score was 6 *SD*s below the mean, raising the possibility that the interaction might simply have been due to the influence of this extremely dissatisfied person. In fact, when we removed this outlier from our analysis, the interaction disappeared. Even when we included this outlier couple, the pattern of means in a 2 × 2 ANOVA still did not support self-verification: Dating women were the least happy when their partners understood their own relatively negative self-perceptions.

Discussion

Happiness depends, as Nature shows,
Less on exterior things than most suppose.
(William Cowper)

The Construction of Satisfaction: A Summary

Intimates' impressions of their partners appeared to reflect a mixture of "reality" and "illusion" (see Figure 19.1). Actors' impressions converged moderately with their partners' self-perceptions, suggesting that some degree of mutual understanding characterizes most close relationships. Individuals who thought highly of themselves also were held in high regard by their partners. Similarly, the within-couple correlations revealed that the attributes partners believed were most self-descriptive were also seen as defining traits by actors. Surprisingly, mutual understanding was not any more evident among married than dating couples.

Intimates also appeared to take considerable license in constructing impressions of their partners. Constructed representations—what intimates saw in their partners that their partners did not see in themselves—appeared to reflect their tendency to see their partners as they wished to see them, through the filters provided by their ideals and rosy self-images. Higher ideals and more positive self-perceptions predicted more idealized impressions. Actors' models of the ideal partner also appeared to structure their impressions of specific attributes, as the within-person correlations between ideals and perceptions illustrate.

As a further testament to the idealized nature of intimates' constructions, both married and dating individuals generally saw their partners even more positively than their partners saw themselves. (The only exception was that dating men

did not exceed their partners' self-ratings in their depictions, perhaps because dating women's self-views were already exceptionally positive.) Intimates' depictions of the typical partner also accentuated their own partners' many unique virtues.

Such positive illusions were most likely to characterize satisfying dating and even marital relationships. As the projected illusions findings illustrate, intimates were happier in their relationships when they saw virtues in their partners that their partners did not see in themselves. The more idealized the construction, the greater the satisfaction. Being the target of such idealized constructions also predicted greater satisfaction, as the reflected illusions findings illustrate. Intimates were happier in their relationships when their partners looked beyond the reality of their self-perceived attributes and saw the best in them.

Is Idealization an Illusion?

The central challenge in understanding the role of "illusions" in romantic relationships is identifying appropriate benchmarks or baselines for "reality." After all, distinguishing fact from fiction requires some knowledge of reality. However, in the interpersonal domain, few gold standards exist for measuring objective truths. We turned to subjective realities—individuals' own personal views of their virtues and faults—as a proxy for truth.

Actors' impressions did appear "illusory" in light of their partners' realities. Individuals generally saw virtues in their partners that their partners claimed not to see in themselves. But can this definition of "reality" be trusted? Perhaps individuals are actually being overly humble in their self-depictions, describing themselves less virtuously than they actually believe themselves to be. Using such modest (and insincere) self-depictions as "reality" baselines would then overestimate the evidence for illusions and their benefits. That is, the apparent benefits of illusions might actually represent the benefits of having a humble, self-effacing partner.

However, several points argue against this humility account of illusions. First, considerable evidence suggests that biases in self-report lean toward self-aggrandizement rather than self-effacement (e.g.,

Taylor & Brown, 1988). As an illustration of this bias, both married and dating respondents depicted themselves much more favorably than they depicted the typical partner. Individuals also tended to see their own attributes as ideal, again suggesting that their self-depictions were less than humble. Finally, intimates were generally happier when their partners held themselves in high regard.

Perhaps individuals' perceptions of their partners only appear illusory because actors and partners rely on different contexts and experiences as the bases for their impressions. For example, in judging his warmth, Bill might consider how warmly he acts toward Hillary, how warmly he acts toward his coworkers, and how warmly he acts toward his friends. In judging Bill's warmth, Hillary might only consider how warmly he acts toward her. Using Bill's (cross-situational) self-concept as a "reality" baseline for assessing the constructed nature of Hillary's (situation-specific) impressions might then overestimate the evidence for illusions.

However, individuals depicted themselves in the context of completing a questionnaire about their relationships. Therefore, when Bill rated his warmth, his behavior toward Hillary should have been utmost in his mind. Finally, greater familiarity did not weaken the evidence for illusions among married couples, despite the greater opportunity for them to observe their partners across many contexts. In light of these arguments, actors' illusions do not simply appear to be "cognitive errors" in judgment (resulting from actors' and partners' reliance on different contexts for judgment).

Self-deception or other-deception? Satisfied intimates in our research seemed to be deceiving themselves, projecting their images of the ideal partner onto their own partners. However, is it possible that satisfied intimates are actually trying to deceive a more public audience (i.e., the investigator), despite their anonymous reports? That is, can a general social desirability bias account for the current findings?

According to this account, the illusion–satisfaction relation might be a simple artifact of certain people's tendencies to depict themselves and their relationships in a desirable light. Such a bias might stem from intentional distortions or

habitual tendencies to use high (vs. low) points on a scale. However, ratings of the typical partner likely captured such habitual tendencies to respond to scaled items in particular ways. And when we controlled for intimates' perceptions of the typical partner, projected and reflected illusions still predicted greater satisfaction.

Also, the evidence for the interpersonal benefits of illusions argues against a social desirability account of the illusions–satisfaction relation. A skeptic would have to argue that people pair or match on social desirability to explain why intimates are happier when their partners idealize them. Finally, the benefits of idealization were apparent on more "behavioral" criteria even when we controlled for intimates' tendency to present their relationships in a favorable light, as indexed by reports of satisfaction. That is, idealizing a partner (projected illusions) and being idealized (reflected illusions) predicted relatively less conflict in both samples, even when we controlled for relationship satisfaction, an extremely conservative analysis.

What is the "real" causal model? Lest the reader accuse us of deceiving ourselves, however, we must emphasize again that our cross-sectional data cannot test the causal assumptions underlying our models. For instance, although we have characterized illusions as leading to satisfaction, the relation between illusions and satisfaction is more likely reciprocal in nature. Satisfaction may promote idealization as well as result from it. Similarly, intimates' ideals might stem from their perceptions of their partners' attributes as well as guiding these perceptions. So-called "causal models" cannot distinguish between these causal alternatives.

Maintaining Idealism: Models of Self and Other

Do individuals love from strength or weakness? Freud (1922) argued that individuals project the qualities they wish to see in themselves onto their partners (e.g., Karp et al., 1970). Idealizing a partner essentially depends on dissatisfaction with oneself. For instance, Dion and Dion (1975) found that individuals with low self-esteem admired their partners more than individuals with high self-esteem. Also, individuals with more negative self-models, such as intimates with a pre-occupied attachment style, appear most likely to idealize their partners (Feeney & Noller, 1991). Similarly, Mathes and Moore (1985) argued that individuals with low self-esteem seek to fulfill their ideal selves by falling in love with someone they think has the qualities they lack.

The opposite argument is that idealization and satisfying relationships depend on positive models of self (e.g., Erikson, 1968; Reis & Shaver, 1988; Rogers, 1972). For instance, individuals with higher self-esteem tend to be involved in more stable relationships (Hendrick, Hendrick, & Adler, 1988). In the current research, self-perceptions were closely tied to ideals and impressions of one's partner, suggesting that self-models play a role in structuring models of others. Individuals with more positive self-images had higher ideals, and more positive perceptions of their partners. Conversely, individuals with more negative self-perceptions had weaker hopes for ideal partners and were less generous in their depictions of their actual partners. Such interrelations among models of self and other are not surprising in light of symbolic interactionist and attachment theorists' arguments that perceptions of the self as worthy of love are strongly tied to positive beliefs about the availability of others and their dispositions in relationship contexts (see Baldwin, 1992).

Intriguingly, intimates' hopes for the ideal partner appeared to have a stronger influence on their perceptions than more general working models of typical partners. Within an attachment theory framework, such generalized expectancies about others are thought to be rooted in individuals' early experiences with attachment figures and structure their later construals of their adult close relationships (e.g., Kobak & Hazan, 1991). However, consistent with our findings, adult children of divorce appear to have pessimistic expectations about others in general and the institution of marriage (i.e., general working models), but they are still hopeful and optimistic about the possibilities for their own romantic relationships (Carnelley & Janoff-Bulman, 1992). If individuals are motivated to maintain confidence in the face of the risks of interdependence, ideals may function as a more satisfying guide for perceptions than general expectations. After all, seeing a partner as nearly ideal should leave a person feeling much more secure than believing this person is susceptible to the many faults afflicting most others.

Is Love Blind? Positive Illusions and Relationship Well-Being

The current findings follow on the heels of the large literature arguing that optimism or idealism is critical for mental health (e.g., Greenwald, 1980; Janoff-Bulman, 1989; Taylor & Brown, 1988; Weinstein, 1980). From this perspective, happiness rests on people's ability to see a sometimes stern reality in the best possible light (e.g., Taylor & Brown, 1988; Taylor, Collins, Skokan, & Aspinwall, 1989). For example, individuals typically underestimate their faults while embellishing their virtues (Alicke, 1985; Brown, 1986). Individuals are similarly idealistic in predicting their futures, overestimating the likelihood of desirable events while underestimating the likelihood of negative events (Weinstein, 1980). People also choose objects of social comparison in a way that serves to accentuate their own virtues while minimizing their faults (e.g., Wood, 1989). Rather than being accurately attuned with the harsher realities of life, happy individuals tend to see their worlds in ways that support their optimism and idealism.

Similarly, satisfied intimates see their partners in ways that support their hopes and fantasies, embellishing their partners' virtues and obscuring their faults. Idealization may have this beneficial effect because ideals provide a template for constructing a sense of conviction that resolves the tension between one's commitments and doubts (e.g., Murray & Holmes, 1993, 1994). From an attachment perspective, seeing one's partner as (nearly) ideal may foster a sense of internal peace that dampens doubts and secures satisfaction through the comfort derived from the thought of possessing a caregiver who mirrors one's hopes. Also, idealizing a partner may be self-affirming (or self-fulfilling) if intimates draw their partners into their own self-images (e.g., Aron et al., 1991; Tesser, 1988).

Conversely, idealized intimates may be happier in their relationships because their partners treat them as special individuals, thereby encouraging intimates to live up to these idealized images (e.g., Snyder & Swann, 1978; Snyder, Tanke, & Berscheid, 1977). Also, if actors see their partners' behaviors through the rosy filters provided by their ideals, their inclination toward "attributional charity" might minimize the potential for overt conflict (e.g., Rusbult, Verette, Whitney, Slovik, & Lipkus, 1991). Finally, positive reflected appraisals might eventually undermine partners' self-criticisms, thereby bolstering their sense of self-worth. In these ways, unconditional admiration may provide the foundation for relationship satisfaction and intimacy, as well as assuring intimates that their partners truly care for them (Reis & Shaver, 1988).

Idealism versus understanding. Unconditional positive regard—seeing the best in partners despite their imperfections—appears to be an integral part of satisfying romantic relationships (Reis & Shaver, 1988). In contrast to this perspective, one might have expected actual understanding (i.e., self-verification) to predict greater satisfaction precisely because intimates would then know and understand one another's actual virtues and faults and still accept and love one another (Swann et al., 1994). After all, it might be disconcerting for individuals to believe that their partners are only in love with an "illusion." Despite these arguments, individuals were not more satisfied when their partners' perceptions of them mirrored their own self-images.

In the critical case of individuals who have relatively low self-regard, intimates still were more satisfied if their partners saw the best in them despite their own self-doubts. Also, even in marriage, being idealized predicted greater satisfaction regardless of whether we focused on abstract interpersonal qualities or more objective qualities, such as those used by Swann et al. (1992, 1994).

Hidden Realities: A Sleeper Effect?

Is idealization the key to enduring satisfaction? Or might intimates' illusions only leave them vulnerable to disappointment once the rigors of greater interdependence make the reality of their partners' virtues and faults impossible to ignore? When illusions do fade, does understanding the partner's real attributes then prove to be the key to lasting happiness?

If illusions rest on intimates' simple denial of disappointing realities, such idealism may well forecast future difficulties. For example, individuals typically ignore apparent negativity and make decisions to marry largely on the basis of their positive feelings about their partners. In fact, apparent negativity, such as premarital conflict, is virtually independent of feelings of love and satisfaction at the point of marriage (Braiker & Kelley, 1979; Kelly, Huston, & Cate, 1985; Markman, 1979). However, such blatant compartmentalization in the service of idealization is not without its costs: Conflict and negativity prior to marriage, although initially divorced from satisfaction, predict later declines in satisfaction (Kelly et al., 1985; Markman, 1981).

Similarly, early on in relationships, intimates are often unaware of incompatibilities on dimensions critical for satisfaction, such as desires for intimacy and autonomy (Christensen & Heavey, 1993). Viewing their partners through the filter of their ideals, individuals may simply assume compatibility on these dimensions even when latent conflicts exist. However, such hidden realities may have an insidious effect on intimates over time, eventually eroding their illusions and dampening satisfaction. In contrast, understanding such differences in personalities or desires early on might preempt later relationship difficulties by facilitating mutual adjustment.

But if intimates simply interpret somewhat disappointing realities in the best possible light, without denying negativity, such positive illusions may ensure later satisfaction (e.g., Taylor et al., 1989). Seeing their partners' faults in the best possible light may provide intimates with the security and optimism necessary to confront difficulties in their relationships. In addition to providing constructive motivation, illusions may create resources of goodwill and generosity that prevent everyday hassles from turning into significant trivia (Holmes & Murray, in press). Intimates might even create elements of the idealized reality they perceive by treating their partners as special, unique individuals (e.g., Snyder & Swann, 1978; Snyder et al., 1977). In these ways, idealizing a partner may provide an effective buffer against the inevitable vicissitudes of time.

NOTES

Sandra L. Murray, John G. Holmes, and Dale W. Griffin, Department of Psychology, University of Waterloo, Waterloo, Ontario, Canada. Dale W. Griffin is now at the School of Cognitive and Computing Sciences, University of Sussex, Falmer, Brighton, United Kingdom.

This research was prepared with the support of a Social Sciences and Humanities Research Council of Canada (SSHRC) doctoral fellowship to Sandra L. Murray and SSHRC research grants. We thank Michael Ross and Mark Zanna for their comments on an earlier version of this article. We also thank Harry Reis for his comments on various aspects of this research and for suggesting Shaw's pithy quote. We are especially grateful to Alisa Lennox, Teresa Pizzamiglio, Renata Snidr, and Stephen Taylor for their assistance in conducting this research.

Correspondence concerning this article should be addressed to Sandra L. Murray, who is now at Department of Psychology, SUNY Buffalo, Buffalo, New York 14260. Electronic mail may be sent to smurray@buffalo.edu.

REFERENCES

Alicke, M. D. (1985). Global self-evaluation as determined by the desirability and controllability of trait adjectives. *Journal of Personality and Social Psychology, 49*, 1621–1630.

Aron, A., Aron, E. N., Tudor, M., & Nelson, G. (1991). Close relationships as including other in the self. *Journal of Personality and Social Psychology, 60*, 241–253.

Baldwin, M. W. (1992). Relational schemas and the processing of social information. *Psychological Bulletin, 112*, 461–484.

Berscheid, E., & Walster, E. H. (1978). *Interpersonal attraction* (2nd ed.). Reading, MA: Addison-Wesley.

Bowlby, J. (1977). The making and breaking of affectional bonds. *British Journal of Psychiatry, 130*, 201–210.

Bowlby, J. (1982). *Attachment and loss* (Vol. 1). London: Hogarth Press.

Braiker, H. B., & Kelley, H. H. (1979). Conflict in the development of close relationships. In R. L. Burgess & T. L. Huston (Eds.), *Social exchange in developing relationships* (pp. 135–168). San Diego, CA: Academic Press.

Brehm, S. S. (1988). Passionate love. In R. J. Sternberg & M. L. Barnes (Eds.), *The psychology of love* (pp. 232–263). New Haven, CT: Yale University Press.

Brehm, S. S. (1992). *Intimate relationships*. New York: McGraw-Hill.

Brickman, P. (1987). *Commitment, conflict, and caring*. Englewood Cliffs, NJ: Prentice Hall.

Brown, J. D. (1986). Evaluations of self and others: Self-enhancement biases in social judgment. *Social Cognition, 4*, 353–376.

Buunk, B. P., & Van Yperen, N. W. (1991). Referential comparisons, relational comparisons, and exchange orientation: Their relation to marital satisfaction. *Personality and Social Psychology Bulletin, 17*, 709–717.

Carnelley, K. B., & Janoff-Bulman, R. (1992). Optimism about love relationships: General vs. specific lessons from one's personal experiences. *Journal of Social and Personal Relationships, 9*, 5–20.

Christensen, A., & Heavey, C. L. (1993). Gender differences in marital conflict: The case of the demand/withdraw interaction pattern. In S. Oskamp & M. Costanzo (Eds.), *Gender issues in contemporary society* (pp. 113–141). Newbury Park, CA: Sage.

Cohen, J., & Cohen, P. (1983). *Applied multiple regression/correlation analysis for the behavioral sciences*. Hillsdale, NJ: Erlbaum.

Dion, K. L., & Dion, K. K. (1975). Self-esteem and romantic love. *Journal of Personality, 43*, 39–57.

Erikson, E. H. (1968). *Identify: Youth and crisis*. New York: Norton.

Feeney, J. A., & Noller, P. (1991). Attachment style and verbal descriptions of romantic partners. *Journal of Social and Personal Relationships, 8*, 187–215.

Fletcher, G. J. O., Fincham, F. D., Cramer, L., & Heron, N. (1987). The role of attributions in the development of dating relationships. *Journal of Personality and Social Psychology, 53*, 481–489.

Freud, S. (1922). *Group psychology and the analysis of the ego*. New York: Liveright.

Gergen, K. J., Hepburn, A., & Fisher, D. C. (1986). Hermeneutics of personality description. *Journal of Personality and Social Psychology, 50*, 1261–1270.

Greenwald, A. G. (1980). The totalitarian ego: Fabrication and revision of personal history. *American Psychologist, 35*, 603–618.

Griffin, D. W., & Ross, L. (1991). Subjective construal, social inference and human misunderstanding. *Advances in Experimental Social Psychology, 24*, 319–359.

Gurman, A. S. (1978). Contemporary marital therapies: A critique and comparative analysis of psychoanalytic, behavioral and systems theory approaches. In T. Paulino, Jr., & B. McCrady (Eds.), *Marriage and marital therapy* (pp. 445–566). New York: Brunner/Mazel.

Hackel, L. S., & Ruble, D. N. (1992). Changes in the marital relationship after the first baby is born: Predicting the impact of expectancy disconfirmation. *Journal of Personality and Social Psychology, 62*, 944–957.

Hall, J. A., & Taylor, S. E. (1976). When love is blind: Maintaining idealized images of one's spouse. *Human Relations, 29*, 751–761.

Hendrick, S. S., Hendrick, C., & Adler, N. L. (1988). Romantic relationships: Love, satisfaction, and staying together. *Journal of Personality and Social Psychology, 54*, 980–988.

Holmes, J. G., & Boon, S. D. (1990). Developments in the field of close relationships: Creating foundations for intervention strategies. *Personality and Social Psychology Bulletin, 16*, 23–41.

Holmes, J. G., & Murray, S. L. (in press). Interpersonal conflict. In E. T. Higgins & A. Kruglanski (Eds.), *Social psychology: Handbook of basic mechanisms and processes.* New York: Guilford Press.

Holmes, J. G., & Rempel, J. K. (1989). Trust in close relationships. In C. Hendrick (Ed.), *Review of personality and social psychology: Close relationships* (Vol. 10, pp. 187–219). Newbury Park, CA: Sage.

Humphreys, L. G. (1990). Erroneous interpretation of difference scores: Application to a recent example. *Intelligence, 14*, 231–233.

Janoff-Bulman, R. (1989). Assumptive worlds and the stress of traumatic events: Applications of the schema construct. *Social Cognition, 7*, 113–136.

Johns, G. (1981). Difference score measures of organizational behavior variables: A critique. *Organizational Behavior and Human Performance, 27*, 443–463.

Johnson, D. J., & Rusbult, C. E. (1989). Resisting temptation: Devaluation of alternative partners as a means of maintaining commitment in close relationships. *Journal of Personality and Social Psychology, 57*, 967–980.

Karp, E. S., Jackson, J. G., & Lester, D. (1970). Ideal-self fulfillment in mate selection: A corollary to the complementary need theory of mate selection. *Journal of Marriage and the Family, 32*, 269–272.

Kelly, C., Huston, T. L., & Cate, R. M. (1985). Premarital relationship correlates of the erosion of satisfaction in marriage. *Journal of Social and Personal Relationships, 2*, 167–178.

Kenny, D. A., & DePaulo, B. M. (1993). Do people know how others view them? An empirical and theoretical account. *Psychological Bulletin, 114*, 145–161.

Kobak, R. R., & Hazan, C. (1991). Attachment in marriage: Effects of security and accuracy of working models. *Journal of Personality and Social Psychology, 60*, 861–869.

Leary, T. (1957). *Interpersonal diagnosis of personality.* New York: Ronald Press.

Levinger, G. (1983). Development and change. In H. H. Kelley, E. Berscheid, A. Christensen, J. H. Harvey, T. L. Huston, G. Levinger, E. McClintock, L. A. Peplau, & D. R. Peterson (Eds.), *Close relationships* (pp. 315–359). San Francisco: Freeman.

Markman, H. J. (1979). Application of a behavioral model of marriage in predicting relationship satisfaction of couples planning marriage. *Journal of Consulting and Clinical Psychology, 47*, 743–749.

Markman, H. J. (1981). Prediction of marital distress: A five-year follow-up. *Journal of Consulting and Clinical Psychology, 49*, 760–762.

Markus, H., & Zajonc, R. B. (1985). The cognitive perspective in social psychology. In G. Lindzey & E. Aronson (Eds.), *Handbook of social psychology* (3rd ed., Vol. 1, pp. 137–230). New York: Random House.

Mathes, E. W., & Moore, C. L. (1985). Reik's complementarity theory of romantic love. *Journal of Social Psychology, 125*, 321–327.

McCall, G. J. (1974). A symbolic interactionist approach to attraction. In T. L. Huston (Ed.), *Foundations of interpersonal attraction* (pp. 217–235). San Diego, CA: Academic Press.

Murray, S. L., & Holmes, J. G. (1993). Seeing virtues in faults: Negativity and the transformation of interpersonal narratives in close relationships. *Journal of Personality and Social Psychology, 65*, 707–722.

Murray, S. L., & Holmes, J. G. (1994). Story-telling in close relationships: The construction of confidence. *Personality and Social Psychology Bulletin, 20*, 663–676.

Murstein, B. I. (1967). Empirical tests of role, complementary needs, and homogamy theories of marital choice. *Journal of Marriage and the Family, 29*, 689–696.

Murstein, B. I. (1971). Self-ideal-self discrepancy and the choice of marital partner. *Journal of Consulting and Clinical Psychology, 37*, 47–52.

Pelham, B. W., & Swann, W. B. (1989). From self-conceptions to self-worth: On the sources and structure of global self-esteem. *Journal of Personality and Social Psychology, 57*, 672–680.

Reis, H. T., & Shaver, P. (1988). Intimacy as an interpersonal process. In S. W. Duck (Ed.), *Handbook of personal relationships* (pp. 367–389). New York: Wiley.

Rogers, C. R. (1972). *Becoming partners: Marriage and its alternatives.* New York: Delacorte.

Rosenberg, M. (1965). *Society and the adolescent self-image.* Princeton, NJ: Princeton University Press.

Rubin, Z. (1973). *Liking and loving: An invitation to social psychology,* New York: Holt, Rinehart & Winston.

Rusbult, C. E., Verette, J., Whitney, G. A., Slovik, L. F., & Lipkus, I. (1991). Accommodation processes in close relationships: Theory and preliminary research evidence. *Journal of Personality and Social Psychology, 60*, 53–78.

Snyder, M., & Swann, W. B. (1978). Behavioral confirmation in social interaction: From social perception to social reality. *Journal of Experimental Social Psychology, 14*, 148–162.

Snyder, M., Tanke, E. D., & Berscheid, E. (1977). Social perception and interpersonal behavior: On the self-fulfilling nature of social stereotypes. *Journal of Personality and Social Psychology, 35*, 656–666.

Swann, W. B., De La Ronde, C., & Hixon, J. G. (1994). Authenticity and positive strivings in marriage and courtship. *Journal of Personality and Social Psychology, 66*, 857–869.

Swann, W. B., Hixon, J. G., & De La Ronde, C. (1992). Embracing the bitter "truth": Negative self-concepts and marital commitment. *Psychological Science, 3*, 118–121.

Taylor, S. E., & Brown, J. D. (1988). Illusion and well-being: A social psychological perspective on mental health. *Psychological Bulletin, 103*, 193–210.

Taylor, S. E., Collins, R. L., Skokan, L. A., & Aspinwall, L. G. (1989). Maintaining positive illusions in the face of negative information: Getting the facts without letting them get to you. *Journal of Social and Clinical Psychology, 8*, 114–129.

Tesser, A. (1988). Toward a self-evaluation maintenance model of social behavior. *Advances in Experimental Social Psychology, 21*, 181–228.

Van Lange, P. A. M., & Rusbult, C. E. (1995). My relationship is better than—and not as bad as—yours is: The perception of superiority in close relationships. *Personality and Social Psychology Bulletin, 21*, 32–44.

Weinstein, N. D. (1980). Unrealistic optimism about future life events. *Journal of Personality and Social Psychology, 39*, 806–820.

Weiss, R. L. (1980). Strategic behavioral marital therapy: Toward a model for assessment and intervention. In J. P. Vincent (Ed.), *Advances in family intervention, assessment and theory* (Vol. 1, pp. 229–271). Greenwich, CT: JAI Press.

Wiggins, J. S. (1979). A psychological taxonomy of trait-descriptive terms: The interpersonal domain. *Journal of Personality and Social Psychology, 37*, 395–412.

Wood, J. V. (1989). Theory and research concerning social comparisons of personal attributes. *Psychological Bulletin, 106*, 231–248.

Cognition and Emotion in Ongoing Relationships

Like everyone else, Raleigh Hayes saw the world, and the people with whom he was obliged to share it, through the kaleidoscope of his own colored designs. As the years turned the viewer round and round, the bits of glass fell into new patterns, but the perspective remained limited to Raleigh's eye.

— Michael Malone

The past is a palimpsest . . . Early memories are always obscured by accumulations of later knowledge.

— Pat Barker

I can't remember which one of us is me.

— Robert Weber, New Yorker cartoon caption,

Man sitting next to his wife

Few matters in life occupy our thoughts and emotions more than relationships do. A substantial portion of everyday mental activity, both within and outside conscious awareness, concerns our relationships, whether those relationships are past or future, ongoing or longed for, desired or dreaded. Even the most superficial examination of popular literature, music, and film could not fail to acknowledge the centrality of relationships in everyday cognition and emotion. Social–psychological research is not so much concerned with the contents of these thoughts and emotions as with their influence on the nature and development of a relationship, and, conversely, with the impact of interactions and relationships on cognitive and emotional processes. The articles reprinted in this section reflect this focus.

Social cognizers are often described as motivated tacticians. As Fiske (1992) pithily expressed this concept, "thinking is for doing"—that is, social-information processing operates in the service of attaining one's goals. Because many social cognitive processes are "designed to address key issues in the development and maintenance of relationships, as well as to capitalize on relational interdependence in dealing with major life tasks" (Reis & Downey, 1999, p. 99), Reis and Downey paraphrased Fiske by suggesting that "thinking is for relating." Some of our most important and influential mental representations concern other persons who are significant in our lives, as well as the nature of our relationships with those people—what Baldwin (1992) calls relational schemas. The many ways in which these schemas affect the spontaneous thoughts and feelings that arise during interaction, which in turn affect how we behave with partners, have provided a seemingly limitless font of intriguing questions for researchers interested in relationship cognition.

As is the case for social cognition, there is an intrinsic link between emotion and relationships: Emotional behavior influences relationships, and relationships in turn influence emotional behavior. Charles Darwin (1899), the father of evolutionary theory, recognized this link in what is generally regarded as the first systematic study of human emotion. In this work, Darwin highlighted the social communicative function of emotion, outlining its role in the survival of species. Contemporary emotion theorists continue to emphasize the interpersonal nature of emotion. For example:

"Emotions, even though their hallmark is the internal state of the individual—the viscera, the gut—are above all social phenomena. They are the basis of social interaction, they are the products of social interaction, their origins, and their currency" (Zajonc, 1998, pp. 619–620).

Even casual scrutiny makes plain the centrality of relationships to emotion: Few entities are capable of eliciting as much joy, anger, excitement, sadness, gratitude, despair, pride, guilt, anxiety, and jealousy as our close partners. To some theorists, in fact, the emotion-eliciting potential of a relationship is its fundamental and defining characteristic (e.g., Berscheid & Ammazzalorso, 2001). The nature of a relationship is a key element in many of the most important processes traditionally studied by emotion researchers—for example, empathy, emotional expression and suppression, emotional contagion, and socioemotional development over the life span (the period that begins with the important relationship between caregiver and child early in life through the problems of affective engagement and disengagement in late life, as social contacts diminish).

The articles reprinted in this section illustrate several of the processes discussed above. In the first article, Aron, Aron, Tudor, and Nelson describe a process they call "including the other in the self." These authors argue that there is more to cognition in close relationships than simply paying close attention to our partners and thinking about them a lot. With increasing closeness Anna also becomes cognitively interdependent with Dave, merging her mental representations of him with her mental representations of herself, so that information processing about Dave (but not about superficial acquaintances) becomes closely linked to her self-cognition. Aron et al. report three clever experiments, each of which uses a task known to demonstrate theoretically important differences between self-cognition and other-cognition (thinking about non-close others). By showing that cognition about a close other—in these studies, one's close friend, mother, or spouse—resembles self-cognition more than it resembles other-cognition, this research demonstrates that closeness affects not only *what* we think about others but also *how* we think about them.

Ickes and Simpson bring a motivational perspective to one very important cognitive process in close relationships, empathic accuracy. There is little doubt that most people want close friends to understand their thoughts, feelings, hopes, fears, intentions, and desires. (The ability to correctly infer another person's inner mental experiences is called empathic accuracy, to distinguish it from empathy—the process of attempting to take another's perspective—and sympathy—or compassionate concern for the well-being of another.) Although empathic accuracy is often beneficial, Ickes and Simpson argue that under certain circumstances, it may be harmful for Dave to accurately perceive the specific content of Anna's thoughts and emotions. Ickes and Simpson's discussion of these circumstances, and of the mechanisms underlying accuracy-based harm, illuminates our understanding of how people cope with the inevitable threats that occur in relationships. Ickes and Simpson's paper also provides a useful discussion of the inherent difficulties of measuring empathic accuracy.

Transference is an intriguing process first identified and later elaborated by psychoanalytically oriented psychologists such as Sigmund Freud and Harry Stack Sullivan. This phenomenon is the subject of Andersen, Reznik, and Manzella's article. The concept of transference may be appreciated by recalling a time when a new acquaintance reminded you of someone with whom you once had a close relationship. When this occurs, it may be difficult to avoid reacting to the new person in the same manner as you reacted to the earlier partner. Andersen and her colleagues have devised an elegant paradigm for subtly yet potently evoking transference reactions in the lab. Their research shows that representations of significant others may—when experimentally activated or when chronically accessible, and even without any conscious awareness—transfer to new partners and situations. In the study reprinted here, when a previously unknown interaction partner was portrayed as possessing several traits similar to those of a significant other, mood, motives, and evaluations of the new partner tended to reflect the self as experienced with that significant other. Their research helps elucidate a familiar yet conceptually ill-understood point: Behavior in current relationships may be influenced, often profoundly so, by experiences in past relationships.

In the final article, Gabriel and Gardner consider how gender differences in relationship-relevant affect and cognition may reflect men's and women's differing orientations toward social relations. They propose that it is *not* that one sex is more independent or interdependent than the other, as some would claim; rather, the sexes differ in the focus of their interdependence. Women's self-construals, they argue, tend to feature relational interdependence—close dyadic relationships with specific others. Men, on the other hand, tend to be more collectively oriented, focusing primarily on group membership and identity. The three studies Gabriel and Gardner report illustrate the diversity of phenomena that this important conceptual distinction may help clarify. Another noteworthy highlight of their work is methodological diversity—spontaneous responses to the prompt "I am . . .," differential memory for the details of a hypothetical student's diary, role-playing in a series of interpersonal dilemmas—adding to our confidence in the validity and generality of their conclusions.

REFERENCES

Baldwin, M. W. (1992). Relational schemas and the processing of social information. *Psychological Bulletin, 112*, 461–484.

Berscheid, E. (1994). Interpersonal relationships. *Annual Review of Psychology, 45*, 79–129.

Berscheid, E., & Ammazzalorso, H. (2001). Emotional experience in close relationships. In M. Hewstone & M. Brewer, (Eds.), *Blackwell handbook of social psychology* (Vol. 2: Interpersonal processes, G. Fletcher & M. Clark [Eds.], pp. 308–330). Oxford, UK: Blackwell.

Darwin, C. (1899). *The expression of the emotions in man and animals*. New York: D. Appleton.

Reis, H. T., & Downey, G. (1999). Social cognition in relationships: Building essential bridges between two literatures. *Social Cognition, 17*, 97–117.

Zajonc, R. B. (1998). Emotions. In D. T. Gilbert, S. T. Fiske, & G. Lindzey (Eds.), *The handbook of social psychology* (4th ed.; Vol. 2, pp. 591–632). New York: McGraw-Hill.

Suggestions for Further Reading

Andersen, S. M., & Chen, S. (2002). The relational self: An interpersonal social-cognitive theory. *Psychological Review, 109*, 619–645. An up-to-date and comprehensive review of Andersen's theory, with broad discussion of existing research, conceptual underpinnings, and generalizability.

Aron, A., & Aron, E. N. (1997). Self-expansion motivation and including other in the self. In S. Duck (Ed.), *Handbook of personal relationships: Theory, research, and interventions* (2nd ed., pp. 251–270). Chichester, England: John Wiley & Sons. An update on theory and research regarding "inclusion of other in the self."

Bugental, D. B., & Goodnow, J. J. (1998). Socialization processes. In W. Damon & N. Eisenberg (Eds.), *Handbook of child psychology: Vol. 3, Social, emotional, and personality development* (5th ed.; pp. 389–462). New York: Wiley. A thoughtful and informative discussion of the role of relationships in socialization, especially of emotion.

Canary, D. J., & Dindia, K. (Eds.). (1998). *Sex differences and similarities in communication: Critical essays and empirical investigations of sex and gender in interaction*. Mahwah, NJ: Erlbaum. For those interested in sex differences in relationships, this volume includes a diverse set of essays based on empirical research, illustrating what is known and not known, and how sex differences and similarities are conceptualized by serious scholars.

Ickes, W. (Ed.). (1997). *Empathy accuracy*. New York: Guilford. This clear and engaging collection of chapters examines the evidence for, and consequences of, accuracy in understanding the emotions of others.

Hatfield, E., Cacioppo, J. T., & Rapson, R. L. (1994). *Emotional contagion*. New York: Cambridge University Press. Emotional contagion refers to the transmission of emotion from one person to another. This accessible volume provides a comprehensive account of relevant research and theory.

Fletcher, G. F. O., & Fitness, J. (Eds.). (1996). *Knowledge structures in close relationships: A social psychological approach* (pp. 325–344). Hillsdale, NJ: Erlbaum. A review of many different approaches to the study of mental representations and cognitive processes in close relationships.

Knee, C. R. (1998). Implicit theories of relationships: Assessment and prediction of romantic relationship initiation, coping, and longevity. *Journal of Personality and Social Psychology, 74*, 360–370. How (and not just what) one thinks about relationships—whether one believes that good relationships are a matter of destiny or work—is the focus of this intriguing research.

Pennebaker, J. (Ed.). (1995). *Emotion, disclosure, and health.* Washington, DC: APA Press. An interesting collection of essays about the ways in which the disclosure and nondisclosure of emotion in relationships can affect health and well-being.

Sprecher, S. (1999). "I love you more today than yesterday": Romantic partners' perceptions of changes in love and related affect over time. *Journal of Personality and Social Psychology, 76*, 46–53. How we perceive temporal changes in our relationships does *not* map onto the manner in which those relationships do (and do not) in reality change over time. This study examines the evidence for this important distinction.

Discussion Questions

1. What does "including the other in the self" mean? Specifically, how does this process operate? For example, do we literally acquire our partners' traits, do we experience "ownership" of their traits, or what?

2. Among your various relationship partners, who best fills the role of someone you might cognitively "include" in yourself? Discuss how your cognition about this person differs from your cognition about others.

3. When is empathic accuracy beneficial to a relationship and when might it be harmful?

4. Discuss an instance from your experience in past relationships when empathic accuracy, either by yourself or your partner, was damaging to the relationship, at least in the short term. How might this instance have been handled better?

5. Describe the process by which resemblances between a new acquaintance and a past relationship partner may trigger "schema-consistent" emotion and cognition. Describe an instance in which you had this sort of reaction to another person, or in which another person responded to you in this way.

6. What sorts of cues can trigger transference in everyday interaction? What sorts of reactions are likely to occur? Discuss how this process may help or hinder the development of new close relationships.

7. Describe other behaviors that may be explained by Gardner and Gabriel's distinction between relational and collective interdependence.

8. Explain the distinction between relational interdependence and collective interdependence. What processes might be responsible for this difference between men and women?

Managing Empathic Accuracy in Close Relationships

William Ickes and Jeffry A. Simpson

To understand all is to forgive all.

— French Proverb

To understand all is to forgive nothing.

— English Epigram

These two quotations express the major thesis and antithesis to be explored in this chapter. The first quotation suggests that empathic accuracy and understanding are good for relationships. If each partner fully comprehends the other's thoughts, feelings, hopes, fears, intentions, and desires, there is presumably no offense that cannot be forgiven. In contrast, the second quotation suggests that empathic accuracy and understanding can be bad for relationships. If each partner fully comprehends the other's point of view and subjective experience, there is presumably no offense that ever *can* be forgiven.

We propose that there is some truth in both of these assertions, with the first having more generality than the second. We further suggest that the intrinsic tension between these two viewpoints impels individuals to find ways to "manage" empathic accuracy in their close relationships. As we hope to demonstrate through a review of relevant theory and research, empathic accuracy must be carefully managed because of its potential to hurt as well as to heal, to cause injury as well as to avoid or ameliorate it. Our goal in this chapter is to shed some light on the processes by which perceivers attempt to navigate through the perilous waters of knowing what they should know—and *not* knowing what they should not know—about their partners' thoughts and feelings.

Before we undertake this task, however, we begin by reviewing the methodological background for the study of empathic accuracy in close relationships. We first consider the measurement of empathic accuracy in both marital adjustment research and in dyadic interaction research. We then examine the question of whether empathic accuracy tends to be good or bad for close relationships. After concluding that empathic accuracy usually has positive effects on the perceived quality of long-term relationships, we next consider some important exceptions to this rule. We then consider the processes by which and the conditions in which empathic *in*accuracy should occur in close relationships. Finally, we sketch the outlines of a preliminary process model that suggests how empathic accuracy is managed in close relationships in the service of both personal and relational goals.

The Measurement of Empathic Accuracy in Close Relationships

For decades, researchers in a number of disciplines have attempted to develop a reliable and valid measure of empathic accuracy. Clinical and counseling psychologists have attempted to assess empathic accuracy in two kinds of relationships: the client–therapist relationship and the relationship between marriage partners (Ickes, 1993). Measures of empathic accuracy have also been developed by communication researchers, developmental psychologists, and personality and social psychologists. Because a comprehensive review of the measurement work in each of these areas is beyond the scope of this chapter, we will focus on the measurement of empathic accuracy in marital adjustment research and in recent research on dyadic interaction.

Marital Adjustment Research

Since the 1950s, clinical and counseling psychologists have attempted to measure the empathic accuracy of couples involved in distressed and nondistressed marriages. As Sillars and his col-leagues have noted, much of the early research was "based on the symbolic interactionist argument that understanding facilitates the flexibility and mutual responsiveness required for coordinated action" (Sillars, Pike, Jones, & Murphy, 1984, p. 345). This line of reasoning suggested that understanding (i.e., empathic accuracy) should be greater in nondistressed marriages than in distressed ones.

Nearly all of the studies in the marital adjustment area have used paper-and-pencil rating tasks that require spouses to provide both self-ratings and inferences about their partner's ratings on various psychological dimensions. A convenient way of designating the possible perceptions and inferences that spouses could report was proposed by Corsini (1956). In Corsini's notational system, (1) HH and WW designate the husband's and wife's self-perceptions, (2) HW and WH designate the husband's and wife's perceptions of each other, (3) HWW and WHH, respectively, designate the husband's inference regarding the wife's self-perception and the wife's inference regarding the husband's self-perception, and (4) HWH and WHW, respectively, designate the husband's inference regarding his wife's perception of him and the wife's inference regarding her husband's perception of her.

A decade later, in their influential book *Interpersonal Perception*, Laing, Phillipson, and Lee (1966) reformulated Corsini's notational system to emphasize differences in the type of perspective involved (i.e., direct perspective, metaperspective, meta-metaperspective). According to their analysis, "*understanding* can be defined as the conjunction between the metaperspective of one person and the direct perspective of the other" (p. 38, italics in the original). The following examples all illustrate cases in which the first spouse understands the second:

Perceiver's metaperspective	*Target's direct perspective*
HWW (H's view of W's view of W) is congruent with WW (W's view of W)	
HWH (H's view of W's view of H) is congruent with WH (W's view of H)	
WHW (W's view of H's view of W) is congruent with HW (H's view of W)	
WHH (W's view of H's view of H) is congruent with HH (H's view of H)	

This logic led researchers to design studies that operationally defined understanding as the aggregated similarity across items of one spouse's self-rating (i.e., the target's direct perspective) and the other spouse's inference regarding this rating (i.e., the perceiver's metaperspective). The actual content of the rating items varied substantially from study to study. Some investigators (e.g., Dymond, 1954; Newmark, Woody, & Ziff, 1977) used Minnesota Multiphasic Personality Inventory (MMPI) items with a true/false response format. Other investigators used adjective Q-sorts (e.g., Corsini, 1956), items derived from Leary's (1957) Interpersonal Check List (e.g., Knudson, Sommers, & Golding, 1980; Luckey, 1960), sets of role expectations (e.g., Stuckert, 1963; Taylor, 1967), or rewardingness ratings of various marital behaviors (e.g., Christensen & Wallace, 1976). Still others used bipolar adjective rating scales (e.g., Murstein & Beck, 1972; Neimeyer & Banikiotes, 1981), judgments of partner affect and intentions (e.g., Guthrie & Noller, 1988; Noller, 1980, 1981; Noller & Venardos, 1986), or salience and importance ratings of marital conflict issues (e.g., Sillars et al., 1984).

Though creatively applied, these paper-and-pencil methods for assessing understanding in marital dyads were often plagued by statistical and interpretive problems. Furthermore, they were not well suited to studying the specific processes involved in understanding a partner's actual thoughts and feelings in natural, ongoing social interactions. These limitations provided the impetus for a more naturalistic measure of empathic accuracy.

Dyadic Interaction Research

An alternative to these methods was recently developed by Ickes and his colleagues (see Ickes, Bissonnette, Garcia, & Stinson, 1990; Ickes, Stinson, Bissonnette, & Garcia, 1990; Ickes & Tooke, 1988). Their approach enables researchers to measure understanding in a way that is more consistent with how it naturally occurs in dyadic interactions, that is, as the ability to make accurate, on-line inferences about the specific content of the successive thoughts and feelings of one's interaction partner. Although this procedure was originally used in laboratory studies of unstructured dyadic interactions between strangers (Ickes, Stinson, et al., 1990; Stinson & Ickes, 1992), it has now been adapted for use in both clinically relevant settings (Marangoni, Garcia, Ickes, & Teng, 1995) and in settings involving dating or married couples (Simpson, Ickes, & Blackstone, 1995).

In the original application of the procedure, the members of each dyad are led to a "waiting room" where they are left together in the experimenter's absence. While the subjects are ostensibly waiting for the experiment to begin, their interaction is unobtrusively videotaped. When the experimenter returns at the end of the observation period, the subjects are partially debriefed and are asked to participate in a second phase of the study, one that involves an assessment of their thoughts and feelings during the interaction.

If they give their consent, the subjects are then led to separate cubicles where they each view a videotape of the interaction in which they have just participated. During their first viewing of the videotape, their task is to stop the tape at each point of the interaction when they had a specific thought or feeling and to record its content on a standardized coding form. This procedure results in a written, time-logged listing of each participant's *actual thought/feeling entries*. The subjects are then instructed to view the videotape a second time, during which the tape is stopped for them at each point in the interaction when their partner reported having had a specific thought or feeling. Their task during the second viewing is to accurately infer the content of their partner's thoughts and feelings and to provide a written, time-logged listing of these *inferred thought/feeling entries*. When both subjects have completed these tasks and responded to posttest questionnaires, they are fully debriefed, thanked, and released.

The data collected through this procedure are used to compute a global measure of empathic accuracy. The computation of this measure requires similarity judgments to be made by trained, independent raters. Using a software program created by Bissonnette and Trued, the actual thought/feeling entries and the corresponding inferred thought/feeling entries are presented as paired stimuli on the screen of a microcomputer. Independent raters judge the similarity of each actual–inferred pair on a 3-point scale ranging from 0 (*essentially different content*) through 1 (*similar, but not the same, content*) to 2 (*essentially the same content*). The internal consistency of the raters' judgments tends to be high, typically ranging from .85 to .95, with a mean alpha coefficient of .90 in previous studies.

Once the reliability of the similarity judgments has been established, the data are averaged across raters to obtain mean content accuracy scores for each of the actual and inferred thought/feeling pairs. To create a global (i.e., aggregated) measure of empathic accuracy, the mean ratings are summed across all of the thought/feeling inferences in a given subject's protocol, and these summed values are then divided by the maximum number of accuracy points that could be obtained for a given number of inferences. The resulting percentage measure of empathic accuracy, which controls for individual differences in the total number of inferences made, can range from .00 (reflecting total inaccuracy) to 1.00 (reflecting perfect accuracy).

Empathic Accuracy: Is it Good or Bad for Relationships?

Is empathic accuracy good or bad for relationships? At first glance, the answer to this question seems obvious. To the casual observer who relies on conventional wisdom, the apparent answer is, "Of course empathic accuracy is good for relationships; if everyone just understood each other better, the world would be a wonderful place."

Upon reflection, however, there may be circumstances in which an accurate understanding of the thoughts and feelings of one's relationship partner could actually harm or destabilize the relationship. Thus, while accurate understanding should be good for relationships as a general rule, too much understanding in certain contexts may have deleterious consequences. In what follows, we review some theory and research that will help

us disentangle the general rule from its important exceptions.

The Rule: Empathic Accuracy is Good for Relationships

Many studies in the marital adjustment literature have documented a positive association between marital adjustment and understanding of the attitudes, role expectations, and self-perceptions of one's spouse (see Sillars & Scott, 1983, for a review). This claim is based on studies by Christensen and Wallace (1976), Corsini (1956), Dymond (1954), Ferguson and Allen (1978), Guthrie and Noller (1988), Laing et al. (1966), Luckey (1960), Murstein and Beck (1972), Newmark et al. (1977), Noller (1980, 1981), Noller and Venardos (1986), and Stuckert (1963). Additional evidence for a positive association between marital adjustment and understanding has been reported by Gottman et al. (1976), Gottman and Porterfield (1981), Kahn (1970), Katz (1965), Knudson et al. (1980), Madden and Janoff-Bulman (1981), Navran (1967), and Neimeyer and Banikiotes (1981).

Collectively, these studies support the view that, as a rule, more understanding (i.e., greater empathic accuracy) is good for relationships. The generality of this rule has recently been questioned, however, in articles by Noller (Noller, 1984; Noller & Ruzzene, 1991) and by Sillars (Sillars, 1985; Sillars et al., 1984; Sillars & Scott, 1983). For example, in some of the early studies that focused on judgments of spouses' self-rated traits, attitudes, and role expectations, the relationship between understanding and marital adjustment held only when the wife was the respondent and the husband's perceptions were being predicted (Corsini, 1956; Kotlar, 1965; Murstein & Beck, 1972; Stuckert, 1963; see also Barry, 1970). Similarly, research examining the judgments of spouses' intentions has revealed that distressed wives typically display less understanding than do nondistressed wives and husbands (Noller & Ruzzene, 1991). Such findings suggest that the association between understanding and marital adjustment is more complicated than earlier theorists and researchers supposed.

In addition, recent empirical and theoretical work indicates that circumstances may exist in which greater understanding might actually *reduce* partners' satisfaction with their relationships. Circumstances of this type are considered in the following section.

The Exceptions: When Empathic Accuracy is Bad for Relationships

To date, the most integrative theoretical work on the question of when empathic accuracy might be bad for relationships has been done by Sillars and his colleagues. They have sought to identify the conditions under which greater understanding increases conflict and dissatisfaction in relationships (Sillars, 1981, 1985; Sillars & Parry, 1982; Sillars et al., 1984; Sillars, Pike, Jones, & Redmon, 1983; Sillars & Scott, 1983). In a recent review, Sillars (1985) suggested three such conditions:

1. *Irreconcilable differences.* When the partners' thoughts and feelings involve irreconcilable differences that cannot be resolved through greater clarification of each others' respective views about an issue, greater empathic accuracy should increase the level of conflict and dissatisfaction in the relationship (Aldous, 1977; Kursh, 1971).
2. *Benevolent misconceptions.* When benevolent misconceptions facilitate the stability and satisfaction that partners experience in their relationship, enhanced understanding that alters or destroys these misconceptions should destabilize the relationship through the decreased satisfaction of one or both partners (Levinger & Breedlove, 1966).
3. *Blunt, unpleasant truths.* When the partner's words and actions cause the perceiver to experience pain and distress because they appear to express blunt, unpleasant "truths" rather than tactful and benign interpretations of the perceiver's character, motives, or behavior, increased understanding of the partner's thoughts and feelings should impair relationship stability and satisfaction (Aldous, 1977;

Rausch, Barry, Hertel, & Swain, 1974; Watzlawick, Weakland, & Fisch, 1974).

What do these three conditions have in common? They all represent cases in which greater empathic accuracy leads to insights that are not only painful and distressing to one or both partners, but also raise doubts about the strength and permanence of their relationship. This simple generalization is appealing because it seems to encompass most of the situations in which increased empathic accuracy is bad for relationships. Unfortunately, however, it also borders on being tautological (i.e., empathic accuracy is bad *for* a relationship when it leads partners to have negative feelings *about* each other or about the relationship itself). To move beyond this simple and almost circular generalization, we need to consider the cognitive dynamics that could generate such effects.

Cognitive Dynamics that Operate when Empathic Accuracy Harms Relationships

In this section, we speculate about some of the cognitive dynamics that might operate in situations in which increased empathic accuracy harms relationships. We first discuss cognitive dynamics that have a *subjective* flavor, that is, those that primarily reflect the perceiver's experience as an individual. We then consider cognitive dynamics that have a more *intersubjective* flavor, that is, those that represent the perceiver's experience as a partner in the relationship.

Cognitive Dynamics Reflecting the Perceiver's Experience as an Individual

Greater empathic accuracy should hurt relationships when perceivers arrive at insights about the target's thoughts and feelings that cause one or both partners to experience pain or distress, thereby shaking their confidence in the relationship. One way to understand this phenomenon is through attributional processes. According to correspondent inference theory (Jones & Davis, 1965), the strong *hedonic and personal relevance* of a romantic partner's thoughts and feelings should lead most perceivers to make strong, correspondent inferences (i.e., internal attributions) about the target's motives for expressing—or even harboring—the kinds of thoughts and feelings that could cause *me*, personally, to experience such distress. When the source of their personal distress is ambiguous or unclear, perceivers should tend to attribute their partners' threatening thoughts and feelings to the partners' negative traits, motives, or intentions. This outcome often occurs in quarrels in which both partners infer that the other harbors highly negative thoughts and feelings about them. When both partners make this inference, they are both likely to attribute to each other motives to injure or give offense, even when such motives are not present (cf. Gottman et al., 1976; Noller, 1980; Noller & Venardos, 1986).

The dynamics underlying cognitive dissonance may also influence how perceivers view both the target and the perceiver–target relationship. According to cognitive consistency theories such as Heider's (1946, 1958) balance theory and Festinger's (1957) theory of cognitive dissonance, the cognition that "my partner's thoughts and feelings upset me and cause me to question our relationship" should be inconsistent with the cognition that "my partner is supposed to care about my well-being, and our relationship is supposed to be one in which I feel safe and secure." The cognitive dissonance produced by this inconsistency can, in some instances, generate relationship instability by leading one partner to question whether the other partner is a truly caring and supportive person and whether their relationship is a viable one.

These tendencies should be exacerbated if the partner is perceived as being the unique source of these painful and unpleasant thoughts or feelings. According to Kelley's (1967) covariation model, perceivers should be particularly likely to make negative attributions about their partner's character and motives when they believe that (1) their partner is unique in harboring such upsetting thoughts and feelings (i.e., consensus is low), (2) their partner has these thoughts and feelings consistently rather than just occasionally (i.e., consistency is high), and (3) their partner's thoughts and feelings are not similarly upsetting

to other people (i.e., distinctiveness is high). Considering how frequently conflict can arise in close relationships and the highly intimate, personal nature of such conflict, the propensity for both partners to make such negative attributions about each other should be high (Peterson, 1983).

Cognitive Dynamics Reflecting the Perceiver's Experience as a Relationship Partner

Other cognitive dynamics involve the perceiver's identification and sense of connectedness with the target, reflecting what Heider (1958) called a "unit relation" and what others (e.g., Hatfield, 1982; McDonald, 1981) have referred to as "we-ness." Aron, Aron, Tudor, and Nelson (1991) have proposed that these dynamics are based in cognitive representations of the self and other as overlapping constructs. The cognitive "confounding" of self and other is fraught with complex implications that cannot be fully addressed here. However, the results of a number of recent studies can be used to illustrate its effects.

Projection, Assumed Similarity, and the Illusion of Understanding

One set of studies concerns the perceiver's tendency to overestimate the other's similarity to the self as a function of the cognitive confounding of self and other. Researchers have described this tendency using terms such as *projection* (Sillars, 1985; Sillars, Weisberg, & Burggraf, 1990) and *assumed similarity* (Kenny, 1994). As Sillars and Scott (1983) have noted, "familiarity increases confidence in one's understanding of another person (Posavec & Pasko, 1971; Obitz & Oziel, 1972; Clatterbuck & Turner, 1978; Lester, 1978), and this confidence may extend to areas in which understanding is not present (Shapiro & Swensen, 1969)" (p. 161). The resulting *illusion of understanding*, which derives more from the relationship itself than does the *false consensus bias* in attribution (see Ross, Greene, & House, 1977; and also Dawes & Mulford, in press), may be responsible for the fact that marital satisfaction tends to be more strongly correlated with spouses' assumed agreement than with their actual agreement (e.g., Burggraf, Stafford, & Yost, 1989; Byrne & Blaylock, 1963; Harvey, Wells, & Alvarez, 1978; Knudson et al., 1980; Levinger & Breedlove, 1966; Williamson, 1975).

Two studies by Sillars and his colleagues (1984) suggest how this "projective" process might occur. Sillars et al. studied spouses' perceptions of issues that created conflict in their marriage. They found that perceived agreement was *positively* correlated with self-reported marital satisfaction, cohesion, consensus, and affection, whereas actual understanding (with response similarity partialed out) was *negatively* correlated with these measures. These effects, which held for both the husband and the wife as perceivers, are consistent with the view that when partners cannot resolve a conflict through deeper clarification of their respective thoughts and feelings about the issue (i.e., when irreconcilable differences exist), more accurate insights about each other's thoughts and feelings can actually escalate conflict and dissatisfaction in the relationship.

Indeed, the illusion of understanding, which stems largely from perceived agreement, may develop in part as a defense *against* such painful insights about one's partner's thoughts and feelings. Moreover, it can be bolstered by spouses' frustrations about repeatedly failing to resolve their differences through trying to understand each other better. To preserve commitment and happiness in their relationship, one or both partners may delude themselves into thinking that they agree on certain issues when, in fact, they do not. While these delusions could be held by only one partner, they are often shared by both.

A Preliminary Study of Motivated Inaccuracy

A recent study by Simpson, Ickes, and Blackstone (1995) was explicitly designed to test the idea that empathic *in*accuracy can, in some conditions, serve the goal of relationship maintenance. In Phase 1 of this study, the members of 82 heterosexual dating couples completed questionnaires that assessed their (1) perceived interdependence

or "closeness" (Berscheid, Snyder, & Omoto, 1989) and (2) their perceived insecurity about the long-term stability of their relationship (Fei & Berscheid, 1977). Then, in Phase 2, each couple viewed and rated a series of slides depicting opposite-sex persons who supposedly were participants in a local "dating pool." Specifically, the male partner rated six women as prospective dates based on their physical attractiveness and sexual appeal, and the female partner rated six men as potential dates on the same dimensions. After each slide appeared on the viewing screen, the partner making the rating reported his or her numerical evaluation out loud (using a 10-point scale), in front of his or her dating partner. The partners then discussed each stimulus person for about 30 seconds, focusing on what they liked or disliked about the person. Approximately half of the couples viewed a set of less attractive stimulus persons, and half saw a set of highly attractive ones. While rating and discussing the slides, each couple's interaction was unobtrusively videotaped.

During Phase 3, the partners viewed a videotape of their rating-and-discussion session in separate rooms, and recorded all of the specific thoughts and feelings they had experienced during the session. Each participant then viewed the videotape again, this time for the purpose of inferring the content of the *partner's* thoughts or feelings at each point when one had actually occurred. Empathic accuracy scores were calculated by having independent coders rate how closely each *inferred* thought or feeling corresponded to the *actual* thought or feeling reported by the partner. Four months later, each partner was contacted by telephone and interviewed to determine whether the dating relationship was still continuing or whether it had ended.

We predicted that *motivated inaccuracy* would be particularly evident in those dating couples (1) who were faced with a situational threat to their relationship (i.e., having to evaluate attractive, opposite-sex persons as potential dates), (2) who had a close, interdependent relationship, and (3) who were insecure about the future of that relationship. The results confirmed these predictions, revealing that the couples who had this constellation of attributes were significantly less accurate at reading

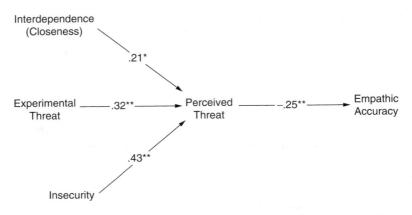

FIGURE 20.1 ■ Empirical model in which perceived threat mediated the relations between dyadic interdependence, insecurity, and experimental threat (predictors) and empathic accuracy (criterion) in the study by Simpson et al. (1995). Copyright 1995 by the American Psychological Association. Adapted by permission.

each other's thoughts and feelings than even opposite-sex strangers had been in an earlier study by Ickes, Stinson, et al. (1990). Moreover, at the 4-month follow-up, these same couples were more likely to still be dating in comparison to the other couples in the study. In fact, none of the highly close and insecure couples who evaluated attractive alternatives had broken up. This finding is important because it suggests that motivated inaccuracy might have helped to protect and stabilize these highly threatened relationships.

To explore the psychological processes underlying these effects, Simpson et al. conducted a set of path analyses. These analyses indicated that the effects reported above were mediated by the degree to which the partners felt that their relationship was threatened during the rating-and-discussion task (see Figure 20.1). Additional analyses indicated that the mediating effect of perceived threat on empathic accuracy was not an artifact of either the amount of stress evident in the *perceivers'* own thoughts or feelings (rated by independent observers) or how easily the *partners'* thoughts and feelings could be inferred from their overt behavior (also rated by observers). In light of these findings, Simpson et al. (1995) concluded that there are, in fact, circumstances in which partners are motivated to *in*accurately infer each other's thoughts and feelings in order to protect both

themselves and their relationship from the distress and instability that more accurate inferences would engender.

Potential Sources of Empathic Inaccuracy

Clearly, not all of the empathic inaccuracy that occurs in close relationships is motivated by goals such as the maintenance of the relationship or of one's own self-esteem; much of the partners' inaccuracy is both unintended and unwanted. To put the phenomenon of motivated inaccuracy into a larger theoretical perspective, it is useful to ask what kinds of factors should, in general, impair empathic accuracy in close relationships.

Distal Factors: The Individual

Several factors intrinsic to the individual partners should reduce empathic accuracy. At the most fundamental level, the target person's inability or unwillingness to *express* the content of his or her thoughts and feelings through verbal and nonverbal channels should impair empathic accuracy, as should the perceiver's inability or unwillingness to correctly *interpret* the target's behavioral cues.

Individual differences in the target's motivation to clearly express thoughts and feelings in behavior may stem from dispositions such as the need to disclose (Miller, Berg, & Archer, 1983), the need for privacy (Altman, 1975), internal correspondence (Ickes & Teng, 1987), or Machiavellianism (Christie & Geis, 1970), to name just a few. On the other hand, individual differences in the perceiver's motivation to correctly interpret the target's behavioral cues probably derive less from stable dispositions than from more transient goals and motives. Individuals enter interactions with different, and sometimes multiple, interaction goals (Gilbert, Jones, & Pelham, 1987). Their goals may be relatively egocentric (e.g., to make a good impression, to persuade, deceive, or seduce) or relatively altruistic (e.g., to try to understand a partner's perspective and offer sympathy and support). A perceiver's most important or salient goal(s) in a given interaction should determine the type(s) of information that he or she attends to, processes, or ignores (see Zadny & Gerard, 1974). For example, if forcing one's will on the other person is the preeminent goal of an interaction, partners should be disinclined to direct their attention toward behavioral cues that would increase their empathic accuracy. In general, the stronger the perceiver's motivation to achieve a particular goal, the stronger should be the influence of that goal upon the perceiver's empathic accuracy.

Stress—both acute and chronic—should also impair empathic accuracy. Worries and concerns that arise in the context of both short- and long-term life stressors (e.g., problems related to health, work, and finances) should draw an individual's attention and cognitive effort away from deciphering those behavioral cues in everyday interaction that help to convey the true content of a partner's thoughts and feelings (Schroder, Driver, & Streufert, 1967).

Distal Factors: The Relationship

Interpersonal perception in close relationships is a particularly complex topic to study for at least two reasons. First, each partner serves as both a stimulus and a response for the other during interactions. Second, partners in close relationships often are the most knowledgeable yet the least objective observers of one another (Sillars, 1985).

During the initial stages of relationship development, the personalizing knowledge gained through mutual self-disclosure usually erodes partners' reliance on simple social stereotypes when they make inferences about each other in specific contexts. Furthermore, as partners develop relationship-specific ways of communicating with and trying to understand each other, they gradually become more accurate at inferring each other's dispositions, including specific thoughts and feelings (Graham, 1994; Knapp, 1978; Morton, Alexander, & Altman, 1976; Stinson & Ickes, 1992).

The inferential advantages conferred by greater knowledge of one's partner may, however, be offset by perceptual biases that originate from knowing the partner *too* well. Sillars (1985) has proposed that three features of close relationships can short-circuit accurate empathic understanding: excessive familiarity with the partner, high levels of behavioral interdependence, and strong emotional involvement. We agree with Sillars that these three features can contribute to perceptual biases in close relationships. However, they should impair empathic accuracy only in certain circumstances. Some of these circumstances are specified below; others will be discussed in a subsequent section describing our model of empathic inaccuracy in close relationships.

Familiarity frequently breeds overconfidence in inferential tasks, and this is especially true when interactants know each other very well (Shapiro & Swensen, 1969). If overconfidence extends into domains in which partners know little about one another, greater familiarity can result in less understanding. This outcome may occur because partners who know each other well may be less motivated to seek out new and potentially diagnostic information about the other that could improve empathic understanding (see Berger & Calabrese, 1975; Pavitt & Cappella, 1979). Excessive familiarity also can reduce empathic understanding by solidifying old impressions that partners have of each other that are no longer valid (cf. Weick, 1971).

High levels of emotional involvement (which we will refer to as *emotional investment*) should—in some circumstances—also attenuate empathic accuracy in close relationships. It is important to emphasize that emotional investment does *not* refer to the frequency or intensity with which partners experience emotions in their relationship on a daily basis. Instead, emotional investment reflects the extent to which a relationship has the potential to elicit strong positive or negative emotions (see Berscheid, 1983). The full impact of emotional investment on a relationship is most apparent when important long-term plans or goals that require the cooperation of the partner are blocked (Berscheid et al., 1989) or when a relationship ends (Simpson, 1987).

Sillars (1985) has speculated that strong emotional investment should reduce empathic understanding for two reasons. First, it should activate self-serving biases (Weary-Bradley, 1978), which often lead to erroneous inferences about the actions and intentions of others. Second, emotional investment should interfere with complex inferential thinking (Schroder et al., 1967; Suedfeld & Tetlock, 1977), perhaps by restricting the acquisition of new information or by channeling the retrieval of old information.

To summarize, relationship partners venture into interactions with different levels of empathic ability and "readability." They also have different motives, different interaction goals, and different degrees of emotional investment in their relationship. These relatively distal factors provide the context in which more proximal, situationally-based factors affect empathic accuracy.

Proximal Factors: The Situation

What kinds of situational contexts should undermine empathic accuracy? Three classes of situations can be identified: (1) those that draw the perceiver's attention away from behavioral cues that are relevant to the inferential task, (2) those that require difficult, novel, or unfamiliar inferences to be made, and (3) those that have the potential to destabilize the partners' relationship.

It is obvious that empathic accuracy should suffer when features of the situation divert the perceiver's attention away from verbal and nonverbal cues that might be valid indicators of a partner's covert thoughts and feelings. When individuals are distracted during interactions (e.g., by being absorbed in their own thoughts about what to say; see Brenner, 1973; Lord & Saenz, 1985), they have poor memory for the behavior of their interaction partners. Because the accurate encoding of information is a critical stage in the process of interpersonal perception, situations that channel the perceivers' attention away from their partners' behavior should produce lower empathic accuracy. In addition, perceivers' empathic accuracy should decline when the situation directs their attention toward invalid behavioral cues and away from more valid ones.

Situations that render inferences more difficult to make even when relevant behavioral cues have been encoded should also reduce empathic accuracy (cf. Osborne & Gilbert, 1992). When perceivers are asked to make accurate trait inferences about targets while simultaneously engaging in a second task that requires controlled and effortful information processing, they fall prey to systematic inferential errors (see, e.g., Gilbert & Krull, 1988; Gilbert, Pelham, & Krull, 1988). Specifically, cognitively "busy" perceivers successfully encode but then fail to use valid information about the situational constraints on a target's behavior. Thus, potentially diagnostic information is noticed and remembered, but it is not used to correct or adjust mistaken initial inferences. This reasoning suggests that when perceivers must deal with one or more competing tasks that require deliberate, controlled, and effortful cognitive processing, their empathic accuracy should be impaired—often in the direction of making overly dispositional attributions about the causes of their partners' behavior.

Perhaps the most interesting class of situations are those having the potential to destabilize or subvert the partners' relationship. As noted earlier, Sillars (1985) identified three interaction contexts in which greater empathic accuracy might have a negative impact on relationships: (1) when the partners have irreconcilable differences about an important issue, (2) when the perpetuation of benevolent misconceptions helps to maintain the relationship, and (3) when the emergence of unpleasant truths could weaken or destroy the relationship. For couples who find conflict aversive and threatening, motivated *in*accuracy should be likely to occur in these contexts. On the other hand, for conflict-habituated couples, motivated inaccuracy may not occur. Instead, like George and Martha in Edward Albee's play *Who's Afraid of Virginia Woolf?*, conflict-habituated couples may take a perverse pleasure in torturing themselves and their partners with such unpleasant truths—with little or no loss of empathic accuracy. For couples in which one partner is conflict-habituated and the other is conflict-averse, only the conflict-averse partner may use motivated inaccuracy as a defense against threats to the relationship.

In addition to destabilizing forces that are *internal* to relationships, destabilization can be instigated by *external* sources as well (Thibaut & Kelley, 1959). Conversations with one's partner about attractive alternatives to the relationship (Simpson et al., 1995), discussions about the quality of one's relationship based on feedback from external experts (e.g., therapists), and interactions about important career decisions that could have negative consequences for the relationship (e.g., partners discussing the prospect of taking jobs in different cities) all represent situations that could destabilize and harm close relationships. For conflict-avoidant couples, the temptation to not even discuss such disruptive influences should be strong. When these issues *are* confronted, however, empathic inaccuracy should serve as a secondary—though often imperfect—line of defense against their destabilizing impact.

A Model of Empathic Inaccuracy in Close Relationships

When and how do individuals monitor, regulate, and manage empathic accuracy in their close relationships? Our model begins with the premise that individual-level distal factors (e.g., the perceivers' ability to decipher the valid cues conveyed by their partners, and their partners' ability to convey cues diagnostic of their internal states) set the range—the upper and the lower boundaries—of empathic accuracy in a given interaction. In other words, the minimal and maximal level of empathic accuracy that can occur in an interaction is initially constrained by the degree to which each

partner has the basic skills, abilities, and motivation needed to accurately read and send relevant behavioral cues.

Within these initial constraints, however, many interesting variations can occur. The variations we regard as most fundamental are captured by the part of our model depicted in Figure 20.2. The first assumption of the model, portrayed at the top of the figure, is that empathic accuracy is managed differently in some situations than in others. Specifically, in situations in which the partner's thoughts and feelings are perceived as likely to cause the perceiver distress, empathic accuracy can vary greatly depending on (1) the clarity or ambiguity of the cues signaling the partner's thoughts and feelings, and (2) the degree to which the perceiver feels highly threatened by the consequences that would likely result from accurately inferring the partner's thoughts and feelings. These relations are depicted in the left and middle sections of Figure 20.2.

On the other hand, in situations in which the partner's thoughts and feelings seem unlikely to cause the perceiver distress, empathic accuracy should be moderate, reflecting both the mundane, taken-for-granted aspect of these situations and the lack of significant threat experienced by either of the perceivers. These relations are depicted in the right section of Figure 20.2.

Empathic Accuracy in Nonthreatening Contexts

To examine the logic of the model, let us begin by considering the right side of Figure 20.2. We assume that relationship members should—in most circumstances—be motivated to accurately infer each other's thoughts and feelings. By the phrase "in most circumstances," we mean routine, mundane interactions in which the partners perceive little or no threat to their relationship. In such circumstances, empathic accuracy should typically provide useful and constructive insights into the partner and/or the issues being discussed. These insights should help the perceiver to clarify potential misunderstandings, avert future conflicts, and perhaps facilitate satisfaction and closeness in the

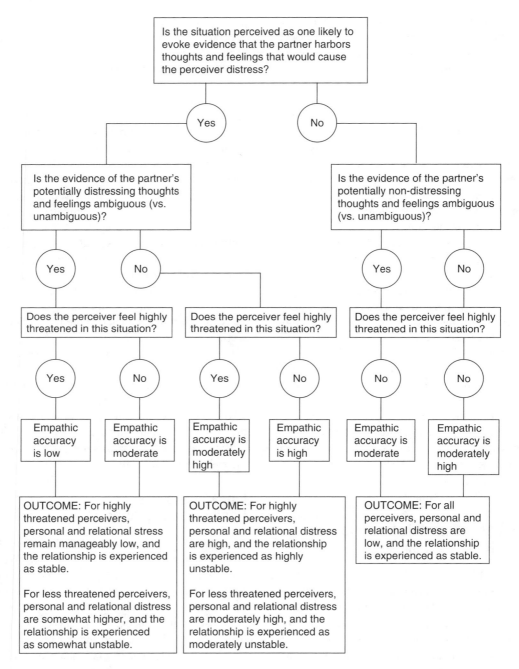

FIGURE 20.2 ■ Theoretical model of the conditions in which relationship partners are motivated to either accurately infer or *in*accurately infer each other's thoughts and feelings.

relationship. Thus, as long as the thoughts and feelings harbored by each partner are not likely to have negative consequences for the stability and happiness of the relationship, accurate empathic understanding should remain an important interaction goal.

Because the motivation to be accurate may be undermined somewhat by the routine, taken-for-granted nature of the interaction in these situations, the perceivers' level of empathic accuracy should typically be moderate, rather than high. Moreover, because neither perceiver has substantial cause to feel threatened by the possible consequences of accurately inferring the partner's thoughts and feelings, both perceivers should achieve levels of empathic accuracy that are relatively similar, rather than discrepant. Finally, both perceivers should experience little if any personal distress in these mundane, nonthreatening situations, and the relationship should remain stable and relatively free of stress as well.

Empathic Accuracy in Threatening Contexts

Although most day-to-day interactions are mundane and nonthreatening, partners occasionally will encounter situations capable of eliciting thoughts and feelings that could harm their relationship. For partners who perceive the situation as potentially threatening, the first line of defense should be to avoid or extricate themselves from situations of this type. This strategy for managing empathic accuracy is not depicted in Figure 20.2, but it fits into the model as a second decision point following the perceiver's initial assessment that the situation could evoke evidence that the partner harbors potentially threatening thoughts and feelings. At this stage, perceivers have the option either to steer clear of the threatening situation (avoiding it, if possible, or escaping from it, if not) or to enter or remain in the situation and try to deal with its threatening implications.

Table 20.1 offers a few representative examples of ways in which perceivers might avoid or escape from situations in which they are likely to discover that their partners harbor threatening thoughts and feelings. This strategy for managing empathic accuracy presupposes that perceivers are, at some level, aware of the probable "danger zones" in their relationship—areas in which painful revelations about their partners' thoughts and feelings might occur. Presumably, the perceivers' motivation to avoid or escape such danger zones stems from the belief that it is better to avoid confronting your worst fears than to have your worst fears confirmed and then have to deal directly with the consequences of that knowledge. For perceivers who (1) have the contrasting belief-structure (i.e., that it is better to confront one's worst fears directly)

TABLE 20.1. Representative Examples of Ways Partners Can Avoid or Escape Threatening Situations

1. Steering the conversation away from "danger zone" topics that are likely to evoke evidence that the partner harbors thoughts and feelings that threaten the relationship and the perceiver's self-esteem.

2. Refusing to enter or, alternatively, exiting situations (i.e., lunch with the partner and the partner's former lover) in which deliberate or inadvertent evidence of the partner's relationship-threatening thoughts and feelings is likely to emerge.

3. Backing away from any confrontations that are likely to evoke evidence that the partner harbors thoughts and feelings that threaten the relationship and the perceiver's self-esteem.

4. Resisting the temptation to question the partner's friends and associates about issues such as the partner's past history, where and how the partner spends time away from home, or attitudes and sentiments which the partner may have expressed only to them.

5. Resisting the temptation to read without permission the partner's private diary, appointment book, or personal correspondence with others.

6. Resisting the temptation to spy on the partner by covertly tracking his or her movements, or by having someone else do so.

7. Resisting the temptation to set up "acid test" situations in which the partner might be trapped in a lie or otherwise forced to reveal thoughts or feelings that have previously been concealed.

and/or (2) cannot avoid or extricate themselves from the potentially threatening situation, the dynamics depicted in the left and middle sections of Figure 20.2 become relevant.

For partners who are either unwilling or unable to avoid or extricate themselves from situations in which such danger zones exist, the next line of defense should be to shift away from an "accuracy" set. Whether this strategy for managing empathic accuracy is a viable one should depend, however, on whether the evidence of the partner's threatening thoughts and feelings is ambiguous or unambiguous. If the evidence is unambiguous (e.g., the partner confesses to being in love with someone else), the sheer clarity of the partner's thoughts and feelings should force both perceivers to achieve at least a moderately high level of empathic accuracy, although accuracy should be somewhat lower for the more-threatened perceiver (Figure 20.2, middle portion).

The outcomes of experiencing these unpleasant insights should also differ for highly threatened versus less-threatened perceivers. For highly threatened perceivers, both personal and relational distress should be high and the relationship should become unstable. For less-threatened perceivers, both personal and relational distress should be somewhat lower. This last prediction is based on the assumption that if the perceiver does not feel threatened by unambiguous evidence that the partner harbors thoughts and feelings that would cause the perceiver distress, the perceiver's emotional investment in the relationship must be low; accordingly, the experience should not create as much distress as it does for a more highly invested and highly threatened perceiver.

If the evidence of the partner's threatening thoughts and feelings is ambiguous, motivated *in*accuracy should be most clearly evident, especially in highly threatened perceivers (Figure 20.2, left portion). For such perceivers, the motivation to shift away from an "accuracy" set should be strong. The kinds of defense mechanisms identified by Freud and others (denial, repression, rationalization, intellectualization) should be most fully deployed in this case, as these perceivers try to avoid confronting the most threatening implications of

the thoughts and feelings that are harbored by their partners. The empathic accuracy of highly threatened perceivers should therefore be low (i.e., motivated *in*accuracy), but their strategy of perceptual–inferential defense should be at least temporarily successful in preserving a low level of personal and relational distress and in keeping the relationship stable. For less-threatened perceivers, who can better afford to scrutinize their partner's thoughts and feelings, less motivated inaccuracy should be evident. Although empathic accuracy should be more moderate in this case, the consequence of this greater insight into the partner's thoughts and feelings should be a somewhat higher level of personal and relational distress.

What Inferential Processing Failures Underlie Motivated Inaccuracy?

Exactly when during the inferential process is empathic accuracy likely to falter? Any attempt to answer to this question is clouded by two basic features of interpersonal perception. First, the motivations, abilities, and actions of *both* interaction partners must be simultaneously considered in the search for the origins of inaccuracy. Second, because each partner serves as both a sender *and* a receiver of information, the task of locating the specific source(s) of inaccuracy becomes even more difficult. Given these complexities and the current lack of research on "on-line" empathic accuracy, we cannot offer definitive answers about the origins of empathic inaccuracy. We can, however, offer a few educated guesses.

To make accurate inferences about targets, perceivers first must have access to valid behavioral cues that signal the target's real thoughts and feelings. For highly threatened perceivers, motivated inaccuracy could arise if threatening elements within the partners' current situation cause the targets to alter or mask their behavioral cues. For example, targets might—either intentionally or unintentionally—conceal their actual thoughts and feelings by altering their verbal and nonverbal expressions. Or targets might become so engrossed in the complexities of the situation—thinking about their own reactions to the situation, pondering the reactions of their partner, contemplating the myriad possible outcomes that might follow the interaction, and so on—that their behavioral cues become conflicted, ambiguous, and difficult to interpret.

Although concealment or masking could be a possible source of empathic inaccuracy, evidence from the Simpson et al. (1995) study suggests that it does not provide a complete account. When independent observers in the Simpson et al. study rated the extent to which each partner's actual thoughts and feelings were easy to infer from his or her behavior in the laboratory interaction, the results indicated that the verbal and nonverbal behavior of partners who were the most invested and who experienced the most threat were *not* more difficult to decipher than the behavior of partners who were less invested and who reported less threat. Although these results could be specific to the paradigm used by Simpson et al., they suggest that empathic inaccuracy may originate from later stages of the inference process.

Assuming that perceivers are exposed to valid behavioral cues, they then must engage in three cognitive tasks in order to make accurate inferences about their interaction partners (see Gilbert & Krull, 1988). First, they must *encode* the cues that might be diagnostic of the target's underlying dispositions. Second, they must accurately *characterize* the target (i.e., make an accurate inference about the target based on his or her behavioral cues). Third, they must *correct* or adjust this initial inference in light of situational constraints in the interaction setting.

Encoding and characterization tend to be automatic processes that require relatively little cognitive effort, particularly when valid behavioral cues are expressed through nonverbal channels (Gilbert & Krull, 1988). Even when perceivers are immersed in a second task that depletes their cognitive resources, they still often encode and characterize relevant behavioral cues with a reasonable degree of accuracy (Gilbert, Pelham, et al., 1988). On the other hand, the correction stage requires more cognitive effort and controlled processing, and it is at this final stage that accuracy often goes awry (Gilbert, Krull, & Pelham, 1988). Because the suppression of one's personal perspective during an interaction takes considerable cognitive effort and can undermine comprehension of one's partner's perspective (cf. Wegner & Giuliano, 1982; Wicklund, 1975), errors should occur frequently during stressful interactions at this final stage of controlled, "corrective" inference making.

The reader should note that studies of accuracy in trait inference differ in several significant ways from studies of "on-line" empathic accuracy. First, in the research paradigms used by Gilbert and his colleagues, the perceivers and targets do not know each other. Second, the perceivers are asked to infer the targets' global traits—not the content of their successive thoughts and feelings during a period of interaction. Third, targets are presented on videotape instead of being "live" interactants. These differences make it difficult to pinpoint the exact stage of information processing from which empathic inaccuracy derives. Nevertheless, research on the inferential accuracy of traits in strangers may offer some preliminary clues about where future research on the empathic inaccuracy of relationship partners should be directed.

Summary and Conclusions

In this chapter, we have proposed a theoretical model that specifies the conditions in which the partners in a close relationship should be motivated to either accurately infer or inaccurately infer each other's thoughts and feelings. The model presumes that, in nonthreatening situations, perceivers should be motivated to accurately infer their partner's thoughts and feelings, although the strength of this motivation should be mitigated somewhat by the routine, taken-for-granted nature of the interactions that occur in these situations. Consistent with the general "rule" that empathic accuracy should be good for (and frequently occur in) close relationships, the model predicts that in the more mundane, nonthreatening contexts that comprise the vast majority of interactions in daily life, empathic accuracy should be associated with greater relationship stability and satisfaction.

On the other hand, in threatening but ambiguous situations that have the potential to destabilize and destroy the relationship, the model proposes that the relation between empathic accuracy and relationship stability/satisfaction should reverse. Consistent with the empirical "exceptions" to the general rule, the model predicts that greater empathic accuracy in such contexts should actually impair relationship stability and satisfaction— and, in many cases, the perceiver's own self-esteem as well. To defend against this possibility, perceivers in these contexts should display motivated inaccuracy, with this effect being most evident for those perceivers experiencing the highest levels of perceived threat.

Our model does not address whether motivated inaccuracy stems primarily from automatic versus controlled mental processing. Although research is just beginning to explore this issue, we suspect that many of the inferential errors that occur in close relationships involve controlled processing. For example, threatened perceivers may engage in "exposure control" by selectively attending to certain behavioral cues displayed by their partners while totally disregarding or ignoring others (Zadny & Gerard, 1974). Alternatively, threatened perceivers may exert "mental control" by deliberately trying *not* to adopt the perspective of their partner during a stressful interaction. Paradoxically, the perceiver's motivated inaccuracy might itself be subverted in cases where the attempt to consciously suppress the partner's perspective is undermined by opponent processes associated with thought suppression (Wegner, 1994).

Two important qualifications bear repeating. First, we do not believe that motivated inaccuracy is evoked by *all* situations that have the potential to undermine well-established relationships (see Figure 20.2, top). Second, we do not believe that the subtle and not-so-subtle delusions that are evoked by threatening situations will invariably be maintained over time. The meaning and implications of some destabilizing situations may be so stark and unambiguous (e.g., discovering one's partner *in flagrante delicto*) that accurate inferences cannot be sidestepped and the harsh glare of reality simply cannot be denied. Furthermore, if a relationship is to remain stable and healthy, it cannot be based on a long history of empathic inaccuracy. Clearly, inaccuracy loses its adaptive value if

inferential errors become so extreme that partners no longer understand each other and the relationship dissolves. Inaccuracy also should be maladaptive if, over time, it impedes partners from taking the steps necessary to correct existing problems in the relationship or to diffuse external threats.

We introduced this chapter with a proverb and an epigram that offer contrasting views about the merits of understanding in relationships: "To understand all is to forgive all" and "To understand all is to forgive nothing." Both views may be correct—but only conditionally so. The key to which one is correct in a given situation hinges on what it is that the perceiver might understand. If what the perceiver might understand does not threaten to destroy a valued relationship, then understanding may well lead to forgiveness. However, if what the perceiver might understand threatens the very existence of the relationship, the perceiver may be faced with two options—to try very hard *not* to understand (motivated inaccuracy), or to understand but not forgive.

REFERENCES

Aldous, J. (1977). Family interaction patterns. *Annual Review of Sociology, 3*, 105–135.

Altman, I. (1975). *The environment and social behavior: Privacy, personal space, territory, and crowding.* Pacific Grove, CA: Brooks/Cole.

Aron, A., & Aron, E. N. (in press). Self-expansion motivation and including other in the self. In S. W. Duck, K. Dindia, W. Ickes, R. M. Milardo, R. Mills, & B. Sarason (Eds.), *Handbook of personal relationships: Theory, research, and interventions* (2nd ed.). Chichester, England: Wiley.

Aron, A., Aron, E. N., Tudor, M., & Nelson, G. (1991). Close relationships as including the other in the self. *Journal of Personality and Social Psychology, 60*, 241–253.

Barry, W. A. (1970). Marriage research and conflict: An integrative review. *Psychological Bulletin, 73*, 41–54.

Berger, C. R., & Bradac, J. J. (1982). *Language and social knowledge: Uncertainty in interpersonal relations.* London: Edward Arnold.

Berger, C. R., & Calabrese, R. J. (1975). Some explorations in initial interaction and beyond: Toward a developmental theory of interpersonal communication. *Human Communication Research, 1*, 99–112.

Berscheid, E. (1983). Emotion. In H. H. Kelley, E. Berscheid, A. Christensen, J. Harvey, T. L. Huston, G. Levinger, E. McClintock, L. A. Peplau, & D. R. Peterson, *Close relationships* (pp. 110–168). San Francisco: Freeman.

Berscheid, E., Snyder, M., & Omoto, A. M. (1989). The relationship closeness inventory: Assessing the closeness of interpersonal relationships. *Journal of Personality and Social Psychology, 57*, 792–807.

Brenner, M. (1973). The next-in-line effect. *Journal of Verbal Learning and Verbal Behavior, 12*, 320–323.

Burggraf, C. S., Stafford, L., & Yost, S. (1989). *Conversational memory, understanding, and marital satisfaction.* Paper presented at the annual meeting of the Speech Communication Association, San Francisco.

Byrne, D., & Blaylock, B. (1963). Similarity and assumed similarity between husbands and wives. *Journal of Abnormal and Social Psychology, 67*, 636–640.

Christensen, L., & Wallace, L. (1976). Perceptual accuracy as a variable in marital adjustment. *Journal of Sex and Marital Therapy, 2*, 130–136.

Christie, R., & Geis, F. L. (1970). *Studies in Machiavellianism.* New York: Academic Press.

Clatterbuck, G. W., & Turner, G. O. (1978). *Short-term and long-term effects of information, physical attractiveness and uncertainty reduction in relationship development.* Paper presented at the meeting of the International Communication Association, Chicago.

Corsini, R. J. (1956). Understanding and similarity in marriage. *Journal of Abnormal and Social Psychology, 52*, 327–332.

Dawes, R. M., & Mulford, M. (in press). The false consensus effect and overconfidence: Flaws in judgment, or flaws in how we study judgment? *Organizational Behavior and Human Performance.*

Dymond, R. (1954). Interpersonal perception and marital happiness. *Canadian Journal of Psychology, 8*, 164–171.

Fei, J., & Berscheid, E. (1977). *Perceived dependency, insecurity, and love in heterosexual relationships: The eternal triangle.* Unpublished manuscript, University of Minnesota.

Ferguson, L. R., & Allen, D. R. (1978). Congruence of parental perception, marital satisfaction, and child adjustment. *Journal of Consulting and Clinical Psychology, 46*, 345–346.

Festinger, L. (1957). *A theory of cognitive dissonance.* Palo Alto, CA: Stanford University Press.

Gilbert, D. T., Jones, E. E., & Pelham, B. W. (1987). Influence and inference: What the active perceiver overlooks. *Journal of Personality and Social Psychology, 52*, 861–870.

Gilbert, D. T., & Krull, D. S. (1988). Seeing less and knowing more: The benefits of perceptual ignorance. *Journal of Personality and Social Psychology, 54*, 193–202.

Gilbert, D. T., Krull, D. S., & Pelham, B. W. (1988). Of thoughts unspoken: Social inference and the self-regulation of behavior. *Journal of Personality and Social Psychology, 55*, 685–694.

Gilbert, D. T., Pelham, B. W., & Krull, D. S. (1988). Cognitive busyness: When person perceivers meet persons perceived. *Journal of Personality and Social Psychology, 54*, 733–740.

Gottman, J. M., Notarius, C., Markman, H., Bank, S., Yoppi, B., & Rubin, M. E. (1976). Behavior exchange theory and marital decision making. *Journal of Personality and Social Psychology, 34*, 14–23.

Gottman, J. M., & Porterfield, A. L. (1981). Communicative competence in the nonverbal behavior of married couples. *Journal of Marriage and the Family, 43*, 817–824.

Graham, T. (1994). *Gender, relationship, and target differences in empathic accuracy.* Unpublished masters thesis, University of Texas at Arlington.

Guthrie, D. M., & Noller, P. (1988). Married couples' perceptions of one another in emotional situations. In P. Noller & M. A. Fitzpatrick (Eds.), *Perspectives on marital interaction* (pp. 153–181). Cleveland, OH: Multilingual Matters.

Harvey, J. H., Wells, G. L., & Alvarez, M. D. (1978). Attribution in the context of conflict and separation in close relationships. In J. H. Harvey, W. J. Ickes, & R. F. Kidd (Eds.), *New directions in attribution research* (Vol. 2, pp. 235–260). New Brunswick, NJ: Erlbaum.

Hatfield, E. (1982). Passionate love, companionate love, and intimacy. In M. Fisher & G. Stricker (Eds.), *Intimacy* (pp. 267–292). New York: Plenum.

Heider, F. (1946). Attitudes and cognitive organization. *Journal of Psychology, 21*, 107–112.

Heider, F. (1958). *The psychology of interpersonal relations.* New York: Wiley.

Ickes, W. (1993). Empathic accuracy. *Journal of Personality, 61*, 587–610.

Ickes, W., Bissonnette, V., Garcia, S., & Stinson, L. (1990). Implementing and using the dyadic interaction paradigm. In C. Hendrick & M. Clark (Eds.), *Review of personality and social psychology: Research methods in personality and social psychology* (Vol. 11, pp. 16–44). Newbury Park, CA: Sage.

Ickes, W., Stinson, L., Bissonnette, V., & Garcia, S. (1990). Naturalistic social cognition: Empathic accuracy in mixed-sex dyads. *Journal of Personality and Social Psychology, 59*, 730–742.

Ickes, W., & Teng, G. (1987). Refinement and validation of Brickman's measure of internal–external correspondence. *Journal of Research in Personality, 21*, 287–305.

Ickes, W., & Tooke, W. (1988). The observational method: Studying the interaction of minds and bodies. In S. Duck, D. Hay, S. Hobfoll, W. Ickes, & B. Montgomery (Eds.), *The handbook of personal relationships: Theory, research, and interventions* (pp. 79–97). Chichester, England: Wiley.

Jones, E. E., & Davis, K. E. (1965). From acts to dispositions: The attribution process in person perception. In L. Berkowitz (Ed.), *Advances in experimental social psychology* (Vol. 2, pp. 219–266). New York: Academic Press.

Kahn, M. (1970). Nonverbal communication and marital satisfaction. *Family Process, 9*, 449–456.

Katz, M. (1965). Agreement on connotative meaning in marriage. *Family Process, 5*, 64–74.

Kelley, H. H. (1967). Attribution theory in social psychology. In D. Levine (Ed.), *Nebraska symposium on motivation, 15*, 192–238.

Kelley, H. H., Berscheid, E., Christensen, A., Harvey, J., Huston, T. L., Levinger, G., McClintock, E., Peplau, L. A., & Peterson, D. R. (1983). *Close relationships.* San Francisco: Freeman.

Kenny, D. A. (1994). *Interpersonal perception: A social relations analysis*. New York: Guilford Press.

Knapp, M. L. (1978). *Social intercourse: From greeting to goodbye*. Boston: Allyn & Bacon.

Knudson, R. A., Sommers, A. A., & Golding, S. L. (1980). Interpersonal perception and mode of resolution in marital conflict. *Journal of Personality and Social Psychology, 38*, 251–263.

Kotlar, S. L. (1965). Middle-class marital role perceptions and marital adjustment. *Sociology and Social Research, 49*, 284–291.

Kursh, C. O. (1971). The benefits of poor communication. *Psychoanalytic Review, 58*, 189–208.

Laing, R. D., Phillipson, H., & Lee, A. R. (1966). *Interpersonal perception: A theory and a method of research*. New York: Springer.

Leary, T. F. (1957). *Interpersonal diagnosis of personality*. New York: Ronald Press.

Lester, R. E. (1978). *Beyond initial interaction: Dyadic communication and uncertainty reduction in personal phase relationships*. Paper presented at the meeting of the International Communication Association, Chicago.

Levinger, G., & Breedlove, J. (1966). Interpersonal attraction and agreement. *Journal of Personality and Social Psychology, 3*, 367–372.

Lord, C. G., & Saenz, D. S. (1985). Memory deficits and memory surfeits: Differential cognitive consequences of tokenism for tokens and observers. *Journal of Personality and Social Psychology, 49*, 918–926.

Luckey, E. B. (1960). Number of years married as related to personality perception and marital satisfaction. *Journal of Marriage and the Family, 28*, 44–48.

Madden, M. E., & Janoff-Bulman, R. (1981). Blame, control, and marital satisfaction: Wives' attributions for conflict in marriage. *Journal of Marriage and the Family, 43*, 663–674.

Marangoni, C., Garcia, S., Ickes, W., & Teng, G. (1995). Empathic accuracy in a clinically relevant setting. *Journal of Personality and Social Psychology, 68*, 854–869.

McDonald, G. (1981, November). Structural exchange and marital interaction. *Journal of Marriage and the Family, 43*, 825–839.

Miller, G. R., & Steinberg, M. (1975). *Between people*. Chicago: Science Research Associates.

Miller, L. C., Berg, J. H., & Archer, R. L. (1983). Openers: Individuals who elicit intimate self-disclosure. *Journal of Personality and Social Psychology, 44*, 1234–1244.

Morton, T. L., Alexander, J. F., & Altman, I. (1976). Communication and relationship definition. In G. R. Miller (Ed.), *Explorations in interpersonal communication* (pp. 105–145). Beverly Hills, CA: Sage.

Murstein, B. I., & Beck, G. D. (1972). Person perception, marriage adjustment, and social desirability. *Journal of Consulting and Clinical Psychology, 39*, 396–403.

Navran, L. (1967). Communication and adjustment in marriage. *Family Process, 6*, 173–184.

Neimeyer, G. J., & Banikiotes, P. G. (1981). Self-disclosure flexibility, empathy, and perceptions of adjustment and attraction. *Journal of Counseling Psychology, 28*, 272–275.

Newmark, C. S., Woody, G., & Ziff, D. (1977). Understanding and similarity in relation to marital satisfaction. *Journal of Clinical Psychology, 33*, 83–86.

Noller, P. (1980). Misunderstandings in marital communication: A study of couples' nonverbal communication. *Journal of Personality and Social Psychology, 39*, 1135–1148.

Noller, P. (1981). Gender and marital adjustment level differences in decoding messages from spouses and strangers. *Journal of Personality and Social Psychology, 41*, 272–278.

Noller, P. (1984). *Nonverbal communication and marital interaction*. Oxford: Pergamon.

Noller, P., & Ruzzene, M. (1991). Communication in marriage: The influence of affect and cognition. In G. J. O. Fletcher & F. D. Fincham (Eds.), *Cognition in close relationships* (pp. 203–233). Hillsdale, NJ: Erlbaum.

Noller, P., & Venardos, C. (1986). Communication awareness in married couples. *Journal of Social and Personal Relationships, 3*, 31–42.

Obitz, F. W., & Oziel, J. L. (1972). Varied information levels and accuracy of person perception. *Psychological Reports, 31*, 571–576.

Osborne, R. E., & Gilbert, D. T. (1992). The preoccupational hazards of social life. *Journal of Personality and Social Psychology, 62*, 219–228.

Pavitt, C., & Cappella, J. N. (1979). Coorientational accuracy in interpersonal and small group discussions: A literature review, model, and simulation. In D. Nimmo (Ed.), *Communication yearbook* (Vol. 3). New Brunswick, NJ: Transaction Books.

Peterson, D. R. (1983). Conflict. In H. H. Kelley, E. Berscheid, A. Christensen, J. Harvey, T. L. Huston, G. Levinger, E. McClintock, L. A. Peplau, & D. R. Peterson, *Close relationships* (pp. 360–396). San Francisco: Freeman.

Posavec, E. J., & Pasko, S. J. (1971). Interpersonal attraction and confidence of attraction ratings as a function of number of attitudes and attitude similarity. *Psychonomic Science, 23*, 433–435.

Rausch, H. L., Barry, W. A., Hertel, R. K., & Swain, M. A. (1974). *Communication conflict and marriage*. San Francisco: Jossey-Bass.

Ross, L., Greene, D., & House, P. (1977). The "false consensus effect": An egocentric bias in social perception and attributional processes. *Journal of Experimental Social Psychology, 13*, 279–301.

Schroder, H. M., Driver, M. J., & Streufert, S. (1967). *Human information processing*. New York: Holt, Rinehart & Winston.

Shapiro, A., & Swensen, C. (1969). Patterns of self-disclosure among married couples. *Journal of Counseling Psychology, 16*, 179–180.

Sillars, A. L. (1981). Attributions and interpersonal conflict resolution. In J. H. Harvey, W. J. Ickes, & R. F. Kidd (Eds.), *New directions in attribution research* (Vol. 3, pp. 279–305). Hillsdale, NJ: Erlbaum.

Sillars, A. L. (1985). Interpersonal perception in relationships. In W. Ickes (Ed.), *Compatible and incompatible relationships* (pp. 277–305). New York: Springer-Verlag.

Sillars, A. L., & Parry, D. (1982). Stress, cognition, and communication in interpersonal conflicts. *Communication Research, 9,* 201–226.

Sillars, A. L., Pike, G. R., Jones, T. S., & Murphy, M. A. (1984). Communication and understanding in marriage. *Human Communication Research, 10,* 317–350.

Sillars, A. L., Pike, G. R., Jones, T. J., & Redmon, K. (1983). Communication and conflict in marriage. In K. Bostrom (Ed.), *Communication yearbook* (Vol. 7). Beverly Hills, CA: Sage.

Sillars, A. L., & Scott, M. D. (1983). Interpersonal perception between intimates: An integrative review. *Human Communication Research, 10,* 153–176.

Sillars, A. L., Weisberg, J., & Burggraf, C. S. (1990). Communication and understanding revisited: Married couples' understanding and recall of conversations. *Communication Research, 17,* 500–522.

Simpson, J. A. (1987). The dissolution of romantic relationships: Factors involved in relationship stability and emotional distress. *Journal of Personality and Social Psychology, 53,* 683–692.

Simpson, J. A., Ickes, W., & Blackstone, T. (1995). When the head protects the heart: Empathic accuracy in dating relationships. *Journal of Personality and Social Psychology, 69,* 629–641.

Stinson, L., & Ickes, W. (1992). Empathic accuracy in the interactions of male friends versus male strangers. *Journal of Personality and Social Psychology, 62,* 787–797.

Stuckert, R. (1963). Role perception and marital satisfaction: A configuration approach. *Marriage and Family Living, 25,* 415–419.

Suedfeld, P., & Tetlock, P. (1977). Integrative complexity of communications in international crises. *Journal of Conflict Resolutions, 21,* 169–184.

Taylor, B. A. (1967). Role perception, empathy, and marriage adjustment. *Sociology and Social Research, 52,* 22–34.

Thibaut, J. W., & Kelley, H. H. (1959). *The social psychology of groups.* New York: Wiley.

Watzlawick, P., Weakland, J., & Fisch, R. (1974). *Principles of problem formation and problem resolution.* New York: Norton.

Weary-Bradley, G. (1978). Self-serving biases in the attribution process: A reexamination of the fact or fiction question. *Journal of Personality and Social Psychology, 36,* 56–71.

Wegner, D. M. (1994). Ironic processes of mental control. *Psychological Review, 101,* 34–52.

Wegner, D. M., & Giuliano, T. (1982). The forms of social awareness. In W. Ickes & E. Knowles (Eds.), *Personality, roles, and social behavior* (pp. 165–198). New York: Springer-Verlag.

Weick, K. E. (1971). Group processes, family processes, and problem solving. In J. Aldous et al. (Eds.), *Family problem solving: A symposium on theoretical, methodological and substantive concerns.* Hinsdale, IL: Dryden.

Wicklund, R. (1975). Objective self-awareness. In L. Berkowitz (Ed.), *Advances in experimental social psychology* (Vol. 8, pp. 233–275). New York: Academic Press.

Williamson, L. K. (1975). *Self and other: An empirical study of interpersonal perception in dyadic marital communication systems.* Unpublished doctoral dissertation, Temple University.

Zadny, J., & Gerard, H. B. (1974). Attributed intentions and informational selectivity. *Journal of Experimental Social Psychology, 10,* 34–52.

Close Relationships as Including Other in the Self

Arthur Aron, Elaine N. Aron, Michael Tudor, and
Greg Nelson • University of California, Santa Cruz

The cognitive significance of being in a close relationship is described in terms of including other in the self (in Lewin's sense of overlapping regions of the life space and in James's sense of the self as resources, perspectives, and characteristics). Experiment 1, adapting Liebrand's (1984) decomposed-game procedures, found less self/other difference in allocations of money to a friend than to a stranger, regardless of whether Ss expected other to know their allocations. Experiment 2, adapting Lord's (1987) procedures, found that Ss recalled fewer nouns previously imaged with self or mother than nouns imaged with a nonclose other, suggesting that mother was processed more like self than a stranger. Experiment 3, adapting self-schema, reaction-time procedures (e.g., Markus, 1977), found longer latencies when making "me/not me" decisions for traits that were different between self and spouse versus traits that were similar for both, suggesting a self/other confusion with spouse.

During the 1980s, close-relationship research expanded rapidly, rating its own *Handbook* (Duck, 1988) and its own *Annual Review of Psychology* chapter (Clark & Reis, 1988). Much of the research in this area does not explicitly define what is meant by a close relationship. However, the behavioral, systemic definition offered by Kelley et al. (1983) has been widely influential. It focuses on mutual influence, interdependence, and degree of interconnectedness of activities. This approach recently served as the basis for the development of a measure of interpersonal-closeness behavior (Berscheid,

Snyder, & Omoto, 1989a, 1989b), which focuses on time spent together, diversity of shared activities, and perceived influence of other over one's own decisions. (Maxwell, 1985, also developed a behavioral measure of closeness, which is based on a more general review of the close-relationship literature.)

There has been much less consensus about the cognitive significance of such behavioral interdependence for each person in a close relationship. Yet a number of relevant phenomena have been observed, mostly falling into one of three overlapping categories:

1. *Closeness as a changed resource allocation strategy.* Kelley and Thibaut (1978; Kelley, 1983) saw the cognitive consequences for the members of a close relationship as a transformation of each member's two-person outcome matrix (that is, how rewards or costs to partner are expected to affect self). Specifically, Kelley and Thibaut argued that members of a close relationship each have a pattern of perceived interdependence of outcomes in which partner's and joint benefits are expected in the long run to benefit self. Similarly, Clark and Mills (1979) described a close relationship as having a *communal* character, in which the partners are each motivated to act for the needs of the other, regardless of the expected reciprocal outcome for the self. This general approach is also similar to the empathy model for explaining prosocial behavior and findings showing greater helping for those with whom the person is in a close relationship (e.g., Clark, 1983). Wegner (1980) suggested that empathy may "stem in part from a basic confusion between ourselves and others" (p. 133), which he considered may arise from an initial lack of differentiation between self and caregiver in infancy (Hoffman, 1976).

2. *Closeness as a changed actor/observer perspective.* Several current social psychological approaches emphasize differences between the perspective people have of their own versus others' behavior; some of the associated research suggests that such differences are less when other is in a close relationship to self. For example, actor–observer discrepancies in attributional processes (Jones & Nisbett, 1971) appear to be less when other is in a close relationship to self (e.g., Sande, Goethals, & Radloff, 1988). Another approach emphasizes the categorization of self and close other(s) into a single cognitive category (e.g., Hogg & Turner, 1987), extending ideas originally developed in the context of the in-group/out-group distinction in intergroup relations. A number of other findings also suggest a change in perspective regarding memory processes. Brenner (1973) found that memory of a mate's or romantic partner's performance in a laboratory task was intermediate between memory of one's own and memory of a stranger's performance. Bower and Gilligan (1979) found that associating trait adjectives with remembered episodes in one's mother's life facilitated later recall equally well as when they were associated with remembered episodes in one's own life and that a comparison between associating traits with Walter Cronkite versus with self yielded much better recall for the self condition. Festinger, Pepitone, and Newcomb (1952) found that ability to distinguish who said what when remembering a group interaction is poorer when one is ego involved in the group interaction. The more general idea that people in close relationships experience a sense of we-ness (e.g., Hatfield, 1982; McDonald, 1981), an idea reminiscent of Heider's (1958) concept of a cognitive "unit relation," is also relevant.

3. *Closeness as vicariously sharing other's characteristics.* This idea is traditionally emphasized in Freudian notions of identification. Although identification is mainly associated with parent–child closeness, it has also been used in other contexts. For example, Bank and Kahn (1982) used identification to describe lifelong sibling relationships, and Reik (1944) argued that people seek romantic partners who possess those characteristics lacking in their own ego ideal to attain those characteristics indirectly. In conceptually related social psychological work, Tesser (1988) showed that under conditions in which one is not competing with one's partner, one is more likely to reflect the pleasure of a partner's achievement if that partner is "close." And Deutsch and Mackesy (1985) interpreted the established findings of self–partner

similarities in close relationships as because of mutual influence on each other's self-schemata, creating an overlap of traits between them.

In the preceding attempt to extract the existing literature's understanding of cognition in close relationships, we found either approaches that emphasize interaction in close relationships, with cognition as a secondary focus, or approaches that emphasize social cognition more generally, with cognition relevant to close relationships as a secondary focus. These approaches represent a considerable diversity of methodologies and theoretical orientations. Yet, although it has not been recognized or articulated, there is a remarkable overarching communality of theme: In each case, these approaches yield results or descriptions regarding close relationships that fall on a continuum, with their findings about self-cognition or typical descriptions of self-cognition at one end and their findings or typical descriptions of cognitions about strangers at the other. These in-between results and descriptions arise, we think, because much of our cognition about the other in a close relationship is cognition in which the other is treated as self or confused with self—the underlying reason being a self/other merging or, as Aron and Aron (1986) put it, "including others in the self" (p. 19).

Of course, this general idea has been expressed by a variety of theorists. For example, the idea of close relationships as including other in the self is elegantly expressed in Levinger and Snoek's (1972) Venn diagrams, an adapted version of which is shown in Figure 21.1. A more complex version was proposed by Lewin (1948, p. 90), who diagrammed relationships within the life space in terms of differing degrees of overlap between the differentiated region that represents the self and the region that to the self represents the partner.

This general notion of overlapping selves involves an understanding similar to what Greenwald and Pratkanis (1984) call the "collective" aspect of self. It is also related to Ickes, Tooke, Stinson, Baker, and Bissonnette's (1988) idea of "intersubjectivity," which Ickes and his colleagues made vivid by citing Merleau-Ponty's (1945) description

of a close relationship as a "double being" and Schutz's (1970) reference to two people "living in each other's subjective contexts of meaning" (p. 167). In a similar vein, Bakan (1966) wrote about "communion" in the context of his expansion on Buber's (1937) "I-thou" relationship.

The principle is that in a close relationship, the person acts as if some or all aspects of the partner are partially the person's own. (There may in addition be some sense of a general increase of fusion of self and other.) Aron and Aron (1986) emphasized that three aspects of self seem to be involved in this process: resources, perspectives, and characteristics. This categorization relies in part on James's (1890/1948) influential division of the "empirical self" into material, social, and spiritual—the latter meaning typical styles of thinking or what Greenwald and Pratkanis (1984) described as self-processes or procedural knowledge. These three categories of aspects of self correspond in a general way to the three categories of cognitive implications of closeness suggested in the previous literature, as reviewed earlier. Specifically, to the extent a partner is perceived as part of one's self, allocation of resources is communal (because benefiting other is benefiting self), actor/observer perspective differences are lessened, and other's characteristics become one's own.

This approach is also generally consistent with much current work on intimacy, a concept often considered virtually synonymous with closeness

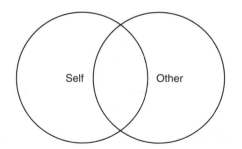

FIGURE 21.1 ■ Pictorial representation of including other in the self in a close relationship. Adapted from *Attraction in Relationship: A New Look at Interpersonal Attraction* (p. 5) by G. Levinger and J. D. Snoek, 1972, Morristown, New Jersey: General Learning Press. Copyright 1972 by Levinger and Snoek. Adapted by permission.

(e.g., Helgeson, Shaver, & Dyer, 1987). For example, Reis and Shaver's (1988) integration of previous research findings emphasized the centrality of the exchange of self-relevant information, and McAdam's (1988) integration argued that most definitions of intimacy "converge on the central idea of *sharing that which is inmost* with others" (p. 18).

More generally still, a wide variety of thinkers on close relationships use metaphors such as *union* and *attachment*. Bataille (1962) expressed it dramatically: "Between one being and another there is a gulf, a discontinuity" (p. 12). "What we desire is to bring into a world founded on discontinuity all the continuity such a world can sustain" (p. 19). Jung (1925/1959) emphasized the role of relationship partners as providing unavailable aspects of self, so as to help make the self whole. Maslow (1967) took it for granted that "beloved people can be incorporated into the self" (p. 103). And McCall (1974) described attachment as "incorporation of . . . [the other's] actions and reactions . . . into the content of one's various conceptions of the self" (p. 219). Finally, the related notion of "possessing" the other (you are mine; I am yours) has been part of classic systematic treatments of love (e.g., Berl, 1924; Freud, 1921/1951; Grant, 1976). As Reik (1949) put it, when we love we desire "to own the other person" (p. 73).

The present research effort was originally suggested by Aron and Aron's (1986) self-expansion model, which holds that people are motivated to enter and maintain close relationships to expand the self by including the resources, perspectives, and characteristics of the other in the self. The model is primarily motivational; previous research on the model (Aron, Aron, & Allen, 1989; Aron, Dutton, Aron, & Iverson, 1989; McKenna, 1989; Paris, 1990; Rousar, 1990) has examined its implications in this context. Nevertheless, the model also clearly implies that a cognitive inclusion of other in the self actually occurs and shapes the way information is processed about the development, maintenance, and dissolution of relationships. However, this article is not specifically focused on the self-expansion model, but on the general paradigm of viewing close relationships in terms of including other in the self.

The precise nature of what it means to have included other into self, in terms of cognitive structure, is probably multifold. For example, cognitive representations of self and other might contain common elements or might occupy overlapping regions of a cognitive matrix, and access to them might follow similar pathways. However, before sorting out these particulars of how including other in the self comes about or even about its precise cognitive structure, the first step is to consider whether an inclusion of other in the self—in the general sense we have described of a lessened self/other distinction influencing behavior and cognition—actually occurs when examined with studies specifically designed for the purpose and using very diverse methodologies. It was to this end that the present research was addressed.

The experiments reported in this article focused on each of the three general aspects of the partner that Aron and Aron (1986) and others suggest to be included in the self in close relationships: resources, perspective, and characteristics. In each case, we took a particular successful existing research paradigm that emphasized self/other differences and adapted it to test whether the self/other difference was reduced when self and other were in a close relationship. Also, different types of close relationships (friendship, parent–child, marriage) were used in the several experiments.

Experiment 1

We argued earlier that to the extent other is included in the self, other's resources are self's resources. Thus, people in a close relationship should make less of a distinction between self and other when allocating resources between self and other. Furthermore, because this lessened self/other difference is suggested to result from perceiving other's resources as one's own (as opposed to expecting direct reciprocation of benefits), it should occur regardless of whether self believes other will be aware of the choices self makes.

Experiment 1 explored these proposals using a modified version of a procedure originally developed by Liebrand (1984). Liebrand's decomposed-game procedure was intended to extract the key elements of typical social psychology game interaction tasks. On a computer screen, subjects were presented with a series of binary choices involving allocating money to themselves or another person. Each choice was between two scenarios, each scenario involving an allocation to self and other. For example, the first computer screen might show Alternative A as self gaining $14.50 and other losing $3.90 and Alternative B as self gaining $16.00 and other losing $7.50. The series of choices included a balanced set of alternatives presented in a randomized order.

Using this procedure, Liebrand (1984) found that people classified into different groups on the basis of their relative allocations to self and other behaved in the ways predicted from his theory in laboratory 7-person and 20-person social dilemma situations involving real money and a considerable amount of experimental realism. In another study, Liebrand, Jansen, Rijken, and Suhre (1986) found that subjects in different groupings behaved in predicted ways regarding reciprocation of an other's strategy and emphasis on morality (vs. power) in a series of ratings of self and other. Other researchers (e.g., Kuhlman & Marshello, 1975) also used simplified game procedures with successful results.

Our adaptation of Liebrand's (1984) procedure did not use his classifications, but instead emphasized differences between experimental conditions in which identifications of who the other was and whether the other would know the subject's choices were systematically manipulated. Following the logic noted earlier, we expected that the difference between self- and other-allocations would be least when other was their best friend, intermediate when other was a friendly acquaintance, and greatest when other was a stranger. We also expected that the pattern would be largely unaffected by whether subjects assumed other would or would not know the subject's choices.

Method

Twenty-four students participated in the experiment in return for research participation credit for a lower division psychology course. The computer presentation was based on a 24-choice version of the decomposed-game procedure provided to us

by Liebrand in the form of a Pascal program on a computer disk. We modified the program slightly, so that the entire series was presented six times (each time with the 24 choices in a different random order). Prior to each series, subjects were instructed about whom to think of as the other in their choices—either their best friend, a particular friendly acquaintance, or a stranger—and whether they should assume this other would or would not know their allocation choices. Thus, each subject completed an entire set of 24 binary choices six times, making a 3 (other is close friend, friendly acquaintance, or stranger) × 2 (other would or would not know subject's choices) within-subject design. Six sequences were used: They included all the permutations of the 3 × 2 design that also fitted the requirement (to minimize subjects' confusion) that subjects first always completed a friend, an acquaintance, and a stranger series (the order of the three varying over subjects), all three with other knowing (or other not knowing), then completed the remaining three series, keeping friend, acquaintance, and stranger in the same order, for other does not know (or other does know). Subjects were randomly assigned to sequences with the restriction that each of the six sequences was completed by two men and two women.

Results and Discussion

None of the various tests for order or gender interactions with the main independent variables were significant. Thus, all further analyses were combined over order and gender, yielding a 3 × 2 repeated measures analysis of variance. The dependent variable was allocations to self minus allocations to other. (Using alternative measures—allocations to other alone, to self alone, or Liebrand's, 1984, "angle vector" measure—all yielded the same patterns of means and statistical significance as the self-minus-other measure used here.)

Means are shown in Table 21.1. There was a clear main effect for type of other, $F(2, 21) = 14.60$, $p < .01$. Bonferroni ts (Dunn's test) confirmed the predicted pattern of least difference between self and best friend, intermediate difference between self and friendly acquaintance, and greatest difference between self and stranger.

TABLE 21.1 Mean Allocations to Self Minus Allocations to Other

	Target person		
Condition	Best friend	Friendly acquaintance	Stranger
Experiment 1			
Other will know	−2.95	6.14	12.76
Other will not know	−0.54	8.50	13.72
Follow-up			
Other will know	−1.05		15.16
Other will not know	−0.74		18.81

Note. The conditions varied regarding whether other would or would not know subject's allocations. For Experiment 1, $n = 24$. Follow-up involved real money ($n = 13$).

Also as expected, neither the main effect nor interaction was statistically significant (both $Fs < 1$) for whether or not the other was assumed to know the subject's choices.

That these results were consistent with the expected pattern was particularly encouraging as a first examination of the utility of the inclusion-of-other-in-self approach to closeness because a continuum over three levels of closeness had been demonstrated. Nevertheless, the procedures used were somewhat abstract. Although scores on the Liebrand measure and related procedures have correlated with appropriate behaviors under somewhat more realistic conditions, on the surface at least the procedure is fairly far removed from interactions involving real and significant resources. Furthermore, the manipulation of whether other knows may have been weak, and there was no check of whether it was understood by the subjects.

Follow-Up Experiment Using Real Money

To address these issues, we attempted to replicate the experiment under more realistic conditions—specifically, using allocations of real money to real others—plus giving more emphasis to the instructions involving the manipulation of other knows or not, and we included checks on whether subjects understood the manipulation instructions.

The procedures used were identical to the original experiment except for the following five changes. First, subjects were informed at the outset that their choices involved real money, and various tactics were used to assure that subjects believed the payment would be made. (Subjects at the end of the study were paid an average of $8.84 and the money sent to friends averaged $5.10 per friend.) Second, to simplify the experiment, the friendly acquaintance conditions were not included. Third, we used an elaborate procedure to make the manipulation for other would know or other would not know more realistic. At the outset, each subject addressed an envelope to his or her best friend living out of town. The experimenter then carefully explained to the subject that after the experiment this best friend would be mailed a check with a letter breaking the total amount into (a) the amount the subject allocated to the best friend in the condition in which the subject was told the friend would know how much was allocated to the friend, (b) an amount allocated to the friend by another subject who did not know this friend (this would be another subject's stranger-will-know condition), and (c) an amount consisting of the sum of own friend-will-not-know and another subject's stranger-will-not-know conditions, which would be described in the letter as coming from two subjects in the experiment. (The letters and checks were all subsequently sent as promised.) Fourth, to reemphasize the reality of the situation, the instructions prior to each series actually included the name of either their best friend or, in the stranger condition, the best friend of another subject (we checked to be sure the subject did not know this person). Finally, fifth, checks were made on whether the subject understood and believed the instructions. After each series, the instructions included a question about whether on the previous series, the other would or would not know how much the subject had allocated to him or her. (Every subject gave the correct answer on each trial to this question.) Subjects were also telephoned a week later, before their friends were sent the letters and money. (All said they had understood and believed what they had been told during the experiment.)

As in the main experiment, there were no significant order or gender effects or interactions. And again, as shown in the middle rows of Table 21.1, the pattern of means was as predicted. There was a main effect for best friend versus stranger, $F(1, 12) = 25.55$, $p < .001$, with no significant main or interaction effect for whether other would or would not know their choices (both $Fs < 1$).

These data show that the suggested pattern holds using more realistic conditions. They also give some added support to the assumption that subjects actually understood and believed that the other would or would not know their decisions.

Experiment 2

As noted in the Introduction, one aspect of including other in the self in a close relationship is viewing the world from the perspective of the other (Aron & Aron, 1986); several theoretical notions and some data support this view. For example, Nisbett, Caputo, Legant, and Marecek (1973, Study 3) found that the extent that people were willing to make dispositional attributions about their friends was less the longer their relationship with the close friend ($r = -.45, p < .01$). Another, more recent study of actor/observer attributional differences, conducted by Sande et al. (1988), bears even more directly on the inclusion-of-other-in-self approach. These researchers first demonstrated an actor/observer difference in which people more often attributed to themselves than to others both poles of pairs of opposite traits (serious/carefree, energetic/relaxed, etc.) when given a choice of the first, the second, both, or neither. They then proceeded to show that this self/other distinction was less when other was liked than when other was disliked. (Sande et al.

also compared familiar versus unfamiliar others. There was a difference between familiar and unfamiliar when both were liked, but not when both were disliked.) We replicated Sande et al.'s procedure in our own lab, modifying it to permit a comparison of self to others that represented different degrees of liking (as opposed to liking versus disliking). The 24 subjects we tested (using the 11 adjective pairs in Sande et al.'s Experiment 2) chose both poles for a mean of 4.50 adjective pairs for themselves, 3.46 for their best friend, and 2.71 for a friendly acquaintance, $F(2, 46) = 6.02, p < .01$.

However, none of the existing studies relate as directly to closeness as might be desired for the present purposes (which they were not intended to serve). Furthermore, we felt that showing a decrease in a different and perhaps less obvious actor/observer discrepancy would be a stronger demonstration of the usefulness of the idea that in a close relationship the other's perspective is included in the self. Lord's (1980, 1987) paradigm seemed to fit this description. Lord showed that nouns remembered by constructing imagined scenes in which the self interacts with the object the noun represents are recalled less well than nouns remembered by constructing such scenes involving someone else.

Specifically, Lord (1980, Experiment 2; 1987) presented subjects with a series of 60 concrete nouns (taken from Craik & Tulving's 1975 experiment) projected on the screen for 10 s each, during which time subjects were instructed to "form as vivid and interesting a mental image as possible of yourself [or a target person] *interacting* with" (1987, p. 447) what the noun referred to (for example, a mule). After the 10 s, the screen went blank, and subjects wrote down their image for 20 s before the next slide appeared. Subjects followed along on a sheet that told them for each slide what target person to associate with the slide (the order of target persons was randomized over subjects). After the entire series was presented, the sheet and the images they wrote down were removed, and subjects were given 5 min to write down, in any order, as many of the nouns as they could recall. Lord found that nouns imaged interacting with self were recalled significantly less well than nouns imaged interacting with a well-known other such as Johnny Carson or then-President Ronald Reagan.

Lord (1980, 1987) interpreted these results in terms of a figure/ground difference between one's experience of self and other when acting in the world. Of course, if this difference were entirely perceptual (as suggested, for example, by Storms's 1973 study), then there would be no reason to expect that even a person with whom one was extremely close would be perceived differently than a prominent entertainment or political personality. However, we reasoned that if this figure/ground difference represented a different way of understanding and appreciating the world, then if other were included in one's inner world, other should become more like ground and less like figure—that is, more like the self. Thus, this figure/ground idea seems to capture very well the notion of including other's perspective in the self.

Actually, in Lord's original study (1980, Experiment 2), one of the targets that subjects used was their father. The mean recall of father-associated nouns was intermediate between self and Walter Cronkite, as the inclusion-of-other-in-self paradigm would suggest, but this difference was not statistically significant. However, we felt that father was not an ideal operationalization of a close other (nor had Lord intended it as such, of course), because college-student subjects in general may not be very close to their father (Youniss & Smollar, 1985), particularly in an era in which a great many of them may have been raised in mother-only households. Thus, we reasoned that if a target person were closer, the difference between a media personality and the close person might prove significant.

Therefore, Experiment 2 attempted to replicate Lord's (1980, 1987) procedures using as targets the subject's self, a prominent entertainment personality, and their mother—a person who should be highly close for most subjects. And because college-age women are likely to be closer to their mother than are college-age men (Youniss & Smollar, 1985), only women were used. To further ensure closeness, we used only women who had

been living at home with their mother in the last 1.5 years (the study was conducted in the fall quarter with first- and second-year students). The singer and movie actress Cher was selected as the entertainment personality, since she was a woman and about the same age as most of the subjects' mothers. Cher had performed in several successful recent movies and had won an Academy Award that year. None of the lower division undergraduate women we pretested had any difficulty forming an image of Cher.

Method

Twenty female students served as subjects in return for research participation credit for their introductory psychology course. All procedures were identical to those used by Lord (1987), except that the three target persons, as noted in the previous paragraph, were self, mother, and Cher. Also, at the outset, subjects were asked if they were familiar with Cher and how she looked. (All said they were.)

Results and Discussion

Order of presentation did not interact with target person. The pattern of means for the different target persons was as predicted, with Cher (8.95 nouns recalled) greater than mother (7.15 recalled), $t(19) = 2.43$, $p < .05$. Also, the difference between mother and self (6.80 recalled) was so small that it was not statistically significant ($t < 1$).

Follow-Up Experiment

One potential alternative explanation is that more nouns were recalled in the Cher condition because she is a more vivid image than one's mother. We were also interested in whether the degree of mother/nonclose other difference would correlate with degree of perceived closeness to mother and whether any such relation could be sorted out from degree of perceived familiarity with or similarity to mother.

Thus, we conducted a follow-up experiment in which subjects formed images of self, mother, and, instead of Cher, "a female friend or relative of your mother's who is about your mother's age and to whom you are not very close." Also, at the end of this experiment, subjects completed a brief questionnaire in which they indicated how close, familiar, and similar they felt to their mother, each recorded on a 13-point scale ranging from *very distant* to *very close* (or *very unfamiliar* to *very familiar*, etc.) The experiment was conducted during a regular class meeting of a summer session lower division psychology class. Everyone in the class volunteered to participate (2 subjects, however, were not included because their mothers were deceased). In all other respects (instructions, nouns, times, randomization of target-person orders, etc.), the procedures were identical to the original experiment.

Of the 14 subjects who participated, 7 had lived with their mother within the last 2 years. The pattern of means for these 7 subjects was about the same as for the original experiment: friend of mother (6.86 nouns recalled) greater than mother (4.86 recalled), $t(6) = 2.90$, $p < .05$; no significant difference between mother and self (5.14 recalled; $t < 1$).

The mother/mother's friend difference in nouns recalled tended to be strongly correlated with rated closeness to mother ($r = .56$, $p < .10$), but only weakly correlated with similarity ($r = 13$) or familiarity ($r = .16$) with mother.

The possibility that the results of these experiments were due to familiarity bears some further discussion. Although Lord did not conceptualize his results as due to familiarity, the idea has played a role in other studies, including the Sande et al. (1988) study noted earlier. The low correlation of rated mother familiarity with the Cher/mother differences in words recalled makes such explanations unlikely, but does not completely rule them out—both because of the small sample size, which makes the difference between the correlations only marginally significant, and because self-ratings of familiarity may not be accurate. On the other hand, one possible explanation for why familiarity might create differences in the Lord task is that a familiar other would require less effort to image and therefore nouns associated with the familiar other would be less well recalled. This explanation, however, seems unlikely to us because it should be easiest to form a vivid

image of the entertainment personality who is known primarily as an image object (indeed this is why the follow-up experiment was conducted). Another possible familiarity explanation is that one's mother is easier to image because she has been observed more often in familiar surroundings. However, this explanation also seems unlikely because in the follow-up experiment, the comparison was to mother's friend, who presumably would have been viewed in the same familiar settings as the mother.

In any case, these follow-up results together with the original Experiment 2 data suggest, once again, that subjects treated someone with whom they were in a close relationship more as if that person were somehow themselves. Moreover, this result is particularly interesting because it is about a nonobvious phenomenon that emphasizes the figure/ground difference between self's and other's perspective.

Experiment 3

The third aspect of the other suggested to be included in the self in a close relationship is the other's characteristics. A number of studies support the idea that the self is a highly organized cognitive structure, in part by demonstrating that in a reaction-time situation, traits that are highly self-descriptive are recognized as self-descriptive more quickly than are traits that are of neutral self-descriptiveness (e.g., Markus, 1977). Similarly, Kuiper (1981) demonstrated that adjectives that were very true and very untrue of self were recognized as such more rapidly than terms that were more intermediate. One standard procedure in these kinds of studies is that people rate a list of adjectives for their descriptiveness of themselves, take part in a distracting filler task, then make a series of me/not me reaction-time choices (or yes/no choices regarding self-relevance). The effect of faster reaction times for recognizing self-descriptive traits as true of self has been labeled a *descriptiveness effect*.

However, another line of research using similar methods (e.g., Mueller, Ross, & Heesacker, 1984;

Ross, Mueller, & de la Torre, 1986) found that traits that are distinctive to self are recognized as self-descriptive more slowly than traits that are shared with others in general (e.g., most students). This has been called a *distinctiveness effect*. One study by Mueller, Thompson, and Dugan (1986) demonstrated that both the descriptiveness and distinctiveness effects operated independently (i.e., additively).

A possible explanation of the distinctiveness effect is that the cognitive structure of the self overlaps with the cognitive structure about the other (or, in the studies in the previous paragraph, overlaps with the cognitive structure held for people in general). Thus, when a trait is descriptive of self but not other, there is a bit of confusion in deciding whether it actually represents the self. We take this line of reasoning one step further. In the case of a close relationship, in which we suggest other's traits are included in the self to a substantial extent, there should be a greater overlap of cognitive structures—hence more confusion and slower response times.

Experiment 3 examined this suggestion of slower reaction times for traits distinctive from close others. We adapted procedures from the various studies cited earlier of response times to self-referent traits. Subjects first rated a series of trait adjectives for their descriptiveness of themselves, their spouse, and an entertainment personality. After a distracting intermediate task, they made a series of me/not me reaction-time choices to these trait words. The prediction was that there would be most confusion, thus longer response latencies, for trait words that were different between self and spouse.

Testing this prediction required dividing traits into groups according to whether they were descriptive or not of self, spouse, and the entertainment personality. Of the eight possible combinations of true and false of each of the three people, four combinations were of interest: (a) traits that were rated as true of self and spouse but not of entertainment personality (TTF), (b) traits that were true of self, false of spouse, and true of the entertainment personality (TFT), (c) traits that were false of self and spouse but true of the entertainment personality (FFT), and (d) traits that were false of self, true of

spouse, and false of the entertainment personality (FTF). (The other four combinations—TTT, FFF, TFF, and FTT—were not of interest because they confounded whether a trait was true or false of spouse with whether it was true or false of the entertainment personality.) The prediction was that subjects would have more confusion, hence slower reaction time, for the traits in which they differed from spouse: (b) TFT and (d) FTF.

Method

Subjects were married graduate students attending a social psychology seminar at a freestanding psychology professional school. The research was presented as a nonrequired opportunity to experience social cognition research methods. There were 17 students in the seminar, of which all 13 who were married agreed to participate. Their mean age was 38.4; they had been married a mean of 6.45 years.

Participants first completed an initial questionnaire as they were waiting for the seminar to begin. Sometime after (allowing 15 min to 2 hr of seminar interaction, functioning as a distracting task), students were called out of the seminar individually and sent to another room where they completed the reaction-time portion of the task at a computer terminal.

The initial questionnaire had subjects rate on separate pages each of three target persons for how much each of 90 traits applied to that person. The trait adjectives were selected from Anderson's (1968) norms. They included 20 with likableness ratings above 4.5, 30 with ratings between 2.0 and 3.8, and 30 with ratings below 1.7. The 90 were randomly ordered on the page. Subjects responded to each item on a 7-point scale from *extremely like* (1) the target person to *unlike* (7). The target persons were self, spouse, and Bill Cosby. Questionnaires using the three possible orders of target persons were randomly assigned to subjects.

The computer instructions explained to subjects that they would be presented with a series of descriptors. Their task was to decide as quickly as possible for each trait whether that trait applied to themselves or not by pressing the A key for "me" or the L key for "not me." Ten example adjectives were given, then the set of 90 adjectives was presented three times, each time in a different random order. Each adjective remained on the screen until the subject pressed one of the keys. The computer recorded responses and latencies.

Results and Discussion

Adjective ratings were divided at the median, so that those with ratings of 4 or higher were considered not descriptive (or false) of the target person and those less than 4 as descriptive (or true) of the target person. Next, the adjectives for each subject were divided into categories according to their pattern of trues and falses for the three target persons. Ten (2 men and 8 women) of the 13 subjects had usable responses to at least one of the traits in each of the four critical categories. Average response latencies to traits in each of these four categories were then computed for each of these subjects.

Table 21.2 contains the mean response latencies in each category. A 2×2 repeated measures analysis of variance yielded a main effect for true versus false, $F(1, 9) = 7.82$, $p < .05$, but no significant interaction, $(F < 1)$. This main effect indicates that subjects were faster at responding to traits that were true of themselves than ones that were false of themselves. This is consistent with previous research (Kuiper, 1981; Mueller et al., 1986). Because there was no interaction, the overall analysis relevant to our predictions about including the other in the self could be collapsed into a t test for dependent means between response latencies to traits in which self and spouse were similar (TTF and FFT) versus not similar (TFT and FTF). The result, $t(9) = 2.21$, $p < .05$,

indicates that subjects were slower responding to traits that differed between self and spouse. This finding is consistent with the prediction and can be interpreted as showing that self and spouse are more closely integrated cognitively than are self and the entertainment personality.

We also analyzed the data for response errors. (A response was counted as an error if the way the subject had rated it as self-descriptive or not on the questionnaire received the opposite corresponding me or not me key press.) The analyses for response errors (means are shown in Table 21.2) yielded the same pattern of findings as the response latency data: a true-versus-false-of-self main effect, $F(1, 9) = 14.85$, $p < .01$; no significant interaction $(F < 1)$ and a significant difference between traits in which self was similar versus different from spouse, $t(9) = 2.45$, $p < .05$. This last finding means that there were more errors in responding to traits on which self and spouse differed—again consistent with the notion that self and spouse are more closely integrated cognitively, leading to confusions, than are self and the entertainment personality.

The question of the possible role of familiarity arises again here, as it did in discussing the results of Experiment 2. Familiarity might seem particularly salient in this case because familiarity is used to explain the findings in other studies for self-and-other-trait-rating reaction times (e.g., Kuiper & Rogers, 1979). Also, Srull and Gaelick (1983) used familiarity to explain their findings, which are conceptually related to the present study. Srull and Gaelick assessed the degree of

TABLE 21.2 Mean Response Times and Errors for Traits Differing in Their Descriptiveness of Self and Spouse

Descriptiveness	Trait			
	Response time (ms)		Proportion of errors	
	Same	Different	Same	Different
For self				
True	1,023	1,096	.069	.177
False	1,094	1,150	.252	.438
Total	1,059	1,123	.161	.308

Note. Same and different refer to descriptiveness of trait for self and spouse.

symmetry between similarity ratings when self versus other is the reference point (how similar is other to you vs. how similar are you to other). In one of their studies, they found that symmetry was greater when the self/other similarity ratings were for mother or father than when they were for a media personality. In their study, familiarity was a quite reasonable explanation because the greater information available about a familiar other makes it easier (as compared with a stranger) for unique differences to come to mind when other is the focus and harder for unique differences to come to mind when self is the focus.

In the present case, the potential influence of familiarity would seem to be less clear. One reasonable possibility might be that familiar/familiar comparisons could be more difficult, making decisions slower, with more errors. Note, however, that this way of thinking implies that when deciding on whether a trait is true or not of themselves, subjects implicitly made a comparison with their spouse.

Thus, this kind of familiarity explanation implies a rather special cognitive relationship between self and other that goes beyond the models of mere familiarity proposed in some previous studies.

In sum, Experiment 3 seems to provide yet another illustration of the potential hypothesis-generating value of considering that in a close relationship, people process information as if the other is partially included in the self. The present experiment is especially interesting because it applied the reaction-time social-cognition approach to a topic that had in the past been studied mainly in the context of clinical theory and personality testing. And even among studies that focus on reaction-time or memory differences in relation to own and other's traits, it was the first to look directly at implicit comparisons or self/other confusions when making only self-ratings—an approach we suspect would not have been generated within the theoretical atmosphere in which most social-cognition studies have been conducted.

General Discussion

Taken together, these various studies, applying a variety of methods and using different types of close relationships, illustrate the utility of viewing close relationships as including other in the self. The results of Experiment 1 and its follow-up experiment suggest that regardless of whether the other will know of self's decision, differences in allocation of money to self and other decrease as other is closer to the self, comparing others who are best friend, acquaintance, and stranger. The results of Experiment 2 and its follow-up suggest that differences in memory that is based on images of self versus others interacting with an object noun to be remembered are less when other is close to self. (Other was varied by comparing images made with mother versus either an entertainment personality or a friend of one's mother.) The results of Experiment 3 suggest that cognitive representations of self and other are more closely interconnected when other is in a close relationship, as shown by patterns of response latencies in making me/not me decisions about traits previously rated as descriptive of self, spouse, or either an entertainment personality or a friend of spouse. Together these findings lend support to the idea that the cognitive implications of being in a close relationship are that other is included in self, taking into account the three central aspects of self originally emphasized by James (1890/1948) and described by Aron and Aron (1986) in terms of resources, perspectives, and characteristics. We want to emphasize that what is important here is not so much the results of each study individually, but of the set as a whole.

The procedures used in the experiments reported here also suggest new ways to look at closeness—as cognitive closeness, rather than objective interaction patterns (Berscheid et al., 1989a, 1989b; Maxwell, 1985). They also provide theoretically meaningful experimental procedures that could serve as criteria for validity testing of measures of closeness. Finally, we hope that this study will inspire a larger number of researchers to respond to Clark and Reis's (1988) call for more experiments that use laboratory methods in the study of ongoing close relationships.

Future research might examine more closely the specific cognitive mechanisms through which other is included in the self. The model of including other in the self as used in the experiments reported here might be best described in Lewin's (1948) terms as overlapping differentiated regions within the life space. A more precise notion, of overlapping prototypes (or schemata) of self and other is also attractive and seems likely to be at least a subclass of the general idea of including other in the self. But as Greenwald and Pratkanis (1984) note, there seem to be more aspects to the self than can be fully accounted for by the cognitive representation approach. One such area of difficulty involves the issue of identity: Do people actually confuse their own identity with the close other (or, alternately, base their identity on that other)? Yet another line of research would focus on the process by which other becomes included in the self (or even by which we see ourselves as included in the other).

A final point about the idea of closeness as including other in the self: In some cases, being in a close relationship might well make one appear to treat the other as more different from self rather than less. For example, Tesser (1988) showed that when self and other are competing for an outcome relevant to one's self-esteem, one is more likely to be jealous of someone with whom one is close than with a stranger (although Tesser's definition of closeness in his various studies overlaps with similarity). More generally, to the extent the other is highly salient in the life space of the individual, other's characteristics are especially available for social comparison. For example, in a marriage in which both partners initially saw themselves as similar in terms of liking the outdoors (because compared with most people, they know they both feel largely the same way), after living together some years, any slight difference between them might repeatedly show itself, for example, one might always want to go camping, but the other might always resist it. Thus, this small difference could become identified in the world of the couple as a major point of conflict. However, such situations arise, in our view, precisely because the self/other merging in close relationships makes any self/other differences both more likely to be noticed and more likely to matter. More generally, we would expect self/other differences in close

relationships to operate like contradictions among one's own behaviors and characteristics. This idea is implicit in cognitive dissonance theorizing. Dissimilarity between self and a friend's attitudes is considered dissonant in the same way that holding opposite attitudes within oneself is considered dissonant—and, we would add, the degree of dissonance should be a function of the closeness of the relationship (i.e., the degree to which the other is included in the self). It is certainly a testable point, as is the implication from a more psychodynamic perspective, that if the other is included in the self and if self/other differences in close relationships function like self/self conflicts, then the closer the relationship, the more self/other differences should be either (a) highly emotionally charged or (b) very uncharged (because of their being integrated into an understanding that sees them no longer really contradictory but as complementary). In other words, in close relationships, we would expect greater variance in emotional charge associated with self/other differences.

Thus, the present experiments only begin to explore the cognitive structure of close relationships in terms of the self. But they are a beginning, we hope, that illustrates the potential utility of the approach as a complement to those that have assisted the study of close relationships up to now.

NOTES

We are grateful to Jennifer Collins, Mary Dundon, Frank Myers, Elena Quintana, Paul Sanders, David Verdugo, and Tanya Webber for their assistance in conducting this research and to Anthony Pratkanis for his suggestions on the article.

Correspondence concerning this article should be addressed to Arthur Aron, Department of Psychology, SUNY Stony Brook, Stony Brook, New York 11794.

REFERENCES

Anderson, N. H. (1968). Likableness ratings of 555 personality-trait words. *Journal of Personality and Social Psychology, 9,* 272–279.

Aron, A., & Aron, E. N. (1986). *Love as the expansion of self: Understanding attraction and satisfaction.* New York: Hemisphere.

Aron, A., Aron, E. N., & Allen, J. (1989, May). *The motivation for unrequited love: A self-expansion perspective.* Paper presented at the Second Iowa Conference on Personal Relationships, Iowa City, IA.

Aron, A., Dutton, D. G., Aron, E. N., & Iverson, A. (1989). Experiences of falling in love. *Journal of Social and Personal Relationships, 6*, 243–257.

Bakan, D. (1966). *The duality of human existence: Isolation and commitment in Western man*. Boston: Beacon Press.

Bank, S. P., & Kahn, M. D. (1982). *The sibling bond*. New York: Basic Books.

Bataille, G. (1962). *Eroticism* (M. Dalwood, Trans.). London: Calder. (Original work published 1957)

Berl, E. (1924). *The nature of love* (F. Rothwell, Trans.). London: Chapman & Hall. (Original work published 1923)

Berscheid, E., Snyder, M., & Omoto, A. M. (1989a). Issues in studying close relationships: Conceptualizing and measuring closeness. In C. Hendrick (Ed.), *Review of personality and social psychology* (Vol. 10, pp. 63–91). Newbury Park, CA: Sage.

Berscheid, E., Snyder, M., & Omoto, A. M. (1989b). The Relationship Closeness Inventory: Assessing the closeness of interpersonal relationships. *Journal of Personality and Social Psychology, 57*, 792–807.

Bower, G. H., & Gilligan, S. G. (1979). Remembering information related to one's self. *Journal of Research in Personality, 13*, 420–432.

Brenner, M. (1973). The next-in-line effect. *Journal of Verbal Learning and Verbal Behavior, 12*, 320–323.

Buber, M. (1937). *I and thou*. New York: Scribners.

Clark, M. S. (1983). Reactions to aid in communal and exchange relationships.·In J. D. Fisher, A. Nadler, & B. M. DePaulo (Eds.), *New directions in helping* (Vol. 1, pp. 281–304). San Diego, CA: Academic Press.

Clark, M. S., & Mills, J. (1979). Interpersonal attraction in exchange and communal relationships. *Journal of Personality and Social Psychology, 37*, 12–24.

Clark, M. S., & Reis, H. T. (1988). Interpersonal processes in close relationships. *Annual Review of Psychology, 39*, 609–672.

Craik, F. I. M., & Tulving, E. (1975). Depth of processing and the retention of words in episodic memory. *Journal of Experimental Psychology: General, 104*, 268–294.

Deutsch, F. M., & Mackesy, M. E. (1985). Friendship and the development of self-schemas: The effects of talking about others. *Personality and Social Psychology Bulletin, 11*, 399–408.

Duck, S. (1988). *Handbook of personal relationships: Theory, research and interventions*. New York: Wiley.

Festinger, L., Pepitone, A., & Newcomb, T. (1952). Some consequences of deindividuation in a group. *Journal of Abnormal and Social Psychology, 47*, 382–389.

Freud, S. (1951). *Group psychology and the analysis of the ego* (J. Strachey, Trans). New York: Liveright. (Original work published 1921)

Grant, V. (1976). *Falling in love: The psychology of the romantic emotion*. New York: Springer.

Greenwald, A. G., & Pratkanis, A. R. (1984). The self. In R. S. Wyer & T. K. Srull (Eds.), *Handbook of social cognition* (Vol. 3, pp. 129–178). Hillsdale, NJ: Erlbaum.

Hatfield, E. (1982). Passionate love, companionate love, and intimacy. In M. Fisher & G. Stricker (Eds.), *Intimacy* (pp. 267–292). New York: Plenum Press.

Heider, F. (1958). *The psychology of interpersonal relations*. New York: Wiley.

Helgeson, V. S., Shaver, P., & Dyer, M. (1987). Prototypes of intimacy and distance in same-sex and opposite-sex relationships. *Journal of Social and Personal Relationships, 4*, 195–233.

Hoffman, M. L. (1976). Empathy, role taking, guilt, and development of altruistic motives. In T. Lickona (Ed.), *Moral development and behavior*. New York: Holt, Rinehart & Winston.

Hogg, M. A., & Turner, J. C. (1987). Intergroup behaviour, self-stereotyping and the salience of social categories. *British Journal of Social Psychology, 26*, 325–340.

Ickes, W., Tooke, W., Stinson, L., Baker, V., & Bissonnette, V. (1988). Naturalistic social cognition: Intersubjectivity in same-sex dyads. *Journal of Nonverbal Behavior, 12*, 58–84.

James, W. (1948). *Psychology*. Cleveland, OH: Fine Editions Press. (Original work published 1890)

Jones, E. E., & Nisbett, R. (1971). The actor and the observer: Divergent perceptions of the causes of behavior. In E. E. Jones, D. Kanouse, H. Kelley, R. Nisbett, S. Valins, & B. Weiner (Eds.), *Attribution: Perceiving the causes of behavior* (pp. 79–94). Morristown, NJ: General Learning Press.

Jung, C. G. (1959). Marriage as a psychological relationship. In V. S. DeLaszlo (Ed.), *The basic writings of C. G. Jung* (R. F. C. Hull, Trans.; pp. 531–544). New York: Modern Library. (Original work published 1925)

Kelley, H. H. (1983). The situational origins of human tendencies: A further reason for the formal analysis of structures. *Personality and Social Psychology Bulletin, 9*, 3–30.

Kelley, H. H., Berscheid, E., Christensen, A., Harvey, J. H., Huston, T. L., Levinger, G., McClintock, E., Peplau, L. A., & Peterson, D. R. (1983). Analyzing close relationships. In *Close relationships* (pp. 20–67). San Francisco: Freeman.

Kelley, H. H., & Thibaut, J. W. (1978). *Interpersonal relations: A theory of interdependence*. New York: Wiley.

Kuhlman, D. M., & Marshello, A. F. J. (1975). Individual differences in game motivation as moderators of preprogrammed strategy effects in prisoner's dilemma. *Journal of Personality and Social Psychology, 32*, 922–931.

Kuiper, N. A. (1981). Convergent evidence for the self as a prototype: The "inverted-U RT effect" for self and other judgments. *Personality and Social Psychology Bulletin, 7*, 438–443.

Kuiper, N. A., & Rogers, T. E. (1979). Encoding of personal information: Self–other differences. *Journal of Personality and Social Psychology, 37*, 499–514.

Levinger, G., & Snoek, J. D. (1972). *Attraction in relationship: A new look at interpersonal attraction*. Morristown, NJ: General Learning Press.

Lewin, K. (1948). The background of conflict in marriage. In G. Lewin (Ed.), *Resolving social conflicts: Selected papers on group dynamics* (pp. 84–102). New York: Harper.

Liebrand, W. B. G. (1984). The effect of social motives, communication and group size on behavior in an *N*-person multi-stage mixed-motive game. *European Journal of Social Psychology, 14*, 239–264.

Liebrand, W. B. G., Jansen, R. W. T. L., Rijken, V. M., & Suhre, C. J. M. (1986). Might over morality: Social values and the perception of other players in experimental games. *Journal of Experimental Social Psychology, 22*, 203–215.

Lord, C. G. (1980). Schemas and images as memory aids: Two modes of processing social information. *Journal of Personality and Social Psychology, 38*, 257–269.

Lord, C. G. (1987). Imagining self and others: Reply to Brown, Keenan, and Potts. *Journal of Personality and Social Psychology, 53*, 445–450.

Markus, H. (1977). Self-schemata and processing information about the self. *Journal of Personality and Social Psychology, 35*, 63–78.

Maslow, A. H. (1967). A theory of metamotivation: The biological rooting of the value-life. *Journal of Humanistic Psychology, 7*, 93–127.

Maxwell, G. M. (1985). Behaviour of lovers: Measuring the closeness of relationships. *Journal of Personal and Social Relationships, 2*, 215–238.

McAdams, D. P. (1988). Personal needs and personal relationships. In S. Duck (Ed.), *Handbook of personal relationships: Theory, research and interventions* (pp. 7–22). New York: Wiley.

McCall, G. J. (1974). A symbolic interactionist approach to attraction. In T. L. Huston (Ed.), *Foundations of interpersonal attraction* (pp. 217–231). San Diego, CA: Academic Press.

McDonald, G. W. (1981). Structural exchange and marital interaction. *Journal of Marriage and the Family, 43*, 825–839.

McKenna, C. (1989). *Marital satisfaction and sensation seeking in the first ten years of marriage: Self-expansion versus boredom.* Unpublished doctoral dissertation, California Graduate School of Family Psychology, San Rafael, CA.

Merleau-Ponty, M. (1945). *Phenomenologie de la perception* [Phenomenology of perception]. Paris: Gallimard.

Mueller, J. H., Ross, M. J., & Heesacker, M. (1984). Distinguishing me from thee. *Bulletin of the Psychonomic Society, 22*, 79–82.

Mueller, J. H., Thompson, W. B., & Dugan, K. (1986). Trait distinctiveness and accessibility in the self-schema. *Personality and Social Psychology Bulletin, 12*, 81–89.

Nisbett, R. E., Caputo, C., Legant, P., & Marecek, J. (1973). Behavior as seen by the actor and as seen by the observer. *Journal of Personality and Social Psychology, 27*, 154–164.

Paris, M. (1990). *Falling in love and the transformation of self-concept.* Unpublished doctoral dissertation, California Graduate School of Family Psychology, San Rafael, CA.

Reik, T. (1944). *A psychologist looks at love.* New York: Farrar & Rinehart.

Reik, T. (1949). *Of love and lust: On the psychoanalysis of romantic and sexual emotions.* New York: Farrar, Straus & Giroux.

Reis, H. T., & Shaver, P. (1988). Intimacy as interpersonal process. In S. Duck (Ed.), *Handbook of personal relationships: Theory, research and interventions* (pp. 367–389). New York: Wiley.

Rosenbaum, M. E. (1986). The repulsion hypothesis: On the nondevelopment of relationships. *Journal of Personality and Social Psychology, 51*, 1156–1166.

Ross, M. J., Mueller, J. H., & de la Torre, M. (1986). Depression and trait distinctiveness in the self schema. *Journal of Social and Clinical Psychology, 4*, 46–59.

Rousar, E. (1990). *Valuing's role in romantic love.* Unpublished doctoral dissertation, Pacific Graduate School of Psychology, Palo Alto, CA.

Sande, G. N., Goethals, G. R., & Radloff, C. E. (1988). Perceiving one's own traits and others': The multifaceted self. *Journal of Personality and Social Psychology, 54*, 13–20.

Schutz, A. (1970). *On phenomenology and social relations.* Chicago: Chicago University Press.

Srull, T. K., & Gaelick, L. (1983). General principles and individual differences in the self as a habitual reference point: An examination of self–other judgments of similarity. *Social Cognition, 2*, 108–121.

Storms, M. D. (1973). Videotape and the attribution process: Reversing actors' and observers' point of view. *Journal of Personality and Social Psychology, 27*, 165–175.

Tesser, A. (1988). Toward a self-evaluation maintenance model of social behavior. In L. Berkowitz (Ed.), *Advances in experimental social psychology* (Vol. 21, pp. 181–227). San Diego, CA: Academic Press.

Wegner, D. M. (1980). The self in prosocial action. In D. M. Wegner & R. R. Vallacher (Eds.), *The self in social psychology* (pp. 131–157). New York: Oxford University Press.

Youniss, J., & Smollar, J. (1985). *Adolescent relations with mothers, fathers, and friends.* Chicago: University of Chicago Press.

Eliciting Facial Affect, Motivation, and Expectancies in Transference: Significant-Other Representations in Social Relations

Susan M. Andersen, Inga Reznik, and
Lenora M. Manzella • New York University

Recent research has demonstrated transference in social perception, defined in terms of memory
and schema-triggered evaluation in relation to a new person. The authors examined schema-
triggered facial affect in transference, along with motivations and expectancies. In a nomothetic
experimental design, participants encountered stimulus descriptors of a new target person that
were derived either from their own idiographic descriptions of a positively toned or a negatively
toned significant other or from a yoked control participant's descriptors. Equal numbers of positive
and negative target descriptors were presented, regardless of the overall tone of the representation.
The results verified the memory effect and schema-triggered evaluation in transference, on the
basis of significant-other resemblance in the target person. Of importance, participants' nonverbal
expression of facial affect when learning about the target person (i.e., at encoding) reflected the
overall tone of their significant-other representation under the condition of significant-other
resemblance, providing strong support for schema-triggered affect in transference, through the use
of this unobtrusive, nonverbal measure. Parallel effects on interpersonal closeness motivation and
expectancies for acceptance/rejection in transference also emerged.

Research has shown that mental representations of significant others are readily activated and applied to new persons in such a way that a new person is interpreted in terms of a significant other. In this way, a new person is likely to be remembered as having characteristics of a pertinent significant other and to be evaluated accordingly (Andersen & Baum, 1994). In particular, a memory effect emerges for information not presented about the new person, but consistent with the representation, so that this information is likely to be remembered; that is, when the significant-other representation is applied to a new person, this memory effect emerges (Andersen & Cole, 1990, Study 3; Andersen, Glassman, Chen, & Cole, 1995) by means of basic principles of social construct activation and application, in terms of social construct theory (Bruner, 1957; Higgins, 1989, 1990, in press; Higgins & King, 1981; Kelly, 1955; Sedikides & Skowronski, 1991; see Andersen & Glassman, 1996). We have argued that this experimental work demonstrates *transference* (Freud, 1912/1958; see discussion of *parataxic distortion* by Sullivan, 1953) in general social perception, in information-processing terms (Andersen & Cole, 1990; Singer, 1988; Wachtel, 1981; Westen, 1988).

In the information-processing model, transference is in part conceptualized as "going beyond the information given" about him or her (Bruner, 1957; Higgins & King, 1981) on the basis of the activation and application of a significant-other representation to a new person (Andersen et al., 1995). This process is also implicated in people's evaluative responses to a new person, when he or she is interpreted according to the significant-other representation; that is, when the overall tone of a significant-other representation is applied to a new person (Andersen & Baum, 1994), as in the theory of schema-triggered affect (Fiske, 1982; Fiske & Pavelchak, 1986; Pavelchak, 1989), affective information linked to the representation is applied to this new person, who is categorized in terms of the representation. This basic process nicely accounts for how new others are evaluated in the context of transference.

Both the memory effect and the schema-triggered evaluation effect in transference provide compelling evidence that significant-other representations are activated and applied to new persons. In our research, we examined the elicitation of *facial affect* in transference, at the exact moment of encoding, at which time the new person's characteristics are encountered, and the significant-other representation may be triggered by relevant features. We also examined interpersonal

closeness *motivation* in terms of wanting to emotionally approach the new person, and *expectancies* about being accepted or rejected by this new person in transference. Overall, the research was designed to extend the literature on transference in terms of these interpersonally relevant outcomes, according to the process of schema-triggered affect.

Clinical Conceptions of Transference

Although we do not endorse Freud's view of transference (as involving unconscious psychosexual conflict and defense; Freud, 1915/1957, 1912/1958), we assume that representations of significant others exist and may be applied to new others. Sullivan's (1953) model of transference, for which he used the term *parataxic distortion*, held that children form personifications of significant others and of the self and dynamisms that link the two; parataxic distortion consists of experiencing a new person as one experiences (or experienced) the significant other and playing out interpersonal patterns learned with the significant other in relation to this new person. Because this occurs as a function of both personifications and dynamisms, the linkage between self and significant-other representations in memory is fundamental (Greenberg & Mitchell, 1983; Mullahy, 1970; see Andersen & Chen, in press; Andersen & Glassman, 1996).

In our work, we adopted this framework, although we assumed that representations of significant others may change in various ways over time rather than remaining invariant (Horney, 1939; Wachtel, 1981). Of course, because the number of theorists positing that experiences with significant others somehow influence subsequent interpersonal relations is large (e.g., Bowlby, 1969; Guidano & Liotti, 1983; Hazan & Shaver, 1987; Horney, 1939; Horowitz, 1989; Luborsky & Crits-Christoph, 1990; Maccoby, 1980; Oatley & Bolton, 1985; Rogers, 1951; Shaver & Rubenstein, 1980; Simpson, 1990; Sroufe & Fleeson, 1986; Wachtel, 1981), our model is in good company and overlaps with other existing models. Its distinction, however, is that it is explicitly social–cognitive and examines the basic process of transference, which may well underlie various other effects that involve the comparison of present relational events with past events, in which the past serves as an analogy for the present (see Gilovich, 1981; Lewicki, 1985; Read & Cessa, 1991).

Social Construct Theory and Transference

In terms of social construct theory, a social construct typically designates a category or type of person (Higgins & King, 1981; Sedikides & Skowronski, 1990, 1991) and thus reflects a grouping of persons used as a point of comparison in assessing others (e.g., Andersen & Klatzky, 1987; Brewer, 1988; Cantor & Kihlstrom, 1987; Fiske & Neuberg, 1990; Hamilton, 1979; Higgins, 1989; Lewicki, 1985; Pratto & Bargh, 1991; Taylor, 1981; Wyer & Martin, 1986). Beyond categories such as these, however, "proper" constructs also exist, as in a "proper" name (Higgins & King, 1981; Smith & Zarate, 1990, 1992). That is, one may represent "Joe," a carpenter one knows, rather than carpenters as a group or a "carpenter-type." A significant-other representation is one such "proper" construct that may be used in social perception (Andersen et. al., 1995). When an individual classifies a new object or person by using such a construct, he or she makes relevant construct-based inferences, often without awareness of doing so (e.g., Banaji & Greenwald, 1992; Bargh, Bond, Lombardi, & Tota, 1986; Kihlstrom, 1987).

Research on transference in social perception is best understood in terms of the notion that an *n*-of-one representation designating an individual person is activated and applied to a newly encountered person in making interpretive judgments about him or her (Andersen & Glassman, 1996; Andersen et al., 1995; see also Smith & Zarate, 1990, 1992). On the basis of prior activation (priming), a match between a new stimulus person and a construct, or both (Andersen et al., 1995; Cantor & Mischel, 1979; Nosofsky, 1986; Tversky, 1977; although see Andersen & Chen, in press), application of the construct to this new person is likely to occur (Higgins, 1989, in press; Higgins & Brendl, 1995; Higgins & King, 1981). In the process, a new person may be experienced in terms of previous experiences with a known

person or an individual-person exemplar (Smith & Zarate, 1990, 1992), in our case, a significant other. (For descriptions of relevant learning and pattern-matching processes, see Gentner, 1983; Ross, Perkins, & Tenpenny, 1990; Schank, 1982; Seifert, McKoon, Abelson, & Ratcliff, 1986; Spellman & Holyoak, 1992.)

The literature on social construct theory clearly indicates that constructs are readily activated by transient contextual cues in the environment, which combine with chronic influences on activation to predict use (e.g., Bargh et al., 1986). Indeed, research on significant-other activation and application has shown that significant-other representations are chronically accessible—or readily used in making sense of new people—especially when some applicability exists (Andersen et al., 1995). Relevant stimulus cues in the new person can thus trigger transference, which we manipulate in our research by means of significant-other resemblance in a new person, although significant-other representations are also likely to be applied quite regularly in interpreting new others (Andersen et al., 1995).

Biased Inferences and Memory in Transference

Going beyond the information given about a new person at encoding in terms of a significant-other representation constitutes a basic definition of the transference phenomenon. This process involves making representation-consistent inferences about a new person at encoding, in such a way that these inferred ideas about the person are more likely to be remembered in relation to him or her. More representation-consistent memory emerges when a new person resembles the participant's own significant other rather than a yoked participant's (Andersen & Baum, 1994) or another representation in memory (Andersen & Cole, 1990; Andersen et al., 1995).

Schema-Triggered Evaluation in Transference

As indicated, the theory of schema-triggered affect suggests that the summary evaluation of a category as a whole comes to be attached to a new person classified in terms of a category (Fiske, 1982; Fiske & Pavelchak, 1986; Pavelchak, 1989). Although many other cognitive models of affect exist (e.g., Averill, 1990; Bower, 1981; Clark & Isen, 1982; Lazarus & Averill, 1972; Ortony, Clore, & Collins, 1988) and many relatively noncognitive models exist as well (e.g., Berkowitz, 1993; Ekman, 1982, 1992; Leventhal, 1984; Zajonc, 1980), the process of schema-triggered affect provides a useful model for how the evaluative tone of a representation may be transferred to a new person (Andersen & Baum, 1994).

When a significant-other representation is applied to a new person, a representation-consistent evaluative response toward the new person is experienced on the basis of significant-other resemblance; no such response emerges when the target resembles a yoked participant's significant other (in a design involving perfect one-to-one participant yoking across conditions; Andersen & Baum, 1994). In other words, a target who resembles a positively toned significant other is liked more than one who resembles a negatively toned significant other, but no such pattern emerges in a yoked-participant control condition. These data demonstrate schema-triggered evaluation in transference and extend research on schema-triggered affect (Fiske & Pavelchak, 1986) into the transference domain.

Facial Affect

Research on the facial expression of affect has shown that perceivers are reliably able to identify emotion in facial expressions, even across cultures (Ekman, 1982, 1992, 1994; Ekman & Friesen, 1978, 1984; Ekman, Friesen, & O'Sullivan, 1988; Frijda, 1988; Scherer & Wallbott, 1994). Available evidence leaves little doubt that affect can be found in facial expression, although self-presentation efforts may contaminate the signal (e.g., DePaulo, 1990). In the absence of self-presentation pressures, however, such as when one does not know that one's facial expressions are being monitored, facial expression appears to provide a reliable index of affective experience, especially if at least one other person is present (Fridlund, 1991). The very brief action of specific facial muscles is

clearly linked to particular emotional expressions conceptually and empirically (Ekman, 1992; see also Batson, Shaw, & Oleson, 1992; Frijda, 1988), and even though debate persists about which emotions are universal (Ekman, 1994; Izard, 1994; Russell, 1994), there is no doubt that the face is a conduit for emotional expression. Facial expression has also been studied in the context of the facial feedback hypothesis, in which intentionally produced facial expressions have been shown to elicit real emotion (e.g., Izard, 1981, 1990; Kraut, 1982; Laird, 1984; Levenson, Ekman, & Friesen, 1990; Strack, Martin, & Stepper, 1988; Tomkins, 1962, 1963; Tourangeau & Ellsworth, 1979; Zajonc, 1980; Zajonc & Markus, 1984; Zajonc, Murphy, & Inglehart, 1989).

In this research, we examined fleeting emotional expression to test the hypothesis that schema-triggered affect is elicited in transference, at the moment of learning about the new person. In other words, as a function of whether the new person does or does not resemble a significant other, emotional responses should be observed at encoding in fleeting facial expressions, as a function of the overall tone of the significant-other representation. More specifically, facial affect should be observable while each bit of information about the new person is learned in the transference context.

Motivation

Our model suggests that a new person who resembles a significant other should activate the significant-other representation and its evaluative and affective aspects, and we extended this notion into the motivational domain in this study. Although motivation has been defined in diverse ways (e.g., Bowlby, 1969, 1973, 1980; Cantor & Kihlstrom, 1987; Deci, 1980; Deci & Ryan, 1985; Higgins, 1989; Horney, 1939; Hull, 1943; Kruglanski, 1989; Lewin, 1935; Maslow, 1970; Rotter, 1966; Sullivan, 1940, 1953), we conceptualized it as interpersonal motivation stored with the significant-other representation in memory, in the linkages between self and other. In other words, we assumed that motivational material about wanting to emotionally approach or avoid the other—that is, to be or not to be emotionally close with the other—is stored with the significant-other representation and can be activated in transference and experienced in relation to a new person, in the same basic process of schema-triggered affect (Andersen & Glassman, 1996; see Fiske & Pavelchak, 1986). Indeed, motivation can be viewed as represented in memory as other constructs are (Bargh, 1990), in such a way that it is activated and used accordingly. This broad conceptualization has received extensive empirical support (e.g., Bargh & Gollwitzer, 1994; see also Bandura, 1982; Cantor & Kihlstrom, 1987; Fiske, 1989; Higgins, 1987, 1989; Higgins & McCann, 1984; Hoffman, Mischel, & Mazze, 1981; Kruglanski, 1989), and motivation is of increasing interest in research on social cognition and on interpersonal relations (e.g., Kruglanski, 1989; Kunda, 1987; Srull, 1983).

In our view, the motivation to approach or to avoid (e.g., Bolles, 1967; Hull, 1943) another person, in the sense of wanting to be close, connected, warm, and open or wanting to be distant and emotionally unavailable, is crucial to significant-other representations because they are infused with affect related to this motivation for connection and the experienced outcomes (see also Aron, Aron, & Smollan, 1992; Aron, Aron, Tudor, & Nelson, 1991; Baldwin, 1992; Murray & Holmes, 1993, 1994; Safran, 1990). Hence, motivational material should be stored with the significant-other representation and activated when the significant-other representation is activated, in a kind of schema-triggered motivation, even though the theory of schema-triggered affect is silent about motivations as "summary" elements triggered when the representation is activated. Because the wish to distance oneself emotionally from someone may emerge even when one likes that person, such motivation is conceptually distinct from evaluation.

Interpersonal Expectancies

In no research on transference have investigators examined expectancies for acceptance or rejection in the context of transference. We assume that the experience of being liked or disliked by the significant other is stored with the significant-other representation, so that when a new person is encountered and the significant-other representation is applied to him or her, the perceiver should expect this new person to like or dislike the perceiver in the same way the significant other does (or did; see also Westen, 1988). One's perception of how positively the significant other evaluates him or her is conceptually distinct from one's own evaluation of the significant other, because one can obviously expect to be rejected and nonetheless love.

Expectancies of acceptance or rejection are of importance because people rely on them in selecting potential partners (Berscheid, Dion, Walster, & Walster, 1971; Downey, Lebolt, & Feldman, in press) and because expectancies, in a broad sense, are likely to play a profound role in how one behaves (Miller & Turnbull, 1986; Olson, Roese, & Zanna, in press). In addition, expectancies may be related to evaluative responses, in that expectancies about how one will feel in the future are related to preferences about what to do next (Wilson, Lisle, Kraft, & Wetzel, 1989) and experiences that fit expectancies lead to faster preference judgments (Wilson et al., 1989; see Fiske & Taylor, 1991). Deliberate actions tend to be based on expectancies (Olson et al., in press; see Darley & Fazio, 1980; Darley & Gross, 1983; Ickes, Patterson, Rajecki, & Tanford, 1982; Jussim, 1986; Miller & Turnbull, 1986; Rosenthal & Rubin, 1978; Trope & Bassok, 1982), which influence performance and are associated with expectancy confirmation (Bandura, 1977, 1986; Cantor & Zirkel, 1990; Snyder, 1992; Snyder & Swann, 1978a, 1978b; Snyder, Tanke, & Berscheid, 1977).

We argue that expectancies for acceptance or rejection of the self are thus stored with the significant-other representation in linkages between the significant other and the self—leading *from* the significant other *toward* the self—that can be activated and applied as predictions about the new person's likely response (as with schema-triggered affect and motivation). In addition, the significant other's evaluative response toward oneself is an outcome or contingency in the relationship that is likely to be involved with strong feelings (Higgins, 1989) and to be important when experienced in new relations.

Method

Overview

In a pretest session held 2 weeks before the experiment, participants named and described both a positively toned significant other and a negatively toned significant other, from their own lives, and completed a set of both positive and negative sentences to describe each person. Before arriving for a presumably unrelated experiment 2 weeks later, participants were randomly assigned to one of four experimental conditions. In each, they learned about a target person, allegedly seated next door, who was portrayed so as to resemble either their positively or negatively toned significant other, or a yoked participant's positively or negatively toned significant other. Participants were perfectly yoked across the experimental and control conditions on a one-to-one basis and were thus exposed to exactly the same target features. Of importance, while participants learned about the target person by reading each sentence-length descriptor about him or her, their facial expressions were videotaped so that these expressions could be rated by trained judges in terms of pleasantness. After learning about the target person, participants completed self-report measures of transient mood, their evaluation of the target person, their motivation to be interpersonally close to him or her, and their expectancies for acceptance or rejection. Recognition memory was also assessed (as in studies by Andersen & Baum, 1994; Andersen & Cole, 1990; Andersen et al., 1995).

Participants and Design

Participants were 80 female undergraduates enrolled in Introductory Psychology at New York University (NYU), who participated in two sessions in partial fulfillment of a course requirement. Because of participant-pool restrictions and the time-intensive nature of this two-session study (in which participants did not know the sessions were related), we restricted the sample to female participants. (Doubling the number of participants

to have sufficient power to test for sex differences was not feasible.) Participants took part in a 2×2 (Participant's Own/Someone Else's Significant Other × Positive/Negative Overall Tone) factorial design, with 20 participants per cell. The gender of the target person was alleged to be that of the particular positive or negative significant other examined. Hence, participants always learned about a target of the same gender as their own significant other of the same overall tone.

Materials and Procedure

Session 1: Generating significant-other names and attributes. For the first session, participants arrived in groups of 2 to 4 for a study about "perceptions of other people." First, participants were asked to name two significant others, each defined as "someone you know very well, have known for a long time, and is very important in your life." One was to be a *positive* significant other, "someone you like very much and feel very good about, someone in whose presence you feel happy and great about yourself, and someone you *want to be close to*, want to share your feelings with, and do not want to distance yourself from"; the other was to be a *negative* significant other, "someone you do not like very much and do not feel very good about, someone in whose presence you feel unhappy and bad about yourself, and someone you do *not* want to be close to, *want to avoid* sharing your feelings with, and want to distance yourself from."

After thinking of these two people and providing a first name (only) for each, as well as a label for the relationship (e.g., "mother," "uncle," "good friend"), participants completed a number of sentences to characterize them (as in Andersen & Baum's 1994 study); that is, participants completed 14 descriptive sentences to describe each person, so as to "uniquely characterize this person and to distinguish him/her from other people." They were also instructed to make sure that half (seven) of the sentences were positive and half (seven) were negative for each significant other, regardless of the overall tone of their relationship with this other. Then participants rank-ordered all features in each list for each significant other according to importance in describing the person until all seven of each valence were ranked. These ranks were later used to select moderately descriptive features of each valence for use as a set of relevant target descriptors in the learning phase of the experiment.

Across all conditions, the same set of features (ranked 4 to 7 from each list) was selected for use in describing a target (number and rank were held constant). After the rating task, participants were shown a list of 42 experimenter-provided adjectives of relatively neutral valence (selected from Anderson's 1968 list, as in Andersen & Baum's 1994 study) and were asked to identify, for each significant other, at least 10 "descriptive" traits, 10 "counterdescriptive" (opposite) traits, and 12 irrelevant or neutral traits. The irrelevant/neutral traits were used as filler items among the target descriptors in the second session.

Participants were then told that the study was over, were partially debriefed, and were thanked for their participation. The experimenter then solicited the participant's participation in some "other experiments in the department," in reality the second session of this study. Virtually all participants agreed.

Session 2: Preliminaries. In the second session of the study, held at least 2 weeks later, participants were greeted individually by a female experimenter, unaware of experimental conditions and different from the experimenter in the earlier session. The experiment was held in a different room on a different floor than was the pretest session. Participants were informed that another participant who would be their interaction partner later in the experiment had arrived earlier and was being interviewed in the room next door. The door to this adjacent room was closed and had a sign nearby that read "Study in Progress."

Participants first completed two preliminary mood measures to assess their pretest affect: the Multiple Affect Adjective Check List (MAACL; Zuckerman & Lubin, 1965) and the Psychiatric Outpatient Mood Scales (POMS; McNair & Lorr, 1964). The MAACL is a widely used, self-report measure of current mood, consisting of 132 mood-related adjectives, in which participants place a check mark next to those describing their

feelings "right now." The POMS is a self-report measure of transient mood, consisting of 52 adjectives again rated by participants in terms of feelings "right now" on a scale ranging from 1 (*Extremely*) to 4 (*Not at all*).

The experiment was then described as a study examining how people interact with each other in a getting-acquainted situation. Specifically, participants were told that the University was considering establishing a "buddy system," in which senior students at NYU would be paired with incoming students as part of the orientation process, and that we were studying how best to match personalities in this kind of a system. Hence, the other student seated next door, whom they would be meeting later in the session, was in the position of a "potential buddy" in the experiment; these instructions were provided to increase the realism and meaningfulness of the situation (Aronson, Ellsworth, Carlsmith, & Gonzales, 1990). Without a person next door and the potential for a future interaction, there might be little reason for affective and motivational involvement.

Participants were further informed that "in this condition of the study," we were interested in the effect of one of the two people having information about the other before an actual meeting and that *they* would therefore be provided with information about the other person before the interaction. This permitted us to present participants with the target descriptors essential to the experiment.

Session 2: The learning trial. The experimenter then left the room and returned with 14 descriptions of the alleged other student. These descriptions were said to be based on an interview by a graduate student who had been asked to provide an impartial, balanced assessment. Fourteen target descriptors were presented in a fixed random order; 8 derived from those listed for a positively toned or negatively toned significant other (ranked 4 to 7 on the positive and the negative lists, respectively). The remaining 6 were derived from the list of irrelevant traits preceded by the word "is."

Participants read each descriptive sentence about the target person from a steno pad positioned upright on a desk, which required them to hold their heads upright so as to read each descriptor while unobtrusively being videotaped. A video camera was hidden in an old oscilloscope sitting on a shelf and surrounded by other old electronic equipment and papers; it was not detected by any participant. One target feature appeared on each page of the steno pad, making it necessary for participants to turn each page to read the next feature. As participants turned the pages of the steno pad, an attached tag with descriptor number was visible to the camera, marking the moment each descriptor was received by the participant and the beginning of the rating "window" (averaging 5 s), during which facial affect was to be rated by judges who were unaware of participants' experimental condition (see Tesser et al., 1988, Study 3).

Session 2: Self-report measures. After the learning task, participants completed the same self-report mood measures (the MAACL and POMS) that they had completed upon their arrival, followed by another self-report questionnaire designed to assess their evaluation of the target person (eight questions; see Andersen & Baum, 1994), motivation to approach or to avoid the person (eight questions), and their expectancies about acceptance/rejection from the other (three questions). The evaluation questions included items such as "How well do you think you will like this person?" and "In general, how positive is your impression of this person?" The motivation questions included, for example, "How much would you want to share your feelings with this person?" and "How much would you want to distance yourself emotionally from this person?" The questions about expectancies for acceptance/rejection included "How much do you think this person would like you?" and "How accepting do you think this person would be of you?"

After responding to these questions, participants completed a recognition-memory test consisting of a series of 20 target descriptors presented in a fixed random order, 8 of which had been presented earlier in the session as target descriptors and 12 of which had not. Of the 8 previously presented statements, 4 were positive and negative features of a significant other (those ranked 5 and 6 in each list), and 4 were irrelevant/neutral features. Of the

12 statements that had not been presented, 6 described the significant other (those ranked 1 to 3 in each list). These latter items constituted the crucial representation-consistent but not presented items that we use to assess the tendency to fill in the blanks about the new person in representation-consistent ways. The other 6 unpresented features were those that had been designated as neutral/irrelevant in advance. Participants rated on a 4-point scale their confidence that each sentence had actually been presented about the target (Andersen & Baum, 1994; Andersen & Cole, 1990, Study 3; Andersen et al., 1995).

At this point, participants were informed that "in this particular condition of the study" they would not meet the potential buddy because we were interested in their impressions while they did not anticipate having to interact with this person. Participants then completed the two mood measures (the MAACL and POMS) again, along with the evaluation, motivation, and expectancy questions. We assumed that removing the anticipation of a real interaction might provide for more accurate assessments (see Andersen & Baum, 1994).

Finally, participants were fully debriefed and were asked to consent to our retaining their videotaped material so as to show it to trained judges. They were then thanked for their participation and excused.

Judges' ratings of participants' facial affect. Two independent judges unaware of participants' condition rated participants' facial expressions for pleasantness during each rating "window" in which the participant read each descriptive sentence about the target. Using a 7-point scale, ranging from 1 (*Not at all pleasant*) to 7 (*Extremely pleasant*), with additional gradations of 0.5, judges rated participant's facial affect. To ensure that both raters viewed exactly the same rating window, judges completed their ratings in the same room on either side of a partition, so that they could not see each other or each other's ratings. A third research assistant operated the videotape equipment, starting it and stopping it so that each segment could be rated. The two judges demonstrated an interrater reliability of .82, estimated by the Spearman-Brown formula (Cronbach, 1970).

Judges' ratings of the nomothetic valence of target features. To assess the objective valence of each target descriptor in the 40 sets of 14 target descriptors used in the study—both when the target resembled the participants' own significant others and when he or she resembled a yoked participant's significant other—we asked two independent judges to rate each descriptor in terms of positivity/negativity, using a scale ranging from −5 to 5. Interjudge reliability was good ($r = .78$). Hence, the ratings of the two judges were averaged for each feature, so that these scores could be examined as an index of the nomothetic, objective valence of the target features to which participants were exposed while their facial affect was assessed.

Results

Check on Positive/Negative Featural Valence

Because participants listed both positive and negative descriptors to characterize each significant other, regardless of the overall tone of the significant-other representation, and then saw equal numbers of positive and negative target features, it made sense to ask judges to assess the "objective" valence of these features, that is, of the descriptive predicates presented about each target. In this way, we sought to verify that participants followed our instructions to list both positive and negative descriptors for each significant other, showing that nomothetic differences in feature valence were present and manipulated in target features across conditions. Therefore, we asked two independent judges to rate the valence of each

feature presented about each target. Judges' ratings were averaged with each other and across the features of each manipulated target for each overall tone and were examined in a 2×2 (Positive/Negative Overall Tone of Target × Positive/Negative Feature) analysis of variance. (Note that exactly the same target features were presented in the two resemblance conditions; hence, the resemblance to the participant's own significant other is not a factor in the analysis).

This analysis yielded a highly reliable main effect that confirmed that the featural valence manipulation was effective, $F(1, 38) = 313.85$, $p < .0001$, with more positive ratings of the positive features ($M = 0.22$) than of the negative ones ($M = -0.01$). Interestingly, no main effect emerged for overall tone; that is, the features of positively toned representations were not seen as reliably more positive than were the features of negatively toned representations, $F(1, 38) = 2.14$, $p = .15$, although the means leaned in this direction. This near-marginal effect led us to assume, conservatively, that we did not perfectly disguise the overall tone of the representation by means of our feature valence manipulation; some of the overall tone may have "leaked out" in the valence of the listed features. On the other hand, the valence manipulation was obviously highly effective, and the fact that no interaction emerged ($F < 2$) suggests that the valence manipulation was equally effective across both overall-tone conditions, minimizing any presence of overall tone in feature valence. The feature-positivity ratings across conditions are shown in Table 22.1. In the experiment, of course, our use of perfect yoking meant that any potential nomothetic differences in overall

TABLE 22.1. Target Feature Valence Assessed by Independent Judges (Nomothetically) by the Overall Tone of the Representation and Feature Valence

Manipulated feature valence	Positively toned representation		Negatively toned representation	
	Positive features	Negative features	Positive features	Negative features
Rated feature valence	.425	.021	.210	−.223

tone were controlled by identical stimuli across the resemblance/nonresemblance conditions.

Representation-Consistent Memory

To ensure that representation-consistent memory occurred when the target resembled the participant's own significant other in relation to when he or she resembled a yoked participant's significant other, we examined participants' average confidence rating that they had been exposed to and learned representation-consistent features about the target person whom they had not in fact seen. We thus conducted a 2 × 2 (Participant's Own/ Someone Else's Significant Other × Positive/ Negative Overall Tone) analysis of covariance (ANCOVA), controlling for participants' average confidence rating that they had learned items that were not representation-consistent (irrelevant) and that were also *not* learned.

As predicted, the analysis yielded a main effect that showed higher confidence ratings for representation-consistent items not learned about the target person when the target had resembled the participant's own significant other ($M = 1.63$) rather than a yoked participant's significant other ($M = 1.38$), $F(1, 75) = 3.92, p = .051$, or $t(75) = 1.93, p < .03$ (one-tailed). These data are shown in Figure 22.1 and replicate data from previous research on transference in social perception by

showing representation-consistent memory about the new person when the target resembled the significant other (Andersen & Cole, 1990; Andersen et al., 1995). No other effects emerged ($Fs < 1$). Hence, the representation-consistent memory effect occurred on the basis of significant-other resemblance in the target person, as in previous work, and the effect occurred both for positively toned (own, $M = 1.77$; yoked, $M = 1.40$) and for negatively toned (own, $M = 1.50$; yoked, $M = 1.35$) significant-other representations (Andersen & Baum, 1994). The data verify the occurrence of transference—in terms of going beyond the information given—in this study.

Representation-Consistent Memory and the Valence of Memory-Test Item

We also examined representation-consistent memory, taking into account the valence of the features in the memory test. We conducted a 2 × 2 × 2 (Participant's Own/Someone Else's Significant Other × Positive/Negative Overall Tone × Positive Feature/Negative Feature) ANCOVA, examining participants' confidence rating for representation-consistent items not presented, while treating featural positivity/negativity in the memory test as a repeated measure and using the same covariate. The analysis yielded the same main effect, $F(1, 76) = 3.83, p = .053$, along with a marginally significant

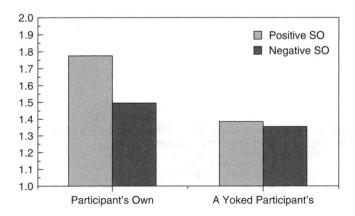

FIGURE 22.1 ■ Average recognition-memory confidence rating about representation-consistent descriptors not presented about the target by significant-other (SO) resemblance and overall tone.

three-way interaction, $F(1, 76) = 2.77, p < .10$. Although only marginal, the effect can be attributed to marginally more representation-consistent memory for positive features when the target resembled the participant's own positively toned significant other ($M = 1.94$) rather than the participant's own negatively toned significant other ($M = 1.47$), an unpredicted finding $t(76) = 1.96$, $p = .057$ (two-tailed). The effect did not hold for negative features (positively toned, $M = 1.61$; negatively toned, $M = 1.52$; $t < 1$, ns) or when participants were exposed to a yoked participant's significant other ($ts < 1$). Hence, positive test items appear to have been somewhat more susceptible to the effect.

Overall, these data show representation-consistent memory favoring the participant's own significant other for both positively and negatively toned significant-other representations, as in prior work (Andersen & Baum, 1994). Moreover, although the effect was apparent only for positive items across both positively and negatively toned significant-other representations, it clearly occurred. The fact that participants were yoked with each other on a one-to-one basis across the two resemblance conditions ruled out the alternative explanation that content differences might account for the effect. The self-generation of the features in the learning task was ruled out as accounting for the phenomenon in prior work (Andersen & Cole, 1990; Andersen et al., 1995).

Representation-Consistent Facial Affect

With regard to the affect that participants expressed in response to each target feature in the learning task, we assessed participants' facial affect while reading each descriptive sentence about the target at the exact moment of encoding. Hence, we assessed judges' average rating of the pleasantness of the participant's facial expression in response to representation-consistent versus irrelevant target features in a 2 × 2 × 2 (Participant's Own/Someone Else's Significant Other × Positive/Negative Overall Tone × Relevant/Irrelevant Target Feature) ANOVA, with feature relevance/irrelevance as repeated measure. On the basis of our extension of the theory of schema-triggered affect, we hypothesized that the overall tone of the significant-other representation would be predictive of participants' facial affect in response to the target features, under the condition of significant-other resemblance and not in the yoked-participant control condition. In other words, we predicted more pleasant facial affect when the target resembled participants' own positively toned significant other rather than their own negatively toned significant other and that no such difference would occur in the yoked-participant control condition, especially for relevant target features.

The analysis yielded a two-way interaction between resemblance and overall tone, as anticipated, although it was only marginally reliable, $F(1, 76) = 3.21, p = .077$. As portrayed in Figure 22.2, and verified by our planned contrast, participants clearly expressed more positive affect, overall, when the target resembled their own positively toned significant other ($M = 4.19$) rather than their negatively toned significant other ($M = 4.01$), $t(76) = 1.73, p = .045$, an effect not shown among control participants ($t < 1$). This suggests schema-triggered facial affect in the transference condition. Although no three-way interaction emerged ($F < 1$), we conducted our contrast separately for relevant and irrelevant target features. As anticipated, the contrast was reliable for relevant target features; participants showed more pleasant affect toward the relevant target features that actually resembled the positively toned significant other ($M = 4.30$) than to those that actually resembled the negatively toned significant other ($M = 4.06$), $t(76) = 1.74, p < .045$, and no such effect emerged in the control condition or for irrelevant features ($ts < 1$).

Interestingly, a main effect emerged for relevance/irrelevance, $F(1, 76) = 9.56, p < .003$, indicating more pleasant facial affect in response to relevant features, whether self-generated or generated by a yoked participant ($M = 4.12$), than in response to neutral predicates ($M = 4.04$). This was qualified by a two-way interaction between relevance/irrelevance and resemblance, $F(1, 76) = 6.91, p < .01$, showing that only when the features of the target person resembled the participant's own significant other did the relevant idiographic

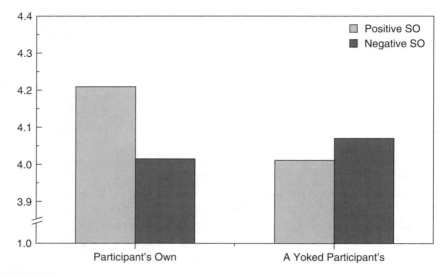

FIGURE 22.2 ■ Judges' ratings of the pleasantness of participants' facially expressed affect at encoding by significant-other (SO) resemblance and overall tone.

features elicit more positive facial affect ($M = 4.18$) than did the irrelevant nomothetic features ($M = 4.03$), $t(39) = 3.30$, $p < .002$, independently of the overall tone of the significant other. This effect did not occur when the target resembled a yoked participant's significant other (relevant features, $M = 4.05$; irrelevant features, $M = 4.04$; $t < 1$), implying more positive facial affect no matter what the overall tone of one's own significant other features in a target person.

Evaluation of the Target

We assessed participants' self-reported evaluative response to the target person by averaging their ratings of the evaluation items (emerging from the factor analysis) just after learning about the target and again after being informed that they would not actually meet the target (under the assumption that ratings made while an interaction was anticipated might differ from those made when it was not; see Andersen & Baum, 1994). The evaluation composite was thus examined in a 2 × 2 × 2 (Participant's Own/Someone Else's Significant Other × Positive/Negative Overall Tone × Time 1/Time 2 Assessment) ANOVA, with time as a repeated

measure. In accord with the theory of schema-triggered affect, we expected a two-way interaction showing that the evaluative tone of the representation was experienced toward the target person, but only under the condition of significant-other resemblance and transference. Indeed, the analysis showed that this interaction was highly reliable, $F(1, 76) = 9.12$, $p = .003$, replicating previous research (Andersen & Baum, 1994). As portrayed in Figure 22.3, our planned contrast showed that participants evaluated the target person more positively when the target resembled their own positively toned significant other ($M = 5.06$) rather than their own negatively toned significant other ($M = 3.61$), $t(76) = 4.59$, $p < .001$, a pattern less apparent, though marginal, when the target resembled a yoked participant's significant other ($M = 4.66$ vs. $M = 4.16$), $t(76) = 1.58$, $p < .07$. The analysis also yielded a reliable main effect for overall tone, $F(1, 76) = 38.28$, $p < .0001$, suggesting that we were not entirely successful in disguising the overall tone by using equal numbers of positive and negative target features in each condition. Nonetheless, the data confirmed our hypothesis. In sum, the overall tone of the significant-other representation was applied to

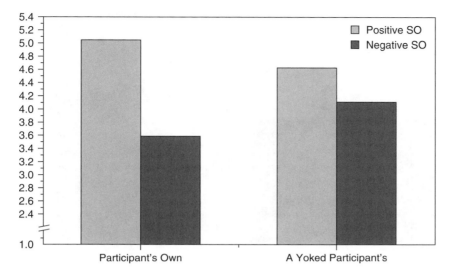

FIGURE 22.3 ■ Average rating given to evaluation-composite items by significant-other (SO) resemblance and overall tone.

the new target person under the condition of significant-other resemblance, and hence schema-triggered evaluation occurred in transference (as shown elsewhere; Andersen & Baum, 1994).

Expectancy About the Target's Evaluation of the Participant

Beyond the participant's evaluation of the target, we assessed participants' expectations about how positively or negatively they thought the new target person would be likely to evaluate them. In this assessment, the evaluation runs in the opposite direction (from the significant other to the self) in relation to our assessment of target evaluation, reported earlier, in which evaluation runs from the self to the significant other. We examined participants' average rating of the expectancy items (from the factor analysis) in the same $2 \times 2 \times 2$ ANOVA, with administration time as a repeated factor. The analysis yielded the predicted two-way interaction, $F(1, 76) = 3.80, p = .05$. As portrayed in Figure 22.4, our planned contrast showed that participants expected the target person to like and accept them more when the target resembled their own positively toned significant other ($M = 4.85$) than when the target resembled

their own negatively toned significant other ($M = 3.83$), $t(76) = 2.46, p < .01$, whereas this was not true in the yoked-control condition ($M = 4.46$ vs. $M = 4.24; t < 1$). These data suggest that a representation-consistent expectation of being liked or disliked by the target person was evoked in the context of significant-other resemblance in which the significant other's evaluative response toward the participant came to be expected *from* the new target person (see Downey et al., in press). Conceptually, expecting to be liked is quite different from liking another person, because one can like another person and not expect to have the affection returned. No other effects emerged, except more positive expectancies when overall tone was positive rather than negative, $F(1, 76) = 8.96, p < .004$. Overall, these data provide evidence that a kind of schema-triggered expectancy for acceptance or rejection is activated in the context of significant other resemblance and transference.

Motivation for Interpersonal Closeness

We also examined the degree to which participants experienced representation-consistent motivations toward the target person, by assessing their desire to emotionally approach the target

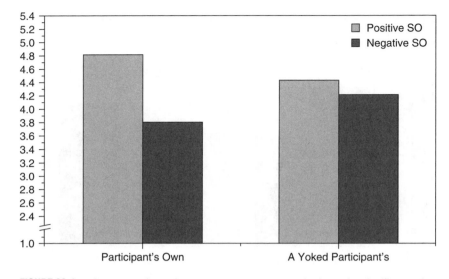

FIGURE 22.4 ■ Average ratings given to expectancy-composite items by significant-other (SO) resemblance and overall tone.

rather than to emotionally avoid him or her. Participants' average rating of the motivation items was examined in the same $2 \times 2 \times 2$ ANOVA, with administration time as a repeated factor. The analysis yielded the predicted two-way interaction, $F(1, 76) = 13.26, p = .0005$. As portrayed in Figure 22.5, our planned contrasts indicated that participants were more motivated to emotionally approach the target who resembled their own positively toned significant other ($M = 3.96$) than the target who resembled their own negatively toned significant other ($M = 2.62$), $t(76) = 3.72$, $p < .001$; this pattern did not hold when the target resembled a yoked participant's positive or negative significant other ($M = 3.43$ vs. $M = 3.40$; $t < 1$). These data demonstrate that the overall tone of the significant-other representation is predictive of the interpersonal approach motivation experienced with a new target person in the context of significant-other resemblance and transference.

Ruling Out the Mediational Role of Facial Affect in a Multiple Regression

One further question of interpretation concerns whether facial affect somehow mediated the interactive effect of resemblance and overall tone in producing schema-triggered evaluation, expectancy, and motivation. Therefore, we conducted a series of multiple regressions for each of these dependent variables. In the first regression for each, the two main effects were entered into the equation, followed by the interaction term. Each analysis yielded a reliable interaction, as in the reported ANOVAs, showing significant change in R^2 attributable to the interaction term, for evaluation ($\beta = .95$; additional variance, 7.4%), $F(1, 76) = 9.12, p = .003$; for expectancy ($\beta = .81$; additional variance, 4.3%), $F(1, 76) = 3.80, p = .055$; and for motivation ($\beta = 1.31$; additional variance, 12.7%), $F(1, 76) = 13.26, p = .0005$. Next, we repeated these analyses, controlling for facial affect (by entering it into the equation first). For both evaluation and motivation, the results showed that the change in R^2 attributable to the interaction remained highly reliable, even when facial affect was covaried out, for evaluation ($\beta = .91$; additional variance, 6.5%), $F(1, 75) = 7.99$, $p = .006$; and for motivation ($\beta = 1.20$; additional variance, 10.3%), $F(1, 75) = 10.91, p = .0015$. In the case of expectancy, however, the interaction term was no longer significant after we controlled for facial affect ($\beta = .59$; additional variance,

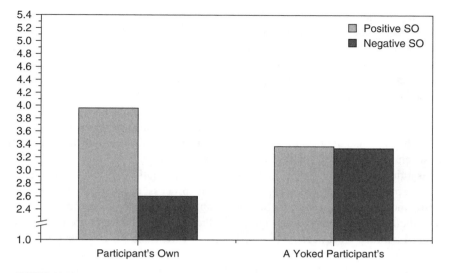

FIGURE 22.5 ■ Average ratings given to motivation-composite items by significant-other (SO) resemblance and overall tone.

2.2%), $F(1, 75) = 2.13$, $p = .15$, which implies that facial affect does, in fact, mediate expectancy for acceptance/rejection. Because the initial interaction term was small in magnitude and diminished only slightly, however, it is probably most accurate to consider this partial mediation rather than complete. Nonetheless, facial affect is clearly a marker of expected outcomes from the other.

Discussion

Research has demonstrated transference in everyday social perception—that is, the activation and application of a significant-other representation to a new individual—resulting in representation-consistent memory and evaluation (Andersen & Baum, 1994; Andersen & Cole, 1990; Andersen et al., 1995). Using a combination of idiographic and nomothetic procedures, as in prior work, we examined the effect of significant-other resemblance in a target person on participants' immediate affective response to learning about the new person, in terms of facial expression. Motivation concerning approaching or avoiding the new person and expectancies about acceptance/rejection from this person were also examined.

Replicating previous findings, the results showed representation-consistent memory as a function of significant-other resemblance (Andersen & Baum, 1994; Andersen et al., 1995) and representation-consistent evaluative responses as well, confirming significant-other activation and application (i.e., transference in social perception). Of more importance, the data showed, as predicted, that participants were more likely to express representation-consistent facial affect under the condition of significant-other resemblance than in the yoked-participant control condition; that is, participants showed more pleasant facial affect in response to relevant significant-other descriptive target features when the target resembled their own positively toned significant other instead of their own negatively toned significant other, and no such pattern held when the target resembled a yoked participant's significant other. Hence, immediate facial affect expressed nonverbally at encoding was driven by the overall tone of the significant-other representation, which suggests that schema-triggered affect (Fiske & Pavelchak, 1986) occurred in facial affect in transference context. The expressed facial affect better reflected the overall tone of the significant-other representation in the significant-other resemblance condition than in the yoked control condition, and this occurred regardless of whether the target features themselves were positive or negative. These data support the notion that representation-based facial affect occurred by means of the process of schema-triggered affect, as we predicted.

Interestingly, the data also demonstrated representation-consistent motivation in relation to the target person as a function of significant-other resemblance; that is, participants wanted to approach and to be more emotionally open with the target who resembled their own positively toned significant other rather than their own negatively toned one, an effect not present in the yoked-participant control condition. Moreover, and again as predicted, the data showed representation-consistent expectancies for acceptance or rejection from the target person on the basis of significant-other resemblance; that is, participants expected to be better liked (i.e., to be more positively evaluated) when the target resembled their own positively toned rather than negatively toned significant other, an effect that did not hold in the yoked-participant control condition.

Finally, although it is conceivable that some of our participants explicitly recognized the features of the targets as being those they had listed earlier (to describe their significant other in the prior session) rather than simply being reminded of their significant other in a more tacit or nonconscious way, we think it improbable that this accounts for obtained effects. It could be argued that participants would be more likely to try to sabotage the experiment rather than to "play along" with it if they recognized the link between the two sessions of the experiment (between the earlier feature listing and the later experiment). Indeed, this could lead participants to correct or even overcorrect for potential bias (Martin, Seta, & Crelia, 1990) in their various ratings, to the extent that they both recognized the features and intuited that a significant-other-consistent response was our hypothesis. There is no a priori reason, however, why participants should have assumed that showing representation-consistent responses in the significant-other condition would reflect well on them. In keeping with this interpretation, in fact, the literature on contextual priming suggests that greater awareness of potential biasing influences tends to lead to contrast effects, not the assimilation effects that we predicted and obtained (e.g., Lombardi, Higgins, & Bargh, 1987; Martin et al., 1990). On the other hand, our data are silent on this issue, and we cannot rule out the role of awareness in obtained effects.

Together, the data can be interpreted in terms of the process of significant-other activation and application in transference—that is, in terms of the experimental literature on transference. They also extend the basic process of schema-triggered affect well beyond the realm of evaluation (Fiske & Pavelchak, 1986) and into the areas of facial affect, expectancies, and motivation.

Schema-Triggered Facial Affect in Transference

Extending the conception of schema-triggered affect (Fiske, 1982; Fiske & Pavelchak, 1986) by focusing on facial affect (see Andersen & Glassman, 1996), these data demonstrated that significant-other-relevant stimulus cues by a target person at the moment of encoding are processed in terms of the overall emotional tone of the significant-other representation. Participants' facial expressions were rated as more pleasant when participants read target features resembling their own positively toned significant other than when they read target features resembling their own negatively toned significant other, a pattern that did not hold when the target person resembled a yoked participant's significant other. Because this facial affect—reflecting the overall tone of the representation—was captured by a hidden camera and was rated by judges unaware of participants' conditions, it serves as an unobtrusive and objective index of affect at the encoding of target features. As such, these data importantly contribute to the literature on transference in social perception by showing that in the context of significant-other resemblance and transference, facial affect consistent with the overall tone of the significant other is elicited. The yoking of participants across conditions controlled for potential content differences.

Schema-Triggered Interpersonal Motivation in Transference

Extending previous work on transference, this study also showed that participants were more motivated to emotionally approach and to be emotionally open with the target person when he or she resembled their own positively toned significant other rather than their own negatively toned significant other, another pattern that did not hold when the target resembled a yoked participant's significant other. Hence, the data suggest that significant-other activation leads not only to representation-consistent facial affect, but also to representation-consistent motivation toward the new person as well. Because this motivational effect cannot be attributed to content differences, the process of schema-triggered affect appears to have led motivations stored with the significant-other representation to be applied to the new target person in the context of significant-other resemblance.

These data are provocative in that they suggest that with a new person who resembles a significant other, people may be motivated to seek the same level of (or lack of) closeness as they have (or have had) with the significant other. The data provide the first evidence we know of that interpersonal closeness motivations are elicited in transference, which is important in part because the desire to be close and connected is thought to be one of the most basic human motivations (e.g., Bowlby, 1969; Helgeson, 1994; Sullivan, 1953; Wiggins, 1992). On the other hand, further work is clearly needed to explore the contention that motivation and goals pursued in relation to the significant other are represented cognitively, much as are other constructs (see Bargh, 1990; Bargh & Barndollar, 1996; Bargh & Gollwitzer, 1994; Kruglanski, 1996), and play out in actual behavior in transference (see Andersen & Glassman, 1996). In any event, our data make it clear that facial affect at encoding did not mediate the effects of significant-other activation and application on interpersonal motivations in transference and that motivation in transference is distinct

from related phenomena involving evaluation and expectancies, as discussed later.

Schema-Triggered Expectancies in Transference

Extending the prior work on transference still further, this research demonstrated that participants' expectancies for acceptance or rejection emerged in transference in a manner consistent with their relationship with their significant other; that is, participants in the own significant-other resemblance conditions expected the same pattern of liking or disliking from the new target that they believed their significant other felt toward them, yet another effect not observed in the yoked-participant control condition. Participants expected the target person to like them more (i.e., to evaluate them more positively) when he or she resembled their own positively toned significant other rather than their own negatively toned significant other. Expectancies based on the significant other's evaluation of the participant were thus applied to a new target person who resembled the significant other, so that the new person was expected to accept or reject the participant in the same way. In view of the known importance of expectancies in interpersonal behavior (e.g., Miller & Turnbull, 1986; Olson et al., in press) and the special relevance of acceptance or rejection by significant persons in one's life in subsequent relationships (e.g., Downey et al., in press), this finding is especially interesting. For example, expectancies about acceptance or rejection may well function as interpersonal contingencies in a relationship with a significant other (e.g., Higgins, 1989; see also Aron et al., 1991; Murray & Holmes, 1993, 1994), and hence, when such contingencies are anticipated in a new relationship, they may lead one to respond in the same way. In addition, because the degree of liking that the target is expected to express toward the participant reflects that stored in memory running from the significant other toward the self—the opposite direction of the liking that the participant feels toward the target and toward the significant other in memory—these expectancies are clearly not identical to participants' evaluation of the other. Indeed, even statistically, expectancies are distinct from both target evaluation and interpersonal closeness motivation. Overall, the data suggest that the general process of schema-triggered affect can cause the acceptance or rejection experienced from the significant other to be expected from a new person in the context of significant-other resemblance.

Schema-Triggered Evaluation in Transference

Our study, of course, replicated prior work showing that participants expressed more liking for the target person when he or she resembled the participant's own positively toned versus negatively toned significant other; this pattern, too, did not emerge when the target resembled the significant other of a yoked participant (Andersen & Baum, 1994). The overall tone of the significant-other representation was thus applied to the target person on the basis of significant-other resemblance, in such a way that participants liked or disliked the other person in accordance with the representation, showing schema-triggered evaluation in transference, an effect unmediated by facial affect at encoding and distinct from motivation and expectancy.

Representation-Consistent Inference and Memory

The representation-consistent memory effect was also replicated (Andersen & Baum, 1994); that is, higher recognition-confidence ratings emerged for representation-consistent descriptors that had not been presented when the target resembled the participant's own significant other rather than a yoked participant's significant other (Andersen & Glassman, 1996; see Andersen & Baum, 1994; Andersen & Cole, 1990; Andersen et al., 1995), reflecting a heightened tendency to go beyond the information given (Bruner, 1957; Higgins & King, 1981). Although this kind of process of filling in the blanks about a new person on the basis of some set of assumptions likely occurs regardless of whatever construct is activated (e.g., Cantor & Mischel, 1977; Higgins & King, 1981), research has shown it is more likely based on significant-other representations than on nonsignificant-other representations, which suggests that significant-other representa-

tions are particularly powerful because of their chronic accessibility (Andersen et al., 1995; see Higgins, 1989, in press). As our study indicates, representation-consistent memory is based far more on participants' own significant other's features than on any yoked participant's significant other's features (Andersen & Baum, 1994; Andersen et al., 1995; Hinkley & Andersen, 1996). Significant-other-based memory is more pronounced when the person resembles the significant other than when he or she does not—that is, when the new person triggers the significant-other representation (Andersen et al., 1995). In other words, relevant stimulus cues in the target person have been shown to combine additively with chronic accessibility in transference (see also Bargh et al., 1986).

On another level, because people describe various others with the personal constructs that they commonly use (Higgins & King, 1981; Kelly, 1955), one alternative explanation for this memory phenomenon is that the items that participants used to describe the significant other were merely those so chronically accessible (frequently used) that they would be used to describe anyone. Fortunately, this factor has been controlled in the previous research just noted that showed more representation-consistent memory based on a significant-other representation than based on a nonsignificant-other representation or a stereotype (Andersen et al., 1995; Chen, Andersen, & Hinkley, 1996); that is, significant-other representations yield more representation-consistent memory than control representations do. In addition, the effect favoring the significant other holds, in comparison to many self-generated features that do not coalesce into any single representation in the participant's memory (used as another control; Andersen et al., 1995). Hence, the memory effect is not accounted for by the simple fact of participants' having called to mind and listed the features before the experiment.

Concluding Comments

In summary, these results replicate and extend previous findings on transference, defined in terms of representation-consistent memory and schema-triggered evaluation (see Andersen &

Baum, 1994; Andersen et al., 1995), by demonstrating representation-consistent facial affect during learning about a target person who resembled one's own significant other rather than a yoked participant's significant other. Facial affect consistent with the overall evaluative tone of the significant-other representation was elicited in the context of significant-other resemblance. The data provide strong evidence—through an unobtrusive, nonverbal measure of facial affect–that schema-triggered affect occurs in transference. Beyond this, the findings also demonstrate that interpersonal closeness motivation toward a new target person is also elicited when the new person resembles one's own positively rather than negatively toned significant other, but not a yoked participant's significant other. In addition, expectancies to be accepted or rejected by the new person are also elicited, just as are actual feelings of liking or disliking the target person on the basis of significant-other resemblance. Overall, the data provide converging evidence for the phenomenon of transference in social perception and extend work on this concept into the domains of facial affect, motivation, and expectancies. These effects can readily be explained in terms of the basic process of schema-triggered affect as it occurs in transference (i.e., based on significant-other activation and application). The findings enable not only the conclusion that people are more likely to infer that a new person possesses more significant-other-descriptive features and to misremember him or her in these terms when the significant-other representation is activated and applied, but also the conclusion that people are more likely to experience relevant "hot" cognitions in the transference context.

NOTES

Susan M. Andersen, Inga Reznik, and Lenora M. Manzella, Department of Psychology, New York University.

We thank Emily Alexopoulos, Steve Florendo, Julia Kalmanson, Tasnim Khomusi, Susan Leonard, Jessica Przygocki, Lisa Rosen, Whitney Shindler, Deniz Sidali, and Serena Stamm for their help with the research. Special thanks are also due to Noah Glassman, Michele Berk, Kathy Balto, Janet Kennedy, and Warner Dick for their comments on a draft of this article.

Correspondence concerning this article should be addressed to Susan M. Andersen, Department of Psychology, New York University, 6 Washington Place, 4th Floor, New York, New York 10003. Electronic mail may be sent via the Internet to andersen@psych.nyu.edu.

REFERENCES

Andersen, S. M., & Baum, A. B. (1994). Transference in interpersonal relations: Inferences and affect based on significant-other representations. *Journal of Personality, 62*, 460–497.

Andersen, S. M., & Chen, S. (in press). Measuring transference in everyday social relations: Theory and evidence using an experimental social–cognitive paradigm. In H. Kurtzman (Ed.), *Cognition and psychodynamics*. New York: Oxford University Press.

Andersen, S. M., & Cole, S. W. (1990). "Do I know you?": The role of significant others in general social perception. *Journal of Personality and Social Psychology, 59*, 384–399.

Andersen, S. M., & Glassman, N. S. (1996). Responding to significant others when they are not there. Effects on interpersonal inference, motivation, and affect. In R. M. Sorrentino & E. T. Higgins (Eds.), *Handbook of motivation and cognition* (Vol. 3, pp. 262–321). New York: Guilford.

Andersen, S. M., Glassman, N. S., Chen, S., & Cole, S. W. (1995). Transference in social perception: The role of chronic accessibility in significant-other representations. *Journal of Personality and Social Psychology, 69*, 41–57.

Andersen, S. M., & Klatzky, R. L. (1987). Traits and social stereotypes: Levels of categorization in person perception. *Journal of Personality and Social Psychology, 53*, 235–246.

Anderson, N. H. (1968). Likability ratings of 555 personality-trait words. *Journal of Personality and Social Psychology, 9*, 272–279.

Aron, A., Aron, E. N., & Smollan, D. (1992). Inclusion of other in the self scale and structure of interpersonal closeness. *Journal of Personality and Social Psychology, 63*, 596–612.

Aron, A., Aron, E. N., Tudor, M., & Nelson, G. (1991). Close relationships as including other in the self. *Journal of Personality and Social Psychology, 60*, 241–253.

Aronson, E., Ellsworth, P. C., Carlsmith, J. M., & Gonzales, M. H. (1990). *Methods of research on social psychology* (2nd ed.). New York: McGraw-Hill.

Averill, J. R. (1990). Emotions as episodic dispositions, cognitive schemas, and transitory social roles: Steps toward an integrated theory of emotion. In D. J. Ozer, J. M. Healy, Jr., & A. J. Stewart (Eds.), *Perspectives in personality: Self and emotion* (Vol. 3, pp. 137–165). Greenwich, CT: JAI Press.

Baldwin, M. W. (1992). Relational schemas and the processing of information. *Psychological Bulletin, 112*, 461–484.

Banaji, M. R., & Greenwald, A. G. (1992). Implicit stereotyping. In M. P. Zanna & J. M. Olson (Eds.), *Psychology of prejudice: The Ontario Symposium* (Vol. 7, pp. 55–76). Hillsdale, NJ: Erlbaum.

Bandura, A. (1977). Self-efficacy: Toward a unifying theory of behavioral change. *Psychological Review, 84*, 191–215.

Bandura, A. (1982). Self-efficacy mechanism in human agency. *American Psychologist, 37,* 122–147.

Bandura, A. (1986). The explanatory and predictive scope of self-efficacy theory. *Journal of Social and Clinical Psychology, 4,* 359–373.

Bargh, J. A. (1990). Auto-motives: Preconscious determinants of social interaction. In E. T. Higgins & R. M. Sorrentino (Eds.), *Handbook of motivation and cognition: Foundations of social behavior* (Vol. 2, pp. 93–130). New York: Guilford.

Bargh, J. A., & Barndollar, K. (1996). Automaticity in action: The unconscious as repository of chronic goals and motives. In P. M. Gollwitzer & J. A. Bargh (Eds.), *The psychology of action: Linking cognition and motivation to behavior* (pp. 457–481). New York: Guilford.

Bargh, J. A., Bond, R. N., Lombardi, W. L., & Tota, M. E. (1986). The addictive nature of chronic and temporary sources of construct accessibility. *Journal of Personality and Social Psychology, 50,* 869–878.

Bargh, J. A., & Gollwitzer, P. M. (1994). Environmental control of goal-directed action: Automatic and strategic contingencies between situations and behavior. In W. D. Spaulding (Ed.), *Integrative views of motivation, cognition, and emotion: Nebraska Symposium on Motivation* (Vol. 41, pp. 71–124). Lincoln: University of Nebraska Press.

Batson, C. D., Shaw, L. L., & Oleson, K. C. (1992). Differentiating affect, mood, and emotion: Toward functionally based conceptual distinctions. In M. S. Clark (Ed.), *Emotion: Review of personality and social psychology* (No. 13, pp. 294–326). Newbury Park, CA: Sage.

Baum, A., & Andersen, S. M. (1995). *Interpersonal roles and everyday transference: Eliciting transient mood states under the condition of significant-other resemblance.* Unpublished manuscript, New York University, Department of Psychology.

Berkowitz, L. (1993). Towards a general theory of anger and emotional aggression: Implications of the cognitive–neoassociationistic perspective for the analysis of anger and other emotions. In R. S. Wyer, Jr., & T. K. Srull (Eds.), *Advances in social cognition* (Vol. 6, pp. 1–46). Hillsdale, NJ: Erlbaum.

Berscheid, E., Dion, K., Walster, E., & Walster, W. G. (1971). Physical attractiveness and dating choice: A test of the match hypothesis. *Journal of Experimental Social Psychology, 7,* 173–189.

Bolles, R. C. (1967). *Theory of motivation.* New York: Harper & Row.

Bower, G. H. (1981). Emotional mood and memory. *American Psychologist, 36,* 129–148.

Bowlby, J. (1969). *Attachment and loss: Volume 1. Attachment.* New York: Basic Books.

Bowlby, J. (1973). *Attachment and loss: Volume 2. Separation: Anxiety and anger.* New York: Basic Books.

Bowlby, J. (1980). *Attachment and loss: Volume 3. Loss: Sadness and depression.* New York: Basic Books.

Brewer, M. (1988). A dual process of impression formation. In T. Srull & R. Wyer (Eds.), *Advances in social cognition* (Vol. 1, pp. 1–35). Hillsdale, NJ: Erlbaum.

Bruner, J. S. (1957). Going beyond the information given. In H. E. Gruber, K. R. Hammond, & R. Jessor (Eds.), *Contemporary approaches to cognition* (pp. 41–60). Cambridge, MA: Harvard University Press.

Cantor, N., & Kihlstrom, J. F. (1987). *Personality and social intelligence.* Englewood Cliffs, NJ: Prentice-Hall.

Cantor, N., & Mischel, W. (1977). Traits as prototypes: Effects on recognition memory. *Journal of Personality and Social Psychology, 35,* 38–48.

Cantor, N., & Mischel, W. (1979). Prototypes in person perception. In L. Berkowitz (Ed.), *Advances in experimental social psychology* (Vol. 12, pp. 3–52). New York: Academy Press.

Cantor, N., & Zirkel, S. (1990). Personality, cognition, and purposive behavior. In L. A. Pervin (Ed.), *Handbook of personality: Theory and research* (pp. 135–164). New York: Guilford.

Chen, S., Andersen, S. M., & Hinkley, K. (1996). *Stimulus applicability and chronic accessibility in significant-other activation and application.* Unpublished manuscript, New York University, Department of Psychology.

Clark, M. S., & Isen, A. M. (1982). Toward understanding the relationship between feeling states and social behavior. In A. Hastorf & A. Isen (Eds.), *Cognitive social psychology* (pp. 73–108). New York: Elsevier North-Holland.

Cronbach, L. J. (1970). *Essentials of psychological testing.* New York: Harper & Row.

Darley, J. M., & Fazio, R. H. (1980). Expectancy confirmation processes arising in the social interaction sequence. *American Psychologist, 35,* 867–881.

Darley, J. M., & Gross, P. H. (1983). A hypothesis-confirming bias in labeling effects. *Journal of Personality and Social Psychology, 44,* 20–33.

Deci, E. L. (1980). Self-determination theory: When mind mediates behavior. *Journal of Mind and Behavior, 1,* 33–43.

Deci, E. L., & Ryan, R. M. (1985). *Intrinsic motivation and self-determination in human behavior.* New York: Plenum.

DePaulo, B. M. (1990). *Nonverbal behavior and self-preservation.* Unpublished manuscript, University of Virginia, Department of Psychology.

Downey, G., Lebolt, A., & Feldman, S. (in press). The impact of early interpersonal trauma on adult adjustment: The mediating role of rejection sensitivity. In D. Cicchetti & S. Toth (Eds.), *Rochester Symposium on Developmental Psychopathology, Vol. VIII: The effects of trauma on the developmental process.* Rochester, NY: University of Rochester Press.

Ekman, P. (Ed.). (1982). *Emotion in the human face* (2nd ed.). New York: Cambridge University Press.

Ekman, P. (1992). Are there basic emotions? *Psychological Review, 99,* 550–553.

Ekman, P. (1994). Strong evidence for universals in facial expression: A reply to Russell's mistaken critique. *Psychological Bulletin, 115,* 268–287.

Ekman, P., & Friesen, W. V. (1978). *Manual for the facial affect coding system.* Palo Alto, CA: Consulting Psychologists Press.

Ekman, P., & Friesen, W. V. (1984). *Unmasking the face* (2nd ed.). Palo Alto, CA: Consulting Psychologists Press.

Ekman, P., Friesen, W. V., & O'Sullivan, M. (1988). Smiles while lying. *Journal of Personality and Social Psychology, 54*, 414–420.

Fiske, S. T. (1982). Schema-triggered affect: Applications to social perception. In M. S. Clark & S. T. Fiske (Eds.), *Affect and cognition: The 17th annual Carnegie symposium on cognition* (pp. 55–78). Hillsdale, NJ: Erlbaum.

Fiske, S. T. (1989). Examining the role of intent: Toward understanding its role in stereotyping and prejudice. In J. S. Uleman & J. A. Bargh (Eds.), *Unintended thought* (pp. 253–283). New York: Guilford.

Fiske, S. T., & Neuberg, S. L. (1990). A continuum model of impression formation from category-based to individuated processes: Influences of information and motivation on attention and interpretation. In M. P. Zanna (Ed.), *Advances in experimental social psychology* (Vol. 23, pp. 1–74). New York: Guilford.

Fiske, S. T., & Pavelchak, M. (1986). Category-based versus piecemeal-based affective responses: Developments in schema-triggered affect. In R. M. Sorrentino & E. T. Higgins (Eds.), *Handbook of motivation and cognition* (pp. 167–203). New York: Guilford.

Fiske, S. T., & Taylor, S. E. (1991). *Social cognition* (2nd ed.). New York: McGraw-Hill.

Freud, S. (1957). Instincts and their vicissitudes. In J. Strachey (Ed. and Trans.), *The standard edition of the complete psychological works of Sigmund Freud* (Vol. 14, pp. 109–140). London: Hogarth Press. (Original work published 1915)

Freud, S. (1958). The dynamics of transference. In J. Strachey (Ed. and Trans.), *The standard edition of the complete psychological works of Sigmund Freud* (Vol. 12, pp. 97–108). London: Hogarth Press. (Original work published 1912)

Fridlund, A. J. (1991). Sociality of solitary smiling: Potentiation by an implicit audience. *Journal of Personality and Social Psychology, 60*, 229–240.

Frijda, N. H. (1988). The law of emotion. *American Psychologist, 43*, 349–358.

Gentner, D. (1983). Structure-mapping: A theoretical framework for analogy. *Cognitive Science, 7*, 155–170.

Gilovich, T. (1981). Seeing the past in the present: The effect of associations to familiar events on judgments and decisions. *Journal of Personality and Social Psychology, 40*, 797–808.

Greenberg, J. R., & Mitchell, S. A. (1983). *Object relations in psychoanalytic theory.* Cambridge, MA: Harvard University Press.

Guidano, V. F., & Liotti, G. (1983). *Cognitive process and emotional disorders.* New York: Guilford.

Hamilton, D. L. (1979). A cognitive-attributional analysis of stereotyping. In L. Berkowitz (Ed.), *Advances in experimental social psychology* (Vol. 12, pp. 53–84). New York: Academic Press.

Hazan, C., & Shaver, P. (1987). Romantic love conceptualized as an attachment process. *Journal of Personality and Social Psychology, 52*, 511–524.

Helgeson, V. S. (1994). Relation of agency and communion to well-being: Evidence and potential explanations. *Psychological Review, 116*, 412–428.

Higgins, E. T. (1987). Self-discrepancy theory: A theory relating self and affect. *Psychological Review, 94*, 319–340.

Higgins, E. T. (1989). Knowledge accessibility and activation: Subjectivity and suffering from unconscious sources. In J. S. Uleman & J. A. Bargh (Eds.), *Unintended thought* (pp. 75–123). New York: Guilford.

Higgins, E. T. (1990). Personality, social psychology, and person–situation relations: Standards and knowledge activation as a common language. In L. A. Pervin (Ed.), *Handbook of personality* (pp. 301–338). New York: Guilford.

Higgins, E. T. (in press). Knowledge activation: Accessibility, applicability, and salience. In E. T. Higgins & A. W. Kruglanski (Eds.), *Social psychology: Handbook of basic principles.* New York: Guilford.

Higgins, E. T., & Brendl, C. M. (1995). Accessibility and applicability: Some "activation rules" influencing judgment. *Journal of Experimental Social Psychology, 31*, 218–243.

Higgins, E. T., & King, G. A. (1981). Accessibility of social constructs: Information processing consequences of individual and contextual variability. In N. Cantor & J. F. Kihlstrom (Eds.), *Personality, cognition and social interaction* (pp. 69–121). Hillsdale, NJ: Erlbaum.

Higgins, E. T., & McCann, C. D. (1984). Social encoding and subsequent attitudes, impressions, and memory: "Context-driven" and motivational aspects of processing. *Journal of Personality and Social Psychology, 47*, 26–39.

Hinkley, K., & Andersen, S. M. (1996). The working self-concept in transference: Significant-other activation and self-change. *Journal of Personality and Social Psychology, 71*, 1279–1295.

Hoffman, C., Mischel, W., & Mazze, K. (1981). The role of purpose in the organization of information about behavior. Trait based vs. goal-based categories in person cognition. *Journal of Personality and Social Psychology, 40*, 211–225.

Horney, K. (1939). *New ways in psychoanalysis.* New York: Norton.

Horowitz, M. J. (1989). Relationship schema formulation: Role-relationship models and intrapsychic conflict. *Psychiatry, 52*, 260–274.

Hull, C. L. (1943). *Principles of behavior.* New York: Appleton-Century-Crofts.

Ickes, W., Patterson, M. L., Rajecki, D. W., & Tanford, S. (1982). Behavioral and cognitive consequences of reciprocal versus compensatory responses to preinteraction expectancies. *Social Cognition, 1*, 160–190.

Izard, C. E. (1981). Differential emotions theory and the facial feedback hypothesis of emotion activation: Comments on Tourangeau and Ellsworth's "The role of facial response in the experience of emotion." *Journal of Personality and Social Psychology, 40*, 350–354.

Izard, C. E. (1990). Facial expressions and the regulation of emotions. *Journal of Personality and Social Psychology, 58*, 487–498.

Izard, C. E. (1994). Innate and universal facial expressions: Evidence for developmental and cross-cultural research. *Psychological Bulletin, 115*, 288–299.

Jussim, L. (1986). Self-fulfilling prophecies: A theoretical review. *Psychological Review, 93*, 429–445.

Kelly, G. A. (1955). *The psychology of personal constructs.* New York: Norton.

Kihlstrom, J. G. (1987). The cognitive unconscious. *Science, 237*, 1445–1452.

Kraut, R. E. (1982). Social presence, facial feedback, and emotion. *Journal of Personality and Social Psychology, 42*, 853–863.

Kruglanski, A. W. (1989). *Lay epistemics and human knowledge: Cognitive and motivational bases.* New York: Plenum.

Kruglanski, A. W. (1996). A motivated gatekeeper of our mind: Need-for-closure effect on interpersonal and group processes. In R. M. Sorrentino & E. T. Higgins (Eds.), *Handbook of motivation and cognition* (Vol. 3, pp. 465–496). New York: Guilford.

Kunda, Z. (1987). Motivated inference: Self-serving generation and evaluation of causal theories. *Journal of Personality and Social Psychology, 53*, 636–647.

Laird, J. D. (1984). The real role of facial response in the experience of emotion: A reply to Tourangeau and Ellsworth, and others. *Journal of Personality and Social Psychology, 47*, 909–917.

Lazarus, R. S., & Averill, J. R. (1972). Emotion and cognition with special reference to anxiety. In C. D. Spielberger (Ed.), *Anxiety: Current trends in theory and research* (Vol. 2, pp. 242–283). New York: Academic Press.

Levenson, R. W., Ekman, P., & Friesen, W. V. (1990). Voluntary facial action generates emotion-specific autonomic nervous system activity. *Psychophysiology, 27*, 363–384.

Leventhal, H. (1984). A perceptual-motor theory of emotion. In L. Berkowitz (Ed.), *Advances in experimental social psychology* (Vol. 17, pp. 117–182). New York: Academy Press.

Lewicki, P. (1985). Nonconscious biasing effects of single instances on subsequent judgments. *Journal of Personality and Social Psychology, 48*, 563–574.

Lewin, K. (1935). *A dynamic theory of personality.* New York: McGraw.

Lombardi, W. J., Higgins, E. T., & Bargh, J. A. (1987). The role of consciousness in priming effects on categorization. *Personality and Social Psychology Bulletin, 13*, 411–429.

Luborsky, L., & Crits-Christoph, P. (1990). *Understanding transference: The CCRT method.* New York: Basic Books.

Maccoby, E. E. (1980). *Social development: Psychological growth and the parent-child relationships.* New York: Harcourt Brace Jovanovich.

Martin, L. L., Seta, J. J., & Crelia, R. A. (1990). Assimilation and contrast as a function of people's willingness and ability to expend effort in forming an impression. *Journal of Personality and Social Psychology, 59*, 27–37.

Maslow, A. (1970). *Motivation and personality* (2nd ed.). New York: Harper & Row.

McNair, D. M., & Lorr, M. (1964). An analysis of mood in neurotics. *Journal of Abnormal and Social Psychology, 69*, 620–627.

Miller, D. T., & Turnbull, W. (1986). Expectancies and interpersonal processes. *Annual Review of Psychology, 37*, 233–256.

Mullahy, P. (1970). *Psychoanalysis and interpersonal psychiatry. The contributions of Harry Stack Sullivan.* New York: Science House.

Murray, S. L., & Holmes, J. G. (1993). Seeing virtues in faults: Negativity and the transformation of interpersonal narratives in close relationships. *Journal of Personality and Social Psychology, 65*, 707–722.

Murray, S. L., & Holmes, J. G. (1994). Storytelling in close relationships: The construction of confidence. *Personality and Social Psychology Bulletin, 20*, 650–663.

Nosofsky, R. M. (1986). Attention, similarity, and the identification–categorization relationship. *Journal of Experimental Psychology: General, 115*, 39–57.

Oatley, K., & Bolton, W. (1985). A social–cognitive theory of depression in reaction to life events. *Psychological Review, 92*, 372–388.

Olson, J. M., Roese, N. J., & Zanna, M. P. (in press). Expectancies. In E. T. Higgins & A. W. Kruglanski (Eds.), *Social psychology: Handbook of basic principles.* New York: Guilford.

Ortony, A., Clore, G. L., & Collins, A. (1988). *The cognitive structure of emotions.* New York: Cambridge University Press.

Pavelchak, M. (1989). Piecemeal and category-based evaluation: An idiographic analysis. *Journal of Personality and Social Psychology, 56*, 354–363.

Pratto, F., & Bargh, J. A. (1991). Stereotyping based on apparently individuating information: Trait and global components of sex stereotypes under attention overload. *Journal of Experimental Social Psychology, 27*, 26–47.

Read, S. J., & Cessa, I. L. (1991). This reminds me of the time when . . . : Expectation failures in reminding and explaining. *Journal of Experimental Social Psychology, 27*, 1–25.

Rogers, C. (1951). *Client-centered therapy.* Boston: Houghton-Mifflin.

Rosenthal, R., & Rubin, D. B. (1978). Interpersonal expectancy effects: The first 345 studies. *Behavioral and Brain Sciences, 1*, 377–415.

Ross, B. H., Perkins, S. J., & Tenpenny, P. L. (1990). Reminding-based category learning. *Cognitive Psychology, 22*, 460–492.

Rotter, J. B. (1966). Generalized expectancies for internal versus external control of reinforcement. *Psychological Monographs, 80* (Whole No. 609).

Russell, J. A. (1994). Is there universal recognition of emotion from facial expression? A review of cross-cultural studies. *Psychological Bulletin, 115*, 102–141.

Safran, J. D. (1990). Toward a refinement of cognitive therapy in light of interpersonal theory: I. Theory. *Clinical Psychology Review, 10*, 87–105.

Schank, R. C. (1982). *Dynamic memory: A theory of reminding and learning in computers and people.* New York: Cambridge University Press.

Scherer, K. R., & Wallbott, H. G. (1994). Evidence for universality and cultural variation of differential emotion response patterning. *Journal of Personality and Social Psychology, 66*, 310–328.

Sedikides, C., & Skowronski, J. J. (1990). Toward reconciling personality and social psychology: A construct accessibility approach. *Journal of Social Behavior and Personality, 5*, 531–546.

Sedikides, C., & Skowronski, J. J. (1991). The law of cognitive structure activation. *Psychology Inquiry, 2*, 169–184.

Seifert, C. M., McKoon, G., Abelson, R. P., & Ratcliff, R. (1986). Memory connections between thematically similar episodes. *Journal of Experimental Psychology: Learning, Memory, and Cognition, 12*, 220–231.

Shaver, P., & Rubenstein, C. (1980). Childhood attachment experience and adult loneliness. In L. Wheeler (Ed.), *Review of personality and social psychology* (Vol. 1, pp. 42–73). Beverly Hills, CA: Sage.

Simpson, J. A. (1990). Influence of attachment styles on romantic relationships. *Journal of Personality and Social Psychology, 59*, 971–980.

Singer, J. L. (1988). Reinterpreting the transference. In D. C. Turk & P. Salvey (Eds.), *Reasoning, inference, and judgment in clinical psychology* (pp. 182–205). New York: Free Press.

Smith, E. R., & Zarate, M. A. (1990). Exemplar and prototype use in social categorization. *Social Cognition, 8*, 243–262.

Smith, E. R., & Zarate, M. A. (1992). Exemplar-based model of social judgment. *Psychological Review, 99*, 3–21.

Snyder, M. (1992). Motivational foundations of behavioral confirmation. In M. P. Zanna (Ed.), *Advances in experimental social psychology* (Vol. 25, pp. 67–114). New York: Academy Press.

Snyder, M., & Swann, W. B., Jr. (1978a). Behavioral confirmation in social interaction: From social perception to social reality. *Journal of Experimental Social Psychology, 14*, 148–162.

Snyder, M., & Swann, W. B., Jr. (1978b). Hypothesis-testing processes in social interaction. *Journal of Personality and Social Psychology, 36*, 1202–1212.

Snyder, M., Tanke, E. D., & Berscheid, E. (1977). Social perception and interpersonal behavior. On the self-fulfilling nature of social stereotypes. *Journal of Personality and Social Psychology, 35*, 656–666.

Spellman, B. A., & Holyoak, B. A. (1992). If Saddam is Hitler, then who is George Bush? Analogical mapping between systems of social roles. *Journal of Personality and Social Psychology, 62*, 913–933.

Sroufe, L. A., & Fleeson, J. (1986). Attachment and the construction of relationships. In W. Hartup & Z. Rubin (Eds.), *Relationships and development* (pp. 51–71). Hillsdale, NJ: Erlbaum.

Srull, T. K. (1983). Organizational and retrieval processes in person memory: An examination of processing objectives, presentation format, and the possible role of self-generated retrieval cues. *Journal of Personality and Social Psychology, 44*, 1157–1170.

Strack, F., Martin, L. L., & Stepper, S. (1988). Inhibiting and facilitating conditions of the human smile: A nonobtrusive test of the facial feedback hypothesis. *Journal of Personality and Social Psychology, 54*, 768–777.

Sullivan, H. S. (1940). *Conceptions of modern psychiatry.* New York: Norton.

Sullivan, H. S. (1953). *The interpersonal theory of psychiatry.* New York: Norton.

Taylor, S. E. (1981). Categorization approach to stereotyping. In D. L. Hamilton (Ed.), *Cognitive processes in stereotyping and intergroup behavior* (pp. 83–114). Hillsdale, NJ: Erlbaum.

Tesser, A., Millar, M., & Moore, J. (1988). Some affective consequences of social comparison and reflection processes: The pain and pleasure of being close. *Journal of Personality and Social Psychology, 54*, 49–61.

Tomkins, S. S. (1962). *Affect, imagery, and consciousness: The negative effects* (Vol. 1). New York: Springer.

Tomkins, S. S. (1963). *Affect, imagery, and consciousness: The negative effects* (Vol. 2). New York: Springer.

Tourangeau, R., & Ellsworth, P. C. (1979). The role of facial response in the experience of emotion. *Journal of Personality and Social Psychology, 37*, 1519–1531.

Trope, Y., & Bassok, M. (1982). Confirmatory and diagnosing strategies in social information gathering. *Journal of Personality and Social Psychology, 43*, 22–34.

Tversky, A. (1977). Features of similarity. *Psychological Review, 84*, 327–352.

Wachtel, P. L. (1981). Transference, schema, and assimilation: The relevance of Piaget to the psychoanalytic theory of transference. *The Annual of Psychoanalysis, 8*, 59–76.

Westen, D. (1988). Transference and information processing. *Clinical Psychology Review, 8*, 161–179.

Wiggins, J. S. (1992). Agency and communion as conceptual coordinates for the understanding and measurement of interpersonal behavior. In W. M. Grove and D. Cicchetti (Eds.), *Thinking clearly about psychology* (pp. 89–113). Minneapolis: University of Minnesota Press.

Wilson, T. D., Lisle, D. J., Kraft, D., & Wetzel, C. G. (1989). Preferences as expectation-driven inferences: Effects of affective expectations on affective experience. *Journal of Personality and Social Psychology, 56*, 519–530.

Wyer, R. S., Jr., & Martin, L. L. (1986). Person memory: The role of traits, group stereotypes, and specific behaviors in the cognitive representation of persons. *Journal of Personality and Social Psychology, 50*, 661–675.

Zajonc, R. B. (1980). Feeling and thinking: Preferences need no inferences. *American Psychologist, 35*, 151–175.

Zajonc, R. B., & Markus, H. (1984). Affect and cognition: The hard interface. In C. E. Izard, J. Kagan, & R. B. Zajonc (Eds.), *Emotions, cognitions, and behavior* (pp. 73–102). Cambridge, England: Cambridge University Press.

Zajonc, R. B., Murphy, S. T., & Inglehart, M. (1989). Feeling and facial efference: Implications of the vascular theory of emotion. *Psychological Review, 96*, 395–416.

Zuckerman, M., & Lubin, B. (1965). *Manual for the Multiple Affect Adjective Check List.* San Diego: Educational and Institutional Testing Service.

Are There "His" and "Hers" Types of Interdependence? The Implications of Gender Differences in Collective Versus Relational Interdependence for Affect, Behavior, and Cognition

Shira Gabriel and Wendi L. Gardner • Northwestern University

In a recent review, S. E. Cross and L. Madson (1997) forwarded that many gender differences in social experience and behavior may be better understood through consideration of gender differences in independence and interdependence. In the current studies, an expansion of the model to include both relational and collective aspects of interdependence was investigated (see R. F. Baumeister & K. L. Sommer, 1997). On the basis of the literature regarding gender differences in affect, behavior, and cognition, it was hypothesized that women would focus more on the relational aspects of interdependence, whereas men would focus more on the collective aspects of interdependence. Five studies in which gender differences in self-construals, emotional experience, selective memory, and behavioral intentions were examined supported the expansion of the model to include both relational and collective aspects of interdependence.

The focus of gender research has recently begun to shift from documenting the existence and extent of gender differences to exploring the origin of those differences (Eagly, 1995). Numerous theories have been advanced to explain the documented gender differences in emotion, motivation, cognition, and social behavior. Prevalent in psychology are theories proposing that gender differences arise from and reflect status differences between men and women (e.g., Geis, 1993; Ridgeway & Diekema, 1992), arise from the different social roles that men and women have traditionally assumed (Eagly, 1987), and exist primarily in the context of social interaction (e.g., Deaux & Major, 1987; West & Zimmerman, 1991). Indeed, many developmental psychologists argue that to some extent children grow up in gender-segregated separate cultures in which different norms exist for social behavior. These different norms are then carried into adult social interaction (e.g., Hoffman, 1972; Maccoby, 1990; Maltz & Borker, 1982; Tannen, 1990).

Recently, Cross and Madson (1997) argued that many empirically demonstrated gender differences can be seen as reflecting fundamental differences in independence and interdependence. Specifically, it was argued that whereas men are relatively more independent, women are relatively more interdependent. Independent and interdependent individuals differ in the extent to which the self is defined as separate from, versus connected to, others (Markus & Kitayama, 1991).

Independent Versus Interdependent Self-Construals

An independent self-construal is thought to arise from a belief in the inherent separateness of individuals (Markus & Kitayama, 1991). The normative goal of an individual who is primarily independent has been posited to be "finding oneself," or discovering and expressing what makes one separate and unique from others (Baumeister, 1998). Accordingly, others are important as standards of reflected appraisals or sources of verification of the self (Markus & Kitayama, 1991).

In contrast, an interdependent self-construal is thought to arise from a belief in the fundamental embeddedness of every individual in a larger social whole (Markus & Kitayama, 1991; Triandis, 1989). The normative goal of interdependent individuals has been posited to be the formation and maintenance of social relationships and the fulfillment of one's place in larger society (Markus & Kitayama, 1991). Individuals with interdependent self-construals are most strongly defined in terms of the public aspects of their lives, with social relationships and roles forming the largest component of self-identity (Lebra, 1976; Markus & Kitayama, 1991). Through this emphasis on social relationships and roles in self-definition, others become directly linked with the self-concept.

For example, implicit in a self-definition of *mother* is the existence of a son or daughter.

Cross and Madson (1997) argued that American culture encourages the development of a more interdependent focus in women and of a more independent focus in men. They theorized that this interdependent focus is then reflected in affect, social behavior, and cognitive processing.

Are Women More Interdependent?

Gender differences in socialization have been detected from infancy onward (Bell & Carver, 1980; Culp, Cook, & Hourley, 1983; Shakin, Shakin, & Sternglanz, 1985). Not only are boys and girls socialized differently, but they are often socialized separately.[1] Children begin to be segregated by gender at a very young age and continue to interact in gender-segregated environments for much of childhood (Maccoby, 1988). Indeed, there is evidence that both parents and the public school system encourage gender-typed activities and sex segregation (Lytton & Romney, 1991; Thorne, 1986).

A great deal of evidence supports the premise that girls' socialization encourages them toward the interdependent tasks of forming and maintaining close relationships. For example, parents emphasize sensitivity to the feelings of others more with girls than with boys (Dunn, Bretherton, & Munn, 1987; Fivush, 1992). Girls' social interactions are characterized more by cooperation, intimate friendships, and efforts to maintain interpersonal harmony, whereas boys' interactions are instead more likely to be characterized by demonstrations of dominance and competitiveness (Maccoby, 1990). Finally, girls are more likely to form pair bonds and report intimacy as an important factor in forming relationships (Broderick & Beltz, 1996; Clark & Bittle, 1992; Jones & Costin, 1995). In sum, girls and boys are socialized differently and often separately; girls are encouraged to emphasize close relationships to a greater extent than boys.

---

[1] Throughout this article, we will refer to "boys" or "girls" if the research participants were under the age of 18.

Thus, it is no surprise that there is evidence that women's self-construals are more relational than men's. For example, when asked to spontaneously describe themselves, girls make more references to close relationships, whereas boys make more references to their general place among large groups of people (McGuire & McGuire, 1982). In an analysis of adolescent self-concept, Rosenberg (1989) found that girls were more likely to value characteristics that related to sensitivity to specific others and interpersonal harmony, whereas boys were more likely to value characteristics related to competitiveness and social dominance. These differences are evident in adults as well; women rate relational aspects of identity as more important to them than do men (Thoits, 1992).

Furthermore, in their review of the literature, Cross and Madson (1997) presented a compelling argument that many gender differences in affect, motivation, and cognition may be a reflection of women's greater interdependence, defined by Cross and Madson as a heightened concern with close relationships. For example, in their review of the literature concerning gender differences in affect, they cited evidence that women described interpersonal problems as a source of distress more than did men (Pratt, Golding, Hunter, & Sampson, 1988; Walker, de Vries, & Trevethan, 1987). Linking hypothesized gender differences in interdependence to motivation, Cross and Madson (1997) argued that in comparison with men, women's behavior was relatively more motivated by the goal of maintaining intimate relationships. They cited evidence that women were more likely to discuss interpersonal topics such as personal feelings and problems, whereas men were more likely to discuss less personal topics such as sports and politics (Aries & Johnson, 1983; Caldwell & Peplau, 1982; Davidson & Duberman, 1982; Fox, Gibbs, & Auerbach, 1985; Heatherington et al., 1993; Johnson & Aries, 1983; McFarland & Miller, 1990). Finally, in evaluating gender differences in cognition, Cross and Madson cited evidence that women attended to information related to relationships more than did men (Josephs, Markus, & Tafarodi, 1992; Ross & Holmberg, 1992) and

that men were more attuned to information related to social dominance (e.g., Maccoby, 1990; Sidanius, Pratto, & Bobo, 1994).

Are Men Less Interdependent?

Although American society may place relatively greater emphasis on the importance of relationships for women, it does not necessarily follow that interdependence, more broadly defined as an awareness and concern with one's connection with others, is unimportant for men. Indeed, an interpretation of men as decidedly noninterdependent would be difficult to reconcile with the thesis that belongingness is a fundamental human need (Baumeister & Leary, 1995). The need to belong has been described as a need for frequent, nonaversive interactions with others that is a characteristic of all human beings. For example, social deprivation affects mental health (Bowlby, 1969, 1973; Harlow, Harlow, & Suomi, 1971), physical health (Kiecolt-Glaser et al., 1984; see Gardner, Gabriel, & Diekman, in press, for review), and the likelihood of suicide (Trout, 1980) for both men and women. Is it possible to reconcile the fundamental importance of belongingness to human functioning with the clear evidence that men appear to be focused on relationships to a far lesser degree than women?

One possible reconciliation could be achieved through an expansion of Cross and Madson's (1997) model to include more than the relational aspect of interdependence; it is possible that men's interdependent needs may be fulfilled differently than women's. In their analysis of belonging as a basic human need, Baumeister and Leary (1995) argued that these needs might be filled in a number of interchangeable ways (i.e., the substitution postulate). Perhaps men and women fulfill their belongingness needs in different ways and thus are focused on different aspects of interdependence.

Brewer and Gardner (1996) described three distinct aspects of self-construal, two of which reflected an interdependent focus. The *personal aspect* was described as the self-construal derived from individual attributes and preferences (e.g., being athletic or intelligent). This aspect corresponds to the independent self as described by Markus and Kitayama (1991) and Cross and Madson (1997). The *relational aspect* of self-construal was described by Brewer and Gardner as being derived from close relationships with specific others (e.g., being Amanda's best friend or Ruben's daughter). This aspect corresponds to the aspect of the interdependent self focused on in Cross and Madson's review. Finally, the *collective aspect* was described as being derived from group memberships and affiliations (e.g., being an American or a member of the Alpha Alpha Alpha sorority). The collective aspect was also considered to reflect a more interdependent focus by Brewer and Gardner and is similar to the concept of social identity as described in both social identity theory and self-categorization theory (Hogg & Abrams, 1988; Turner, Hogg, Oakes, Reicher, & Wetherell, 1987).

The bulk of the literature cited by Cross and Madson (1997) addressed the relational aspect of interdependence, comparing goals, behavior, and emotions involving close, often dyadic relationships with those involving independence or individualism. In a comment on Cross and Madson (1997), Baumeister and Sommer (1997) expanded on Cross and Madson's theory to include the collective aspects of interdependence. Baumeister and Sommer offered an extension of Cross and Madson's analysis of gender differences by arguing that men have the same motivation for connectedness as women, but that motivation is expressed by having a higher number of large group associations instead of more intimate dyadic relationships. In other words, they posited that men and women do not differ in the importance of having an independent or interdependent focus per se, but rather in the aspect of interdependence that is important. Baumeister and Sommer argued that whereas women tend to invest in a number of close, often dyadic relationships, men tend toward investing in a larger sphere of social relationships. From Brewer and Gardner's (1996) perspective, then, women should maintain a more chronically accessible relational focus,

whereas men should maintain a more chronically accessible collective focus.

The expansion of interdependence to include both relational and collective aspects may be necessary to fully describe gender differences in self-construal and social behavior. If interdependence is limited to a focus on close relationships, then women undoubtedly appear to be more interdependent. As Cross and Madson (1997) argued, from an early age, women are more likely to define the self in terms of their close relationships and behave in ways that are supportive of those relationships. Men, on the other hand, do not define themselves in terms of close relationships as readily and often behave in ways that enhance personal status or success rather than in ways that maintain or deepen their relationships.

A reexamination of the literature that includes collective aspects of interdependence, however, reveals that men are strongly attuned toward these group aspects of social relations. For example, although girls tend to describe themselves more in terms of interdependent roles in close relationships, boys actually exceed girls in the collective aspect of interdependence; they describe themselves more in terms of group memberships than do girls (McGuire & McGuire, 1982). On the one hand, from an early age, boys are more likely to congregate in larger groups; for example, they tend to take part in sports activities that rely on teams (Maccoby, 1990). Boys have larger social networks than do girls (Belle, 1989; Berndt & Hoyle, 1985) and more coordinated group activities (Benenson, Apostoleris, & Parnass, 1997). Girls, on the other hand, are more likely to form pair bonds and report intimacy as being an important factor in forming relationships (Broderick & Beltz, 1996; Clark & Bittle, 1992; Jones & Costin, 1995). Indeed, even status- or dominance-oriented behaviors can be reinterpreted to reflect a collective orientation. Baumeister and Sommer (1997) argued that because large groups contain status differences, successful membership in collectives requires an awareness of those differences and a desire to acquire and maintain status. Therefore, many of the behaviors that Cross and Madson interpreted as reflecting chronically accessible independent focus in men could alternatively be seen as reflecting chronically accessible collective focus.

Overview of the Current Studies

The current research was designed to examine the relationship between interdependence and gender and to examine whether an expansion of interdependence to include both relational and collective aspects would be fruitful in understanding gender differences. Are men truly more independent than women, as might be predicted by Cross and Madson (1997)? Or instead, do men and women differ not in independence versus interdependence per se, but rather in the aspect of interdependence that is most valued, as suggested by Baumeister and Sommer (1997)? Finally, how might these differences be reflected in self-construals, emotional experiences, cognition, and social behavior?[2]

Study 1

Cross-cultural differences in independent and interdependent self-construals have commonly been examined using the Twenty Statements Test (Kuhn & McPartland, 1954). In this task, participants are asked to complete 20 statements beginning with the words "I am." Researchers have found that members of interdependent Eastern cultures complete the sentence fragments with more interdependent descriptors than do members of independent Western cultures. Similarly, members of independent Western cultures complete sentence fragments with more independent descriptors than do members of interdependent Eastern cultures (Cousins, 1989; Markus & Kitayama, 1991).

The first experiment was designed to examine any differences in men's and women's self-construals using the Twenty Statements Test (Kuhn

& McPartland, 1954). Male and female participants were asked to supply 20 statements describing themselves. The statements were then coded as describing independent, relational, or collective aspects of the self or as "non-self" (e.g., referring to transient states such as "I am hungry"). If men and women differ in a general emphasis on independence versus interdependence, then men should spontaneously supply more independent self-descriptors than women. However, if men and women differ instead in the aspect of interdependence that is emphasized, then men and women should supply equal numbers of independent self-construals, but men should supply more collective self-descriptors than women, and women should supply more relational self-descriptors than men.

Method

Participants. Participants were 18 male and 18 female European American undergraduates at a large midwestern university who participated in partial fulfillment of a research requirement.

Materials and procedure. Participants were asked to complete 20 sentence fragments beginning with the words "I am" (Kuhn & McPartland, 1954). Demographic information was then collected from the participants; they were debriefed and thanked for their participation.

Results and Discussion

The self-descriptors were coded by two independent coders who were blind to the experimental hypotheses. They coded the statements as being either independent (e.g., "I am intelligent"), relational (e.g., "I am the youngest daughter in my family"), collective (e.g., "I am in a sorority"), or non-self statements (e.g. "I am almost finished with this experiment"). The coders' evaluations matched on 92% of the judgments, with the remaining 8% resolved by discussion. Because of individual differences in the total number of self-descriptors supplied (range = 17–20), proportions for independent, collective, and relational self-descriptors were calculated by dividing the number of each type of self-descriptor by the total number of relevant self-descriptors. These proportions were then

---

[2]Because the focus of Cross and Madson's review was on members of Western culture, and because differences have been found in self-construal between Asian American and European American undergraduates (Gardner, Gabriel, & Lee, 1999), an attempt was made to study only European American participants. This was successful in all but the second study, in which demographic information pertaining to race was not collected.

arcsine transformed to correct for distributional skew. Proportions of relational and collective self-descriptors were summed to provide an index of general interdependent self-descriptors.

First, an analysis was performed on the proportion of interdependent descriptors overall. If men and women differ in their interdependence more generally, then women should spontaneously supply a greater proportion of self-descriptors that mention relationships and groups. A t test using gender was not significant, however ($p > .5$); men ($M = .17$, $SD = .12$) and women ($M = .19$, $SD = .13$) reported an equal number of general interdependent self-descriptors. Thus, there was no evidence that women maintained a more generally interdependent self-construal than did men.

In the next analysis, we examined the expanded model of interdependence by investigating gender differences in the aspect of interdependence that was emphasized in the self-descriptors. A 2 (gender: male, female) × 2 (type of interdependence: relational, collective) analysis of variance (ANOVA) was performed. A main effect was found for type of interdependent self-descriptor, $F(1, 34) = 11.56$, $p < .005$. Across all participants, a higher proportion of relational self-descriptors ($M = .12$, $SD = .90$) was supplied than collective self-descriptors ($M = .06$, $SD = .75$). Importantly, this main effect was qualified by a significant interaction with gender, $F(1, 34) = 13.44$, $p = .001$. As illustrated in Figure 23.1, whereas women provided a higher proportion of relational self-descriptors ($M = .16$, $SD = .90$) than did men ($M = .80$, $SD = .80$), men provided a higher proportion of collective self-descriptors ($M = .80$, $SD = .80$) than did women ($M = .40$, $SD = .50$). These results suggest that the self-construals of men and women differed not in whether they were generally more independent or interdependent, but rather in a differential emphasis on the aspect of interdependence that was most important.

In sum, the findings of Study 1 supported the expanded model of interdependence and Baumeister and Sommer's (1997) hypothesis that men and women possess different foci for their interdependence. Participants in this study showed no

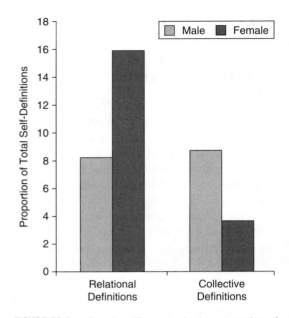

FIGURE 23.1 ■ Gender differences in the proportion of relational and collective self-definitions.

gender differences in the overall proportions of interdependent self-construals that were generated, but did show differences in the type of interdependent self-construals that were generated. Consistent with Cross and Madson's (1997) review, women provided a greater number of self-definitions that included close relationships. However, as Baumeister and Sommer (1997) might have predicted, men provided a greater number of self-definitions that included group memberships, implying that the collective aspect of interdependence may have been more important for them than for women. Importantly, neither men nor women were provided predominantly more interdependent self-descriptors: Most self-descriptors were independent in nature. This is consistent with findings that independence is the default self-construal for both male and female Americans (Gardner, Gabriel, & Lee, 1999).

Although these findings supporting the expanded model of gender differences in interdependence were intriguing, the question of whether and how these differences might be reflected in other gender differences remained. Studies 2 and

3 were therefore designed to assess whether the differences found in men's and women's interdependent self-construals would be mirrored in differences in affect, cognition, and behavioral intentions.

Study 2

Study 2 was designed to investigate gender differences in selective memory for social information. Past research has consistently demonstrated that constructs important to the self often guide information processing and that information relevant to those constructs will be shown a memorial advantage (Gardner, Pickett, & Brewer, in press; Higgins & Tykocinski, 1992; Markus, Smith, & Moreland, 1985). For example, Higgins and Tykocinski (1992), using a "diary" reading paradigm, showed that an individual's chronic self-guides changed the type of information that was later recalled about a target person. Using an adaptation of Higgins and Tykocinski's diary paradigm, Gardner, Pickett, et al. (in press) demonstrated that participants whose need to belong had been temporarily heightened as a result of social rejection selectively remembered more social and fewer individual events from a student's diary. Thus, this selective memory paradigm appears to be sensitive to both chronic and situationally induced processing biases.

This diary-reading paradigm was used for assessing selective memory: Diary entries containing independent, relational, and collective information were presented to participants who were later given an unanticipated recall task. We expected consistent gender differences in selective memory despite the equal frequencies with which the independent, relational, and collective information was presented. Specifically, if men and women were attuned toward the aspects of the social environment that reflected or fulfilled their interdependence needs, then we would expect no gender differences in recall of the independent events, but women would show selective memory for the relational events, and men, for the collective events.

Method

Participants. Participants were 49 male and 47 female undergraduates at a large midwestern university who participated for partial fulfillment of a research requirement.

Materials and procedure. Participants read a computerized "diary" of a student ostensibly as part of an impression formation experiment. The gender of the diary writer was matched to that of the participant. Thus, the content of the diaries was the same for men and women, except women believed the diary was written by a women, whereas men believed it was written by a man. Therefore, any gender references (e.g., fraternities vs. sororities) were gender matched.

Participants were presented with four pages from the diary on a computer screen and were asked to read the events of the diary slowly and carefully in order to form an impression of the person about whom they were reading. After 25 s, participants were free to move to the next screen (i.e., the next page of the diary) by pressing the space bar. Thus, the task was self-paced. Each page contained 6 relevant diary entries presented in a random order on the page; of these entries, 2 described independent behaviors that dealt with events irrelevant to intimate relationships or collectives (e.g., "I went to the dentist and had 3 cavities—ugh"), 2 described relational behaviors (e.g., "My roommate and I went out on the town tonight and had a really great time together"), and 2 described collective behaviors (e.g., "All of us in my fraternity [sorority] have been working really hard on the Greek Week Community Drive—and today we placed first out of all the Greek organizations!").[3] Thus, participants read a total of 8 diary entries of each type and 24 entries in all (see Appendix A for exact items).

The events in the diary were selected to be relatively gender neutral in importance; the relational events dealt with roommates, friends, and romantic partners, and the collective events dealt with campus groups, Greek organizations, and

---

[3]The diary entries were also balanced across valence, with equal numbers of positive and negative behaviors of each type.

college affiliations. For example, a group of five undergraduate student raters did not perceive a man to be more likely than a woman to belong to a student chorus or a Greek organization nor a woman to be more likely than a man to spend time with a roommate or go on vacation with a brother. Finally, where it seemed we could not avoid some differential gender appropriateness in behaviors, we ensured that they were gender matched in both the relational and collective sets (e.g., although one collective item dealt with the diary writer being excited about the university's basketball team going to a championship playoff, which may be seen as more "male," it was matched by a collective item concerning a fear that the student choir was angry at the diary writer, which may be seen as more "female"). All of this ensured that any differences in recall could not be attributed to the fit between an item and the gender of the imaginary diary writer.

After completing the diary task, participants completed two filler tasks. The first task was a brief questionnaire that asked a series of questions concerning their experience with the computer (e.g., did they feel rushed, was it difficult to read the behaviors on the screen?). Participants were given 4 min to answer the items on that questionnaire. Next, in what they were told was a test of verbal abilities, participants were given 8 min to create as many words as possible from the words *crustacean* and *librarian*. After both filler tasks were completed (taking 12 min total), participants were given a surprise memory task in which they were asked to recall as many of the items from the diary as possible.

Results and Discussion

Each participant's total number of items remembered was tallied, and the numbers of independent, relational, and collective items recalled were recorded separately.[4] To correct for any individual

differences in memorial ability, we calculated proportions by dividing the number recalled of each type of event (independent, relational, collective) by the total number of events recalled. Thus, indexes were created for each participant that reflected the proportion of an individual's memory of the diary that was relegated to independent, relational, and collective events. The proportions of relational and collective events were summed to provide an index of the proportion of general interdependent events recalled. Analyses were performed on arcsine transformed data to correct for any skew in the proportions.

To determine whether men and women differed in their overall memory for the general interdependent events, we conducted a t test comparing the recall of men and women for these events. This test was nonsignificant ($p > .5$; $Ms = .70$ vs. .67, $SDs = .12$ vs. .11, for men vs. women, respectively).

To evaluate whether men and women differed in the type of interdependent items remembered, we performed a 2 (gender) $\times$ 2 (interdependent event: relational, collective) ANOVA. A main effect was found for the type of interdependent event recalled, $F(1, 94) = 67.44$, $p < .001$, revealing that relational items ($M = .42$, $SD = .11$) had an advantage in memory as compared with collective items ($M = .27$, $SD = .10$). Importantly, this effect was qualified by a significant interaction with gender, $F(1, 94) = 8.93$, $p < .005$. As Figure 23.2 illustrates, women showed relatively greater selective memory than did men for the relational events ($Ms = .44$ vs. .40, $SDs = .13$ vs. .10, respectively), whereas men showed relatively greater selective memory than women for the collective events ($Ms = .30$ vs. .24, $SDs = .10$ vs. .08, respectively). Once again, the aspects of interdependence that were differentially important for women's and men's self-construals were mirrored in their perceptions and representations of the social world.

In sum, the results of Study 2 were consistent with predictions. No gender differences were found in selective memory for independent items, but gender affected the type of interdependent items that were recalled. As predicted, women

[4]Because of the objective and clear-cut nature of the recall task, a simple tally by one person is sufficient. The research assistant, who was blind to the experimental hypothesis, merely counted the behaviors of each type that were recalled.

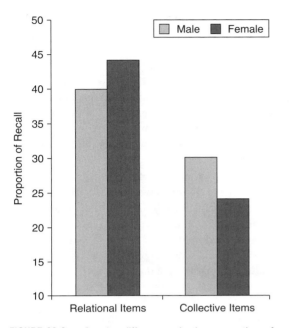

FIGURE 23.2 ■ Gender differences in the proportion of recall relegated to the relational and collective items of another student's diary.

recalled a greater proportion of the relational events than did men; likewise, men recalled a greater proportion of the collective events than did women. As selective memory differences such as these have been interpreted in the past to reflect differences in the chronic or situational representation of the self (Higgins & Tykocinski, 1992), these results are consistent with Study 1, which showed that men and women differ in the emphasis placed on relational versus collective aspects of identity. Further, these results imply that the gender differences in the aspects of interdependence that are emphasized by men and women may act as filters on perceptions of the social world. Because of higher relational interdependence, women may be more likely to attend to and remember information relevant to relationships. Similarly, because of higher collective interdependence, men may be more likely to attend to and remember information that is relevant to groups.

Thus, the first two studies demonstrated that men and women differ in the extent to which they are relational and collective and in terms of their memory for relational and collective emotional events and controlled information. Although these studies have presented a consistent and compelling demonstration of gender differences in interdependent focus, there is one important component that has not yet been addressed, a component that may indeed be at the very heart of interdependence: a willingness to put the good of others above the good of the self.

Study 3

The final study was designed to explore whether gender differences in behavioral intentions would also mirror gender differences in interdependence. Male and female participants were asked how they would behave in situations in which the well-being of others (either a close friend or an important group) was in conflict with their own personal well-being. Given the outcome of the first two studies, we predicted that both genders would be equally likely to indicate that they would benefit themselves overall, but men should be more likely to indicate that they would benefit a collective, and women, a close friend.

Method

Participants. Participants were 68 male and 69 female undergraduates at a large midwestern university who participated on a voluntary basis.

Materials and procedure. Participants were approached in the student union at Northwestern University. The experimenter approached all individuals seated alone. Participants were asked if they would be willing to assist in a research project by reading two scenarios and answering two questions about each scenario. They were told that participation would take about 5 min. Approximately 80% of the people approached agreed to participate.

Participants read two brief scenarios in which they were asked to imagine that they were in a particular situation and that they had to decide what they would feel like doing (desire to behave) and what they would do (behavioral intention). The scenarios were generated with the assistance of two Northwestern undergraduates and were then screened by a group of five Northwestern undergraduates, who were asked to choose those scenarios that best reflected a collective versus a relational dilemma. The behavioral intention question was included to see under what circumstances men and women would neglect their own desires for the good of others.

In addition, it was essential to establish that all of the behaviors (independent, relational, and collective) would be equally compelling and attractive to both men and women. Otherwise, gender differences in behavioral intention might not reflect gender differences in the willingness to put the good of others above the good of the self but gender differences in attractiveness of behaviors. For example, if going to a concert was simply more desirable for one gender than the other, then helping a friend instead of going to a concert might reflect differences in the evaluation of the concert rather than differences in the desire to put the good of others in front of the good of the self. Two methods were used to establish that the behaviors were equally compelling for men and women. First, 25 Northwestern undergraduates (12 women and 13 men) rated their desire to perform the four behaviors (the two independent behaviors and the relational and collective behaviors) independently, that is, when a forced choice was not required between the self and others (e.g., they were asked to rate the desirability of attending a concert by their favorite band). Two repeated measures ANOVAs revealed that the men and women did not differ in how desirable they found the independent and relational events involved in the relational dilemma ($F = .23$) or the independent and collective events involved in the collective dilemma ($F = .30$). Thus, we could be confident that any difference in behavioral intention would be due to gender differences in willingness to put relations or collectives before the self as opposed to gender differences in the desirability of the behaviors. Second, a desire-to-behave question was included in the actual study as an additional check on the attractiveness of behaviors.

The first scenario pitted the good of the individual against the good of a collective. Participants were asked to imagine that they were guarding "the rock" for an organization to which they belonged, and although their shift was over and they had to attend an important review session for a class, their replacement had not shown up. The rock is a well-known rock on campus that university organizations can paint to publicize upcoming events, and dominance of the rock is highly valued by campus organizations. Use of the rock can be reserved ahead of time, but can also be "stolen" by other organizations if left unguarded. Thus, the individual would need to decide between staying and guarding the rock or going to a review session for an exam in a class they desperately needed help in.

The second scenario pitted the good of the individual against the good of a close friend. Participants were asked to imagine that they were on the way to a highly anticipated concert when they spotted a close friend standing on the side of the road next to a car with its hood up. They had to decide whether to stop and drive their friend (who had not seen them) to a service station 20 miles back (and thus miss much of the concert) or attend the concert. After reading each scenario, participants indicated on a 7-point scale ranging from 1 (*benefiting the self*) to 7 (*benefiting others*) which behavior they would be most likely to do (behavioral intention) and which they would feel more like doing (desire to behave). Participants were then debriefed and thanked for their participation with a piece of candy.

Results and Discussion

If men and women differed in independence, then men would be more likely to choose goals that benefited themselves rather than goals that benefited others. To evaluate that possibility, we averaged the responses to both scenarios, and two independent sample t tests were performed on behavioral intention and desire to behave. No differences were found between men and women in either behavioral intention ($p > .9$; $M = 4.31$ and 4.34, $SDs = 1.45$ and $.99$, respectively) or the desire to behave ($p > .4$; $M = 4.02$ and 4.13, $SDs = 1.45$ and 1.30, respectively). Therefore, there were no overall differences between male and female participants in general desire or intention to benefit the self over others.

To ensure that the scenarios presented were equally compelling for men and women, we performed a 2 (gender of participant) × 2 (type of scenario: collective or relational) ANOVA on desire to behave. A main effect was found for type of scenario, $F(1, 114) = 22.71$, $p < .001$. Overall, participants felt more like benefiting themselves in the collective dilemma ($M = 3.2$, $SD = 1.98$) than in the relational dilemma ($M = 4.5$, $SD = 2.07$). This might have been due to students at an academically oriented university evaluating the consequences of receiving a low grade on an exam. Importantly, the interaction between gender of participant and type of behavior was not significant ($p > .85$). Men and women did not differ in the degree to which they felt like benefiting themselves versus others in either the collective or the relational dilemma (for men vs. women, respectively: in the collective dilemma, $Ms = 3.12$ vs. 3.24, $SDs = 2.06$ vs. 1.91; in the relational dilemma, $Ms = 4.40$ vs. 4.60, $SDs = 2.08$ vs. 2.08). This supports our pretest data, which indicated that the scenarios were equally compelling for both men and women.

To determine whether men and women would differ in their actual behavioral intentions, we performed a 2 (gender of participant) × 2 (type of scenario: collective or relational) ANOVA on behavioral intention. A main effect was found for type of scenario, $F(1, 114) = 167.84$, $p < .001$. Overall, participants indicated that they would be more likely to behave in a manner that would benefit themselves in the collective dilemma ($M = 2.91$, $SD = 1.9$) than in the relational dilemma ($M = 5.73$, $SD = 1.53$). Once again, this may be due to students at an academically oriented university evaluating the consequences of receiving a low grade on an exam. More importantly, the interaction between gender of participant and type of behavior was significant, $F(1, 114) = 5.32$, $p < .05$. As illustrated in Figure 23.3, men were more likely than women to place the good of the group above personal gain in the collective dilemma ($Ms = 3.15$ vs. 2.67, $SDs = 2.04$ vs. 1.73, respectively), whereas women were more likely than

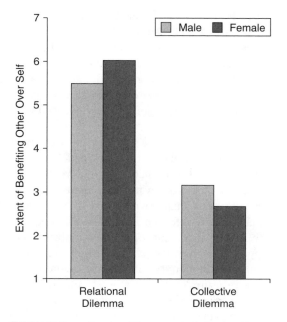

FIGURE 23.3 ■ Gender differences in behavioral intentions to place the good of others before personal gain in relational and collective dilemmas.

men to place the good of their friend over personal gain in the relational dilemma ($Ms = 6.0$ vs. 5.47, $SDs = 1.23$ vs. 1.75, respectively).

To summarize, when put in a behavioral dilemma, men and women did not differ in their general intentions to behave in ways that would benefit themselves versus benefit others. However, women were more likely than men to put their own personal desires aside to assist a friend, whereas men were more likely to put their personal desires aside to help their group. The findings of this study thus imply that gender differences in the relational and collective interdependence are mirrored in behavioral intentions.

General Discussion

We began this research wishing to examine whether an expansion of interdependence to include both relational and collective aspects would add to the prior research concerning gender differences in interdependence. This expansion appears to be a fruitful avenue for understanding the different ways in which men and women view themselves in relation to the larger social world. Across three studies, we found consistent evidence that implied that men and women differ not in a focus on independence versus interdependence per se, but rather in the aspect of interdependence that is focused upon.

Importantly, this work represents an expansion rather than a rejection of Cross and Madson's (1997) model. Recall that Cross and Madson hypothesized that women maintain more relational self-construals than do men and that this relational focus is reflected in gender differences in affect, motivation, and cognition. All three studies supported this hypothesis. Women indeed describe themselves in more relational terms, score higher on a measure of the relational self-construal, report more emotional experiences linked to relationships, appear attuned to information pertaining to the relationships of others, and are motivated to behave in ways that maintain close relationships. The data also clearly point out the fruitful nature of the expansion of the model to include the collective aspect of interdependence proposed by Baumeister and Sommer (1997). Men describe themselves in more collective terms, score higher on a measure of collective self-construal, report more emotional experiences linked to groups, appear attuned to information pertaining to the group memberships of others, and are motivated to behave in ways that support their groups. Furthermore, our data also support Baumeister and Sommer's contention that men and women do not differ in their emphasis on independence: No gender differences were detected in overall interdependence versus independence in any of the studies. Thus, the findings are also parsimonious with previous findings that individualistic dimensions of the self often show cultural but not gender differences, whereas relational aspects of the self often show gender but not cultural differences (Kashima et al., 1995).

The differences in men's and women's interdependence can be readily understood through a social roles interpretation of gender differences (Eagly, 1987). Women's social roles of raising children emphasize relationships. Conversely, men's traditional social roles, such as fighting in wars and working outside the home, may be roles that emphasize groups or collectives. Women's and men's predominance in those roles should cause them to be seen as more relational and collective, respectively. Because people often comply with societal expectations (Eagly, 1987), the differing social roles may explain why women emphasize more relational and men more collective aspects of the social environment.

Although social role theory makes an interesting and compelling argument, evolutionary theory is also consistent with gender differences in aspects of interdependence. For example, women who possessed better relational skills may have been better equipped to care for and protect offspring, and thus their offspring may have had increased odds of survival. Further, Tiger (1969) argued that survival in early societies would necessitate men bonding in task-oriented groups so they could coordinate the complex task of hunting for large prey. That type of large-group bonding may have made it more likely that men would retain genetic tendencies toward group loyalty and collective skills.

In an elaboration of the evolutionary argument, Baumeister and Sommer (1997) argued that relational skills in women and collective skills in men would be beneficial in attracting mates, a primary component of evolutionary theory. The central tenet to their theory was that traditionally, men have acquired status through their place in a larger society. Men with a more collective orientation would be better able to acquire that status. Because status increases men's access to women (Buss, 1995), men with a more collective orientation would have had greater access to women. Women, however, traditionally acquired status through connections to men who had status in society. Therefore, intimate relationships with men both increased a woman's reproductive success and imbued her with power. In addition, men remained in their groups or tribes for life, whereas women changed groups with marriage. Thus, men's success would have depended on their skills in negotiating a social network that surrounded them throughout life, whereas women's success would have depended on their bond to their husband, their primary link to the larger society to which they belonged.

We find both the social roles explanation and the evolutionary account of the gender differences in self-construal and social behavior compelling and intuitively appealing. Future research would be necessary to better identify both the evolutionary and the cultural contributions. We suspect that, as with many social behaviors, both evolutionary and cultural factors may play a role in establishing the gender differences in relational and collective orientations.

Regardless of the underlying causes for the gender difference in interdependence, the implications of that difference are quite compelling. For example, Baumeister and Sommer (1997), in their analysis of the literature, outlined how gender differences in aggression and altruism might be explained by differences in the aspects of interdependence that are emphasized by men and women. A more relational orientation would inhibit direct aggression because direct aggression could hamper (to say the least) a close relationship. However, aggressive behavior may be used to establish status or maintain position in a large collective and thus could be beneficial for an individual with a collective orientation. Likewise, research on altruism has demonstrated that men are more likely than women to help a stranger (Eagly & Crowley, 1986). Baumeister and Sommer argued that the "stranger" often used in the literature is frequently a fellow member of a collective, such as another student at the same university, an age cohort, or a gender-matched person. If strangers are often seen as members of the same collective, then the gender difference in helping behavior can be interpreted as men being more likely than women to help group members, precisely the difference we found in behavioral intentions in Study 3.

In sum, an acknowledgment of gender differences in the importance of different aspects of interdependence may lead to a greater understanding of the ways in which men and women view the social world. This expansion of interdependence to include aspects that men value highly represents

the largest departure of the current theory from conventional theories of gender differences. The analysis of women as being highly relational is central to many theories of gender difference and has enjoyed broad acceptance (e.g., Cross & Madson, 1997; Eagly, 1987; Markus & Oyserman, 1989). It is the treatment of men as being more collective than women that is new and thus has the potential for providing new insights.

The desire to be connected and intimate with other people is primary and essential to the human experience (Baumeister & Leary, 1995). The present research has established that this important component of existence, interdependence, is different for men and women: Women are more focused on the close relationships that they are part of, whereas men are more focused on the groups to which they belong. We believe that understanding these differences in how men and women view themselves and their relationships to others has the potential to illuminate more of the mechanisms that contribute to a wide array of gender differences in social behavior.

NOTES

Authorship on this article was determined alphabetically. We thank Roy Baumeister, Susan Cross, and Alice Eagly for their comments on a draft of this article. We also thank Molly Roebuck for her invaluable assistance in data collection and entry.

Correspondence concerning this article should be addressed to Shira Gabriel or Wendi L. Gardner, Department of Psychology, Northwestern University, 2029 Sheridan Road, Evanston, Illinois 60208-2710. Electronic mail may be sent to s-gabriel@nwu.edu or to wgardner@nwu.edu.

REFERENCES

Aries, E. J., & Johnson, F. L. (1983). Close friendship in adulthood: Conversational content between same-sex friends. *Sex Roles, 9*, 1183–1196.

Baumeister, R. F. (1998). The self. In D. Gilbert & S. Fiske (Eds.), *Handbook of social psychology* (4th ed., Vol. 2, pp. 680–740). Boston: McGraw-Hill.

Baumeister, R. F., & Leary, M. R. (1995). The need to belong: Desire for interpersonal attachments as a fundamental human motivation. *Psychological Bulletin, 117*, 497–529.

Baumeister, R. F., & Sommer, K. L. (1997). What do men want? Gender differences and two spheres of belongingness: Comment on Cross and Madson. *Psychology Bulletin, 122*, 38–44.

Bell, N. J., & Carver, W. (1980). A reevaluation of gender label effects: Expectant mothers' responses to infants. *Child Development, 51*, 925–927.

Belle, D. (1989). Gender differences in children's social networks and supports. In D. Belle (Ed.), *Children's social networks and social supports* (pp. 173–188). New York: Wiley.

Benenson, J. F., Apostoleris, N. H., & Parnass, J. (1997). Age and sex differences in dyadic and group interaction. *Developmental Psychology, 33*, 538–543.

Berndt, T. J., & Hoyle, S. G. (1985). Stability and change in childhood and adolescent friendships. *Developmental Psychology, 21*, 1007–1015.

Bowlby, J. (1969). *Attachment and loss: Vol. 1*. New York: Basic Books.

Bowlby, J. (1973). *Attachment and loss: Vol. 2*. New York: Basic Books.

Brewer, M. B., & Gardner, W. (1996). Who is this "we"? Levels of collective identity and self representations. *Journal of Personality and Social Psychology, 71*, 83–93.

Broderick, P. C., & Beltz, C. M. (1996). The contribution of self-monitoring and gender to preadolescents' friendship expectations. *Social Behavior and Personality, 24*, 35–45.

Buss, D. M. (1995). Evolutionary psychology: A new paradigm for psychological science. *Psychological Inquiry, 6*, 1–30.

Caldwell, M., & Peplau, L. (1982). Sex differences in same-sex friendships. *Sex Roles, 8*, 721–732.

Clark, M. L., & Bittle, M. L. (1992). Friendship expectations and the evaluation of present friendships in middle childhood and early adolescence. *Child Study Journal, 22*, 115–135.

Cousins, S. (1989). Culture and self-perception in Japan and the United States. *Journal of Personality and Social Psychology, 56*, 124–131.

Cross, S. E., & Madson, L. (1997). Models of the self: Self-construals and gender. *Psychological Bulletin, 122*, 5–37.

Culp, R. E., Cook, A. S., & Hourley, P. C. (1983). A comparison of observed and reported adult–infant interactions: Effects of perceived sex. *Sex Roles, 9*, 475–479.

Davidson, L., & Duberman, L. (1982). Friendship: Communication and interaction patterns in same-sex dyads. *Sex Roles, 8*, 809–822.

Deaux, K., & Major, B. (1987). Putting gender into context: An interactive model of gender-related behavior. *Psychological Review, 94*, 369–389.

Dunn, J., Bretherton, I., & Munn, P. (1987). Conversations about feeling states between mothers and their young children. *Developmental Psychology, 23*, 132–139.

Eagly, A. H. (1987). *Sex differences in social behavior: A social-role interpretation*. Hillsdale, NJ: Erlbaum.

Eagly, A. H. (1995). The science and politics of comparing women and men. *American Psychologist, 50*, 145–158.

Eagly, A. H., & Crowley, M. (1986). Gender and helping behavior: A meta-analytic review of the social psychological literature. *Psychological Bulletin, 100*, 283–308.

Fivush, R. (1992). Gender differences in parent–child conversations about past emotions. *Sex Roles, 27*, 683–698.

Fox, M., Gibbs, M., & Auerbach, D. (1985). Age and gender dimensions of friendship. *Psychology of Women Quarterly, 9*, 489–501.

Gardner, W. L., Gabriel, S., & Diekman, A. (in press). Interpersonal processes. In L. Tassinary, J. Cacioppo, & G. Berntson (Eds.), *The handbook of psychophysiology*. Cambridge, England: Cambridge University Press.

Gardner, W. L., Gabriel, S., & Lee, A. (1999). "I" value freedom, but "we" value relationships: Self-construal priming mimics cultural differences in judgment. *Psychological Science, 4*, 321–326.

Gardner, W. L., Pickett, C., & Brewer, M. B. (in press). Social exclusion and selective memory: How the "need to belong" influences memory for social events. *Personality and Social Psychology Bulletin*.

Geis, F. L. (1993). Self-fulfilling prophecies: A social psychological view of gender. In A. E. Beall & R. J. Sternberg (Eds.), *The psychology of gender* (pp. 9–54). New York: Guilford Press.

Harlow, H. F., Harlow, M. K., & Suomi, S. J. (1971). From thought to therapy: Lessons from a primate laboratory. *American Scientist, 59*, 538–549.

Heatherington, L., Daubman, K. A., Bates, C., Ahn, A., Brown, H., & Preston, C. (1993). Two investigations of "female modesty" in achievement situations. *Sex Roles, 29*, 739–754.

Higgins, E. T., & Tykocinski, O. (1992). Self-discrepancies and biographical memory: Personality and cognition at the level of psychological situation. *Personality and Social Psychology Bulletin, 18*, 527–535.

Hoffman, L. W. (1972). Early childhood experiences and women's achievement motives. *Journal of Social Issues, 28*, 129–155.

Hogg, M. A., & Abrams, D. (1988). *Social identifications: A social psychology of intergroup relations and group processes*. London: Routledge.

Johnson, F. L., & Aries, E. J. (1983). Conversation patterns among same-sex pairs of late-adolescent close friends. *Journal of Genetic Psychology, 142*, 225–238.

Jones, D. C., & Costin, S. E. (1995). Friendship quality during preadolescence and adolescence: The contributions of relationship orientations, instrumentality, and expressivity. *Merrill-Palmer Quarterly, 41*, 517–535.

Josephs, R. A., Markus, H. R., & Tafarodi, R. W. (1992). Gender and self-esteem. *Journal of Personality and Social Psychology, 63*, 391–402.

Kashima, Y., Yamaguchi, S., Kim, U., Choi, S., Gelfand, M., & Yuki, M. (1995). Culture, gender, and self: A perspective from individualism–collectivism research. *Journal of Personality and Social Psychology, 69*, 925–937.

Kiecolt-Glaser, J. K., Garner, W., Speicher, C., Penn, G. M., Holliday, J., & Glaser, R. (1984). Psychosocial modifiers of immunocompetence in medical students. *Psychosomatic Medicine, 49*, 13–34.

Kuhn, M. H., & McPartland, T. (1954). An empirical investigation of self-attitudes. *American Sociological Review, 19*, 58–76.

Lebra, T. S. (1976). *Japanese patterns of behavior*. Honolulu: University of Hawaii Press.

Lytton, H., & Romney, D. M. (1991). Parents' differential socialization of boys and girls: A meta-analysis. *Psychological Bulletin, 109*, 267–296.

Maccoby, E. E. (1988). Gender as a social category. *Developmental Psychology, 24*, 513–520.

Maccoby, E. E. (1990). Gender and relationships. *American Psychologist, 45*, 513–520.

Maltz, D. N., & Borker, R. A. (1982). A cultural approach to male–female miscommunication. In J. J. Gumperz (Ed.), *Language and social identity* (pp. 195–216). New York: Cambridge University Press.

Markus, H., & Kitayama, S. (1991). Culture and the self: Implications for cognition, emotion, and motivation. *Psychological Review, 98*, 224–252.

Markus, H., & Oyserman, D. (1989). Gender and thought: The role of self-concept. In M. Crawford & M. Gentry (Eds.), *Gender and thought: Psychological perspectives* (pp. 100–127). New York: Springer-Verlag.

Markus, H., Smith, J., & Moreland, R. L. (1985). Role of the self-concept in the perception of others. *Journal of Personality and Social Psychology, 49*, 1494–1512.

McFarland, C., & Miller, D. T. (1990). Judgments of self–other similarity: Just like other people, only more so. *Journal of Personality and Social Psychology, 16*, 475–484.

McGuire, W. J., & McGuire, C. V. (1982). Significant others in self space: Sex differences and developmental trends in social self. In J. Suls (Ed.), *Psychological perspectives on the self* (Vol. 1, pp. 71–96). Hillsdale, NJ: Erlbaum.

Pratt, M. W., Golding, G., Hunter, W., & Sampson, R. (1988). Sex differences in adult moral orientations. *Journal of Personality and Social Psychology, 56*, 373–391.

Ridgeway, C. L., & Diekema, D. (1992). Are gender differences status differences? In C. L. Ridgeway (Ed.), *Gender, interaction, and inequality* (pp. 157–180). New York: Springer-Verlag.

Rosenberg, M. (1989). The self-concept: Social product and social force. In M. Rosenberg & R. H. Turner (Eds.), *Social psychology: Sociological perspectives* (pp. 593–624). New York: Basic Books.

Ross, M., & Holmberg, D. (1992). Are wives' memories for events in relationships more vivid than their husbands' memories? *Journal of Social and Personal Relationships, 9*, 585–604.

Shakin, M., Shakin, D., & Sternglanz, S. H. (1985). Infant clothing: Sex labeling for strangers. *Sex Roles, 12*, 955–964.

Sidanius, J., Pratto, F., & Bobo, L. (1994). Social dominance orientation and the political psychology of gender: A case of invariance? *Journal of Personality and Social Psychology, 67*, 998–1011.

Tannen, D. (1990). *You just don't understand: Women and men in conversation*. New York: Morrow.

Thoits, P. A. (1992). Identity structures and psychological well-being: Gender and marital status comparisons. *Social Psychology Quarterly, 55*, 236–256.

Thorne, B. (1986). Girls and boys together ... but mostly apart: Gender arrangements in elementary schools. In W. W. Hartup & Z. Rubin (Eds.), *Relationships and development* (pp. 167–184). Hillsdale, NJ: Erlbaum.

Tiger, L. (1969). *Men in groups*. London, England: Nelson.

Triandis, H. C. (1989). The self and social behavior in differing cultural contexts. *Psychological Review, 96*, 506–520.

Trout, D. L. (1980). The role of social isolation in suicide. *Suicide and Life-Threatening Behavior, 10*, 10–23.

Turner, J. C., Hogg, M., Oakes, P., Reicher, S., & Wetherell, M. (1987). *Rediscovering the social group: A self-categorization theory*. Oxford, England: Basil Blackwell.

Walker, L. J., de Vries, B., & Trevethan, S. D. (1987). Moral stages and moral orientations in real-life and hypothetical dilemmas. *Child Development, 58*, 842–858.

West, C., & Zimmerman, D. H. (1991). Doing gender. In J. Lorber & S. A. Farrell, *The social construction of gender* (pp. 13–37). Newbury Park, CA: Sage.

Appendix A

Independent, Relational, and Collective Diary Entries From Study 2

Day 1

My girlfriend [boyfriend] totally flirted with someone else tonight and practically ignored me. I don't know how seriously I should take it.

My intramural soccer team won its final game in the regular season—now we get to compete for the intramural championship.

I received the highest grade in the class on my English paper.

I went to the post office and bought stamps so I could mail out the rent check.

I received a package in the mail from my brother, and it was full of these hilarious pictures from our last vacation together.

I got a haircut I absolutely can't stand.

My Irish heritage is really important to me, but when I went to the student Irish Association they acted like I didn't really belong there, like they thought I didn't fit in.

Day 2

I went to the dentist and had 3 cavities—ugh.

My roommate and I went out on the town tonight and had a really great time together.

I bought an instant lottery ticket and won $19.

My best friend blew me off. We had made weekend plans, but I guess he [she] just totally ignored them.

I forgot to bring the music for a really important practice session for the student choir I sing in (we're going to competition soon)—boy, was everyone mad at me.

I went to the grocery store.

I was elected as one of just a few brothers [sisters] in my fraternity [sorority] to represent us on the Greek council.

Day 3

My roommate and I got into an argument tonight over the room being such a mess—I don't know if we're ever going to stop fighting about the same old stuff.

A $5 bill fell out of my pocket and blew away before I could grab it.

I rode the bus in to work.

I have been running for only a few weeks, but today I ran 2 miles and wasn't even really winded.

I'm usually pretty proud to be a college student, but I was reading an editorial in the student paper—it seems that no matter how hard we try, my university just gets no respect in the business world.

It occurred to me today that my relationship with my girlfriend [boyfriend] is going pretty well—we seem happier than most couples.

All of us in my fraternity [sorority] have been working really hard on the Greek Week Community Drive—and today we placed first out of all the Greek organizations!

Day 4

My fraternity [sorority] did really terribly in the Greek Week skit night—in fact, we probably came in dead last.

I took a long and peaceful walk in the beautiful weather today.

My best friend and I trounced the rest of the dorm in the Ping-Pong championship.

I ordered a cheeseburger and some fries for lunch today.

I forgot all about my older sister's birthday—I think I really let her down, and I don't know if she'll accept my apology.

It looks like my university's basketball team is going to the Final Four!

I overslept and got to my chemistry midterm late; I'm sure I failed.

Deteriorating Relationships

The test of a man or woman's breeding is how they behave in a quarrel.

— George Bernard Shaw

The greatest ordeal in life is marriage—it is the central focus for enlightenment and the natural therapeutic process in the culture.

— Carl Whitaker

Few topics spark more lively interest in ordinary thought and conversation than the question of what makes some relationships thrive while others wither and collapse. Not surprisingly, this has been an immensely popular topic for researchers, too. One reason why researchers have devoted special attention to the study of deteriorating relationships is that the treatment of relationship distress depends on understanding the root causes of poor functioning. As discussed by Berscheid in the opening article of this reader, marital discord—and its concomitant effects on family relationships—not only cause distress to the involved parties and to the people with whom their lives are entwined, but also underlie many of today's most pressing social problems. In light of the harmful effects of discord on individuals, relationships, and societies, researchers have sought to determine how the behavior of satisfied couples differs from the behavior of dissatisfied couples. This body of research spans a vast array of predictor variables and causal influences, including, for example, sociodemographic variables, personality traits and other individual differences, interaction behavior, cognitive and emotional processes, and even genetic makeup.

In its early years, research on what was then called "marital success and failure" was dominated by surveys and interviews that sought to predict marital outcomes from various characteristics of the individual. Terman et al.'s (1938) study of the personality correlates of later marital success in their renowned longitudinal sample of gifted individuals is often cited as the seminal study in the scientific analysis of marriage. Three developments have shaped the field during the intervening decades. First, early studies were largely actuarial and atheoretical, seeking to predict marital success from whichever variables the researchers found compelling. Although such studies continue to make useful contributions, recent research—especially in social psychology—is more theory-driven, seeking to validate theoretical accounts of the processes by which marital relationships change over time. Second, although negative emotion—dissatisfaction, unhappiness, and discord—is a major cause of divorce, it is important to recognize that dissatisfaction and dissolution are not one and the same. Many unsatisfying relationships are stable, and many not-entirely-unhappy marriages end in divorce. Accordingly, many researchers take care to distinguish between theories and findings regarding dissatisfaction versus those regarding instability. Third, observational studies have become increasingly common, wherein the couple's interaction is videotaped to provide a record for subsequent coding and detailed analysis. The rationale for observation is twofold: Certain key marital processes are apparent only when the partners interact with each other; and observed behavior may be more informative about the true state of a relationship than the partners' potentially biased self-reports (Gottman, 1998).

Tolstoy began *Anna Karenina* by observing that "Happy families are all alike; each unhappy family is unhappy in its own way." Whatever merit his observation may have, research has identified several important ways in which satisfying and dissatisfying relationships differ. The articles in this section have been selected to represent the themes mentioned above, as well as some of the more important and enduring findings from this literature. Two of these papers—those by Fincham and by Carstensen, Gottman, and Levenson—compare distressed and nondistressed couples on a series of variables that may help to explain the current state of their marriage. Fincham's article is based on the hypothesis that distress is grounded less in Dave's and Anna's behavior than in their attributions about the cause of each other's behavior. Given that all relationships encounter conflict and disagreement, the very same behaviors can be interpreted in a manner that exacerbates these difficulties, or alternatively, in a manner that minimizes their impact. Fincham's research details how these patterns of attribution differ.

Carstensen and her colleagues are known for their observational studies of marital interaction. In this example of their work, these authors examine partners' expressions of affect during a 15-minute conversation about a "problem area of continuing disagreement in their marriage." The approach in this work is deliberately broad brush: Affective expressions are diverse, allowing the researchers to compare the behavior of happy and unhappy couples, husbands and wives, and middle-aged and older couples (who are rarely studied). Particularly important to their work are the sequences of affect—how Dave responds to the emotion expressed by Anna, and how she, in turn, responds to the emotion expressed by Dave. Many researchers believe that these patterns of emotional engagement are the *sine qua non* of marital functioning.

Geraldine Downey and her colleagues focus their attention on an interesting personality variable, rejection sensitivity, and its role in eliciting from a partner precisely what is most feared—rejection. Rejection-sensitive individuals are prone to perceiving (often inaccurately) that their partners' ambiguous behaviors are indications of possible rejection. As a consequence of rejection sensitivity, Anna may defensively treat Dave in a hostile or distant manner, which, ironically, may elicit actual rejection from him. This pattern of behavior is called a self-fulfilling prophecy because it is Anna's preexisting anxious expectation of rejection that is causally responsible for evoking Dave's rejecting behavior—and not Dave's initial intent, as rejection-sensitive Anna assumes. Downey et al. report two elegant studies to demonstrate the operation of this mechanism—a daily diary study revealing the operation of this process in everyday interaction and an observational study in which observer ratings are used to independently corroborate the hypothesized sequence of events.

The final article in this set, by Michael Johnson, concerns a societal problem of great importance—abuse. Johnson argues for the need to distinguish between two forms of relationship violence: patriarchal terrorism and common couple violence. No one doubts that couple violence is a critical social problem, yet research to date has failed to provide a sufficiently well-validated base of knowledge on which interventions might be designed. One explanation for this limitation may be the failure to differentiate patriarchal terrorism from common couple violence. Johnson discusses several important differences between these forms of abuse, including their causal etiology, severity, impact, and societal implications. He also proposes, and we concur, that this distinction has great significance not only for theory and research, but also for the development of treatments, educational programs, and public policy.

REFERENCES

Gottman, J. M. (1998). Psychology and the study of marital processes. *Annual Review of Psychology, 49*, 169–197.

Terman, L. M., Buttenweiser, P., Ferguson, L. W., Johnson, W. B., & Wison, D. P. (1938). *Psychological factors in marital happiness*. New York: McGraw-Hill.

 # Suggestions for Further Reading

Archer, J. (2000). Sex differences in aggression between heterosexual partners. *Psychological Bulletin, 126*, 651–680. A meta-analysis followed by several valuable commentaries.

Arriaga, X. B., & Oskamp, S. (Eds.). (1999). *Violence in intimate relationships*. Thousand Oaks, CA: Sage. This volume provides a useful introduction to research concerning violence in intimate relationships.

Bradbury, T. N. (Ed.). (1998). *The developmental course of marital dysfunction*. New York: Cambridge University Press. A systematic compilation of information regarding longitudinal studies of the development and deterioration of marriage.

Bradbury, T. N. (2002). Research on relationships as a prelude to action. *Journal of Personal and Social Relationships, 19*, 571–599. In this call to action, Bradbury proposes that relationship research must aim at developing strategies for intervening with distressed couples.

Christensen, A., & Heavey, C. L. (1999). Interventions for couples. *Annual Review of Psychology, 50*, 165–190. A systematic review and commentary on existing research that evaluates contemporary approaches to interventions with couples.

Christensen, A., & Jacobsen, N. S. (2000). *Reconcilable differences*. New York: Guilford Press. Self-help books for unhappy relationships crowd the psychology section in most bookstores. This one is the best of them.

Dutton, D. G. (1998). *The abusive personality: Violence and control in intimate relationships*. New York: Guilford. A thoughtful, insightful analysis of personality factors that predispose individuals toward marital violence.

Epstein, N. B., & Baucom, D. H. (2002). *Enhanced cognitive–behavioral therapy for couples: A contextual approach*. Washington, D.C.: APA Books. This important synthesis of theory, research, and practical suggestions is a "state-of-the-art" summary of what is known about cognitive–behavioral interventions, arguably the predominant model of couples therapy in practice today.

Gottman, J. M. (1994). *What predicts divorce? The relationship between marital processes and marital outcomes*. Hillsdale, NJ: Erlbaum. Gottman has been a pioneering advocate of observational studies of marriage; herein, he summarizes his two decades of research on predicting divorce.

Harvey, J. H., & Wenzel, A. (Eds.). (2002). *A clinician's guide to maintaining and enhancing close relationships*. Mahwah, NJ: Erlbaum. Research on relationship maintenance presented with an eye toward application in clinical settings.

MacDonald, G., Zanna, M. P., & Holmes, J. G. (2000). An experimental test of the role of alcohol in relationship conflict. *Journal of Experimental Social Psychology, 36*, 182–193. An examination of the ways in which alcohol may exacerbate tendencies to deal with conflict in less-than-ideal ways.

Markman, H. J., Renick, M. J., Floyd, F. J., Stanley, S. M., & Clements, M. (1993). Preventing marital distress through communication and conflict management training: A 4- and 5-year follow-up. *Journal of Consulting and Clinical Psychology, 61*, 70–77. This study examines the long-term effectiveness of a well-known premarital program designed to teach partners effective modes of communication and conflict resolution.

Discussion Questions

1. Explain how holding an expectation of rejection, even if the individual is unaware of holding such expectations, can serve as a self-fulfilling prophecy. Can you think of a good example of this process from your personal experience?

2. If sensitivity to rejection can subtly create rejection, how might rejection-sensitive people who do *not* wish to sabotage their relationships go about short-circuiting this process?

3. Summarize in your own words how the happy and unhappy long-term couples in Carstensen, Gottman, and Levenson's research differed.

4. Based on the work of Carstensen and her colleagues, how do you see the interaction of older and middle-aged couples differing? What factors did they not study that you believe might also be important in differentiating between older and middle-aged couples?

5. What are causal attributions, and why do they matter for understanding marital distress?

6. How might you use Fincham's findings to help distressed couples?

7. Explain the difference between "patriarchal terrorism" and "common couple violence." Give a clear example of each.

8. What factors make patriarchal terrorism and common couple violence more or less likely? How do the predictors of these forms of interpersonal violence differ?

Attribution Processes in Distressed and Nondistressed Couples: 2. Responsibility for Marital Problems

Frank D. Fincham • SUNY Buffalo

Attributions for marital difficulties are examined in couples seeking therapy and in a community sample. Seventy-four spouses rated their two most important marital difficulties on several dimensions and indicated the extent to which they blamed their spouse for the difficulties. Distressed spouses were more likely to see their partner and the relationship as the source of their difficulties, to perceive the causes of their difficulties as more global, and to consider the causes as more reflective of their spouses' negative attitude toward them. The results are discussed in terms of the assessment of attributions in relationships, and their implications for marital therapy are outlined.

For some time, cognitive therapists have examined the utility of attribution theory and research for understanding the acquisition, maintenance, and remediation of clinical problems (cf. Fincham, 1983; Forsterling, 1980). Recently, this interest has manifested itself in the area of marital therapy as both practitioners and researchers have begun to emphasize the importance of attributions in marital dysfunction (e.g., Baucom, 1981; Berley & Jacobson, 1984; Doherty, 1981a, 1981b; Epstein, 1982; Fincham, in press; Jacobson, 1984; Revensdorf, 1984). Several writers have utilized the distinction made in attribution theory between internal and extenal causes and have argued that distressed spouses attribute negative partner behavior to internal factors that function to accentuate their negative impact and maintain marital distress (Berley & Jacobson, 1984; Wright & Fichten, 1976). Nondistressed spouses, in contrast, are thought to make external attributions for negative behavior, thereby minimizing its impact. Conversely, distressed spouses are hypothesized to make external attributions for positive partner behavior, whereas nondistressed spouses make internal attributions. It has also been suggested that these attribution patterns mediate behavior exchanges between spouses and thus account for differences in behavioral reciprocity between distressed and nondistressed couples (Berley & Jacobson, 1984: Fincham, in press).

However, despite the appeal of the idea that differences in patterns of attributions for a spouse's behavior underlie variations in patterns of behavior exchange and marital satisfaction, there are only a few studies in this area. Moreover, these studies involve some conceptual difficulties that make interpretation of the results problematic. Jacobson, McDonald, Follette, and Berley (1985), using couples recruited from the community, found that a distressed group (one partner scored below 100 on the Dyadic Adjustment Scale; Spanier, 1976), relative to their nondistressed counterparts, made internal attributions for negative spouse behavior and attributed positive acts to external factors. In contrast, Fincham and O'Leary (1983) and Fincham, Beach, and Nelson (1984) found no differences between couples seeking therapy and happily married community couples in the extent to which they attributed positive or negative spouse behavior internally to the spouse as compared to themselves, others, or circumstances.

The above findings are not only contradictory, but the interpretation of each data set is also problematic. Consider the attribution items that subjects rated in Jacobson et al.'s (1985) study: "She or he was trying to please me," and "She or he wanted to put on a good performance for the camera." The first is considered *internal*, the second *external*. Yet it is possible to argue that the structure of both is identical, as the motivation occurs in the actor and is directed to an external source. What is at issue is the external target; the first attribution is an example of an interpersonal attribution (Newman, 1981a) because it states what the partner is like in relation to the attributor, whereas the second is not. In an alternative attempt to capture the internal–external distinction, Fincham (Fincham & O'Leary, 1983; Fincham et al., 1984) contrasted the spouse with all other causal factors on a single bipolar rating scale. However, this measure is also problematic as it assumes that (a) attributions to

the spouse are only important when contrasted with other potential causes (contextual assumption); (b) attributions to all nonspouse causes have the same psychological meaning (equivalence assumption); and (c) spouse and nonspouse attributions are inversely correlated, such that an increment in one necessarily accompanies a decrement in the other (hydraulic assumption). These assumptions rest on conceptual distinctions that may not be appropriate.

This lack of conceptual clarity has also given rise to measurement problems in social psychological research concerned with intrapersonal attribution processes (Miller, Smith, & Ullman, 1981; Ross, 1977). Although the internal–external distinction retains considerable appeal despite these measurement problems (Ross & Fletcher, in press), its utilization in relationship research creates even greater difficulty. One needs to consider, for instance, whether internal attributions apply only to individual partners or also to properties of the relationship. Similarly, one must determine whether a spouse's influence on his or her partner is external, or whether situational influences reside only outside of the dyad. One solution to this problem is to distinguish conceptually between causes residing in the attributor, his or her spouse, the relationship, and outside circumstances (Fincham, in press). Attributions to each of these causes is therefore measured separately in the present study.

It seems unlikely, however, that the locus of a cause alone fully captures the psychological meaning of the explanations that people give for marital problems or is a sufficient basis for conceptualizing attributional differences between distressed and nondistressed couples. For example, attributing a spouse's lack of punctuality to a factor that may affect many areas of the relationship and may be difficult to change (e.g., "because he or she is selfish and uncaring") carries different implications for the marriage than one that is unlikely to affect other areas of the relationship and has no particular implications for the future (e.g., "he or she misread the train timetable") even though both are internal attributions. These observations suggested that examination of attributional differences with respect to the global–specific and stable–unstable causal dimensions might reveal attribution patterns that are related to marital distress. The expected group differences have been found on the global–specific dimension (distressed spouses see causes as more global for negative spouse behavior and more specific for positive spouse behavior), but not on the stable–unstable causal dimension (Fincham & O'Leary, 1983; Fincham et al., 1984).

In sum, it appears that there is both conceptual confusion about the properties of particular attribution dimensions and, perhaps as a result, empirical uncertainty about attributional differences between distressed and nondistressed spouses. Moreover, examination of the social and clinical psychological literatures suggests that there have been important oversights in the research conducted on attributions in marriage. For instance, Passer, Kelley, and Michela (1978) found that attributions in relationships differ on an underlying dimension defined by the positive/negative nature of the attributor's attitude toward his or her partner. This study suggests that a dimension, potentially of great importance for attributions in marriage, has been overlooked. From the perspective of the clinician, another oversight is that couples seldom describe their difficulties in terms of the specific, concrete spouse behaviors used in previous research. More typically, when entering therapy, couples present and make attributions about global problems. Moreover, the attributions are often overtly evaluative. Indeed, it is the attempt to operationalize general complaints and overcome evaluative attributions that characterizes the early stages of marital therapy (Jacobson & Margolin, 1979).

The present study, therefore, examined causal and evaluative attributions for marital difficulties in distressed and nondistressed couples. It was hypothesized that distressed spouses would (a) differ from their nondistressed counterparts on the internal–external causal dimension when attributions to the spouse were assessed independently of other causes associated with this dimension, (b) see the causes of their difficulties as more global and reflective of their partner's negative attitude toward them, and (c) blame their spouses for the difficulties.

Method

Subjects

Thirty-seven couples participated in the study. The distressed group comprised 18 couples in the early stages of marital therapy. They had been married an average of 7.3 ($SD = 5.2$) years and had a mean gross family income of between $18,000–$21,000 per year. Husbands averaged 31.7 ($SD = 5.2$) years of age, 14.9 ($SD = 3.0$) years of formal education, and had an average score of 85.7 ($SD = 27.2$) on the Marital Adjustment Test (Locke & Wallace, 1959). Wives averaged 30.6 ($SD = 5.9$) years of age, 14.7 ($SD = 2.6$) years of formal education, and had an average score of 77.2 ($SD = 29.8$) on the Marital Adjustment Test.

The nondistressed group consisted of 19 couples recruited from the community. Couples responded to an advertisement in a local newspaper that asked for volunteers to participate in a study on marriage. This group had been married for an average of 11.6 ($SD = 5.8$) years and had an average gross family income of $18,000–$21,000. Husbands averaged 37.1 ($SD = 8.4$) years of age on average, 15.3 (2.6) years of formal education, and had an average score of 98.4 ($SD = 29.1$) on the Marital Adjustment Test. Wives averaged 34.8 ($SD = 5.9$) years of age, 15.3 ($SD = 2.5$) years of education, and scored an average of 109.6 ($SD = 10.6$) on the Marital Adjustment Test. As expected, the couples in therapy were more maritally distressed than the community sample, $F(1, 73) = 11.0, p < .001$.

Materials

Each spouse completed a battery of questionnaires that included the Marital Adjustment Test, a demographic questionnaire, and an areas of difficulty questionnaire. The latter questionnaire measured attributions for the difficulties spouses experienced in their marriage and was specifically designed for this study. It asked respondents to list the two most important difficulties they experienced in their marriage, which were then rated on 7-point scales for severity (*very minor* to *very severe*) and intensity of feeling about each difficulty (*neutral* to *very negative*). The following instructions were given for this task:

> All couples experience some difficulties in their relationship, even if they are only very minor ones. In this questionnaire you are asked to list what you consider to be the two most important difficulties that exist between you and your partner. To assist you in this task we have listed below numerous areas in which couples can experience difficulties. You can choose the items you write down from the areas in this list or you can add your own completely different items. For each item you list please also indicate how much of a difficulty it is in your relationship. The final two questions ask how you feel about each difficulty.

A list of 18 potential difficulties followed (communication, unrealistic expectations of marriage or spouse, decision making/problem solving, children, etc.). The difficulties were derived from lists used to survey the frequency of marital difficulties (Geiss & O'Leary, 1981) and the areas covered by the Spouse Observation Checklist (Weiss & Perry, 1979). Subject-generated stimuli, rather than standard stimuli, were used to ensure that the difficulties rated by each spouse were indeed relevant to their marriage.

The remainder of the questionnaire was similar in format to the Attribution Style Questionnaire (Peterson et al., 1982) used in depression research. Thus, subjects wrote down what they considered to be the major cause of the difficulty and answered seven questions relating to the cause. The first four concerned the locus of the cause. Thus, subjects were asked to indicate the extent to which the cause of the difficulty rested in themselves, their spouse, the relationship, and outside circumstances, respectively. The fifth question required the participants to locate the cause on the global–specific dimension by asking whether the cause affected only this area of difficulty or whether it affected other areas of the marriage. The sixth question asked whether the cause would again be present in

the future when the difficulty was experienced, and thus measured its stability. The last causal question asked subjects to indicate the extent to which the cause was due to their spouse's negative attitude or feelings toward them. Finally, spouses indicated the extent to which they blamed their spouse for the difficulty. All answers were given on 7-point rating scales. The questions for each difficulty were answered on separate pages.

Procedure

The distressed group was referred to the study by practitioners in the community. Only couples who presented for therapy with marital problems and who had not participated in more than three therapy sessions were eligible for the study. Community couples interested in the study telephoned the laboratory in response to a newspaper advertisement. The experimenter briefly outlined the study to the couples and, if they agreed to participate, arranged a single appointment for them to visit the laboratory. When couples arrived at the laboratory, the study was again briefly outlined. Subjects were then given a battery of questionnaires that they completed independently of their spouses. The experimenter remained in the same room as the couple and was available to help spouses in the event that they encountered any difficulties with the task. Such difficulties were infrequent.

Following their completion of the questionnaire battery, couples were given the opportunity to discuss their experiences in completing the task and to ask any questions they might have. All couples were paid $10 for participating in the study.

Results

The difficulties listed by each spouse were examined to determine whether distressed and nondistressed couples differed in their agreement regarding the difficulties they had experienced in their marriage. Three couples in the whole sample (2 nondistressed, 1 distressed) agreed on what constituted their two most important marital difficulties, and only a small percentage of agreement was obtained in the distressed (27.7%) and nondistressed (22.2%) groups regarding individual difficulties. The frequency with which each group listed specific problems was examined, as attributions are a function of both the characteristics of the attributor and the event for which an attribution is made. A series of chi-square analyses showed that the frequency with which specific difficulties were listed by the distressed and nondistressed groups did not differ. This finding suggests that any group differences in attributions are not therefore simply due to distressed and nondistressed spouses rating different problems. Finally, the pattern of ratings obtained on the measures of problem severity and feelings about the problem were similar for each of the two problems. Thus, these ratings were summed to form more stable measures. As might be expected, 2×2 (Group $\times$ Sex) analyses of variance (ANOVAs) revealed that distressed couples rated their difficulties as more severe, $F(1, 70) = 10.63$, $p < .005$, and felt more negative about them, $F(1, 70) = 9.82$, $p < .005$, than did nondistressed couples. No other significant effects were found.

The causes generated by distressed and nondistressed spouses for their problems were not given in sufficient detail to allow reliable categorization and, hence, formal analysis. However, the causes given by the two groups did not appear to systematically differ on the basis of an informal visual inspection. The attribution ratings made regarding each problem were similar. Correlations between corresponding attribution ratings for each difficulty were significant (average $r = .41$; range $= .32–.51$). Hence, the corresponding ratings made for each of the difficulties were summed to form more stable measures. The mean scores obtained on the attribution measures are shown in Table 24.1.

A 2×2 (Group $\times$ Sex) multivariate analysis of variance yielded only a significant group main effect, $F(8, 63) = 4.7$, $p < .001$. Univariate analyses of variance confirmed that this effect, as predicted, was due largely to the fact that distressed spouses, relative to their nondistressed counterparts, were more likely to see their partner, $F(1, 70) = 5.24$, $p < .03$, and the relationship, $F(1, 70) = 12.2$,

TABLE 24.1. Mean Attribution Scores and Standard Deviations of Distressed and Nondistressed Husbands and Wives for Each Attribution Measure

| Measure | Group | | | |
| | Distressed | | Nondistressed | |
	Male	Female	Male	Female
Self				
M	8.61	7.28	8.37	8.16
SD	2.77	2.65	2.41	2.73
Spouse				
M	8.67	9.61	7.68	7.58
SD	2.14	2.33	2.77	3.75
Relationship				
M	7.83	8.22	5.84	5.10
SD	3.09	2.07	3.37	3.73
Circumstances				
M	7.28	8.00	5.89	7.36
SD	4.13	3.38	3.25	4.66
Globality				
M	9.88	11.11	7.89	6.94
SD	2.05	1.81	3.03	3.27
Stability				
M	10.61	10.38	11.21	10.89
SD	2.53	3.31	1.72	2.42
Attitude				
M	6.38	7.38	5.42	4.94
SD	3.19	3.15	2.87	3.54
Blame				
M	7.55	7.55	6.52	7.26
SD	2.17	3.41	3.77	2.90

$p < .001$, as the source of their marital difficulties; to perceive the causes of their difficulties as more global, $F(1, 70) = 25.2$, $p < .001$; and to see the causes as more reflective of their spouses' negative attitude toward them, $F(1, 70) = 9.25$, $p < .01$. As the community sample contained 13 subjects who scored in the distressed range on the Marital Adjustment Test (scores < 100), the above analysis was repeated excluding the data obtained from these subjects. An identical pattern of results was obtained.

A global internal–external index was computed by subtracting the average of the self and circumstance ratings from the spouse attribution. This was examined to determine whether the same pattern of results found in previous research using a bipolar internal–external scale was obtained. A 2×2 (Group $\times$ Sex) ANOVA yielded no significant effects, which is consistent with previous findings. However, when self-attributions only were subtracted from spouse ratings, a significant group main effect again emerged, $F(1, 70) = 8.17, p < .01$; distressed spouses were more likely to see their spouse, rather than themselves, as the source of their difficulties (mean difference = 2.61), as compared to nondistressed spouses (mean difference = −.08).

Finally, it was found that blaming the spouse for the marital difficulties correlated highly with seeing the spouse as the *cause* of the marital difficulties, $r(74) = .61, p < .005$. Spouse blame was also significantly associated with perceiving the relationship as the cause of the difficulties, $r(74) = .30, p < .005$; seeing the cause of the difficulties as reflective of the spouse's attitude, $r(74) = .43, p < .005$; and judging the cause to be global, $r(74) = .31, p < .005$. Rating the self as cause tended to be inversely associated with spouse blame, $r(74) = − .23, p < .025$.

Discussion

The results of the present study provide support for the view that variations in attributional patterns within marriage are related to differences in marital satisfaction. This finding is particularly intriguing because, unlike previous studies, the situations considered here involved actual marital difficulties rather than hypothetical or contrived spouse behaviors. Furthermore, the measures used in this investigation confront some of the conceptual issues regarding the psychological meaningfulness of various distinctions between causes that differ in locus, which means that the results help to clarify the confusion about this problem that has arisen from previous research.

More specifically, the present data revealed differences on only some of the conceptual distinctions that have been suggested regarding the internal–external causal dimension. Distressed spouses, relative to nondistressed spouses, were more likely to see their partner and the relationship as the source of their marital difficulties, but no differences were found between the two groups for self- or circumstance attributions. Thus, little support was found for the assumptions

made by the use of a bipolar scale to measure internal–external attributions in relationships. The fact that members of the distressed group were more likely than were members of the nondistressed group to see their spouses as the cause of their marital difficulties belies the contextual assumption that spouse attributions are only important when contrasted with other (nonspouse) causes.

Although distressed spouses made more relationship attributions than did nondistressed spouses, the interpretation of this finding is problematic. Conceptually, a distinction can be made between attributions that focus on the partner (e.g., "She or he does not trust *me*") and those that are truly dyadic (e.g., "lack of affection between *us*"). The former concerns the perception of the partner in regard to the self and is an interpersonal attribution (cf. Newman, 1981a, 1981b). The latter involves the relationship per se, with each partner making an equal contribution (a relationship attribution). It is unclear which of these is represented by relationship ratings obtained in this study.

In addition to the above differences obtained on the spouse and relationship components of the internal–external dimension, distressed spouses viewed the cause of their difficulties as more global than did nondistressed spouses, but the groups did not differ on the stability causal dimension. The difference on the global–specific dimension and the absence of any significant effect on the stable–unstable dimension is consistent with previous findings (Fincham & O'Leary, 1983; Fincham et al., 1984) and thus replicates results obtained for reactions to hypothetical spouse behaviors. The fact that distressed spouses view causes as global, pervading all areas of their marriage, is also consistent with clinical experience, as couples seldom present specific, circumscribed problems in therapy (Jacobson & Margolin, 1979). The recurrent absence of group differences on the stability dimension is also noteworthy as the perceived stability of a cause theoretically mediates the chronicity of a problem (Abramson, Seligman, & Teasdale, 1978). However, the very fact that couples are in therapy, attempting to alleviate their difficulties, might explain this finding. Presumably, they believe that with some help, the cause of the difficulty can be removed and, hence, does not indicate that it will be present in the future. The stable–unstable dimension may thus only prove important for distressed couples resigned to their difficulties who do not seek therapy. In the community sample, the distressed subgroup indeed saw the causes of their marital difficulties as more stable than did nondistressed spouses, thus providing preliminary support for this viewpoint.

It should be noted that group differences also emerged on the dimension derived from recent social psychological research on interpersonal attribution; distressed spouses were more likely than were nondistressed spouses to view the cause of their difficulties as reflective of their spouse's attitude toward them. The overtly evaluative nature of this rating draws attention to the fact that *causal* ratings for marital difficulties do not represent value neutral judgments. In fact, all of the causal dimensions on which group differences were obtained significantly correlated with spouse blame, although the groups did not actually differ in blame judgments. One implication of this finding is that cognitive interventions based on classical attribution principles used to explain phenomenal causality (e.g., coaching spouses to use covariation as a basis for inferring causality; Baucom, 1981) may prove less appropriate than those that are drawn from the responsibility attribution literature (Fincham & Jaspars, 1980). The quintessence of responsibility is the idea of accountability, which implies that behavior is evaluated on the basis of a set of rules or expectations regarding appropriate behavior. Hence, the view that attributions in marriage are, in fact, responsibility judgments necessarily entails consideration of the couple's expectations, which comprises "much of what happens in good marital therapy" (O'Leary & Turkewitz, 1978, p. 247). Indeed, it is possible to argue that a responsibility attribution framework for therapy integrates several cognitive therapy techniques and that coaching spouses in the rules of responsibility attribution may prove to be a useful tool in working with couples (Fincham, in press).

In sum, the attributional differences found in the present study are consistent with the view that attributions serve to maintain current levels of distress regarding marital difficulties. The present study, however, precludes valid inferences regarding the causal relationship between attributions and marital satisfaction. Indeed, distressed spouses saw their problems as more severe than did nondistressed spouses, and it is quite possible that the attributions made by the distressed group reflect their response to severe and chronic problems. The existence of attribution differences between distressed and nondistressed spouses nonetheless provides some justification for the longitudinal research needed to untangle the causal relationship between attributions and marital distress. Finally, the importance of multidimensional assessment of attributions in evaluating attributional differences between distressed and nondistressed spouses is apparent.

NOTES

This research was funded by a grant from the University of Illinois Research Board.

The author would like to thank Audrey Hokoda for her help in conducting the study and Thomas Bradbury, Garth Fletcher, Jolene Galegher, and Susan Kemp-Fincham for their critical comments on an earlier draft of the article. The cooperation of Milton Adler, Jim Hannum, and Chuck Romig in recruiting distressed couples is also gratefully acknowledged.

Requests for reprints should be sent to Frank Fincham, Department of Psychology, SUNY Buffalo, Buffalo, New York 14260.

REFERENCES

Abramson, L. Y., Seligman, M. E. P., & Teasdale, J. D. (1978). Learned helplessness in humans: Critique and reformulation. *Journal of Abnormal Psychology, 87,* 49–74.

Baucom, D. H. (1981). *Cognitive behavioral strategies in the treatment of marital discord.* Paper presented at the 15th annual convention of the Association for the Advancement of Behavior Therapy, Toronto.

Berley, R. A., & Jacobson, N. S. (1984). Causal attributions in intimate relationships: Toward a model of cognitive–behavioral marital therapy. In P. Kendall (Ed.), *Advances in cognitive–behavioral research and therapy* (Vol. 3, pp. 1–90). New York: Academic Press.

Doherty, W. J. (1981a). Cognitive processes in intimate conflict: I. Extending attribution theory. *The American Journal of Family Therapy, 9,* 1–13.

Doherty, W. J. (1981b). Cognitive processes in intimate conflict: II. Efficacy and learned helplessness. *The American Journal of Family Therapy, 9*, 35–44.

Epstein, N. (1982). Cognitive therapy with couples. *The American Journal of Family Therapy, 10*, 5–16.

Fincham, F. D. (1983). Clinical applications of attribution theory: Problems and prospects. In M. Hewstone (Ed.), *Attribution theory: Social and functional extensions* (pp. 187–203). Oxford, England: Blackwells.

Fincham, F. D. (in press). Attribution in close relationships. In J. H. Harvey & G. Weary (Eds.), *Contemporary attribution theory and research*. New York: Academic Press.

Fincham, F. D., Beach, S., & Nelson, G. (1984). *Attributional processes in distressed and nondistressed couples: 3. Causal and evaluative inferences for spouse behavior.* Manuscript submitted for publication.

Fincham, F. D., & Jaspars, J. M. F. (1980). Attribution of responsibility: From man the scientist to man as lawyer. In L. Berkowitz (Ed.), *Advances in experimental social psychology* (Vol. 13, pp. 81–138). New York: Academic Press.

Fincham, F. D., & O'Leary, K. D. (1983). Causal inferences for spouse behavior in maritally distressed and nondistressed couples. *Journal of Social and Clinical Psychology, 1*, 42–57.

Forsterling, F. (1980). Attributional aspects of cognitive behavior modification: A theoretical approach and suggestions for techniques. *Cognitive Therapy and Research, 4*, 27–37.

Geiss, S. K., & O'Leary, K. D. (1981). Therapist ratings of frequency and severity of marital problems: Implications for research. *Journal of Marital and Family Therapy, 7*, 515–520.

Jacobson, N. (1984). Modification of cognitive processes. In K. Hahlweg & N. Jacobson (Ed.), *Marital interaction: Analysis and modification* (pp. 174–195). New York: Guilford.

Jacobson, N. S., & Margolin, G. (1979). *Marital therapy.* New York: Brunner/Mazel.

Jacobson, N. S., McDonald, D. W., Follette, W. C., & Berley, R. A. (1985). Attribution processes in distressed and nondistressed married couples. *Cognitive Therapy and Research, 9*, 35–50.

Locke, H. J., & Wallace, K. M. (1959). Short marital adjustment and prediction tests: Their reliability and validity. *Marriage and Family Living, 21*, 251–255.

Miller, F. D., Smith, E. R., & Ullman, J. (1981). Measurement of interpretation of situational and dispositional attributions. *Journal of Experimental Social Psychology, 17*, 80–95.

Newman, H. (1981a). Communication within ongoing intimate relationships: An attributional perspective. *Personality and Social Psychology Bulletin, 7*, 59–70.

Newman, H. (1981b). Interpretation and explanation: Influences on communicative exchanges within intimate relationships. *Communication Quarterly, 8*, 123–132.

O'Leary, K. D., & Turkewitz, H. L. (1978). Marital therapy from a behavioral perspective. In T. J. Paolino & B. S. McCrady (Eds.), *Marriage and marital therapy* (pp. 240–297). New York: Brunner/Mazel.

Passer, M. W., Kelley, H. H., & Michela, J. L. (1978). Multidimensional scaling of the causes for negative interpersonal behavior. *Journal of Personality and Social Psychology, 36*, 951–962.

Peterson, C., Semmel, A., von Baeyer, C., Abramson, L. Y., Metalsky, G. M., & Seligman, M. E. (1982). The Attribution Style Questionnaire. *Cognitive Therapy and Research, 6*, 287–300.

Revensdorf, D. (1984). Attribution of marital distress. In K. Hahlweg & N. Jacobson (Eds.). *Marital interaction: Analysis and modification* (pp. 325–336). New York: Guilford Press.

Ross, L. D. (1977). The intuitive psychologist and his shortcomings: Distortions in the attribution process. In L. Berkowitz (Ed.), *Advances in experimental social psychology* (Vol. 10, pp. 173–220). New York: Academic Press.

Ross, M., & Fletcher, G. (in press). Attribution and social perception. In G. Lindzey & E. Aronson (Eds.), *Handbook of social psychology* (3rd ed.). London: Addison-Wesley.

Spanier, G. B. (1976). Measuring dyadic adjustment: New Scales for assessing the quality of marriage and similar dyads. *Journal of Marriage and Family, 38*, 15–28.

Weiss, R. L., & Perry, B. A. (1979). *Assessment and treatment of marital dysfunction.* Eugene: Oregon Marital Studies Program. (Available from R. L. Weiss, Department of Psychology, University of Oregon, Eugene, Oregon 97403)

Wright, J., & Fichten, C. (1976). Denial of responsibility, videotape feedback and attribution theory: Relevance for behavioral marital therapy. *Canadian Psychology Review, 17*, 219–230.

The Self-Fulfilling Prophecy in Close Relationships: Rejection Sensitivity and Rejection by Romantic Partners

Geraldine Downey, Antonio L. Freitas, Benjamin Michaelis, and
Hala Khouri • Columbia University

The authors hypothesized a self-fulfilling prophecy wherein rejection expectancies lead people to behave in ways that elicit rejection from their dating partners. The hypothesis was tested in 2 studies of conflict in couples: (a) a longitudinal field study where couples provided daily-diary reports and (b) a lab study involving behavioral observations. Results from the field study showed that high rejection-sensitive (HRS) people's relationships were more likely to break up than those of low rejection-sensitive (LRS) people. Conflict processes that contribute to relationship erosion were revealed for HRS women, but not for HRS men. Following naturally occurring relationship conflicts, HRS women's partners were more rejecting than were LRS women's partners. The lab study showed that HRS women's negative behavior during conflictual discussions helped explain their partners' more rejecting postconflict responses.

People's beliefs about their significant others are assumed to influence the course of their relationships in important ways (for reviews, see Baldwin, 1992; Bradbury & Fincham, 1990; Hazan & Shaver, 1994; Reis & Patrick, 1996). One class of beliefs—expectations concerning acceptance and rejection—has long been deemed especially vital to people's relationship functioning (e.g., Bowlby, 1969, 1973, 1980; Erikson, 1950; Horney, 1937; Sullivan, 1953). Bowlby (1969, 1973, 1980), for example, theorized that people's internal working models of relationships, incorporating expectations of rejection and acceptance, shape their relationships. In an example of what Merton (1948) termed the *self-fulfilling prophecy*, Sroufe (1990) suggested that rejection expectations can lead people to behave in ways that elicit rejection from others. In this article, we examine whether and how this proposed self-fulfilling prophecy operates in the romantic relationships of people high in rejection sensitivity (RS).

Drawing selectively on attachment and social–cognitive approaches to close relationships, we have conceptualized RS as the disposition to anxiously expect, readily perceive, and overreact to rejection (Downey & Feldman, 1996; Downey, Lebolt, Rincon, & Freitas, 1998; Feldman & Downey, 1994). Because we view anxious expectations of rejection by significant others as being at the core of RS, we have operationalized RS as anxious expectations of rejection in situations that afford the possibility of rejection by significant others. We refer to people who tend to anxiously expect rejection as *high RS* (HRS) and those who more calmly expect acceptance as *low RS* (LRS). Our prior research has documented a link between RS and repeated experiences of rejection from significant others (Bonica & Downey, 1997; Downey, Khouri, & Feldman, 1997; Feldman & Downey, 1994). Such experiences are thought to lead people to form rejection expectancies that are subsequently activated in situations where rejection is possible.

Once activated, anxious expectations of rejection are thought to prompt a readiness to perceive rejection. Accordingly, in both experimental and field studies, HRS people have been found to perceive rejection in ambiguous cues more readily than LRS people (Downey & Feldman, 1996; Downey et al., 1998). In an experiment, college students who anxiously expected rejection felt more rejected than others when told that a stranger with whom they had just finished a friendly conversation opted not to meet with them a second time (Downey & Feldman, 1996, Study 2). In a prospective field study, students who entered romantic relationships anxiously expecting rejection more readily perceived hurtful intent in their new partners' ambiguous behavior (e.g., being cool and distant; Downey & Feldman, 1996, Study 3). When perceived rejection prompts a behavioral overreaction that a significant other finds aversive, it is likely that the significant other will respond in ways that fulfill the HRS person's rejection expectations and that ultimately predict relationship breakup. This article tests this proposition.

Do Self-Fulfilling Prophecies Operate in Close Relationships?

Abundant evidence shows that experimentally induced expectations can evoke confirmatory behavior from strangers (for reviews, see Darley & Fazio, 1980; Hilton & Darley, 1991; Jussim, 1986, 1991; D. T. Miller & Turnbull, 1986; Snyder, 1992). However, demonstrating expectancy confirmation in ongoing relationships has proven more difficult. Because third variables such as preexisting partner characteristics are potential alternative explanations for apparent expectancy confirmation, the effects of such third variables must be ruled out (Jussim, 1991). Well-controlled longitudinal investigations of the impact of people's naturally occurring expectancies on their close relationships are now accumulating. Murray, Holmes, and Griffin (1996a, 1996b) demonstrated that people's idealizations of their romantic partners predicted improvements in their partners' self-images, controlling for the effect of their partners' preexisting self-perceptions. McNulty and Swann (1994) showed that, over time, college students' self-concepts began to conform to their roommates' appraisals of them.

Although Murray et al. (1996a, 1996b) did not examine this issue, people's behavior toward their romantic partners probably mediated the relationship between their idealization of their partners and their partners' self-concepts. Similarly, in McNulty and Swann's (1994) study, students' behavior toward their roommates probably helped account for the increasing congruence between the students' self-concepts and their roommates' appraisals of them. Whereas the role of people's behavior in eliciting cognition-congruent responses from significant others has not yet been demonstrated (for a review, see Jussim & Eccles, 1995), researchers have begun to document the impact of people's relationship cognitions on their behavior toward significant others.

In particular, researchers have focused on establishing the impact of people's relationship cognitions on their behavior during conflicts with romantic partners. This emphasis on conflict is based on findings that conflict behavior has a distinctive utility in predicting important outcomes (e.g., Gottman, 1979, 1993). There is now evidence that relationship cognitions can predict conflict behavior of the type deemed consequential for relationship quality (for a review, see Bradbury & Karney, 1993). However, links between relationship cognitions and conflict behavior appear to be stronger for women than for men. For example, women's, but not men's, negative attributions for a spouse's behavior have been shown to predict their negative, unconstructive behavior toward the spouse during conflictual discussions (Bradbury, Beach, Fincham, & Nelson, 1996; Bradbury & Fincham, 1992, 1993; G. E. Miller & Bradbury, 1995). Similarly, doubts about a spouse's psychological availability were stronger predictors of women's than of men's rejecting behavior toward their spouses during problem-solving discussions (Kobak & Hazan, 1991). Thus, conflicts may be more appropriate situations in which to observe the consequences of women's relationship cognitions than those of men.

Does Conflict Lead to Confirmation of Rejection Expectancies?

Of concern to our present study is whether conflict is a suitable situation in which to examine the hypothesized process through which people's rejection expectancies are fulfilled. Downey (1997) found that HRS people reported feeling more anxious than LRS people in anticipation of conflicts with romantic partners. This conflict-related anxiety did not reflect a generalized anxiety about interactions with romantic partners because no differences in anticipatory anxiety were found for nonconflictual discussions. Thus, by activating HRS people's anxiety, conflicts may potentially trigger the proposed processes leading to rejection.

However, consistent with previously discussed evidence of gender differences in links between

relationship cognitions and conflict behaviors, Downey (1997) found that RS was more strongly associated with women's than with men's pessimism about the course and outcome of conflicts with romantic partners. Specifically, RS was a stronger predictor of concern about rejection during conflict, and of feeling lonely and unloved after conflict, in women than in men. Moreover, HRS women were less confident than HRS men that their efforts to resolve conflicts would be successful. These findings imply that HRS women may be more likely to behave in ways that exacerbate conflicts. Consequently, conflicts may be more likely to reveal the hypothesized processes linking rejection expectations with their fulfillment for women than for men.

Current Studies

This research assessed whether people's anxious expectations of rejection prompt them to behave toward romantic partners in ways that elicit rejection and predict breakup. Toward this end, we tested three specific hypotheses in two studies of dating couples.

Study 1 involved a daily-diary study of dating couples and a 1-year follow-up. We used the follow-up data to test whether RS predicted breakup (Hypothesis 1). This possibility was implied by Downey and Feldman's (1996, Study 4) finding that RS predicted partner dissatisfaction, an established predictor of breakup (e.g., Kayser, 1993; Stephen, 1984). Directly showing that RS predicts breakup would underscore the importance of understanding the mechanisms leading to this outcome.

We used daily-diary data from Study 1 to test whether the cycle leading to the fulfillment of rejection expectations is more evident in conflictual than in nonconflictual situations (Hypothesis 2). Based on the above review, we expected that conflicts would be more strongly linked with rejection expectancy confirmation in HRS women than in HRS men. In Study 2, we used a behavioral observation paradigm developed by Gottman (1979) to test whether people's conflict behavior mediated the relation between their rejection expectancies and their partners' postconflict rejecting reactions (Hypothesis 3).

Study 1

For 4 weeks, both members of participating couples provided daily records of their relationship-relevant cognitions, affects, behaviors, and conflicts. One-year follow-up data on the status of their relationships were used to test whether RS predicts breakup (Hypothesis 1). The daily-diary data were used to test whether conflicts precipitate the hypothesized process where people's rejection expectations elicit confirmatory responses from their partners (Hypothesis 2). Daily-diary designs are well-suited for investigating the effects of naturally occurring conflict on individual couples over time and the differences between couples in response to conflict (Bolger & Schilling, 1991). Because in diary designs participants serve as their own controls, the resulting statistical tests are more powerful than those in conventional between-subject designs. Furthermore, the longitudinal nature of diary designs permits more confident inferences about causal directionality between variables (e.g., between conflict and relationship satisfaction; Bolger & Zuckerman, 1995).

The daily-diary data allowed us to test whether, on days following conflict, HRS people's partners were more likely than LRS people's partners to respond in a rejecting manner, indexed by diminished relationship satisfaction and commitment. We used these measures because they are established predictors of breakup (Stephen, 1984) and because we expected that they would elicit rejecting behavior that is evident to the person. As validation, we tested whether these measures predicted breakup and people's perceptions of their partners' rejecting behavior, indexed by withdrawal, criticism, and reduced affection. As discussed above, we anticipated that partners' responses to conflict would be more strongly predicted by women's rejection expectancies than by those of men.

Relative to LRS people, HRS people were also predicted to view their partners as behaving in a

more rejecting way on the day after a conflict. We expected that the relation between people's RS and their perceptions of postconflict partner rejection would be partially mediated by the partners' self-reported relationship satisfaction and commitment.

Method

Sample and Procedure

Dating couples were recruited through announcements posted on the Columbia University campus to participate for pay in a study of romantic relationships. At least one member of each couple was a student at Columbia University. The study was restricted to couples in committed relationships that had been ongoing for at least 6 months and in which both members of the couple lived in New York City. The mean length of relationship was 18.6 months ($SD = 14.2$). Fifty-eight percent of the men were Caucasian, 20% were Asian American, 7% were African American, 4% were Hispanic, and 11% were from other ethnic backgrounds. The men's mean age was 22 years ($SD = 3.7$). Fifty-three percent of the women were Caucasian, 34% were Asian American, 5% were Hispanic, 3% were African American, and 5% were from other backgrounds. The women's mean age was 21 years ($SD = 2.9$). Participants' ethnicities were unrelated to their RS scores.

Couples who completed the study received $50 in compensation. Each member of a couple who expressed interest in the study was mailed a package containing one consent form, five packets, and five return envelopes. The first packet was a background questionnaire that included questions about demographic characteristics, RS, dating history, dating patterns, and the current dating relationship. The final four packets each consisted of seven identical, structured questionnaires to be completed at the end of each day for a total of 28 days. Participants were asked to return each week's set of diaries as soon as they were completed. Participants were also asked to complete both the background questionnaire and the daily diaries separately from their partners and to refrain from discussing their responses with their partners.

All couples who completed the study were heterosexual. At least one member of each of 108 couples who had been dating for at least 6 months contacted us to express interest in the study. In 76% of the 108 couples, at least one member completed a background questionnaire (75 couples, 6 additional women, and 1 additional man). In 54% (58/108) of couples, both members provided background data and at least 2 overlapping weeks of diary data. In fact, all except 4 male and 4 female partners in these 58 couples completed at least 3 weeks of diaries. Time constraint was the primary reason given by couples who did not complete the diary part of the study.

The RS scores of men and women in the 58 couples who provided at least 2 weeks of diary data did not differ from the scores of their counterparts in couples who completed background questionnaires but provided less than 2 weeks of diary data. The diary analyses reported below are based on these 58 couples. Female partners in these 58 couples completed diaries on 94.2% of days and male partners completed diaries on 94.0% of days. Days on which participants did not complete the diary were treated as missing values. Diary completion rate was not associated with RS in either men or women.

About 1 year after the diary study, we attempted to locate all the couples for whom we had background data to establish if they had broken up. Addresses were obtained from several sources including current university directories and records, Internet directories, and commercial databases. We succeeded in recontacting 53 of the 75 couples. These included 49 of the 58 couples (84%) in which both partners had provided diary data. There were no significant differences in RS between couples who were recontacted and those who were not.

Background Measures

The background questionnaire included the Rejection Sensitivity Questionnaire (RSQ; Downey & Feldman, 1996), global measures of relationship satisfaction and commitment, and demographic questions.

RSQ. The RSQ assesses the anxious-expectations component of RS. A detailed description of

the development and validation of the measure is given in Downey and Feldman (1996).[1] The measure was initially developed from open-ended interviews in which students were asked what they thought would happen and how they would feel in hypothetical situations in which they were requesting something of a significant other, such as a romantic partner, friend, or parent. Answers varied along two dimensions: (a) degree of concern and anxiety about the outcome and (b) expectations of acceptance and rejection.

The final version of the measure consists of 18 hypothetical situations in which rejection by a significant other is possible (e.g., "You ask your friend to do you a big favor"). For each situation, people are first asked to indicate their degree of concern or anxiety about the outcome of each situation (e.g., "How concerned or anxious would you be over whether or not your friend would want to help you out?") on a 6-point scale ranging from 1 (*very unconcerned*) to 6 (*very concerned*). They are then asked to indicate the likelihood that the other person(s) would respond in an accepting fashion (e.g., "I would expect that he/she would willingly agree to help me out") on a 6-point scale ranging from 1 (*very unlikely*) to 6 (*very likely*). High likelihood of this outcome represents expectations of acceptance, and low likelihood represents expectations of rejection.

Following from our expectancy-value model of anxious expectations of rejection, we computed the RSQ scores as follows: A score for each situation was obtained by weighting the expected likelihood of rejection by the degree of anxiety about the outcome of the request. The score for acceptance expectancy was reversed to index rejection expectancy (expectancy of rejection = 7 − expectancy of acceptance). The reversed score was then multiplied by the score for degree of anxiety or concern. A total (cross-situational) RS score for each participant was computed by summing the RS scores for each situation and dividing by the total number of situations.

---

[1]The complete measure is available on the World Wide Web at www.columbia.edu/~gd20.

Downey and Feldman (1996, Study 1) showed that the RSQ is a normally distributed measure that taps a relatively enduring and coherent information-processing disposition. The RSQ test–retest reliability was .83 over a 2–3-week period and .78 over a 4-month period. The anxiety and expectations components of the measure were mildly positively related in a large sample ($r = .18, N = 550$). Downey and Feldman (1996, Study 3) provided evidence that RS was not redundant, in terms of its predictive utility, with established personality constructs to which it is conceptually and empirically related. These include measures of introversion, neuroticism, adult attachment style, social anxiety, social avoidance, and self-esteem.

Although RS is measured continuously, to simplify the analyses we treated it as a dichotomy. People scoring at or above the median (i.e., 8.90 for women and 7.42 for men) were defined as HRS and could be viewed as tending to anxiously expect rejection (scored 1). People scoring below the median were defined as LRS and could be viewed as tending to calmly expect acceptance (scored 0). The results reported below were similar whether RS was treated as a dichotomy or as a continuous measure. Partners' RS scores were not significantly correlated (for the continuous measure, $r = .14, p > .10$; for the dichotomous measure, $r = -.01, p > .10$).

Relationship satisfaction. A scale assessing satisfaction with the relationship was developed by averaging participants' responses to the following three items: (a) "I am satisfied with our relationship," (b) "Our relationship meets my expectations of what a good relationship should be like," and (c) "I could not be happier in our relationship." Participants indicated the extent to which each statement was true of their feelings on an 8-point scale from 0 (*not at all true of my feelings*) to 7 (*completely true of my feelings*). The mean for the three-item scale was 5.74 ($SD = 1.19, \alpha = .91$) for men and 5.47 ($SD = 1.65, \alpha = .95$) for women. In a pilot study ($n = 148$), scores on this scale correlated .73 ($p < .001$) with relationship satisfaction as assessed by the Dyadic Adjustment Scale (Spanier, 1976).

Relationship commitment. Participants responded to the question "How committed are you to the relationship?" on a 1 (*not committed*) to 7 (*very committed*) scale. The mean was 6.51 ($SD = 0.83$) for men and 6.50 ($SD = 0.69$) for women.

Diary Measures

The structured daily diary included questions concerning thoughts and feelings about the couples' relationships, partner behavior, and conflict.

Conflict. Each day, participants were asked to indicate whether they had experienced a conflict or disagreement with their romantic partner that day (the occurrence of any conflict was coded "1"; the absence of any conflict was coded "0"). Women reported conflict on 18% of days, and men reported conflict on 16% of days, $F(1, 58) = 5.11, p < .05$. Members of a couple agreed about whether conflict had occurred on 89% of days. Level of agreement was not affected by people's RS scores. To maximize the independence of data sources, we used women's reports of conflict when examining the effect of women's RS on their partners, and we used men's reports of conflict when examining the effects of men's RS on their partners. RS was not significantly associated with conflict rates over the diary period (HRS women: $M = .21, SD = .41$; LRS women: $M = .16, SD = .37, F[1, 56] = 1.77, p = .19$; HRS men: $M = .16, SD = .36$; LRS men: $M = .16, SD = .37, F[1, 56] = 0.02, p = .89$).

Relationship dissatisfaction. Dissatisfaction with the relationship was assessed with the question, "Overall, how would you describe your relationship today?" Participants responded using a 7-point scale ranging from 1 (*terrific*) to 7 (*terrible*). The daily mean was 2.32 ($SD = 1.15$) for men and 2.36 ($SD = 1.21$) for women, $F(1, 58) = 0.01$, *ns*.

Thoughts of ending the relationship. Participants indicated whether the following statement applied to them that day: "I thought about ending the relationship" ($1 = yes, 0 = no$). The mean was .04 ($SD = .19$) for men and .05 ($SD = .23$) for women, $F(1, 58) = 3.42, p < .10$. This measure was used to index daily levels of commitment.

Perceptions of partner behavior. Participants checked which one of a set of three accepting and two rejecting behaviors their partners had enacted toward them that day. The accepting behaviors were as follows: "My partner made me feel wanted," "My partner was physically affectionate toward me," and "My partner told me s/he loves me." Responses to these items were summed to form an index of accepting behavior (men: $M = 2.02, SD = .97, \alpha = .57$; women: $M = 2.17, SD = 0.99, \alpha = .59, F[1, 58] = 0.05, ns$). The relatively low reliability of this measure is likely to work against our hypothesis.

One rejecting behavior item indexed passive rejection in the form of withdrawal: "My partner was inattentive and unresponsive toward me" (men: $M = .05, SD = .22$; women: $M = .09, SD = .29, F[1, 58] = 0.40, p < .05$). The other item indexed active rejection: "My partner criticized something I said or did" (men: $M = .18, SD = .39$; women: $M = .17, SD = .37, F[1, 58] = 0.18, ns$).

One-Year Follow-Up Contact

The first member of each couple that we contacted was asked whether the couple was still together. Of the 53 couples we contacted, 29% had broken up.

Diary-Data Analyses

This study of male–female couples yielded a data set with two levels of analysis. The within-couple level reflects daily variation over time within a couple or within a focal partner in the couple. The between-couple level reflects differences between couples or between focal members of couples. The within-couple level of analysis could be used to estimate each couple's or couple member's reactivity to conflict (e.g., changes in the male partner's satisfaction with or commitment to the relationship following a conflict) as well as the average level of satisfaction or commitment for each couple or member of a couple. The between-couple level of analysis could be used to examine whether couples that included an HRS person differed in these processes from couples that included an LRS person (e.g., whether couples that included an HRS woman differed from couples that included an LRS woman in the impact of conflict on partner satisfaction; whether members of couples that broke up differed from members of couples that stayed together in average daily satisfaction).

The analyses were conducted using a multilevel or hierarchical linear model approach, which permits the simultaneous analysis of within- and between-couple variation (Bolger & Zuckerman, 1995; Bryk & Raudenbush, 1992; Kenny, Kashy, & Bolger, 1998). In contrast, conventional linear models either aggregate across within-couple data, which results in information loss, or conflate within- and between-couple variation, resulting in incorrect tests of significance (see Kenny et al., 1998).

The diary data analyses we conducted addressed two basic types of questions. The main question was whether the relation between variables measured at the daily level (e.g., between conflict and partners' relationship dissatisfaction) differed for HRS and LRS people. More specifically, we were interested in whether the effect of the previous day's independent variable (e.g., conflict) on today's dependent variable (e.g., partner's relationship dissatisfaction) was contingent on the person's RS. Answering this question using a multilevel approach required specifying two equations, including a within- and a between-couple equation. The within-couple equation specifies that values of the dependent variable for a given couple (e.g., partner dissatisfaction) on a given day, S_t, is predicted by the level of the dependent variable on the previous day, S_{t-1}; the level of the independent variable (e.g., conflict) on the previous day, C_{t-1}; and a residual component of the dependent variable, specific to each day, q_t. The variable q_t is assumed to have a mean of zero and a constant variance across persons and days. The equation is as follows:

$$S_t = a_0 + a_1 S_{t-1} + a_2 C_{t-1} + q_t. \quad (1)$$

Results

Does RS Predict Breakup?

Because showing that RS predicts breakup would underscore the importance of investigating mediating processes, we began by testing this hypothesis. The prediction was supported. Forty-four percent of couples that included a HRS woman had broken up within a year of the diary study, compared with 15% of couples that included an LRS woman, $\chi^2 (1, N = 53) = 5.39, p < .05$. Forty-two percent of couples that included an HRS man had broken up in this 1-year period, compared with 15% of couples that included an LRS man, $\chi^2(1, N = 53) = 4.59, p < .05$. Logistic regression analyses showed that the effect of people's RS on breakup remained significant when their partners' RS, relationship satisfaction, and commitment assessed prior to beginning the diary study were statistically controlled.

Do Partner Relationship Dissatisfaction and Thoughts of Ending the Relationship Predict Breakup?

The next analyses were undertaken with daily-diary data to validate that, by assessing the impact of RS on partners' daily relationship dissatisfaction and thoughts of ending the relationship, we were focusing on outcomes that predicted breakup. Thus, we tested the prediction that the average daily level of relationship dissatisfaction and thoughts of ending the relationship, which we viewed as a daily index of relationship commitment, in male and female partners predicted breakup over the following year. Multilevel analyses revealed support for the predictions for both men and women.

Men and women in relationships that ended during the 1-year follow-up period were more dissatisfied at the daily level than their counterparts in relationships that remained intact—male breakup: $M = 2.84, SD = 1.29$; male intact: $M = 2.12, SD = 1.02, F(1, 47) = 12.51, p < .001$; female breakup: $M = 2.73, SD = 1.40$; female intact: $M = 2.21, SD = 1.07, F(1, 47) = 5.44, p < .05$. Similarly, the daily probability of thoughts of ending the relationship was higher in relationships that subsequently ended than in those that continued for both men and women—male breakup: $M = .08, SD = .27$; male intact: $M = .02, SD = .14, F(1, 47) = 8.33, p < .01$; female breakup: $M = .13, SD = .34$; female intact: $M = .03, SD = .17, F(1, 47) = 23.18, p < .001$.

Impact of Conflict on the Partners of HRS and LRS People

Having established that daily relationship satisfaction and commitment distinguish men and women in relationships that subsequently end from those that remain intact, we then examined processes linking RS with daily levels of partner satisfaction and commitment. We used the multi-level approach described earlier to examine (a) whether conflict had a more negative impact on HRS people's partners than on LRS people's partners and (b) whether HRS and LRS people were aware of their partners' differential responses following conflict. Separate analyses were conducted for men and women.

Does Conflict More Negatively Affect HRS Than LRS People's Partners?

On the day after a conflict, HRS people's partners were expected to experience more relationship dissatisfaction and more thoughts of ending the relationship than LRS people's partners. Conflict effects were expected to be stronger for HRS women's partners than for HRS men's partners. We examined partners' self-reports of (a) relationship dissatisfaction and (b) thoughts of ending the relationship as a function of their previous day's reports of these variables, previous day's conflict, RS, and the interaction between conflict and RS.

Men. The Conflict × Men's RS interaction was not significant either for partners' relationship dissatisfaction, $b = .03, F(1, 47) = 0.02, p = .86$, or for partners' thoughts of ending the relationship, $b = .01, F(1, 47) = 0.09, p = .76$. Thus, HRS and LRS men's partners did not differ significantly in the extent to which conflict affected their relationship satisfaction or commitment.

Women. The hypothesis was supported for women. The results are reported in Table 25.1 (Models 1 and 2). The partners of HRS and LRS women differed significantly more from each other on days that were not preceded by conflict than on days that were preceded by conflict. This is indicated by significant interactions between conflict and women's RS both for partners' relationship dissatisfaction, $b = .34, F(1, 52) = 5.03, p < .05$, and for partners' thoughts of ending the relationship, $b = .08, F(1, 52) = 6.22, p < .05$. The nonsignificant coefficients for RS in Table 25.1 (Models 1 and 2) show that partners of HRS and LRS women did not differ significantly from one

TABLE 25.1 Impact of Women's Rejection Sensitivity (RS) and Yesterday's Conflict on Their Partner's Feelings About the Relationship and Behavior Today (Based on Multilevel Analysis)

			b		
Today's value of dependent variable	Intercept	Yesterday's value of dependent variable	Yesterday's conflict (1 = *yes*, 0 = *no*)	RS (HRS = 1, LRS = 0)	Yesterday's conflict × RS
Model 1 Partner's relationship dissatisfaction (self-report)	1.16	0.48***	−0.12	0.10	0.34*
Model 2 Partner's thoughts of ending the relationship (self-report)	0.03	0.22**	−0.03	−0.01	0.08*
Model 3 Partner's accepting behavior (woman's report)	1.27	0.48***	0.09	−0.23*	−0.27*
Model 4 Partner's withdrawal (woman's report)	0.06	0.10**	−0.03	0.03	0.09*

Note. HRS = high rejection-sensitive; LRS = low rejection-sensitive.
*$p < .05$. **$p < .01$. ***$p < .001$.

another in relationship dissatisfaction or in thoughts of ending their relationships on days that were not preceded by conflict.

Figure 25.1 gives the predicted levels of the current-day's thoughts of ending the relationship for the partners of HRS and LRS women as a function of whether a conflict had occurred on the previous day. Postconflict differences between HRS and LRS women's partners reflect the following pattern: On days that were preceded by conflict, relative to those that were not, HRS women's partners showed significant increases in thoughts of ending the relationship, $b = .05$, $F(1, 52) = 5.90$, $p < .05$. By contrast, LRS women's partners showed nonsignificant declines in thoughts of ending the relationship, $b = −.03$, $F(1, 52) = 1.05$, $p = .31$.

Are HRS and LRS People Aware of Their Partners' Differential Responses to Conflict?

We expected that, compared with LRS people, HRS people would perceive their partners as being less accepting and more rejecting on days following

a conflict. As above, women's RS was expected to have a more pronounced effect than men's RS. Using multilevel analyses, we assessed people's perceptions of their partners' current-day levels of accepting behavior and of rejecting behavior (i.e., withdrawal and criticism) as a function of the previous day's respective perceived partner behavior, previous day's conflict, RS, and the interaction between the previous day's conflict and RS.

Men. The Conflict × Men's RS interaction was not significant for men's perceptions of the following behaviors: partners' accepting behavior, $b = −.10$, $F(1, 47) = 0.84$, $p = .36$; withdrawal, $b = .05$, $F(1, 47) = 2.50$, $p = .12$; or critical behavior, $b = .05$, $F(1, 47) = 0.51$, $p = .48$. Thus, HRS and LRS men's perceptions of their partners' behavior did not differ more on days preceded by a conflict than on days not preceded by a conflict.

Women. The hypothesis was supported for accepting behavior and withdrawal (see Table 25.1, Models 3 and 4), but not for criticism. On days that were preceded by conflict, the differences in HRS

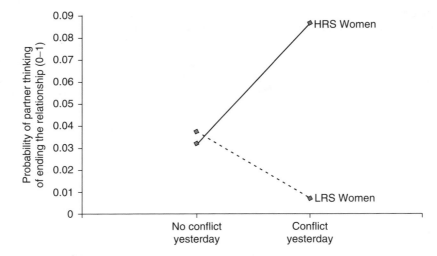

FIGURE 25.1 ■ Partner's likelihood of thinking of ending the relationship as a function of conflict and of woman's rejection sensitivity. Predicted values were based on the following equation for a partner at the mean on thoughts of ending the relationship yesterday ($M = .034$): Partner Thoughts of Ending Relationship$_t$ = .03 + .22 Partner Thoughts of Ending Relationship$_{t-1}$ − .03 Conflict$_{t-1}$ − .01 Rejection Sensitivity + .08 Rejection Sensitivity × Conflict$_{t-1}$. HRS = high rejection-sensitive; LRS = low rejection-sensitive.

and LRS women's perceptions of their partners' behavior were significantly more pronounced than on days that were not preceded by conflict. This is indicated by significant interactions between conflict and women's RS for perceptions of partners' accepting behavior, $b = .27$, $F(1, 52) = 5.00$, $p < .05$, and withdrawal, $b = .09$, $F(1, 52) = 4.03$, $p < .05$. The interaction was not significant, however, for perceptions of partners' criticism, $b = .08$, $F(1, 52) = 1.49$, $p = .23$. As the coefficient for RS in Table 25.1 (Model 4) shows, on days that were not preceded by conflict, HRS and LRS women did not differ significantly in their perceptions of partner withdrawal. However, as the coefficient for RS in Table 25.1 (Model 3) shows, HRS women perceived their partners as being significantly less accepting than did LRS women, even on days that were not preceded by conflict.

Figure 25.2 gives the predicted levels of the current-day's perceived partners' withdrawal for HRS and LRS women as a function of whether a conflict had occurred on the previous day. Postconflict differences between HRS and LRS women's perceptions of their partners' behavior reflected

the following pattern: On days preceded by conflict, HRS women perceived their partners as being significantly more withdrawn, $b = .06$, $F(1, 52) = 4.02$, $p < .05$, than on days that were not preceded by conflict. The pattern was reversed for LRS women's perceptions of their partners' behavior but not to a significant degree, $b = -.03$, $F[1, 52] = 0.72$, $p = .40$.

Discussion

Supporting Hypothesis 1, RS predicted relationship breakup for both men and women, even when controlling for partners' initial level of RS, relationship satisfaction, and commitment. Results from the diary study helped illuminate the processes whereby RS undermines relationships in the case of women but not of men. Specifically, we found that naturally occurring conflicts triggered a process through which women's rejection expectancies led to their partners' rejecting responses, operationalized as partner-reported relationship dissatisfaction and thoughts of ending the relationship.

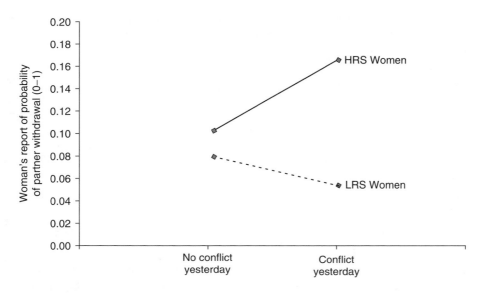

FIGURE 25.2 ■ Woman's report of partner's withdrawal as a function of conflict and woman's rejection sensitivity. Predicted values were based on the following equation for a partner at the mean on withdrawal yesterday ($M = .09$): Partner Withdrawal$_t$ = .06 + .10 Partner Withdrawal$_{t-1}$ − .03 Conflict$_{t-1}$ + .03 Rejection Sensitivity + .09 Rejection Sensitivity × Conflict$_{t-1}$. HRS = high rejection-sensitive; LRS = low rejection-sensitive.

Both of these indexes of rejection predicted breakup for men and for women.

On days preceded by conflict, HRS women's partners were more likely than LRS women's partners to experience relationship dissatisfaction and to think of ending the relationship. Moreover, HRS women's partners felt significantly more negative about their relationships on days preceded by conflict than on days that were not. The pattern was reversed, but to a nonsignificant degree, for the partners of LRS women. These findings are not attributable to the stable effects of partner background characteristics, because these were held constant in within-couple analyses. Nor can they be accounted for by the contaminating effect of prior day's dissatisfaction and thoughts of ending the relationship, which were also held constant in the analyses.

The differential impact of conflict on the partners of HRS and LRS women was evident to the women. On days preceded by conflict, partners were perceived to be less accepting and more withdrawn by HRS than by LRS women.

Overall, Study 1 findings implicate conflicts as critical situations in which to examine the processes leading to the fulfillment of HRS women's rejection expectations. However, there are a number of limitations to the diary approach that qualify the confidence with which such conclusions can be drawn. First, partners' relationship perceptions were not assessed immediately before and after the conflict. Thus, rather than resulting from the conflict per se, the more rejecting responses of HRS women's partners on the day after a conflict may have been caused by the negative interactional residue of a poorly resolved conflict. Second, the daily-diary approach relies on people completing self-reports each day. Poor compliance may have distorted the study results.

Study 2

The first goal of Study 2 was to address the limitations of the diary approach by investigating under more controlled conditions whether conflict had a differential impact on HRS and LRS women's partners. The second goal was to determine whether the negative behavior of HRS women during a conflict would account for their partners' postconflict rejecting responses (Hypothesis 3). In this study, partners' postconflict anger about their relationships was used as an index of rejection because anger is a common reaction to negative interactions and because it has been shown to predict rejecting behavior (e.g., Juvonen, 1991).

To replicate the Study 1 finding that conflict would precipitate rejection by HRS women's partners, we first examined whether HRS women's partners would feel more angry about their relationships following a conflict discussion than would LRS women's partners. Prior evidence that laboratory discussions of conflictual issues improved romantic partners' moods (Bradbury, 1994; Bradbury & Davila, 1997; Veroff, Hatchett, & Douvan, 1992) led us to expect an average pre- to postconflict decline in partner anger. This decline was expected to be significantly more pronounced in LRS women's partners than in HRS women's partners.

Next, we tested whether, during the conflict discussion, HRS women would behave in a more negative way toward their partners than would LRS women. Finally, we tested whether differences in HRS and LRS women's negative conflict behavior would help account for postconflict differences in their partners' anger levels.

Following Jussim (1991), we sought to rule out third-variable explanations for the hypothesized impact of the person's anxious expectations of rejection on the partner's postconflict anger and on the person's own conflict behavior. Potential third-variable explanations included the person's preconflict mood and the partner's own level of RS, current relationship satisfaction and commitment, preconflict anger, and conflict behavior. Thus, we tested whether controlling for these variables altered support for the behavior mediational model.

Method

Sample

Participants were 39 college-age couples in the early stages of dating relationships. The couples had been dating for an average of 3.3 months ($SD = 1.4$), with a minimum of 2 months and a maximum of 6 months. The mean age of both men and women was 20 years. At least 1 member of each couple was a university student. The racial composition of the sample was as follows: 67.4% of the men were Caucasian, 2.2% were African American, 8.7% were Hispanic, 15.2% were Asian American, and 6.5% were from other backgrounds; 57.8% of the women were Caucasian, 2.2% were African American, 2.2% were Hispanic, 22.2% were Asian American, and 15.6% were from other backgrounds.

The study included only couples in which both members reported that the relationship was exclusive. This criterion was used to preclude the possibility that people might feel rejected by and negative towards their partners because of their partners' other romantic involvements.

Procedure

Flyers were posted around the Columbia University campus and in students' mailboxes inviting couples to participate for pay in a study of dating relationships. All participants signed consent forms that included assurances of confidentiality and of the participants' freedom to drop out of the study at any point. Each member of the couple separately completed a background questionnaire that included measures of RS, relationship satisfaction and commitment, exclusivity of the relationship, and demographic information. Forty-eight couples completed the background questionnaires.

One to 2 weeks later, couples came into the laboratory to be videotaped discussing an unresolved relationship issue. On arrival, both members separately completed a measure of their current mood when thinking of their partner and of the relationship.

Participants were then given a list of 19 topics that college dating couples report arguing about (see below). They were asked (a) to choose up to 5 topics of ongoing conflict to discuss during the video session and (b) to indicate the most salient issue. This approach to selecting discussion topics was based on Gottman's (1979) finding that couples become more involved when discussing topics of personal concern than when discussing standard experimenter-assigned topics. The list had been generated from the most common answers to the open-ended question, "What are some of the things you and your dating partner argue about?", provided by 100 participants in a pilot study of college students. These items included "spending time together," "other friendships," "commitment," and "sex."

The researcher then picked a topic that both partners had selected to be the focus of their discussion. In the four couples whose members selected nonoverlapping topics, the researcher randomly selected a topic that one member of the couple had picked as especially salient. HRS and LRS people did not differ in their selection of topics.

Couples were filmed for 20 min. The video camera was set up behind a one-way mirror to reduce distraction. Participants were aware that they were being recorded on video, but they were assured that nobody would be watching them during the interaction period. After 20 min, the camera was turned off and the interaction ended. To assess postdiscussion mood, each partner again completed the mood questionnaire. When finished, participants were asked for a second time for consent to use the video for research purposes and were given the opportunity to question the experimenter about the study. Each participant received $14 in compensation for his or her time.

The laboratory interaction component was completed successfully by 39 couples. Of the remaining 9 couples who had completed the background questionnaire, 3 couples had broken up before being videotaped, 3 couples could not be scheduled for videotaping before leaving campus for the summer, and 2 couples declined to participate in the videotaped discussion. One couple completed the conflict discussion, but their data could not be used because of technical difficulties. The 39 couples on whom interaction data were obtained did not differ significantly from the original 48 couples on RS or on relationship satisfaction or commitment. An additional 23 couples expressed an interest in participating in the study, but did not complete any measures.

The sample included two lesbian couples. These couples were excluded from the analyses examining the impact of men's RS. For the analyses of the impact of women's RS, one member of each lesbian couple was randomly assigned to be the focal woman. Dropping these two couples from the analyses did not alter the findings reported below.

Measures

RSQ. As in Study 1, we treated RS as a dichotomy. People scoring at or above the median were defined as HRS (scored 1), whereas those scoring below the median were defined as LRS (scored 0). Similar results emerged whether RS was treated dichotomously or continuously. Partners' RS scores were not significantly correlated (for the continuous measure: $r = -.11, p > .10$; for the dichotomous measure, $r = -.15, p > .10$).

Relationship *satisfaction.* This measure was described in Study 1. The mean on a 0–7 scale was 5.31 ($SD = 1.29, \alpha = .79$) for men and 5.45 ($SD = 1.30, \alpha = .91$) for women.

Relationship commitment. As in Study 1, commitment was indexed by responses on a 1 (*not committed*) to 7 (*very committed*) scale to the question, "How committed are you to the relationship?" The mean was 6.34 ($SD = 0.84$) for men and 6.03 ($SD = 0.96$) for women.

Mood questionnaire. This questionnaire was used to assess anger about the relationship, which we viewed as an indicator of the partners' rejecting response following conflict. The questionnaire also assessed depression and anxiety about the relationship, the preconflict measures of which were included as covariates in some of the analyses reported below. Participants were asked to rate, on a 0–3 scale, how they felt "right now" when they thought of their partner and their relationship. The mood items were drawn from the Affects Balance Scale (Derogatis, 1975).

The Anger scale consists of feeling resentful, irritated, frustrated, enraged, wary, threatened, and angry at the other person. The Depression scale consists of feeling guilty, hopeless, sad, worthless, depressed, blue, ashamed, and unhappy. The Anxiety scale consists of feeling afraid, nervous, agitated, tense, on edge, and anxious. Alpha reliabilities for Anger, Depression, and Anxiety were respectively .78, .82, and .77 for men and .78, .80, and .65 for women.

Interaction data. Videotaped interactions were coded using the Marital Interaction Coding System—IV (MICS–IV; Weiss & Summers, 1983). To ensure that participants had become comfortable in the laboratory setting, only the final 10 min of the taped session were coded. Coding was done by experienced coders at the University of Oregon Marital Studies Program (for a discussion of the MICS–IV coding scheme, see Weiss & Summers, 1983). This microanalytic coding scheme involves coding each discrete segment of classifiable action that participants engage in during the taped session. The MICS–IV codes encompass both verbal content and nonverbal behavior. HRS and LRS people engaged in the same overall amounts of behavior.

We combined a set of behavior codes to form a negative-behavior composite and calculated the proportion of total behavior that was negative. The codes that made up the negative-behavior composite and their definitions given in the MICS–IV manual were as follows: mindread negative (a statement of fact that assumes a negative mindset or motivation of the partner), voice tone (indicates a hostile or negative voice tone), deny responsibility (a statement that conveys lack of responsibility for a problem), put-down (a verbal statement or nonverbal behavior that demeans and mocks the partner), turn-off (nonverbal gestures that communicate disgust, displeasure, disapproval, or disagreement), and dysphoric affect (an affect that communicates depression or sadness; any self-complaint or whiny voice). No participants engaged in two additional types of negative behaviors coded by the MICS: criticize and threat. The negative-behavior composite accounted for 2% of the total number of behaviors coded for women and 1% for men. The relatively low rates of negative behaviors were to be expected, given that the sample was nondistressed and given that a high proportion of all the coded behaviors were statements relating to the problem being discussed (35%) and inaudible talk (11%). Coders were

unaware of the study hypotheses or of participants' RS scores. Two people coded 20% of the tapes. The interrater agreement between the two coders was 75%.

Results

Because the behavior data were proportional, analyses were performed on behavior data that had been transformed using the arcsin square root transformation (Myers, 1966); means and standard deviations are reported on the basis of untransformed behavior data.

Men

The behavioral mediation hypothesis was not supported for men. The results of an analysis of covariance (ANCOVA) showed that partners of HRS men were not significantly more angry about the relationship following the conflict discussion than partners of LRS men, adjusting for preconflict partner anger (HRS: adjusted $M = .25$; LRS: adjusted $M = .23$, $t[34] = 0.17$, $p = .87$). Men's RS also was not significantly associated with partners' postconflict depression and anxiety. HRS and LRS men did not differ significantly in the negativity of their behavior during the conflict discussion (HRS: $M = .02$, $SD = .02$; LRS: $M = .01$, $SD = .02$, $t[35] = 0.92$, $p = .36$).

Women

The behavioral mediation hypothesis was supported for women. The results of an analysis of variance (ANOVA) showed that partners of HRS women were significantly more angry about the relationship following the conflict discussion than partners of LRS women (HRS: $M = .34$, $SD = .43$; LRS: $M = .11$, $SD = .20$, $t[37] = 2.15$, $p < .05$). HRS and LRS women's partners did not differ significantly in preconflict anger (HRS: $M = .30$, $SD = .40$; LRS: $M = .20$, $SD = .39$, $t[37] = 0.83$, $p = .41$). Adjusting for preconflict anger, the postconflict difference between HRS and LRS women in their partners' anger reflected both a significant pre- to postconflict discussion decline in anger in partners of LRS women, $M = -.11$, $t(36) = 2.10$,

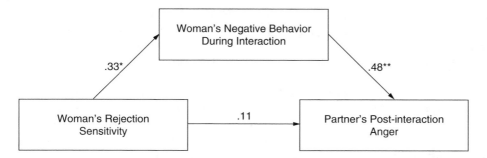

FIGURE 25.3 ■ Does women's negative behavior mediate the impact of their rejection sensitivity on their partner's postinteraction anger? Analyses controlled for partner's preconflict anger. Total effect of women's rejection sensitivity on partner's postinteraction anger was .24*. *$p < .05$; **$p < .01$.

$p < .05$, and a nonsignificant increase in anger in partners of HRS women, $M = .05$, $t(36) = 0.96$, $p = .35$. The effect of women's RS on their partners' postconflict mood was specific to anger. Women's RS was not a significant predictor of their partners' postconflict depression or anxiety.

An ANOVA also revealed that HRS women showed proportionately more negative behavior than LRS women during the discussion (HRS: $M = .04$, $SD = .04$; LRS: $M = .01$, $SD = .02$; $t[37] = 2.97$, $p < .001$). This difference remained significant when partners' preconflict anger was entered as a covariate, $t(36) = 2.81$, $p < .01$.

To assess how much of the association between women's RS and their partners' postconflict anger was explained by the women's negative behavior during the conflict, we conducted a path analysis. First, we regressed the partners' postconflict anger on their preconflict anger and on the women's RS. The b for RS was .24, $t(37) = 2.14$, $p < .05$. When women's negativity during the interaction was controlled, the b for the women's RS declined from .24 to .11. This latter coefficient is the direct effect of the women's RS on their partners' change in anger. The indirect effect of women's RS on their partners' change in anger is $.24 - .11 = .13$. Thus, the women's negative behaviors accounted for 54% (.13/.24) of the effect of women's RS on their partners' change in anger. These results are presented in Figure 25.3.

We recomputed the various analyses with a number of control variables to rule out potential third-variable explanations for the impact of women's RS on their behavior and on their partners' postconflict anger. Controlling for partners' RS, global relationship satisfaction or commitment, or their negative behavior during their interactions did not alter the results. Similarly, the results were not altered by controlling for the women's relationship satisfaction or commitment, or preinteraction negative mood.

Discussion

These results support the behavioral mediation hypothesis (Hypothesis 3) for women, but not for men. First, although the partners of HRS and LRS women did not differ significantly in preconflict anger, the partners of HRS women were significantly more angry about their relationships after conflict than were the partners of LRS women. These postconflict differences reflected a nonsignificant increase in the anger of HRS women's partners and a significant decline in the anger of LRS women's partners, which is consistent with prior research (Bradbury, 1994; Bradbury & Davila, 1997; Veroff, Hatchett, & Douvan, 1992).

Second, HRS women behaved more negatively than LRS women during the conflict discussion. Third, HRS women's greater negativity during their discussions helped account for why their partners were more angry than LRS women's partners after their discussions. These results held irrespective of the women's preinteraction negative mood, relationship satisfaction and commitment, their partners' relationship satisfaction and commitment, RS, preinteraction negative mood, and negative behavior during the interaction. Consistent with Study 1's findings, men's RS predicted neither their conflict behavior nor their partners' postconflict anger.

General Discussion

Our two studies join other recent studies (McNulty & Swann, 1994; Murray et al., 1996a, 1996b) in answering Jussim's call for evidence that people's expectations influence, rather than merely reflect, the reality of their ongoing relationships (Jussim, 1991; Jussim & Eccles, 1995). Moreover, our research moves beyond documenting expectancy confirmation and into delineating the intermediary behavioral processes. Specifically, our results provide evidence for Sroufe's (1990) proposal, derived from attachment theory, that rejection expectations can lead people to behave in ways that elicit rejection from others. Using research designs that permitted us to rule out plausible alternative hypotheses for the relation between rejection expectancies and their confirmation, we showed that women who anxiously expected rejection behaved in ways during conflict that elicited a rejecting response from their romantic partners.

Role of Relationship Beliefs in Close Relationships

Our studies elucidate a process whereby one person's relationship beliefs, presumably formed on the basis of that person's prior relational experience, can lead a couple to become locked into destructive interactional patterns. Our results also point to a process whereby a person's maladaptive relationship beliefs can be maintained, whatever their initial origin. Moreover, our findings suggest how one person's relationship history could help shape the quality of the partner's experiences in subsequent relationships. Specifically, the destructive or healthy interactional processes set in motion by one person's relationship beliefs may alter the relationship beliefs of that person's partner

in ways that influence the partner's subsequent relationships. These possibilities need to be tested directly in subsequent research.

The particular relationship beliefs that we focused on, beliefs about whether significant others will be supportive or rejecting in times of need, are widely acknowledged to shape and be shaped by relationship experiences (e.g., Bowlby, 1969, 1973, 1980; Hazan & Shaver, 1994). An objective of our work on rejection sensitivity was to provide a precise and, consequently, testable account of these beliefs and of their role in people's relationships. Guided by social–cognitive theory, we conceptualized the legacy of rejection in terms of the moment-to-moment thoughts, feelings, and action plans that are the immediate antecedents of social interaction (e.g., Andersen & Glassman, 1996; Baldwin, 1992; Dweck & Leggett, 1988; Heider, 1958; Higgins & Bargh, 1987; Kelley, 1979; Mischel, 1973; Mischel & Shoda, 1995). Specifically, we conceptualized rejection sensitivity as the disposition to anxiously expect, readily perceive, and overreact to rejection from significant others. Our findings underscore the value of merging our social–cognitive perspective on what individuals bring to and take from relationships with the interpersonal perspective on relationships (Christensen & Heavey, 1990; Coyne, 1976; Gottman, 1979), which emphasizes the social interaction occurring in relationships.

Self-Fulfilling Prophecy in Naturally Occurring Relationships

A review of existing studies of self-fulfilling prophecy in ongoing relationships led Jussim (1991) to conclude that the evidence is weaker and less consistent than commonly assumed (see also Jussim & Eccles, 1995). Results from our diary study support an explanation for the equivocal nature of this evidence that is consistent with Mischel and Shoda's (1995) explanation for why personality dispositions are generally equivocal predictors of behavior. Mischel and Shoda (1995) have proposed that whether an individual's personality disposition (e.g., RS) becomes activated in ways that influence behavior depends reliably on the psychological meaning of the situations that the individual encounters. Thus, for example, situations where rejection is perceived to be a possibility (e.g., conflict) should activate anxious expectations of rejection in HRS women to a greater extent than the average situation. Consequently, Mischel and Shoda's (1995) dynamic account of personality predicts a pattern of weak and inconsistent results from studies of expectancy confirmation that aggregate across expectancy-relevant and expectancy-irrelevant situations.

The diary methodology allowed us to capitalize on naturally occurring, within-person variation in situations deemed likely to activate rejection expectancies (i.e., conflicts) and to compare expectancy realization in these situations with expectancy realization in situations unselected for their expectancy-activating potential. There was no evidence of expectancy realization in nonconflict situations, which we view as proxying for the aggregation approach in that no distinction is made between expectancy-relevant and expectancy-irrelevant nonconflict situations. However, expectancy realization occurred in the specific context of conflict, which was known to activate rejection expectancies in HRS women. These findings highlight the importance of expectancy-relevant situations in revealing expectancy realization. By implication, studies of self-fulfilling prophecy hypotheses in ongoing relationships can yield evidence of expectancy confirmation only to the extent that participants are exposed to situations that activate their pertinent expectations.

Issues for Future Research

Although answering the questions of whether and why rejection expectancies are realized, our findings also raised important questions.

What explains the gender differences in our findings? Whereas our results reveal the potential of interpersonal conflict as a critical situation for observing the realization of rejection expectancies, they also delineate its boundaries. Conflicts with romantic partners were appropriate situations in which to examine the confirmation of rejection expectations in women, but not in men. Perhaps gender differences in the meaning of conflicts and

disagreement with intimate partners account for this finding. Consistent with this possibility, the prospect of disagreement and conflict has been found to elicit stronger rejection concerns in HRS women than in HRS men (Downey, 1997). Similarly, adult attachment research has shown links between relationship arguments and abandonment anxiety for women, but not for men (Collins & Read, 1990).

Why might intimate conflicts have different meanings for men and women? Cross and Madson (1997) recently proposed that maintaining harmonious intimate relationships is a more integral part of the self-concept in women than in men. If that is true, then one implication is that events that threaten closeness and connection with significant others, including private conflicts and disagreement, should activate rejection concerns in HRS women to a greater extent than in HRS men. What type of events may signify rejection to HRS men to a greater extent than to HRS women? Baumeister and Sommer (1997) have argued that whereas connection with significant others may be relatively more integral to the self-concepts of women than of men, the status and esteem in which men are held by the larger social group may be relatively more integral to men's self-concepts. Thus, HRS men may be particularly likely to perceive rejection in events that threaten the loss of societal respect or in events that challenge their confidence that others respect them (e.g., if their partners make them look foolish in front of their friends or undermine their belief that others respect them). This speculation is consistent with Downey and Feldman's (1996) finding that HRS men, but not HRS women, were characterized by sexual jealousy and by efforts to monitor and control their partners' social contacts. These behaviors can readily be interpreted as reflecting attempts to control a partner's behavior to maintain the respect of one's social group. Not surprisingly, such behavior contributed to partner dissatisfaction.

These observations suggest that the relation between women's RS and their rejection-eliciting hostility should be particularly evident in situations that activate concerns about loss of a close, intimate relationship. In contrast, the relation between men's RS and their rejection-eliciting jealous and controlling behavior should be evident in situations that activate concerns about loss of social status.

Why do HRS women behave in ways that elicit rejection? A possible explanation suggested by self-verification theory (Swann, 1983) is that HRS women, like everyone else, are motivated to maintain predictability and thus a sense of control over their lives. Thus, the goal of maintaining predictability might prompt women who anxiously expect rejection to act in ways that help ensure partner rejection. One way of achieving this goal is to select partners who are likely to act rejectingly, such as someone who is unlikely to show sustained relationship satisfaction or commitment. Yet, our findings cannot be completely explained by HRS women selecting partners who are prone to behave rejectingly. The longitudinal nature of the diary and observational studies made it possible to statistically adjust for pertinent preexisting partner characteristics, such as satisfaction and commitment.

Although partner selection cannot completely explain why women with anxious expectations of rejection tend to get rejected, the desire to maintain predictability may still motivate women who anxiously expect rejection to behave in rejection-eliciting ways during conflict. However, Ayduk, Downey, Testa, Yen, and Shoda (in press) have found evidence that is more consistent with viewing the hostile behavior of women who anxiously expect rejection as an overreaction to perceived rejection (see also, Collins, 1996). In an experiment using a priming paradigm (Bargh, Raymond, Pryor, & Strack, 1995), thoughts of rejection automatically facilitated thoughts of hostility in HRS women to a greater extent than in LRS women. By contrast, hostile thoughts did not facilitate thoughts of rejection, as should have occurred if HRS women's hostile behavior was intended to elicit rejection. Rather than having an explicit instrumental goal, HRS women's aggression is probably a behavioral expression of feelings of hurt, anger, despair, and hopelessness (Ben-David, 1993; Eskin & Kravitz, 1980).

Are there alternative responses to rejection cues? Above, we suggested that HRS women tend to interpret rejection cues as evidence that rejection has occurred. Thus, feeling that they have

nothing left to lose, their hostility may be an expression of revenge or frustration. An alternative response of HRS women in situations where they fear rejection may be to interpret rejection cues as triggers to engage in behaviors such as self-silencing (Jack, 1991; Jack & Dill, 1992) or acting ingratiatingly (Downey, Bonica, & Rincon, in press), which are intended to prevent rejection. Both of these forms of behavior may help them prevent overt rejection in the short run. But, in the long run, such behavior in HRS women may lead to both depression and diminished relationship satisfaction for both partners as problems in the relationship never get constructively resolved.

What are the consequences of violated expectations? Our research focused on demonstrating that rejection expectancies are fulfilled by prompting behavior that elicits confirmatory social feedback. By implication, altering people's rejection expectations should alter their behavior and consequently alter the quality of feedback they receive. In support of this inference, Rabiner and Coie (1989) found that when peer-rejected children were led to expect acceptance from peers they were about to meet, these children were subsequently better accepted than peer-rejected children not led to expect acceptance, and that the girls (but not boys) induced to expect acceptance were observed to behave more positively toward their peers. These experimental results convey the importance of delineating the naturally occurring circumstances that alter people's rejection expectations.

Yet, the malleability of people's expectations about relationships undoubtedly depends on how ingrained and generalized their expectations are and on the goals served by maintaining consistency (Swann, 1997). Generalized expectations of rejection that are based on prolonged childhood rejection by parents and peers are probably less responsive to contradictory feedback than specific expectations about romantic relationships formed on the basis of rejection in a recent relationship (Bowlby, 1969).

Conclusions and Caveats

Several caveats should be noted when interpreting the results of Studies 1 and 2. First, both studies were restricted to college dating couples in committed and satisfying relationships. Indeed, very little negativity was expressed during the Study 2 conflict discussion. We examined only committed relationships to help ensure that RS was an antecedent rather than a consequence of relationship difficulties. Future research will need to establish whether our findings generalize to distressed relationships. The applicability of our findings to marital relationships also needs to be examined.

Second, the findings suggest that HRS women's anxious expectations of rejection lead to relationship breakup in part because HRS women behave in ways that erode their partners' relationship satisfaction and commitment. Alternatively, as perceived rejections accumulate, HRS women may become increasingly dissatisfied with the relationship, prompting them to end it. Or, having become convinced that their partner will inevitably leave them, HRS women may act preemptively to end the anxiety-laden waiting period and to avoid overt rejection. Our studies did not examine the precise causes of the breakups or who initiated them. A more complete understanding of the relation between RS and relationship longevity requires following people throughout a relationship and recording the breakup process.

These caveats notwithstanding, our results confirm that women's expectancies help create their own reality in romantic relationships. During conflicts, women's expectations of rejection led them to behave in ways that elicited confirmatory reactions from their romantic partners. Moreover, even when controlling for a partner's relationship satisfaction and commitment, rejection sensitivity proved a potent predictor of relationship breakup. Eventually, then, as conflicts accumulate, the realities of HRS women's relationships may merge more closely with their expectations.

NOTES

Geraldine Downey, Antonio L. Freitas, Benjamin Michaelis, and Hala Khouri, Department of Psychology, Columbia University. Antonio L. Freitas is now at the Department of Psychology, Yale University.

This research was supported by grants from the National Institute of Mental Health (R29-MH51113) and the Harry Frank Guggenheim Foundation and by a W. T. Grant faculty scholar award.

We thank Rebecca Shansky for her competent help in conducting these studies. We also gratefully acknowledge the contributions of Niall Bolger, Thomas Bradbury, Carol Dweck, Scott Feldman, Tory Higgins, Sheri Levy, Walter Mischel, and Yuichi Shoda.

Correspondence concerning this article should be addressed to Geraldine Downey, Department of Psychology, Columbia University, Schermerhorn Hall, Room 406, Mail Code 5501, 1190 Amsterdam Avenue, New York, New York 10027. Electronic mail may be sent to gdowney@psych.columbia.edu.

REFERENCES

Andersen, S., & Glassman, N. (1996). Responding to significant others when they are not there: Effects on interpersonal inference, motivation, and affect. In R. Sorrentino & E. T. Higgins (Eds.), *Handbook of motivation and cognition: Vol. 3. The interpersonal context* (pp. 262–321). New York: Guilford Press.

Ayduk, O., Downey, G., Testa, A., Yen, Y., & Shoda, Y. (in press). Does rejection elicit hostility in rejection-sensitive women? *Social Cognition*.

Baldwin, M. W. (1992). Relational schemas and the processing of social information. *Psychological Bulletin, 112*, 461–484.

Bargh, J. A., Raymond, P., Pryor, J. B., & Strack, F. (1995). Attractiveness of the underling: An automatic power → sex association and its consequences for sexual harassment and aggression. *Journal of Personality and Social Psychology, 68*, 768–781.

Baumeister, R., & Sommer, K. L. (1997). What do men want? Gender differences and two spheres of belongingness: Comment on Cross and Madson (1997). *Psychological Bulletin, 122*, 38–44.

Ben-David, S. (1993). The two facets of female violence: The public and the domestic domains. *Journal of Family Violence, 8*, 345–359.

Bolger, N., & Schilling, E. A. (1991). Personality and problems of everyday life: The role of neuroticism in exposure and reactivity to daily stressors. *Journal of Personality, 59*, 355–386.

Bolger, N., & Zuckerman, A. (1995). A framework for studying personality in the stress process. *Journal of Personality and Social Psychology, 69*, 890–902.

Bonica, C., & Downey, G. (1997). *Peer rejection sensitizes children to expect rejection*. Unpublished manuscript, Columbia University, New York.

Bowlby, J. (1969). *Attachment and loss: Vol. 1. Attachment*. New York: Basic Books.

Bowlby, J. (1973). *Attachment and loss: Vol. 2. Separation*. New York: Basic Books.

Bowlby, J. (1980). *Attachment and loss: Vol. 3. Loss, sadness, and depression*. New York: Basic Books.

Bradbury, T. N. (1994). Unintended effects of marital research on marital relationships. *Journal of Family Psychology, 8*, 187–201.

Bradbury, T. N., Beach, S. R., Fincham, F. D., & Nelson, G. M. (1996). Attributions and behavior in functional and dysfunctional marriages. *Journal of Consulting and Clinical Psychology, 64*, 569–576.

Bradbury, T. N., & Davila, J. (1997). *Husband and wife affect before and after conflict discussions*. Unpublished data, University of California, Los Angeles.

Bradbury, T. N., & Fincham, F. D. (1990). Attributions in marriage: Review and critique. *Psychological Bulletin, 107*, 3–33.

Bradbury, T. N., & Fincham, F. D. (1992). Attributions and behavior in marital interactions. *Journal of Personality and Social Psychology, 63*, 613–628.

Bradbury, T. N., & Fincham, F. D. (1993). Assessing dysfunctional cognitions in marriage: A reconsideration of the Relationship Belief Inventory. *Psychological Assessment, 5*, 92–101.

Bradbury, T. N., & Karney, B. R. (1993). Longitudinal study of marital interaction and dysfunction: Review and analysis. *Clinical Psychology Review, 13*, 15–27.

Bryk, A., & Raudenbush, S. W. (1992). *Hierarchical linear models*. Newbury Park, CA: Sage.

Christensen, A., & Heavey, C. L. (1990). Gender and social structure in the demand/withdraw pattern of marital interaction. *Journal of Personality and Social Psychology, 59*, 73–81.

Collins, N. (1996). Working models of attachment: Implications for explanations, emotion, and behavior. *Journal of Personality and Social Psychology, 71*, 810–832.

Collins, N., & Read, S. (1990). Adult attachment, working models, and relationship quality in dating couples. *Journal of Personality and Social Psychology, 58*, 644–663.

Coyne, J. C. (1976). Depression and the response of others. *Journal of Abnormal Psychology, 85*, 186–193.

Cross, S. E., & Madson, L. (1997). Models of the self: Self-construals and gender. *Psychological Bulletin, 122*, 5–37.

Darley, J., & Fazio, R. (1980). Expectancy confirmation processes arising in the social interaction sequence. *American Psychologist, 35*, 867–881.

Derogotis, L. (1975). *Affects Balance Scale*. Towson, MD: Clinical Psychometrics Research Unit.

Downey, G. (1997, May). *Rejection sensitivity and intimate relationships*. Paper presented at the annual meeting of the American Psychological Society, Washington, DC.

Downey, G., Bonica, C., & Rincon, C. (in press). Rejection sensitivity and conflict in adolescent romantic relationships. In W. Furman, B. Brown, & C. Feiring (Eds.), *Adolescent romantic relationships*. New York: Cambridge University Press.

Downey, G., & Feldman, S. (1996). Implications of rejection sensitivity for intimate relationships. *Journal of Personality and Social Psychology, 70*, 1327–1343.

Downey, G., Khouri, H., & Feldman, S. (1997). Early interpersonal trauma and adult adjustment: The mediational role of rejection sensitivity. In D. Cicchetti & S. Toth (Eds.), *Rochester Symposium on Developmental Psychopathology:*

Vol. VIII. The effects of trauma on the developmental process (pp. 85–114). Rochester, NY: University of Rochester Press.

Downey, G., Lebolt, A., Rincon, C., & Freitas, A. L. (1998). Rejection sensitivity and children's interpersonal difficulties. *Child Development, 69*, 1072–1089.

Dweck, C. S., & Leggett, E. L. (1988). A social–cognitive approach to personality and motivation. *Psychological Review, 95*, 256–273.

Erikson, E. (1950). *Childhood and society*. New York: Norton.

Eskin, M., & Kravitz, M. (1980). *Child abuse and neglect*. Washington, DC: U. S. Department of Justice.

Feldman, S., & Downey, G. (1994). Rejection sensitivity as a mediator of the impact of childhood exposure to family violence on adult attachment behavior. *Development and Psychopathology, 6*, 231–247.

Gottman, J. M. (1979). *Marital interaction: Experimental investigations*. New York: Academic Press.

Gottman, J. M. (1993). The roles of conflict engagement, escalation, and avoidance in marital interaction: A longitudinal view of five types of couples. *Journal of Consulting and Clinical Psychology, 61*, 6–15.

Hazan, C., & Shaver, P. (1994). Attachment as an organizational framework for the study of close relationships. *Psychological Inquiry, 5*, 1–22.

Heider, F. (1958). *The psychology of interpersonal relations*. New York: Wiley.

Higgins, E. T., & Bargh, J. A. (1987). Social cognition and social perception. *Annual Review of Psychology, 38*, 369–425.

Hilton, J., & Darley, J. (1991). The effects of interaction goals on person perception. In M. N. Zanna (Ed.), *Advances in experimental social psychology* (Vol. 24, pp. 235–267). San Diego, CA: Academic Press.

Horney, K. (1937). *The neurotic personality of our time*. New York: Norton.

Jack, D. C. (1991). *Silencing the self: Women and depression*. Cambridge, MA: Harvard University Press.

Jack, D. C., & Dill, D. (1992). The Silencing the Self Scale: Schemas of intimacy associated with depression in women. *Psychology of Women Quarterly, 16*, 97–106.

Jussim, L. (1986). Self-fulfilling prophecies: A theoretical and integrative review. *Psychological Review, 93*, 429–445.

Jussim, L. (1991). Social perception and social reality: A reflection-construction model. *Psychological Review, 98*, 54–73.

Jussim, L., & Eccles, J. (1995). Naturally occurring interpersonal expectancies. In N. Eisenberg (Ed.), *Social development: Review of personality and social psychology* (Vol. 15, pp. 74–108). Thousand Oaks, CA: Sage.

Juvonen, J. (1991). Deviance, perceived responsibility, and negative peer reactions. *Developmental Psychology, 27*, 672–681.

Kayser, K. (1993). *When love dies: The process of marital disaffection*. New York: Guilford Press.

Kelley, H. (1979). *Personal relationships: Their structure and processes*. Hillsdale, NJ: Erlbaum.

Kenny, D., Kashy, D., & Bolger, N. (1998). Data analysis in social psychology. In D. Gilbert, S. Fiske, & G. Linzey

(Eds.), *Handbook of social psychology* (4th ed., pp. 233–265). New York: McGraw-Hill.

Kobak, R., & Hazan, C. (1991). Attachment in marriage: Effects of security and accuracy of working models. *Journal of Personality and Social Psychology, 60*, 861–869.

McNulty, S. E., & Swann, W. E., Jr. (1994). Identity negotiation in roommate relationships: The self as architect and consequence of social reality. *Journal of Personality and Social Psychology, 67*, 1012–1023.

Merton, R. K. (1948). The self-fulfilling prophecy. *Antioch Review, 8*, 193–210.

Miller, D. T., & Turnbull, W. (1986). Expectancies and interpersonal processes. *Annual Review of Psychology, 37*, 233–256.

Miller, G. E., & Bradbury, T. N. (1995). Refining the association between attributions and behavior in marital interaction. *Journal of Family Psychology, 9*, 196–208.

Mischel, W. (1973). Toward a cognitive social learning reconceptualization of personality. *Psychological Review, 80*, 252–283.

Mischel, W., & Shoda, Y. (1995). A cognitive–affective system theory of personality: Reconceptualizing situations, dispositions, dynamics, and invariance in personality structures. *Psychological Review, 102*, 246–268.

Murray, S. L., Holmes, J. G., & Griffin, D. W. (1996a). The benefits of positive illusions: Idealization and the construction of satisfaction in close relationships. *Journal of Personality and Social Psychology, 70*, 79–98.

Murray, S. L., Holmes, J. G., & Griffin, D. W. (1996b). The self-fulfilling nature of positive illusions in romantic relationships: Love is not blind, but prescient. *Journal of Personality and Social Psychology, 71*, 1155–1180.

Myers, J. L. (1966). *Fundamentals of experimental design.* Boston: Allyn & Bacon.

Rabiner, D., & Coie, J. (1989). Effects of expectancy inductions on rejected children's acceptance by unfamiliar peers. *Developmental Psychology, 25*, 450–457.

Reis, H. T., & Patrick, B. C. (1996). Attachment and intimacy: Component processes. In E. T. Higgins & A. W. Kruglanski (Eds.), *Social psychology: Handbook of basic principles* (pp. 523–563). New York: Guilford Press.

SAS Institute. (1989). *SAS/STAT user's guide* (Version 6, 4th ed., Vol. 2). Cary, NC: Author.

Snyder, M. (1992). Motivational foundations of behavioral confirmation. In M. P. Zanna (Ed.), *Advances in experimental social psychology* (Vol. 25, pp. 67–114). San Diego, CA: Academic Press.

Spanier, G. B. (1976). Measuring dyadic adjustment: New scales for assessing the quality of marriage and similar dyads. *Journal of Marriage and the Family, 38*, 15–28.

Sroufe, L. A. (1990). An organizational perspective on the self. In D. Cicchetti & M. Beeghly (Eds.), *The self in transition: Infancy to childhood. The John D. and Catherine T. MacArthur Foundation Series on Mental Health and Development* (pp. 281–307). Chicago: University of Chicago Press.

Stephen, T. D. (1984). Symbolic interdependence and post-breakup distress: A reformulation of the attachment construct. *Journal of Divorce, 8*, 1–16.

Sullivan, H. S. (1953). *The interpersonal theory of psychiatry.* New York: Norton.

Swann, W. B., Jr. (1983). Self-verification: Bringing social reality into harmony with the self. In J. Suls & A. G. Greenwald (Eds.), *Psychological perspectives on the self* (Vol. 2, pp. 33–66). Hillsdale, NJ: Erlbaum.

Swann, W. B., Jr. (1997). The trouble with change: Self-verification and the self. *Psychological Science, 8*, 177–180.

Veroff, J., Hatchett, S., & Douvan, E. (1992). Consequences of participating in a longitudinal study of marriage. *Public Opinion Quarterly, 56*, 315–327.

Weiss, R. L., & Summers, K. (1983). Marital Interaction Coding System III. In E. Filsinger (Ed.), *Marriage and family assessment* (pp. 35—115). Beverly Hills, CA: Sage.

Emotional Behavior in Long-Term Marriage

Laura L. Carstensen • Stanford University

John M. Gottman • University of Washington

Robert W. Levenson • University of California, Berkeley

In exploring the emotional climate of long-term marriages, this study used an observational coding system to identify specific emotional behaviors expressed by middle-aged and older spouses during discussions of a marital problem. One hundred and fifty-six couples differing in age and marital satisfaction were studied. Emotional behaviors expressed by couples differed as a function of age, gender, and marital satisfaction. In older couples, the resolution of conflict was less emotionally negative and more affectionate than in middle-aged marriages. Differences between husbands and wives and between happy and unhappy marriages were also found. Wives were more affectively negative than husbands, whereas husbands were more defensive than wives, and unhappy marriages involved greater exchange of negative affect than happy marriages.

We had two primary goals in this research. The first was to explore differences in emotional expression in intimate relationships in middle-aged and older marriages. The second was to test the generalizability to middle-aged and older couples of findings from earlier research investigating the influence of gender and marital satisfaction on emotional interaction in young married couples. The study was based on the analysis of videotaped interactions of happy and unhappy couples discussing conflicts in their relationships (see also Levenson, Carstensen, & Gottman, 1993). By pursuing our research questions in both happy and unhappy marriages, we were able to examine the pervasiveness of age and gender differences across these very different types of couples. In the following sections, we elaborate our rationale and hypotheses for the research.

Emotion and Aging

Early theories of old age depicted emotion as dampened, rigid, and flat (Banham, 1951; Looft, 1972). Yet, a growing body of empirical evidence is painting quite a different picture. Findings from several laboratories suggest age-related improvement in the control of emotion (Lawton, Kleban, Rajagopal, & Dean, 1992) and emotional understanding (Labouvie-Vief & DeVoe, 1991; Labouvie-Vief, Hakim-Larson, DeVoe, & Schoeberlein, 1989). Self-reported intensity of emotion is comparable for old and young people (Levenson, Carstensen, Friesen, & Ekman, 1991; Malatesta & Kalnok, 1984), and some research suggests that emotion becomes increasingly salient with age (Carstensen, 1992; Carstensen & Turk-Charles, 1994; Fredrickson & Carstensen, 1990; Hashtroudi, Johnson, & Chrosniak, 1990). This evidence, in tandem with findings that older people experience relatively low rates of psychological disorders (George, Blazer, Winfield-Laird, Leaf, & Fischback, 1988), suggests that emotion may represent a life domain in which functioning is well preserved or even improves with age.

If improved functioning does indeed characterize emotion in old age, it is important to undertake examination of the mechanisms underlying such change. Theoretical arguments have been advanced that older people proactively design their environments in the service of emotion regulation (Carstensen, 1993; Lawton, 1989; Schulz, 1985). In socioemotional selectivity theory, for example, Carstensen (1991, 1993) argued that because emotion becomes more salient with age, people mold social interactions to maximize emotional benefits. However, we know of almost no studies of older adults that have examined emotion expressed within a social context. If older people do "manage" social interactions toward the optimization of positive affect, one should see evidence of this in the interactional dynamics surrounding discussion of emotionally charged topics.

The marital relationship offers an ideal context in which to examine emotion. First, emotions experienced in the context of marriage run the gamut from joy to contempt, and the negotiation of affectively laden issues is required in the best of marriages. Second, a growing body of research, based on cross-sectional and longitudinal findings, suggests that—after a decline in marital satisfaction in midlife—marriages become increasingly positive as the partners enter old age (Brubaker, 1990; Guilford & Bengtson, 1979; Levenson et al., 1993). Thus, long-term marriages

theoretically represent social relationships that involve both positive and negative affect and show age-related change in a positive direction. By examining the expression of specific emotions, emotional exchanges, and emotional sequences in discussions of marital conflicts, one should be able to identify age-related differences in the strategies used in negotiating emotional interactions.

Gender Differences in Marital Interactions

Our earlier research (Gottman & Levenson, 1988; Levenson, Carstensen, & Gottman, 1994; Levenson & Gottman, 1983), as well as research from other laboratories (Christensen & Heavey, 1990; Notarius & Johnson, 1982; Schaap, 1982), suggests that there are reliable gender differences in marital behavior. Women are more confronting and more expressive emotionally and both more negative and more positive than men. Men are less expressive emotionally and are, in the face of conflict, more likely than women to be defensive and withdrawn and to engage in "stonewalling" behavior (i.e., nonexpressiveness when experiencing strong negative emotion).

However, these findings are based almost exclusively on research with relatively young couples. Virtually no research has addressed whether or not similar interactional patterns are present in older married couples. It is possible that the behavioral patterns observed in younger couples characterize only new marriages. Over time, gender-linked patterns may be over-shadowed by idiosyncratic patterns of individual couples. It is also possible that gender differences diminish with age. Several researchers (e.g., Gutmann, 1987; Hyde & Phillis, 1979; Keith & Brubaker, 1979) have suggested that men and women become more similar as they age. If such convergence occurs in the realm of emotional expression, then the oft-reported finding that wives are more likely to engage in conflict and husbands are more likely to withdraw might not hold in older marriages.

Overview of the Use of Observational Methods in Research on Marriage and Marital Satisfaction

The application of observational methods to research on marriage began in the early 1970s, addressing the fundamental question of how satisfied and dissatisfied couples differed in their resolution of conflict. In more than 50 studies conducted in the United States and cross nationally during the next two decades, observational methodology has revealed consistent differences between satisfied and dissatisfied couples (for reviews, see Gottman, 1979; Markman & Notarius, 1987; Schaap, 1982, 1984; Schaap, Buunk, & Kerkstra, 1988; Weiss & Heyman, 1990; Weiss & Summers, 1983).

Previous observational research has produced a number of consistent results. First, negative emotional behavior, such as expressed anger, sadness, contempt, and other negative emotions, appears to be the best discriminator between satisfied and dissatisfied marriages (see Schaap et al., 1988, for a review). Second, sequences of emotion expressed during marital interaction differentiate happy from unhappy couples. When the expression of negative affect by one spouse is reciprocated by negative affect from the other spouse, a pattern termed *negative affect reciprocity*, couples are likely to be dissatisfied. The temporal sequential stability or continuance of negative affective states across time also characterizes dissatisfied marriages. Third, differences between satisfied and dissatisfied couples are most pronounced when couples engage in attempts to resolve conflict (Gottman, 1979).

How representative of marriage were these observational studies, and how generalizable were their conclusions? Krokoff (1987) pointed out that the mean age of couples in past marital interaction studies was 29.94 years, whereas the mean age of the U.S. population is 44.70 years (and rising). Hence, these observational studies were primarily studies of relatively young couples in relatively new marriages. Their generality to middle-aged and older couples remains an open question.

We are aware of only two observational studies that have been conducted with older couples. One was an unpublished dissertation by Illig (1977), and the other was a published study by Zietlow and Sillars (1988). Zietlow and Sillars studied 59 couples during marital discussions. They found that "aging couples are characteristically happy, although inexpressive by modern standards" (p. 241). The emotional quality of the discussions of the older couples they studied differed as a function of the salience of the topic. When the couples discussed nonsalient topics, they were quite cordial; when they discussed salient topics, they were quite confronting. Both Illig (1977) and Zietlow and Sillars (1988) noted that the interactions of older couples had more temporal sequential predictability than the interactions of younger couples, particularly greater negative reciprocity.

These studies represent the first use of observational methods with older couples, but they are not without problems. Zietlow and Sillars (1988) recruited all of their couples from one Lutheran church in Milwaukee, which probably limits the generality of the results. Neither their study nor Illig's (1977) investigation assessed or controlled for marital satisfaction. Given the real possibility that couples in their age groups differed in marital satisfaction, it is impossible to know whether the reported findings were characteristic of different age groups, of happy or unhappy marriages, or of both.

The Present Study

Our aim in the present study was to explore affect expression and reciprocity in long-term marriages using a detailed observational system that allowed for the coding of specific emotions. First, we asked whether patterns of affect and affect reciprocity were more positive in older than in middle-aged couples. We hypothesized that older couples would express more positive emotions and fewer negative emotions during conflict discussions than would middle-aged couples. Second, we asked whether relationships that negative affect and negative affect reciprocity have been found to have with marital unhappiness in previous research with younger marriages would also be found in middle-aged and older marriages. If negative affective expression diminishes or loses its aversive quality over the years, then it might not be as strongly related to marital dissatisfaction. Finally, we asked whether gender differences observed in young marriages would still be obtained in later-life marriages.

Method

Participants

Constructing the experimental sample. A three-stage sampling procedure was used to recruit couples from communities surrounding Berkeley, California (see Levenson et al., 1993, for a complete description of the procedure). After establishing characteristics of older couples in the local community in terms of marital satisfaction, ethnicity, and socioeconomic status through a random telephone survey, we established recruitment goals (e.g., a certain percentage of old, unhappy, White, and blue-collar couples) that would represent the population of interest. A large sample of participants ($N = 960$) was then recruited by means of newspaper, radio, bulletin boards, and placards on city buses. These participants were screened by telephone and questionnaire responses to determine their suitability for the experiment. Screened participants were selected on the basis of recruitment goals for participation in the laboratory experiment.

Recruitment eligibility included length of marriage, age, and marital satisfaction criteria. To ensure that all couples were in long-term marriages, we required that middle-aged couples be married for at least 15 years, with the older spouse between 40 and 50 years of age. Older couples had to be married for at least 35 years, with the older spouse between 60 and 70 years old. To ensure representation of both relatively happy and relatively unhappy couples in the sample, we recruited comparable numbers of happy and unhappy couples in both middle-aged and older subsamples. In addition, we required that the difference between

spouses' marital satisfaction scores be no more than 20 points so that the spouses in a couple would not differ substantially in their feelings about the marriage. Because older couples were determined to be happier, on average, than middle-aged couples during telephone screening, we initially used different marital satisfaction cutoffs in recruiting the two subsamples. However (as described later), so as not to confound marital satisfaction with age, we conducted all data analyses using satisfaction groupings based on the median satisfaction score for the entire sample.

Additional criteria for participation were as follows: (a) Neither spouse had retired; (b) English was the native language or language customarily spoken at home; (c) the age difference between spouses was no more than 5 years; and (d) neither spouse was alcoholic (as indicated by scoring below 7 on the Michigan Alcoholism Screening Test; Selzer, 1971). The rationale for these additional satisfaction and age criteria was to make our sample representative of the modal long-term marriage, in which couples are relatively close in marital satisfaction and age, and to avoid having spouses fall into different satisfaction or age groups.

The final laboratory sample consisted of 156 couples assigned to one of four groups according to age and marital satisfaction using the grand average of both spouses' scores on two measures of marital satisfaction, the Locke-Williamson measure (Burgess, Locke, & Thomes, 1971) and the Locke-Wallace measure (Locke & Wallace, 1959). For the entire sample, the mean for this aggregated score was 111.5 ($SD = 17.0$) and the median was 115.1 (range $= 42.8-160.0$). This median score was used to make the final assignments to experimental groups as follows: (a) middle-aged satisfied ($n = 35$), (b) middle-aged dissatisfied ($n = 47$), (c) old satisfied ($n = 43$), and (d) old dissatisfied ($n = 31$).

Sample demographics. For middle-aged couples, the mean ages were 44.3 ($SD = 2.9$) for husbands and 43.3 ($SD = 2.9$) for wives. For older couples, the mean ages were 63.6 ($SD = 2.9$) for husbands and 62.2 ($SD = 3.2$) for wives. For the middle-aged satisfied group, the mean aggregated satisfaction score was 122.7 ($SD = 5.8$) and the mean duration of marriage in years was 21.3 ($SD = 3.4$); for the middle-aged dissatisfied group, 98.7 ($SD = 13.7$) and 20.9 ($SD = 3.4$); for the old satisfied group, 125.1 ($SD = 8.5$) and 40.4 ($SD = 3.9$); and, for the old dissatisfied group, 99.3 ($SD = 15.3$) and 39.8 ($SD = 3.1$).

The resulting sample was 85.9% White, 5.8% African American, 2.6% Hispanic, 2.6% Asian, and 2.2% with spouses of different races. Experimental groups were recruited such that they matched the general demographic balance of the geographic area (as determined by the random telephone survey) for older couples in terms of religion, ethnicity, and socioeconomic status (Levenson et al., 1993). Also, the groups themselves were matched for religion, ethnicity, and socioeconomic status.

Confounding of age and marital duration. One particular feature of our sampling strategy requires separate mention, namely, our decision to focus on long-term first marriages in these two age groups. We focused our investigation on these kinds of marriages because they are most representative of marriages in the current middle-aged and older cohorts and because we were particularly interested in learning about couples who had married in early adulthood and had managed to stay together ever since. One implication of this decision was that we would be confounding age with duration of marriage.

It is important to recognize that, in this regard, our sample is a reasonable proxy for marriages in the real world, where age and length of marriage are also typically confounded. Of course, it would have been possible to separate age and marital duration, but doing so would have meant recruiting a sample of couples who would be very unrepresentative of marriages in at least one of the age cohorts. For example, had we required that both older and middle-aged couples be married for 15 years, the resulting sample would have been composed of middle-aged couples who married in their 20s and 30s and older couples who married in their 40s and 50s. Thus, age at the time of marriage would have been confounded with current age. Furthermore, unless we recruited older couples who married for the first time in their 40s and 50s (a highly

unrepresentative group), we would probably be studying remarriages in our older sample versus first marriages in our middle-aged sample, another serious confound. We ask readers to be aware that, when we mention age differences, these may result from differences in the duration of marriage as well.

Procedure

The procedures used in this experiment were modeled after those developed by Levenson and Gottman (1983). Couples came to the laboratory after having not spoken to each other for at least 8 hr. Recording devices for obtaining physiological measures were attached, and couples engaged in three conversational interactions: (a) discussing the events of the day, (b) discussing a problem area of continuing disagreement in their marriage, and (c) discussing a mutually agreed on pleasant topic. Before the problem area interaction, couples completed the Couple's Problem Inventory (Gottman, Markman, & Notarius, 1977), in which they rated the perceived severity of 10 marital issues on a scale ranging from 0 to 100. Using these ratings, the experimenter helped couples pick a topic that both spouses had rated highly, interviewed them about the topic, and helped them focus on the key area of disagreement. In our experience, this interview serves to make the ensuing discussion more personal and less abstract.

Each conversation lasted for 15 min, preceded by a 5-min silent period. A split-screen video recording was made of the entire session. Couples were paid $150 for participating in the laboratory experiment, which consisted of the interaction session and two subsequent sessions in which spouses separately viewed the video recording and provided ratings of how they were feeling during the interaction.

Apparatus

Two remotely controlled high-resolution video cameras that were partially concealed behind darkened glass were used to obtain frontal views of each spouse's face and upper torso. These images were combined into a single split-screen image with a video special effects generator and were recorded on a VHS videocassette recorder. Two lavaliere microphones were used to record the spouses' conversations.

Data Reduction

A team of coders using the Specific Affect Coding System (SPAFF; Gottman & Krokoff, 1989; SPAFF Version 2.0, Gottman, 1989), which dismantles affect into specific positive and negative emotions and includes codes for both speakers and listeners, coded the problem area discussions. SPAFF is a cultural informant system in which coders, working with videotapes, consider a gestalt consisting of verbal content, voice tone, context, facial expression, gestures, and body movement. SPAFF treats the stream of behavior as continuous (rather than segmenting it into time blocks or turns at speech), and, thus, codes can be given at any time. The code best describing the affect of a spouse is indicated on a computerized dial until a change in behavior occurs such that another code better reflects the affective state of the spouse.

For speakers, the positive affect codes are *interest, affection, humor, validation* (i.e., acknowledgment of partner's feelings), and *joy*. The negative affect codes are *anger, contempt, disgust, belligerence, domineering, defensiveness, fear/tension/worry, sadness*, and *whining*. There is also a neutral speaker code. For listeners, codes are *positive, negative*, and *neutral*. These codes are based on the facial expressions of the listener. There is an additional code for listener disengagement called *stonewalling*.

Reliability for SPAFF codes is based on the second-by-second concordance of observers throughout the 15-min (900-s) interaction period. When more than one code appears during a 1-s period, reliability is based on the code indicated for the longer period of time in milliseconds. The statistic used to calculate reliability was Cohen's kappa, which controls for agreement by chance alone and provides a single reliability index for the entire coding system (Bakeman & Gottman, 1986). For this study, the overall mean kappa was 0.64, and the mean z score (kappa divided by the standard deviation of kappa) was 19.25 (the mean z score must exceed 1.96 for agreement to be

significantly greater than chance). The mean kappa for listener codes was 0.71, and the z score was 16.92 ($p < .001$). For speaker codes, the kappa was 0.60 and the z score was 15.02 ($p < .001$). To control for differences among couples in the total number of codes given, we converted SPAFF data for any given spouse in any given couple to percentages of the total number of speaker and listener codes expressed by that spouse and his or her partner (i.e., the sum of the 15 speaker codes and 4 listener codes for both spouses).

Results

Overview

SPAFF codes were examined at both specific and relatively global levels. First, to describe differences in the profiles of affect by age, marital satisfaction, and gender while preserving the detail provided by the 15 specific affect speaker codes and 4 listener codes, we entered the SPAFF codes into an overall multivariate analysis of variance (MANOVA). Second, to test a small number of conceptually interesting hypotheses about affect sequences, we collapsed the specific SPAFF speaker and listener codes into 3 global codes (positive, negative, and neutral) and submitted these codes to sequential analysis. (In the findings discussed subsequently, the .05 rejection level was used, unless otherwise noted.)

Specific Affect

SPAFF codes were analyzed by means of 2 (age: middle-aged vs. older couples) × 2 (satisfaction: happy vs. unhappy) × 2 (spouse: husband vs. wife) MANOVAs and analyses of variance (ANOVAs); spouse was treated as a repeated measure. An overall MANOVA was computed for the 14 nonneutral speaker codes and the 3 nonneutral listener codes (because the data were expressed as percentages of codes, for any given spouse, of the total number of codes expressed by both spouses, the neutral code was omitted to avoid linear dependency in the analysis). This was followed by univariate ANOVAs for the 15 speaker and 4 listener codes and for 3 global speaker codes: total speaker positive (sum of percentages of interest, affection, humor, validation, and joy), total speaker negative (sum of percentages of anger, contempt, disgust, belligerence, domineering, defensiveness, fear/tension/worry, sadness, and whining), and total speaker emotion (sum of percentages of positive and negative speaker codes).

The overall MANOVA revealed significant main effects of age, $F(17, 136) = 4.25, p < .001$; satisfaction, $F(17, 136) = 2.13, p = .009$; and spouse, $F(17, 136) = 5.37, p < .001$. None of the interactions in the overall MANOVA were significant. Means and F values for the univariate age, satisfaction, and spouse main effects are presented in Table 26.1.

Age effects. In terms of speaker behaviors, elderly couples were coded as being more affectionate than middle-aged couples. Middle-aged couples were coded as displaying more interest, humor,

anger, disgust, belligerence, and whining than older couples. There were no age differences in listener behaviors.

Because we had previously found that older couples rated their marital problems as less severe than those of middle-aged couples (Levenson et al., 1993), we thought it important to establish that age differences found in emotional behavior did not merely reflect age differences in problem severity. Thus, for those behaviors for which significant age differences had been found, we reran our analyses using the average rated severity of marital problems as a covariate (these ratings had been obtained before the problem area discussion by means of the Couple's Problem Inventory [Gottman et al., 1977]).

Age-related differences in affection, $F(1, 146) = 6.45, p = .012$; interest, $F(1, 146) = 10.41, p = .002$; humor, $F(1, 146) = 8.42, p = .004$; disgust,

TABLE 26.1. Specific Affect Coding System Emotional Coding for Couples

Measure	Age			Satisfaction			Spouse		
	Middle	Old	F^a	Unhappy	Happy	F^a	Husband	Wife	F^a
Global speaker codes									
Total speaker emotion	18.43	16.61	3.14	18.77	16.37	6.04*	16.60	18.53	12.26***
Total speaker positive	4.82	4.81	< 1	4.01	5.61	10.26**	4.94	4.68	< 1
Total speaker negative	13.61	11.81	1.58	14.76	10.76	14.72***	11.66	13.85	14.91***
Specific speaker and listener codes									
Neutral	8.05	8.99	< 1	7.61	9.38	5.00*	8.47	8.53	< 1
Humor	1.33	0.97	4.91*	0.98	1.35	5.09*	1.19	1.13	< 1
Affection	0.69	1.24	8.14**	0.71	1.19	5.64*	0.86	1.04	2.00
Validation	2.55	2.51	< 1	2.16	2.90	4.60*	2.72	2.34	2.91
Interest	0.23	0.07	10.11**	0.15	0.16	< 1	0.16	0.15	< 1
Joy	0.02	0.01	< 1	0.01	0.02	< 1	0.00	0.03	4.29*
Anger	2.04	1.13	7.20**	2.14	1.08	10.53**	1.17	2.04	17.81***
Disgust	0.14	0.03	9.54**	0.12	0.06	1.85	0.07	0.11	1.28
Contempt	1.20	0.98	< 1	1.43	0.75	13.85***	0.81	1.38	16.04***
Whining	0.99	0.65	5.19*	0.85	0.81	< 1	0.53	1.13	31.30***
Sadness	0.60	0.43	1.30	0.66	0.38	5.02*	0.37	0.67	9.15**
Tension	1.94	2.41	3.04	2.17	2.16	< 1	2.13	2.20	< 1
Domineering	0.98	1.13	1.17	1.36	0.74	8.16**	0.97	1.13	< 1
Belligerence	1.93	0.89	18.54***	1.74	1.14	4.00*	1.29	1.58	3.57
Defensiveness	3.79	4.16	1.01	4.29	3.64	2.20	4.32	3.61	6.75**
Listener neutral	14.77	14.93	< 1	13.86	15.83	6.61*	15.31	14.38	4.27*
Listener positive	2.54	2.73	< 1	2.04	3.22	14.11***	2.45	2.82	3.97*
Listener negative	5.86	6.54	1.89	7.36	5.00	10.61**	5.78	6.59	4.90*
Listener stonewalling	0.35	0.19	1.69	0.36	0.19	1.85	0.34	0.21	1.88

Note. Data are expressed, for any given spouse, as percentages of the total number of specific speaker and listener codes expressed by that couple. For speaker codes, the spouse column refers to the speaking spouse. For listener codes, the spouse column refers to the nonspeaking spouse.
[a]Degrees of freedom = (1, 152).   * $p < .05$.   ** $p < .01$.   *** $p < .001$.

$F(1, 146) = 5.54, p = .020$; and belligerence, $F(1, 146) = 10.37, p = .002$, survived this test. The age difference in whining approached significance, $F(1, 146) = 3.74, p = .055$, whereas the age difference in anger was no longer significant, $F(1, 146) = 0.87$.

Gender effects. In terms of speaker behaviors, wives were coded as showing more total emotion, negative emotion, anger, joy, contempt, whining, and sadness. Husbands were coded as being more defensive than wives. In terms of listener behavior, husbands were coded as being more neutral listeners than wives; wives were coded as being both more positive and more negative listeners than husbands.

Significant Satisfaction × Spouse interaction effects were found for several affect codes. In general, for these codes, wives were more emotional than husbands in unhappy marriages, but not in happy marriages. This was true for total speaker emotion $F = 4.93, p < .03$; negative speaker emotion, $F(1, 152) = 4.02, p < .04$; contempt, $F(1, 152) = 6.42, p < .04$; and negative listener emotion, $F(1, 152) = 6.86, p < .01$. The mean percentages of total speaker emotion were 20.32 for unhappy wives and 17.21 for unhappy husbands, $t(152) = 3.05, p < .003$; they were 16.00 for happy wives and 16.74 for happy husbands. The mean percentages of negative speaker emotion were 16.41 for unhappy wives and 13.11 for unhappy husbands, $t(152) = 2.49, p < .01$; these percentages were 10.22 for happy wives and 11.29 for happy husbands. The mean percentages of contempt were 1.89 for unhappy wives and 0.97 for unhappy husbands, $t(152) = 3.95, p < .0001$; these percentages were 0.87 for happy wives and 0.64 for happy husbands. The mean percentages of negative listener emotion were 8.27 for unhappy wives and 6.46 for unhappy husbands, $t(152) = 2.09, p < .04$; they were 4.91 for happy wives and 5.10 for happy husbands.

Both a two-way Satisfaction × Spouse effect $F = 5.16, p < .02$, and a three-way Age × Satisfaction × Spouse interaction effect, $F = 4.58, p < .03$, were found for the neutral speaker code. However, follow-up t tests revealed no differences between spouses in the various types of couples.

Satisfaction effects. In terms of speaker behavior, happy couples were coded as showing more positive emotion and as being more neutral, more humorous, more affectionate, and more validating than unhappy couples. Unhappy couples were coded as showing more emotion overall and more negative emotion and as being more angry, contemptuous, sad, domineering, and belligerent than happily married couples. In terms of listener behavior, happy couples were coded as being more neutral and more positive listeners than unhappy couples; unhappy couples were coded as expressing more negative listening behavior than happy couples.

Affect Sequences. In attempts to understand marital interaction, assessing the occurrence of single episodes of affect often does not tell the entire story. Rather, when one spouse expresses a certain type of affect, the type of affect expressed by the other spouse in response is often very informative. Unfortunately, with a coding system such as SPAFF, which has a large number of possible specific affect codes, the number of possible specific affect sequences is very large $[(2N)^2$ for N codes given to each spouse, i.e., 1,444 potential sequences]. To control for Type I error, we decided to limit the number of sequential analyses conducted by collapsing the 15 specific speaker codes and 4 listener codes into 3 global affect codes (positive, negative, and neutral). On an a priori basis, we selected five theoretically interesting sequences of global affect to analyze: (a) *negative start-up* (neutral affect by one spouse followed by negative affect by the other spouse; Patterson, 1982), (b) *negative continuance* (negative affect by one spouse followed by negative affect by the other spouse; Gottman, 1979; Patterson, 1982), (c) *deescalation* (negative affect by one spouse followed by neutral affect by the other spouse), (d) *positive continuance* (positive affect by one spouse followed by positive affect by the other spouse; Gottman, 1979), and (e) *neutral continuance* (neutral affect by one spouse followed by neutral affect by the other spouse).

The sequential analyses proceeded in three steps. First, the SPAFF speaker and listener codes were collapsed into positive, negative, and neutral

TABLE 26.2. Specific Affect Coding System Speaker and Listener Coding: Affect Sequences

Measure	Age			Satisfaction			Spouse		
	Middle[a]	Old[a]	F	Unhappy[a]	Happy[a]	F	Husband[a]	Wife[a]	F
Negative start-up (neutral–negative)	0.70	0.54	1.20[b]	0.49	0.76	2.78[b]	0.52	0.74	3.10[c]
Negative continuance (negative–negative)	1.71	1.59	< 1[c]	1.98	1.32	5.98[c*]	1.72	1.58	< 1[c]
Deescalation (negative–neutral)	1.11	.88	1.25[b]	1.10	.90	< 1[b]	1.06	.94	< 1[c]
Positive continuance (positive–positive)	2.60	2.76	< 1[d]	2.65	2.70	< 1[d]	2.46	2.89	3.98[d*]
Neutral continuance (neutral–neutral)	1.75	1.93	< 1[b]	1.86	1.82	< 1[b]	1.93	1.75	2.47[b]

Note. The spouse column refers to the antecedent behavior (i.e., the spouse whose behavior initiated the sequence). [a]z-score estimates of the strength of sequential connections. [b]Degrees of freedom (df) = (1, 152). [c]df = (1, 151). [d]df = (1, 146). *$p < .05$.

affect categories. Second, we computed z-score estimates of the strength of the sequential connection of each of the five sequences as initiated by each spouse. Third, we conducted 2 (age: middle-aged vs. older couples) × 2 (satisfaction: happy vs. unhappy) × 2 (spouse initiating the sequence: husband vs. wife) ANOVAs using the z scores for the five sequences as initiated by each spouse; we treated spouse as a repeated measure. Means and F values for the age, satisfaction, and spouse main effects are presented in Table 26.2.

Age effects. There were no main effects by age and length of marriage in affect sequences. However, there was a significant Age × Satisfaction interaction for negative start-up. Decomposing this interaction revealed that older unhappy couples were less likely to manifest negative start-up sequences than any of the other groups, $F(1, 152)$ = 4.62, $p = .031$. The mean (z) negative start-ups were as follows: older unhappy couples, 0.11, and older happy couples, 0.85, $t(152) = -2.70$, $p = .008$; middle-aged unhappy couples, 0.74 (vs. older unhappy couples), $t(152) = -2.30$, $p = .022$; and middle-aged happy couples, 0.65 (vs. older unhappy couples), $t(152) = -1.95$, $p = .05$.

Gender effects. Wives engaged in more positive continuance than husbands. A significant Satisfaction × Spouse interaction for deescalation revealed that husbands were more likely to deescalate than wives in unhappy marriages, but there were no spousal differences in happy marriages, $F(1, 151)$

= 9.26, $p = .022$. Mean (z) deescalations were 1.34 for unhappy husbands and 0.87 for unhappy wives, $t(151) = 1.96$, $p = .048$; means were 0.78 for happy husbands and 1.01 for happy wives, $t(151) = -0.61$, ns.

Satisfaction effects. Unhappy couples engaged in more negative continuance than happy couples.

Discussion

Findings from this project provide evidence for both stability and change in the nature of the marital relationship as it unfolds in later adulthood. Using a microanalytic emotional coding system, we documented considerable variation across couples in the ways that they discussed and attempted to resolve a problematic area in their relationship. In some ways, the patterns we observed in these middle-aged and older couples were highly similar to those seen in younger couples. In particular, interactional patterns associated with gender and level of marital satisfaction were evident even after many years of marriage. Nonetheless, we observed important differences in the realm of emotional expression related to the ages of the spouses and the duration of their marriages. Older couples, who in our study had also been married longer, expressed less negativity and more affection than middle-aged couples, even after differences in the severity of marital problems had been controlled. Thus, there is evidence suggesting an age-related positive affective trend within this highly intimate social relationship. In the following sections, we discuss in greater detail specific results by age, satisfaction, and gender.

Age

In this research, we used an experimental paradigm designed to elicit emotional interchange and studied the discussion of a marital problem, which is likely to generate negative affect. In a number of ways, the interactions of middle-aged couples were more emotional than those of older couples. We remind readers that we cannot disentangle age from length of marriage, and either could account for the findings. In terms of specific negative affect, middle-aged couples displayed higher levels of anger, disgust, belligerence, and whining than older couples. Possibly reflecting the attention-grabbing properties of negative affect (Hansen & Hansen, 1988; Pratto & John, 1991), the level of expressed interest was also higher in middle-aged couples. In terms of specific positive affect, middle-aged couples also displayed more humor than older couples.

For older couples, lower levels of negative affect could be seen as reflecting reduced engagement in the task or a general lessening of emotional intensity, or they could simply reflect the fact that older couples have less severe marital problems. However, we reject these interpretations on the basis of three findings. First, neither overall levels of emotion nor specific levels of tension, domineeringness, or contempt differentiated middle-aged and older couples, arguing against the notion that older people were simply not involved in the task. Second, the older couples expressed more of one kind of emotion than middle-aged couples: affection. This greater expression of affection in older couples argues against an overall dampening of emotional vitality. Third, even when age differences in the severity of marital problems were statistically controlled, old couples were less emotionally negative and more affectionate than middle-aged couples.

These results are consistent with the notion that older people actively use strategies that limit the experience of negative affect. Recall that all couples were discussing a conflict in their relationship. However, in doing so, older couples managed to express higher levels of affection and lower levels of negative affect toward their partner. Negative emotions were certainly expressed, but they were interwoven with affection. Thus, even when discussing areas of substantial disagreement with considerable potential for generating negative affect, elderly couples were more likely to communicate their positive feelings for each other.

Our analysis of affective sequences revealed one other age-related difference. Older unhappy couples were less likely to engage in sequences in which one spouse's neutral affect was followed by the other spouse's negative affect (i.e., negative start-up) than were any of the other three experimental groups. One of our overarching goals in undertaking this research has been to learn more about couples who have stayed together for long periods of time, but are not satisfied with their marriages. This finding suggests that these couples may have learned to "leave well enough alone" by staying in affectively neutral interactive sequences and avoiding escalation to negative affect.

Collectively, these findings provide observational evidence in support of self-report data indicating that people control their emotions better with age (cf. Lawton et al., 1992). Although cross-sectional comparisons render conclusions about changes with age highly speculative, our profile of findings is also consistent with Guilford and Bengtson's (1979) longitudinal evidence for increasing positivity and decreasing negativity in marriage in late life. Placed within a broader life span model, these findings are consistent with socioemotional selectivity theory's (Carstensen, 1991, 1993) notions that emotion regulation assumes increasing importance with age and that people take active steps to avoid negative emotional experiences by negotiating the emotional course of social interactions. By recording specific affect and affect exchanges, we were able to show that, within the context of the marital relationship, older people use strategies that optimize emotional experiences and minimize negative emotional experiences.

Greater affection expressed by elderly couples during conflict resolution is consistent with other kinds of data we have obtained from these same couples. On questionnaires, elderly couples reported less disagreement than middle-aged couples across a wide range of issues (Levenson et al., 1993). In the domains of physiology and affective self-ratings, older couples, relative to middle-aged couples, evidenced lower levels of autonomic arousal, which we interpreted as being consistent with more positive emotional states (Levenson, Ekman, & Friesen, 1990), and rated their own affect as being more positive during conflict resolution (Levenson et al., 1993).

Satisfaction

Our finding of greater amounts of negative affect and negative continuance sequences in unhappy marriages than in happy marriages is consistent with a large literature (see Schaap et al., 1988, for a review), including our own previous studies with younger couples (Gottman, 1979; Levenson & Gottman, 1983, 1985). Moreover, the results of the present study generally suggest that this close relation between negative affect and marital unhappiness is maintained even in long-term marriages in middle age and old age. Although it might have been predicted that negative affective expression in unhappy marriages would diminish over the years (whether as a result of age or length of marriage), such that it no longer would be a distinguishing feature of long-term unhappy marriages, the present findings indicate that this is not the case. Even in marriages that have lasted more than 35 years, the link between marital unhappiness and expression of negative affect remains strong. However, our finding that older unhappy couples were less likely to engage in negative start-up sequences than other couples suggests that the former have achieved some control over the emergence of negative affect.

Without in any way diminishing the importance of global measures of emotion, one advantage of using a coding system such as SPAFF is its ability to move beyond global categories, such as positive and negative affect, to allow examination of the specific types of affect that characterize unhappy

and happy marriages. In this sample, unhappy marriages were marked by a wide range of specific negative emotions including anger, contempt, sadness, and domineeringness.

The positive emotions of humor, affection, and validation were more likely to emerge in happy marriages than in unhappy marriages, even in a potentially hostile context such as discussing a marital conflict. Listener positivity and neutrality, often highly functional in helping to regulate conflictive interactions and in keeping the level of negative affect from escalating precipitously, were also more prevalent in happy marriages than in unhappy ones. Possibly indicative of this tighter control of negative affect, happy couples in this sample were less likely than unhappy couples to manifest sequences of negative affective continuance (negative affect followed by negative affect), a sequence that, if not regulated, can quickly lead to negative affect escalation.

Gender

In terms of emotional behavior, wives were clearly more emotionally expressive than husbands. Wives showed greater emotion overall, greater negative emotion, more anger, more contempt, more sadness, more whining, more joy, and more positive and negative affect as listeners. Also, they were more likely to engage in positive affect continuance. The two behaviors that husbands manifested at higher levels than wives were defensiveness (which may, in fact, represent emotional restraint or self-protection) and, in unhappy marriages, the affect sequence of deescalation (which may suggest a preference for nonemotional interaction). Taken as a whole, these results are consistent with a large literature on marital interaction in relatively young marriages that has found women to be more confronting and more affectively negative than men, who tend to be more defensive and more likely to try to escape from conflict (Christensen & Heavey, 1990; Gottman & Krokoff, 1989; Gottman & Levenson, 1988; Notarius & Johnson, 1982; Schaap, 1982).

In several areas, spousal differences were found only in unhappy marriages. For total speaker emotion, negative speaker emotion, contempt, and negative listener emotion, wives expressed more emotion than husbands only in unhappy couples. Thus, it appears that gender differences in negative emotion are particularly exacerbated in unhappy marriages.

In terms of notions that gender differences decrease with age (e.g., Gutmann, 1987; Hyde & Phillis, 1979; Keith & Brubaker, 1979), we found no interactions between gender and age. These findings, together with those of Zietlow and Sillars (1988), suggest that gender differences in marital interactive behavior are maintained in later stages of the life cycle. One caveat, however, is that our older couples are still relatively young. In addition, because we hope to examine marital interaction before and after retirement, our sample was limited to couples who had not yet retired. Thus, it certainly is possible that gender differences will lessen as our couples progress into later life, spending more time together (Gilford, 1984), coping with increasing frailty (especially of husbands; Troll & Bengtson, 1982), and moving through other late life transitions. We remain optimistic that observational research will provide an excellent modality by which to study gender differences. Unlike self-reports, which can be influenced by demand characteristics and other reporting biases, we expect that gendered behavior is less likely to be under the conscious awareness of the actor and thus less likely to be actively modulated.

Conclusion

This study has begun a process of applying observational methods of coding marital behavior to the interactional processes of a sample of marriages that are of much longer duration and whose spouses are much older than those that have typically been studied in the marital interaction literature. Both differences and similarities as a function of age were revealed. In terms of differences, important disparities between the emotional qualities of marriages in middle age and old age were found. Notably, in older marriages, the resolution of important conflicts was less negatively emotional and more affectionate than in middle-aged marriages. In terms of similarities, emotional

differences between husbands and wives and between happy and unhappy marriages that have been found in other studies of younger couples were also found in these older couples. Most significant, the greater negative affect expressed in unhappy marriages than in happy marriages and the greater likelihood of wives to be affectively negative and husbands to be defensive and neutral were also found with these older cohorts.

NOTES

Laura L. Carstensen, Department of Psychology, Stanford University; John M. Gottman, Department of Psychology, University of Washington; Robert W. Levenson, Department of Psychology, University of California, Berkeley.

We wish to acknowledge National Institute on Aging Grants AG08816 and AG07476 and Research Scientist Award 1K02MH00257.

Correspondence concerning this article should be addressed to Laura L. Carstensen, Department of Psychology, Stanford University, Stanford, California 94305; John M. Gottman, University of Washington, Department of Psychology, NI-25, Seattle, Washington 98195; or Robert W. Levenson, Department of Psychology, 3210 Tolman Hall, University of California, Berkeley, California 94720.

REFERENCES

Bakeman, R., & Gottman, J. M. (1986). *Observing interaction: An introduction to sequential analysis.* New York: Cambridge University Press.

Banham, K. M. (1951). Senescence and the emotions: A genetic theory. *Journal of Genetic Psychology, 78*, 175–183.

Brubaker, T. H. (1990). Families in later life: A burgeoning research area. *Journal of Marriage and the Family, 52*, 959–981.

Burgess, E. W., Locke, H. J., & Thomes, M. M. (1971). *The family.* New York: Van Nostrand Reinhold.

Carstensen, L. L. (1991). Selectivity theory: Social activity in life-span context. In K. W. Schaie (Ed.), *Annual review of gerontology and geriatrics* (Vol. 11, pp. 195–217). New York: Springer.

Carstensen, L. L. (1992). Social and emotional patterns in adulthood: Support for socioemotional selectivity theory. *Psychology and Aging, 7*, 331–338.

Carstensen, L. L. (1993). Motivation for social contact across the life span: A theory of socioemotional selectivity. In J. Jacobs (Ed.), *Nebraska Symposium on Motivation* (Vol. 40, pp. 209–254). Lincoln: University of Nebraska Press.

Carstensen, L. L., & Turk-Charles, S. (1994). The salience of emotion across the adult life span. *Psychology and Aging, 9*, 259–264.

Christensen, A., & Heavey, C. L. (1990). Gender and social structure in the demand/withdraw pattern of marital conflict. *Journal of Personality and Social Psychology, 59*, 73–81.

Fredrickson, B. L., & Carstensen, L. L. (1990). Choosing social partners: How old age and anticipated endings make people more selective. *Psychology and Aging, 5*, 335–347.

George, L. K., Blazer, D. F., Winfield-Laird, I., Leaf, P. J., & Fischback, R. L. (1988). Psychiatric disorders and mental health service use in later life: Evidence from the Epidemiologic Catchment Area Program. In J. Brody & G. Maddox (Eds.), *Epidemiology and aging* (pp. 189–219). New York: Springer.

Gilford, R. (1984). Contrasts in marital satisfaction throughout old age: An exchange theory analysis. *Journal of Gerontology, 39*, 325–333.

Gottman, J. M. (1979). *Marital interaction: Experimental investigations*. New York: Academic Press.

Gottman, J. M. (1989). *The Specific Affect Coding System (SPAFF)*. Unpublished manuscript, University of Washington, Seattle.

Gottman, J. M., & Krokoff, L. J. (1989). The relationship between marital interaction and marital satisfaction: A longitudinal view. *Journal of Consulting and Clinical Psychology, 57*, 47–52.

Gottman, J. M., & Levenson, R. W. (1988). The social psychophysiology of marriage. In P. Noller & M. A. Fitzpatrick (Eds.), *Perspectives on marital interaction* (pp. 182–200). Clevedon, England: Multilingual Matters.

Gottman, J. M., Markman, H., & Notarius, C. (1977). The topography of marital conflict: A sequential analysis of verbal and nonverbal behavior. *Journal of Marriage and the Family, 39*, 461–477.

Guilford, R., & Bengtson, V. (1979). Measuring marital satisfaction in three generations: Positive and negative dimensions. *Journal of Marriage and the Family, 39*, 387–398.

Gutmann, D. (1987). *Reclaimed power: Toward a new psychology of men and women in later life*. New York: Basic Books.

Hansen, C. H., & Hansen, R. D. (1988). Finding the face in the crowd: An anger superiority effect. *Journal of Personality and Social Psychology, 54*, 917–924.

Hashtroudi, S., Johnson, M., & Chrosniak, L. (1990). Aging and qualitative characteristics of memories for perceived and imagined complex events. *Psychology and Aging, 5*, 119–126.

Hyde, J. S., & Phillis, D. (1979). Androgyny across the lifespan. *Developmental Psychology, 15*, 334–336.

Illig, D. P. (1977). *Distributional structure, sequential structure, multivariate information analysis, and models of communicative patterns of elderly and young married and friendship dyads in problem-solving situations*. Unpublished doctoral dissertation, Pennsylvania State University, University Park.

Keith, P. M., & Brubaker, T. H. (1979). Male household roles in later life: A look at masculinity and marital relationships. *Family Coordinator, 28*, 497–502.

Krokoff, L. J. (1987). Recruiting representative samples for marital interaction research. *Journal of Social and Personal Relationships, 4*, 317–328.

Labouvie-Vief, G., & DeVoe, M. (1991). Emotional regulation in adulthood and later life: A developmental view. In *Annual review of gerontology and geriatrics* (Vol. 11, pp. 172–194). New York: Springer.

Labouvie-Vief, G., Hakim-Larson, J., DeVoe, M., & Schoeberlein, S. (1989). Emotions and self-regulation: A life span view. *Human Development, 32*, 279–299.

Lawton, M. P. (1989). Environmental proactivity and affect in older people. In S. Spacapan & S. Oskamp (Eds.), *Social psychology of aging* (pp. 135–164). Newbury Park, CA: Sage.

Lawton, M. P., Kleban, M. H., Rajagopal, D., & Dean, J. (1992). Dimensions of affective experience in three age groups. *Psychology and Aging, 7*, 171–184.

Levenson, R. W., Carstensen, L. L., Friesen, W. V., & Ekman, P. (1991). Emotion, physiology, and expression in old age. *Psychology and Aging, 6*, 28–35.

Levenson, R. W., Carstensen, L. L., & Gottman, J. M. (1993). Long-term marriage: Age, gender and satisfaction. *Psychology and Aging, 8*, 301–313.

Levenson, R. W., Carstensen, L. L., & Gottman, J. M. (1994). The influence of age and gender on affect, physiology, and their interrelations: A study of long-term marriage. *Journal of Personality and Social Psychology, 67*, 56–68.

Levenson, R. W., Ekman, P., & Friesen, W. V. (1990). Voluntary facial action generates emotion-specific autonomic nervous system activity. *Psychophysiology, 27*, 363–384.

Levenson, R. W., & Gottman, J. M. (1983). Marital interaction: Physiological linkage and affective exchange. *Journal of Personality and Social Psychology, 45*, 587–597.

Levenson, R. W., & Gottman, J. M. (1985). A valid procedure for obtaining self-report of affect in marital interaction. *Journal of Consulting and Clinical Psychology, 53*, 151–160.

Locke, H. J., & Wallace, K. M. (1959). Short marital-adjustment and prediction tests: Their reliability and validity. *Marriage and Family Living, 21*, 251–255.

Looft, W. R. (1972). Egocentrism and social interaction across the life span. *Psychological Bulletin, 78*, 73–92.

Malatesta, C. Z., & Kalnok, M. (1984). Emotional experience in younger and older adults. *Journal of Gerontology, 39*, 301–308.

Markman, H. J., & Notarius, C. I. (1987). Coding marital and family interaction: Current status. In T. Jacob (Ed.), *Family interaction and psychopathology: Theories, methods, and findings* (pp. 329–390). New York: Plenum.

Notarius, C. I., & Johnson, J. (1982). Emotional expression in husbands and wives. *Journal of Marriage and the Family, 44*, 483–489.

Patterson, G. R. (1982). *Coercive family process*. Eugene, OR: Castalia Press.

Pratto, F., & John, O. P. (1991). Automatic vigilance: The attention-grabbing power of negative social information. *Journal of Personality and Social Psychology, 61*, 380–391.

Schaap, C. (1982). *Communication and adjustment in marriage*. Lisse, The Netherlands: Swets & Zeitlinger.

Schaap, C. (1984). A comparison of the interaction of distressed and nondistressed married couples in a laboratory situation: Literature survey, methodological issues, and an empirical investigation. In K. Hahlweg & N. S. Jacobson (Eds.), *Marital interaction: Analysis and modification* (pp. 133–155). New York: Guilford Press.

Schaap, C., Buunk, B., & Kerkstra, A. (1988). Marital conflict resolution. In P. Noller & M. A. Fitzpatrick (Eds.), *Perspectives on marital interaction* (pp. 203–244). Clevedon, England: Multilingual Matters.

Schulz, R. (1985). Emotion and affect. In J. E. Birren & K. W. Schaie (Eds.), *Handbook of the psychology of aging* (2nd ed., pp. 531–543). New York: Van Nostrand Reinhold.

Selzer, M. L. (1971). The Michigan Alcoholism Screening Test: The quest for a new diagnostic instrument. *American Journal of Psychiatry, 127*, 1653–1658.

Troll, L., & Bengtson, V. (1982). Intergenerational relations throughout the life span. In B. B. Wolman (Ed.), *Handbook of developmental psychology* (pp. 890–911). Englewood Cliffs, NJ: Prentice-Hall.

Weiss, R. L., & Heyman, R. E. (1990). Observation of marital interaction. In F. Fincham & T. Bradbury (Eds.), *The psychology of marriage* (pp. 87–117). New York: Guilford Press.

Weiss, R. L., & Summers, K. J. (1983). Marital interaction coding system—III. In E. Filsinger (Ed.), *Marriage and family assessment* (pp. 85–115). Beverly Hills, CA: Sage.

Zietlow, P. H., & Sillars, A. L. (1988). Life-stage differences in communication during marital conflicts. *Journal of Social and Personal Relationships, 5*, 223–245.

Patriarchal Terrorism and Common Couple Violence: Two Forms of Violence Against Women

Michael P. Johnson • The Pennsylvania State University

> You must go through a play of ebb and flow and watch such things as make you sick at heart.
>
> —Nguyen Du (1983)

This article argues that there are two distinct forms of couple violence taking place within families in the United States and other Western countries. A review of evidence from large-sample survey research and from qualitative and quantitative data gathered from women's shelters suggests that some families suffer from occasional outbursts of violence from either husbands or wives (common couple violence), while other families are terrorized by systematic male violence (patriarchal terrorism). It is argued that the distinction between common couple violence and patriarchal terrorism is important because it has implications for the implementation of public policy, the development of educational programs and intervention strategies, and the development of theories of interpersonal violence.

We are all too familiar with stories of women who are finally murdered by husbands who have terrorized them for years. In addition, the authors of the 1985 National Family Violence Survey estimate that over six million women are assaulted by their husbands each year in the United States. But are these really the same phenomenon?

This article argues that there are, in fact, two distinct forms of couple violence taking place in American households. Evidence from large-sample survey research and from data gathered from women's shelters and other public agencies suggests that a large number of families suffer from occasional outbursts of violence from either husbands or wives or both, while a significant number of other families are terrorized by systematic male violence enacted in the service of patriarchal control.

Sociological Perspectives on Violence Against Women in the Family

There are two major streams of sociological work on couple violence in families, one that is generally referred to as the *family violence perspective*, and the other of which may be called the *feminist perspective* (Kurz, 1989).

Work in the family violence perspective grew out of family scholars' interest in a variety of family conflict issues, and is generally traced to the early work of Straus (1971) and Gelles (1974). They came together in the early 1970s to develop a research agenda based on the use of interviews to elicit information regarding family violence from large random samples of the adult population of the United States, conducting national surveys in 1975 and 1985. Methodologically, work in this tradition has relied primarily on quantitative analysis of responses to survey questions, utilizing the strengths of random sample surveys in the production of estimates of prevalence, and causal analyses that rely on multivariate statistical techniques. Theoretically, the focus has been largely on commonalities among the various forms of family violence, such as the surprising frequency of violence, the instigating role of stress, and public adherence to norms accepting the use of some violence within the family context.

In contrast, research from the feminist perspective began with a narrower focus on the issue of wife beating, developing a literature that focuses on factors specific to violence perpetrated against women by their male partners (Dobash & Dobash, 1979; Martin, 1981; Roy, 1976; Walker, 1984). Methodologically, feminist analyses have relied heavily upon data collected from battered women, especially those who have come into contact with law enforcement agencies, hospitals, or shelters. Theoretically, the emphasis has been upon historical traditions of the patriarchal family, contemporary constructions of masculinity and femininity, and structural constraints that make escape difficult for women who are systematically beaten.

I do not wish to give the impression that the differences between these two literatures are absolute, although the often-rancorous debates that have gone on between the two groups of scholars seem at times to suggest that there is absolutely no overlap in methodology or theory (e.g., Dobash & Dobash, 1992, pp. 251–284). The truth is that family violence researchers do acknowledge the role of patriarchy in wife abuse (Straus, Gelles, &

Steinmetz, 1980, pp. 242–243), and do make use of qualitative data obtained from battered wives (Gelles, 1974). On the other side, many feminist researchers utilize quantitative data (Yllo & Bograd, 1988) and acknowledge the role of factors other than the patriarchal structure of society in precipitating violence against wives (Martin, 1981). As will be seen in the next section, however, family violence researchers and feminist researchers do clearly disagree on some very important issues, and a case can be made that their differences arise from the fact that they are, to a large extent, analyzing different phenomena.

Violence Against Women in U.S. Families: Patriarchal Terrorism and Common Couple Violence

The findings of the two literatures discussed above lead to strikingly different conclusions regarding a number of the central features of family violence for which they both provide information (gender symmetry/asymmetry, per-couple frequency of violence, escalation of violence, and reciprocity of violence). While these findings suggest to each group of scholars that the other misunderstands the nature of such violence, they suggest to me that these groups are in fact studying two distinctly different phenomena.

The first form of couple violence, which I will call *patriarchal terrorism*, has been the focus of the women's movement and of researchers working in the feminist perspective. Patriarchal terrorism, a product of patriarchal traditions of men's right to control "their" women, is a form of terroristic control of wives by their husbands that involves the systematic use of not only violence but economic subordination, threats, isolation, and other control tactics.

There are a number of difficult and important terminological issues here. The pattern of violence that I have just described is often referred to with terms such as *wife beating, wife battery*, and *battered women*. I have chosen to avoid these terms for two reasons. I avoid the restrictive term *wife* in order to acknowledge recent literatures that suggest that such a phenomenon may be involved in heterosexual dating relationships (Cate, Henton, Koval, Christopher, & Lloyd, 1982; Stets & Pirog-Good, 1987) and perhaps even in some lesbian relationships (Renzetti, 1992). I have chosen not to switch to a simple nongendered alternative, such as *partner*, because I am convinced that this pattern of violence is rooted in basically patriarchal ideas of male ownership of their female partners.

The terminology of *the battered wife* is also objectionable on the grounds that it shifts the focus to the victim, seeming to imply that the pattern in question adheres to the woman rather than to the man who is in fact behaviorally and morally responsible for the syndrome. The term *patriarchal terrorism* has the advantage of keeping the focus on the perpetrator and of keeping our attention on the systematic, intentional nature of this form of violence. Of course, the term also forces us to attend routinely to the historical and cultural roots of this form of family violence.

The second form of couple violence, which I will call *common couple violence*, is less a product of patriarchy, and more a product of the less-gendered causal processes discussed at length by Straus and his colleagues working in the family violence tradition (Straus & Smith, 1990). The dynamic is one in which conflict occasionally gets "out of hand," leading usually to "minor" forms of violence, and more rarely escalating into serious, sometimes even life-threatening, forms of violence.

Gender Symmetry/Asymmetry

The importance of the distinction between common couple violence and patriarchal terrorism is most forcefully illustrated in the heated debate over the extent to which women are perpetrators of couple violence. One of the surprising findings of Straus and his colleagues' national surveys was that women were evidently as likely to utilize violence in response to couple conflict as were men. One family violence researcher unfortunately chose to refer to these women's use of violence against their partners as "the battered husband syndrome" (Steinmetz, 1978a), suggesting that women's violence against men represented the same sort of phenomenon as the male violence

that was being reported to women's shelters across the country. The feminist scholars strongly disagreed (Adams, Jackson, & Lauby, 1988; Berk, Loseke, Berk, & Rauma, 1983; Dobash & Dobash, 1992, pp. 251–284; Dobash, Dobash, Wilson, & Daly, 1992; Fields & Kirchner, 1978; Pleck, Pleck, Grossman, & Bart, 1978; Wardell, Gillespie, & Leffler, 1983). Unfortunately, this debate has been structured as an argument about *the* nature of family violence, with both sets of scholars overlooking the possibility that there may be two distinct forms of partner violence, one relatively gender balanced (and tapped by the survey research methodology of the family violence tradition), the other involving men's terroristic attacks on their female partners (and tapped by the research with shelter populations and criminal justice and divorce court data that dominates the work in the feminist tradition).

The Steinmetz (1978) article that introduced the term *battered husband* to the literature relied primarily on data from large-scale survey research to make a case for the position that women are just as violent as men in intimate relationships, and that there was therefore a need for the development of public policy that would address the needs of men who were battered by their wives or lovers. Results from the Conflict Tactics Scale (CTS) used in the National Family Violence Surveys (NFVS)—both the 1975 study upon which Steinmetz relied and the 1985 replication—do indicate almost perfect symmetry in the use of violence by men and women against their partners. (For a thorough methodological critique of the CTS, see Dobash & Dobash, 1992, and Dobash et al., 1992. For earlier responses to many of those criticisms, see Straus, 1990a, 1990b. Although I am in essential agreement with many of the criticisms of the CTS, data presented below indicate that the patterns of violence discovered in shelter samples and national samples differ dramatically, even when violence is assessed with the CTS in both settings. This provides strong evidence that the differences are not due merely to the deficiencies of the CTS.) For *any* use of violence, the 1975 national figures for men and women were 12.1% and 11.6%, respectively;

in 1985, the comparable figures were 11.3% and 12.1%. For *serious* violence (a subset of the figures for any use of violence, including only acts judged to have a high probability of producing serious injury, such as hitting with a fist), the 1975 figures were 3.8% for men, 4.6% for women; in 1985, the comparable figures were 3.0% and 4.4% (Straus & Gelles, 1990, p. 118). In all cases, the gender differences are less than 2%.

These findings contrast dramatically with those from shelter populations, from hospitals, and from the courts. For example, Gaquin (1978) reported that National Crime Survey data (United States) for the period 1973–75 indicate that 97% of assaults on adults in the family were assaults on wives. Analyses of police files in the U.S. and Britain show similar patterns (Dobash & Dobash, 1992, p. 265; Martin, 1981, pp. 13–14). Kincaid's (1982, p. 91) analysis of family court files in Ontario, Canada, found 17 times as many female as male victims, and Levinger's (1966) study of divorce actions in Cleveland, Ohio, found 12 times more wives than husbands mentioning physical abuse (37% vs. 3%). Fields and Kirchner (1978, p. 218) reported that Crisis Centers in the New York City public hospitals counseled 490 battered wives and only two battered husbands during the last half of 1977.

The most likely explanation for these dramatic differences in the gender patterns of violence in the national surveys and in statistics collected by public agencies is not that one or the other methodology misrepresents the "true" nature of family violence, but that the two information sources deal with nearly nonoverlapping phenomena. The common couple violence that is assessed by the large-scale random survey methodology is in fact gender balanced, and is a product of a violence-prone culture and the privatized setting of most U.S. households. The patriarchal terrorism that is tapped in research with the families encountered by public agencies is a pattern perpetrated almost exclusively by men, and rooted deeply in the patriarchal traditions of the Western family.

Per Couple Frequency

With regard to the frequency of couple violence in "violent" families, we are fortunate to have data using the same data collection instrument (the CTS) with survey samples and shelter samples. According to Straus (1990b), among women who report to NFVS researchers that they have been assaulted by their husbands in the previous year, the average number of such assaults per woman was six ($n = 622$); for those in the sample who had used the services of a shelter, the average was 15.3 ($n = 13$).

In dramatic contrast, Straus cited studies of shelter populations in Maine (Giles-Sims, 1983) and Michigan (Okun, 1986), utilizing the same series of survey questions, that find an average annual number of incidents per woman in the 65 to 68 range! Although Straus argued that the NFVS probably "underrepresents" certain types of violence against women (among the 622 assaulted women in the sample, only four had been assaulted as many as 65 times), he evidently continued to think of this as just another point on a continuum of violence, referring to the missed cases as "cases of extreme violence" (Straus, 1990b, p. 85). Although Straus recognized and discussed the possibilities raised by this "underrepresentation" for resolving differences between the conclusions of shelter research and survey research, and even referred to the possibility of a "qualitatively different experience," he does not seem to have taken the next step, to suggest that perhaps we are dealing with decidedly different phenomena and should adopt a terminology that would mitigate against the mistaken assumption that common couple violence is merely less severe or less frequent than patriarchal terrorism.

Escalation

The two literatures also appear to uncover dramatically different patterns of behavior in terms of escalation. The evidence from the NFVS suggests that so-called minor violence against women does not escalate into more serious forms of violence. Feld and Straus (1990) reported data relevant to this question based on a 1-year follow-up survey of 420 respondents from the 1985 NFVS. My own reanalysis of their published data shows almost no tendency to escalation. For example, among husbands who had perpetrated no acts of minor or severe violence in Year 1 (the year prior to the 1985 interview), 2.6% had moved to severe violence in Year 2. Among those who had committed at least one act of only minor violence, only 5.8% had moved to severe violence; among those who had used severe violence in Year 1, only 30.4% had been that violent in Year 2. Thus, these data indicate that not only is there virtually no tendency to escalation (fully 94% of perpetrators of minor violence do not go on to severe violence), but that in most (70%) of the cases of severe violence there is, in fact, a deescalation. Data on frequency show much the same pattern.

A very different pattern is observed in research with shelter populations. According to Pagelow (1981), "one of the few things about which almost all researchers agree is that the batterings escalate in frequency and intensity over time" (p. 45).

Why does patriarchal terrorism escalate while common couple violence does not? Common couple violence is an intermittent response to the occasional conflicts of everyday life, motivated by a need to control in the specific situation (Milardo & Klein, 1992), but not a more general need to be in charge of the relationship. In contrast, the causal dynamic of patriarchal terrorism is rooted in patriarchal traditions, adopted with a vengeance by men who feel that they must control "their" women by any means necessary. As one husband responded to his wife's protests regarding a violent episode during their honeymoon, "I married you so I own you" (Dobash & Dobash, 1979, p. 94). Escalation in such cases may be prompted by either of two dynamics. First, if his partner resists his control, he may escalate the level of violence until she is subdued. Second, even if she submits, he may be motivated not only by a need to control, but by a need to display that control, yielding a pattern observed by Dobash and Dobash (1979, p. 137), in which no amount of compliance can assure a wife that she will not be beaten:

> For a woman simply to live her daily life she is always in a position in which almost anything she does may be deemed a violation of her wifely duties or a challenge to her husband's authority and thus defined as the cause of the violence she continues to experience. (p. 137)

Reciprocity and Initiation of Violence

On the issue of reciprocity, the NFVS analysts report a pattern in which two-thirds of the families in which the husband has been violent also involve a violent wife, and in which "women initiate violence about as often as men" (Stets & Straus, 1990, p. 161).

Research with shelter populations provides quite a different picture. Pagelow, for example, reported that only 26% of her respondents say they fight back; another 16% indicate that they had once tried, but stopped when it made things worse (Pagelow, 1981, p. 66). She also suggested, although she is not entirely clear (Pagelow, 1981, pp. 65–66), that none of her respondents had initiated the violence in the incidents on which they reported. Giles-Sims's (1983, pp. 49–50) data for a shelter population show dramatic lack of reciprocity in the use of violence, as reported in response to the CTS. The five most severe forms of violence were roughly twice as likely to have been used by the men as the women, and in some cases the differences are even more dramatic (e.g., 84% of the men had beat up their spouse, as compared with 13% of the women), and this in spite of the fact that "the men had almost all abused the women seriously enough to cause injury. In many cases the beatings had been life threatening" (Giles-Sims, 1983, p. 50). The feminist scholars also point out that when women murder they are 7 times more likely than men to have acted in self-defense (Martin, 1981, p. 14). We may sum up the feminist research with testimony to the United States Commission on Civil Rights to the effect that "most women who have been violent towards their husbands have done so only as a last resort, in self-defense against longstanding terror and abuse from their husbands" (United States Commission on Civil Rights, 1978, pp. 450–453, cited in Dobash & Dobash, 1992, p. 257).

Patriarchal Terrorism and Common Couple Violence

The interpersonal dynamic of violence against women uncovered by the researchers working in the feminist tradition is one in which men systematically terrorize their wives, thus the term *patriarchal terrorism*. In these families, the beatings occur on average more than once a week, and escalate in seriousness over time. The violence is almost exclusively initiated by the husband, most wives never attempt to fight back, and, among those who do, about one-third quickly desist, leaving only a small minority of cases in which the women respond, even with self-defensive violence. These patterns have led researchers in the feminist tradition to conclude that violence against women in the family has its roots in the patriarchal structure of the U.S. family. The central motivating factor behind the violence is a man's desire to exercise *general* control over "his" woman.

It is important not to make the mistake of assuming that this pattern of general control can be indexed simply by high rates of violence. Although the average frequency of violence among cases of patriarchal terrorism may be high, there may well be cases in which the perpetrator does not need to use violence often in order to terrorize his partner. Feminist theorists and shelter activists argue that since patriarchal terrorism has its roots in a motive to exercise general control over one's partner, it is characterized by the use of multiple control tactics (Dobash & Dobash, 1979). The Duluth Domestic Abuse Intervention Project (Pence & Paymar, 1993) has developed a useful graphic representation of this pattern that captures the importance of not becoming overly focused on the violent control tactics that are only part of an overall pattern (see Table 27.1). The patriarchal terrorist will use any combination of these tactics

TABLE 27.1. Tactics of Power and Control

Using Coercion and Threats	Using Intimidation
Making and/or carrying out threats to do something to hurt her • threatening to leave her, to commit suicide, to report her to welfare • making her drop charges • making her do illegal things	Making her afraid by using looks, actions, gestures • smashing things • destroying her property • abusing pets • displaying weapons
Using Emotional Abuse	**Using Isolation**
Putting her down • making her feel bad about herself • calling her names • making her think she's crazy • playing mind games • humiliating her • making her feel guilty	Controlling what she does, who she sees and talks to, what she reads, where she goes • limiting her outside involvement • using jealousy to justify actions
Minimizing, Denying, and Blaming	**Using Children**
Making light of the abuse and not taking her concerns about it seriously • saying the abuse didn't happen • shifting responsibility for abusive behavior • saying she caused it	Making her feel guilty about the children • using the children to relay messages • using visitation to harass her • threatening to take the children away
Using Male Privilege	**Using Economic Abuse**
Treating her like a servant • making all the big decisions • acting like the "master of the castle" • being the one to define men's and women's roles	Preventing her from getting or keeping a job • making her ask for money • giving her an allowance • taking her money • not letting her know about or have access to family income

Note. Slightly adapted from Pence and Paymer (1993).

that will successfully (a) control his partner and (b) satisfy his need to display that control.

Researchers in the family violence perspective describe a dramatically different pattern of violence, one in which the complexities of family life produce conflicts that occasionally get "out of hand" in some families, incidents occurring in those families an average of once every 2 months. The violence is no more likely to be enacted by men than by women, and violent incidents are initiated as often by women as by men. In this common couple violence, there appears to be little likelihood of escalation of the level of violence over time. I would argue that this type of violence is usually not part of a pattern in which one partner is trying to exert general control over his or her partner. Although it is possible that a relatively infrequent, nonescalating use of violence is in some cases part of a generally successful use of other control tactics (the "success" precluding the need to use frequent or extreme violence), I will argue next that it is more likely that the national surveys that uncover this pattern reach only populations in which violence is a relatively isolated reaction to conflict (common couple violence), while studies using data from shelters and other public agencies reach primarily victims of violent, but multifaceted, strategies of control (patriarchal terrorism).

Survey Samples and Shelter Samples

The debate that has arisen between the feminist researchers and the family violence researchers continues to be framed as a contention over the validity of two radically different descriptions of the nature of couple violence in the United States. The feminists have argued that the description of violence against women that is derived from family violence research is seriously flawed and simply cannot be reconciled with the results of feminist research.

I disagree, arguing that such apparent inconsistencies would be expected if the two literatures are dealing with different phenomena. I propose that the dramatic differences in the patterns of violence described by these two research traditions arise because the sampling decisions of the two traditions have given them access to different, largely nonoverlapping populations, experiencing different forms of violence.

The Sampling Biases of Surveys and Shelters

Sampling bias in survey research comes in large part from the fact that even the best designed survey projects are unable to gather information from the total target sample, and nonrespondents may differ in important ways from respondents. For example, men who systematically terrorize their wives would hardly be likely to agree to participate in such a survey, and the women whom they beat would probably be terrified at the possibility that their husband might find out that they had answered such questions. Support for the argument that such families are not represented in the survey data may be found in the fact that among the 182 victims of so-called "wife beating" in the 1985 survey research sample, only four had been assaulted 65 times or more (the average for shelter populations). In contrast, if Straus and his colleagues are correct, and occasional family violence is normative in the sense of being expected and tolerated, if not accepted, then many, if not most, families involved in common couple violence may well agree to participate in a survey on family life.

What about the data sources for most of the feminist research—shelters, hospital emergency rooms, and the criminal and divorce courts? Certainly there are equally serious biases in these sources of data. It is likely, for example, that most families in which couple violence is only intermittent, an unusual response to family conflict, do not need or want such services. The woman or man who is struck or pushed by his or her partner a few times a year will not in most cases report the incident to the police, or go to a shelter, or file for divorce, or need to seek medical treatment. Such sources of data are therefore heavily biased in the direction of providing access only to cases of patriarchal terrorism, and, even among those cases, biased in the direction of the most egregious cases.

The biases of shelter samples, although hard to document, are perhaps obvious. The biases of random sample surveys, however, may require a bit of documentation.

Do the Survey Numbers Seem to Include Patriarchal Terrorism?

Violence data. Straus (1990b) reported that, in the 1985 NFVS, four women reported a frequency of assaults equal to or above the average for shelter populations. If we assume a symmetrical distribution of frequency of violence for shelter populations, the total population should be projected from double that figure, or eight. The projection to the total U.S. population yields an estimate of about 80,000 women whose beatings fall into a frequency range comparable to that of shelter populations, and who might therefore seriously consider the possibility of moving to shelter housing.

We can compare this figure with an estimate of the number of women actually requesting housing in shelters in the United States. Although the National Coalition on Domestic Violence cannot provide such statistics, this source suggested that I contact the Pennsylvania Coalition on Domestic Violence for the best available statistical data; another source suggested Minnesota. In 1985–86, Pennsylvania shelters housed or turned away 6,262 different women (Pennsylvania Coalition Against Domestic Violence, 1995). Extrapolating that figure to the total U.S. population (i.e., multiplying by 19.20), we get an estimate of 120,230 women who actually tried to use shelter housing, a number roughly 1.5 times the 80,000 that the NFVS suggests might even consider such housing. The Minnesota data provide an even more dramatic contrast. According to the Minnesota Department of Corrections (1987), in 1985, 8,518 women were housed or turned away from shelters. Extrapolating to the U.S. population (i.e., multiplying by 57.72), we get an estimate of 491,659 women to compare with the NFVS estimate of 80,000.

If we take the shelter data as representing the absolute minimum number of women who consider using shelter services each year (they include, after all, only those women who not only considered such action, but took it), we would

estimate that the NFVS reaches one-sixth to two-thirds of the victims of patriarchal terrorism in its target sample. However, given the difficulty most women find making the decision to seek help (Kirkwood, 1993), most shelter activists assume that there are at least five terrorized women in the community for every one that seeks shelter, suggesting that the NFVS may collect data from only 1/13 to 1/7 of such couples in its target sample.

Data on use of shelter services. There is another potential source of data on patriarchal terrorism in the NFVS. Straus (1990b) reported that there were 13 women in the NFVS who had used shelter services. That figure extrapolates to about 128,600 women nationwide. Unfortunately, the survey wording, referring to the use of the services of a women's shelter, is ambiguous. Most so-called women's shelters in the U.S. actually function as comprehensive resources for women who have been victimized by patriarchal terrorism (many also address issues of sexual assault and child sexual abuse). Most of the women who use the services of such organizations do not actually move into a shelter facility. I will, therefore, compare the figure of 128,600 derived from the NFVS with an estimate from shelters of the number of women who contact them annually regarding domestic violence.

The Pennsylvania Coalition Against Domestic Violence reported 41,425 domestic violence contacts with different women in 1985–86, which extrapolates to 795,360 nationwide. If we assume rough comparability of "domestic violence contacts" in the shelter data and "used the services of a women's shelter" in the NFVS data, we must conclude that the NFVS successfully interviewed about one-sixth of the users of shelter services in its target sample. The Minnesota Department of Corrections reported shelter contacts with 36,189 women in 1985, which extrapolates to about 2.1 million women nationwide, 16 times the extrapolation from the NFVS.

Certainly, there are a great many problems with the statistical manipulations presented above. Pennsylvania and Minnesota are certainly unusual states, having been in the forefront of the shelter movement. In addition, the meaning of "using the services of a shelter" and "shelter contacts" may be different in the two data sources, and there may be hidden problems of distinguishing multiple contacts with the same woman from contacts with different women. The extrapolations from the NFVS and shelter statistics are so divergent, however, that it is unlikely that any of these problems would alter the conclusion that the NFVS simply does not provide valid information regarding the prevalence or nature of patriarchal terrorism.

Thus, I would argue that the sampling biases of shelter research and "random" sample research put them in touch with distinct, virtually nonoverlapping populations of violent families. On the one hand, shelter samples include only a small portion of the women who are assaulted at least once by their partner in any particular year. (For 1985, the NFVS estimate is six million such women, while the shelter extrapolations suggest that at most two million women contacted shelters, many fewer seeking services that would make them likely to show up in a shelter research sample.) Of course, this select group is likely to include only women who feel they must enlist help to escape from a man who has entrapped them in a general pattern of violence and control, that is, victims of patriarchal terrorism.

On the other hand, the extrapolations from the NFVS and the Minnesota and Pennsylvania shelter data indicate that survey research reaches only a small fraction of the women who experience severe violence or who make use of the services of shelters. The vast majority of NFVS respondents who experience couple violence have not contacted shelters and have not experienced the level of violence likely to lead them to consider seeking shelter. This select group thus includes only cases in which the women are not generally afraid of their partner—because they have not experienced a general pattern of control—that is, women who are victims of common couple violence.

Summary

Certainly, the case for two forms of violence, one relatively nongendered, the other clearly patriarchal, is not ironclad. However, I am not the first scholar to suggest the possibility that there are multiple forms of couple violence. In fact, at about the time she was developing her case for the "battered husband syndrome," Steinmetz (1978b) published an excellent article making a distinction that is quite similar to the distinction between patriarchal terrorism and common couple violence. More recently, Lloyd and Emery (1994) have emphasized variability in their review of the literature on couple violence. They present nine "tenets" that explicate the interpersonal and contextual dynamics of aggression in intimate relationships. Two of those nine tenets focus on the likelihood of multiple forms of couple violence, and in both cases, the authors are able to cite relevant data to support their position (Lloyd & Emery, 1994, pp. 37–40).

Nevertheless, since the heart of the distinction between common couple violence and patriarchal terrorism is one of motivation, the evidence presented above can only be suggestive. What is required is research that can provide insight into motivation. One way to get at motivation would be to gather information concerning a range of conflict and control tactics from each couple. Patriarchal terrorism is presumed to involve acts of violence that are embedded in a larger context of control tactics. Common couple violence is presumed to show a less purposive pattern, erupting as it does from particular conflicts rather than from a general intent to control one's partner. A second approach to motivation is in-depth interviewing of couples who are involved in violence, eliciting interpretations of the psychological and interpersonal causes of specific incidents or patterns of control. The goal is to go beyond the behavioral description of particular acts to develop a narrative of each incident's development, as presented and interpreted by perpetrators and targets of violence. Both of these sorts of data are commonly collected in the work with shelter samples. However, we also need this kind of data from samples that target populations that are more likely to include examples of both forms of violence.

Let me conclude with a partial list of the reasons for my belief that the distinction between common couple violence and patriarchal terrorism is important. The first, and most important, has to do with the role of scientific understanding in the shaping of social policy. The issue is perhaps best illustrated in the debate regarding the gender symmetry/asymmetry of couple violence. The failure to make a distinction between patriarchal terrorism and common couple violence has led some analysts to make the logical error of leaping from (a) the description of a few case studies of terrorism perpetrated against men and (b) frequency estimates of common couple violence against men from survey research to (z) the conclusion that there is a widespread "battered husband" syndrome. This erroneous conclusion may be used in campaigns against funding for women's shelters (Pleck et al., 1978), opponents arguing that shelters should not be funded unless they devote equal resources to male and female victims. Although it is indisputable that *some* men are terrorized by their female partners (I have worked with some at my local shelter), the presentation of survey data that tap only common couple violence as evidence that men are terrorized as frequently as women produces a dangerous distortion of reality.

A similar distortion occurs when stories of patriarchal terrorism against women are used to describe the nature of family violence, while numbers that probably apply only to common couple violence (survey extrapolations) are used to describe its prevalence. If the arguments presented above are correct, random sample surveys cannot produce estimates of the prevalence of patriarchal terrorism. We must develop methods of collecting and extrapolating effectively from shelter, hospital, police, and court data.

A second major problem arises when educational and therapeutic efforts targeted at prevention and intervention are governed by the assumption of one form of couple violence. For example, in women's studies texts and in training manuals at women's centers, one often finds the statement that couple violence always escalates. Unacceptable as any one incident of violence in a relationship may be, if the arguments above are correct, it is certainly not the case that escalation is an inevitable part of male violence, let alone an inevitable part of the violence in lesbian relationships, which is almost certainly more likely to be common couple violence, which does not generally escalate. Thus, advice that is based on a mistaken assumption of impending terrorism may do some women a great disservice. One can also imagine similar scenarios of misinterpretation and misplaced advice in family counseling or other therapeutic relationships. As in most areas of intervention, family practitioners will be most effective if they work with a set of alternative interpretive frameworks rather than with a single-minded assumption that every case of violence fits the same pattern.

The third area in which problems may be created by the conflation of different forms of violence is in theoretical interpretation. If the two forms of violence have different psychological and interpersonal roots, then theory development will either have to proceed along different lines for each, or move in the direction of synergistic theories that explicate the conditions under which particular combinations of the same causal factors might produce qualitatively different patterns of violent behavior. For example, we are beginning to try to develop an understanding of the dynamics of lesbian couple violence, a phenomenon that must seem somewhat mysterious if we assume that all violence within couples follows the pattern found in patriarchal terrorism. If we were to assume a unitary phenomenon, we would develop a theory of lesbian violence that focused heavily on the conditions under which some lesbians might fall into patriarchal family forms. It may be more reasonable to assume that the bulk of violence in lesbian relationships is of the common couple variety and involves causal processes that are very similar to those involved in nonlesbian common couple violence, having little to do with the taking on of patriarchal family values.

Alternatively, using the synergistic approach to theory development, we might note that (a) some, if not all, of the causal factors involved in patriarchal terrorism may also be involved in common couple violence and vice versa, (b) many of these factors are best conceptualized as continuous variables, and (c) although some of them are sex-linked, there is probably considerable overlap in the gender distributions (Taylor, 1993). The following partial list of causal factors may be used to illustrate these three points: (a) motivation to control, (b) normative acceptability of control, (c) inclination to use violence for control, (d) physical strength differences that make violence effective, (e) inclination to expressive violence, (f) victim deference, and (g) structural commitment to the relationship. All could conceivably be involved in the generation of particular cases of either patriarchal terrorism or common couple violence, each can be conceived as a continuous variable, and all are likely to be at least imperfectly linked to gender. The behavior described in this paper as patriarchal terrorism, however, may develop only from the co-occurrence of high values on some particular subset of the causal variables. If all other combinations of the same variables produce either no violence at all or a pattern recognizable as common couple violence, this complex combination of weakly gender-linked, continuous variables would produce a strongly gender-linked pattern of two types of couple violence. Under such conditions, even relatively weak links of the various factors to gender might produce empirical patterns of patriarchal terrorism that occur almost exclusively among men in heterosexual relationships, accompanied by the occasional occurrence of a similar pattern among women—even in lesbian relationships—and in gay male couples.

Finally, we have to ask, "How on earth could two groups of social scientists come to such different conclusions about something as unsubtle as family violence?" We owe it to the families that are the focus of our work not to get so caught up in the defense of our initial positions that we fail to see important insights that can be gained from our disagreements. The social policy, educational, and therapeutic implications of what we do are too important for us to allow our deep moral aversion to violence to blind us to important distinctions. Yes, all family violence is abhorrent, but not all family violence is the same. If there are different patterns that arise from different societal roots and interpersonal dynamics, we must make distinctions in order to maximize our effectiveness in moving toward the goal of peace in our private lives.

NOTE

I owe thanks to Kathleen Barry and our colleagues in Vietnam, who started me off in this direction. Kathleen Barry, Donna Hastings, Stephen Marks, Bob Milardo, Marylee Taylor, and anonymous *JMF* reviewers gave me invaluable comments on early drafts.

REFERENCES

Adams, D., Jackson, J., & Lauby, M. (1988). Family violence research: Aid or obstacle to the battered women's movement. *Response, 11*, 14–16.

Berk, R. A., Loseke, D. R., Berk, S. F., & Rauma, D. (1983). Mutual combat and other family violence myths. In D. Finkelhor, R. Gelles, G. Hotaling, & M. A. Straus (Eds.), *The dark side of families: Current family violence research* (pp. 197–212). Newbury Park, CA: Sage.

Cate, R. M., Henton, J. M., Koval, J., Christopher, F. S., & Lloyd, S. (1982). Premarital abuse: A social psychological perspective. *Journal of Family Issues, 3*, 79–90.

Dobash, R. E., & Dobash, R. P. (1979). *Violence against wives*. New York: Free Press.

Dobash, R. E., & Dobash, R. P. (1992). *Women, violence and social change*. New York: Routledge.

Dobash, R. P., Dobash, R. E., Wilson, M., & Daly, M. (1992). The myth of sexual symmetry in marital violence. *Social Problems, 39*, 71–91.

Feld, S. L., & Straus, M. A. (1990). Escalation and desistance from wife assault in marriage. In M. A. Straus & R. J. Gelles (Eds.), *Physical violence in American families* (pp. 489–505). New Brunswick, NJ: Transaction Publishers.

Fields, M. D., & Kirchner, R. M. (1978). Battered women are still in need: A reply to Steinmetz. *Victimology, 3*, 216–226.

Gaquin, D. A. (1978). Spouse abuse: Data from the National Crime Survey. *Victimology, 2*, 632–643.

Gelles, R. J. (1974). *The violent home: A study of physical aggression between husbands and wives*. Newbury Park, CA: Sage.

Gelles, R. J., & Straus, M. A. (1988). New York: Simon & Schuster.

Gelles, R. J., & Straus, M. A. (1991). Second National Family Violence Survey: Survey methodology (3rd rev.). In R. J. Gelles & M. A. Straus (Eds.), *Physical violence in American families, 1985* (2nd release) [Computer file]. Durham, NH: University of New Hampshire Family Research Laboratory [Producer]. Ann Arbor, MI: Inter-University Consortium for Political and Social Research [Distributor].

Giles-Sims, J. (1983). *Wife-battering: A systems theory approach*. New York: Guilford.

Kincaid, P. J. (1982). *The omitted reality: Husband-wife violence in Ontario and policy implications for education*. Maple, Ontario: Learners Press.

Kirkwood, C. (1993). *Leaving abusive partners*. Newbury Park, CA: Sage.

Kurz, D. (1989). Social science perspectives on wife abuse: Current debates and future directions. *Gender and Society, 3*, 489–505.

Levinger, G. (1966). Sources of marital dissatisfaction among applicants for divorce. *American Journal of Orthopsychiatry, 36*, 803–807.

Lloyd, S. A., & Emery, B. C. (1994). Physically aggressive conflict in romantic relationships. In Dudley Cahn (Ed.), *Conflict in close relationships* (pp. 27–46). Hillsdale, NJ: Lawrence Erlbaum.

Martin, D. (1981). *Battered wives*. Volcano, CA: Volcano Press.

Milardo, R. M., & Klein, R. (1992). *Dominance norms and domestic violence: The justification of aggression in close relationships.* Paper presented at the Pre-Conference Theory Construction and Research Methodology Workshop. National Council on Family Relations annual meeting, Orlando, FL.

Minnesota Department of Corrections. (1987). *Minnesota program for battered women: Advocacy program: Data summary report (through 1986)*. St. Paul, MN: Author.

Nguyen Du. (1983). *The tale of Kieu* (Translated and annotated by Huynh Sanh Thong). New Haven: Yale University Press.

Okun, L. (1986). *Woman abuse: Facts replacing myths*. Albany: State University of New York Press.

Pagelow, M. (1981). *Woman-battering: Victims and their experience*. Newbury Park, CA: Sage.

Pence, E., & Paymar, M. (1993). *Education groups for men who batter: The Duluth model*. New York: Springer.

Pennsylvania Coalition Against Domestic Violence. (1995). Personal correspondence.

Pleck, E., Pleck, J. H., Grossman, M., & Bart, P. B. (1978). The battered data syndrome: A comment on Steinmetz' article. *Victimology, 2*, 680–683.

Renzetti, C. M. (1992). *Violent betrayal: Partner abuse in lesbian relationships*. Newbury Park, CA: Sage.

Roy, M. (Ed.). (1976). *Battered women: A psychosocial study of domestic violence*. New York: Van Nostrand Reinhold.

Steinmetz, S. K. (1978a). The battered husband syndrome. *Victimology, 2*, 499–509.

Steinmetz, S. K. (1978b). Wife-beating: A critique and reformulation of existing theory. Bulletin of the *American Academy of Psychiatry and the Law, 6*, 322–334.

Stets, J. E., & Pirog-Good, M. A. (1987). Violence in dating relationships. *Social Psychology Quarterly, 50*, 237–246.

Stets, J. E., & Straus, M. A. (1990). Gender differences in reporting marital violence and its medical and psychological consequences. In M. A. Straus & R. J. Gelles (Eds.), *Physical violence in American families* (pp. 151–180). New Brunswick, NJ: Transaction Publishers.

Straus, M. A. (1971). Some social antecedents of physical punishment: A linkage theory interpretation. *Journal of Marriage and the Family, 33*, 658–663.

Straus, M. A. (1990a). The Conflict Tactics Scales [sic] and its critics: An evaluation and new data on validity and reliability. In M. A. Straus & R. J. Gelles (Eds.), *Physical violence in American families* (pp. 49–73). New Brunswick, NJ: Transaction Publishers.

Straus, M. A. (1990b). Injury and frequency of assault and the "representative sample fallacy" in measuring wife beating and child abuse. In M. A. Straus & R. J. Gelles (Eds.), *Physical violence in American families* (pp. 75–91). New Brunswick, NJ: Transaction Publishers.

Straus, M. A., & Gelles, R. J. (1990). Societal change and change in family violence from 1975–1985 as revealed by two national surveys. In M. A. Straus & R. J. Gelles (Eds.), *Physical violence in American families* (pp. 113–131). New Brunswick, NJ: Transaction Publishers.

Straus, M. A., Gelles, R. J., & Steinmetz, S. K. (1980). *Behind closed doors*. Newbury Park, CA: Sage.

Straus, M. A., & Smith, C. (1990). Family patterns and primary prevention of family violence. In M. A. Straus & R. J. Gelles (Eds.), *Physical violence in American families* (pp. 507–526). New Brunswick, NJ: Transaction Publishers.

Taylor, M. C. (1993). Personal correspondence.

United States Commission on Civil Rights. (1978). *Battered women: Issues of public policy*. Washington, DC: Author.

Walker, L. E. (1984). *The battered woman syndrome*. New York: Springer.

Wardell, L., Gillespie, D. L., & Leffler, A. (1983). Science and violence against wives. In D. Finkelhor, R. J. Gelles, G. T. Hoteling, & M. A. Straus (Eds.), *The dark side of families: Current family violence research* (pp. 69–84). Beverly Hills, CA: Sage.

Yllo, K., & Bograd, M. (Eds.). (1988). *Feminist perspectives on wife abuse*. Newbury Park, CA: Sage.

How to Read a Journal Article in Social Psychology

Christian H. Jordan and Mark P. Zanna • University of Waterloo

How to Read a Journal Article in Social Psychology

When approaching a journal article for the first time, and often on subsequent occasions, most people try to digest it as they would any piece of prose. They start at the beginning and read word for word, until eventually they arrive at the end, perhaps a little bewildered, but with a vague sense of relief. This is not an altogether terrible strategy; journal articles do have a logical structure that lends itself to this sort of reading. There are, however, more efficient approaches—approaches that enable you, a student of social psychology, to cut through peripheral details, avoid sophisticated statistics with which you may not be familiar, and focus on the central ideas in an article. Arming yourself with a little fore-knowledge of what is contained in journal articles, as well as some practical advice on how to read them, should help you read journal articles more effectively. If this sounds tempting, read on.

Journal articles offer a window into the inner workings of social psychology. They document how social psychologists formulate hypotheses, design empirical studies, analyze the observations they collect, and interpret their results. Journal articles also serve an invaluable archival function: They contain the full store of common and cumulative knowledge of social psychology. Having documentation of past research allows researchers to build on past findings and advance our understanding of social behavior, without pursuing avenues of investigation that have already been explored. Perhaps most importantly, a research study is never complete until its results have been shared with others, colleagues and students alike. Journal articles are a primary means of communicating research findings. As such, they can be genuinely exciting and interesting to read.

That last claim may have caught you off guard. For beginning readers, journal articles may seem anything but interesting and exciting. They may, on the contrary, appear daunting and esoteric, laden with jargon and obscured by menacing statistics. Recognizing this fact, we hope to arm you, through this paper, with the basic information you will need to read journal articles with a greater sense of comfort and perspective.

Social psychologists study many fascinating topics, ranging from prejudice and discrimination, to culture, persuasion, liking and love, conformity and obedience, aggression, and the self. In our daily lives, these are issues we often struggle to understand. Social psychologists present systematic observations of, as well as a wealth of ideas about, such issues in journal articles. It would be a shame if the fascination and intrigue these topics have were lost in their translation into journal publications. We don't think they are, and by the end of this paper, hopefully you won't either.

Journal articles come in a variety of forms, including research reports, review articles, and theoretical articles. Put briefly, a *research report* is a formal presentation of an original research study, or series of studies. A *review article* is an evaluative survey of previously published work, usually organized by a guiding theory or point of view. The author of a review article summarizes previous investigations of a circumscribed problem, comments on what progress has been made toward its resolution, and suggests areas of the problem that require further study. A *theoretical article* also evaluates past research, but focuses on the development of theories used to explain empirical findings. Here, the author may present a new theory to explain a set of findings, or may compare and contrast a set of competing theories, suggesting why one theory might be the superior one.

This paper focuses primarily on how to read research reports, for several reasons. First, the bulk of published literature in social psychology consists of research reports. Second, the summaries presented in review articles, and the ideas set forth in theoretical articles, are built on findings presented in research reports. To get a deep understanding of how research is done in social psychology, fluency in reading original research reports is essential. Moreover, theoretical articles frequently report new studies that pit one theory against another, or test a novel prediction derived from a new theory. In order to appraise the validity of such theoretical contentions, a grounded understanding of basic findings is invaluable. Finally, most research reports are written in a standard format that is likely unfamiliar to new readers. The format of review and theoretical articles is less standardized, and more like that of textbooks and other scholarly writings, with which most readers are familiar. This is not to suggest that such articles are easier to read and comprehend than research reports; they can be quite challenging indeed. It is simply the case that, because more rules apply to the writing of research reports, more guidelines can be offered on how to read them.

The Anatomy of Research Reports

Most research reports in social psychology, and in psychology in general, are written in a standard format prescribed by the American Psychological Association (1994). This is a great boon to both readers and writers. It allows writers to present their ideas and findings in a clear, systematic manner. Consequently, as a reader, once you understand this format, you will not be on completely foreign ground when you approach a new research report—regardless of its specific content. You will know where in the paper particular information is found, making it easier to locate. No matter what your reasons for reading a research report, a firm understanding of the format in which they are written will ease your task. We discuss the format of research reports next, with some practical suggestions on how to read them. Later, we discuss how this format reflects the process of scientific investigation, illustrating how research reports have a coherent narrative structure.

Title and Abstract. Though you can't judge a book by its cover, you can learn a lot about a research report simply by reading its title. The title presents a concise statement of the theoretical issues investigated, and/or the variables that were studied. For example, the following title was taken almost at random from a prestigious journal in social psychology: "Sad and guilty? Affective influences on the explanation of conflict in close relationships" (Forgas, 1994, p. 56). Just by reading the title, it can be inferred that the study investigated how emotional states change the way people explain conflict in close relationships. It also suggests that when feeling sad, people accept more personal blame for such conflicts (i.e., feel more guilty).

The abstract is also an invaluable source of information. It is a brief synopsis of the study, and packs a lot of information into 150 words or less. The abstract contains information about the problem that was investigated, how it was investigated, the major findings of the study, and hints at the theoretical and practical implications of the findings. Thus, the abstract is a useful summary of the research that provides the gist of the investigation. Reading this outline first can be very helpful, because it tells you where the report is going, and gives you a useful framework for organizing information contained in the article.

The title and abstract of a research report are like a movie preview. A movie preview highlights the important aspects of a movie's plot, and provides just enough information for one to decide whether to watch the whole movie. Just so with titles and abstracts; they highlight the key features of a research report to allow you to decide if you want to read the whole paper. And just as with movie previews, they do not give the whole story. Reading just the title and abstract is never enough to fully understand a research report.

Introduction. A research report has four main sections: introduction, method, results, and discussion. Though it is not explicitly labeled, the introduction begins the main body of a research report. Here, the researchers set the stage for the study. They present the problem under investigation, and state why it was important to study. By providing a brief review of past research and theory relevant to the central issue of investigation, the researchers place the study in an historical context and suggest how the study advances knowledge of the problem. Beginning with broad theoretical and practical considerations, the researchers delineate the rationale that led them to the specific set of hypotheses tested in the study. They also describe how they decided on their research strategy (e.g., why they chose an experiment or a correlational study).

The introduction generally begins with a broad consideration of the problem investigated. Here, the researchers want to illustrate that the problem they studied is a real problem about which people should care. If the researchers are studying prejudice, they may cite statistics that suggest discrimination is prevalent, or describe specific cases of discrimination. Such information helps illustrate why the research is both practically and theoretically meaningful, and why you should bother reading about it. Such discussions are often quite interesting and useful. They can help you decide for yourself if the research has merit. But they may not be essential for understanding the study at hand. Read the introduction carefully, but choose judiciously what to focus on and remember. To understand a study, what you really need to understand is what the researchers' hypotheses were, and how they were derived from theory, informal observation, or intuition. Other background information may be intriguing, but may not be critical to understand what the researchers did and why they did it.

While reading the introduction, try answering these questions: What problem was studied, and why? How does this study relate to, and go beyond, past investigations of the problem? How did the researchers derive their hypotheses? What questions do the researchers hope to answer with this study?

Method. In the method section, the researchers translate their hypotheses into a set of specific, testable questions. Here, the researchers introduce the main characters of the study—the subjects or participants—describing their characteristics (gender, age, etc.) and how many of them were involved. Then, they describe the materials (or apparatus), such as any questionnaires or special equipment, used in the study. Finally, they describe chronologically the procedures of the study; that is, how the study was conducted. Often, an overview of the research design will begin the method section. This overview provides a broad outline of the design, alerting you to what you should attend.

The method is presented in great detail so that other researchers can recreate the study to confirm (or question) its results. This degree of detail is normally not necessary to understand a study, so don't get bogged down trying to memorize the particulars of the procedures. Focus on how the independent variables were manipulated (or measured) and how the dependent variables were measured.

Measuring variables adequately is not always an easy matter. Many of the variables psychologists are interested in cannot be directly observed, so they must be inferred from participants' behavior. Happiness, for example, cannot be directly observed. Thus, researchers interested in how being happy influences people's judgments must infer happiness (or its absence) from their behavior—perhaps by asking people how happy they are, and judging their degree of happiness from their responses; perhaps by studying people's facial expressions for signs of happiness, such as smiling. Think about the measures researchers use while reading the method section. Do they adequately reflect or capture the concepts they are meant to measure? If a measure seems odd, consider carefully how the researchers justify its use.

Oftentimes in social psychology, getting there is half the fun. In other words, how a result is obtained can be just as interesting as the result itself. Social psychologists often strive to have participants behave in a natural, spontaneous manner, while controlling enough of their environment to pinpoint the causes of their behavior. Sometimes, the major contribution of a research report is its presentation of a novel method of investigation. When this is the case, the method will be discussed in some detail in the introduction.

Participants in social psychology studies are intelligent and inquisitive people who are responsive to what happens around them. Because of this, they are not always initially told the true purpose of a study. If they were told, they might not act naturally. Thus, researchers frequently need to be creative, presenting a credible rationale for complying with procedures, without revealing the study's purpose. This rationale is known as a *cover story*, and is often an elaborate scenario. While reading the method section, try putting yourself in the shoes of a participant in the study, and ask yourself if the instructions given to participants seem sensible, realistic, and engaging. Imagining what it was like to be in the study will also help you remember the study's procedure, and aid you in interpreting the study's results.

While reading the method section, try answering these questions: How were the hypotheses translated into testable questions? How were the variables of interest manipulated and/or measured? Did the measures used adequately reflect the variables of interest? For example, is self-reported income an adequate measure of social class? Why or why not?

Results. The results section describes how the observations collected were analyzed to determine whether the original hypotheses were supported. Here, the data (observations of behavior) are described, and statistical tests are presented. Because of this, the results section is often intimidating to readers who have little or no training in statistics. Wading through complex and unfamiliar statistical analyses is understandably confusing and frustrating. As a result, many students are tempted to skip over reading this section. We advise you not to do so. Empirical findings are the foundation of any science and results sections are where such findings are presented.

Take heart. Even the most prestigious researchers were once in your shoes and sympathize with you. Though space in psychology journals is limited, researchers try to strike a balance between the need to be clear and the need to be brief in describing their results. In an influential paper on how to write good research reports, Bem (1987) offered this advice to researchers:

> No matter how technical or abstruse your article is in its particulars, intelligent nonpsychologists with no expertise in statistics or experimental design should be able to comprehend the broad outlines of what you did and why. They should understand in general terms what was learned. (p. 74)

Generally speaking, social psychologists try to practice this advice.

Most statistical analyses presented in research reports test specific hypotheses. Often, each analysis presented is preceded by a reminder of the hypothesis it is meant to test. After an analysis is presented, researchers usually provide a narrative description of the result in plain English. When the hypothesis tested by a statistical analysis is not explicitly stated, you can usually determine the hypothesis that was tested by reading this narrative description of the result, and referring back to the introduction to locate an hypothesis that corresponds to that result. After even the most complex statistical analysis, there will be a written description of what the result means conceptually. Turn your attention to these descriptions. Focus on the conceptual meaning of research findings, not on the mechanics of how they were obtained (unless you're comfortable with statistics).

Aside from statistical tests and narrative descriptions of results, results sections also frequently contain tables and graphs. These are efficient summaries of data. Even if you are not familiar with statistics, look closely at tables and graphs, and pay attention to the means or correlations presented in them. Researchers always include written descriptions of the pertinent aspects of tables and graphs. While reading these descriptions, check the tables and graphs to make sure what the researchers say accurately reflects their data. If they say there was a difference between two groups on a particular dependent measure, look at the means in the table that correspond to those two groups, and see if the means do differ as described. Occasionally, results seem to become stronger in their narrative description than an examination of the data would warrant.

Statistics *can* be misused. When they are, results are difficult to interpret. Having said this, a lack of statistical knowledge should not make you overly cautious while reading results sections. Though not a perfect antidote, journal articles undergo extensive review by professional researchers before publication. Thus, most misapplications of statistics are caught and corrected before an article is published. So, if you are unfamiliar with statistics, you can be reasonably confident that findings are accurately reported.

While reading the results section, try answering these questions: Did the researchers provide evidence that any independent variable manipulations were effective? For example, if testing for behavioral differences between happy and sad participants, did the researchers demonstrate that one group was in fact happier than the other? What were the major findings of the study? Were the researchers' original hypotheses supported by their observations? If not, look in the discussion section for how the researchers explain the findings that were obtained.

Discussion. The discussion section frequently opens with a summary of what the study found, and an evaluation of whether the findings supported the original hypotheses. Here, the researchers evaluate the theoretical and practical implications of their results. This can be particularly interesting when the results did not work out exactly as the researchers anticipated. When such is the case, consider the researchers' explanations carefully, and see if they seem plausible to you. Often, researchers will also report any aspects of their study that limit their interpretation of its results, and suggest further research that could overcome these limitations to provide a better understanding of the problem under investigation.

Some readers find it useful to read the first few paragraphs of the discussion section before reading any other part of a research report. Like the abstract, these few paragraphs usually contain all of the main ideas of a research report: What the hypotheses were, the major findings and whether they supported the original hypotheses, and how the findings relate to past research and theory. Having this information before reading a research report can guide your reading, allowing you to focus on the specific details you need to complete your understanding of a study. The description of the results, for example, will alert you to the major variables that were studied. If they are unfamiliar to you, you can pay special attention to how they are defined in the introduction, and how they are operationalized in the method section.

After you have finished reading an article, it can also be helpful to reread the first few paragraphs of the discussion and the abstract. As noted, these two passages present highly distilled summaries of the major ideas in a research report. Just as they can help guide your reading of a report, they can also help you consolidate your understanding of a report once you have finished reading it. They provide a check on whether you have understood the main points of a report, and offer a succinct digest of the research in the authors' own words.

While reading the discussion section, try answering these questions: What conclusions can be drawn from the study? What new information does the study provide about the problem under investigation? Does the study help resolve the problem? What are the practical and theoretical implications of the study's findings? Did the results contradict past research findings? If so, how do the researchers explain this discrepancy?

Some Notes on Reports of Multiple Studies

Up to this point, we have implicitly assumed that a research report describes just one study. It is also quite common, however, for a research report to describe a series of studies of the same problem in a single article. When such is the case, each study reported will have the same basic structure (introduction, method, results, and discussion sections) that we have outlined, with the notable exception that sometimes the results and discussion section for each study are combined. Combined "results and discussion" sections contain the same information that separate results and discussion sections normally contain. Sometimes, the authors present all their results first, and only then discuss the implications of these results, just as they would in separate results and discussion sections. Other times, however, the authors alternate between describing results and discussing their implications, as each result is presented. In either case, you should be on the lookout for the same information, as outlined above in our consideration of separate results and discussion sections.

Reports including multiple studies also differ from single study reports in that they include more general introduction and discussion sections. The general introduction, which begins the main body of a research report, is similar in essence to the introduction of a single study report. In both cases, the researchers describe the problem investigated and its practical and theoretical significance. They also demonstrate how they derived their hypotheses, and explain how their research relates to past investigations of the problem. In contrast, the separate introductions to each individual study in reports of multiple studies are usually quite brief, and focus more specifically on the logic and rationale of each particular study presented. Such introductions generally describe the methods used in the particular study, outlining how they answer questions that have not been adequately addressed by past research, including studies reported earlier in the same article.

General discussion sections parallel discussions of single studies, except on a somewhat grander scale. They present all of the information contained in discussions of single studies, but consider the implications of all the studies presented together. A general discussion section brings the main ideas of a research program into bold relief. It typically begins with a concise summary of a research program's main findings, their relation to the original hypotheses, and their practical and theoretical implications. Thus, the summaries that begin general discussion sections are counterparts of the summaries that begin discussion sections of single study reports. Each presents a digest of the research presented in an article that can serve as both an organizing framework (when read first), and as a check on how well you have understood the main points of an article (when read last).

Research Reporting as Storytelling

A research report tells the story of how a researcher or group of researchers investigated a specific problem. Thus, a research report has a linear, narrative structure with a beginning, middle, and end. In his paper on writing research reports, Bem noted that a research report:

> . . . is shaped like an hourglass. It begins with broad general statements, progressively narrows down to the specifics of [the] study, and then broadens out again to more general considerations. (1987, p. 175)

This format roughly mirrors the process of scientific investigation, wherein researchers do the following: (1) start with a broad idea from which they formulate a narrower set of hypotheses, informed by past empirical findings (introduction); (2) design a specific set of concrete operations to test these hypotheses (method); (3) analyze the observations collected in this way, and decide if they support the original hypotheses (results); and (4) explore the broader theoretical and practical implications of the findings, and consider how they contribute to an understanding of the problem under investigation (discussion). Though these stages are somewhat arbitrary distinctions—research actually proceeds in a number of different ways—they help elucidate the inner logic of research reports.

While reading a research report, keep this linear structure in mind. Though it is difficult to remember a series of seemingly disjointed facts, when these facts are joined together in a logical, narrative structure, they become easier to comprehend and recall. Thus, always remember that a research report tells a story. It will help you to organize the information you read, and remember it later.

Describing research reports as stories is not just a convenient metaphor. Research reports *are* stories. Stories can be said to consist of two components: A telling of what happened, and an explanation of why it happened. It is tempting to view science as an endeavor that simply catalogues facts, but nothing is further from the truth. The goal of science, social psychology included, is to *explain* facts, to explain *why* what happened happened. Social psychology is built on the dynamic interplay of discovery and justification, the dialogue between systematic observation of relations and their theoretical explanation. Though research reports do present novel facts based on systematic observation, these facts are presented in the service of ideas. Facts in isolation are trivia. Facts tied together by an explanatory theory are science. Therein lies the story. To really understand what researchers have to say, you need consider how their explanations relate to their findings.

The Rest of the Story

> There is really no such thing as research. There is only search, more search, keep on searching. (Bowering, 1988, p. 95)

Once you have read through a research report, and understand the researchers' findings and their explanations of them, the story does not end there. There is more than one interpretation for any set of findings. Different researchers often explain the same set of facts in different ways.

Let's take a moment to dispel a nasty rumor. The rumor is this: Researchers present their studies in a dispassionate manner, intending only to inform readers of their findings and their interpretation of those findings. In truth, researchers aim not only to inform readers, but also to *persuade* them (Sternberg, 1995). Researchers want to convince you their ideas are right. There is never only one explanation for a set of findings. Certainly, some explanations are better than others; some fit the available data better, are more parsimonious, or require fewer questionable assumptions. The point here is that researchers are very passionate about their ideas, and want you to believe them. It's up to you to decide if you want to buy their ideas or not.

Let's compare social psychologists to sales clerks. Both social psychologists and sales clerks want to sell you something; either their ideas, or their wares. You need to decide if you want to buy what they're selling or not—and there are potentially negative consequences for either decision. If you let a sales clerk dazzle you with a sales pitch, without thinking about it carefully, you might end up buying a substandard product that you don't really need. After having done this a few times, people tend to become cynical, steeling themselves against any and all sales pitches. This too is dangerous. If you are overly critical of sales pitches, you could end up foregoing genuinely useful products. Thus, by analogy, when you are too critical in your reading of research reports, you might dismiss, out of hand, some genuinely useful ideas—ideas that can help shed light on why people behave the way they do.

This discussion raises the important question of how critical one should be while reading a research report. In part, this will depend on why one is reading the report. If you are reading it simply to learn what the researchers have to say about a particular issue, for example, then there is usually no need to be overly critical. If you want to use the research as a basis for planning a new study, then you should be more critical. As you develop an understanding of psychological theory and research methods, you will also develop an ability to criticize research on many different levels. And *any* piece of research can be criticized at some level. As Jacob Cohen put it, "A successful piece of research doesn't conclusively settle an issue, it just makes some theoretical proposition to some degree more likely" (1990, p. 1311). Thus, as a consumer of research reports, you have to strike a delicate balance between being overly critical and overly accepting.

While reading a research report, at least initially, try to suspend your disbelief. Try to understand the researchers' story; that is, try to understand the facts—the findings and how they were obtained—and the suggested explanation of those facts—the researchers' interpretation of the findings and what they mean. Take the research to task only after you feel you understand what the authors are trying to say.

Research reports serve not only an important archival function, documenting research and its findings, but also an invaluable stimulus function. They can excite other researchers to join the investigation of a particular issue, or to apply new methods or theory to a different, perhaps novel, issue. It is this stimulus function that Elliot Aronson, an eminent social psychologist, referred to when he admitted that, in publishing a study, he hopes his colleagues will "look at it, be stimulated by it, be provoked by it, annoyed by it, and then go ahead and do it better . . . . That's the exciting thing about science; it progresses by people taking off on one another's work" (1995, p. 5). Science is indeed a cumulative enterprise, and each new study builds on what has (or, sometimes, has not) gone before it. In this way, research articles keep social psychology vibrant.

A study can inspire new research in a number of different ways, such as: (1) it can lead one to conduct a better test of the hypotheses, trying to rule out alternative explanations of the findings; (2) it can lead one to explore the limits of the findings, to see how widely applicable they are, perhaps exploring situations to which they do not apply; (3) it can lead one to test the implications of the findings, furthering scientific investigation of the phenomenon; (4) it can inspire one to apply the findings, or a novel methodology, to a different area of investigation; and (5) it can provoke one to test the findings in the context of a specific real-world problem, to see if they can shed light on it. All of these are excellent extensions of the original research, and there are, undoubtedly, other ways that research findings can spur new investigations.

The problem with being too critical, too soon, while reading research reports is that the only further research one may be willing to attempt is research of the first type: redoing a study better. Sometimes this is desirable, particularly in the early stages of investigating a particular issue, when the findings are novel and perhaps unexpected. But redoing a reasonably compelling study, without extending it in any way, does little to advance our understanding of human behavior. Although the new study might be "better," it will not be "perfect," so *it* would have to be run again, and again, likely never reaching a stage where it is beyond criticism. At some point, researchers have to decide that the evidence is compelling enough to warrant investigation of the last four types. It is these types of studies that most advance our knowledge of social behavior. As you read more research reports, you will become more comfortable deciding when a study is "good enough" to move beyond it. This is a somewhat subjective judgment, and should be made carefully.

When social psychologists write up a research report for publication, it is because they believe they have something new and exciting to communicate about social behavior. Most research reports that are submitted for publication are rejected. Thus, the reports that are eventually published are deemed pertinent not only by the researchers who wrote them, but also by the reviewers and editors of the journals in which they are published. These people, at least, believe the research reports they write and publish have something important and interesting to say. Sometimes, you'll disagree; not all journal articles are created equal, after all. But we recommend that you, at least initially, give these well-meaning social psychologists the benefit of the doubt. Look for what they're excited about. Try to understand the authors' story, and see where it leads you.

NOTE

Preparation of this paper was facilitated by a Natural Sciences and Engineering Research Council of Canada doctoral fellowship to Christian H. Jordan. Thanks to Roy Baumeister, Arie Kruglanski, Ziva Kunda, John Levine, Geoff Mac-Donald, Richard Moreland, Ian Newby-Clark, Steve Spencer, and Adam Zanna for their insightful comments on, and appraisals of, various drafts of this paper. Thanks also to Arie Kruglanski and four anonymous editors of volumes in the series, *Key Readings in Social Psychology* for their helpful critiques of an initial outline of this paper. Correspondence concerning this article should be addressed to Christian H. Jordan, Department of Psychology, University of Waterloo, Waterloo, Ontario, Canada N2L 3G1. Electronic mail can be sent to chjordan@watarts.uwaterloo.ca.

REFERENCES

American Psychological Association (1994). *Publication manual* (4th ed.). Washington, D.C.

Aronson, E. (1995). Research in social psychology as a leap of faith. In E. Aronson (Ed.), *Readings about the social animal* (7th ed., pp. 3–9). New York: W. H. Freeman and Company.

Bem, D. J. (1987). Writing the empirical journal article. In M. P. Zanna & J. M. Darley (Eds.), *The compleat academic: A practical guide for the beginning social scientist* (pp. 171–201). New York: Random House.

Bowering, G. (1988). *Errata*. Red Deer, Alta.: Red Deer College Press.

Cohen, J. (1990). Things I have learned (so far). *American Psychologist, 45*, 1304–1312.

Forgas, J. P. (1994). Sad and guilty? Affective influences on the explanation of conflict in close relationships. *Journal of Personality and Social Psychology, 66*, 56–68.

Sternberg, R. J. (1995). *The psychologist's companion: A guide to scientific writing for students and researchers* (3rd ed.). Cambridge: Cambridge University Press.

Author Index

Subject Index